A2

AQA(A)

Psychology

Erika Cox

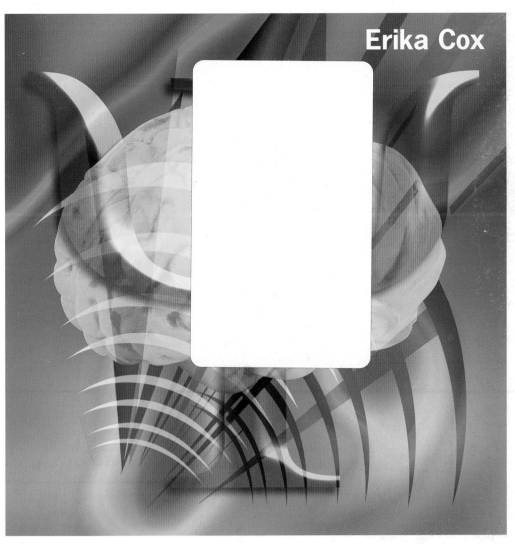

Philip Allan Updates, an imprint of Hodder Education, an Hachette UK company, Market Place, Deddington, Oxfordshire OX15 0SE

Orders

Bookpoint Ltd, 130 Milton Park, Abingdon, Oxfordshire OX14 4SB
tel: 01235 827720
fax: 01235 400454
e-mail: uk.orders@bookpoint.co.uk
Lines are open 9.00 a.m.–5.00 p.m., Monday to Saturday, with a 24-hour message answering service. You can also order through the Philip Allan Updates website: www.philipallan.co.uk

© Philip Allan Updates 2009

ISBN 978-0-340-98519-9

First printed 2009
Impression number   5   4   3   2   1
Year   2014   2013   2012   2011   2010   2009

Design by Juha Sorsa
Printed in Italy

Hachette UK's policy is to use papers that are natural, renewable and recyclable products and made from wood grown in sustainable forests. The logging and manufacturing processes are expected to conform to the environmental regulations of the country of origin.

P1424

Contents

Unit 4: Psychopathology, psychology in action and research methods

Introduction

This textbook has been written to meet the requirements of the new AQA (A) A2 Psychology specification. It provides comprehensive, accessible and up-to-date coverage of all the relevant topic areas. However, you may find it interesting to follow up some of the topics covered, and learn something about other areas of psychology, by reading around the subject — for example, you might be interested in subscribing to *Psychology Review*, a quarterly magazine aimed at A-level psychology students, also published by Philip Allan Updates.

This book builds on what has been covered at AS, with discussions of a range of further topics in which psychologists are interested. In Unit 3, these are drawn from biological, cognitive, social and developmental psychology. In Unit 4, there are sections on psychopathology and applied psychology, and a section on research methods, which elaborates on what has been covered at AS.

As with the AS psychology textbook, there are a number of emboldened specialised terms, which have been defined in the text on the first occasion that they appear.

Psychology is research-based, so you will find a large number of studies in this book. These include classical studies, carried out some time ago but which are still regarded as important today, and some recent research that has provided useful insight into psychological issues.

About the exam

Assessment objectives

The examination has three assessment objectives:
- AO1 — knowledge and understanding of psychological theories and research
- AO2 — analysis and evaluation of psychological material, and the ability to apply psychological knowledge to unfamiliar situations
- AO3 — understanding and application of ethical principles in research; understanding and evaluating the processes involved in planning, carrying out and reporting research; and the ability to explain and evaluate methodology

These assessment objectives are weighted differently, with AO2 given the most weight in Unit 3 and AO3 given the most weight in Unit 4. To achieve the highest grades, you will need to do well on all three objectives.

The unit tests

Unit 3 is tested in a 1½-hour exam. There will be one essay question on each of the eight topics covered in the unit, but you will only need to answer three.

Unit 4 is tested in a 2-hour exam. The first topic is psychopathology, with one question on each of three disorders, of which you must answer one. The next topic is applied psychology, and again there will be three questions, one on each topic, of which you need to answer one. These questions are in the form of essays, which are often made up of several parts; you will need to answer all the parts of your chosen question. The final question is compulsory and takes the form of a description of a study, with a set of short questions relating to various research issues. This last question is more heavily weighted than the two essay questions.

In both Units 3 and 4, the number of marks available for each question is given. This should help you to not spend too much time on an answer to a question that is only worth a few marks and conversely not to rush an answer to a question that is worth a lot of marks. In both units, the quality of written communication (QWC) will be assessed along with the content of your answers.

You may find it useful to get a copy of the specification; your teacher may be able to give you one, or a copy can be downloaded from www.aqa.org.uk. The specification is useful in that it tells you exactly what you need to know for the exam. For example, if a theorist or a piece of research is not named in the specification, then you cannot be asked a question in the exam that relates explicitly to that theorist/ research.

Understanding exam questions

Process words in exam questions are those that tell you how to approach each question. It is important to pay attention to these words, as well as the topic a question addresses, so that you focus your answer in the way required. For example, if a question only requires AO1 skills, you will not gain any marks for including AO2 skills.

Process words include the following:

Outline — this requires you to give brief information and so is an AO1 term (see 'Assessment objectives', above), as it does not ask for any evaluation.

Identify — this is also an AO1 term, and requires brief information. It is used with subsections of questions that are worth only 1 or 2 marks and can be answered in two or three words.

Discuss — this requires you to give information and comment on it, i.e. to outline and evaluate, so it is a term that covers both AO1 and AO2 skills. The AO2 aspect could include commenting on the strengths and limitations of a theory, and/or positive and negative criticisms of research studies.

Explain — this is an AO2 term, elaborating on the information you provide. An example could be explaining the differences between two competing theories that seek to explain a particular phenomenon.

Evaluate — this is also an AO2 term, which covers such skills as commenting on the strengths and limitations of a theory, and/or positive and negative criticisms of research studies.

Revision tips

- Organise your notes into the different topics covered in the exam so that they are easy to use when you come to revise.
- Use the specification to check that you have notes on everything on which you can be asked questions.
- Plan your revision time. Be realistic about how much time can be spent on revision, and allow for time off to relax.
- Make sure you continue to take exercise, eat healthily and get enough sleep during the revision period. It is difficult to revise and sit exams when you are feeling under the weather.
- Try to think positively about the exams, i.e. as a way of demonstrating what you know, rather than a hurdle to be crossed. Changing the way we think about something so that we take a more positive view is called cognitive restructuring and can contribute to reducing stress. It may help to know that examiners use positive marking; they are looking for something for which they can give credit, rather than for points that you have got wrong, which they ignore.
- Revising for short periods of half an hour or so with breaks in between is more effective than attempting to revise for a longer period — for example, 2 hours at a time, without a break.
- Reading and re-reading information in a textbook and class notes is useful, but memory research has demonstrated that we remember more when we actively engage with material, compared with the more passive activity of reading. One way to do this is to try answering past questions. There are samples on the AQA website, and you can always try making up your own questions using these as a guide.
- Remember to revise not only basic information about theories and research, but also evaluation of this material. This will be needed to gain high AO2 marks, but is often overlooked in revision. A lot of evaluation is contained in the book, and you may also think of additional points yourself.
- Practise writing timed answers under exam conditions. This will help you to get a feel for the time you should allow for each question, so you are less likely to get your timing wrong in the exam. Remembering to focus precisely on what the question is asking may also help you to answer in the exam the question that has been set, and not a question that you hoped would be there.
- Drawing up a detailed, colour-coded revision timetable does not count as revision, however pretty it is. In psychology, this is known as displacement activity, where we put off doing something important that we are not keen to do by doing something unimportant instead.

AQA(A)
A2 Psychology

Unit 3
Topics in psychology

In this chapter, we will be looking at:
- biological rhythms
  - circadian, infradian and ultradian rhythms
  - the disruption of biological rhythms
- sleep states
  - the nature of sleep
  - explanations of sleep
  - lifespan changes in sleep
- disorders of sleep
  - insomnia
  - sleep walking
  - narcolepsy

Biological rhythms

A biological rhythm is a pattern of physiological processes, sometimes accompanied by psychological changes, which repeats itself on a regular basis over a specific period of time. In this section we will look at three kinds of biological rhythms: circadian, infradian and ultradian.

Description	Length of cycle
Circadian	Approximately 24 hours
Infradian	Longer than a day, for example monthly
Ultradian	More than once within a day

Circadian rhythms

This term comes from the Latin 'circa', meaning 'about' and from 'dies', meaning 'day'. There are many biological rhythms that vary regularly, following this pattern.

For example, heart rate, urine secretion, metabolic rate, respiration (breathing) and temperature are all highest at around 4 p.m. and lowest at around 4 a.m. Hormone levels also vary; pro-lactin, which stimulates milk production in females, rises in the middle of the night.

Circadian rhythms are maintained by external cues (Zeitgebers) such as light and dark

However, sleep is the most obvious example of a circadian rhythm, as we normally follow a regular 24-hour cycle of sleeping and waking. The regular pattern of sleep and waking is maintained by exogenous (external) factors, cues such as light and dark, or mealtimes; these are known as Zeitgebers (German for 'time givers'), and light appears to be the most important factor. The role of Zeitgebers was established in a classic study by the French explorer Michel Siffre (see Box 1.1).

Box 1.1   Siffre (1972)

Aim: To establish the role of light as a Zeitgeber in the cycle of sleep and waking.

Procedure: Siffre spent 7 months underground. He had adequate food and opportunities to take exercise and was always able to contact others by phone, but had no cues as to whether it was day or night. Changes in his pattern of sleep and waking were observed.

Results: After a time, he showed a 25-hour cycle of sleeping and waking.

Conclusion: The pattern of sleep and waking remains even when there are no external cues. However, the natural length of the cycle is 25 hours.

The results of this study suggest that as well as external cues, there must be endogenous (internal) factors, known as **pacemakers**, which maintain this rhythm when external Zeitgebers cannot be used.

The principal internal mechanism or **biological clock** that governs circadian rhythms appears to be the **supra-chiasmatic nuclei (SCN)** of the **hypothalamus** (Figure 1.1). SCN lesions have been shown to disrupt circadian rhythms (Ibuka and Kawamura 1975) and there is a correlation between cyclical changes in behaviour and the activity of neurons in that area of the brain (Rusak and Groos 1982). Other clocks, such as temperature changes, may regulate specific

Figure 1.1 *The brain physiology of arousal and sleep*

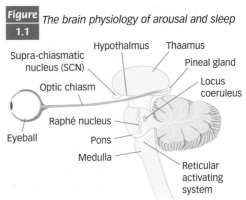

- Hypothalmus
- Thaamus
- Supra-chiasmatic nucleus (SCN)
- Pineal gland
- Optic chiasm
- Locus coeruleus
- Eyeball
- Raphé nucleus
- Pons
- Medulla
- Reticular activating system

1

rhythms, but the SCN appears to have some controlling function. This makes sense, since the SCN receive nerve input directly from the retina of the eye, so can respond to the Zeitgebers of light and darkness. This information is passed to the **pineal gland**, which manufactures **melatonin**, a hormone that regulates many of the body's systems and is involved in bringing about sleep.

As well as this system of control, the SCN may also govern circadian rhythms by means of the secretion of **neuromodulators**, chemicals that affect the behaviour of neurotransmitters. Ralph et al. (1990) found that grafted SCN, even when they had not formed connections with other areas of the brain, were nonetheless able to establish circadian rhythms within a few days. Moreover, in a study of hamsters, Hard and Ralph (1998) found that if the animal receiving the graft had a slightly different cycle from the donor, the donor cycle was adopted.

However, a person can adapt their biological rhythms if necessary, for example if they work permanently at night, although the time it takes to do so varies from person to person and some people may never fully adapt.

Infradian rhythms

Infradian rhythms, where the cycle is longer than a day, include the menstrual cycle (28 days), testosterone secretion in males (21 days) and seasonal mating.

The most researched of these is the **menstrual cycle**. This relates to activity in the endocrine system that prepares the womb for the possibility of conception after egg cells are released. Several hormones are involved, coordinated by the **pituitary gland**. This gland may be influenced by levels of light and the secretion of melatonin, a view supported by research (see Box 1.2).

Box 1.2	Reinberg (1967)

Aim: To investigate the influence of light on biological rhythms.

Procedure: A young woman spent 3 months in a cave, with no external source of light, the only light available being a miner's lamp. The effects on the sleep/waking cycle and the infradian cycle of menstruation were noted.

Results: As in the Siffre study (Box 1.1), the woman's day lengthened, in this case to 24.6 hours. Her menstrual cycle shortened to 25.7 days. At the end of the study, it took almost a year for her menstrual cycle to return to normal.

Conclusion: The lack of light as a Zeitgeber resulted in changes both to the circadian rhythm of the sleep/waking cycle and to the infradian rhythm of menstruation, which was slow to adapt to the previous pattern even when light was restored.

The menstrual cycle may also be influenced by smell. It has been found that when a group of young women spend a lot of time together, their menstrual cycles tend to synchronise and so follow the same timing. Russell et al. (1980) showed that synchronisation could be produced simply by transferring samples of underarm sweat from one woman to another.

The phenomenon of **premenstrual syndrome (PMS)** is associated with hormonal changes during the menstrual cycle. This refers to the negative psychological effects experienced by up to 60% of women 4–5 days before a period. The symptoms may include irritability, depression, headaches, insomnia, lethargy and sometimes changes in appetite; both an increase and a decrease have been reported. Some researchers, for example Dalton (1964), have suggested that during this part of the menstrual cycle, women are more likely to have accidents, carry out crimes, commit suicide and to have reduced scores on IQ tests.

Clare (1985) points out that there is no detectable and consistent hormonal abnormality that differentiates those women who suffer from PMS from those who do not. Moreover there are often methodological problems with studies that have reported a link between PMS and aggression, accidents and so on. A small number of women do seem to be vulnerable to behavioural and emotional changes due to menstruation, but these have not been consistently linked with any particular phase of the menstrual cycle.

Ultradian rhythms

These rhythms are shorter than a day and include changes within a 24-hour period in heart rate and the secretion of hormones. Most of the research in this area has investigated the stages of sleep; this will be looked at in a later section.

Summary

- Physiological and psychological processes generally show a rhythm or **cycle** that recurs over a period of time.
- **Circadian rhythms** are repeated approximately over 24 hours. The sleep/waking cycle is an example and is governed by external **Zeitgebers** and internal **pacemakers** involving the **SCN** of the **hypothalamus** and the **pineal gland**.
- **Infradian rhythms** recur over a period longer than a day. The **menstrual cycle** is an example.
- **Ultradian rhythms** recur over a period shorter than a day. The most researched example is the **stages of sleep**.

The disruption of biological rhythms

There has been a lot of research into what happens when biological rhythms are disrupted. This disruption can take two forms: **desynchronisation**, when different rhythms adapt at different rates, and **flattening**, when the amount of variation is decreased. Shift work and jetlag disrupt circadian and other biological rhythms; these are a source of stress as people have difficulty in making the rapid adjustments that are required, consequently there has been a considerable amount of research on both.

Shift work

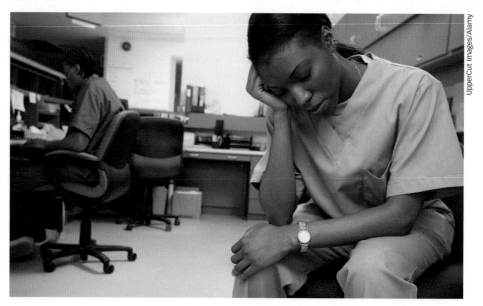

Shift work can cause sleep disturbances that lead to accidents caused by sleepiness

In the short term, working rotating shifts can cause sleep disturbances, fatigue, stress, irritability, errors and accidents. For example, in a hospital-based survey, Gold et al. (1992) found that nurses who worked rotating shifts were twice as likely to fall asleep while driving to work as those who worked only day or evening shifts and were twice as likely to report an accident or error at work due to sleepiness. Costa (1999) has summarised the serious long-term effects of shift work (see Box 1.3).

Box 1.3   Costa (1999)

Research has shown that the long-term effects of shift working include:
- difficulties in social and family relationships
- the development of peptic ulcers
- chronic fatigue, anxiety and depression
- cardiovascular problems, for example hypertension and ischaemic heart disease
- consequences for women's health, for example pregnancy difficulties

The severity of the effects varies, depending on individual factors, such as age, personality and physiological characteristics; on the working situation, such as workload schedules; and on social conditions, such as the number and age of children, housing and commuting to work.

However, it has been estimated that around 20% of all workers have to leave shift work after a short time because of serious problems.

To some extent, the problems associated with shift work can be reduced by making changes in the workplace (see Box 1.4).

| Box 1.4 | Blakemore (1988) |

Aim: To investigate possible improvements in health and productivity through changing the pattern of shift working.

Procedure: Workers in a chemical company in Utah were studied. The company operated a three-shift system, in which employees worked a day shift for a week, then a night shift and then an evening shift, before starting the cycle again. The effects of lengthening the period between shift changes and rotating the shifts in the opposite direction, i.e. clockwise, in line with the body's preference for a longer rather than a shorter day, were assessed.

Results: Both the health and the productivity of the workers improved.

Conclusion: It is possible to modify the effects of shift work.

Conversely, a shorter shift system can also be beneficial. Williamson and Sanderson (1986) found that bringing in a more rapidly rotating system, where workers never worked for more than three consecutive nights, led to improved health. Pisarski et al. (2008) also found that the negative effects on the health of shift workers could be reduced if they felt they had social support and some control at work.

Other ways of addressing these problems have focused on measures that may help to reset the body clock. Exposure to light can go some way towards helping shift workers overcome adjustment problems. Dawson and Campbell (1991) found that exposing workers to 4 hours of bright light on the first night of shift work could help people to adjust. There has also been a lot of interest in **chronobiotics**, substances that can readjust the timing of biological rhythms. Several studies, for example Touitou and Bogdan (2007), have found that the hormone **melatonin** can be used effectively in this way. However, while some modification is possible, there is as yet no way of eliminating completely the adjustment problems arising from shift work.

Jetlag

When we travel across different time zones, for example, if we fly to the USA, the Zeitgebers — the external cues that help to regulate circadian rhythms — give us information that conflicts with our internal biological clock, with the result that we feel tired when others are awake, get hungry at the wrong times and so on. It may take up to 10 days for our bodies to adjust. Some rhythms, such as temperature, adjust more quickly than others, such as ACTH production. There are also individual differences in how easily people adapt; some never do so completely.

guichaoua/Alamy

Those who frequently experience jetlag can suffer from long-term effects

The immediate effects of jetlag can include headache, sleepiness, irritability and difficulty in concentrating; these are usually overcome after a few days. However, for those who frequently experience jetlag, such as pilots and cabin crew, there may be long-term effects (see Box 1.5).

Box 1.5 | Cho (2001)

Aim: To investigate the long-term effects of frequent jetlag.

Procedure: Participants were 20 healthy women who had worked for at least 5 years as flight attendants. Participants who were allowed only a few days rest between flights were compared with those allowed longer recovery periods.

Results: Those who had little recovery time between flights performed worse on memory tests. They showed slower reaction times and made more mistakes. Brain scans showed that they had significant shrinkage of the right temporal lobe of the brain, and this was correlated with high levels of the stress hormone cortisol, which affects the immune system.

Conclusion: Repeated jet lag, with insufficient recovery time between flights, can lead to reduced cognitive ability and brain damage.

Cho et al. (2000) also found that cabin crew had problems with working memory, which became apparent after several years of the disruption of circadian rhythms associated with their work.

It may take up to 10 days for our bodies to adjust from the effects of jetlag

One way of dealing with the immediate effects of jetlag is to try to stay awake longer. As shown earlier, in the absence of external cues (Zeitgebers), the body adjusts to a slightly longer cycle of around 25 hours, so extending the waking part of the cycle is more effective than trying to shorten it. This also explains why jetlag is less of a problem flying from east to west, and so lengthening the day, than from west to east.

As with shift work, **melatonin** can be effective in treating the immediate effects of jet lag (Herxheimer and Petrie 2002). However, it needs to be taken at the right time — at around the time of day that a traveller wants to fall asleep when he or she arrives at the destination — or it may make the problems worse. It may also interact badly with other medication, such as the blood-thinning drug Warfarin.

Summary

- Working **rotating shifts** disrupts circadian rhythms and so produces problems in the short term, but also has **long-term health implications**.
- Changing **working practices** can help to reduce the effects of shift working. **Exposure to light** and the use of **melatonin** have also been found to be effective, but cannot altogether overcome the problems.

- The adjustment of circadian rhythms when crossing time zones causes the short-term effects of **jetlag**.
- There are more serious **physiological effects** for people who experience this regularly without sufficient recovery periods.
- In the short term, jetlag can be reduced by **staying awake longer**. **Melatonin** can also be helpful.

Sleep states

Physiological changes that occur during sleep have been well documented, and researchers have been interested in the mechanisms that bring about these changes. Another area of interest has been the question of why we need to sleep, and a number of explanations have been put forward. A further question is how sleep changes across the lifespan. We will be looking at all these aspects of sleep research in this section.

The nature of sleep

Stages of sleep

While the cycle of sleeping and waking has a circadian rhythm, there are also stages within sleep that are based on a 90-minute ultradian cycle. These have been recorded using different methods, shown in Figure 1.2.

Figure 1.2 Figure 1.2 Methods of recording the stages of sleep

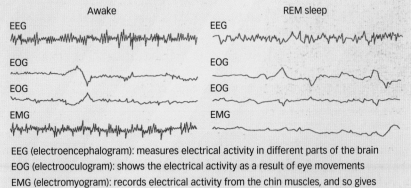

EEG (electroencephalogram): measures electrical activity in different parts of the brain
EOG (electrooculogram): shows the electrical activity as a result of eye movements
EMG (electromyogram): records electrical activity from the chin muscles, and so gives information abut muscle tension

One particular kind of sleep that has been of interest to psychologists is **rapid eye movement (REM)** sleep. People experience several periods of this in the course of a night's sleep, during which the eyes make rapid movements that produce intense EOG activity. In an early study, Dement and Kleitman (1957) found that REM sleep shows a distinctive pattern of brain activity and that it is predominantly associated with dreaming. Following on from this, the different kinds of sleep we experience have been categorised (see Box 1.6).

Box 1.6 Rechtschaffen and Kales (1968): the stages of sleep

Stage 0: wakefulness, this is identified by the presence of low-amplitude, high-frequency beta waves in the EEG. As we relax, these are replaced by alpha waves, which are higher in amplitude but slower in frequency (8–12 cycles per second).

Stage 1: this is characterised by the appearance of theta waves in the EEG; these are slower (4–7 cycles per second) and more irregular. Breathing and heart rate slow down, body temperature falls and muscles relax. There may also be slow eye rolling shown on the EOG.

Stage 2: this usually occurs after about a minute and is characterised by brief bursts of high frequency EEG activity, known as sleep spindles, which last about 1 second. There are also K-complexes, which represent the brain's response to stimulation, either external, such as a noise in the room, or internal, such as a muscle movement. Very slow (1–3 cycles per second), high-amplitude delta waves start to appear. The EOG shows little activity and the EMG is reduced still further.

Stage 3: this occurs after about 20 more minutes. There is between 20% and 50% delta activity in the EEG.

Stage 4: sleep follows shortly, when delta activity has increased to over 50% of the total and become even slower. Heart rate, blood pressure and body temperature are at their lowest and the muscles are relaxed. At this stage, people are difficult to wake and do not respond readily to external stimuli, so this is seen as a deeper form of sleep; it lasts for about 40 minutes.

Stages 3 and 4 are known as slow-wave sleep and stages 1–4 as non-REM (NREM) sleep.

Having descended what is known as the sleep staircase into deeper and deeper sleep, the sleeper then starts to climb back through stages 3 and 2; this is followed by REM sleep. The EEG pattern here resembles that in the waking, relaxed state with a high level of alpha activity. There are also PGO spikes, which are short bursts of high frequency, large amplitude activity from the pons, thalamus and visual cortex. Heart rate, blood pressure and breathing rate increase and become more irregular; rapid eye movements occur, where the eyes flick from side to side. The EMG record shows that in spite of these signs of activity, the muscles are in a state of virtual paralysis, apart from occasional twitches of the toes and fingers. This is when people are hardest to wake. It is also known as paradoxical sleep, since the brain is alert but the body is not. After about 10 minutes, we return to stage 2 and descend the sleep staircase again.

Figure 1.3 *EEG, EOG and EMG recordings in the various stages of sleep*

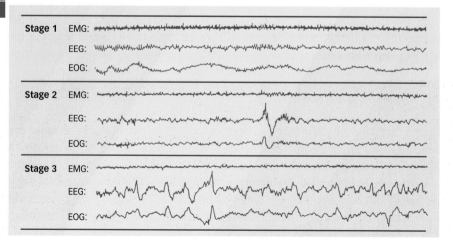

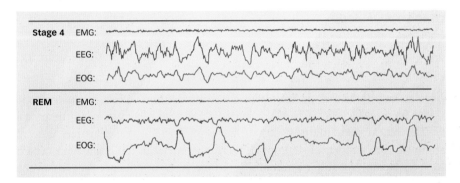

During the night, we usually experience around five sleep cycles, each of which lasts about 90 minutes. Stages 3 and 4 only occur in the first two cycles and the periods of REM get longer in the course of the night.

Figure 1.4 *Characteristic profile of a night's sleep.*

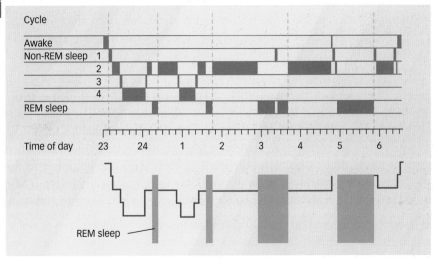

The exact pattern of sleep varies from person to person and can also vary in the same person on different nights. As we will see later, there are also changes in the pattern of sleep with age.

Summary

- The **stages of sleep** show a cycle of approximately **90 minutes**.
- Brain activity during sleep is recorded in several ways: **EEG**, **EOG** and **EMG**.
- The different stages show different patterns of **alpha**, **delta** and **theta** waves.
- **REM** sleep is the hardest kind of sleep to wake up from and is predominantly associated with **dreaming**. The other stages are **NREM** sleep.
- The stages of sleep show some variation between **individuals** and with **age**.

Mechanisms of sleep

Research into the mechanisms of sleep has looked at neurochemicals, circulating sleep-inducing chemicals and at neurological mechanisms involved in sleep, i.e. sleep centres and circuits.

We have already looked at the link with circadian rhythms; when it gets dark the eyes send messages to the SCN of the hypothalamus and from there to the pineal gland. The pineal gland starts to secrete melatonin, which makes us feel drowsy. Melatonin in turn influences neurons in the **raphé nuclei** in the brain stem, which produce the neurotransmitter **serotonin**. Serotonin in turn influences activity in the nearby **reticular activating system (RAS)** (see Figure 1.1).

The RAS is concerned with arousal. Early research has shown that low levels of activity in the RAS are associated with the onset of sleep. Moruzzi and Magoun (1949) and French (1957) found that a sleeping cat could be woken by stimulation of the RAS. More recent research seems to indicate that the RAS is involved with movement rather than arousal. In the context of sleep, serotonin is an inhibitory transmitter and lesions of the raphé nuclei, which are known to produce sleeplessness, will produce an almost complete loss of brain serotonin. Drugs that reduce levels of serotonin in the brain prevent sleep and those that increase levels of serotonin reverse this effect.

A different system appears to govern REM sleep. Jouvet (1967) found that destruction of the **locus coeruleus**, located in the pons, eliminates REM sleep. The locus coeruleus produces the neurotransmitters **noradrenaline** and **acetylcholine**. REM sleep occurs when there are increases in activity in acetylcholine systems and ends when there are increases in activity in noradrenaline systems. This can be linked to the finding that **monoamine oxidase inhibitors (MAOIs)** also eliminate REM sleep. These are drugs used to treat depression and increase levels of noradrenaline and serotonin.

Other research has focused on the idea that substances that promote sleep or wakefulness might be produced, accumulating in the blood during wakefulness and being destroyed during sleep. Support for this comes from Monnier and Hosli (1964), who were able to extract **delta-sleep-inducing-peptide (DSIP)** from rabbits, which induced sleep when injected into rats. Pappenheimer et al. (1975) obtained **Factor S** from the cerebrospinal fluid of sleep-deprived goats, which had the same effect; this has also been found in human urine (Garcia-Arraras and Pappenheimer 1983). However, the role of these chemicals is still unclear, as they have other effects as well, such as raising body temperature and stimulating the immune system.

There are further problems with this theory. Mukhametov (1984) has shown that in dolphins the two halves of the brain sleep separately, which

Summary

- The **hypothalamus, pineal gland** and **RAS** are involved in **NREM** sleep, which is influenced by the neurotransmitter **serotonin**.
- The **locus coeruleus** governs **REM** sleep. The neurotransmitters **acetylcholine** and **noradrenaline** are involved.
- Other chemicals may also be important in regulating sleep.

they would not be able to do if sleep was being produced by chemicals in a shared blood supply. Even more convincingly, conjoined twins, who also share the same blood supply, show different patterns of sleep.

Explanations of sleep

A number of theories have been put forward to explain why we sleep. Some of them are concerned with sleep in general, while others focus only on a particular kind of sleep. Evolutionary theories and restoration theories are important examples of the ideas that have been suggested.

Evolutionary explanations of sleep

Evolutionary theory aims to explain behaviour in terms of how it may be adaptive. In this context, **adaptive** refers to how a behaviour may promote survival long enough for an individual to breed and pass on their genes to the next generation. On the principle of **natural selection**, members of a species with characteristics that promote survival will be more successful in passing on their genes than individuals who do not share those characteristics.

Meddis (1975) suggested that sleep may be adaptive in terms of safety, drawing on the fact that some species sleep for longer than others and at different times. For example, predators such as lions, which are unlikely to be attacked by other animals and can quickly and easily meet their nutritional needs, sleep for long periods. In contrast, sheep, which have little defence against predators and need to spend a long time feeding to gain enough nutrition, only sleep for about 2 hours a day, in the form of brief naps. The amount of time spent asleep is therefore related to an animal's need for and method of obtaining food and its exposure to predators.

In a similar theory, in that it emphasises the adaptive nature of sleep, Webb (1982) has suggested that sleep is an instinctual behavioural response, related to the need to conserve energy by not expending energy when it is unnecessary or even counter-productive. It would be adaptive to keep out of danger when danger is most likely to occur and there is nothing to be gained by exposure.

This idea leads to the notion known as the **hibernation theory of sleep function** that sleep in humans has evolved because it promotes survival by preventing unnecessary energy expenditure, as we are much less likely to find food at night than during the day. It keeps us out of harm's way by immobilising us at night, when we are vulnerable.

Evolutionary theories are limited in that they attempt to explain differences in sleep patterns and durations, rather than the phenomenon of sleep itself. A major difficulty with this approach is that it has an explanation for completely opposite phenomena. For example, sleeping for longer or for shorter periods could both be seen as adaptive in a species in danger from predators. Sleeping for longer periods would conserve energy necessary to deal with predatory attacks and help to avoid attack. On the other hand, sleeping for shorter periods would mean alertness and so being better prepared to avoid predators.

As with most evolutionary theories, these ideas are impossible to test directly and are purely speculative. Evolutionary theory tends to be better at offering explanations of behaviour than in producing testable hypotheses.

Restoration theories of sleep

It seems reasonable, as evolutionary theories suggest, that safety and energy conservation could be two of the functions of sleep, but it is possible that it also serves other functions. Oswald (1966) has suggested that the purpose of sleep is to restore reserves of energy and repair the brain and body after the events of the day. This theory suggests that NREM sleep restores bodily processes, for example hormone levels, while REM sleep restores brain processes, for example by stimulating the synthesis of proteins.

Restoration theory of sleep explains why babies spend more time asleep

There are several lines of evidence to support Oswald's approach. First, it could explain why babies spend more time asleep than older people, since they would need more REM sleep to assist the development of the central nervous system. Second, people who have been given ECT, where an electric shock is given to the brain as a treatment for depression, show an increase in REM sleep for a period of 6–8 weeks afterwards (Grunhaus et al. 1994), which is about how long it would take to replace half the brain's protein. There is also evidence that we spend longer in NREM sleep after a physically demanding day (see Box 1.7).

Box 1.7 | **Shapiro (1981)**

Aim: To investigate the effect of physical exercise on sleep.

Procedure: Participants were athletes, aged 18–26, who took part in an ultra-marathon, a 92-kilometre road race. Sleep recordings were made on the four nights following the race.

Results: The athletes showed a significant increase in sleep time — 1½ hours longer on the two nights immediately following the race — and specifically in deeper levels of NREM (slow-wave) sleep. Stage 4 sleep accounted for 45% of the total sleep time, where normally this is around 25%. The proportion of REM sleep decreased.

Conclusion: The extra time spent in slow-wave sleep allowed the body to recover from the exertion of the race.

However, if restoration theories are correct, it might be expected that not taking any exercise should result in a shorter time spent asleep, but this does not appear to be the case. Ryback and Lewis (1971) found that healthy people who spent 6 weeks resting in bed showed no change to their sleep patterns.

A variation of restoration theory has suggested that sleep is not only a physiological restorative, for example allowing cell renewal to take place and neurotransmitter levels to be adjusted, but may also serve a similar psychological function. Kales et al. (1974) have shown that insomniacs have far more psychological problems than healthy people. This suggests that psychological problems could arise through a lack of the sleep, which would allow psychological restoration. However, this is correlational evidence, so could equally be interpreted in terms of insomniacs having difficulty sleeping because of their psychological problems.

Lifespan changes in sleep

There is variation across the lifespan in both the total amount of sleep a person experiences and in the proportion of time spent in the different stages of sleep.

Figure 1.5 Changes in sleep across the lifespan

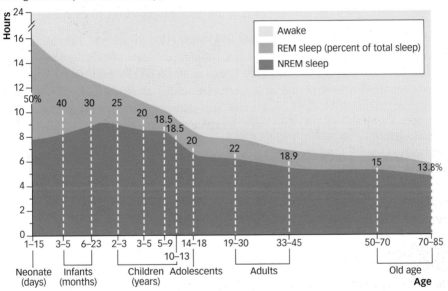

Floyd et al. (2007) carried out a study of the amount of REM sleep across the lifespan. In a sample whose ages ranged from 18 to over 90, they found that REM sleep decreased by about 0.6% each decade. In the mid-70s, however, there was a small increase in REM sleep, while total sleep time decreased.

A more detailed analysis of a number of studies into changes in sleep across the lifespan has also been carried out (see Box 1.8).

Box 1.8   Obayon et al. (2004)

Aim: To carry out a meta-analysis of studies of the changes in sleep across the lifespan.

Procedure: An analysis was made of the findings of 65 studies of changes in sleep patterns across the lifespan, in which participants were aged from 5 to 102 years old.

Results: In children and adolescents, the total sleep time decreased significantly from typical levels only in studies carried out on school days. In adults, total sleep time and the percentages of slow wave and REM sleep all decreased significantly with age. Sleep latency (the period before falling asleep), the percentages of stage 1 and stage 2 sleep and waking up after falling asleep all increased significantly with age. However, after the age of 60, only sleep efficiency, i.e. the percentage of time between falling asleep and waking that is actually spent asleep, continued to decrease significantly.

Conclusion: There are a number of changes in the patterns of sleep across the lifespan.

Newborn infants sleep for around 16 hours a day, half of which is REM sleep. This drops to about 12 hours at 12 months old, a third of which is REM sleep. It has been suggested by Empson and Clarke (1970) that REM sleep is important for memory consolidation. This could account for the prominence of REM sleep in infants and young children, given the amount of new information they take in each day.

Obayon (2004) also noted that there are few studies that investigate sleep in school-aged children and adolescents, making it difficult to draw conclusions about the sleep of these age groups. In one study, Loessl et al. (2008) investigated the amount of sleep reported over a period of 2 weeks by school students aged 12–18. They found that the majority slept on average less than the 9 hours per night recommended for this age group, with even less sleep on school nights. However, few reported daytime sleepiness or impaired cognitive functioning, suggesting little effect of sleep deprivation on people of this age.

Morphy et al. (2007) found a significant correlation between age and insomnia, which we look at in the next section. Older people also appear to be more susceptible to the effects of sleep disturbance than younger people (see Box 1.9).

Box 1.9   **Koller (1983)**

Aim: To compare the health of workers working changing shifts and day workers.

Procedure: Workers in an oil refinery provided information about absence due to sickness, morbidity, severity of diseases and subjective complaints, which gave them an overall health score. The health scores of shift and day workers were compared.

Results: Older workers had lower health scores, but the pattern of deterioration differed for shift and day workers. In the shift workers, there was a steep decrease during the early years at work, a continued slight decrease in middle age, followed by a further sharp decrease. In day workers, there was little decrease up to middle age, followed by a sharper drop. The permanent shift workers showed an increase in absence through illness, in particular with gastro-intestinal problems and heart disease. They also reported more sleep disturbances.

Conclusion: Older workers are more vulnerable to the effects of sleep problems caused by the disruption of circadian rhythms involved in shift work.

Summary

- **Evolutionary theories** of sleep suggest that sleep is **adaptive**. Sleep patterns differ in different species and this difference is related to the need for obtaining food and avoiding predators. It also serves the function of conserving energy. While this kind of explanation seems feasible, these ideas **cannot be tested** directly.
- **Restoration theories** suggest that the purpose of sleep is to restore the brain and the body. There is evidence to support this view.
- Sleep may also be important in restoring **psychological functioning**.
- There are changes in both the amount of sleep and the proportion of REM sleep across the **lifespan**.

Disorders of sleep

Many of us have occasionally had a night where sleep was difficult, perhaps because we were worried about an exam the next day or have been disturbed by noises from the street outside. However, there are a number of sleep disorders that are not only distressing but also may threaten the individual's health. Some of these will be looked at in this section.

Insomnia

Insomnia can be defined as the chronic inability to get enough sleep due to difficulty in falling asleep, frequent waking during sleep and/or early morning waking. Kao et al. (2008) found that difficulty getting to sleep was the most commonly reported symptom, followed by early morning waking and difficulty staying asleep. Morphy et al. (2007) found that of over 2,000 English adults who took part in a questionnaire survey, 37% reported symptoms, though this may be something of an overestimate, since the data came only from those who chose to return the completed questionnaire and so may be biased. Several studies carried out in western Europe and North America have reported an incidence of around 20%. As well as being frustrating and unpleasant, insomnia creates a range of problems, such as daytime sleepiness and difficulties in concentration, memory and with personal relationships.

Insomnia can be divided into primary and secondary insomnia. **Primary insomnia** is psychophysiological in origin and linked to hyperarousal, though the precise mechanisms involved are not clear. **Secondary insomnia**, the more common type, is the result of psychiatric or organic illness, or the effect of prescription or illicit drugs, alcohol, or any combination of these factors.

Primary insomnia

Primary insomnia has been linked to **personality factors**. Wang et al. (2001) compared patients with chronic primary insomnia and healthy controls. The insomniacs scored higher on scales measuring neuroticism, anxiety and impulsivity.

They suggested that this could be the result of aberrant functioning of the hypothalamus, or a neurotransmitter imbalance. The results and conclusions are consistent with the findings of other studies in this area (see Box 1.10).

Box 1.10 | Kales et al. (1983)

Aim: To assess personality characteristics of patients with chronic insomnia.

Procedure: The Minnesota Multiphasic Personality Inventory (MMPI) was used to draw up personality profiles. The results of 428 insomniacs and 100 healthy controls were compared.

Results: Unlike the controls, the insomniac profiles demonstrated neurotic depression, chronic anxiety, inhibition of emotions and an inability to express anger.

Conclusion: The results are consistent with the idea that handling stress and conflict through internalising emotions has physiological effects and is a major factor in insomnia.

There appears to be general agreement that a tendency towards the internalisation of emotions and the occurrence of stressful life events play a major role in the development of chronic insomnia.

It also seems that some insomniacs overestimate their sleep problems. Mercer et al. (2002) found that some greatly overestimate the time it takes them to fall asleep and underestimate how long they have slept. They may believe that they have spent much of the night awake, even though EEG recordings show that they have in fact been sleeping. Perlis et al. (2001) have suggested that this may arise as a result of a fault in the mechanisms that normally erase our memories during the transition from wakefulness to sleep, blurring the distinction between sleep and wakefulness and so creating a false perception of having been awake.

Secondary insomnia

Dejanovic et al. (2003) suggest that there are four different kinds of causes of secondary insomnia:

Causes of secondary insomnia

Environmental factors, including stress, emotional arousal, noise, shift work (and night work in general) and intercontinental flights from east to west or west to east. Narcotics, alcohol and drugs also come under this heading.

Organic problems, such as chronic pain.

Mental disorders, such as anxiety, depression and bipolar disorder.

Causes specific to sleep, of which perhaps the most important is a breathing disorder, obstructive sleep apnoea.

They suggest that primary insomnia should only be diagnosed when there is no other obvious cause.

Insomnia can be linked to **anxiety** disorders. In a study of medical students, Jiang et al. (2003) found that the life events experienced by insomniacs and controls were similar. The groups differed, however, in their tolerance of stressors. There is also a strong link between insomnia and clinical **depression**, of which early-morning waking is a typical symptom. In depressed patients, patterns of sleep nearly always change. There is typically an increase in REM sleep, REM sleep is entered more quickly than normal and there is a higher frequency of rapid eye movements.

Much of the research in this area is correlational, so it is not clear whether depression causes insomnia, or is a result of it. It is possible that depression can lead to insomnia and insomnia can lead to depression. There is evidence that both anxiety and depression can be a cause of insomnia (see Box 1.11).

Box 1.11   ## Jansson-Fröjmark and Lindblom (2008)

Aim: To investigate the relationships between depression, anxiety and insomnia.

Procedure: A sample of 3,000 participants completed a survey on anxiety, depression and insomnia and a follow-up survey a year later.

Results: There was a strong interrelationship between anxiety, depression and insomnia. Both anxiety and depression as measured on the first survey were predictive of the development of new cases of insomnia on the follow-up survey. Measures of insomnia on the first survey were also predictive of new cases of depression and anxiety in the follow-up survey.

Conclusion: There is a bi-directional relationship between anxiety, depression and insomnia; while insomnia can lead to anxiety and depression, these conditions can also lead to insomnia.

A major cause of insomnia is **obstructive sleep apnoea** (from the Greek, meaning 'without breath'). This occurs when the upper airway is temporarily blocked when a person is asleep, in spite of the respiratory muscles trying to inhale. The sleeper stops breathing for anything from a few seconds to more than a minute. Eventually a partial reawakening is triggered and the sleeper gasps in some air. This can happen over 100 times in one night. People with sleep apnoea rarely wake up during these episodes, but the effects the next day are sleepiness, irritability and other signs of sleep deprivation. The main symptom apart from the effects of sleep deprivation is snoring, which affects the vast majority of sufferers.

It is a serious condition, since it is associated with an increased probability of developing **hypertension** and **heart disorders**. It has also been associated with an increased risk of motor accidents, as a result of daytime sleepiness. Mulgrew et al. (2008) found that drivers with sleep apnoea were significantly more likely than controls to be involved in motor vehicle crashes and that the crashes they were involved in were more serious.

Sleep apnoea is more likely to affect older people, obese individuals and men rather than women. It is more likely to affect older people as the soft tissues in the upper airways become slacker as we get older. However, children can also suffer from sleep apnoea. In a large-scale study in Iceland, Martikainen et al. (1994) found that 3% of children aged from 6 months to 6 years had sleep apnoea.

Obesity is the most powerful predictor of sleep apnoea in adults, since fat deposits in the neck constrict the upper airways. Stradley and Crosby (1991) found that neck circumference, rather than general obesity, was a strong predictor of sleep apnoea. The relationship between obesity and sleep apnoea can also be a vicious cycle.

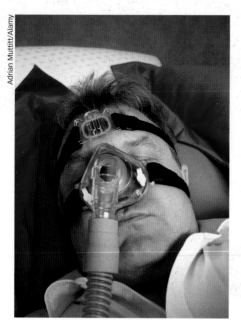

Obesity can trigger sleep apnoea, but sleep apnoea is also associated with physiological abnormalities that promote weight gain. Added to this, sleep apnoea sufferers may snack on sugar-rich foods like chocolate and fizzy drinks to try to overcome their daytime sleepiness, so making things worse.

There are also physiological characteristics of facial anatomy that influence whether or not a person will develop the disorder, suggesting a genetically-determined predisposition; those who have long faces, longer soft palates and narrower airways are more vulnerable. Dematteis et al. (2001) found that 11 of 14 members of one family suffered from sleep apnoea, linked to an abnormality of the pharynx.

Sleep apnoea can be treated successfully using **continuous positive airway pressure (CPAP)**. A machine is used, mainly by patients at home, which delivers a stream of compressed air via a hose to a nasal pillow, nose mask or full-face mask, keeping the airway open under air pressure so that unobstructed breathing becomes possible.

Sleep apnoea can be treated with CPAP, which helps keep the airway open

Summary

- **Primary insomnia** has been linked to **personality** characteristics, in particular the internalisation of emotions and to **hyperarousal**. Sufferers may also have **distorted beliefs** about how much they sleep.
- **Secondary insomnia** is more common. It is caused by **environmental factors**, **organic problems**, **mental disorders** or causes specific to sleep, especially **obstructive sleep apnoea**.
- **Depression** and **anxiety** are common in people suffering from insomnia; these conditions can cause insomnia, as well as being the result of it.
- **Sleep apnoea** is commonly a cause of insomnia. It is more common in older, male and obese people and may also be genetically predetermined. It can cause long-term **health problems**, but can be treated successfully.

Sleep walking

Sleep walking is known to specialists as **somnambulism** and is one of the **parasomnias**, a group of disorders that also includes nightmares and night terrors. Sleep walking takes place during NREM sleep — it would not be possible during REM sleep, as the muscles are then paralysed — and actions are carried out without the person having any conscious awareness of what they are doing.

People can carry out quite complex behaviours while sleep walking. Gunn and Gunn (2007) report people lining up all their shoes on the windowsill, rearranging furniture, or climbing out of a window in the middle of the night. Martin (2003) relates an anecdote of a lady waking up with the feeling that there was someone else in the room; she heard a thud and fainted with terror. When she awoke, she found that her butler, while sleep walking, had laid the table for 14 people on her bed.

Sleep walking is relatively common in children and is usually benign and self-limiting. All that is usually necessary is to reassure the parents, make sure that steps are taken so that children cannot hurt themselves and wait for it to pass. It has been suggested that cognitive behavioural therapy may help childhood sufferers, but there has been only limited research into its effectiveness. Sleep walking reaches a peak in pre-adolescence and is relatively rare in adults. It is estimated to affect around 2% of the adult population worldwide. It is less common in older people and affects men and women equally.

Somnambulists can carry out complex tasks when sleep walking

Sleep walking is more likely to occur if the person is very tired, so **stress**, anxiety and any other factor that disturbs sleep may trigger sleep walking. Soldatos and Kales (1990) suggest that in adults it may be the result of underlying pathology, in particular stress or **depression**. It may also be the result of **trauma**. For example, Kurtz and Davidson (1973) report a case of somnambulism in an 11-year-old child who underwent a trauma following the injury of his father in an Israeli security operation. Ohayon (1999) identified several factors associated with sleep walking, which include: being between 15–24 years old; a subjective sense of choking or blocked breathing at night; sleep talking; and being involved in a road accident within the previous year. There is also some evidence that it may run in families (see Box 1.12).

Box 1.12 Hublin et al. (1997)

Aim: To investigate possible genetic effects in sleep walking.

Procedure: In a Finnish study, over 11,000 participants aged 33 to 60 years, including 1,045 monozygotic (MZ) and 1,899 dizygotic (DZ) twin pairs were studied. They were asked about the frequency of sleep walking, both in childhood and in adulthood.

1

Results: For sleep walking in childhood, there was a concordance rate of 0.55 for MZ and 0.35 for DZ twin pairs. For adults, the concordance rate was 0.32 for MZ and 0.06 for DZ twin pairs. Less than 1% of those who reported never having walked in their sleep in childhood did so as adults. Of those who reported walking in their sleep often or sometimes in childhood, 25% of men and 18% of women reported sleep walking as adults. In adult sleep walkers, 89% of men and 85% of women had a history of sleep walking in childhood. The genetic influence was calculated as 66% in men and 57% in women in childhood sleep walking and 80% in men and 36% in women in adult sleep walking.

Conclusion: The greater similarities between MZ than between DZ twins and the figures linking childhood and adult sleep walking suggest that there is a substantial genetic effect in sleep walking, both in adults and in children.

Most of the activities carried out during sleep walking are unproblematic when a person is awake, but when they occur during somnambulism, they could be potentially dangerous to the sleep walker or other people. Although the risk is slight, cases have been reported where sleepwalkers have hurt themselves or others (see Box 1.13).

Box 1.13　Broughton et al. (1994)

The case of Ken Parks took place in Canada in the 1980s. He was married with a young daughter and got on well with his in-laws. However, as a result of anxiety about gambling problems he only slept between 4–6 hours a night. To settle his debts, he embezzled money from work, lost his job and was charged with theft. He and his wife agreed that he should tell his in-laws everything.

The night before this was due to happen, he fell asleep in front of the television and the next thing he claimed to remember was looking at his mother-in law's face and seeing a knife in his hands and that he was bleeding. He drove straight to the police station, where he said: 'I think I have killed some people.' The police reconstructed what must have taken place. He had got up from the sofa, driven 14 miles to the house of his parents-in-law, strangled (but not killed) his father-in-law and stabbed his mother-in-law to death.

He was acquitted of the murder and attempted murder, as it was argued that he had been sleep walking during the entire episode and therefore had not acted voluntarily. This claim was strengthened by the fact that his story never varied and because he seemed genuinely upset by what had happened.

This kind of incident is thankfully rare but, rather more worryingly, increasing numbers of '**sleep driving**' cases are being reported, in which somnambulists get in their cars and drive, sometimes long distances, ignoring lanes, stoplights and stationary objects and after waking up have no memory of what they did.

Sleep walkers rarely seek medical help, but if the sleep walking is associated with anxiety, it can be treated with **anxiolytic drugs**, such as benzodiazepines (for example Diazepam). In a small-scale case study, Kennedy (2002) found that the relaxation achieved in **hypnosis** could be effective in reducing anxiety and through this the frequency of sleep walking. It has the advantage of being a relatively simple, non-invasive and inexpensive treatment. Sleep walking may also be associated with depression, in which case **SSRIs** such as Prozac can be effective. Some chronic sleep walkers suffer from **sleep-disordered breathing (SDB)**; Guilleminault et al. (2005) report that if this is treated, either by nasal continuous positive airway pressure (CPAP) or surgery, the sleep walking stops completely.

Summary

- Sleep walking is relatively common in **children**, but affects only around 2% of **adults**.
- It is associated with **stress**, **depression** and **trauma**. There may also be some **genetic** basis.
- On rare occasions, sleep walkers may harm others. **Sleep driving**, however, is being increasingly reported.
- Sufferers may be treated with **anxiolytics**, **hypnosis**, **SSRIs** or — in the case of breathing difficulties — with **CPAP**.

Narcolepsy

Narcolepsy affects about 0.05% of the population, around 1 in 2,000 people. In narcolepsy, problems in the brain mechanisms that control sleep and waking allow REM sleep to break through into waking consciousness. Symptoms include excessive daytime sleepiness and sufferers may experience **cataplexy**; they suddenly lose muscle tone so their arms and legs go limp, or they may collapse or fall as though they have suddenly fallen asleep. However, they remain conscious, so it is as if they are asleep and awake at the same time. Cataplectic attacks can last for a few seconds or for several minutes and may occur several times a day. The attacks appear to be triggered by emotions, such as fear or amusement, or by sexual arousal. In contrast to the normal sleep cycle, where REM sleep does not occur for an hour or so after falling asleep, narcoleptics experience REM sleep soon after falling asleep. This limits the amount of NREM sleep they get, which accounts for their daytime sleepiness. They also experience sleep paralysis, either at the start or at the end of a night's sleep, which may be accompanied by hallucinations.

However, the symptoms experienced by narcoleptics vary considerably, for example in the amount of sleepiness they experience. Some have disabling cataplexy, whereas others have no cataplexy at all, or only rare episodes. Usually patients with unexplained sleepiness, sleep-onset REM, sleep paralysis and hallucinations are diagnosed as narcoleptic even if they do not experience cataplexy, and the same disease process seems to be at work, whether or not patients experience cataplexy.

There is a strong genetic component in the development of narcolepsy. De Lecea et al. (1998) identified two peptides, synthesised only in the hypothalamus and which are now referred to as **hypocretins**, hypocretin-1 and hypocretin-2, sometimes also referred to as **orexins**. They are derived from a single gene and the disorder is the result of mutations in the genes synthesising these peptides or their receptors;

Parkes and Lock (1989) report that the genetic defect in narcolepsy has been located on the short arm of chromosome 6.

Thannickal et al. (2000) proposed that damage to the hypocretin system might be the cause of narcolepsy, i.e. that hypocretin-producing cells in the lateral hypothalamus are selectively destroyed in people who are genetically susceptible. This was supported in their study that examined the dead brains of narcoleptics and compared them with the brains of controls. They found a huge loss of hypocretin neurons in the brains of narcoleptics — on average a 93% reduction — compared with controls. This suggests that giving injections of hypocretin could help to alleviate the symptoms and John et al. (2000) found it indeed to be effective in reducing cataplexy in dogs, providing it was given in a carefully judged amount and in a specific area.

However, a genetic abnormality is not necessarily expressed, in other words carrying a gene for narcolepsy does not necessarily mean that a person will develop the disorder. The extent of genetic influence in the development of narcolepsy has been explored (see Box 1.14).

Box 1.14   Ohayon et al. (2005)

Aim: To establish the extent of genetic influence on the development of narcolepsy.

Procedure: A survey was carried out, using telephone interviews of 157 narcoleptics, 263 of their first-degree relatives and a matched group of controls. In addition 68 spouses of narcoleptics were also surveyed.

Results: Among the first-degree relatives of narcoleptics, 10.8% were also narcoleptic, with a much lower rate among controls. They were also more at risk than controls for other sleep disorders, such as sleep talking and sleep apnoea.

Conclusion: Genes are an important factor in narcolepsy.

The influence of environmental factors on the development of narcolepsy has also been investigated (see Box 1.15).

Box 1.15   Picchioni et al. (2007)

Aim: To assess the effects of environmental factors on the development of narcolepsy.

Procedure: Participants were 63 narcoleptics and 63 non-narcoleptic controls. They completed a questionnaire to assess the frequency and timing of stressors and infections.

Results: Several stressors, including a major change in sleeping habits, carried a significant risk. Among the infectious diseases that were investigated, only flu infections and unexplained fevers carried a significant risk. For both kinds of risk factors, exposure before puberty increased the risk of developing narcolepsy.

Conclusion: Environmental factors are important in the risk of developing narcolepsy.

It has also been suggested that a high body mass index (BMI) and a compromised immune system may play a part in the development of narcolepsy. However, it is not clear whether the associations that have been found between these factors and narcolepsy are a result of the disorder, rather than a cause.

Summary

- **Narcolepsy** is a relatively rare disorder as a result of problems with the mechanisms of sleep and waking. Some narcoleptics also experience **cataplexy**.
- There is a strong **genetic** component related to peptides called **hypocretins**.
- **Environmental factors** such as **stress** are also important.

Chapter 2

Perception

In this chapter, we will be looking at:

- theories of perceptual organisation
  - Gregory's theory
  - Gibson's theory
- the development of perception
  - depth and distance perception
  - visual constancies
  - the development of perception in infants
  - cross-cultural studies of perception
  - the nature–nurture debate in perception
- face recognition and visual agnosias
  - Bruce and Young's theory of face recognition
  - prosopagnosia

We first need to define what is meant by perception. Information reaches the sense organs from the outside world and generates signals in the form of electro-chemical changes, which are then transmitted by nerve fibres to the brain. A certain amount of immediate processing at the level of the sense organs is carried out before this information is transmitted. Perception refers to these sensations being organised and interpreted by the brain, enabling us to make sense of the outside world.

Perception relates to all the senses, but we will be focusing in this chapter on visual perception. This is the dominant sense in human beings and far more is known about it than the other senses.

Theories of perceptual organisation

There are several theories of perception, which vary in terms of the relative importance given to different kinds of processing. Some psychologists emphasise the importance in explaining perception by starting with the analysis of sensory inputs. This information is then transmitted to higher levels of analysis, so that sensory information builds up to a mental representation. This is data-driven or **bottom-up processing**, since perception is driven by sensory data. This is a broadly nativist or 'nature' approach, since it suggests that everything necessary for perception could be in the stimulus or built into the perceptual processing systems.

Other theorists claim that sensory information is not enough to explain perception, since this information is fragmentary and may be ambiguous. They emphasise the importance of stored knowledge in processing sensory information. This is called context-driven or **top-down processing**, since knowledge and expectations work downwards to influence how we interpret sensory inputs. This is an empiricist, or 'nurture' approach, since it stresses the role of prior experience in perception.

Gregory's theory

Gregory (1966) takes a top-down approach to explaining perception. He claims that we construct our perceptions 'from floating, fragmentary scraps of data signalled to the senses and drawn from the brain memory banks, themselves constructions from the snippets of the past'. Gregory's theory is a **constructivist** model because it claims that we actively construct our perception of reality, drawing on past knowledge and experience. What we perceive goes beyond the often incomplete sensory information received through the sense organs. We may also select which aspects of the visual input we attend to. Gregory suggests that we form a **perceptual hypothesis**, make a 'best bet' about what we see and then check this hypothesis against the available data.

The idea of **perceptual set** provides some evidence for these ideas. This refers to a bias to interpret visual stimuli in a particular way, depending on the context. For example, Bruner and Minturn (1955) found that participants were more likely to perceive the fourth item in this sequence:

$$E \; C \; D \; B \; A$$

as a B and in this sequence:

$$16 \; 15 \; 14 \; 13 \; 12$$

as 13, although they are identical.

There is evidence from **cross-cultural studies** that perception is influenced by experience and we will be returning to this later in the chapter.

Some **visual illusions** offer support for context-dependent ideas. For example the Zollner illusion and Titchener's circles (Figure 2.1) demonstrate the effect of context on what we perceive. In the Zollner illusion, the long diagonal lines are parallel and the central circles of Titchener's illusion are the same size, but the context leads us to perceive otherwise. The checkerboard illusion, where the squares marked A and B are identical, is a good example of both context and brightness constancy.

Figure 2.1 (a) Zollner illusion; (b) Titchener's circles; (c) checkerboard illusion

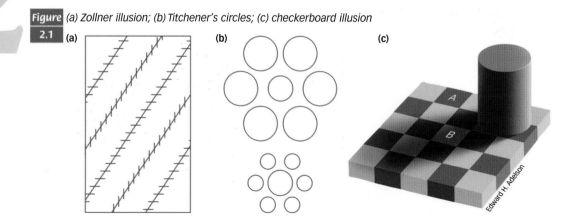

We attempt to make sense of some visual illusions in the same way that we normally make sense of our visual environment, but in the case of illusions, these attempts are misleading. Some illusions are examples of inappropriate perceptual hypotheses that are not confirmed by the data.

In the Ponzo illusion (Figure 2.2), the upper horizontal line appears longer than the lower one, although they are the same length. This can be explained in terms of our past experience of using depth cues provided by perspective. For example,

Figure 2.2 Ponzo illusion

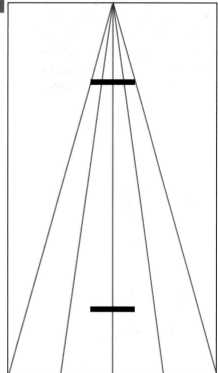

we know that the railway sleepers lying across a track are of equal length. Those farther away appear shorter, but the perceptual system takes into account the distance of an object from the person perceiving it and we automatically compensate for this in making sense of what we see. This is called **size constancy** and we will be looking at this in more detail in a later section.

Similarly, in the Müller-Lyer illusion (Figure 2.3), the left vertical line appears shorter than the right one, although they are the same length. Gregory suggests that we interpret the figure in terms of our knowledge and exprience of the world and see the two sets of lines as two three-dimensional figures representing corners. The receding corner on the left is seen as further away, so size constancy adjusts for this, resulting in us seeing the line on the left as longer.

Gregory's theory assumes that our knowledge of the world influences what we perceive. If this is the case, it would be expected that people with different experiences might perceive illusions

Figure 2.3 *The Müller-Lyer illusion*

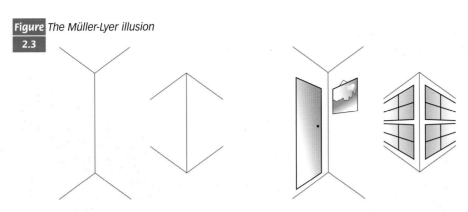

differently. Segall et al. (1963) tested people from a number of different cultures on the Müller-Lyer illusion and found that those least susceptible were the Bete people who live in a dense rainforest environment, with relatively few corners.

While there is evidence to support Gregory's theory and it is appealing in that it provides an explanatory framework suggesting how we integrate bottom-up information from our senses with top-down information based on experience, there are some problems. His interpretation of the Müller-Lyer illusion in terms of misplaced size constancy has been challenged by other research. Delboeuf (1892) used variants of the Müller-Lyer illusion, shown in Figure 2.4.

In these variants, the illusion still works and it is difficult to see how this could be explained in terms of corners. An alternative interpretation, put forward by Day (1989), suggested that we see the illusion as a result of **perceptual compromise**; we judge the length of the lines as a compromise between their actual length and the length of the overall figure. This is a simple explanation, with everything required for perception being present in the stimulus, with no need to draw on stored knowledge.

Figure 2.4 *Modified Müller-Lyer figures*

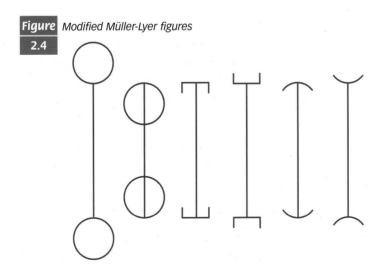

A more general problem with Gregory's theory is that knowledge may not lead us to modify our perceptions. For example, even when we know that the two lines of the Müller-Lyer are the same length, the illusion still persists. We are not able to change our perceptual hypothesis in the light of additional information as Gregory suggested. Simply knowing that a perception is inaccurate cannot remove the illusion; clearly 'visual knowledge' is incorporated at an unconscious level. It has been argued that Gregory underestimates the richness of the information that reaches our senses by his use of deliberately impoverished stimuli; this is the focus of Gibson's theory, which is looked at next.

Summary

- Sensory information must be processed and organised by the brain for perception to take place.
- Gregory's **constructivist** theory takes a **top-down approach**, suggesting that perception draws on **stored knowledge**.
- We form **perceptual hypotheses** that are then checked against sensory data.
- **Visual illusions**, seen as inappropriate hypotheses, lend support to Gregory's theory. It is also supported by the phenomenon of **perceptual set** and by **cross-cultural studies**.
- Gregory's theory cannot explain some perceptual phenomena.

Gibson's theory

Gibson's (1955) theory of **direct perception** contrasts with Gregory's theory in that it proposes that incoming sensory information is rich and contains everything needed for perception without any integration of stored knowledge. There is no need for any kind of processing, since the information we receive about size, shape, distance and so on is sufficiently detailed to allow us to interact directly with the environment. No interpretation needs to take place and no hypotheses need to be formed. For Gibson, sensation is perception. This approach is in tune with bottom-up theories of perception, although strictly speaking it is not a bottom-up theory, since Gibson claims no processing is necessary for perception to take place.

Gibson developed his theory as a result of his experience in training pilots. During the Second World War, he was asked to provide training films for pilots and in particular to focus on the problems experienced by pilots on take-off and landing. These two manoeuvres require skill and concentration and Gibson became interested in researching just what information pilots had available to them at these times; he called this information **optic flow patterns**.

Gibson pointed out just how much information was available. The point to which the pilot is moving is **invariant** (static within the display) but all around that point is a moving display giving a great deal of unambiguous information about speed, direction and altitude. He also stressed the importance of **texture gradients**; for example, the textured nature of stones on a beach is more apparent at close range

Figure 2.5 *Optic flow patterns as a pilot approaches a landing strip*

and less so further away. This is a rich source of cues about depth and distance without any need for analysis.

Gibson emphasises the dynamic nature of perception. We do not perceive a sequence of static images, but rather a dynamic ever-changing scene with aspects of the environment being seen from different perspectives as we (and they) move about. Because of this movement, there are continuous changes in what Gibson calls the **ambient optic array** — all the transmitted and reflected light rays from the environment — and these changes provide us with new information.

Gibson called his theory an **ecological approach**, since it emphasises the direct contact between the perceiver and meaningful aspects of the environment. He sees this as adaptive, in terms of promoting survival. This seems plausible in the area of instinctive, visually-guided behaviour. Bruce et al. (1996) give the example of a frog trying to catch a fly with its tongue. All it needs to do is to sense a small flying object and to use that sensory information to guide the tongue to catch it. It can just sense and react. It does not need to develop perceptual hypotheses, which would in any case be counter-productive, since an immediate response is required if it is to catch the fly.

The frog simply needs to sense and react to catch the fly

Arco Images GmbH/Alamy

Another aspect of this approach is Gibson's concept of **affordances**, which relates to the function of different aspects of the environment — the possible uses something affords, such as for shelter or use as a tool.

The main strength of Gibson's theory is its ecological approach, in that it relates to the perceptual experience of people and animals in real-life situations. He is right to point out that we spend a lot of our time in motion, producing moment-by-moment changes in the optic array, which increase the richness of sensory data available to us. This is in stark contrast to the impoverished visual information in the artificial setting of many laboratory experiments. For example, Gibson sees the illusions that are so easily explained by Gregory's theory as essentially coming about as the result of deliberately ambiguous information in artificial situations. Day's explanation of the Müller-Lyer illusion, mentioned previously, is a good example of an explanation that does not draw on stored knowledge; everything is there in the stimulus. However, many visual illusions do seem to rely on stored knowledge to be perceived.

There is a serious problem with Gibson's claim that no processing is needed to analyse the visual world. According to Hampson and Morris (1996), neurophysiological studies have shown that quite a lot of processing of the visual input occurs before perception can take place. Gibson's theory also has problems in explaining the influence of perceptual set, mentioned earlier, and cannot explain cultural influences on perception, for example the study of the Bete people referred to in the section on Gregory's theory. We will be looking at cultural differences in perception in more detail later in this chapter.

The links made between animals and humans may not be entirely appropriate. Many animals seem to be preprogrammed to attend and respond to particular aspects of their environment that are relevant to such activities as homing behaviour. A lot of human behaviour, on the other hand, is governed by higher-order cognitive processes, such as remembering and planning, between stimulus and response. The parallel between humans and other animals seems particularly weak in relation to the notion of affordances. Clearly we need to draw on relevant cultural knowledge to understand that a pen affords writing and a washing machine affords cleaning clothes.

Gibson's theory seems better at explaining some aspects of perception than others. This can be related to the distinction drawn by Fodor and Pylyshyn (1981) between 'seeing' and 'seeing as'. They illustrate this with the example of a man lost at sea who sees the Pole Star. If he sees it as just another star ('seeing'), he will be just as lost as ever. If he sees it as the Pole Star ('seeing as'), it is a potential navigational aid that could help him to find his way. Gibson's theory is better at explaining 'seeing' than 'seeing as'. The theories of Gregory and Gibson are therefore not necessarily mutually exclusive. It seems reasonable to conclude that they are explaining different aspects of perception.

One theory that attempts to combine the best of both approaches is Neisser's cyclic theory (see Figure 2.6). In Neisser's theory, top-down and bottom-up processes are

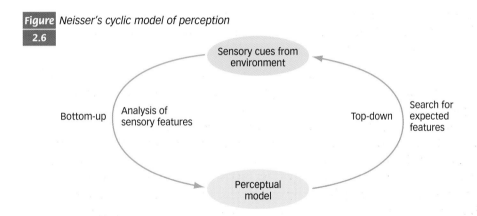

Figure 2.6 *Neisser's cyclic model of perception*

Sensory cues from environment

Bottom-up

Analysis of sensory features

Top-down

Search for expected features

Perceptual model

used in a continuing cycle in perception. He proposes that perception starts with **schemas**; these are ideas and expectations of what we expect to see in a particular context. Schemas influence the way we explore our perceptual environment as we seek to confirm our expectations. We sample the information available in the environment in an initial analysis of the sensory cues and on this basis we form a **perceptual model**, that is, a mental representation of a likely object or event.

The perceptual model is then used to initiate an active search of the sensory cues in the environment. If sensory cues confirm the perceptual model, there is an **elaborative effect**, i.e. details are added to the model. If not, the model is revised and there is a **corrective effect**. Perception therefore involves a continuous process of checking and rechecking sensory data in line with the perceptual model we have formed. Neisser calls his model an **analysis-by-synthesis** theory, since perception involves extracting information about aspects of the environment (analysis) and generating a perceptual model (synthesis) as a cyclical process.

A major strength of Neisser's model is that it attempts to show the interaction of top-down and bottom-up processing; we have already seen that both have a part to play in perception. There is much in common with Gregory's idea of perceptual hypotheses, although according to Neisser's model, the hypotheses we form are much more general than those proposed by Gregory. Another positive point is that it makes links to attention, in that the process of checking sensory data is directed towards aspects of the environment that are relevant to the perceptual model we have formed.

However, there are some limitations to the model. As with the models of Gregory and Gibson, it does not specify the neural mechanisms involved and so provides a broad framework rather than a detailed explanation of how a perception is built up. There is also the issue of the point in the cycle at which perception can be said to have taken place; does this happen with the initial hypothesis, or not until the perception is fully confirmed? There are further problems when it comes to trying to test this theory in a natural environment; given the cyclical nature of perception, it is difficult to see how this could be done.

2

Summary

- Gibson's theory of **direct perception** claims there is enough information in the **ambient optic array** for no processing to be necessary for perception.
- **Affordances** — the function of objects in the environment — are also perceived directly, though this may be more true of animals than humans.
- The main strength of the theory is its **ecological approach**, pointing up the artificiality of many **laboratory experiments**.
- It is challenged by **neurophysiological evidence** that processing takes place and is better at explaining 'seeing' than 'seeing as'.
- The theories of Gregory and Gibson may be explaining **different aspects of perception**.
- Neisser's **cyclical model** attempts to bring together the theories of Gregory and Gibson. However, there are issues about the **depth of analysis**. The theory is **difficult to test**.

The development of perception

In this section, we will be looking at the development of various aspects of perception, in particular depth and distance perception and the visual constancies and what studies of infants and across cultures can tell us about their perceptual development.

Depth and distance perception

Although the retinal image is two-dimensional, humans perceive the world in three dimensions. The retina of each eye receives slightly different information, as each eye is in a different position on the face. However, the brain builds up the information from both eyes into a single three-dimensional perception. This ability to see objects in three dimensions is depth perception, and the cues we use can be **monocular**, using information from just one retinal image, or **binocular**, using information from both retinal images together.

There are a number of monocular cues. One is **linear perspective**. Lines appear to converge as they get further away, for example railway lines stretching into the distance, which influences perceived distance. Another cue is **relative size**. For example, if you can see a tree and a cat and they both produce retinal images of the same size, you can infer that the tree is further away, as you know that a tree is larger than a cat. There is also **interposition**. An object that blocks the full view of another object is perceived to be in front of it.

If you look out of the window from a moving car or train, objects that are closer appear to move across your field of vision more quickly than those that are further away. This is **motion parallax** and provides a further monocular cue to distance. As we noted earlier in the section on Gibson's theory, the **texture** of objects such as cobbles on a street also appears to be smoother when they are further away than close to.

A shadow is a cue that an object is three-dimensional

Only three-dimensional objects cast **shadows**, so a shadow can be a cue that an object is three-dimensional, thus providing a cue to depth. Relative **brightness** and **colour** cues provide information about distance. Objects closer to us reflect more light to the eyes than those further away, and the colour of closer objects is perceived as more intense.

A final cue is **accommodation**. The lenses of the eyes change shape when we focus on objects at different distances. They become thicker when the object is close to and flatten when it is further away. So we are able to assess distance by attending to the degree of pull exerted by the muscles controlling lens thickness.

One binocular cue is **convergence**; when we focus on closer objects, the eyes turn inward to a greater extent, so that when you try to focus on the end of your nose, the eyes converge so much that you become cross-eyed. The degree of convergence provides the brain with information about distance.

Stereopsis is the process the brain uses to put together the information from the two retinal images to create a single three-dimensional image. This provides more information about distance because of **retinal disparity**, the degree of difference between the images received by each eye.

Visual constancies

We recognise objects in spite of variations in the information that reaches our eyes. For example, we may see a cup from the side or from the top, close to us or further away and in bright or dim light. All these views provide different retinal information, but the cup is still seen as a cup. The ability to perceive an object as unchanging, in spite of changes in the sensory information that reaches the eyes, is known as perceptual **constancy**.

There are a number of visual constancies. For example, with **shape constancy**, we tend to see an object as the same shape in spite of changes in the angle from which we see it. For example, a door that is ajar projects a trapezoid image, but we still perceive it as rectangular.

In **colour constancy**, an object is perceived as the same colour when viewed in different light conditions. We seem to be able to compensate for darkness and even for coloured light shining on an object and still make reasonably accurate judgements about its colour. For example, colours appear much the same whether or not you are wearing sunglasses.

We see objects as having more or less constant brightness in spite of changes in lighting conditions. This is **brightness constancy**. If illumination is constant, white things reflect more light than black things. However, snow still appears white even when it is in deep shadow, and coal still appears black in bright sunlight.

We have already referred to **size constancy** in the discussion of Gregory's theory of perception, perceiving an object as the same size when we see it at different distances. As we look at a person walking away from us, the retinal image of the person becomes smaller, but we do not perceive them as actually getting smaller. Instead, our perceptual system interprets the apparent change in size in terms of the change in location of a person of constant size.

Summary

- Although the retinal image is two-dimensional, we see the world in **three dimensions**.
- **Monocular cues** to **depth** and distance perception include linear **perspective**, **relative size**, **interposition**, **motion parallax**, **brightness** and **colour** cues and **accommodation**.
- **Convergence** and **stereopsis**, coming about through **retinal disparity**, are **binocular cues**.
- **Visual constancy** refers to our ability to see things as unchanging in spite of variation in the sensory information that reaches our eyes. This includes constancies of **shape**, **colour**, **brightness** and **size**.

The development of perception in infants

A great deal of research has been carried out to investigate the development of perception in infants. At birth, visual perception is the least developed of the senses; much of the visual system matures after birth. For example, cells in the retina are not as densely packed as they will be after several months, and the muscles of the lens, which allow us to adjust our focus to varying distances of objects, are weak although by 3 months infants can focus as well as adults (Clavadetscher et al. 1988).

Visual acuity is limited. Courage and Adams (1990) found that newborns perceive objects at a distance of 20 feet about as clearly as adults do at 660 feet; this improves steadily during the first year. Unlike adults, who see nearby objects most clearly, newborns' vision is equally unclear across a range of distances, so that the mother's face, even when seen from close to, is a blur. They are not yet good at discriminating colours, but by 2 months they can discriminate colours across the entire spectrum.

Research with infants is difficult, since they are not yet able to communicate with us, but psychologists have developed some ingenious methods for establishing infants' perceptual abilities. A major breakthrough came with Fantz's idea of observing how much time babies spend looking at different visual stimuli. He reasoned that if babies consistently look at some things rather than others, they must be able to perceive differences between them and developed a 'viewing chamber' to investigate the development of infants' visual perception.

Using this apparatus, babies are presented with two stimuli at a time and the length of fixation on each stimulus is recorded by observing the infant's direction of gaze and corneal reflection, i.e. the reflection of the stimulus over the cornea of the eye. This method is known as **forced-choice preferential looking**. It has been used to assess infants' **visual acuity**.

Up to the age of 1 month, infants only show a visual preference for stripes over a grey square when shown the thickest set of stripes in Figure 2.7, which suggests that they are not yet able to discriminate between the two. Acuity gradually improves until at 6 months they are able to discriminate the finest set of stripes from a grey square.

Figure 2.7 *Stimuli to test the development of visual acuity in infants*

A classic study investigated **depth perception** in infants (see Box 2.1).

Box 2.1   Gibson and Walk (1960)

Aim: To investigate depth perception in infants.

Procedure: The researchers developed a 'visual cliff', consisting of a central board laid across a heavy sheet of plate glass, supported about a metre above the floor. On one side, there was a checkerboard surface directly below the glass, while on the other the checkerboard surface was at floor level, creating a deep visual drop. Babies aged from 6 months to 1 year were placed on the central board and their mothers were asked to encourage them to crawl across both the visually solid and the visual cliff sides.

Results: All 27 infants crawled over the visually solid side, but only 3 crawled over the visual cliff side. This was in spite of it being perfectly safe and some infants reaching out and patting the glass above the drop.

Conclusion: By 6 months, babies have depth perception.

The visual cliff

Another study looked at infants' ability to use monocular cues to judge depth in pictures (see Box 2.2).

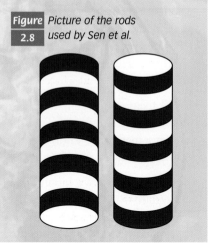

Figure 2.8 *Picture of the rods used by Sen et al.*

A further method used in the study of infants' abilities is the **familiarisation/novelty preference technique**. An infant who has seen the same stimulus a number of times loses interest in it, a process known as **habituation**. When infants are then shown the same stimulus together with a new stimulus, they are more likely to look at the new stimulus. This suggests that the infant has learned about the previously familiarised stimulus and can discriminate it from the new stimulus. This method has been used to investigate **size constancy** in infants (see Box 2.3).

Summary

- The **visual system** is immature at birth and continues to develop over the early months.
- **Visual acuity** improves in the first months after birth.
- The 'visual cliff' study demonstrated **depth perception** in 6-month-old infants. They are also capable of using **pictorial depth cues**.
- Babies only 2 days old show **size constancy**.

Cross-cultural studies of perception

Cross-cultural studies have identified a variety of cultural differences in perception. There is evidence to show that the ways in which we perceive the world are influenced by cultural factors.

Several studies have used visual illusions to investigate cultural differences in perception. Probably the earliest study in this area was carried out by Rivers (1901), who found that Murray Islanders were less susceptible than English participants to the Müller-Lyer illusion (Figure 2.3). A similar study carried out by Segall et al. (1963), made several comparisons (see Box 2.4).

Box 2.4 | **Segall et al. (1963)**

Aims: To compare the susceptibility to visual illusions of members of different cultures.

Procedure: Three African cultures, the Batoro and Bayankole who live in open country and the Bete who live in dense rainforest, together with Filipinos, South Africans of European descent and Americans, were tested on the Müller-Lyer illusion and the horizontal-vertical illusion, where the vertical line appears longer, although the two lines are the same length.

Results: The non-European Africans and Filipinos were less susceptible to the Müller-Lyer illusion than the other groups. On the horizontal-vertical illusion, the Batoro and Bayankole were the most susceptible and the Bete the least susceptible.

Figure 2.9 *Horizontal-vertical illusion*

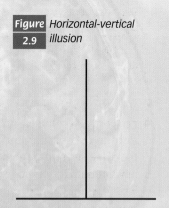

Conclusion: The results for the horizontal-vertical illusion can be explained in terms of the open country where the Batoro and Bayankole live. This makes it possible to see for long distances, so vertical objects are important indicators of distance and so an important part of visual experience. The opposite is true of the Bete who live in dense rainforest.

Based on these findings, which highlighted the importance of context on perception, Segall et al. (1963) put forward the **carpentered world hypothesis**. It was suggested earlier that the Müller-Lyer illusion could be interpreted as two three-dimensional figures representing corners. Segall suggested that people in Western cultures live in an environment full of straight lines, in which most retinal images of lines meeting at an angle can realistically be interpreted, using shape constancy, as right angles; we add the extra dimension of depth that is not actually there and so are susceptible to illusions such as the Müller-Lyer. People who live in an environment that does not trigger this kind of interpretation are therefore less susceptible to this illusion.

Some studies have supported Segall's hypothesis. For example, in a study of Native Americans, Annis and Frost (1973) found that the Cree who lived in a non-carpentered environment were good at making judgements about whether two lines were parallel, irrespective of the angle at which the lines were shown; while Cree living in a carpentered environment were good at judging vertical and horizontal lines, they were less good when the lines were at other angles. However, the results of a study by Jahoda (1966), which tested Ghanaians, and one by Gregor and McPherson (1965), with Australian Aborigines, were not in line with what this hypothesis would predict. Illusions have not been the only method of investigating cultural differences in perception. Pictorial material has also been used (see Box 2.5).

Box 2.5 Hudson et al. (1960)

Aim: To investigate pictorial depth perception in African cultures.

Procedure: People from several African cultures were shown pictures similar to this and asked questions about it, such as which animal was nearer to the man and at which animal the man was aiming his spear.

Results: The participants believed that the elephant was closer to the man and that the man was aiming his spear at the elephant.

Conclusion: People from these cultures did not see the picture as a two-dimensional representation of a three-dimensional scene. They did not perceive depth in this picture.

However, the methodology of the Hudson et al. study is open to question. One problem is the relative lack of depth cues in Hudson's material. You may remember that there are a number of potential sources of information about depth other than those used by Hudson. Serpell (1976) described a study by Kingsley et al. in which texture gradients were added to Hudson's pictures. This made it more likely that the Zambian children who were tested would give answers to pictorial material based on a three-dimensional interpretation. The nature of the presentation is also problematic. Deregowski (1972) found that the Me'en of Ethiopia were better at recognising pictorial representations on cloth, which they were used to, rather than unfamiliar paper, and when there were no distractions such as borders.

Figure 2.10 *Top views of an elephant — 'split elephant' and top-view perspective*

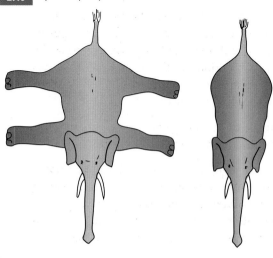

Serpell went on to suggest it could be that cultural differences in perception might instead be stylistic preferences. Deregowski (1972) found that several cultures preferred the 'split elephant' to the top-view perspective (Figure 2.10), though one person was not keen on the split elephant, which seemed to him to be jumping around dangerously.

There are also conventions in pictorial representation that differ between cultures; these conventions could be confusing to someone from another culture. For example, Duncan et al. (1973) tested rural African children on pictures such as the one shown in Figure 2.11.

Figure 2.11 Conventions in Western pictorial representation

Here, the Western conventions, such as the use of stars in the picture to show the person has been stunned and the curved lines to indicate a staggering movement, were not understood by the African children. In the same way, a Western observer would not understand that in ancient Egyptian art, a figure with feet apart depicts a live person, while one with feet together means the person is dead.

Summary

- There are differences between cultures in susceptibility to **visual illusions**. One explanation is the **carpentered world hypothesis**, though research evidence is ambiguous.
- Studies using **pictures** have found differences in **depth perception**. However, there are **methodological issues** with these studies. The results could also be interpreted in terms of differing **stylistic preferences** and **pictorial conventions**.

The nature–nurture debate in perception

The nature–nurture debate is an issue in many areas of psychology. The extreme 'nature' position takes the view that human characteristics and abilities are genetically determined and innate — we are born with them and they will emerge as the result of maturation. The extreme 'nurture' position, on the other hand, proposes that little is innate — perhaps just a few simple reflexes — and that human development is shaped almost entirely by environmental influences.

However, such extreme positions are rare, since it is clear that both genes and environment, in interaction with each other, are important to development.

In the area of perception, the question is more to do with identifying what perceptual abilities seem to be preprogrammed, either being present at birth or emerging independently of experience as an infant matures, and in what ways perception is shaped by our experience of developing within a particular environment. Research into infants' abilities and cross-cultural research can provide useful information.

As we saw in the section on the development of infant abilities, there is considerable evidence on the 'nature' side of the argument. The visual system matures, to a large extent, after birth, improving infants' ability to focus and their visual acuity over the early months; this appears to follow a regular pattern in which the environment plays little part. Slater's study demonstrated size constancy (Box 2.3) in 2-day-old infants, who would have had little time to learn from experience, particularly given that they were likely to have been asleep for most of the 2 days.

Other aspects of infant perception and in particular preferences also seem to be innate. Using variations of Fantz's technique, mentioned earlier, several studies have found that infants when only 2–3 days old prefer moving stimuli to stationary ones and three-dimensional objects to photographs of the same objects. These preferences would make sense, since they would supply information about the real world the infant experiences.

Further evidence that infants are born with an ability to discriminate and a predisposition to attend to certain aspects of their visual environment comes from Bushnell (2003), who found that infants just 12 hours old would spend more time looking at their mother's face when she was paired with a stranger with a generally similar face. This would make sense from an evolutionary point of view, since it would be adaptive in terms of promoting survival.

There is, however, evidence that some aspects of perception may be acquired through experience. As shown in the study by Sen et al. (Box 2.2), the ability to use **pictorial depth cues** is absent at 5 months, but has been developed by 7 months, when the child has had more experience of the environment. Baillargeon (1993) reports studies showing that babies are beginning to understand about **interposition** — mentioned earlier in the section on depth perception — by about 2 months. By around 5–6 months they are beginning to realise that two touching objects are two objects and not one, and by around 6–8 months they have learned about support and gravity, for example that an object hanging off the end of a table should fall. This was the age of the babies tested on the 'visual cliff' in the Gibson and Walk study (Box 2.1). Campos et al. (1992) carried out a 'visual cliff' experiment with younger babies and found that when infants first start to crawl, they will happily cross the 'deep' side, suggesting that experience of moving about is necessary for a wariness of heights to develop.

Cross-cultural research also supports a 'nurture' argument; if there are differences between cultures, the development of perception cannot simply be the result of maturation. Cultural differences reported in studies of susceptibility to visual illusions, such as Segall et al. (Box 2.4), support the view that visual perception is affected by the physical environment in which a person develops. Studies using pictorial material, such as Hudson et al. (1960) suggest that cultural conventions also have an influence.

Overall, it appears that some aspects of visual perception are innate and while not fully present at birth, will develop following a regular pattern as an individual matures. Other aspects rely on experience of both the physical world and the cultural context within which development takes place.

Summary

- The **nature–nurture debate** relates to the extent to which characteristics are **innate** or the result of **experience**.
- In infants, some aspects of visual perception are innate and develop through **maturational processes**. Others develop through experience.
- Cross-cultural studies show that visual perception is influenced by the **physical** and **cultural environment**.

Face recognition and visual agnosias

Being able to recognise familiar faces is of great importance to us; imagine what it would be like not to be able to recognise your mother, best friend or partner. Humans have an amazing ability to recognise faces. Standing (1973) showed participants 10,000 faces over a period of 5 days, then showed them pairs of faces, one of which they had been shown previously and one of which was new. They could identify the faces they had been shown 95% of the time. Psychologists are interested in explaining the systems that underlie this ability.

Usually, when we fully recognise a face we also recall other information about the person, including their name. For example, when we meet a friend, we may recall that his name is Chris, that he works for a law firm and that he plays the guitar. Any theory of face recognition must therefore include our ability to put a name to a face and remember personal details.

Different areas of the brain are involved in different aspects of face recognition. Regions of the **temporal lobes** of the cortex specialise in face recognition and in rare cases damage to this area can lead to **prosopagnosia**, the inability to recognise familiar faces. This disorder will be looked at in more detail later in this chapter. A subcortical area called the **limbic system**, where emotional responses to familiar faces are generated, is also involved. Problems in this area can lead to **Capgras syndrome**; patients with this syndrome recognise familiar people, but the emotions associated with the person are missing. Patients may deal with this mismatch between face and emotion by believing that those close to them have been replaced by impostors, or even by aliens. Blount (1986) refers to the case of a man who was so convinced that his father had been replaced by a humanoid robot that he slit his father's throat to find the wires.

Bruce and Young's theory of face recognition

Prosopagnosia and Capgras syndrome are extreme examples of what can happen when the face recognition system fails to function properly; less extreme cases can also shed light on the system. Young et al. (1986) asked volunteers to keep a diary

of any errors they made in person recognition. The findings suggested that there must be at least three separate systems involved in face recognition:

- Stored representations are held in a **face-recognition** system.
- A **semantic** system holds information about people, such as where they live, their jobs and interests.
- A third system stores **names**.

On the basis of this and other research into face recognition, Bruce and Young (1986) developed a model of face recognition.

In this model, each box represents a separate processing mechanism or store, with arrows representing the flow of information between them. Working down the right-hand side of the model, information is first encoded. This information is **expression-independent**, first because we recognise faces irrespective of their expression and second because there is clinical evidence that faces and emotional expression are processed separately. Some patients can recognise faces but not emotions, while others can recognise emotions but not faces.

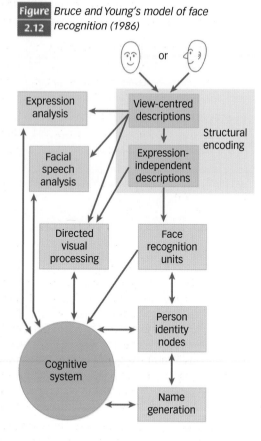

Figure 2.12 *Bruce and Young's model of face recognition (1986)*

Recognising hair colour is one aspect used to help find someone in a crowded room

This structural encoding stimulates the **face recognition units (FRUs)**. The closer the correspondence between the face that is seen and information stored in a FRU, the stronger the activation will be. The FRUs are linked to both the **cognitive system** and to **person identity nodes (PINs)**. Face recognition makes available other information about the person from which identification can be made, such as their job or their hobbies. Information from the cognitive system to the PIN is included because we may often recognise someone using information other than their face, perhaps their voice or the way they walk. The PIN is the point at which recognising a person can be said to have taken place; after this **name generation** can occur.

The **directed visual processing** unit is included because we can choose to focus on certain aspects of a face. For example, if we are meeting a friend in a crowded bar, we may choose to look for someone with their hair colour. The **facial speech analysis** unit is included because there is clinical evidence that lip reading is a separate ability from face recognition, as some patients with brain damage can read lips but not recognise faces, while others can recognise faces but not lip read. This model can help to explain errors in person recognition (see Box 2.6).

Box 2.6   Young et al. (1986)

Aim: To identify the kinds of errors made in person recognition and to use this to model what happens in face recognition.

Procedure: Volunteers were asked to keep a diary of any errors made in person recognition.

Results: Most of the 1,008 incidents recorded fell into four main categories:
- Failure to recognise a familiar person. This typically happened when the person's appearance had changed, perhaps if they had grown a beard.
- Misidentifying one person as another. People thought they recognised a stranger. This was most likely to happen in poor viewing conditions.
- Recognising a person, but not being able to place them or remember their name. This was most likely to happen when the person was an acquaintance seen in an unfamiliar context, for example a familiar shop assistant seen in a doctor's surgery.
- Inability to remember someone's name. Even when the name was forgotten, some personal details were recalled, such as the person's job or where they were usually seen.

Conclusion: There are at least three separate systems involved in face recognition: a face recognition system, a semantic system that includes general information about people you know and a name system.

Using the Bruce and Young model, failure to recognise a familiar person because of a change in their appearance would come about as a result of there being insufficient stimulation of a FRU for the face to be recognised. For the second kind of error, misidentifying one person as another would happen because the person misidentified was sufficiently like the familiar person to activate a FRU inappropriately. Recognising a person but not being able to place them or remember their name would suggest that the relevant FRU has been activated, but the stimulation has not been sufficient to activate the cognitive system or the PIN and so retrieve more information about the person. Finally, inability to remember someone's name would suggest a problem at the final stage between the PIN and the name generation system.

The Bruce and Young model has triggered further research in this area. Burton et al. (1990) have used it to develop a model that can be simulated by a computer. Like the Bruce and Young model, this model has three separate groups of interlinked units, one for FRUs, one for PINs and one for semantic information. However, unlike the Bruce and Young model, semantic information is linked to PINs but not to FRUs. Recognition occurs when activation in the relevant PIN reaches a given threshold; this excitation is then transmitted to other parts of the system.

Figure 2.13 *Interactive activation model of face recognition. Burton et al. (1990)*

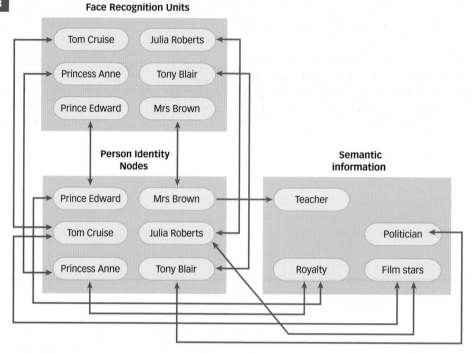

This model has been successful in replicating some of the findings of research into face recognition, for example **semantic priming**. Bruce and Valentine (1988) found that people recognised a familiar face more quickly if they had been primed by being shown another familiar associated face, for example the queen would be recognised more quickly if participants had first been shown a picture of Prince Charles. It has also simulated the **distinctiveness effect**, where people recognise a distinctive face more quickly than a more typical face. Distinctive faces share fewer features than more typical faces and this difference in shared features was incorporated into the model. When the model was run, the PINs for distinctive FRUs were more quickly and more strongly activated than those for more typical faces.

Unlike the Bruce and Young model, this one suggests there is no need for a separate name store. Burton and Bruce (1992) pointed out that unlike most semantic information about a person, their name is connected to only one PIN. For example, knowing that a person works for a law firm is information that applies to many people, but a person's name is likely to be a unique link between the name and the PIN. When the model was run, it was found that names received the least activation of all the semantic information units, which could account for the difficulty people have in remembering them.

Summary

- The Bruce and Young model of face recognition proposes three different interlinked systems: **FRUs**, **PINs** and **name generation**.
- **Structural encoding** stimulates the **FRUs**, which are linked to both the **cognitive system** and the **PINs**.
- The **PIN** is the point at which recognition takes place. After this, **name generation** can occur.
- The model has stimulated **further research**, for example the interactive activation model of Burton et al., which uses **computer simulation**.
- This model can account for a range of findings in face-recognition research.
- It suggests that a separate name generation module is not necessary.

Prosopagnosia

The agnosias ('failure to know') are a group of disorders of visual perception. The visual system is intact, but objects cannot be identified from drawings or by sight. However, if an object can be held, it can be identified, so the problem is a visual rather than a language difficulty. One special form of this is prosopagnosia (from '*prosopon*', the Greek for 'face'). People with prosopagnosia cannot recognise familiar faces and sometimes cannot even recognise their own face in a mirror. They can however recognise friends and family from their voices, so the problem is not that people have been forgotten.

It has been suggested that the problem arises through a more general difficulty in making fine discriminations, but research evidence challenges this idea. For example, De Renzi (1986) reports the case of a prosopagnosic man who could make fine discriminations between people's handwriting. Similarly, McNeil and Warrington (1991) report the case of a 51-year-old male patient with severe prosopagnosia. He became a farmer and learned to recognise and name many of his sheep, but could not recognise familiar people. Both these cases suggest that prosopagnosia is a face-specific disorder. However, some prosopagnosics also have difficulty in making discriminations in other categories, such as birds, fruit or cars. The theory now widely accepted links prosopagnosia with bilateral brain damage to the area where the occipital and temporal cortex meet, although cases have been reported where scans have identified damage only on one side. Lopera and Ardila (1992) carried out a detailed case study for more than 5 years (see Box 2.7).

Box 2.7	Lopera and Ardila (1992)

FE suffered head injuries in a car accident and was in a coma for 2 weeks. A CT scan showed occipito-temporal damage on the right side.

On recovering consciousness, he could not recognise his wife and children by their faces, only by their voices. He said that all faces looked the same: 'I see the mouth, nose, eyes, everything, but it doesn't have any meaning for me; even when I look at myself in the mirror, I just see the eyes, the mouth and so on, but nothing else; I can't even imagine how I was before.'

He experienced hypoemotionality (a lack of emotional feeling) for visual stimuli, but an increased emotional response to music. He could not discriminate flowers (although he had been interested in flowers before the accident), fruit (even by taste), animals and cars. He had total retrograde amnesia for the 6 months after the accident and mild anterograde amnesia, i.e. difficulty in remembering new information.

He was assessed again 5 years later. He had now returned to work part time. In spite of some improvement in the ability to match faces, he still experienced a lack of emotion to visual stimuli and a total failure in recognising faces and in learning new faces. He still had severe memory deficits.

Given the variation in the location and extent of brain damage and the range of symptoms shown by prosopagnosics, an explanation of the cause of prosopagnosia is difficult. Warrington and James (1967) interpret prosopagnosia as a perceptual problem where people have difficulty in making discriminations within a particular visual category. There is some support for this viewpoint from the other discrimination problems experienced by FE, but it only takes into account some of the symptoms; as with some other cases of prosopagnosia, FE had problems other than with face recognition.

Hypoemotionality is an interesting feature of the Lopera and Ardila study. It is not usually mentioned in cases of prosopagnosia, though there are some reports; Lopera and Ardila suggest that it may sometimes be overlooked. They point out that face recognition is closely related to emotional memory and that hypoemotionality may be related to the inability to assign individuality to familiar faces.

Summary

- Prosopagnosia is the inability to recognise **familiar faces**.
- Damage to areas of the **temporal** and **occipital lobes** of the brain are associated with the disorder.
- Patients may also experience other symptoms, such as **memory loss** and **hypoemotionality**.
- Explanation is difficult on account of **variation** in brain damage and symptoms.

Chapter

Relationships

In this chapter, we will be looking at:
- romantic relationships
  - the formation of relationships
  - the maintenance of relationships
  - the breakdown of relationships
- human reproductive behaviour
  - sexual selection
  - evolutionary explanations of parental investment
  - parent-offspring conflict
- the effects of early experience on adult relationships
  - childhood experiences on adult relationships
  - adolescent experiences on adult relationships
- relationships in different cultures

With rare exceptions, we all have a need for the company of others; this is known as **affiliation**. However, a relationship goes beyond simple affiliation; it is not the case that anyone could just as easily become a friend or partner as anyone else. We have many different relationships in our lives, but we will be looking here at **dyadic relationships**, those between two people. We will look at romantic relationships and in particular theories that seek to explain the basis on which relationships are formed, how relationships are maintained and what leads to them breaking down.

Romantic relationships

The formation of relationships

There are several theories that provide a framework to explain the underlying factors that influence the formation of relationships, and we will look here at the role of reward and need satisfaction and stage and filter theories.

Topics in psychology

Reward and need satisfaction theory

Reinforcement is a central concept in **operant conditioning**. We associate behaviour with its consequences; if the consequences of a behaviour are positive, the behaviour is likely to be repeated. Byrne and Clore (1970) applied this general principle in explaining the formation of relationships. We tend to like people whose behaviour is rewarding to us. **Classical conditioning** also plays a part, as we learn to associate a person with certain characteristics or behaviours that lead to rewards.

Reinforcement in a relationship can take many different forms. Foa and Foa (1975) proposed eight categories; a partner can provide us with: help, information, goods, love, money, respect, sex and status, or indeed any combination of these possible reinforcers.

In a similar theory, Argyle (1994) suggests that we are likely to form a relationship with someone who fulfils our social needs. These include our need for self-esteem, which is met by the approval of the other person; our need for dependency is met by comfort being offered; dominance needs are met by a measure of control over the other person and sexual needs are met by making love.

There is evidence to support the role of conditioning in relationship formation (see Box 3.1).

Box 3.1 **May and Hamilton (1980)**

Aims: To investigate the effect of pleasant music on personal judgements.

Procedure: While listening to either pleasant, unpleasant or no music, 30 female undergraduates were asked to make a series of personal judgements of attractive and unattractive males, using photographs.

Results: They evaluated the attractive males more positively than the unattractive males, but made more positive evaluations of personal character in the 'pleasant music' condition than in either of the other conditions.

Conclusion: Through classical conditioning, the pleasant music was associated with the photos, leading to more positive evaluations.

However, it could be argued that the May and Hamilton study, like much of the research into this approach to relationship formation, lacks **ecological validity**. It was carried out in a laboratory, in different conditions from those in which we make judgements in everyday life. Making an assessment of someone from a photograph is different from meeting someone in person, where a range of other information is available.

Another major limitation of this kind of theory is that while it may help to explain why a relationship has been formed, it cannot be used to predict who will form a relationship with whom. It is difficult, if not impossible, to assess what different people in different situations will find rewarding.

Another issue is that the argument it presents is basically circular. Why do people form relationships? Because relationships bring rewards. How do we know that respect, love, money and so on constitute rewards? Because people form relationships to gain them.

This theory gives little weight to gender and cultural differences, which raises the issue of generalisation of the principles to all relationships. For example, Lott (1994) suggested that in many cultures, women are socialised into being more concerned with meeting the needs of their partner than their own, so we cannot assume that men and women are reinforced in the same ways and that they find the same things rewarding. The notion of access to reinforcers being the key factor in relationship formation may also be more true of cultures such as the UK, which focus on the rights, needs and responsibilities of the individual, than of cultures such as Korea, where the social focus is the group rather than the individual. There may also be subcultural differences; for example, Hays (1985) found that in student friendships as much value was attached to giving rewards as to receiving them.

Stage and filter theories

These theories see relationships as passing through a series of stages, so their focus is not entirely on the formation of relationships, but they nonetheless have something to say about it. Based on a comparison of couples who had been in a relationship for less than 18 months and those whose relationship was of longer standing, Kerckhoff and Davis (1962) proposed that relationships pass through a series of filters, which progressively narrow down our choice of partner. Their first, second and third filters are relevant to the formation of relationships:

- The first filter relates to **demographic similarity**, that is, similarity of race, religion and social class. This determines the potential friends and partners we are likely to meet and so limits what Kerckhoff (1974) calls 'the field of availables'.
- The second filter relates to **similarity of psychological characteristics**, for example shared values. Kerckhoff and Davis found that it was this factor that was most closely related to the probability of the relationship becoming stronger.
- The third filter relates to the **complementarity of emotional needs**, and it is this that is associated with whether or not the relationship becomes a longer term commitment; it was found to be more important for couples who had been together for more than 18 months.

Murstein (1976) has also proposed a stage theory of relationships:

Murstein's stimulus-value-role (SVR) theory

Stimulus stage: couples are first influenced by physical attributes, for example looks.

Value stage: the match between their attitudes and values becomes important.

Role stage: couples are concerned with whether their performances of the roles they have adopted in the partnership complement each other and so form the basis for a satisfactory relationship.

The factors of most significance at each stage will play a role throughout the partnership, but are of particular importance to the stage that the relationship has reached.

As in the filter theory of Kerckhoff and Davis (1962), the 'value' stage of relationship formation focuses on similarity, and this is also a feature of the last stage theory we will look at, the processes in the development of a relationship outlined by Lewis (1972). In this model, the first stage combines the first two filters of the Kerckhoff and Davis model; the fifth stage can be compared with Murstein's 'role' stage and the third filter of Kerckhoff and Davis:

Processes in the development of relationships (Lewis 1972)

1 Perceiving similarities: sociocultural, values and interests.

2 Achieving pair rapport: deep liking develops; there is greater ease of communication and satisfaction with the relationship.

3 Inducing self-disclosure: the process of 'falling in love', which leads to a degree of intimacy beyond 'liking'. Increasingly more personal and private matters are shared and discussed.

4 Role-taking (empathy): those who show greatest role accuracy, based on self-disclosure and observation of the other person, make greater progress towards a dyadic relationship.

5 Achieving interpersonal role-fit: observed personal similarity; complementarity of roles and needs.

6 Achieving dyadic crystallisation: the life of the individual becomes ever more entwined with that of their partner and the relationship becomes more committed. At the same time, boundaries are set, i.e. areas that are 'me' and not 'us'.

As with the other stage theories we have looked at, it is only the early stages of the Lewis model that offer information about the formation of relationships. However, it has the advantage of breaking down the stages of development in rather more detail and links both feelings and thoughts with the development of a relationship.

Stage theories have much to offer. They tend not to be based on studies that are artificially set up, but rather on observations of and interviews with individuals in relationships; they therefore tend to be high in ecological validity. They often have high face validity, in that we can relate them to our own experience of relationships changing over time. They can integrate earlier research (for example the determinants of attraction) into models with wider applicability and explanatory power and have suggested ideas that have stimulated a great deal of research. They may also be useful as 'tools for thought' by professionals helping couples with relationship problems.

However, some stage theories do not address adequately the question of what exactly is meant by a 'stage'? For example, are there distinct and qualitatively different types of behaviour and emotions at different stages? Do later stages depend on coping successfully with earlier stages? Do these earlier stages disappear during later stages, or do they continue, as Murstein's SVR theory suggests, in the background? Can stages be returned to?

The evidence supporting stage theories also tends to be weak. For example, Perlman and Duck (1987) report that there is little evidence to suggest that relationships necessarily go through the same stages in the same order. There may be considerable variation in couples in terms of when different aspects of relationship formation come to the fore, so stages may instead be better thought of as phases.

The later stages of all these theories suggest factors, in particular the linking of disclosure, intimacy and empathy in Lewis' model, which may be important in the maintenance of a relationship. This will be looked at in the next section.

Summary

- **Reward and need satisfaction theories** of the formation of relationships draw on **conditioning** principles. We are more likely to form relationships with those who offer us rewards, such as goods, money or approval.
- Research in this area tends to have **low ecological validity**.
- These theories have difficulty in predicting with whom a relationship will be formed and are somewhat circular. They do not take **gender** and **culture** into account.
- **Stage** and **filter theories** suggest relationships are formed through a series of stages.
- Some theories are **detailed** and take both **feelings** and **thoughts** into account. While they have **intuitive appeal**, there are questions around what is meant by a stage. There is **little supporting evidence** for stage theories.

The maintenance of relationships

Maintenance theories are concerned with the reasons why people who have formed a relationship choose to remain in the relationship, or leave it. Economic theories are an extension of reward/need satisfaction theories, discussed in the previous section, while other theories consider relationships in which individuals are more concerned with the needs of the other person than their own.

The **social exchange theory**, proposed by Thibaut and Kelley (1959), suggests that whether or not a relationship is maintained depends on the benefits a person believes he or she gets from the relationship and the costs that it involves. The benefits include some of the factors mentioned in relation to reward/need satisfaction theories, such as love, money and status. Costs can include the time and effort it takes to maintain a relationship and possibly financial considerations. If both partners feel that the benefits

TopFoto

A relationship is likely to be maintained when both partners feel the benefits outweigh the costs

outweigh the costs, then the relationship is likely to be maintained. The theory assumes that people will want to maximise the benefits of a relationship, while minimising its costs. The benefits are weighed against the costs and it is the outcome of this calculation that determines the level of commitment to a relationship that people will make.

An important aspect of this theory is the comparison of a relationship (**comparison level** or **CL**) with what we expect from a relationship on the basis of our previous experience, our views of what relationships should be like and what we expect to gain from them. We also make a comparison with what an alternative relationship might have to offer (**comparison level for alternatives** or **CL alt**). Relationships are seen as dynamic, in that making comparisons is a continuous process. It is possible that what you expect from a relationship (the CL) might change because other people seem to be getting more from their relationships than you. Your CL alt may change if you meet someone who seems to have a lot to offer. There is research that supports this theory (see Box 3.2).

Box 3.2   Rusbult and Zembrodt (1983)

Aim: To investigate why relationships are maintained or come to an end.

Procedure: In a longitudinal study, 30 students, each in a heterosexual relationship, completed questionnaires every 17 days, over a period of 7 months. During this time, 10 had ended their original relationship.

Results: The students had weighed up the rewards and costs of the relationship and their investment in it. For those who stayed in their relationship, increases in rewards led to increased satisfaction with the relationship, while changes in costs had little impact. The existence of an attractive alternative influenced the decision to end the relationship.

Conclusion: There is some support for the principles of social exchange theory, though costs are not as important as rewards. CL alt shapes the decision to remain in or end the relationship.

Equity theory is a modification of exchange theory, in that it focuses on what people see as equitable in a relationship, fair rather than equal. Walster et al. (1978) suggest that we try to establish equity between the outcomes for both people in a relationship in terms of the effort each puts in. If both people receive the same outcome, but one has put in more effort, the relationship is seen as inequitable. However, if one person has put in less effort, but also receives a lower outcome, the relationship may be seen as equitable.

Theories of this kind see relationships as based on self-interest and so can be seen as reductionist and oversimplified; as Argyle (1994) points out, couples tend to think in terms of rewards and costs only when the relationship is beginning to break down. There is also a great deal of variety in relationships that is not really reflected in this kind of approach. A distinction has been drawn, for example Mills and Clark (1982), between this kind of exchange-oriented relationship and **communal relationships**, which are more altruistic and concerned more with the needs of the other person than is suggested by economic theories.

The differences between these two kinds of relationship can be seen early on. For example, Kerckhoff and Davis (1962) found that disclosure in an exchange relationship was on a reciprocal basis; disclosure from one partner was 'repaid' by disclosure from the other. On the other hand, in communal relationships, disclosure was made freely, without anything being expected in return. Once a communal relationship has been established, it can be characterised by the giving of gifts — in the broadest sense — without gifts being given in return. Indeed, Mills and Clark (1982) found that in communal relationships, 'exchange' acts could be seen as negative. At the same time, however, costs and benefits can still be relevant in a communal relationship, if one partner feels that he or she does all the giving and receives little or nothing in return.

Other approaches have aimed to identify factors that predict whether or not a relationship is maintained. One factor is **similarity**, for example, in a study of long-term married couples, Cattell and Nesselrode (1967) found that these partners had similar personalities, for example both were extroverts. Similarly, Cohen et al. (1984) found that those most likely to stay married were similar with regard to the tolerance of quarrels, exhibitions of intimacy, activities, impulsivity and susceptibility to boredom.

Interaction between partners has also been investigated. In a review of studies of factors associated with marital satisfaction, Duck (1992) found that happy couples give more positive and consistent non-verbal cues, express more agreement and approval of each other, talk more about their relationship and are willing to compromise. Smyer (1982) identified a further factor in a study that found that well-developed **social networks** can help to maintain a marriage. Research has also identified some of the maintenance and repair **strategies** people use (see Box 3.3).

Couples that share activities are more likely to stay married

---

| **Box 3.3** | **Dindia and Baxter (1987)** |

Aim: To identify the strategies couples use to maintain and repair a relationship.

Procedure: A sample of 50 married couples was interviewed about the strategies they use to keep a relationship going and to deal with problems.

Results: A total of 49 different strategies were identified:
- Maintenance strategies included doing things together, spending time together with friends and talking about their day.
- Repair strategies included talking about problems within the relationship, or one partner giving the other an ultimatum.

Conclusion: Couples use a range of strategies to maintain a relationship.

3

Summary

- **Social exchange theory** proposes that we maintain a relationship where the **benefits** outweigh the **costs**. We compare the relationship with what we expect from a relationship (**CL**) and what alternative relationships might offer (**CL alt**).
- **Equity theory** is a development of this, in terms of what is seen as fair in a relationship.
- There is some supporting evidence, but some relationships are **communal**, where each partner focuses more on the needs of the other.
- Factors that promote the maintenance of a relationship include **similarity**, **positive interaction** and a supportive **social network**.
- Couples use **strategies** to maintain and repair a relationship.

The breakdown of relationships

Relationships bring many benefits. For example, Cochrane (1996) found that people were significantly more likely to die earlier when single than when married and even more so if divorced. Similarly, Cramer (1994) found that married people have lower rates of mental disorder than single people. However, in spite of these benefits, many relationships do come to an end and we will look here at some of the reasons that have been identified.

Some of the material in the previous section is relevant to relationship breakdown. For example, according to **social exchange theory**, if a partner in a relationship comes to believe that the costs outweigh the benefits, and particularly if an alternative relationship seems to offer more, they are more likely to leave the relationship. According to **equity theory**, the same is true if the relationship comes to be seen as inequitable and even communal relationships can break down if the relationship is seen as one-sided. However, there is research that focuses specifically on relationship breakdown.

Duck (1992) has identified a range of factors that are linked to the likelihood of a relationship breaking down:

Factors linked to relationship breakdown (Duck 1992)

- marriages in which the partners are very young
- early parenthood
- being in a lower socioeconomic group
- poor education
- partners are of a different race or religion
- one or both partners have parents who themselves divorced
- a greater number of sexual partners before marriage

Although these factors are associated with relationship breakdown, they cannot be seen as direct causes. However, several interpersonal factors that may lead to the dissolution of a relationship have been identified:

Interpersonal reasons for relationship breakdown (Baron and Byrne 1997)

- People may think they agree more than they do. There may be conflict if this emerges when problems arise.
- Differences in the way people interact, for example the extent to which they are able to express their feelings, may cause tensions in a relationship.
- Jealousy.
- People may change their attitudes or values. This is a particular problem when the change involves something that is important to the other person, including politics or religion.
- The relationship may become routine or boring. Even if only one partner becomes bored, the couple will then develop different goals, leading to possible relationship breakdown.
- Lack of sexual satisfaction.

Rusbult and Zembrodt (1983) have described four possible reactions to problems within a relationship that are linked to whether or not the relationship is likely to break down. These vary along two dimensions: constructive/destructive and active/passive. Different combinations lead to different strategies:

According to Rusbult (1987), the strategy to be used will depend on the degree of satisfaction a person has experienced in the relationship. Those who are generally satisfied will tend to react in a constructive way. They may use the active strategy of voice: they will talk about their concerns and suggest ways in which the problems might be addressed. Alternatively, the more passive option is loyalty, waiting for the situation to improve. Those who are less satisfied are likely to use the more destructive strategies of exit by leaving the relationship, or neglect, perhaps waiting for the relationship to come to its inevitable end. Exit and neglect are the strategies associated with relationship breakdown; possible differences in the strategies used by different groups of people have been explored (see Box 3.4).

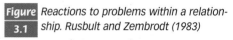

Figure 3.1 *Reactions to problems within a relationship. Rusbult and Zembrodt (1983)*

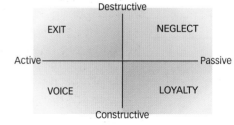

Box 3.4   Rusbult et al. (1986)

Aim: To investigate possible differences in response to dissatisfaction with a relationship between males and females and in relation to sexual orientation.

Procedure: A set of three studies examined the responses to dissatisfaction in a relationship of university students, heterosexual adults, gays and lesbians.

Results: In all three studies, greater psychological femininity was associated with voice and loyalty responses and greater psychological masculinity with exit and neglect responses.

Conclusion: There is a link between strategies used and psychological gender across age groups and in both heterosexual and same-sex relationships.

3

Other factors may also influence the choice of options (see Box 3.5).

Box 3.5   Yovetich and Rusbult (1994)

Aim: To investigate a possible link between speed of response to a relationship problem and the choice of strategy used.

Procedure: Students were asked to role-play likely responses to problems, for example 'I'd be better off without you!' The amount of time they were given to consider their responses varied from less than 10 seconds and up to 30 seconds.

Results: Those who had more time to think about their responses were more likely to use constructive options.

Conclusion: Spontaneous reactions can be destructive to a relationship, while taking time to consider a response is likely to lead to a more constructive approach.

The Yovetich and Rusbult study is interesting in proposing a further factor that could influence whether a relationship is maintained or breaks down. However, it could arguably be said to have low ecological validity, since it looked at role-play rather than real situations. As it only tested students, generalisability is also questionable.

Attribution theory, which looks at the ways in which we assess the causes of behaviour, has also been used to look at strategies that maintain a relationship (and so is relevant to the section on the maintenance of relationships), or lead to its breakdown. There are three relevant distinctions:

1 **Internal** (the person acts in a particular way because of personal characteristics) vs **external** (the person behaves that way because of the situation).
2 **Global** (the person acts that way across different situations) vs **specific** (the person acts that way in this particular situation).
3 **Stable** (the person always acts that way) vs **unstable** (this is unlike the person's usual behaviour).

Bradbury and Fincham (1990) suggested that couples have different patterns of attribution, a relationship-enhancing pattern where the couples are satisfied in their relationship and a distress-maintaining pattern where this is not the case.

Figure 3.2 *Patterns of attribution, Bradbury and Fincham (1990)*

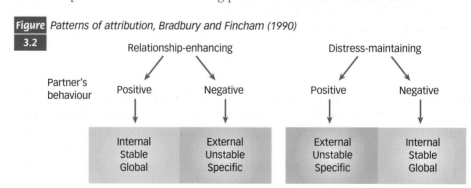

For example, if Kate's partner brings her flowers, she can interpret this in relationship-enhancing terms: he is a kind and thoughtful person (**internal**), who often brings her flowers (**stable**) and shows his thoughtfulness in many ways (**global**). Alternatively, she may make distress-enhancing attributions: he just happened to pass a flower shop (**external**), he does not usually bother with bringing her gifts (**unstable**), so he must be feeling guilty about something (**specific**).

Stages of breakdown in a relationship

Relationship breakdown is a process rather than an event to which Duck (1982) has suggested there are four phases:

Phases of relationship breakdown (Duck 1982)

Intra-psychic stage: one of the partners decides he or she does not want to continue the relationship. He or she thinks about negative aspects of the relationship, the costs of withdrawal and a possible alternative relationship. It is called 'intra-psychic' because these thoughts are not shared with anyone.

Dyadic phase: the other partner is involved. Negotiations and attempts to repair the relationship take place and the costs of ending it are assessed.

Social phase: the dissatisfied partner decides he or she wants the relationship to end. The state of the relationship is discussed with the couple's family and friends, who may be asked to try to help to repair the relationship.

Grave-dressing phase: the end of the relationship is inevitable. Others are made aware of each partner's version of events as part of getting over the relationship breakdown.

A similar approach has been taken by Lee (1984), who has suggested that there are five stages in relationship breakdown:

Five stages of relationship breakdown (Lee 1984)

1 **Dissatisfaction** is experienced.

2 There is **exposure** of this dissatisfaction.

3 **Negotiation** about this dissatisfaction takes place.

4 **Attempts at resolution** take place.

5 There is **termination** when the relationship breaks down.

The two accounts are in some ways similar. In both the Lee and Duck models, the first two stages are identical. However, the third and fourth stages of Duck's model then look at the wider social context of the relationship, while Lee's focuses only on the couple whose relationship is breaking down. This difference can perhaps be accounted for by Lee's focus exclusively on premarital relationships. There is support for stage models from research (see Box 3.6).

> **Box 3.6** | **Lee (1984)**
>
> **Aim:** To explore the application of stages in relationship breakdown.
>
> **Procedure:** A survey was carried out of 112 couples experiencing relationship breakdown.
>
> **Results:** Exposure and negotiation were the most emotionally exhausting stages. Couples who moved straight from dissatisfaction to termination had poorer relationships with their partner once the relationship was over. When movement through the stages was long and drawn-out, couples reported feeling more attracted to their partner, but also more fear and loneliness during the negotiation and resolution stages.
>
> **Conclusion:** There is quite a lot of variation in the experience of relationship breakdown depending on how the stages are negotiated.

Stage models are intuitively appealing, in that we can relate their ideas to our own and others' experience of relationship breakdown. They are also useful in describing breakdown as a process rather than an event. Both models could be useful to relationship counsellors, in terms of identifying which stage a relationship crisis has reached and so deciding how best to offer help. However, both models start from the point where dissatisfaction has occurred, without identifying reasons why this has happened, so could be seen as not giving a complete picture of relationship breakdown. In addition, as we have seen with other relationship theories, relationships vary widely, so any particular one may not fit easily into either model.

Summary

- Researchers have identified a range of **demographic** and **interpersonal factors** associated with the likelihood of a relationship breaking down.
- The choice of **strategies** — active vs passive, and constructive vs destructive — used to respond to problems in a relationship has been linked to the likelihood of the relationship being maintained or breaking down.
- **Psychological femininity** has been associated more with **constructive** strategies and **masculinity** with **destructive** strategies.
- **Attribution theory** suggests that there is a link between patterns of attribution about a partner's behaviour and relationship maintenance or breakdown.
- **Stage theories** describe the stages through which a couple passes as a relationship breaks down. There is some **support** for these accounts, but they can be seen as **incomplete** and do not take into account **variation in relationships**.

Human reproductive behaviour

Evolutionary accounts of relationships take a different approach from what we have looked at in the previous section. **Darwin's theory of evolution** starts from the premise that the characteristics of any organism are important in terms of survival and successful reproduction. Within a species, physical characteristics vary; some individuals will have characteristics that are **adaptive**, in that they promote survival long enough for successful reproduction to take place, so those individuals' genes are passed to the next generation. Individuals with less adaptive characteristics are less likely to survive long enough to reproduce, so their genes will be lost from the gene pool; this is referred to as **natural selection**.

The term **fitness** is used to refer to an individual's ability to survive and produce offspring who will be able to survive (referred to as **viability**) and produce offspring (referred to as **fecundity**).

Evolutionary psychology is concerned with innate patterns of behaviour. It focuses on understanding the function of mechanisms that were laid down in the distant past — the **environment of evolutionary adaptation (EEA)** — which were adaptive at that time in terms of promoting fitness, although they may not necessarily be adaptive now. This approach has been described by Tooby and Cosmides (1992) as a kind of **reverse engineering**; in the same way that we could use our knowledge of mechanical principles and observations of how a car operates to work out how and why it was designed in that particular way, we can use our knowledge of evolutionary principles and past environmental conditions to identify the functions of characteristics and behaviours, in terms of promoting survival and reproduction in human prehistory, that remain with us today.

Evolutionary theory has been widely used to account for the behaviour of humans and non-human animals. It proposes that the mind consists of a number of specialised mechanisms or **modules**, each of which has developed through natural selection to solve specific problems faced by our ancestors, such as acquiring a mate or raising children. It has also claimed that these modules are universal. In this section, we will be looking in particular at what this kind of approach has to say about our selection of a sexual partner and the behaviour of parents in relation to their children.

Evolutionary psychology seeks to explain human reproductive behaviour in terms of how particular behaviours may be adaptive in maximising the chances of producing viable offspring, who will produce offspring to carry on an individual's genes. However, since the reproductive roles of men and women are different, so too are their mental modules. To understand these differences, we need to look first at **anisogamy**, i.e. the differences in the gametes (sperm and ova) in males and females. This represents a fundamental difference between males and females, in that males produce a large number of small, mobile sperm, while females produce larger, relatively immobile eggs, in quite small numbers.

The number of offspring that a female can produce is limited by the number of eggs she can produce. Although she may be able to increase the quality of her offspring by mating with other males while maintaining a relationship with a mate who provides resources, she cannot increase the number of offspring by mating with several males. The male, on the other hand, can increase his reproductive success by mating with several females. This means that males and females have different reproductive priorities, in terms of the strategies that are most likely to lead to reproductive success.

A comparison can be made here between mating effort and parental effort. On the basis of anisogamy, it would be expected that for the male, most of his reproductive effort would be taken up by competing with other males for females and persuading females to mate with him (**mating effort**). The male does not need to make parental effort, in terms of caring for offspring, since his part in the reproductive process is quickly accomplished, compared to the female's commitment to gestation. Even if a mating is unsuccessful, or the young he has fathered fail to survive, he has not lost much since his role is so small. Making a large parental effort would limit his opportunities for mating with other females and so his reproductive success. However, for females reproductive effort will largely be taken up in the production and care of offspring (**parental effort**). While she could theoretically leave the male to look after the offspring and seek additional matings, this would be a risky strategy, since if the male failed to look after them — and as we have seen, making parental effort is not the optimal strategy for reproductive success for the male — the considerable investment she had made in producing them would be lost. As they are limited in number, the eggs a female can produce are a more precious resource than a male's sperm.

The difference in priorities for males and females is clear. The male will be more interested in quantity of offspring, to maximise the chances that at least some of them will be viable, and is likely to leave their care to the female. On the other hand, the female will be more committed to raising successfully the relatively few offspring she is able to produce.

A further factor is the mating pattern of a species and the pattern for which humans are adapted. **Monogamy** refers to one female mating exclusively with one male as long as the bond lasts. In **polygamy**, one member of one sex will mate with several members of the other sex. This can take the form of polygyny, where one male has several mates, or — much less frequently — polyandry, where one female has several mates. The final pattern is **polygynandry** (or **promiscuity**), where no pair bonds are formed, but males and females come together briefly to mate. The likelihood of a member of a species showing a particular pattern has been shown in a study by Harcourt et al. (1981) to correlate with the relative weight of the testes. Species such as the gorilla, where males have exclusive access to several females, have smaller testes in relation to their body weight than species such as the chimpanzee, where several males mate with a receptive female. This can be explained in terms of competition for mates in the

Steve Bloom Images/Alamy

Male gorillas have exclusive access to several females

chimpanzee, where the male's sperm has to compete with the sperm of other chimpanzees and increased sperm production would make a male more competitive. A gorilla, on the other hand, needs to produce only enough sperm to ensure fertilisation of the females to which only he has access and so has smaller testes.

Short (1991) applied these ideas to humans and came to the conclusion that 'we are basically a polygynous primate, in which polygyny usually takes the form of serial monogamy'. This is actually quite a common pattern, particularly in Western societies; it is not unusual for men to have a series of partners before deciding to make their lives with one person. However, Short's account relates only to men and it is not uncommon for women to show a similar pattern in relationships, so perhaps polygynandry would be a more accurate description.

The different systems are also reflected in the maximum number of recorded offspring in a lifetime in different species. In kittiwakes, a monogamous species, the numbers (male = 26; female = 28) are virtually identical. According to the *Guinness World Records*, the numbers for humans are 888 for a male and 69 for a female. The male was Moulay Ismael the Bloodthirsty, Emperor of Morocco and the female a Russian, who produced her children in 27 pregnancies. Though the accuracy of these figures for humans has been questioned in Einon (1988), this kind of difference — even if it is more limited than the *Guinness World Records* suggests — provides some support for the claim that humans may be a polygynous or polygynandrous species.

A further argument for innate differences in reproductive strategies comes from Symons (1979), who claimed that gay men are more likely to have a series of short-term relationships, while lesbians tend to form lasting partnerships. While homosexuality is not a reproductively successful strategy, these findings suggest that males have an inherited tendency to be polygynous and females to be monogamous. In the next section, we will look at the influence of these differences on sexual selection and parental investment.

Summary

- **Evolutionary theory** has been used to explain a variety of human behaviours.
- **Anisogamy** refers to the different forms that gametes take in the male and the female. These differences have implications for **mating effort** and **parental effort**.
- Patterns of mating in different species include monogamy, polygamy and polygynandry (promiscuity). There is some support for the idea that human **males** are genetically **promiscuous** and human **females** are **monogamous**.
- This difference has implications for **sexual selection** and **parental investment**.

Sexual selection

According to Darwin (1871), sexual selection is a special form of natural selection. Variation in physical and psychological characteristics affects access to mates. For males, access to more mates leads to the possibility of a greater number of offspring and access to higher quality mates implies better care. Thus both quantity and quality of mates influence how many viable offspring are produced, who will, in turn, go on to reproduce successfully.

Intrasexual selection refers to competition — usually between males — leading to the development of traits that increase competitive ability. **Intersexual selection** relates to mate selection based on either physical or behavioural characteristics. If the characteristics that promote successful reproduction are carried in the genes, genes coding for them will be passed on to the next generation. Individuals without them would have less reproductive success, so their genes would be lost from the gene pool.

In humans, males compete for females and females select males. At the most basic level this can be seen in the competition of sperm to fertilise eggs; the element of competition is inevitable as there are many more sperm available than there are eggs to be fertilised. The female has to be selective in her choice of mate because she is limited in the number of eggs and offspring she can produce. It therefore makes sense for her to select the 'fittest' mate as a sexual partner, in terms of both genetic quality and in the sense of resources offered, including likely contribution to parental care.

A male can potentially fertilise a huge number of females. A male's genes are more likely to be carried on if he fertilises as many females as possible and any adaptation that allows him to do so will be favoured by sexual selection. This assumes that the decrease in the chances of offspring survival in one-parent rather than two-parent care is more than made up for by the number of extra opportunities the male has for fertilising females. This difference in priorities has been supported by research (See Box 3.7).

Box 3.7	**Clark and Hatfield (1989)**

Aim: To investigate male/female differences in mating behaviour.

Procedure: On an American college campus, an attractive stranger approached participants of the opposite sex, engaged them in conversation and asked (a) to go out with them (b) to go back to their home or (c) to have sex with them.

Results: While 50% of both men and women agreed to a date, only 6% of females, compared to 69% of males, agreed to go back to their home. None of the women, compared to 75% of the men, agreed to have sex.

Conclusion: The findings are consistent with evolutionary ideas about differences in optimal reproductive strategies in males and females.

The Clark and Hatfield study has been replicated many times, with similar results. However, although these results are consistent with evolutionary ideas, it could be argued instead that physical vulnerability could account for the difference in the percentage agreeing to sex. However, the reasons given for refusal — they did not know the person well enough; they already had a girl/boyfriend — did not differ between males and females. The results could also be linked to cultural stereotypes, with social attitudes towards women having sex with someone they had only just met being more negative than towards men who do the same thing.

The different priorities of men and women lead to different criteria in the selection of a mate. For males, one important factor in the attractiveness of females appears to be the ratio of the circumference of the waist to the hips (see Box 3.8).

Box 3.8 **Singh (1993)**

Aim: To investigate the waist-to-hip ratio (WHR) in terms of attractiveness in females.

Procedure: The measurements of the Miss America Pageant winners and Playboy centrefolds over the previous 50 years were studied.

Results: Although factors like physique and body weight varied across the years, a WHR of around 0.7 was a consistent feature of female attractiveness.

Conclusion: A WHR of 0.7 differentiates women from pre-pubertal females and signals that they are not already pregnant. It is associated with better health status and therefore potentially better reproductive capacity. This preference in men is therefore adaptive in maximising reproductive potential.

It could perhaps be argued that this preference is culturally based, but the consistency across many years, given the many cultural changes that take place over so long a period, lends some support to an evolutionary interpretation. This interpretation is also supported by a later study, carried out by Pawlowski and Dunbar (2005), of Polish women who had given birth to one child. They found that there was a correlation between the closeness of the WHR of 0.7 and one measure of biological fitness, specifically the child's birth weight, a variable that significantly affects infant survival rate. A further study has investigated more general priorities in choosing a mate in males and in females (see Box 3.9).

Box 3.9 **Buss (1989)**

Aim: To investigate the priorities of males and females in choosing a sexual partner.

Procedure: More than 10,000 people in 37 cultures on six continents and five islands were asked what their priorities were in choosing a sexual partner.

Results: Men were much more likely to rate youth and good looks as extremely important, while females favoured a cluster of factors, which included good financial prospects, ambition, industriousness, older age and emotional maturity

Conclusion: Priorities for males and females differ and appear to be universal.

In evolutionary terms, these differences in preferences make sense. The reproductive success of men is likely to be increased if they mate with younger, healthy women, rather than older and/or less healthy women. Youth indicates that the woman is still fertile, while attractiveness is a rough guide to health. In looking for a good provider, women can help to ensure that their pregnancies are successful and that their offspring survive to sexual maturity.

Dunbar (1995) approached the same issue in a study using content analysis of a 'lonely hearts' column. He found that men were more likely to ask for attractiveness and offer resources, for example 'own house/car' and women were more likely to offer attractiveness and ask for resources, for example 'professional man'.

However, while these findings lend some support to the evolutionary position, the characteristics identified as being more important to males and to females are not necessarily those that are the most important to either. For example, Buss found that kindness and intelligence were consistently rated by both men and women as more important than either good looks or financial status, and a survey by Kenrick and Simpson (1997) found that kindness, understanding and intelligence were top of the list for both men and women. Moreover, the findings of studies have not always been consistent with evolutionary ideas (see Box 3.10).

Box 3.10	Strassberg and Holty (2003)

Aim: To assess evolutionary ideas about male/female differences in mate selection.

Procedure: Using two large internet-dating bulletin boards, four 'female seeking male' adverts were posted, each with different key words.

Results: Over 500 email responses were collected over 6 weeks. The most popular advert was one in which the woman described herself as 'financially independent…successful… ambitious'. This was 50% more popular than the next most popular, where key words were 'lovely…very attractive…slim'.

Conclusion: This does not support the claim made by evolutionary psychology that in choosing a sexual partner, males would focus more on attractiveness than resources.

A further problem with the argument that Buss and others put forward is its focus on only one level of explanation. Historical and cultural influences may also affect our choice of a partner. For example, it could be that a man may seek an attractive partner because this will enhance his social status. Similarly, women may try to obtain resources through men because they have traditionally been cut off from economic opportunities. However, if a female's preference for financial resources is a result of economic inequality, it might be expected that financially successful women would not have this preference. Wiederman and Allgeier (1992) found that, on the contrary, such women show an even more marked preference for wealthy men.

Eagly (1992) has put forward a similar cultural explanation for human mate selection criteria. She points out that in all the cultures that have been studied, males are socially dominant, and suggests that if females were the dominant sex, then the preferred attributes of the opposite sex would be reversed. She argues that the choices found in this kind of research therefore depend not on evolutionary forces but cultural and social ones. There is no way of testing this suggestion directly, since there are no societies in which females are socially dominant. However, this kind of reversal is found in some animals. For example, in the seahorse, it is the male who is responsible for parental care, having a special pouch that holds infant seahorses as they mature. In this species, brightly-coloured females compete for dull-coloured males.

To counter these arguments, Dunbar et al. (1999) have argued that evolution may have shaped cultural practice, which in turn reinforces patterns of behaviour that are determined by evolutionary forces; cultural and evolutionary forces are not independent influences.

There is also the issue of individual differences. Not all men are promiscuous and some women are, a reversal of the pattern evolutionary psychology would predict. There are sound evolutionary reasons for women to be unfaithful, for example to gain male protection, or to improve the genetic quality of her offspring with a better quality mate. Similarly, a man may be faithful because infidelity may lead to him losing his sexual partner with no guarantee of gaining another. In other words, patterns of behaviour that are diametrically opposed to what evolutionary theory has predicted can also be explained in evolutionary terms.

It seems that the same theory can explain whatever male or female behaviours are observed, which means that the theory may have poor predictive value. It cannot be falsified and therefore according to Popper (1959) it has no value as a scientific theory and so is of limited use in explaining human behaviour. It is also the case that other explanations — for example, relating to historical, cultural and social values — may be just as valid.

Summary

- **Sexual selection** takes place on the basis of characteristics that optimise human reproduction. There are two components: **intrasexual** selection and **intersexual** selection.
- Males and females have different **reproductive potential**. It would be expected that **males** would attempt to mate with **many females** and select **young, attractive** females as a guide to fertility.
- **Females** would select **one mate** on the basis of **resources** being offered to maximise the chances of her offspring reaching maturity.
- There is **research evidence** consistent with these predictions. However, **historical** and **cultural factors** could also explain the findings.
- This kind of explanation has been criticised for being **unfalsifiable** and having **little predictive value**.

Evolutionary explanations of parental investment

The selection of an appropriate mate is only one part of the process of maximising the chances of an individual's genes being carried forward to future generations. In many species, care of the young by one or both parents is essential if the young are to stand a chance of surviving to maturity and breeding.

Trivers (1972) used the term 'parental investment' to mean 'any investment by the parent in an individual offspring that increases the offspring's chance of surviving

In many species, care of the young by both parents is essential for offspring survival

(and hence reproductive success) at the cost of the parent's ability to invest in other offspring'. In practice, it is difficult to define terms like 'cost to parents' and 'off-spring's chance of surviving' in ways that can be measured, so this is not an easy area to investigate.

In some species, including insects and some species of fish, little or no parental care is given, since offspring are produced in such large numbers that it is likely that some individuals, and therefore their parental genes, will survive. Other species, of which humans are an example, are characterised by slower development, fewer offspring, a higher survival rate, a higher proportion of learned behaviour and a longer lifespan. Considerable parental investment is therefore needed.

The brain size of humans makes lengthy parental care necessary if the offspring are to reach maturity and also reproduce. The size of the human brain has tripled over the last 2 million years, so the size of the skull has had to increase to accommodate it. At the same time, the size of the human pelvis is determined by our walking on two legs. The increased size of the skull made childbirth more difficult and to compensate for this and make it possible for the baby's head to pass through the narrow birth canal, birth takes place when the infant is still relatively immature. If we were like other primates, the gestation period for humans would be 21 months, by which time an infant's head would be too large to pass through the pelvic canal. So while most animals become independent within a matter of months, humans remain dependent for much longer.

One advantage of increased brain size is that it allows for learning, such as adapting behaviour to the requirements of a particular environment. This in turn means that few behaviours are completely genetically determined and 'hard-wired' into the system. A period of prolonged care and education of the young — in terms of selection of relevant environmental events — is therefore necessary for appropriate learning to take place.

In general, women tend to make a greater parental investment than men. In the past, breastfeeding made them the more likely parent to care for very young children and so continue to provide parental care while it was needed. Women therefore provide not only the most prenatal investment, but also the most postnatal investment. This makes evolutionary sense, in that if a woman has made a considerable investment in a child before it is born, it makes sense for her to continue to provide for it, given her limited reproductive capability.

Differences between species in the parental care offered is associated with the different mating systems, looked at in the previous section, which offer a general guide as to whether and by whom parental care is offered. Human males, as noted earlier, seem to have a tendency to be serial monogamists; in monogamous species, both parents are likely to offer parental care. For the female, offering care makes sense because of the relatively large investment she has made in producing the offspring. In males, offering parental care can help to ensure the survival of offspring he has fathered, and this would outweigh the additional opportunities for mating that would be possible if this care were not offered. However, parental care is also influenced by other factors that may lead to less parental investment being made by men.

One factor in parental investment that leads to more parental care being offered by mothers is **paternity uncertainty**. Because fertilisation in humans is internal, females always know who their offspring are, but males can never be entirely certain; if they offer parental care they may be caring for offspring who carry none of their genes. Indeed, Fisher (1992) referred to several large-scale surveys that indicate that on average, in married couples with children, about 10% of children have a genetic father different from the official family father. If a man is to offer parental care, he needs to be as certain as possible that a child is his.

In all cultures, women typically tend to invest more time and energy than men in childrearing. Buss (1999) noted that maternal relatives other than the mother make a greater investment than paternal relatives. In addition, Daly and Wilson (1982) found that 80% of comments on a child's resemblance to a parent referred to a similarity with the father, while only 20% referred to the mother. This could be interpreted as reassurance about paternity. However, it is also possible that it reflects a naturally-selected tendency for human offspring to resemble their fathers; this would provide protection against infanticide by the father and a way of extracting paternal care from him.

The **Trivers-Willard hypothesis** (Trivers and Willard 1973) is relevant here. This looks at the variance in reproductive success in species where this is greater for males than for females. In such species, some males will have great reproductive success and others none, whereas females will not show the same extremes. Where this difference in variance holds true, males in good condition will have a greater chance than females in good condition of leaving viable offspring, since their reproductive success is likely to be greater. Therefore parents who are in good condition should show a bias towards producing sons (who will in turn have a greater likelihood of reproductive success) than daughters. Those in poor condition should show a bias towards producing daughters. Trivers and Willard suggested that this idea could be extended to human societies, using wealth and socioeconomic status (which varies more for males than for females) as an indicator of condition. There is some evidence to support this hypothesis (see Box 3.11).

Box 3.11   Mueller (1993)

Aim: To investigate the Trivers-Willard hypothesis in relation to the proportion of sons and daughters in different socioeconomic groups.

Procedure: An analysis was carried out of the sons-to-daughters ratio of eminent men. The sample included elite American and German men, using information from the American and German *Who's Who*, and British industrialists, using the *Dictionary of Business Biography*.

Results: In all three sample groups, the ratio of sons to daughters was significantly greater than would be expected from the ratio for the populations as a whole.

Conclusion: There is some support for the Trivers-Willard hypothesis in relation to human sex ratios.

The mechanism that brings about this skewing is unclear, but is likely to be mediated by hormone production in the parents. However, other mechanisms could include differential mobility or differential survival of the X and Y sperm, or differential mortality of male and female embryos. Within this framework, it would also be predicted that not all children would be cared for equally and that male and female children would be treated differently depending on social status. It might be expected that high-status parents would invest more in sons and low-status parents in daughters (see Box 3.12).

Box 3.12   Gaulin and Robbins (1992)

Aim: To compare parental investment in sons and daughters in high- and low-income families.

Procedure: Breastfeeding was used as a measure of parental investment. A further measure was birth spacing, i.e. the time between the birth of one child and the birth of the next, on the basis that a shorter period before the birth of another child would represent a smaller investment in the existing child.

Results: In low-income families, more than 50% of the daughters but less than 50% of the sons were breastfed. In high-income families, over 90% of sons compared to 60% of daughters were breastfed. In low-income families, birth spacing was on average 4.3 years after the birth of a daughter and 3.5 years after the birth of a son. In high-income families, the results were reversed: 3.2 years for daughters and 3.9 years for sons.

Conclusion: Both measures support the claim that parental investment is linked to the sex of a child, which in turn is linked with status.

However, while the results of studies in this area are consistent with an evolutionary explanation, there are the same problems, in particular that direct testing is not possible and so it may be that alternative interpretations are possible.

Summary

- The difference in optimal strategies for reproductive success in males and females influence the degree of **parental investment** each offers.
- Across cultures, females make a higher degree of investment than males. One factor in this difference is **paternity uncertainty**.
- The **Trivers-Willard hypothesis** suggests that parental investment will differ for **sons** and **daughters**, the pattern changing according to **socioeconomic status**. There is research evidence to support this idea.

Parent-offspring conflict

Given that parents and children both have the priority of optimising the chance of their genes being carried on to future generations; it seems curious that there should ever be conflict between them. To understand why this might happen, we need to look at **inclusive fitness**, a term introduced by Hamilton (1964). 'Fitness' is defined not only in terms of the reproductive success of the individual, but also the success of the individual's kin, with whom a proportion of genes are shared. A parent has approximately 50% of their genes in common with their child and around 25% with a grandchild and so has an interest, in evolutionary terms, in the survival of kin with whom they share genes, proportional to their genetic similarity. This is the basis on which parent-offspring conflict may arise. The concept of parent-offspring conflict was originally developed by Trivers (1974).

There are fitness implications in the choice of a mate, both for the person forming the relationship and for their parents. As parents and offspring are not genetically identical, the traits of a mating candidate that maximise the inclusive fitness of parents do not necessarily maximise that of the offspring.

For the offspring, forming a permanent relationship with someone of lower mating quality than yourself is not a sound reproductive strategy, since it means giving up the opportunity of a relationship with someone with superior genes. An important criterion for selecting a mate (spouse) is therefore good genes. For the parents, there are fewer benefits from good genes. They share 50% of their genes with their children, but only 25% with their grandchildren, so although good genes are beneficial to offspring and parents, the parents receive fewer fitness benefits from high genetic quality of a son- or daughter-in-law than their offspring. Evolutionary theory would therefore predict that good looks — an indicator of genetic quality — would be more valued by the offspring than the parents.

However, in-laws and spouses provide not only their genes, but also the material resources and social support that are necessary for survival and reproduction. Parents would be expected to prefer their offspring's mates to have qualities that maximise the fitness of all their kin. Trivers (1974) pointed out that a good marriage with an unrelated family can provide economic benefits to kin of the parents, beyond those enjoyed by the offspring making that marriage; for example resources when food is short and support in disputes with others. Evolutionary theory would therefore predict that parents would place more emphasis on the family background of a potential son- or daughter-in-law than their offspring.

There is some support for this idea from ethnographic studies. In cultures where parents play some part in their offspring's selection of a mate, the criteria on which possible partners are selected emphasise qualities that would maximise inclusive fitness, offering benefits not only to the son or daughter but also to the wider circle of kin. For example, Murstein (1974) reports that in Japan, factors considered to be important in a son-in-law include the family's economic position and status. According to Abdel-Rahim et al. (1988), similar criteria apply in Korea, together with academic achievement. In a study of Hindu women living in the UK, participants claimed that their family would never accept a son-in-law from outside their caste or culture (Bhopal 1997).

This is not to say that there is complete disagreement between parent and offspring about what is desirable in a mate; indeed, there is likely to be considerable overlap. However, the priorities of parent and offspring are likely to differ. This has been tested empirically (see Box 3.13).

Box 3.13 Apostolou (2008)

Aim: To compare priorities in the choice of a marriage partner and a son- or daughter-in-law.

Procedure: A survey was completed by 292 participants, 115 women and 177 men, all of whom were or had been in a long-term relationship and had at least one child. They were asked to rate a set of characteristics in (1) a potential son- or daughter-in-law and (2) a future husband or wife. The ratings of female participants for a son-in-law and a husband were compared and those of male participants for a daughter-in-law and a wife.

Results: For females, 'similar religious background' was more important in a son-in-law than in a husband and 'good looks' were valued more in a husband than in a son-in-law. For males, 'good looks' were valued more in a wife than in a daughter-in-law.

Conclusion: In most cases, preferences were similar, but there are differences in priorities when choosing an in-law and a spouse.

The Apostolou study supports the idea that parents receive fewer benefits from the genetic quality of a son- or daughter-in-law, indicated by good looks, and have therefore evolved to prefer this trait less than their offspring. However, there are problems with this study. As all the participants were parents, with an average age in their 40s, they could not be said to be representative of people making a first marriage. It may also be that 'good looks' are valued differently at a younger age, thus skewing the findings. If so, the difference in relation to mate and in-law choice may be even greater than the results suggest. It is possible that becoming a parent may influence a person's mating preferences, so that in-law and mating preferences could appear to be more similar than they actually are.

Trivers (1974) suggested that other possible areas of parent-offspring conflict may arise in **pregnancy**. As with mate choice, the interests of the mother and the foetus overlap to a large extent. It is in the interest of the mother to provide sufficient resources for the foetus, but not to the extent of compromising her future reproductive potential. It is in the interest of the foetus to attract as many maternal resources as possible without damaging the mother's health during pregnancy. However, their interests are not identical.

A number of events during pregnancy have been explained in terms of parent-foetus conflict. For example Profet (1992) explains morning sickness as a way in which the foetus protects itself from toxins in food, to which the mother has become immune, but which threaten the foetus through the shared blood supply. Similarly, pre-eclampsia is a disorder of pregnancy in which the mother's blood pressure becomes extremely high for a while and can be life-threatening. Haig (1993) explains this in terms of the foetus sending cells into the mother's arteries, which dilate them; this has the benefit of delivering more resources, carried in the mother's blood, to the placenta.

Summary

- Parent-offspring conflict can be explained in terms of **inclusive fitness**.
- There is considerable overlap between offspring and parent in the choice of a partner and son- or daughter-in law. However, **good genes** are more of a priority for offspring, and qualities that serve the wider circle of kin, indicated by **family background**, in a parent.
- There is some **empirical support** for this claim, although the findings are not clear-cut
- Parent-offspring conflict can also explain events in **pregnancy**.

The effects of early experience on relationships

This section will look at the differences in relationships and, to begin with, how experiences in childhood and adolescence affect relationships. Much of the material covered earlier in this chapter focused on Western relationships, so the findings cannot necessarily be generalised to other cultures. For example, the principles of exchange may not apply so well in non-Western cultures. The chapter will therefore conclude by looking at the nature of relationships in different cultures.

Childhood experiences and adult relationships

A lot of research in this area has focused on the effects of the quality of early attachment on later relationships. You may remember that in his **attachment theory**, Bowlby (1907–90) proposed that infants are innately predisposed to develop an attachment — a strong emotional bond — usually with the mother. On the basis of this first attachment, they form an **internal working model (IWM)** of relationships that is applied to all future relationships. He also claimed that if this attachment had not formed in the critical period of the first 5 years, it could no longer be formed and this would lead to long-term and irreversible consequences for the child's development.

Ainsworth et al. (1978) developed the **Strange Situation** technique to classify the quality of an infant's attachment and identified three patterns of attachment:

Strange Situation: patterns of attachment

Type A: insecure (anxious-avoidant), where the child is not particularly concerned when left alone by the mother and does not seek comfort when she returns.

Type B: secure, where the child is upset when the mother leaves the room, but is easily comforted when she returns.

Type C: insecure (anxious-ambivalent), where the child is upset when the mother leaves, but is not easily comforted on her return and combines attempting to be close to her with pushing her away.

Bowlby's attachment theory claims that infants are predisposed to make a strong emotional bond, usually with the mother

Main and Solomon (1990) later identified a fourth type, **Type D**: disorganised, where the child seems dazed and confused and does not seem to have any coherent way of dealing with separation and reunion. This technique has been used to investigate a possible link between infant attachment and interpersonal relationships as children get older.

To explore the nature of adult relationships in relation to early attachment, Main and Goldwyn (1994) developed the **Adult Attachment Interview (AAI)**, which classifies adults into three groups:

AAI groups

Dismissing: childhood experiences and current personal relationships are seen as unimportant.

Autonomous: relationships, both past and current, are seen as important.

Preoccupied-entangled: the importance of past experience is recognised, but past issues are unresolved.

They found a link between early attachment type and adult relationships, with '**dismissing**' being associated with the infant **Type A** classification, '**autonomous**' with **Type B** and '**preoccupied-entangled**' with **Type C**.

This pattern is reflected in the way mothers interact with infants. Vondra et al. (1995) found that dismissing mothers tended to be controlling, and their children were likely to be Type A (anxious-avoidant). Autonomous mothers were sensitive to their infants' needs, with the infants likely to be Type B (secure) and preoccupied mothers tended to be unresponsive and to have Type C (anxious-ambivalent) infants. There is thus an **intergenerational transmission** of relationship quality from infancy to adulthood, with an individual's own experience of early attachment being carried forward into the way he or she interacts with his or her children, in turn affecting the nature of the child's attachment.

Further evidence comes from Quinton and Rutter (1988), who investigated the parenting offered by women who had been raised in institutions. During interaction with their children, they were less sensitive, warm and supportive than a control group. However, it does not follow that poor parenting skills necessarily result from a lack of an early attachment, but may arise from other aspects of institutional care. Quinton and Rutter identified factors such as teenage pregnancy, having an unsupportive partner, or one with whom the relationship had broken down. They also found considerable variation in mothering skills in the group they studied, with some being sensitive mothers in spite of their difficult early experiences. The AAI has also been used to examine peer and family relationships in adolescence and early adulthood (see Box 3.14).

Box 3.14	Kobak and Sceery (1988)

Aim: To investigate a link between adult attachment type and peer and family relationships.

Procedure: The AAI was used to categorise 53 college students as dismissing, autonomous or preoccupied-entangled. Self-report and peer ratings were used to assess the quality of their relationships with others.

Results: The secure group was rated as low in anxiety and hostility and felt confident in relationships and well supported by others. In comparison, the dismissing group was rated as high on hostility and reported that their relationships were more distant; they felt lonely and did not feel well-supported by their family. The preoccupied-entangled group felt well supported by their family, but were rated as high in anxiety and lacking in confidence in their relationships.

Conclusion: Early attachment, as reflected in adult attachment types, can affect the nature of relationships in young adults.

A possible link between early attachment and adult romantic relationships has also been explored (see Box 3.15).

Box 3.15 Hazan and Shaver (1987)

Aim: To investigate a possible link between the quality of mothering experienced as an infant and the experience of adult romantic love.

Procedure: Ainsworth's three basic types were used to write descriptions of three types of corresponding adult attachment. On this basis, a 'love quiz' was published in a newspaper and readers were asked to pick which description of adult romantic relationships best applied to them. They were also asked to complete an adjective checklist to describe the kind of parenting they had received as children. The first 620 replies were analysed.

Results: There was a significant correlation between attachment classification, based on the checklist and the choice of participants' description of adult relationships.

Conclusion: There is a link between early attachment experience and the nature of romantic relationships formed as an adult.

Table 3.1 *Attachment type, parenting and adult relationships (Hazan and Shaver 1987)*

Attachment style	Type of parenting	Adult relationships: self-description
Securely attached	Readily available, responsive	I find it relatively easy to get close to others and am comfortable depending on them and having them depend on me. I don't often worry about being abandoned or about someone getting too close to me.
Anxious-avoidant	Unresponsive, rejecting, inattentive	I am somewhat uncomfortable being close to others; I find it difficult to trust them completely, and difficult to allow myself to depend on them. I am nervous when anyone gets too close and, often, love partners want me to be more intimate than I feel comfortable being.
Anxious-ambivalent	Anxious, fussy, out of step with child's needs; only available/responsive some of the time	I find that others are reluctant to get as close as I would like. I often worry that my partner doesn't really love me or won't want to stay with me. I want to merge completely with another person, and this desire sometimes scares people away.

The Hazan and Shaver study suggests that the experience of attachment in early childhood has an impact on adult relationships. However, there are problems with this study; the sample was self-selecting and so not necessarily representative. In addition, people were asked to provide data based on experiences that had happened many years previously, which may not have been entirely reliable. Finally, it is possible that respondents were not completely truthful.

Based on the AAI, a further study carried out by Collins and Read (1990) has explored in more detail the nature of the dimensions along which adult attachments differ. Three dimensions were established — the extent to which a person:

● is comfortable with closeness
● feels that he or she can depend on others
● is anxious that he or she will be unloved or abandoned

They found that for women, being comfortable with closeness was the best predictor of a good relationship with a dating partner, while being low in anxiety about being unloved or abandoned was the best predictor for men.

However, research has not always found a clear link between infant attachment and later relationships. Furman et al. (2002) found that the quality of adolescent friendships predicted features of their romantic relationships, but relationships with parents — as measured by the AAI — did not. This could be explained in terms of the interpersonal theory of personality and personal relationship processes put forward by Sullivan (1953). This theory proposes that mature relationships are related not only to attachment, but also to affiliation (characterised by wanting to spend time with another person), care-giving (offering support, for example by making someone feel good about themselves) and sexual behaviour. Furman et al. argue that affiliation is more important than attachment in friendships and that sexual behaviour, which is part of mature relationships, develops from the intimate exchanges, for example sharing personal information, which is a characteristic of friendship. On this basis, it makes sense that attachment type is only a limited predictor of adult romantic relationships.

It would be unwise to assume, on the basis of these studies, that there is a straightforward link between early attachment and later relationships, since attachment is only one experience in childhood. There has been research into other early experiences that may impact on adult relationships. Indeed, Zimmermann (2000) found that early attachment was not a good predictor of later relationships; life events and in particular serious parental illness and divorce were more influential. Richards (1995) found that children whose parents divorced had more distant relationships with their parents and other relatives as adults. Again, there were individual differences in terms of the impact of divorce, resulting from a number of possible factors, such as the sex of the children, the amount of parental contact and the nature of the relationship between the parents.

Adolescent experiences and adult relationships

Researchers have also been interested in the effect of **adolescent experience** on peer relationships in adulthood. Adolescence is often a difficult time for young people as they develop from childhood to adulthood. In his theory of lifespan development, Erikson (1968) suggests that adolescence is a period when children seek to establish their individual identity; research in Western industrial cultures, for example Grotevant (1998), shows that this is a time when in order to achieve this, they distance themselves from parents and shift focus to their peers. They not only need to make this kind of psychological adjustment, but also to come to terms with the changes in their bodies at puberty.

The timing of puberty has been shown to have an immediate effect on interactions with peers. For example, Simmons et al. (1979) found that early-maturing boys tended to be more confident in peer relationships than late-maturing boys, while early-maturing girls tended to be less popular with other girls, but more popular with boys, than late-maturing girls. The timing of puberty can also have an effect on relationships as an adult. Clausen (1975) found that at 33, most late-maturing boys were less self-confident than the early maturers and more in need of support and help from others, while Jones (1957) found that early-maturing boys were more responsible, cooperative and sociable as adults. In contrast, Simmons et al. (1983) found that early maturing girls were more confident and popular as adults than those that matured late.

Summary

- Links have been made between **infant attachment** types and adults' experience of **relationships with family and peers**, including romantic relationships.
- Difficult early childhood experiences are associated with later poor **parenting**, though there is a lot of **individual variability**.
- **Life events**, such as death of a parent or divorce, are also relevant to the quality of later relationships.
- The timing of **puberty** is associated with immediate effects on peer relationships, which can continue into adulthood.

Relationships in different cultures

In cross-cultural research, Hsu (1971) differentiates between individualist and collectivist cultures. In **individualist** cultures, the emphasis is on the goals and needs of the individual and the importance of personal choice. Priority is given to personal achievement and self-reliance; the USA is a good example of this kind of culture. In **collectivist** cultures, the emphasis is on the goals and needs of the social group and the duty of the individual towards the group to which they belong; priority is given to the unity and welfare of the group. This is more typical of non-Western cultures, such as India. This is a broad distinction, since there are subcultural variations within any culture, but is nonetheless one that may help to explain differences in behaviour between people living in different societies. Moghaddam et al. (1993) have used this distinction to suggest that Western relationships are dominated by different concerns from non-Western relationships.

Cultural differences in relationships

Western relationships are characterised as:
- voluntary (individuals select their own partners)
- individualistic (the partnership is the concern of the two people involved)
- temporary (the partnership lasts until either partner wishes to finish it)

Eastern relationships are characterised as:
- involuntary (individuals do not select their own partners)
- communal (the partnership is the concern of the wider social group)
- permanent (the partnership is seen as being for ever)

Both kinds of relationship offer benefits but also have costs. In an individualist culture, people have more personal freedom, but they are more likely to suffer from loneliness and are at greater risk of divorce. In a collectivist culture, social support is provided by the extended family and loneliness and divorce are less likely. However, at the same time, personal freedom is more limited and there could be a risk of powerful members of the social group controlling those who are less dominant.

The distinction drawn between different kinds of relationship in terms of culture is reflected in the criteria seen to be important in selecting a partner. Dion and Dion (1988) found that people from individualist cultures tended to stress the importance of personality compatibility in choosing a mate. Those from collectivist cultures were more likely to mention socially valued characteristics, such as financial resources and social status. Hofstede (1980) has pointed out that the priorities identified by members of collectivist cultures are logical, given that young people in these cultures may have limited economic freedom. Economic interdependency with their family or small social group makes these factors important; particularly when — as in many collectivist cultures — material resources are scarce. This links well with some of the material in the section on parent-offspring conflict, for example the point raised by Trivers (1974) that a good marriage with an unrelated family can provide economic benefits to kin of the parents beyond those enjoyed by the offspring making that marriage; for example resources when food is short and support in disputes.

In Western individualist cultures, romantic love is seen as the basis for marriage, with each person making their own choice of partner. However, the passionate love popularly shown in Hollywood movies is a Western, individualistic concept when considered as a basis for marriage. India — a collectivist culture — also has a thriving film industry portraying this kind of love, but it does not correspond to what happens in real life. Marriage within collectivist cultures is often arranged. The term **'arranged marriage'** may be associated in Western cultures with unwilling teenage girls being forced into marriages with men they have never met. There are extreme cases where this happens, but these are forced rather than arranged marriages. In arranged marriages, families often select possible partners from among those with a similar social background, with the individual making a choice from among these possibilities. Romantic love is not seen as a prerequisite for these marriages, but this does not mean that they are entirely without love.

In arranged marriages, families select possible partners from among those of similar backgrounds

Sternberg (1986) has suggested that there are different kinds of love, typified by the presence, absence and proportions of three basic components. This can be represented graphically as sides of a triangle that represents the amount of love.

The shape of the triangle changes in relation to the proportion of each kind of love in a relationship.

Using Sternberg's components, passion would be the most prominent component as a basis for Western marriages, with commitment being the major feature of an arranged marriage. In a good marriage, the other components will also develop in time and there is evidence for this in arranged marriages (see Box 3.16).

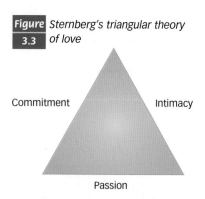

Figure 3.3 *Sternberg's triangular theory of love*

Commitment · Intimacy · Passion

Box 3.16 Gupta and Singh (1992)

Aim: To compare the development of love in arranged and love marriages.

Procedure: A sample of 50 couples in Jaipur in India, some in arranged marriages and some in love marriages, completed Rubin's Love Scale, a questionnaire used to assess different components of love, at various points of time after their marriage.

Results: Those in arranged marriages felt less love at the start of their marriage than those in love marriages. However, this love increased over the first 5 years of marriage and was maintained at this new high level over the following 5 years. For those in love marriages, the degree of love started at a higher level and was maintained over the first 5 years. However, over the following 5 years, it had fallen well below the level experienced by those in arranged marriages.

Conclusion: Love is likely to develop and be maintained in arranged marriages, but is likely to decrease after an initial period in love marriages.

However, some criticisms can be made of the Gupta and Singh study. Since this was a natural experiment, it is likely that the two sets of couples differed systematically in ways other than the type of marriage they had made. In addition, it is highly probable that those marrying for love were in relationships that were, at the time of marriage, substantially more developed than those of couples whose marriages were arranged. It is possible that the lack of an increase in love after marriage in the non-arranged marriages simply reflects the greater maturity of these relationships compared to the arranged marriages.

The individualist/collectivist distinction itself is not without its problems. If we consider the choice of partner, in the arranged marriage system, there can be a large element of choice, even though the choice is restricted. At the same time, it is questionable whether people within a Western individualist culture have a completely free choice without influence from outside pressures.

Another issue is what happens when people change cultures, for example Asians coming to live in Britain. According to Goodwin (1995), it is not unusual for immigrants to fall into two groups, those who wish to maintain traditional values, which stress the role of the family and community in the choice of a partner, and those who adopt the values of their new society, where there is more freedom of choice. Hanassab and Tidwell (1989) claim that whichever position is taken, there are likely to be problems, with individuals feeling torn between two cultural traditions.

It should also be remembered that societies change, sometimes slowly but often dramatically, affecting the values and traditions of people living within those societies, often giving rise to tensions (see Box 3.17).

Box 3.17   Goodwin (1995)

Aim: To investigate the effects of cultural change on relationships.

Procedure: Research into relationships was carried out in Russia, after the fall of the Communist regime. People of different ages and backgrounds were interviewed.

Results: Individualistic relationships were found among the young and affluent. More collectivist attitudes were found among older people and manual workers. The speed with which new individualistic values were being adopted was seen as the cause of problems between different sections of society.

Conclusion: Times of change may bring about a shift in values, including attitudes towards relationships. Rapid change, in particular, can lead to tensions within a society.

While there seems to be a general trend towards adopting individualistic values, there are also cultures where religious values have reversed this and promoted a move towards more collectivist values, for example in Iran (Tashakkori and Thompson 1991).

The individualist/collectivist distinction is useful in illustrating ways in which relationships vary across different cultures, but it has its limitations. Perhaps most importantly, within any culture there are subcultures (the UK is a good example), which may show variations in the way in which relationships are formed. Research is needed to provide a more detailed picture of cultural variation.

Summary

- **Individualist** and **collectivist** cultures differ in their values and priorities and these variations are reflected in their patterns of relationships. Both kinds of culture have advantages and limitations for the individual.
- Individualist cultures tend to see **love** as a prerequisite for marriage, while collectivist cultures expect love to develop within marriage. There is evidence to support this difference.
- Questions arise as to what happens when people change cultures and when a culture itself changes.
- The distinction between individualist and collectivist cultures is useful, but has limitations, particularly in relation to **subcultural differences**.

Chapter

Aggression

Aggression is not an easy term to define. Baron (1977) has proposed one possible definition:
- the **aggressor** must have the intention to harm the victim
- the **victim** must be another living thing
- the **victim** must be motivated to avoid such treatment

This is not altogether satisfactory; for example, it might be argued that planning an aggressive action, even if it is not carried out, could be seen as aggressive. Furthermore, does using force to stop a fight, and so prevent further harm to someone who is being hurt, count as aggression? Nevertheless, this definition does at least provide a framework for investigating aggression.

A number of theorists have put forward ideas to explain aggression. For example, Freud used the term Thanatos, to refer to what he saw as the **death instinct**, to explain aggressive behaviour. Lorenz (1965) also suggested that we have an aggressive instinct that generates energy. This energy needs to be discharged through aggressive behaviour. Others have taken a more directly **biological** approach, proposing that aggression can be explained in terms of brain mechanisms, hormones and genes. These ideas will be looked at in more detail later in the chapter. Many theorists have tried to explain aggression in terms of the **social context** within which it takes place; some of these ideas will be looked at first.

Social psychological approaches to explaining aggression

There are a number of theories that take this approach, including **Social Learning Theory (SLT)** and **deindividuation theory**.

Social Learning Theory (SLT)

SLT is based on the principles of **operant conditioning**, which suggests that we learn through associating a behaviour with its consequences. If a behaviour has a positive outcome, through either positive or negative **reinforcement**, the behaviour is likely to be repeated. SLT, put forward by **Bandura** in the 1960s, takes this a step further, claiming that we not only learn to behave in a particular way as a result of the consequences of our own behaviour, but also through **observational learning** and **modelling**: we observe the behaviour of others and if it has positive consequences, we may adopt the behaviour ourselves. **Vicarious reinforcement** occurs when we observe another person being rewarded for a particular behaviour and this makes it more likely that we will model that behaviour. Bandura carried out a series of studies using a Bobo doll to demonstrate the effects of observational learning and modelling on aggressive behaviour (see Box 4.1).

Box 4.1	Bandura et al. (1963)

Aim: To examine the effects on children's behaviour after they have observed aggressive behaviour in an adult model.

Procedure: In a playroom, with a range of toys, children watched an adult attacking a large inflatable Bobo doll in unusual ways, for example hitting it with a hammer and saying 'Pow!' One group saw the adult rewarded for his behaviour, a second group saw him punished and for a third group, the behaviour had no consequences. The adult then left the playroom and the children entered it. The behaviour of the children was observed. All the children were later offered rewards to behave as the adult model had done and their behaviour was again observed.

Results: During the first observation, the first and third groups of children attacked the Bobo doll in similar ways to the adult. The children who had seen him punished did not. (see Figure 4.1) During the second observation, all three groups modelled the adult's behaviour.

Conclusions: Children can learn particular behaviours through observational learning, even when there is no reinforcement. Behaviour that is seen to be punished is unlikely to be modelled immediately, but it has been learned, since the second group of children could produce similar behaviour when they were encouraged to do so.

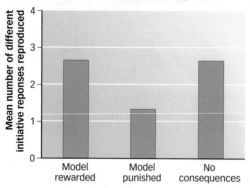

Figure 4.1 The mean number of imitated aggressive behaviours exhibited by children after observing models being rewarded, punished or receiving no feedback for aggression

There are problems with the Bandura et al. study in that it might be limited in terms of what it can tell us about real-life aggression. It could be criticised for having low **ecological validity**, since it is not often that children are exposed to such a simple demonstration of behaviour and its consequences, nor one in which aggression is rewarded. The children were put into an unfamiliar situation, which might have created **demand characteristics**; they could well have been looking for cues as to how they were supposed to behave in this situation. Moreover, the ways in which a Bobo doll can be played with are limited; it is difficult to see what else you could do with it other than hit it. Nonetheless it does suggest that we may learn behaviours in the way that Bandura suggests.

On the basis of this and other studies, Bandura concluded that there are several factors that make it more likely that a person will model the behaviour they have observed. They include:

- The model being similar to themselves, for example being the same gender or age.
- The model being seen as having desirable characteristics, for example being warm and friendly, or an admired celebrity.
- The individual having low self-esteem.
- Observation being direct, for example, when the model is seen in action rather than on film.

SLT also differs from operant conditioning in that there is a **cognitive** element in observational learning and modelling. A person does not simply model behaviour that they have seen reinforced, but processes this information in terms of whether the behaviour is appropriate for them and in what circumstances.

Bandura suggested that there are three main sources of models: the family, the sub-culture and the mass media. The effects of the **media** have been a focus of a great deal of interest, and the idea that people and especially children may be affected by films and television has gained wide public acceptance. There are examples in the press of murders that are said to have been inspired by films. For example, in 1994 the film *Natural Born Killers* was released, in which a young boy and girl kill her abusive family and set off on the road, becoming public celebrities in the course of the film. Soon after its release, a 14-year-old boy in France killed a 13-year-old girl, claiming that he wanted to be famous like the characters in *Natural Born Killers*, one of several murders said to have been inspired by the film.

This is anecdotal evidence and so is limited in what it can tell us, but research into the effects of the media, and in particular the effects of television violence and violent computer games, have been widely researched. In contrast to Bandura's Bobo doll studies, many have been more naturalistic field studies (see Box 4.2).

| Box 4.2 | Friedrich and Stein (1973) |

Aim: To investigate the effect on young children of watching violent cartoons.

Procedure: Children in a nursery school were observed over a period of 3 weeks, in order to establish a baseline measure of aggression. Over the next 4 weeks, they were shown either violent cartoons, non-violent cartoons or prosocial cartoons, in which characters were kind and helpful. Their behaviour during this time and for the following 2 weeks was observed.

Result: Children who were initially above average in terms of aggressive behaviour were affected by the violent cartoons and showed more aggressive behaviour. Other children were not affected.

Conclusion: Watching violent cartoons can lead to a rise in aggressive behaviour, but only for children who are already aggressive. There are interactive effects between the individual and the situation.

The Friedrich and Stein study has the advantage of focusing on naturally occurring behaviour and looking at individual differences. It lends some support to SLT, in that some children showed evidence of observational learning. At the same time, it is possible that the outcome was affected by demand characteristics. The conclusion drawn suggests that it may be something of an oversimplification to propose a straightforward cause-and-effect relationship between being exposed to television violence and aggressive behaviour, in that some children were affected and some were not.

The Friedrich and Stein study looked at the short-term effects of being exposed to media violence. It has been calculated that the average 16-year-old in Western cultures has witnessed around 13,000 violent murders on television, so the longer term effects of such constant exposure have also been investigated (see Box 4.3).

| Box 4.3 | Williams (1985) |

Aim: To investigate the possibility of long-term effects of television violence.

Procedure: In this natural experiment, taking advantage of a naturally occurring event, children's behaviour was monitored in a town in British Columbia before and after it was able to receive television.

Results: Two years after the arrival of television, children were found to be more aggressive than previously, both verbally and physically. There was no increase in aggression over this period in communities who already had television.

Conclusion: Television violence is associated with an increase in children's aggressive behaviour, the effects of which can be long term.

While the Williams' study has high ecological validity, it also has limitations. For example, it would be interesting to know the amount of television violence the children had been exposed to. Were there individual differences in children's responses, as suggested by the Friedrich and Stein study? Did those who watched more television show more aggression than those who watched less? Furthermore it is not known what other societal changes took place over the period of the study, which could perhaps have influenced the rise in aggressive behaviour. It is interesting that a similar longitudinal study, carried out by Charlton et al. (1998) on St Helena in the South Atlantic, found no rise in aggression after the introduction of television, so clearly other factors can modify the effects of television.

There has been a lot of interest in the possible effects on aggression of playing violent video games. Over recent years, the violent content in video games has become increasingly realistic and graphic. While watching television is relatively passive, video games require more active participa-

There is interest in the possible relationship between playing video games and aggressive behaviour

tion. Players adopt roles in which they control actions within the game and decide the direction it should take, and in doing so, they may be rewarded for violent acts against fictitious video game characters or other online players (see Box 4.4).

Box 4.4   Polman et al. (2008)

Aim: To compare the effects of actively playing and passively watching a violent video game on aggressive behaviour.

Procedure: A sample of 57 children, aged 10–13, either played a violent video game, watched the same game, or played a non-violent video game. Levels of aggression were measured by asking their schoolmates about aggressive behaviour of the participants during play sessions at school.

Results: Boys who had played the violent video game behaved more aggressively than those who had only watched it. For girls, there was no difference in behaviour between the three groups.

Conclusion: For boys, but not for girls, active participation in a violent video game results in more aggressive behaviour than merely watching it.

The Polman et al. study was small scale, but nonetheless it suggests again that a straightforward cause-and-effect relationship between exposure to violence in the media and demonstrating aggressive behaviour is too simplistic. In particular, the effects of being actively involved in playing a violent video game add a further dimension to the ideas of SLT. It also confirms the findings of Bandura et al. (1963) that gender is a variable, which is looked at in greater detail in the section on biological theories of aggression.

Other research also challenges the view that exposure to violent video games is a major factor in aggressive behaviour. In a pair of studies involving violent video games, Ferguson et al. (2008) found that males were more aggressive than females, again supporting the idea of a biological basis to aggression, but that neither exposure to violent video games in the laboratory nor previous real-life exposure to such games was found to be a good predictor of aggression. In their second study, they established an association between exposure to family violence and later committing a violent crime, but no such association with exposure to video-game violence. This again challenges the view that media violence has negative effects.

On the other hand, this study supports Bandura's idea of the **family** as a source of models that may be even more important than the media. There is considerable research evidence to support the idea, known as the **intergenerational transmission of violence**, that a child raised in a violent family is more likely to be aggressive as he or she grows up. A number of studies have found that children who witness aggression between parents are more likely to be violent within their own adult relationships. For example, in a study of university students, Breslin et al. (1990) found that for both men and women, there was a strong correlation between witnessing physical parental aggression when they were children and being themselves aggressive in their relationships. However, families share genes as well as environments, so an alternative interpretation of the findings is possible.

A major longitudinal study carried out in Canada found that 8% of children aged 4–11 had witnessed physical aggression in their families. Onyskiw (2000) investigated whether any effects of this experience were already apparent in childhood (see Box 4.5).

Box 4.5	Onyskiw (2000)

Aim: To carry out a large-scale study to investigate a possible link between witnessing parental aggression and aggression in childhood.

Procedure: A sample of over 11,000 children aged 4–11 took part in this study. For all the children, mothers completed questionnaires about both parents and child. The older children also completed their own questionnaires.

Results: Children who witnessed aggression more frequently were themselves more aggressive. Aggression was also associated with a lack of maternal responsiveness and with children who were sad, withdrawn and depressed. Across all age groups, boys were more physically aggressive.

Conclusion: There is some support for the claim made by SLT that aggressive behaviour can be learned within the family. At the same time, other characteristics, in particular gender, emotional variables and the quality of mothering, influenced the outcome.

The Onyskiw study is useful in that it used a large sample to demonstrate that aggressive behaviour can be learned within the family. It again highlights the idea that factors other than witnessing aggression need to be taken into account. However, Onyskiw reported that in the case of both mothers and children completing questionnaires, there was some divergence in what was reported, reducing the reliability of the findings.

One aspect of SLT is the proposal that modelling of behaviour is more likely when the model is perceived to be similar to the observer, for example the same sex. The theory would therefore predict that the same-sex parent would be a stronger model than the opposite-sex parent, and there is some support for this. In a study of students, Jankowski et al. (1999) found that students were significantly more likely to be aggressive towards their partners when they had witnessed as children aggression in the same-sex parent than when aggression was shown by the opposite-sex parent.

There is also support for the influence of the **subculture** on aggression. In interviews with young offenders, Halliday-Boykins and Graham (2001) found a link between offending and growing up within a violent community. This issue has also been investigated more closely in relation to the effect of the subculture on children (see Box 4.6).

Box 4.6   Werner (2001)

Aim: To investigate a possible relationship between peer influence, aggression and later antisocial behaviour.

Procedure: Two large samples of 9-year-old children, one of highly aggressive individuals and the other of children who were low in aggression, were asked who their three best friends were. These children were also assessed for aggression. Changes in levels of aggression of the sample children were assessed after a year.

Results: Those children who had highly aggressive friends had become more aggressive themselves and in the case of boys, more physically aggressive. They were also more likely to show other kinds of antisocial behaviour, such as disruptive behaviour.

Conclusion: Peers can influence the development of aggression in children.

It should be borne in mind that children choose their friends, so it could be that children who are already more aggressive make friends with other aggressive children. Even so, the findings are worrying, given that Dishion, Patterson and Griesler (1994) found that childhood aggression was a good predictor of future antisocial behaviour, including delinquency, crime and substance abuse.

The element of **cognition** in SLT has also been supported. Dodge et al. (1997) found that children who had witnessed parental aggression were more likely than controls to see aggression as a legitimate social response; not only their behaviour but also their beliefs had been influenced by what they had observed.

The social learning theory explanation of aggression has been extremely influential, and there is evidence to support the idea that modelling, particularly in children, can explain some aggressive behaviour. It takes environmental and cognitive factors, as well as individual differences, into account. However, it also seems to be the case that it cannot provide a complete explanation. Other factors, and in particular a possible genetic component and gender differences, may also play a part.

Summary

- **Social learning theory** suggests that we may acquire behaviours as the result of **observational learning and modelling**.
- There is some support for Bandura's proposal that the **media**, the **family** and the **subculture** are sources of models, though research findings have suggested that other factors are also likely to be involved.
- There is also support for the **cognitive** element of SLT.

Deindividuation

Another social psychological theory of aggression is deindividuation. This term refers to losing a sense of personal identity, perhaps by becoming part of a group, or by wearing a costume or mask. When we become anonymous, we may behave in ways quite different from how we would normally behave as identifiable individuals, and this may be expressed as aggression. Everyday observation of group behaviour — for example at football matches or demonstrations — suggests that people often behave more violently in groups than as individuals.

An early suggestion as to why this might be was put forward by Le Bon (1895), who suggested that when we become anonymous, our control over our own behaviour may become weakened. We are less concerned with observing social norms and

Deindividuation theory suggests that people often behave more violently in groups

with how our behaviour will be evaluated by others and are less likely to think about the consequences of what we do. Our inhibitions are lowered and aggressive behaviour, as well as other antisocial behaviour such as vandalism, becomes more likely. The effect of anonymity on behaviour has been investigated experimentally (see Box 4.7).

Box 4.7   Diener et al. (1976)

Aim: To investigate the influence of anonymity on antisocial behaviour.

Procedure: In a field study, the behaviour of 1,300 children at Halloween was observed when they were doing 'trick or treat', going from house to house asking for sweets or money.

Results: Children who were in large groups and wearing costumes and masks, which made it impossible for them to be identified, were more likely than other children to steal sweets and money.

Conclusion: There is an association between anonymity and antisocial behaviour.

However, while the Diener et al. study lends some support to the idea that deindividuation can lead to antisocial behaviour, it is a correlational study and so cannot establish the direction of causation. It is possible, as the theory suggests, that those children who were wearing disguises behaved more aggressively because they could not be identified. It is also possible, however, that those children who were more aggressive were the ones who chose to wear costumes and so make themselves anonymous. Zimbardo (1969) proposed that anonymity was the key factor leading to deindividuation and carried out a study focusing on this idea (see Box 4.8).

Box 4.8   Zimbardo (1969)

Aim: To investigate anonymity as a possible cause of aggression.

Procedure: In a study similar to that carried out by Milgram on obedience, participants took part in what was described as a study into the effects of punishment on obedience. They were asked to give electric shocks to the 'learner' (actually a confederate of the experiment) for wrong answers in a learning task, though in fact no shocks were delivered. The participants could see the 'learner', who appeared to be in great discomfort, through a one-way mirror. Half of the participants sat in a darkened room, wore bulky coats and hoods that hid their faces, were only spoken to as a group and were not addressed by name. The other participants wore ordinary clothes, had large name tags and were introduced to each other by name. All participants were given information about the 'learner', either positive (that she was warm and sincere) or negative (that she was conceited or critical). The degree of 'shocks' given by each group was compared.

Results: Participants in the 'anonymous' condition gave twice as much shock than those in the control condition. Those in the control condition, but not those in the 'anonymous' condition, decreased the level of shocks given when they had been given positive information about the 'learner'.

Conclusion: The anonymity of the hooded participants led to deindividuation, which in turn led to aggressive behaviour.

A more recent study has also demonstrated that anonymity can lead to aggression (see Box 4.9).

Box 4.9   Ellison et al. (1995)

Aim: To investigate anonymity as a possible cause of aggression.

Procedure: A confederate driver pulled up in front of other cars at a traffic light. He remained stationary when the lights turned green and recorded the hooting behaviour of the driver behind him. In some cases, these drivers were in open-top cars and so were identifiable, while others were in closed-top cars and so were anonymous.

Results: The 'anonymous drivers' were quicker to hoot their horns and hooted more frequently and for longer.

Conclusion: Anonymity can lead to aggressive behaviour.

There is some evidence, therefore, that the deindividuation brought about by anonymity can lead to aggressive behaviour. However, the main problem with this theory of aggression is that deindividuation does not always lead to aggressive behaviour and so can only account for some instances. There have been conflicting findings in research in this area, with some studies finding that the anonymity that creates deindividuation increases aggression, some finding that it has no effect and some even finding that it reduces aggression. For example, Gergen et al. (1973) found that a group of participants who spent an hour together in a dark room made physical contact with each other and a large majority were sexually aroused, whereas a similar group, who spent an hour in the room with normal lighting, did not experience these effects.

Deindividuation often occurs in group situations, and we will return to it again in this context later in the chapter.

Summary

- The theory of deindividuation suggests that **anonymity** leads to aggression.
- While there is some empirical support for this idea, anonymity can have different effects.

Institutional aggression

An institution can be defined as any organisation that seeks to benefit itself, others or both. This definition includes such diverse organisations as sports and professional groups, government, the military and cults. In any of these institutions, there is a synergistic interaction of individuals, which means that such an organisation has the potential to be more damaging than individuals working destructively on their own. Whitaker (2000) argues that all organisations have the potential for aggression, whether physical or psychological, since their goals may be against the interests of outsiders. Aggression can also be used against members of the organisation who challenge its goals and actions.

Social Identity Theory (SIT) is relevant to institutional aggression. Tajfel (1978) proposed that our identity has two components: personal identity and social identity. **Personal identity** refers to our perception of our individual traits and relationships, which are unique to us, whereas **social identity** is created as a result of our membership of different groups. We tend to put people into categories and this also applies to ourselves. For example, you may define yourself as a girl, a student, a Baptist or a member of a hockey team. Since we all strive for a positive self-image, we emphasise the positive aspects of the groups to which we belong, on the basis that if the group is seen positively, we can also see ourselves positively as a member. One way of enhancing the positive aspects of the groups to which we belong (**ingroups**) is to think less positively of groups to which we do not belong (**outgroups**) and to overemphasise the differences between the two. This leads to biases in the way we see and behave towards other people. These effects have been demonstrated experimentally (see Box 4.10).

Box 4.10	**Tajfel (1970)**

Aim: To investigate the effect of group membership on behaviour towards another group.

Procedure: Schoolboys were divided into groups using clearly arbitrary criteria such as the toss of a coin. There was no contact between group members; all that each boy knew about the others taking part was whether or not they were members of the same group. Their task was individually to allocate points (later to be converted into money) either to members of their own group or the other group.

Results: There was a strong tendency for the boys to allocate more points to their own group. They were also likely to maintain the differentials between the groups, even where this meant allocating fewer points in total to their own group.

Conclusion: Group membership is in itself sufficient to lead to ingroup favouritism and negative outgroup bias.

Tajfel carried out a series of these experiments, known as **minimal group** studies, because the basis of dividing people into groups was essentially random. These had similar findings, even when participants knew that allocation to groups was not based on any important distinction.

Within an organisation, individual members are therefore likely to see membership of the group as part of their social identity and take a correspondingly negative view of those outside the group, laying the foundation for possible aggression against them. This theory will be returned to in the final section of this chapter.

If any organisation is to function effectively, there has to be some inhibition of an individual's personal behaviour and values in favour of the group ethos, in other words a degree of **conformity** within the group. An individual group member may need to check his or her personal impulses and be guided by the social and cultural forces of the environment relating to the group. He or she may act as a group member in a way that is different from the way he or she would act as an individual and in pursuit of the organisation's aims; this may well be aggressive. This links in with the idea of **deindividuation**, discussed earlier, as a group member becomes less an individual and more a part of a larger whole. It also relates to the idea of being in an **agentic state**, when an individual feels controlled by others, in this case the organisation, and so lacks a sense of personal responsibility for his or her behaviour.

Some institutions, in particular the military, have aggression as one of their aims. Soldiers are trained not only to protect, but also to harm and destroy. This training may create an ethos in which aggressive behaviour may be demonstrated in contexts other than those for which it was originally intended. Whitaker (2000) gives the example of the US Marine Corps. When a man has completed his paratrooper training he is awarded his wings, a medal that is pinned to his uniform. However, there have been a number of cases of what is known as 'blood winging', where, in spite of the practice being officially forbidden, the medal is pinned directly to the marine's chest. This could be at least in part explained in terms of **desensitisation**, where emotions are blunted as a result of repeated exposure to an emotional stimulus, in this case a lowered sensitivity to the pain of others. A similar idea has been put forward to account for children's decreasing response to violence in the media; over time, a higher level of violence becomes necessary to elicit the same response.

In another military context, Eisler (1996) describes the training of Nazi SS officers who manned the mass extermination camps. They were given puppies to raise, which they had to feed, play with and care for. They were then instructed to kill the puppies without showing any signs of emotion. The aim of this part of the training programme was to produce men who had a reduced ability to respond to feelings, other than 'hard' feelings, such as anger and hate, and so could carry out the job to which they had been assigned.

An alternative way of explaining behaviour such as 'blood winging' is **emergent norm theory**, proposed by Turner and Killian (1973). This theory suggests that behaviour such as aggression is more likely to be shown in a group because the group develops norms to which the individual then conforms. In a military organisation, aggression is a necessary part of being a soldier and so becomes one of the norms of the group.

Institutional aggression can also come about through a system within the organisation of **shared beliefs** involving violence, which has characterised many cults. A cult can be defined as a religious or political group with unorthodox and extremist views, whose members often live outside conventional society. Typically, a cult has a charismatic leader, who demands complete obedience from his or her followers, both in terms of their beliefs — often achieved by controlling the access of cult members to information other than that provided by the leader — and their behaviour.

One example is the Aum Shinrikyo doomsday cult in Japan. This quasi-religious group carried out an attack in the Tokyo underground system in 1995, using the nerve gas Sarin. The attack killed 12 commuters, seriously injured 54 and 980 others were less seriously affected. The cult's leader Shoko Asahara created a belief system based on Shiva, the Hindu god of destruction, and was on a mission of destruction to 'cleanse' the world in preparation for a new world order. Members of the cult who questioned any of its beliefs or principles were themselves 'cleansed' by being beaten.

Similarly, Charles Manson was the leader of 'the Family'. Influenced by the Book of Revelation in the New Testament, Manson believed that there were coded messages on The Beatles' *White Album* and in particular the song *Helter Skelter*, predicting a race war that would lead to the extermination of all white people in America. Manson and his followers planned to retire to an underground city in Death Valley during this time, to emerge at the end of the conflict to rule the remaining blacks, whom Manson believed would be incapable of running the world. He and members of the Family carried out murders, including that of the actress Sharon Tate, which were intended to precipitate race war.

Summary

- Institutional aggression can be related to **Social Identity Theory**, which suggests we define ourselves partly in terms of group membership and have negative views about other groups.
- **Conformity** to the norms of the institution can lead to **deindividuation** and the sense of being in an **agentic state**.
- In organisations where violence is one of the goals, **desensitisation** can take place, leading to aggression being carried over into other situations.
- **Emergent norm theory** suggests that within the group, norms develop to which we then conform.
- Cults have a **shared belief system**, which may involve violence towards those outside the group.

Biological explanations of aggression

We have looked so far at social explanations of aggression, either in terms of an individual's social experience or in relation to institutions. However, there is also a good deal of research that has looked at the biological basis of aggression and the mechanisms that may lead to it being expressed.

Neural and hormonal mechanisms in aggression

One approach to explaining aggression in physiological terms is with reference to brain anatomy. The **limbic system** of the brain is an area associated with emotional arousal and response, with the amygdala and septum being key areas. There is evidence that the **prefrontal cortex**, a part of the cortex involved in planning and the conscious control of behaviour, is involved in inhibiting aggressive behaviour.

The relevance of the **amygdala** in mediating violence was first established as a result of work by Kluver and Bucy (1939), who found that monkeys who had their temporal lobes removed were extremely docile. Later research indicated that this behaviour was mediated by the amygdala, as its removal produced similar effects. In animals, electrical stimulation of the amygdala produces aggressive behaviour, and there is evidence that it plays the same role in human behaviour. In 1966, a sniper called Charles Whitman killed 14 people and wounded 31 others from the University of Texas Tower, before he was killed by a police marksman. He left a note asking that his brain be examined for possible dysfunction. A post mortem revealed that he had a tumour pressing into his amygdala. Albert et al. (1993) report that aggression in humans increases with tumours in the medial hypothalamus and septal region and with seizure activity in the amygdala.

Measures of brain functioning such as the EEG have long suggested that violent criminals have impaired neurological processes, but the recent advancement of neuroimaging techniques has

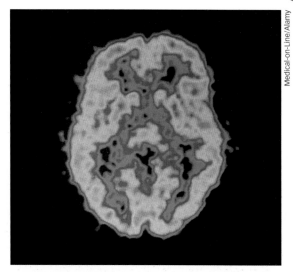

Neuroimaging techniques such as PET scans have allowed researchers to examine violent offenders' brains

allowed researchers to examine violent offenders' brains in more detail. Raine et al. (1997) used PET scans to carry out a study to compare brain activity in 41 convicted violent offenders to activity in 41 age-matched controls. They found that the people convicted of murder had reduced activity in the **prefrontal cortex** and abnormal activity in subcortical regions such as the amygdala and thalamus. This finding fits well with previous research showing that damage to the prefrontal cortex impairs decision making and increases impulsive behaviour. However, while the study provides good evidence that impaired brain functioning may underlie some types of violent aggression; participants in the 'violent' group were at the extreme end of an aggression continuum and may not be typical of most aggressors. There are many examples of people with prefrontal cortex damage who do not commit violent acts, so brain abnormality of this kind cannot provide a complete answer as to why people are aggressive.

There is evidence that exposure to media violence can modify brain functioning. In a study using fMRI imaging, Weber et al. (2006) found that while playing a violent video game, participants showed suppressed activity in the amygdala and the anterior cingulate gyrus, both areas associated with emotion.

Studies of the brain have also helped to explain why men are, in general, more aggressive than women. Gur et al. (2002) found that compared to men, women had proportionally larger frontal brain regions, which exert inhibitory control over behaviour in relation to the size of the amygdala, hippocampus and other limbic areas associated with emotional arousal. This suggests that women may be better able to control emotional responses than men.

It has been suggested that the hormone **testosterone** may mediate aggression, and this link has been well established in non-human animals, such as mice. In humans, males of all ages, races and cultures are generally more physically aggressive than females. Males usually have higher levels of testosterone than females, and testosterone is a major influence on male sexual development. Some studies have shown a correlation between high testosterone levels and aggression. For example, Kalat (1998) found that young men aged 15–25, an age at which testosterone levels are at their highest, demonstrate the highest levels of aggression, as measured by crime statistics. However, this is again correlational evidence, and so cannot tell us the direction of the effect. It could also be explained in other ways, for example as a result of the psychological changes that take place in adolescence and the challenges faced by young adults making life decisions at this time.

It has also been suggested that the understanding of what constitutes aggression could be extended to include its expression in characteristics such as assertiveness and competitiveness, and there is some evidence that high testosterone levels in males are related to this kind of social aggression. For example, men with high testosterone levels are often more successful in professions that thrive on competition, such as running a company or following a career in sport. However, as discussed at the beginning of the chapter, aggression is difficult to define and this kind of broad definition is not generally accepted.

There are problems with making a straightforward link between testosterone levels and aggression. For example, aggression does not increase at puberty when testosterone levels rise, or when testosterone is administered to support sexual activity in hypogonadal males. It is possible that rather than high levels of testosterone leading to aggressive behaviour, other factors may have an effect. Klinesmith (2006) found that handling a gun, associated with aggressive behaviour, caused testosterone levels, assessed from saliva samples, to rise. This kind of explanation might also be applied to the findings of Kalat, mentioned previously. Moreover, the correlations found between testosterone levels and aggression are usually small. In a large meta-analysis of 45 studies, Book et al. (2001) found a correlation of only +0.14. It has also been suggested that females are not necessarily less aggressive than males; rather, they may express aggression differently, for example by causing others psychological distress. Testosterone levels are therefore not a good predictor of aggression.

There is evidence to suggest that the neurotransmitter **serotonin** plays a key role in mediating violent and aggressive behaviour. Kyes et al. (1995) found that lowering serotonin levels in vervet monkeys increases their aggressive behaviour, whereas raising serotonin levels reduces aggression and increases peaceable interactions like grooming. Serotonin has also been implicated in human aggression. For example, medication that boosts the functioning of the serotonergic systems (physiological systems that use serotonin) has been shown to reduce hostility and violent outbursts in aggressive psychiatric patients. Moreover, Virkkunen et al. (1987) found that people with a history of impulsively violent behaviour, such as arsonists, violent criminals and people who die by violent methods of suicide (which can be thought of as aggression against oneself), showed low levels of serotonin in their cerebrospinal fluid. Similarly, Moffitt et al. (1998) carried out a large-scale study, with 781 men and women aged 21 years old, into the relationship of serotonin levels and aggression, as assessed through self-reports and records of court convictions and found a relationship for men but not for women. However, these findings are correlational, so the direction of the effect is unclear. It may be that aggressive behaviour affects serotonin levels rather than vice versa.

Bernhardt (1997) has suggested that it is the combination of high levels of testosterone and low levels of serotonin that lead to aggression. He notes that testosterone is linked more strongly to dominance than aggression and that low serotonin activity is associated with being overly responsive to aversive stimuli. Thus when a high-testosterone man is put into a situation where dominance is frustrated, low serotonin levels make it more likely that he will respond in an aggressive way to the situation. This fits well with the finding that both the amygdala and the hypothalamus are associated with both testosterone and serotonin.

Summary

- The **limbic system** and the **prefrontal cortex** have been implicated in aggressive behaviour.
- While a link between **testosterone** and aggression is well established in non-human animals, there is limited evidence for a direct relationship in humans.
- Aggression is related to low levels of **serotonin**.
- High levels of testosterone in combination with low levels of serotonin may help to account for aggression.

Genetic factors in aggressive behaviour

Jacobs et al. (1965) made an early attempt to link genes to violent behaviour, when they found that a large number of men in prison had XYY sex chromosomes instead of the normal XY. This led them to suggest that men born with an extra Y chromosome might have inherited a predisposition to violence. Although this idea attracted a lot of attention at the time, further examination of XYY males revealed that they did not necessarily display any particularly violent tendencies, and further examination showed that they were mainly imprisoned for crimes against property (for example burglary) rather than for violent crime. Moreover, XYY males are relatively common (about 1 in 1,000 males), the majority of whom do not commit violent crimes, while some men with the normal XY chromosomal pattern are violent, so this chromosomal abnormality falls short of explaining violent behaviour.

In later research, Brunner et al. (1993) identified a mutation in the gene coding for the enzyme monoamine oxidase A (MAOA) in male members of a Dutch family who all showed abnormal aggressive behaviour, and separate research by Shih et al. (2000) has shown that mice deficient in MAOA also show high rates of aggression. MAOA is involved in the metabolising of serotonin, and as detailed in the previous section, aggression has been linked to low levels of serotonin. However, aggressive behaviour is not confined to individuals with this mutation, so again it can only be a partial explanation. A longitudinal study provides some evidence that aggression may, to a degree, be innate rather than learned (see Box 4.11).

Topics in psychology

4

Box 4.11	**Stevenson and Goodman (2001)**

Aim: To investigate a possible link between childhood temperament and later aggression.

Procedure: A total of 828 randomly selected children were assessed at age 3 in 1969–70 for behaviours such as temper tantrums, bedwetting, poor concentration and an inability to get along with their siblings. Family and social circumstances were also assessed.

Results: As adults, 81 were later convicted of crimes, 26 of them violent. There was a significant link between the behaviours assessed at age 3 and violent tendencies as adults. There was no link with adverse family circumstances.

Conclusion: Differences in temperament as a child can give some indication of a tendency to violence as an adult. As this is not linked to adverse family circumstances, it provides some support for the view that differences in aggression are innate.

However, as the researchers point out, levels of offending in this sample were low. Although problems in early childhood might indicate a risk of criminality, there is not enough evidence to claim that they can reliably predict violent behaviour. Evidence for a genetic component to aggression also comes from twin studies (see Box 4.12).

Box 4.12	**McGue et al. (1992)**

Aim: To investigate the contribution of genes to aggression.

Procedure: The aggression scale on the Multi-Dimensional Personality Questionnaire was used to assess levels of aggression in 54 pairs of MZ twins and 79 pairs of DZ twins.

Results: There was a correlation of +0.43 for MZ twins and +0.30 for DZ twins.

Conclusion: The higher correlation for MZ twins suggests that genetic factors play a part in aggression.

While the McGue et al. study suggests that genes have a role in aggression, other interpretations of the findings are possible. For example, the greater similarity of the scores of MZ twins than those of DZ twins may result from MZ twins being treated both within and outside the family in a more similar way than DZ twins. Although the MZ/DZ difference is significant, it is also relatively small, which suggests that factors other than genes also play a part. However, the role of genes is supported in a similar study by Vernon et al. (1999), who found a larger difference between MZ and DZ twins. An adoption study carried out by van den Oord et al. (1994) again found high heritability in aggression.

However, there is little agreement in the findings across studies of how large the genetic contribution is. In a review of studies of aggression, Rhee and Waldman (2002) claim that depending on which study you look at, the genetic contribution can be anything from 0% to 75%, and these differences can be related to how aggression is defined, how it is assessed and the age of participants.

Assessment is a major issue. Children are usually assessed through the questioning of parents and teachers, while the assessment of adolescents and adults depends on official records, such as arrests, convictions and school records, or the self-report of the individual person being investigated. However, there is often little agreement between different sources (see Box 4.13).

Box 4.13 Achenbach et al. (1987)

Aim: To investigate consistency between different ways of assessing aggression.

Procedure: In a meta-analysis of 119 studies, using 269 samples, the degree of correlation between ratings of aggression of participants aged 18 months to 19 years provided by parents, teachers, mental health workers, peers and the participants themselves was calculated.

Results: The mean correlation between all sources of ratings was statistically significant, but in some cases rather low:

- pairs of parents: +0.6
- parent and teacher: +0.28
- participant and other sources: +0.22

The correlations were significantly lower for adolescents than for children aged 6–11.

Conclusion: There is considerable variation in the assessment of aggression depending on the source of the information and the age of the person being assessed.

Assessment raises a further problem in twin studies. Several studies (for example McCartney et al. 1990) have found that parents tend to overestimate the similarity of MZ twins and underestimate the similarity of DZ twins, when compared with the estimates made by the twins themselves.

While the nature of the assessment and the age of the person being assessed make it difficult to calculate the genetic component to aggression, psychologists agree that genes probably have a role in aggression because violent behaviour tends to run in families. However, with a complex behaviour like aggression, it is especially difficult to separate genetic and environmental contributions. Perhaps the most plausible conclusion is that it is possible to inherit a predisposition to violence, but modelling aggressive behaviour observed in the home and from other sources is also likely to be an important factor.

Summary

- There is limited evidence for a **genetic** explanation of aggression.
- **Twin** and **adoption** studies provide some support.
- It is difficult to establish the contribution of genes because of problems of **assessment**.

4

Aggression as an adaptive response

Evolutionary explanations of human aggression

In a general way, evolutionary theory can explain human aggression, and in particular gender differences. In our evolutionary past, aggression would have been adaptive for males, in terms of making hunting more productive, protecting territory and controlling mating, therefore making it more likely that the individual would survive to reproduce. However, particular focus has been given in this kind of theory to explaining male aggression in relation to jealousy and infidelity in sexual relationships.

For both males and females, infidelity can be adaptive. For a male, additional sexual partners increase reproductive success. For a female, mating with a male with better genes than her current mate can lead to an improvement in the quality of her offspring. However, for both males and females, the infidelity of a partner threatens their own fitness. A male with an unfaithful mate may put resources into offspring who are not genetically his, while for a female an unfaithful male may divert resources from her and her offspring. For these reasons, jealousy, and therefore mate guarding, are natural responses.

A key issue here is **paternity uncertainty**. Because fertilisation in humans is internal, while females always know who their offspring are, males can never be entirely certain. In terms of reproductive success, infidelity in a partner is more costly to a male than to a female, whose offspring — whoever they are fathered by — will still carry her genes. To maximise the possibility of their genes being carried on to the next generation and beyond, males need to be as certain as possible that they have indeed fathered any offspring to whom care is given, rather than making a parental investment in infants to whom they are not genetically related.

Anxieties about paternity can be linked to cultural attitudes and practices of men in relation to women. Daly and Wilson (1996) have indicated some of the ways in which men in different cultures have tried to increase paternal certainty. They may attempt to restrict the access of other men to females, for example by female circumcision and in particular infibulation, which makes intercourse impossible for a woman and guarantees her virginity. Similarly, the veiling of women in some Muslim countries and not allowing them to travel without a male relative serves the same purpose.

Other cultural attitudes and practices relate to physical violence towards unfaithful women; if they are unfaithful, they will put themselves at risk. As an extreme example, in some cultures, adulteresses are stoned to death, but some degree of violence of men against their partners whom they suspect of infidelity happens worldwide and in some cases has been

TopFoto

In our evolutionary past, aggression would have been adaptive for men in terms of hunting and protecting territory

condoned as reasonable. Pinker (1997) cites a case in America as recently as 1974 in which a man who killed his wife when he found her with a lover was not considered guilty of a crime. Gender differences towards infidelity have also emerged in a study by Buckle et al. (1996), who examined the reasons given for divorce between 1974 and 1989 in samples from Canada, England and Wales; adultery was given as a reason by over 40% of men, but only around 10% of women.

According to evolutionary theory, the emotion of jealousy in males in response to sexual infidelity is an adaptive response to the risk that parental investment may be 'wasted' on offspring who do not carry their genes. In females, who are certain that their offspring are genetically theirs, it would be expected that jealousy should be related to the fact that a male partner may be investing resources elsewhere that could be devoted to herself and her offspring. Research has investigated possible gender differences (see Box 4.14).

Box 4.14 Buss (1992)

Aim: To investigate the nature of jealousy in men and women.

Procedure: Both men and women were asked if they would be more jealous if their partner had sex with someone else or if they formed a deep emotional attachment to another person.

Results: Of the men, 60% said they would be more jealous if their partner had a sexual relationship with another person. Of the women, 85% said they would be more jealous if their partner formed a deep emotional attachment to someone else. These subjective measures were supported by physiological measures, such as heart rate and galvanic skin response (GSR).

Conclusion: If a man is to make a parental investment in children, he would need to be sure that they were genetically his, and this would be compromised by his partner having a sexual relationship with another person. A woman would want a commitment from her partner to help ensure that any children produced would survive until maturity. A deep emotional attachment to another person would be more of a threat to this than sexual infidelity.

However, the validity of these findings has been questioned. Harris (2002) found similar results to those of Buss when the same procedure was followed, but when participants recalled personal experiences of a partner's actual infidelity, there was no significant difference between men and women; both focused more on emotional infidelity. There was no correlation between how they responded to hypothetical infidelity (as in the Buss study) and their reactions to actual infidelity.

Harris and Christenfeld (1996) further suggest that the differences found in studies such as those of Buss can be explained in terms of how men and women interpret infidelity, rather than being the result of innate emotional differences. Men may believe that women have sex only when in love and so interpret sexual infidelity as the partner being in love with someone else. Women may believe that men can have sex without love, so should be less bothered by sexual infidelity, as it does not imply that a partner has fallen in love. They carried out a survey of 137 undergraduate students, the results of which supported this view.

If evolutionary ideas about jealousy are correct, it would also be expected that because of paternal uncertainty, jealousy would be a stronger emotion in men than in women. It has been suggested that this can be seen in the comparison of figures for violent crimes between spouses (see Box 4.15).

Box 4.15 **Daly and Wilson (1988)**

Aim: To compare the motives of men and women who killed their partners.

Procedure: Data were collected on spousal homicide in Canada over a 9-year period, including the motives for them recorded by the police. The motives were classed as argument, jealousy, anger/hatred and 'other'.

Results: In more cases, the husband was the killer; there were 812 cases in which a husband killed his wife, compared with 248 cases where a wife killed her husband. The percentage of cases in which the motive for the killing was recorded as jealousy was 24% for husbands, compared to only 7.7% for wives.

Conclusion: Jealousy appears to be a stronger motive for violence in men than in women.

It is worth noting that it may well be that in the Daly and Wilson study, jealousy as a motive may be underestimated, since both argument and anger/hatred could contain an element of sexual jealousy.

Summary

- A key factor in gender differences towards infidelity is **paternal uncertainty**.
- There is some support for the prediction of evolutionary theory that **males** would be more jealous of a partner's **sexual infidelity** and **females** of an **emotional attachment**.
- **Jealousy** appears to be a stronger motive for **violence** in men than in women.

Group displays of aggression

We looked earlier at reasons why aggression may be shown by institutions. We will look in this section at groups and aggression, where some of the same factors may apply, together with other influences, in rather more informal groups, in particular sports fans and players and lynch mobs.

Sports events

While most sporting events pass off without incident, there are numerous examples of spectators showing violent behaviour, for example throwing stones or bottles during a football game or being verbally abusive to players or the referee. There have also been occasions where violence was more serious. For example, a 'friendly' international in Dublin in 1995 between the Republic of Ireland and England had to be abandoned after 27 minutes when the English fans rioted. Probably the most serious example, in which English football fans have been involved, took place at the Heysel stadium in Brussels in 1985, when 39 fans were killed during rioting before the European Cup Final between Juventus and Liverpool, which resulted in England being banned from European competition. Sport is intended to promote friendly rivalry, but it seems it can instead create antagonism and precipitate violence.

Aggression is an important and acceptable component of some sports, with aggression in players socially sanctioned. Many sportsmen have

In 1985 at the Heysel stadium in Brussels, 39 fans were killed when football violence turned into a devastating riot

nicknames that focus on their aggressive tendencies, for example the British boxers Nigel 'Dark Destroyer' Benn and Ricky 'Hitman' Hatton, the Mexican boxer Marco Antonio 'Baby Face Assassin' Barrera and the former English footballer who played for Nottingham Forest and Manchester City, and who is now an England coach, Stuart 'Psycho' Pearce. In sports such as boxing and football, a certain amount of controlled aggression is accepted and even admired as being necessary for success. It has been argued that watching aggressive sports could make spectators less aggressive through **catharsis**. This idea proposes that watching aggressive behaviour provides an outlet for violent emotions and so acts as a form of release. After all, most fans do not act aggressively. However, there is evidence to the contrary.

Box 4.16 | **Goldstein and Arms (1971)**

Aim: To compare levels of aggressive emotions before and after different sporting events.

Procedure: Interviews were conducted with 150 male spectators before and after a football match and a control group of 81 males who had watched a gymnastics competition.

Results: Aggressive emotions increased significantly in those who had watched the football game, but not in those who had watched gymnastics.

Conclusion: Watching a sport in which play involves aggression raises levels of aggressive emotions. This does not happen with an equally competitive but non-aggressive sport.

A similar before-and-after study was carried out by Arms et al. (1979), comparing spectators of an ice hockey event (realistic aggression), professional wrestling (stylised aggression, where the aggression shown is often acted rather than genuine) and swimming (competitive but non-aggressive), using three different measures of aggression. They found increased levels of aggression for the groups who had watched ice hockey or wrestling, but not for those who watched swimming, so the effect seems to hold true even when the aggression is not entirely genuine.

4

Social Identity Theory (SIT), which was discussed earlier, could provide at least a partial explanation of the aggression experienced and shown by sports fans. In team sports such as football and ice hockey, being a fan of a particular team would form part of a person's social identity. Negative outgroup bias would lead to hostility towards players and fans of opposing teams, heightened by the teams being in competition with each other. In non-team sports, when there is international competition, identifying oneself as a member of a particular nation would have a similar effect. There is some evidence for this. In a study by Branscombe and Wann (1992), participants watched a boxing match between an American and a Russian; participants who had previously identified themselves as proud to be American, but not those who had little national pride, showed increases in blood pressure while watching the match, suggesting greater identification with the competition.

Social Learning Theory (SLT), discussed at the start of the chapter, has also been used to explain aggression in a sporting context. We learn by observing others' behaviour and its outcome, with one source of models being subculture. If a social norm of aggression has developed within a group of supporters and other fans are perceived as gaining satisfaction from behaving aggressively towards supporters of competing teams or nations, then aggressive behaviour is likely to be modelled.

Within a group of spectators, **deindividuation** is also likely to play a part. Among a group of fans, the individual becomes anonymous and responsibility for aggressive behaviour becomes shared among the group, rather than being focused on an individual; this is known as **diffusion of responsibility**.

Disinhibition is also relevant; watching other people behave aggressively may make aggression come to be seen as an appropriate behaviour, so we lose the inhibitions we have about behaving in this way and remove the restraints we normally impose on our own behaviour.

Aggression has also been linked to physiological **arousal**. In a study by Zillmann and Bryant (1974), participants in whom arousal had been heightened through physical exercise were more aggressive when insulted than those in a lower state of arousal. In the context of sports events, there is arousal in the anticipation of the event and as a result of anxiety about winning and losing. There is also evidence that noise heightens arousal (Quigley et al. 2003), as does being in a crowd (Tripathi 2004), both of which apply to sporting events. These sources underpin the arousal produced by the flow of play. Afterwards, this arousal may find its outlet in aggression. For example, in a football match, if your team has won, aggression against supporters of the losing team may be a way of consolidating the victory. If your team has lost, aggression against supporters of the other team is an act of revenge. Dissipating arousal in this way is more likely at sports events where aggression appears to have become accepted as the norm.

A further reason for aggressive behaviour at sports events is provided by the **frustration-aggression hypothesis**, developed by Dollard et al. (1939). In its basic form, the hypothesis states that frustration always leads to aggression and aggression is always the result of frustration. Frustration is defined here as a goal-directed activity that is prevented from being achieved. In the context of sport, spectators are likely to experience frustration when, for example, their team fails to take advantage of a goal-scoring opportunity, and this is likely to lead to aggression. While this may apply to supporters of both sides in the course of a match, the frustration-aggression hypothesis cannot explain aggression in supporters of the winning side, where arousal may be a better explanation. The frustration-aggression hypothesis will be returned to in the final section.

A cognitive theory of aggression involves what is known as '**priming**'. In cognitive experiments, an individual recognises a word or picture more quickly if he or she has previously been shown the word or picture, or one that is closely related to it in meaning. For example, a picture of Prince Charles will be more quickly recognised if a picture of the queen has previously been shown. A particular schema, in this case 'the royal family', was made accessible and therefore easily triggered by the initial picture. The effect of priming in relation to sport has been investigated (see Box 4.17).

Box 4.17 **Wann and Branscombe (1990)**

Aim: To investigate the effect of priming in relation to sport.

Procedure: Participants (46 males and 40 females) were asked to carry out a task in which they were shown sets of four words, for example 'hockey is fast exciting' and 'baseball is enjoyable challenging' and asked to underline three that could form a sentence. They were randomly assigned to two conditions. In one, some sentences related to aggressive sports, for example hockey, and in the other to non-aggressive sports, for example baseball. After a short distracter task, they read a deliberately ambiguous description of a man called Donald and rated him on personality characteristics, some of which related to aggression and suggested what his hobbies and interests might be, choosing from among aggressive sports, non-aggressive sports and hobbies unrelated to sport, for example music.

Results: There were significantly higher hostility ratings from those whose sentences had related to aggressive sports, and these participants were more likely to choose aggressive sports as being among Donald's interests.

Conclusion: Priming is effective in preparing people to see hostility in others.

The Wann and Branscombe study shows that the effects of priming can explain hostility, even when there are no aggressive models and no heightened arousal. It is suggested that some sporting events, such as boxing and football, are associated with aggression, and so people attending them are already primed for aggression. They may therefore be more likely to interpret the ambiguous conduct of others at these events as hostile and looking for trouble and so behave aggressively. It is worth noting that while aggressive schemas may be activated simply by being at a sporting event that is associated with aggression, they can also be triggered by the behaviour of players. In a survey of hockey matches, Smith (1978) found that 75% of spectators' aggressive outbursts took place following a violent display by the players.

Not all spectators of an aggressive sport act aggressively, and research has looked at **individual differences** in this tendency. In a Canadian study of spectators at a hockey game, Harrell (1981) found that attitudes to violence in the game affected hostility. Those who were tolerant of violence were more likely to behave aggressively than those who were not. This could be related to the idea of desensitisation, mentioned earlier. It may also be the case that more aggressive sports attract people who are already more aggressive.

We have looked so far at aggression in spectators, but research has also investigated aggression in players at sports events. The phenomenon of **home-team advantage** is well established. For example, in a survey of the outcome of sporting events, Schwartz and Barsky (1977) found that the home team won 53% of the time in baseball matches, 60% of American football matches and 64% of basketball and ice hockey matches. They further established that improved home performance was associated with a greater percentage of offensive play.

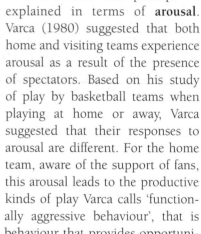

It is not only spectators who show aggression at sports events; research has also investigated violent behaviour in players

This difference can perhaps be explained in terms of **arousal**. Varca (1980) suggested that both home and visiting teams experience arousal as a result of the presence of spectators. Based on his study of play by basketball teams when playing at home or away, Varca suggested that their responses to arousal are different. For the home team, aware of the support of fans, this arousal leads to the productive kinds of play Varca calls 'functionally aggressive behaviour', that is behaviour that provides opportunities for getting ahead in the game. For the visiting team, it leads to 'dysfunctional aggressive behaviour', such as committing fouls on the opposition. The unsupportive behaviour of the crowd towards a visiting team, such as whistling at players who commit personal fouls, might well anger team members and lead to the kind of aggression shown in dysfunctional aggressive play. There is some empirical support for this idea (see Box 4.18).

Box 4.18 McGuire et al. (1992)

Aim: To compare the aggressive play of home and visiting teams.

Procedure: Data were collected from the 1987/88 season of ice hockey games. Thirteen different kinds of aggressive behaviour were identified and levels of aggression of home and visiting teams were compared.

Results: Home teams were more aggressive in games that they won and visiting teams were more aggressive in games that they lost.

Conclusion: Levels of aggression are related to success in ice hockey matches. Aggression is productive for the home team, but not for the visiting team.

A study by Courneya and Carron (1990) supports the idea that this difference is related to the spectators; they found that the home team advantage disappeared for softball teams when there were no spectators present.

Summary

- There is little evidence that sports events create **catharsis**, but rather that they may make aggression more likely.
- Several theories have suggestions to explain spectator aggression at sports events. They include **social theories**, for example SIT, SLT, deindividuation, disinhibition and the frustration-aggression hypothesis; **biological accounts** such as arousal; and the **cognitive explanation** of priming.
- There are **individual differences** in whether or not aggression is shown at sporting events.
- The **home-team advantage** in team sports can be linked to the different kinds of aggression shown by players at home and away games.

Lynch mobs

'Lynching' describes murder, usually by hanging, carried out by a group of people — a lynch mob — who are often a marginalised group in society and who see their actions as a form of non-legal execution. Although lynching has taken place in various parts of the world, and with members of different ethnic groups as victims, it is usually associated with the murder of African-Americans by whites in the southern states of America before the civil rights movement in the 1960s; few people taking part in lynchings have ever been convicted.

Sometimes the reason underlying a lynching was sexual, where a black man was believed to have attacked a white woman, but more often the cause seems to have been economic. The American Civil War (1861–65) was the result of 11 southern slave states declaring secession from the USA. After the war was lost, many whites in the southern states were badly affected and found it difficult to make a living. If a black farmer was lynched, his land then became available. Similarly, in 1930s America, in the grip of the Depression, blacks could be hired for less money than whites and there was anger among unemployed lower-class whites who felt they were losing out in competition with blacks. During this decade, 114 lynchings took place in America; 90% of the victims were black.

Social Identity Theory, discussed earlier, is relevant here, particularly as skin colour readily identified groups. **Diffusion of responsibility**, also mentioned previously, may play a role. Leader et al. (2007) found that the level of violence used by a lynch mob was related to the number of people in the mob, so the greater the number in the group, the less any one individual would feel personal responsibility.

Other theories also have something to offer. **Relative deprivation theory** suggests that when people feel that they are deprived in relation to another group, they become hostile against the group with whom they are comparing themselves. This hostility can then express itself in aggressive behaviour such as lynching. In the Depression, blacks' easier access to paid work could lead to unemployed whites seeing themselves as deprived relative to blacks. **Realistic group conflict theory**, proposed by Sherif (1966), states that hostility between groups comes about when there is a conflict of interests, which again would be the result of whites' perceived competition with blacks for work.

A major and more generally applicable theory in this area is the **frustration-aggression hypothesis**. The original hypothesis was later modified by Miller and Dollard (1941), who claimed that aggression is just one form of learned response to frustration. We may learn, either through our own experience or through observation of others, that when someone is blocking a goal, aggression is often effective in removing the blockage and so is rewarding. These ideas link to operant conditioning (direct experience) and SLT (observation of others).

Another key term here is **drive**, a motivational state that seeks expression in behaviour as the result of a need; for example, a hungry animal will have a drive to feed. When there is no opportunity for the behaviour to take place, frustration is experienced. **Cues** in the environment determine what response to a situation is made. The theory claims that as frustration increases, the drive increases in strength. Where aggression is rewarded, i.e. the goal is reached, the drive is reduced and the individual experiences catharsis.

Miller and Dollard (1941) noted the effects of being part of a crowd. What they called **crowd intensification** relates to individuals having stronger responses as part of being in a crowd than they would on their own. Some of the reasons for this have already been discussed; for example the **deindividuation** experienced as a crowd member reduces individual responsibility for behaviour. Individuals may also feel anxious about appearing different from other group members and so behave as others do to reduce this **anxiety**. You may remember this from the study of conformity carried out by Asch (1951), where members of a group agreed to obviously wrong answers given by

Figure 4.2 *The lynch crowd model, Miller and Dollard (1941)*

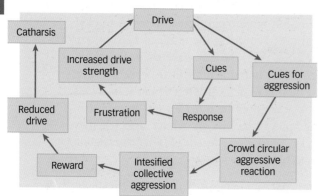

other group members, many of whom said they did so because they did not want to create a bad impression by seeming different from the others. Intensification can also be linked to the physical **arousal** created by the proximity of others, the noise made by a crowd of people and so on. Dollard and Miller (1941) related these ideas explicitly to lynch mob behaviour.

They illustrated this account with reference to a specific lynching that took place in 1933. A young black farm worker was believed to have had a sexual relationship with a white girl. It was believed that she tried to finish the relationship and threatened to tell some white men what had happened, so he killed her. He was charged with rape and murder and apparently confessed, even though there was no evidence of rape and a level of doubt that he had in fact committed the murder. A group of around 100 men tortured him for several hours and finally killed him. They then dragged his body behind a truck to where a crowd of several thousand mutilated his body further, finally leaving him hanging from a tree.

An explanation of a lynching (Miller and Dollard 1941)

Drive: against the general background of the Depression and the deprivation that was experienced as a result, whites who were outnumbered by blacks feared continued competition for work and physical assault. This primary drive of fear turned to anger at the rape and murder of a white woman by a black man. Miller and Dollard characterised the local mood as 'the niggers are getting out of hand — if one can rape and murder and get away with it, others will do the same thing'.

Cues: word got around that there were horrendous injuries to the body. This would suggest an aggressive response to fit the nature of the crime.

Response: people experienced the competing responses of anger and the wish to take revenge on the young man, but fear of punishment if they acted alone.

Frustration: as they were afraid to respond to their anger, they were frustrated, thus increasing their anger still further.

Increased drive strength: with increasing anger, aggression became a more likely response than fear. Some individuals started to express anger, providing cues for others.

Increased cues for aggression: the prisoner was taken to a less secure jail. A deputy sheriff said that 'the mob will not be bothered before or after the lynching'. A local radio station announced 'a lynching party to which all white people are invited'.

Crowd circular aggressive reaction/intensified collective aggression: the man was tortured and killed and then further mutilated by a larger mob, including men, women and children. The crowd then made general attacks on blacks, which only stopped when the National Guard arrived. In the crowd, people behaved more aggressively than might have been expected of them as individuals.

NB: in this example, the sequence of events did not end with catharsis, but rather with the fear of punishment.

The kind of approach taken by Miller and Dollard (1941) has the strength of including a range of ideas that have been demonstrated in other contexts and so can contribute to our understanding of the behaviour of a lynch mob; for example, learning from our own experience and that of others and the deindividuation that develops when we are in a group are well-established ideas. The idea of cues influencing responses has also been supported.

Building on the frustration-aggression hypothesis of Dollard et al. (1939), Berkowitz (1974) proposed **aggressive cue theory**, in which he proposed that the relationship of frustration to aggression is mediated by cues in the environment. Frustration triggers anger, but whether this is translated into aggression depends on the existence of relevant situational cues. These cues can be the observation of aggression by others, or by the mere presence of objects such as guns, which are associated with violence. As Berkowitz (1968) stated: 'Guns not only permit violence, they stimulate it as well. The finger pulls the trigger, but the trigger may also be pulling the finger.' This idea was tested in a classic study by Berkowitz and LePage (1967), who found that participants gave others more electric shocks when a revolver and a shotgun were in the room than when they were not. This is known as the **weapons effect**.

However, some criticisms can be made of this approach. First, the work of Miller and Dollard (1941) is somewhat limited in terms of using secondary materials, for example reports of events, rather than systematic observation. Details of events that may have had an influence on the outcome would therefore not be available to them. On the other hand, given the nature of lynching, it is difficult to see how a more structured approach would be possible. Second, they also make a general characterisation of crowds as 'irrational' and 'patently dangerous', which presents a somewhat one-sided view. Lynch mobs are by definition dangerous, but it seems unwise to generalise this description more widely, as crowd violence is actually quite rare.

Summary

- Miller and Dollard explain the behaviour of lynch mobs in terms of the more generally applicable **frustration-aggression hypothesis**.
- **Drive** is a motivational force that needs to be expressed in behaviour and cues in the environment serve to determine the response to a drive state.
- **Crowd intensification** refers to people having stronger responses when they are part of a crowd, as in a lynch mob.
- While the theory is supported in that it includes many **well-established ideas**, it is limited by the **method** used to investigate it and the rather **general approach** to explaining behaviour.

Chapter 5

Eating behaviour

In this chapter, we will be looking at:
- eating behaviour
  - attitudes to food
  - the success and failure of dieting
- biological explanations of eating behaviour
  - neural mechanisms in eating behaviour
  - evolutionary explanations of food preference
- eating disorders
  - psychological explanations of anorexia nervosa
  - biological explanations of anorexia nervosa

At first sight, eating behaviour seems unproblematic. When we get hungry we eat, and if we eat a reasonably varied diet, we will get the nutrients we need to stay healthy. However, there is a range of factors that affect food choices and eating behaviour, and eating disorders such as anorexia nervosa and obesity are widespread. We will be looking in this chapter at some of these issues.

Eating behaviour

There are several factors that influence what we choose to eat. We all have personal preferences, but we will look here at what influences attitudes to food, including culture, mood and health concerns. We will also look at dieting, in terms of what is effective and ineffective in leading to sustained weight loss.

Attitudes to food

Cultural influences

At birth, we have few genetically programmed food biases; infants show a positive response to sweet tastes and a negative response to bitter and strong tastes. In our culture, up to around 2 years of age we seem to regard everything as potentially edible. From around 2–5, however, young children are **neophobic**, i.e. unwilling to try novel foods. This is true of all young animals and makes evolutionary sense,

Young children are unwilling to try new foods

in that avoiding unfamiliar foods that might be harmful would promote survival. To an extent, this wariness persists into adulthood. For example, Pliner et al. (1994) found that people expected novel foods to be less palatable than familiar ones, and beliefs about their palatability predicted their willingness to taste them.

Through cultural influences, especially as a result of growing up in a family within a particular culture, we acquire a set of beliefs and attitudes that lead us to categorise substances as food or not food. Culture plays a large part in what potential foods are seen as acceptable. For example, in the UK, snakes, otters and cats — although edible — are not classified as food. Insects such as witchety grubs are seen as food by Australian Aboriginals, but would not be thought of as such in the UK. According to Foster and Anderson (1978), 'no group, even under conditions of extreme starvation, utilises all available nutritional substances as food'.

We learn what is regarded as food within our culture and develop attitudes to food and food preferences through **exposure** to different kinds of food. Flight et al. (2008) compared two groups of Australian high school students, aged 12–18 years, from remote rural areas and cosmopolitan city areas. The city students had greater exposure to cultural diversity than the rural students and were significantly more familiar with different foods. Moreover, they were also significantly less neophobic and more willing to try unfamiliar foods.

Social Learning Theory (SLT) suggests that, together with the family, the **media** are an important source of cultural information. They are particularly influential when behaviours are modelled by people who are similar to ourselves. A study carried out by Stoneman and Brody (1981) has demonstrated that one way in which our attitudes towards food are shaped is through television advertisements. They found that children expressed a preference for advertised foods when the children in the advertisements were racially similar rather than racially different from themselves.

One major cultural factor in food choices is **religion**, with dietary laws being based on religious writings and fundamental beliefs. Many religious customs and laws can be traced to early concerns for health and safety in eating foods, when methods of preservation that we now take for granted, such as freezing, were not available. The Jewish dietary laws of *Kashrut*, meaning 'proper' or 'correct', are based on writings in the Old Testament of the Bible and the Torah. Land animals that do not have cloven hooves and that do not chew the cud, such as pigs and rabbits, may not be eaten, they are considered unclean and are forbidden, as is seafood, such as lobster and shrimps. The Jewish dietary laws regard grapes as a fruit of idolatry, so wine and products made from grapes are forbidden, except under special conditions. In Islam, eating is a matter of faith for those who follow the dietary laws of *Halal*, a term for all permitted foods. Prohibited foods include pork and birds of prey, and alcohol is also forbidden; failure to eat correctly reduces spiritual awareness. Hindus do not eat any foods that they believe will reduce spiritual growth; many are strict vegetarians, but among those who do eat meat, pork and fowl are avoided and beef is forbidden, as the cow is thought of as sacred. However, other products from the cow, such as milk, yoghurt and butter, are thought to promote purity of the mind, spirit and body. Many Christian sects follow a vegetarian diet, based on writing in the book of Genesis in the Bible. For example, the Seventh-day Adventist Church encourages a vegetarian diet, but includes milk and eggs, while for Mormons, grains, fruits, vegetables and nuts should take the place of meat.

That food has an important cultural significance is demonstrated by the food habits of people who move from one culture to another. For example, in a study of Chinese-American women, Liou and Contento (2001) found that the degree of acculturation in terms of accepting and conforming to US norms was reflected in food preferences, with less acculturated women maintaining a traditionally Chinese diet. Similarly, in a study of Italian-Canadians, Laroche et al. (1998) found that ethnic identity, defined in terms of retaining the attitudes, values and behaviours of the culture of origin, was strongly related to eating traditional Italian foods. There are also cultural differences in attitudes to different classes of food (see Box 5.1).

Box 5.1   Bryant and Dundes (2008)

Aim: To investigate cultural differences in attitudes to fast food.

Procedure: A survey was carried out of college students from Spain and the USA to explore their attitudes towards fast food. They were asked about the importance of convenience, value, i.e. the amount of food for the money spent, and the nutritional status of food and their attitudes to fast food establishments.

Results: There were striking differences between the two groups of students. The food's nutritional status had significantly less importance for Americans than for Spaniards, while value and convenience were much more of a priority. Half the Spaniards surveyed but less than a fifth of the Americans objected to the proliferation of fast food establishments in their own countries.

Conclusion: Students from different cultural backgrounds show significant differences on a range of measures of attitudes to fast food.

This is likely to be related, in some degree, to the nature of the food being investigated. Fast food of the kind investigated here is an American invention and part of US culture, so while Americans might see it as an expression of their culture, Spaniards might well see it as a threat to theirs.

Summary

- Young children are **neophobic** and must learn to eat new foods. Exposure to new foods is important in willingness to try them.
- The **media** can play a role in influencing attitudes to food.
- The **dietary laws** of religions influence the foods eaten by practitioners.
- People who move to a different culture may continue the dietary traditions of their former culture to maintain their **ethnic identity**.

Mood

There appears to be no doubt that mood affects what we choose to eat and eating affects mood. According to Gibson (2006), eating a meal typically lowers arousal and reduces irritability, while inducing calmness and a positive emotional state. However, this depends on the size of the meal and what is eaten, as eating can also create a negative mood.

There has been considerable interest in **emotional eating** or comfort eating, i.e. eating as a way of dealing with negative emotions, rather than as a response to hunger. One aspect is the food choices people make in this situation (see Box 5.2).

Box 5.2   Michel (2007)

Aim: To investigate the circumstances that lead to emotional eating and its relationship to food choices.

Procedure: Participants were 617 13- and 14-year-olds. Data were collected on the circumstances in which they would eat for emotional reasons and the kinds of food they would choose.

Results: Girls tended to eat when they were depressed and boys when they were anxious. For both, emotional eating was associated with feeling stressed. Both boys and girls were likely to eat salty, high-calorie foods, such as crisps, and sweet, high-calorie foods, such as cake and ice cream. Boys, but not girls, were also likely to eat fruit and vegetables.

Conclusion: Adolescents can use (often unhealthy) food as a way of dealing with negative emotions.

However, emotional eating is not necessarily linked to negative mood (see Box 5.3). There is a physiological basis for the choice of sweet and fatty foods when a person's mood is negative, since these kinds of food affect the **neurotransmitters** dopamine and serotonin, the latter in particular raising mood and alleviating stress. Christenson and Brooks suggest that using food to bring this about can be interpreted in terms of self-medication.

Box 5.3   Christensen and Brooks (2006)

Aim: To investigate the effect of mood on food choices.

Procedure: Participants were asked to read a sad vignette and a happy vignette and to relate the events they read about to their own experience. They were then asked whether or not they would be likely to eat after experiencing the events described in the vignettes and what types of food they would choose.

Results: Both men and women believed they were more likely to eat following a happy event than after a sad event. Men believed they were significantly more likely to eat than did women. In men, the likelihood of eating sweet foods did not significantly change as their mood changed. However, women believed they were more likely to consume sweet foods following a sad event.

Conclusion: People's beliefs about food preference are affected by mood. There are gender differences in emotional eating, both in terms of the nature of the mood and in the food choices made.

Emotional eating in the absence of hunger can be problematic, since using food in this way may lead to overeating. Given the food choices made, emotional eating could increase the risk of obesity, with its attendant health risks; we will be looking at this in more detail later in the chapter. This suggests that interventions to help young people deal with negative emotions in a more effective way could be useful.

As well as mood influencing food choices, there is evidence that the **media** may promote certain kinds of foods as a way of enhancing mood. Pettigrew (2007) carried out a thematic analysis of a number of hours of children's television programmes. One of the themes she identified was the promotion of the idea that certain foods, many of them poor from a health point of view, would not only make you more popular, but also lift your mood.

Research has also investigated whether the kinds of food preferred for emotional eating actually do produce the desired mood-enhancing effect. Macht and Mueller (2007) investigated the effect of chocolate on mood. They asked participants to watch film clips to induce a negative mood, a positive mood or a neutral mood. They found that chocolate had an immediate effect on lifting negative mood, but had no effect if the person was in a positive or neutral mood. Mood enhancement only occurred if the chocolate was sweet. However, even when chocolate raised a negative mood, the effects were short-lived, lasting only about 3 minutes. On the basis of their findings, Macht and Mueller concluded that the kind of immediate but short-term effect created by chocolate could contribute to the habit of eating to cope with stress.

For some individuals, emotional eating can take the form of binge eating, and it has been suggested that this pattern may be linked to difficulty in understanding and coping with emotions. In a study of 695 undergraduates, Whiteside et al. (2007) found that binge eating was strongly associated with difficulty in identifying and making sense of emotional states and having only a limited range of strategies to deal with emotions. For people who show this kind of emotional eating, helping them to develop the skills to cope with emotions in ways other than eating would be useful.

Summary

- Eating normally lowers arousal and creates a **positive emotional state**.
- **Emotional eating**, often of unhealthy foods, refers to eating not in response to hunger but as a way of dealing with a **negative emotional state**, particularly when people lack the skills to cope with emotions in other ways.
- It can be effective in the short term, as these foods affect **neurotransmitters** that raise mood.
- It can also take place in response to a positive mood.
- The **media** promote some foods as having mood-enhancing properties.

Health concerns

The government and health professionals have produced guidelines as to what constitutes a healthy diet. We are told to eat a well-balanced diet if we want to stay healthy. This should include complex carbohydrates, including whole grains, plenty of fruit and vegetables, as well as small amounts of protein, including oily fish, with limited amounts of fats, sugary foods and salt.

The government have issued guidelines to advise us of the type and portions of food that constitute a healthy diet

Following this eating plan will reduce the risk of heart disease, stroke, high blood pressure, some cancers and conditions associated with obesity, for example Type 2 diabetes. These guidelines are heavily promoted, but to what extent do they guide people's food preferences?

There is evidence that people who are more concerned with their health respond positively to these guidelines in terms of the food choices they make (see Box 5.4).

Aim: To investigate the effect of food labelling on food choice in relation to degree of health concern.

Procedure: Thirty-six participants aged 18–53 tasted and rated three different kinds of food: three cheeses, three yoghurts and three koerrtas, a tofu-based food. The fat content in each case was virtually identical, but one was labelled as 'higher', one 'normal' and one 'lower' in fat content. They were asked to rate each on how pleasant they tasted and how likely they were to buy them. They were also asked to assess how influenced they were by health concerns.

Results: Overall, foods labelled 'lower' were rated as slightly less pleasant. However, for the yoghurts, participants reported that they were more likely to buy the 'lower' fat ones. Participants who claimed to be more influenced by health concerns in their food choices rated the 'higher' foods as less pleasant. They were less likely to buy the 'higher' labelled yoghurts and cheeses than those for whom this was less important.

Conclusion: A high degree of concern about health can influence both the perception of how pleasant food tastes and the choice of food in relation to fat content.

This suggests that health concerns are likely to be a factor in food choice. Other studies have produced similar findings. For example, Liou (2001) found a positive correlation between health concerns and choosing reduced-fat foods. However, in both these studies, as with much research in this area, the data are in the form of self-report. What people say they would buy might not necessarily correspond with what they actually buy.

There is also evidence that reading the information on food labels before making a purchase is more about health concerns, in terms of checking for harmful ingredients, than general food information. Jauregui (2008) found that concerns included calorific value and caution about additives, cholesterol and fat.

Given the link between health concerns and food choices, a number of interventions have been carried out to provide information about healthy eating and its implications as a way of improving nutritional choices. Allen et al. (2007) used a simulated fast-food restaurant setting and asked adolescents to choose a meal from a fast-food menu. The nutritional make-up of their choices was analysed for calorific value, fat, cholesterol, sodium, carbohydrates, protein and fibre. There was then a 30-minute nutrition education session, after which participants were asked again to choose a meal from the same menu. The nutritional make-up of this meal was compared with the meal chosen before the education session. There was a significant positive difference in the make-up of the second meal. However, it cannot be concluded that these choices reflected the choices the young people would actually make in this kind of restaurant, nor that, even if the change in choices was applied in a real-life situation, they would be permanent and reflect a lasting change in attitudes.

Nicklas et al. (2001) reported that many children eat over the recommended amount of sugary and fatty foods and less than the recommended minimum of vegetables and grains, raising their risk of illness and obesity. The Health Select Committee Report on Obesity (2004) predicted that children born in the early twenty-first century will have a shorter life expectancy than their parents due to diet and obesity. There is growing concern about childhood obesity and this is a strong predictor of adult obesity. As we shall see later, while heredity plays some part in obesity, food choices are likely to be even more important, so there have been several initiatives to raise children's awareness of health issues and help them to make good nutritional choices (see Box 5.5).

Box 5.5   **Tapper et al. (2003)**

Aim: To develop a programme to encourage healthy eating in children.

Procedure: The programme, planned for primary school children, was based on three basic principles:
- Repeated exposure to the taste of a food increases liking for it.
- Social learning theory suggests that a child is more likely to imitate a model who is liked and admired.
- Rewarding behaviour as soon as it occurs can effectively change behaviour, particularly if the behaviours themselves are enjoyable.

As a source of models, a video was created about four older children, the Food Dudes, who appeared to gain super powers from eating fruit and vegetables. The Food Dudes were engaged in battle against the Junk Punks. Children were encouraged to taste fruits and vegetables repeatedly so that they could develop a liking for them and were rewarded with items such as Food Dudes stickers and pens for eating the required amounts. A similar programme using an animated video of characters called Jarvis and Jess was developed for use with nursery-age children. The programme was tested in a number of schools.

Results: The programmes have been shown to increase significantly children's consumption of fruit and vegetables both at home and at school. The effects have been shown to last up to 15 months after their introduction.

Conclusion: The programmes have been successful in influencing attitudes to food and healthy food choices in children across the age range for which they were designed. A programme that is fun and geared to a particular age range can be effective in changing attitudes towards food and food choices.

There are difficulties, relating to culture, in promoting healthy eating, since as we have seen, the foods people eat can be part of their culture. James (2004) carried out a study of African-American attitudes to food, and in particular those relating to healthy eating. The study demonstrated that people felt that eating healthily meant giving up part of their cultural heritage and trying to conform to the dominant culture.

Participants reported that friends and relatives were usually not supportive of making changes in the diet. Some of the findings about resistance to healthy eating may also be relevant more generally; for example it was believed that healthy foods did not taste nice and were expensive. However, more positively, there was a belief that change was possible and that some demographic groups might be more motivated than others to make changes, i.e. women, men with health problems, young adults, the elderly and people diagnosed with a severe, life-threatening disease.

Summary

- People who are more concerned with health issues respond more positively to **guidelines** on healthy eating. However, the results of research in this area do not necessarily reflect real-life food choices.
- Given concerns about **childhood obesity** and related health risks, **education** may help to influence children's choices, particularly when the programmes used are entertaining.
- Eating healthily may be resisted if it means giving up a part of a person's **cultural heritage**.

The success and failure of dieting

Obesity affects a large number of people and appears to be on the increase. Weight is assessed in terms of body mass index (BMI), which is calculated by dividing a person's weight in kilograms by their height in metres squared. A person who is 1.6 m (5'3") tall and weighs 65 kg (10st. 3lb) would therefore have a BMI of 25.39. A BMI of 25–30 is classed as overweight, while a BMI greater than 30 is classed as obese.

Using these definitions, the World Health Organization (WHO) reported in 2006 that nearly 55% of the adult population of the UK was overweight; almost 25% were obese. Around 30% of children were overweight, of which 50% were obese.

This is of great concern, not least because obesity has serious health implications. People who are overweight are more likely to develop Type 2 diabetes, to have high blood pressure (a major factor in heart failure), an increased risk of stroke and high cholesterol levels (also a risk factor for heart attack and stroke). Obesity is also implicated in infertility, osteoarthritis, sleep apnoea (discussed in Chapter 1) and the development of some cancers. It may also have psychological effects, for example low self-esteem and depression.

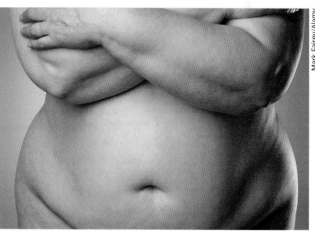

Obesity has serious health implications including diabetes, infertility and heart disease

Most advice on losing weight focuses on dieting, i.e. restricting calorie intake. If over a sufficient period of time a person consumes fewer calories than they burn through activity, they will lose weight. When calories are restricted, the body needs to draw on stored body fat for the calories it needs to function, so in the short term, dieting can indeed be effective. Perri and Fuller (1995) summarised a number of diet studies from the 1970s to the mid-1990s and found that weight-loss programs consistently resulted in participants losing an average of 5%–10% of their weight. Similarly, in a large-scale study of 1,120 adults, French et al. (1999) found that the duration of calorie reduction in weeks predicted the amount of weight loss 4 years later.

Louis-Sylvestre et al. (2003) reported epidemiological evidence that suggests that dieting can be made more effective by eating frequent but smaller meals, so that the same amount of calories is consumed in the course of a day. In France, a fourth meal — the 'goûter' — is commonly eaten in the afternoon by most children and many adults. Missing this meal soon leads to an increase in BMI. Moreover, people who eat 'goûter' regularly have a higher carbohydrate intake (with a correspondingly lower intake of calories from other sources) and a higher metabolic rate than other adults, leading to calories being burned off more quickly.

Psychological factors are also important in the effectiveness of dieting. McManus et al. (2001) found that a diet with a moderate rather than a low fat content was more effective in bringing about weight loss, in that the diet was more palatable, so participants were more likely to stick to it. Blair et al. (1989) found that successful dieters were those with high self-efficacy, i.e. the belief that they were capable of achieving what they set out to do. Shannon et al. (1990) also highlighted the role of self-efficacy, in particular when this was promoted by friends and family of the dieter.

However, over a period of time a restricted-calorie diet becomes less effective, as the body will start to draw on reserves from muscles. If you lose muscle mass, your metabolic rate slows and you burn fewer calories, so weight loss slows. Moreover, one pound of fat burns just two calories a day to maintain itself, while one pound of muscle burns 30 to 50 calories a day, so the reduction in muscle mass means fewer calories are burned.

While diets can lead to weight loss in the short term, the new weight is seldom maintained. Several studies have investigated weight regain after a restricted-calorie diet. For example, Swanson and Dinello (1970) carried out a study that followed obese patients who had lost weight on a restricted-calorie diet. Of those who were followed for less than two years, 23% had gained back more weight than they had lost, while of those who were followed for more than two years, 83% had gained back more weight than they lost. Mann et al. (2007) carried out a meta-analysis of 14 studies that followed participants for at least four years after a diet. The average weight loss on these diets was 14 kg (30.8 lb) and by the long-term follow-up, participants had gained back all but 3 of those kilograms (6.6 lb).

The poor long-term outcome of diets has also been shown by Jeffery and Wing (1995). They carried out a diet study over a period of 2.5 years, comparing a group of people who had dieted with a control group who did not take part in a diet. They found that at the end of this period, the controls did not show a statistically significant weight gain and their weight change was only marginally different from that of the dieters. The dieters had kept off an average of only 1.7 kg (3.7 lb). It seems that in the long term, dieters do not fare notably better than non-dieters. However, there is evidence that a healthy diet combined with exercise can be effective in maintaining weight reduction (see Box 5.6).

Unit 3

| Box 5.6 | Skender et al. (1996) |

Aim: To assess the effects of exercise on maintaining weight loss after dieting.

Procedure: Participants were 127 men and women who were at least 14 kg overweight. They were randomly assigned to one of three experimental conditions: diet only, exercise only and a combination of diet and exercise. They were followed up after 1 and 2 years. The diet was a low-calorie eating plan aimed at producing a 1 kg/week weight loss. Exercise involved training in walking and a supervised home-based programme of up to five exercise periods per week.

Results: After 1 year, there were no significant weight differences among the three groups, with all participants losing similar amounts of weight. After 2 years, the diet-only group regained weight, reaching on average 0.9 kg above baseline. However, the combination group regained weight to 2.2 kg *below* baseline and the exercise-only group regained weight to 2.7 kg *below* baseline.

Conclusion: Dieting is associated with weight loss followed by a regain of weight when the diet ends. Exercise leads to better maintenance of weight loss.

Similarly, in a longitudinal study of people who maintained their weight loss of 13.6 kg (29.9 lb) for at least a year, Klem et al. (1997) found that 90% used regular physical activity as a strategy to maintain the loss. As well as physical activity, a further factor in preventing weight regain is the nature of the food eaten after a diet is stopped. Leser et al. (2002) found that there was less weight regain with a lower percentage fat intake.

There are several reasons why restricted-calorie diets do not work in the longer term. One reason can be related to **set point theory**, which suggests that we have an optimum weight that the body seeks to maintain. When insufficient calories are taken in to maintain this weight, the body responds by slowing metabolism to reduce energy consumption. When people reach their target weight on a calorie-controlled diet, they generally go back to 'normal' eating, but with a lower metabolic rate will put on weight until the original set point is reached.

There is evidence that some people are **genetically predisposed** to put on weight when there are ample supplies of food readily available, making weight-loss diets relatively ineffective. This could be explained in evolutionary terms. In our evolutionary past, those individuals who stored fat when food was plentiful would have the resources to survive and reproduce — and so pass on their genes, including those for storing fat — when food was scarce. There have been a number of studies that have tried to establish the heritability of obesity. For example, in a UK study of 4-year-old twins carried out by Koeppen-Schomerus et al. (2001), heritability was assessed as 0.64 in boys and 0.61 in girls. However, this study relied on mothers' reports of weight, which might be inaccurate. In a survey of studies carried out to determine the heritability of obesity, Maes et al (1997) reported that this varied between 0.50 and 0.80, suggesting that genes may be at least as important as environmental factors. However, while there is clearly a genetic component to obesity, genes are not the only influence and cannot explain the recent rapid increase in obesity in many countries; factors such as the ready availability of palatable but high-calorie foods are likely to play a part.

It is widely accepted that a predisposition to obesity in humans is polygenetic, i.e. it depends on multiple genes, one of which is the **ob gene** ('ob' for 'obese'), discovered through research on mice. The ob gene product is a protein called **leptin**, which acts on the hypothalamus, a part of the brain associated among other things with eating behaviour. If a large amount of leptin is produced, the hypothalamus responds by reducing appetite and speeding up the body's metabolism. If this gene is defective and the amount of leptin is reduced, the hypothalamus might be induced to continually signal a need for food. It may be that overweight people are less sensitive to leptin and so eat when they are not hungry. There is some evidence for this. Baicy et al. (2007) tested morbidly obese adults with a mutation in the ob gene. The participants were shown food-related stimuli and their brain activity was recorded using fMRI scanning. It was found that leptin replacement in these adults led to a reduction in brain activation in areas linked to hunger and increased activation in areas linked to satiety.

Another gene thought to be associated with obesity is **UCP2.** Fleury et al. (1997) suggested that the gene product may act to raise body temperature, requiring an increased use of calories. On the other hand, a malfunction of the gene could increase the likelihood of fat stores being laid down — and hence obesity — as lower calorie expenditure is needed.

A further factor may be **gastrointestinal hormones** and in particular **ghrelin**. Levels normally rise before meals and decrease after eating, although the normally rapid drop after eating is not shown in those who are obese. Moreover, ghrelin has been shown to increase following weight loss as the result of a diet, thus stimulating eating and promoting weight gain.

Psychological factors are important on the effects of dieting. Wing et al. (2008) found that people suffering from **depression** were more likely to regain any weight lost. Adam and Epel (2007) suggested that **stress** could also play a role. Stress hormones encourage the formation of fat-cell formation and so lead to weight gain. A restricted-calorie diet is itself a stressor and one reason why it may be difficult to adhere to a diet is our use of food to deal with stress, the emotional eating referred to earlier. Some foods such as chocolate — many of them high in calories — encourage the production of **endorphins**, naturally produced biochemicals that not only reduce the perception of pain but also act as sedatives and so reduce feelings of stress. It is also possible that the association between certain foods, such as chocolate or cake and comfort, has been learned. If we were given them in childhood when we were feeling sad, we have learned to associate them with feelings of love, security and happiness, but they are counterproductive if a person is trying to lose weight through dieting.

Summary

- **Obesity** is on the increase and poses many **health risks**.
- A **calorie-restricted diet** is effective in reducing weight in the short term, particularly if the individual has **high self-efficacy**. Eating **more but smaller meals** may be effective in weight control.
- **Weight regain** after dieting is a problem, but can be reduced by **exercise**.
- **Set point theory** suggests the body responds to weight loss by lowering the **metabolic rate** and so making further weight loss more difficult.
- Dieting may be less effective for those who are **genetically predisposed** to put on weight. **Gastrointestinal hormones** such as ghrelin are also involved in weight loss and gain.
- Psychological factors such as **stress** and **depression** may also lead to dieting being less effective.

Biological explanations of eating behaviour

We have looked so far at broadly psychological factors that affect eating behaviour, with some brief reference to biological factors. In this section, we will look more closely at biological factors and in particular neural mechanisms, together with what evolutionary theory has to offer in relation to food preferences.

Neural mechanisms in eating behaviour

The main area of the brain associated with hunger and satiation is the **hypothalamus**. Its role in eating was established in general terms at the beginning of the twentieth century, when it was found that tumours near the hypothalamus caused **hyperphagia**, i.e. overeating. More precise methods of studying the brain, in particular stereotactic procedures used in animal research, allowed precise damage, known as a **lesion**, to be caused to a specific part of the brain. The reasoning here was that the function of this precise area could be deduced through a change in behaviour when it was destroyed. Much of the research into the neural mechanisms of eating behaviour is still carried out on animals, on the principle that these systems are similar to those of humans.

Different parts of the hypothalamus appear to be responsible for different aspects of eating. The **lateral hypothalamus (LH)** is a feeding centre, which stimulates eating behaviour. Anand and Brobeck (1951) found that rats with lesions to the

LH showed **aphagia**; they would stop eating, even when palatable food was readily available, and would starve to death. The **ventromedial hypothalamus (VMH)** is a satiety centre, which stops feeding behaviour. Hetherington and Ranson (1942) found that rats with lesions to the VMH would overeat until they became grossly fat. Later research showed that VMH hyperphagia has two phases. To begin with the animal overeats for several weeks until it is obese; it then eats in such a way to maintain its new body weight. If it is then deprived of food, it will overeat until it has regained the weight it has lost. If it is force-fed, it will reduce its food intake until the extra weight gained through force-feeding has been lost.

The influence on hunger and satiety of these two hypothalamic areas has also been shown in humans; for example, Quaade (1971) successfully lesioned the LH of obese patients to reduce eating. If the LH was stimulated electrically, they reported feeling hungry. In a different approach, Reeves and Plum (1969) carried out a post mortem on a patient who had doubled her weight in two years and found a tumour in her VMH, suggesting that this had impaired the sensation of satiety.

However, the complete picture of hunger and satiety is rather more complex than straightforward 'start' and 'stop' mechanisms; this is already suggested by the eating patterns shown in hyperphagic rats, mentioned earlier. Research carried out on rats by Teitelbaum and Stellar (1954) found that appetite could be recovered after LH lesions. Furthermore, this area of the hypothalamus is involved not only with hunger but also with drinking, temperature change and sexual activity. Systems other than the hypothalamus are also likely to be involved in hunger. For example, Zeigler and Karten (1974) found that damage to nerves involved in chewing and swallowing had a similar effect to LH lesions.

A further complication is that while a rat with VMH damage eats more than normal, it will only do so if food is readily available. If it has to work to obtain food, for example by pressing a lever, it will actually eat less than a normal animal. The same appears to be true of humans (see Box 5.7).

Box 5.7   Schachter (1971)

Aim: To assess the relationship between obesity, eating behaviour and access to food.

Procedure: Twenty obese participants and 20 controls of normal weight were tested. They were asked individually to sit at the experimenter's desk and fill in a variety of personality questionnaires. On the desk there were several items, including a bag of almonds. The experimenter helped himself or herself to a nut and invited the participant to do the same. The nuts were either shelled or unshelled.

Results: Of the controls, roughly the same number ate and did not eat nuts, whether or not they had been shelled. Of the obese participants, 19 ate the shelled nuts, but only one ate the unshelled nuts.

Conclusion: Obese people are motivated to eat more than those of normal weight only when access to food is easy.

It is believed that the LH and the VMH function in response to a set point, an optimal weight that the body seeks to maintain; **set point theory** was mentioned in the previous section. This can be related to the behaviour of the hyperphagic rats in the Hetherington and Ranson study. The hypothalamic systems work to maintain a reasonably constant level of satiety, 'switching on' and 'switching off' eating behaviour appropriately. To do this, the systems need to know the state of the body's energy reserves. Two possible sources of this information are changes in blood glucose levels and the amounts of fat in the body.

Originally blood glucose levels were seen to be the most important factor. **Glucostatic theory** proposes that when blood glucose levels drop below their set point, we are hungry and motivated to eat. When they rise again to their set point, we become satiated. Since glucose is the primary food of the brain, this theory seems logical. Russek (1971) provided evidence that detectors of blood glucose levels might be found in the liver. In an investigation of hunger in dogs, glucose was injected either into the bloodstream or directly into the liver; the dogs stopped eating only when the injection was into the liver. Furthermore, if neural connections between the liver and the brain are blocked, an injection of glucose into the liver no longer has this effect. This seems to suggest that the liver assesses the situation and then sends signals to the brain.

Another set point theory is **lipostatic theory**, related to body fat. Fats are stored in adipocytes, which make up the fatty (adipose) tissue of the body. As the level of fats in the adipocytes fall, we are motivated to eat to adjust the level and as it rises we are motivated to stop eating. There is support for this theory in that most people maintain a relatively constant weight. Taken together, glucostatic theory can explain feeding motivation in the short term and lipsostatic theory in the long term.

The role of a protein called **leptin**, which acts as a hormone, has also been investigated. This was mentioned briefly in the previous section. It is normally produced by the adipocytes, in proportion to the amount of fat they contain. It travels via the bloodstream to the hypothalamus where it acts to decrease food intake. Halaas et al. (1995) found that in obese mice that lacked the leptin gene, leptin injections dramatically reduced the amount of food eaten and body weight. Other research has shown it is also important in humans. Farooqi et al. (2007) carried out a study of two people with congenital leptin deficiency. They were shown images of food before and after 7 days of leptin replacement therapy and fMRI imaging was used to measure their brain responses. The results suggested that leptin acts on neural circuits governing food intake to reduce the perception of food as rewarding and increase the response to satiety signals produced while food was being eaten.

While neural mechanisms are important in hunger and satiation, psychological factors — as we saw at the beginning of the chapter — also play a part. We shall return to the role of both physiological and psychological factors in food behaviour when we discuss the eating disorder anorexia nervosa in the final section.

Summary

- The **hypothalamus** plays a major role in hunger and satiation, although how this functions is complex.
- There is support for the idea that feeding systems work to maintain body weight at a **set point**.
- **Glucostatic theory** suggests that the hypothalamus responds to blood glucose levels. **Lipostatic theory** suggests that information is provided by the levels of fat in the adipocytes. The two systems may work together.
- The hormone **leptin** is also important in feeding behaviour.

Evolutionary explanations of food preference

As animals evolve, there is a tendency for them to grow bigger, sometimes referred to as Cope's law. For example, eohippus — the forerunner in the Eocene period (about 45 million years ago) of the modern horse — was only the size of a small dog. The same principle has been shown in human development. This increase in size has evolutionary consequences. The metabolic rate of an animal increases with body weight, with the effect that as the size of the ancestors of modern humans increased, the requirement for intake of calories increased, but the rate of input of calories per unit of body mass fell. They therefore needed to adapt their behaviour to enable them to take in the extra calories required.

There were various options; one would be to increase the absolute amount of food eaten, a strategy adopted by the ancestors of gorillas, who ate increasing quantities of low-calorie plant material as they developed. However, most primates are unable to deal with the large amounts of cellulose involved in a herbivorous diet and chimps and early humans opted for a more mixed diet. Teaford and Ungar (2000) point out that diversifying their diet would be adaptive in terms of making them well suited for living in different environments. **Optimal foraging theory (OFT)** proposed by MacArthur and Pianka (1966) is also relevant here. It accounts for the feeding strategies of animals, claiming that they aim to maximise their energy intake in terms of calories, while spending the least amount of time and effort possible doing so. A shift to **meat eating** would have avoided the digestive problems associated with a purely plant-based diet and would fulfil the principles of OFT, since meat is highly calorific. Evidence for this kind of explanation comes from observation of modern hunter-gatherer societies. Hawkes et al. (1982) studied the Achè hunter-gatherers in the Amazonian forests of eastern Paraguay. Their findings support an optimal foraging theory explanation, since hunters appear to balance the time spent hunting potential prey with the energy returns the prey offers; for example, they do not pursue some small birds, rodents and reptiles where the nutritional returns would be poor in terms of the time and effort expended. However, while meat makes up to 45% of the Achè diet, they also eat plants, which offer lower nutritional rewards. Hawkes explains this in terms of risk reduction; there is a high risk of failure inherent in hunting, and these risks can be mitigated by collecting other types of food as well.

Foley (1987) also points out that larger animals take longer to mature sexually, so offspring are costly to produce and need longer periods of care; this would make being part of a larger social group important for care and protection. The social interactions required for effective hunting and for maximising the benefits of group living in raising offspring would require a larger brain, which in itself would require high-calorie foodstuffs. Cartwright (2000) reports that in humans, about 22% of the basal metabolic rate is devoted to maintaining a healthy brain, even though the brain itself represents only about 2% of body mass. Meat would provide this sort of energy-rich food and hunting would both be facilitated by making it a social endeavour and would in its turn reinforce cooperation and sharing within the group. The initial increase in human brain size about 2 million years ago seems to coincide with the switch from a herbivorous diet to one including a large proportion of meat.

The studies of Hawkes et al. (1982) have also shed light on the relevance of social factors in hunting. The Achè share among the group the food obtained by hunting, but there is no relationship between the contribution made by an individual to the size of the kill and the share of it they and their immediate family receive. This suggests that there are non-nutritional reasons for the way that the food is shared, for example to secure alliances, to enhance status and perhaps gain access to sexual partners and so increase reproductive success. Hawkes et al. found some support for this last possibility, in that the preferred sexual partners of the females of the tribe were the men who were the best hunters.

Another factor in food preference is a liking for things that taste sweet. In evolutionary terms, a preference for **sweetness** would be adaptive for two reasons. First, sweet things contain large numbers of calories, so a sweet taste would act as a readily-detectable signal of nutrients that would provide an easily accessible source of energy. Second, sweet things are rarely poisonous, so a sweet taste would signal safety. In evolutionary terms, those individuals with a preference for a sweet taste would be more likely to survive and pass on their genes — including those coding for a preference for sweetness — to the next generation. Steiner (1987) has shown that the facial expressions of newborn babies indicate acceptance and pleasure to a sweet taste and rejection and disgust to a bitter taste. This makes sense in evolutionary terms, as in nature bitter tastes tend to signal the presence of a harmful substance. Moreover, human breast milk is sweet, and this may be a factor in an infant's ready acceptance of it as a food.

A preference for cooked food may be adaptive in evolutionary terms, making relatively indigestible food easier to digest

A preference for **cooked food** may also be adaptive in evolutionary terms. Cooking food clearly has benefits: it makes some relatively indigestible foods more digestible, it facilitates energy release from foods by making fewer digestive demands and it also reduces the wear and tear on teeth. Wobber et al. (2008) carried out a study to investigate whether great apes, i.e. chimpanzees, bonobos, gorillas and orangutans, preferred cooked to raw food. They found that they preferred meat, sweet potatoes and carrots if they were cooked, although they showed no preference between cooked and raw apples and regular potatoes. This preference was shown even with foods they had not come across before. Brewer (1978) also noted that chimpanzees in the wild show a preference for seeds that have been cooked by wild fires over zraw seeds. This suggests that the preference was established in the ancestors of modern humans before the control of fire developed, but given the benefits of cooked food, it is likely to have spreadquickly soon after.

Summary

- The shift to **meat eating** occurred around 2 million years ago. It can be explained in terms of **optimal foraging theory** and is linked to the increase in **brain size** of our ancestors at that time.
- Studies of **modern hunter-gatherers** support optimal foraging theory. They also highlight the relevance of **social factors** to hunting.
- A preference for foods that taste **sweet** would have been adaptive in signalling **safety** and a source of **high-calorie** nutrition.
- A liking for **cooked food** also offers **adaptive** advantages.

Eating disorders

Eating disorders include anorexia nervosa, bulimia nervosa and obesity, all of which are widespread. In this section, we will focus on anorexia nervosa and the reasons that have been suggested to underlie its development.

Anorexia nervosa means 'nervous loss of appetite'. Sufferers do feel hungry, but do not respond to hunger by eating. They are very thin, with their weight being at least 15% below what is regarded as normal. They are likely to share a number of characteristics:

Typical characteristics of anorectics

- a fear of gaining weight or becoming fat
- a distorted body image — they see themselves as fatter than they are
- denial that they have a problem
- perfectionism
- an obsession with food and its preparation, while attempting to hide the fact that they are not eating it

- avoidance of high-calorie food
- hyperactivity, for example excessive exercising
- in females, amenorrhoea — one diagnostic criterion is three missed periods

Some of these characteristics may apply also to non-anorectics, but this gives an idea of the general overall pattern. Some anorectics also binge and vomit; it is thought that this applies to between 30–50% of sufferers. Around 90% are female and the typical age of onset of the disorder is between 13 and 18, although cases as young as 8 have been reported and some anorectics are much older than 18 when the disorder starts. Anorexia also seems to be on the increase among males, around half of whom are homosexual. The Diagnostic and Statistical Manual DSM-IV claims that the incidence of anorexia is between 0.5% and 1% among young females. The top two social classes (professional and managerial) are overrepresented, as are certain professions; Garfinkel and Garner (1982) claim that dancers and models account for around 7% of cases.

Around 20% of anorectics have one episode but make a full recovery. For about 60% there is a pattern of weight gain and relapse over several years. The remaining 20% are severely affected and usually need to be hospitalised. The mortality rate in this group is more than 10%; anorectics die from starvation, suicide or electrolyte imbalance. Hsu (1990) reports that anorexia is fatal in between 5–15% of cases.

As with other disorders, a range of explanations has been proposed. Some stress the importance of social and psychological factors, while others focus on biological factors. We will discuss in this section some of the suggestions that have been made.

Psychological explanations of anorexia nervosa

Several psychological explanations of anorexia have been put forward and make a contribution to our understanding of the disorder.

The **psychodynamic approach** has several suggestions to make. As the disorder is much more common in adolescent girls, it is possible that anorexia is related to the development of adult sexuality. Freud (1889) claimed that 'the well-known anorexia nervosa of girls seems to be a melancholia occurring where sexuality is undeveloped'. For Freud, eating can be a substitute for sexual expression, so eating disorders could be a way of repressing sexual impulses. It may express a fear of adult sexuality, with eating being symbolic of sexual penetration. It could also express a fear of becoming pregnant or even of oral impregnation (Kaufman and Heiman 1964). One of the symptoms of anorexia is amenorrhoea, which has the effect of returning the body to a prepubescent state, so avoiding the issue of adult sexuality.

While in therapy many patients with eating disorders report being sexually abused as children, so an eating disorder may be a response to early traumatic experiences.

For example, Carter et al. (2006) found that 48% of the 77 anorectics they studied reported childhood sexual abuse. Similarly, in a study of gay and bisexual men, Feldman and Meyer (2007) found that those who reported childhood sexual abuse were significantly more likely to be anorexic than those who had not suffered abuse. Sexual abuse may lead people to reject their own bodies in adolescence, so anorexia may express their unconscious desire to destroy their own bodies.

However, this interpretation raises a number of problems. Although most people who develop anorexia are adolescent females, this is by no means always the case; the idea of avoiding sexuality and adult responsibilities by stopping menstruation would have difficulty in explaining the development of anorexia in older people and could not explain anorexia in males. It is also the case that many women who are sexually abused in childhood do not go on to develop anorexia and many people who have not been sexually abused do develop it.

Freud's ideas are often difficult to test in a rigorous and scientific way, but some research in this area also casts doubt on his interpretation. For example, Halmi et al. (1977) found that in almost 40% of anorectics, menstruation ceased *before* significant weight loss occurred, so the weight loss could not be an unconscious attempt to bring about amenorrhoea; this is more likely to be the result of an underlying endocrine problem. There are also problems with suggesting a direct link between childhood trauma and the development of an eating disorder. Of the 18 patients with an eating disorder studied by Piran et al. (1985), eight had shown symptoms of depression at least a year before developing the disorder, suggesting that any link would be indirect.

Family systems theory offers a further psychodynamic explanation. Minuchin et al. (1978) suggested that some families place constraints on children to the extent that they cannot develop their own identity and are not allowed to become independent; they experience **enmeshment** within the family. This is a particular issue in adolescence because according to Erikson (1902–79), establishing one's own identity is the developmental issue at this period in a person's life. Blos (1967) suggested that a young child goes through a period of **individuation** when he or she starts to separate from the caregiver and become a more independent toddler, with a second period of **reindividuation** in adolescence. If adolescents are prevented from asserting themselves within the family, one way of gaining some control is through developing an eating disorder. Minuchin et al. also claimed that enmeshed families find it hard to resolve conflicts. This would create anxiety, which could be dealt with using ego defence mechanisms. Parents could deal with anxiety by taking care of the anorexic child and, by doing so, continue to play an important role in their child's life and so create a further barrier against the child's independence.

Another approach within the psychodynamic tradition focuses more specifically on the relationship between mother and child when the child was very young and on the child's later need for independence. It also relates this directly to food. In a study of 64 anorexic patients and their mothers, Bruch (1973) found that typically the mother did not respond appropriately to the child's needs. For example, food was only offered when the mother was hungry, or at the 'correct' time. Thus when issues of dominance and independence emerged, they centred on food.

Kallucy et al. (1977) found some evidence for high levels of parental conflict in the families of anorectics, and Hsu (1990) found that families with an anorexic child tend to be ambitious and to ignore or deny conflicts. However, Archibald et al. (2002) suggested that instead of unhealthy family relationships leading to unhealthy eating attitudes and behaviours, it is also possible that these behaviours contribute to more negative relationships within the family. In a large-scale study over 2 years, they found that there was no direct effect of parent-adolescent relationships on unhealthy eating, but for adolescent girls, unhealthy eating behaviours and attitudes predicted less positive parent-adolescent relationships. It is therefore possible that parental conflicts may be the *result* of having an anorexic child, rather than a cause of anorexia. Moreover, a number of studies (for example Halmi 1992) have not found evidence of the kind of pathology in the families of anorectics that theories of this nature suggest. Twin studies (for example Rutherford et al. 1993) have found that genetic factors appear to play a much more important role in the development of anorexia than family environment. This kind of explanation does not account for the higher incidence of anorexia in girls, nor for the development of the disorder later in life, and, as with all psychodynamic ideas, it rests on an interpretation of the facts and is difficult to test directly.

The behaviourist perspective offers an alternative psychological explanation of anorexia. From an **operant conditioning** perspective, avoiding food may be reinforcing, since it is a way of gaining attention, and the resulting slimness may be admired by others. Using a **classical conditioning** model, anorectics may have learned to associate eating with anxiety, because they see eating too much as making people overweight and unattractive. They would therefore avoid eating to reduce anxiety. Anorexia can therefore be seen as a weight phobia, brought about by social norms. Advertising puts across the message that 'slim is beautiful', and dieting in Western cultures is often seen as 'normal'. Garner et al. (1980) found that Playboy centrefolds and contestants in the Miss America Pageant had become thinner over the preceding 20 years, while the average weight for women over the same period had increased. Similarly, Wade and Tavris (1993) reported that Miss Sweden of 1951 was 5 feet 7 inches tall and weighed 151 pounds, while Miss Sweden of 1983 was 5 feet 9 inches tall and weighed only 109 pounds.

However, while this kind of explanation could help to explain why unhealthy eating patterns are maintained once they are established, they do not explain why some people who are exposed to these media influences develop eating disorders while others do not. They also have difficulty in explaining characteristics of anorexia such as distorted body image and the willingness to pursue the goal of thinness even if it leads to death.

Social theories explain anorexia in terms of the limited options available to women and girls in Western patriarchal societies. Anorexia can be seen as a hunger strike against a culture that oppresses women, an attempt to assert personal control, or an avoidance of sexual exploitation. This approach can explain why women and girls are more likely to develop anorexia. The fashion and entertainment industries promote an ideal size that is impossible for most women to maintain; Seid (1994) has reported that while male fashion models are usually normal weight, female models generally weigh about 85% of expected body weight and so meet one of the criteria for a diagnosis of anorexia, the result of attempting to attain the ideal body size and shape promoted by men. However, this approach has difficulty in explaining anorexia in men and cannot really explain characteristics of anorexia such as distorted body image and hyperactivity. Nor has it been established that anorexia is more common in patriarchal societies.

Overall, psychological and social theories cannot really offer an explanation for the typical symptoms of anorexia, but they do help us to understand why most women in the developed world feel too fat and may attempt to diet to very low weights.

Summary

- The **psychodynamic approach** has suggested that anorexia signifies a retreat from **adult sexuality**.
- Within this approach, **family systems theory** relates it to **enmeshment** within the family, with anorexia as a way of establishing **independence**. A related idea makes a link between the **mother–child relationship** and **control**.
- The behaviourist approach sees anorexia as a **learned behaviour** in response to **cultural factors**.
- **Social theorists** suggest that anorexia is a response to the **disempowerment** women experience in Western patriarchal societies.
- All these theories may have something to offer, but none can explain all the characteristics of the disorder.

Biological explanations of anorexia nervosa

One possibility is that anorexia may have a **genetic** basis. One way of investigating this has been through **family studies**, on the principle that if the cause is genetic, if one member of the family is anorexic, there should be a higher incidence among other family members, especially close relatives, than among unrelated people.

DSM-IV states that there is an increased risk of an eating disorder among first-degree relatives of sufferers, i.e. parents, brothers and sisters and children. This approach has usually relied on interviewing family members about both current and past generations. However, this is problematic, in that it asks untrained people to draw conclusions about the mental health of others, and when asking about past generations relies on the accuracy of people's memory. This has been overcome to some extent by looking at medical records, but this can only be done where people have presented for treatment. At the same time, a higher incidence among close family members does not necessarily mean that the cause is genetic, since close family members are likely to share the same physical and psychological environment.

Another approach is **twin studies**, which have looked at the concordance of the disorder between monozygotic twins (MZ, who have 100% of their genes in common) and dizygotic twins (DZ, who share about 50% of their genes). If the underlying cause is genetic, there should be a higher **concordance** in MZ twins, i.e. a greater probability of both twins sharing the disorder, than in DZ twins. These studies provide some evidence that genes may make a contribution. For example, Holland et al. (1984) found a concordance of 56% for MZ twins, but only 7% for DZ twins. A more recent and much larger study carried out by Klump et al. (2001) used a different statistical technique, but had similar findings. However, since the concordance rate for MZ twins was well below 100%, there must be factors other than genes that influence the development of anorexia, so this approach can be criticised for being reductionist, in terms of only taking one factor, i.e. genes, into account. For example, it could be that the greater similarity between MZ twins could in part be explained by them being treated more similarly than DZ twins, since they look more alike, i.e. an environmental explanation. The **diathesis-stress model** of mental disorders may be useful here. This proposes that there may be a genetic vulnerability or predisposition to develop a disorder (diathesis), but its development has an environmental trigger, i.e. a stressful event.

A further biological approach looks at the role of **neurotransmitters**. As discussed earlier, the hypothalamus is important in regulating eating behaviour. The lateral hypothalamus, which stimulates eating behaviour, works on the neurotransmitters noradrenaline and dopamine, so low levels could be insufficient to stimulate eating, even though hunger is experienced. Halmi and Yum (2007) report that there is substantial evidence that **noradrenaline** influences feeding behaviour and that there are disturbances of the noradrenaline system in anorectics. However, they point out that it is not clear whether these disturbances are a cause of anorexia or an effect of it. Moreover, since eating behaviour is highly influenced by other neurotransmitters and neuropeptides, as well as noradrenaline, it is likely that anorexia arises from a complex interaction of these various neurotransmitters and neuropeptides.

Another neurotransmitter involved in feeding behaviour is **serotonin**. Barbarich (2002) reports that high levels of serotonin are typical of both anorectics and of people suffering from obsessive compulsive disorder and suggests that characteristics of anorexia such as the obsession with food and the compulsion to achieve perfection may result from a dysfunction of the serotonergic system. This seems reasonable, but again, there is the issue of cause and effect. It is perhaps worth noting that in 'normal' starvation the pattern of neuroendocrine changes is distinctly different from that in anorexia, leading to lethargy and hunger, not hyperactivity and food refusal.

It has been suggested that anorexia can be explained in relation to **evolution**. The **reproductive suppression hypothesis (RSH)** proposed by Anderson and Crawford (1992) focused on the lack of menstruation in female anorectics and suggested that this was an evolutionary adaptation to slow down sexual maturation when there are starvation cues and so a probability of poor reproductive success. However, the RSH does not explain the function of distorted body image and hyperactivity, why wealthy well-fed women and girls — those who seem to be most susceptible to developing anorexia — might expect poor reproductive success, or why sufferers include men and postmenopausal women.

An alternative evolutionary explanation, the **Adapted to Flee Famine Hypothesis (AFFH)**, has been put forward by Guisinger (2003). Anorectics frequently feel they have boundless energy, exercise excessively and feel that they are well, so it could be that instead of an underlying physiological cause leading to weight loss, losing at least 15% of body weight triggers these characteristics. With this degree of weight loss, a person's body is subjected to the equivalent of a famine; some people have inherited a genetic ability to respond to such low body weight in an adaptive way, as developing these characteristics would make it possible for them to leave areas where food is scarce. Normally, when a person or animal begins to lose weight, the body responds in such a way as to conserve energy and increase desire for food. If starvation continues, people become obsessed with eating, lethargic and depressed. In most environments, these adaptations would facilitate survival in times of food shortage. However, if extreme weight loss was the result of a lack of local food resources, it would have been adaptive to try to find food elsewhere. In this case the normal responses of conserving energy would be maladaptive. The ability to stop foraging locally, feeling restless and energetic and denying that you are dangerously thin would be adaptive in terms of facilitating a search for food further afield. Such symptoms of anorexia as ignoring food, hyperactivity and denial of starvation, including distorted body image, would be adaptive in terms of surviving famine conditions. There is evidence to support this hypothesis, but also contradictory evidence:

The AFFH evidence

Food refusal is found in many species and in circumstances when feeding would compete with other activities. For example, Mrosovsky and Sherry (1980) found that many species stop eating, even though food is readily available, when they migrate. However, anorectics have a great resistance to feeding even though food is readily available and there is no competing activity.

Many animals show **hyperactivity** when food is short. For example, Epling and Pierce (1992) found that rats that were starved in the laboratory would then ignore their food and exercise excessively. However, hyperactivity is not always shown by anorectics.

In anorexia, hyperactivity and food refusal are experienced as desperate **compulsions**.

There is evidence that **genes** make a significant contribution to the development of anorexia, so **natural selection** may have been involved in the development of the traits associated with anorexia.

Most of the **biochemicals** involved in appetite and activity facilitate the migration suggested by the hypothesis, since they promote activity and satiety. However, some biochemicals that promote appetite, for example ghrelin, are elevated in people with anorexia.

This theory is interesting in accounting for a range of the common symptoms of anorexia, which other theories find difficult to explain. However, as shown previously, there are some pieces of evidence that do not fit easily.

Summary

- There is evidence from family and twin studies that **genes** play a role in anorexia, but this cannot provide a complete explanation.
- **Biochemical abnormalities** are involved in anorexia, but the nature of the relationship between these irregularities and the disorder is not clear.
- The **evolutionary approach** has put forward the **reproductive suppression hypothesis**, but this cannot account for all the characteristics of anorexia.
- This approach has also put forward the **Adapted to Flee Famine hypothesis**. There is some support for this idea, but again, it is not a perfect fit.

Chapter

Gender

In this chapter, we will be looking at:
- psychological explanations of gender development
  - Kohlberg's theory
  - gender schema theory
  - psychological androgyny
  - gender dysphoria
- biological influences on gender
  - the role of hormones and genes
  - evolutionary explanations of gender roles
  - the biosocial approach to gender development
- social contexts of gender role
  - the influence of parents, peers and the media
  - cross-cultural studies of gender role

Psychological explanations of gender development

We first need to consider the terms 'sex' and 'gender'. Quite often, 'sex' is used to talk about biological aspects of being male or female, while 'gender' refers to social characteristics, for example the kinds of behaviour associated with being male or female. However, this is an artificial distinction, since biological and social factors are likely to interact, so many researchers now use the two terms interchangeably.

There are several psychological theories that seek to explain gender development, i.e. understanding of our own gender and its implications. They vary in the weight they give to cognitive and to social factors. We will be looking in this section at cognitive explanations and return to social influences towards the end of the chapter.

Kohlberg's theory

Kohlberg's (1966) theory of gender development proposes that children come to understand and adopt gender roles as a result of a developing understanding of the social world. **Gender role** refers to the attributes, behaviours and attitudes that are associated with being male or female and so takes the form of **gender stereotypes**, i.e. general ideas about what boys are like and what girls are like. In Kohlberg's view, boys think 'I am a boy, therefore I want to do boy things, therefore the opportunity to do boy things (and to gain approval for doing them) is rewarding'. A boy therefore actively seeks out and organises information in the social environment about male gender roles and then behaves in accordance with that information.

Kohlberg believed that children develop a sense of **gender identity** — a sense of being male or female and its implications — through a series of stages, in each of which their thinking is qualitatively different from the last, with approximate ages being attached to each stage. There are three stages:

A boy actively seeks information about male gender roles and then behaves in accordance with it

Kohlberg's stages of gender development

Stage 1: gender labelling
Children can identify themselves and other people as boys or girls, mummies or daddies, but do not yet understand that gender is stable over time, nor that it is unaffected by superficial changes, such as clothing or the length of a person's hair.

Stage 2: gender stability (around 3 years)
Children recognise that gender is stable over time, but do not yet understand that it is unaffected by superficial changes in appearance or choice of activities, such as knitting or playing football.

Stage 3: gender constancy (around 6–7 years)
Children understand the unchanging nature of gender across time and in different situations.

In this theory, Kohlberg was much influenced by Piaget's theory of cognitive development, which is discussed in Chapter 8. For Piaget, younger children are dominated by their perceptions; he believed it was not until the age of 6 or 7 that children were capable of **conservation**, for example understanding that the amount of water in a beaker remains the same when it is poured into a beaker of a different shape. Before this age, children are likely to say that there is more water in a tall, narrow beaker than there was in the original shorter, wider beaker from which it has been poured because they focus on height, rather than taking the width of the container into account. Similarly, Kohlberg believed that it was only around this age that children reached a full understanding of gender, when they understood that gender was not affected by superficial changes in appearance.

The theory predicts that children's understanding of the unchanging nature of gender develops with age and that children with a more advanced understanding should pay more attention to same-sex models as a way of developing their own gender roles. There is some evidence to support these ideas (see Box 6.1).

Box 6.1   Slaby and Frey (1975)

Aim: To investigate the development of children's understanding of gender in relation to the attention they give to same-sex models.

Procedure: A structured gender concept interview was carried out with 55 children, aged 2–5. It included questions relating to gender labelling, for example 'Is this a girl or a boy?' (showing a girl/boy doll), questions on gender stability, for example 'When you grow up, will you be a mummy or daddy?' and questions on gender consistency, for example 'Could you be a [opposite of child's sex] if you wanted to be?' Several weeks later, the children watched a short film showing a man and a woman carrying out parallel activities on different sides of the screen. The amount of time children's eyes were fixed on each side of the screen was measured.

Results: Children's answers to the questions reflected the developmental sequence with age that Kohlberg proposed. Those with a more advanced understanding of gender constancy showed more selective attention to their own sex. This was particularly true of boys.

Conclusion: Gender development appears to follow the sequence Kohlberg suggested, with those with a more advanced understanding seeking information about gender role from same-sex models.

However, the kinds of questions used in this study have been criticised, since they may not be easy for very young children to understand. For example, the question: 'If you have children of your own when you grow up, will you be a mummy or a daddy?' is not only grammatically complex, but also assumes that children understand that in the context of 'have children' means 'give birth to'.

Attempts have been made to simplify the procedure by using drawings and photographs. Emmerlich et al. (1977) found that children were less likely to show gender constancy when drawings were used. They typically do better with photographs (for example Bem 1989), but do best when they are asked questions about themselves. It is possible that children learn gender constancy about themselves before they are able to apply it to other people; it is also possible that drawings and photographs confuse the issue; after all, drawings can be changed.

There is little evidence for a link between the appreciation of gender constancy and gender role. For example, a review by Ruble and Martin (1998) found that research tended to demonstrate that understanding of gender role appeared much earlier than Kohlberg's theory suggests. In a study by Ruble et al. (2007), this understanding was related to the gender stability stage, rather than when children had achieved gender constancy. This early understanding has also been shown in a study of gender stereotypes of very young children (see Box 6.2).

Box 6.2   **Kuhn et al. (1978)**

Aim: To investigate young children's understanding of gender role.

Procedure: Children aged 2½ to 3½ were shown paper dolls called Michael and Lisa. They were asked whether Michael or Lisa would be likely to make statements such as: 'I like to help mummy', 'I like to fight' and 'I need some help'.

Results: Boys and girls shared some beliefs about gender roles, for example that girls like to help mummy, talk a lot and ask for help and that boys like to play with cars and help daddy. Boys also have beliefs about girls that girls do not share, for example that girls cry. Similarly, girls have beliefs about boys that boys do not share, for example that boys fight. Boys and girls also have beliefs about positive aspects of themselves not shared by the other sex. For example, girls (but not boys) believe that girls look pretty and never fight, while boys (but not girls) believe that boys like to work hard and are loud.

Conclusion: Gender-role stereotypes are held by very young children and include positive beliefs about their own sex and negative ones about the other sex.

This kind of evidence challenges Kohlberg's view that there should be little gender-appropriate behaviour before gender constancy is achieved, and overall research evidence for the link the theory suggests, between achieving gender constancy and the development of gender-typed behaviour, is not strong. While there is support for the kind of staged development Kohlberg suggests, most of the evidence suggests that gender-typed behaviour emerges strongly when gender labelling is achieved, and as Bandura and Bussey (1999) claim, children at this much earlier stage are already modelling themselves on same-sex models.

Gender schema theory

Kohlberg's idea that cognition is important in gender development has been taken up by gender schema theory, developed by Bem (1981). This theory suggests that children develop schemas, in this case gender stereotypes, that help them make sense of and organise information. Schemas are areas of knowledge gained from past experience, which cut down on and therefore simplify the processing of new information and make it more efficient. However, they can lead to distortion when new information does not fit an existing schema. Gender is a powerful schema that can affect the way that children interpret gender-related information.

6

According to Martin and Halverson (1981), there are two key schemas:

- the **ingroup/outgroup schema**: a broad categorisation of attributes and behaviours that relate either to boys or to girls
- the **own-sex schema**: characteristics and behaviours that relate to the child's ingroup

The environment provides information about what toys or activities are masculine or feminine, which is organised in the ingroup/outgroup schema. This in turn determines what information is processed into the own sex schema. This theory differs from Kohlberg's in that it proposes that schemas start to develop as soon as gender labelling is achieved, rather than gender constancy.

These ideas about schemas have been supported by research (see Box 6.3).

Box 6.3	**Martin and Halverson (1983)**

Aim: To investigate the role of schemas in gender-role understanding.

Procedure: Children aged between 5 and 6 were shown pictures of children carrying out activities that were either gender-consistent (for example boys playing with trucks) or gender-inconsistent (for example girls sawing wood). They were asked to recall the pictures a week later.

Results: During recall, children tended to change the sex of children in the gender-inconsistent pictures.

Conclusion: Memory is distorted to fit in with existing gender schemas.

Liben and Signorella (1993) had similar results using pictures of adults. These studies suggest that the influence of gender schemas is so strong that counter-stereotypical information may be distorted to fit in with the existing schemas.

This theory has the advantage of fitting better with research that shows that children's understanding of gender, in the form of the development of gender stereotypes, takes place much earlier than Kohlberg's theory suggests. It also gives more weight than Kohlberg's theory to social aspects of gender development, since it emphasises the importance of social learning in gender development. It can also help to explain why parents have such difficulty when they attempt to challenge gender stereotypes, for example that only girls play with dolls and only boys with cars, since schemas govern what people pay attention to, what they try to find out more about, what they interact with and what they remember.

The theory can also explain why younger children tend to have more rigid stereotypes than older children. Martin (1989) asked children to predict how much characters in a story would like to play with stereotypically masculine and feminine toys. Younger children based their answers purely on the character's gender, while older children took into account additional information, for example about the character's interests. This suggests that the younger children's thinking reflected a relatively simplistic gender schema, while the older children's thinking was more flexible, allowing them to draw on different sources of information simultaneously.

Summary

- **Kohlberg** suggests that children's understanding of gender goes through **stages**. Full understanding develops at around 6 or 7.
- There is support for his belief that **cognition** is important. However, understanding appears to develop earlier than the theory suggests.
- **Gender schema theory** also emphasises the importance of **cognition**. It claims that children develop strong gender schemas as soon as they can label themselves as a boy or a girl.
- This theory is supported by **research**. It also has good **explanatory power**.

Psychological androgyny

Most gender research is based on a dichotomy between males and females and has investigated differences between the two sexes. This research tends to assume that a person can be either masculine or feminine, but not both. However, Bem (1974) suggests that it is possible that a person could be highly masculine, i.e. have well-developed masculine characteristics, and at the same time highly feminine. Bem uses the term androgyny — from the Greek *andros* ('man') and *gyne* ('woman') — to refer to this. She suggests that differentiation of gender roles merely serves to prevent both men and women from developing as full and complete human beings. She points out that this approach can be contrasted with gender schema theory, according to which sex-typed individuals process information on the basis of gender, rather than using alternative information. The thinking of an androgynous person is relatively unconstrained by cultural stereotypes of gender appropriateness.

Bem suggests that the benefits of androgyny come about through the integration of masculine and feminine characteristics, for example it is possible for an individual to be both compassionate (a stereotypically feminine characteristic) and assertive (characteristically masculine), and these complementary qualities can help a person to deal more appropriately with a situation. She gives the example of the ability to fire an employee, if the circumstances require it, but with sensitivity for the human feelings aroused by such an act.

Bem developed the **Bem Sex Role Inventory (BSRI)** to measure androgyny. This contains 20 stereotypically socially desirable feminine traits, for example compassionate, 20 stereotypically masculine traits, for example assertive, and 20 neutral items, for example honest. Respondents rate each item in terms of how well it applies to them on a scale of 1 (never/almost never true) to 7 (always/almost always true). The androgyny score is worked out using a formula that combines the masculinity and femininity scores. Boldizar (1991) has developed a similar scale for children aged 9–13, the **Children's Sex Role Inventory (CSRI)**.

The development of androgyny can be related to childhood experiences. In a study of 6-year-old children, Weisner and Wilson-Mitchell (1990) found that while all the children had knowledge of gender-typed schemas, those children in families that were committed to sexual equality and encouraged a questioning attitude towards society and lifestyle choices were less likely to be influenced by sexual stereotypes relating to occupations, for example that nurses are female and firefighters are male.

Bigler and Liben (1990) showed that it is possible to influence gender stereotyping in children and thus promote androgyny. Teaching primary school children about occupations, based not on gender but on interests and skills, reduced occupational stereotyping. In comparison with a control group, children who had received this teaching were better able to remember counter-stereotypical material on a later memory test.

Attitudes to androgyny appear to vary with age. In a sample of people aged from 12 to over 80, Strough et al. (2007) found that the oldest men in their sample were more likely than younger men to think positively about androgyny, while the opposite was true of the oldest women. They link these trends not with age as such, but with the development of feminism, which appears to have had more influence on younger women than older ones.

A great deal of research has been carried out to investigate the benefits of androgyny. One area with which it has been linked is self-esteem (see Box 6.4).

Box 6.4   Spence and Helmreich (1979)

Aim: To investigate a possible association between androgyny and self-esteem.

Procedure: Using the BSRI, participants were divided into those who were high on masculinity; high on femininity; high on androgyny (both) and undifferentiated (low on both). Self-esteem was also measured.

Results: Self-esteem was highest for those high on androgyny, followed by those high on masculinity, then those high on femininity. The undifferentiated group had the lowest self-esteem.

Conclusion: The combination of good traits, both masculine and feminine, is related to high self-esteem.

A study of adolescent girls carried out by Buckley and Carter (2005) had similar findings. However, since the research is correlational, it cannot be assumed that androgyny is the cause of higher self-esteem.

Androgyny also appears to have other advantages. For example, Cheng (2005) found that androgynous individuals were better able to cope with **stress**. This was supported by Damon (2008), who found that androgynous women were better able to cope with sexual trauma than more feminine women. It has also been linked with general **wellbeing**. Davison (2000) found that among older women, who are often at the receiving end of both sexism and ageism in our society, those who scored high for androgyny also reported higher levels of subjective wellbeing than less androgynous women. Similarly, Isaac and Shah (2004) found that androgyny was related to better marital adjustment. Links have also been suggested between androgyny and **creativity**. For example, Hittner and Daniels (2002) found that androgynous individuals were more creative in areas such as literature, theatre and film-making.

While there is some evidence to support Bem's view that androgyny brings advantages, her claim that the benefits of androgyny come about through the integration of masculine and feminine characteristics has been questioned. While Lefkowitz and Zeldow (2006) found that androgyny was associated with good **mental health**, Woo and Oei (2006) found that it was the strength of masculine characteristics that predicted good mental health, with androgyny making no contribution. A study by Choi (2004) into **self-efficacy**, i.e. people's belief in their own abilities, in this case both academic and more generally, had similar findings. This suggests that in some areas, it is the extent to which people have high levels of masculine characteristics that is important, rather than the integration of masculine and feminine characteristics that Bem suggests.

Summary

- Much gender research looks at gender role **differentiation**. Androgyny suggests we can have high levels of **both masculine and feminine characteristics**.
- Androgyny can be measured by the **BSRI**.
- Its development is related to **childhood experience** within the family and can be encouraged by **teaching**.
- There is evidence that androgyny brings **benefits**, such as high self-esteem, the ability to cope with stress and creativity.
- In some cases, it may be that high levels of **masculine characteristics** make an important contribution, rather than androgyny.

Gender dysphoria

Gender dysphoria is also known as **gender identity disorder**, although sometimes the term gender dysphoria is used only for extreme cases of the disorder. According to DSM-IV, the current version of the *Diagnostic and Statistical Manual*, which is used for diagnosing mental disorders, an individual with gender dysphoria has a strong and continuing sense of wanting to be (or in fact a feeling that they belong to) the other sex. They feel persistently distressed in their current gender role.

A person may also have a disorder such as **androgen insensitivity syndrome (AIS)**, where although they have male XY chromosomes, they have failed to respond normally to testosterone while in the womb. In this case, they may have been wrongly assigned as females when they were born; if so, they may also experience gender dysphoria. However, these cases are rare and do not apply to most people who have been diagnosed with gender dysphoria.

The Gender Identity Research and Education Society (GIRES) estimates that there are about 15,000 people in the UK receiving some form of medical help for gender dysphoria, about 1 in 4,000 of the whole population. It is more than twice as common in men as in women. In children, five times as many boys as girls have some degree of gender identity disorder, although not everyone diagnosed as a child goes on to develop the condition in its extreme form.

6

For some people, gender dysphoria may take a mild form, when they occasionally feel they belong to the other sex, and this may be expressed in **transvestism**, i.e. cross-dressing. For others — **transsexuals** — the feeling of being in the wrong body can dominate their lives, leading to them seeking gender reassignment surgery. They may develop an anxiety disorder, leading to clinical depression and some may even attempt suicide. They have normal male (XY) or female (XX) chromosomes for their sex; as yet, no physical characteristics have been identified that can reliably lead to a diagnosis.

Gender dysphoria can be treated with sex hormones and in some cases by **gender reassignment surgery**; this is a drastic measure, since after the surgery people will no longer be able to have children. However, after a thorough psychological and medical evaluation of the individual, hormone treatment can be followed later by surgery, which gives the individual the appearance of the gender to which they feel they belong. They can then apply for their new gender to be legally recognised. Most people function well — psychologically, socially and sexually — after treatment. A study carried out by Smith et al. (2005) found that only 2 of the 162 transsexuals studied regretted having reassignment surgery.

It is not entirely clear what causes the condition, although the evidence points to a largely biological rather than a psychological explanation. We will be looking in more detail at both these kinds of influence on gender development later in the chapter. One piece of evidence comes from research carried out by Cohen-Kettenis and Gooren (1999), who found that children showed cross-sex typed behaviour — for example a boy dressing up in his mother's clothes, playing with girls' toys and preferring to play with girls rather than boys — early on, when there would have been limited time for social factors to have had an effect. There may be a **genetic** component (see Box 6.5).

Box 6.5	**Green (2000)**

Aims: To investigate whether gender dysphoria, in the form of both transsexualism and transvestism, has a genetic basis.

Procedure: Data were collected, using interviews and medical records, on ten siblings or parent-child pairs.

Results: Overall, seven pairs showed concordance for either transsexualism or transvestism, including one set of MZ twins, three sets of non-twin brothers, one brother and sister pair, one set of sisters and one father and son. There was also one transsexual father with a transvestic son, one transvestic father with a transsexual son, and one transvestic father with a transsexual daughter.

Conclusion: Genes may play a part in the development of gender dysphoria.

This was a small-scale study, so care should be taken in generalising the results as an explanation of the causes of gender dysphoria. Furthermore, there is not a lot of research into the role of genes in the development of gender dysphoria, but what research there is has not always supported the idea of a genetic basis. For example,

Garden and Rothery (1992) carried out a case study of 13-year-old MZ twin girls, one of whom was transsexual, while the other had no gender identity problems. This suggests that the disorder cannot be entirely explained by a simple genetic mechanism. Other factors, such as social experience during childhood, need to be taken into account.

Another biological explanation suggests that there may be atypical development of the **hypothalamus**, involved in the early development of sex differences within the brain, which controls the production of sex hormones throughout life, causing parts of this structure to take on the characteristics of the other sex. There are differences between males and females in size and cell number of various nuclei in the preoptic area of the hypothalamus. Sexual differentiation in the brain continues throughout early childhood, with a rapid increase in the number of cells in this particular area taking place in both girls and boys up until the age of about 4 years. This is followed by a rapid decrease of these cells in girls, but not in boys, so that as young adults, men have about twice as many cells as women. If this process is abnormal, the result can be a 'female' brain in a male body, or vice versa. Swaab et al. (1995) found that this area of the hypothalamus was smaller in male-to-female transsexuals and further evidence that this could not have come about as the result of adult sex hormones. On the basis of studies carried out with rats, they suggest that the difference comes about as a result of interaction between genes and hormones during development.

A similar study by Kruijver et al. (2000) carried out post-mortem studies of this area of the hypothalamus. They found that in the brains of male-to-female transsexuals, or males that had adopted the female role, this area was identical to the pattern found in ordinary women. Similarly, in two brains of female-to-male transsexuals, this part of the brain corresponded to what is normally found in males. This research too offers support for the idea that there is a biological basis to gender dysphoria. However, these investigations were carried out post mortem and it cannot be assumed that abnormal brain characteristics *cause* gender dysphoria; they may instead have come about through taking on the identity of the other sex. As there is such a large degree of development during childhood, it may be that in addition to genetic factors, environmental and social factors could have an important influence on brain development.

The **H-Y antigen** may also be implicated. This is a protein, determined by the **SRY** gene (**S**ex-determining **R**egion of the **Y** chromosome), which is active in the development of male anatomical structures. Males should therefore be H-Y antigen positive and females H-Y antigen negative. In a study of 11 male-to-female and 11 female-to-male transsexuals, Eicher et al. (1980) reported that 8 of the male-to-female transsexuals were H-Y antigen negative and 9 of the female-to-male transsexuals were H-Y antigen positive. Other studies have also reported that a large number of male transsexuals have abnormally low levels of H-Y antigen. However, the findings have been mixed; for example, they were not replicated in a study by Wachtel et al. (1986).

6

It may be that there is a biological basis to gender dysphoria for many transsexuals, but for some it may arise as the result of social experience. Support for this idea comes from Jones and Tinker (1982), who suggested that gender dysphoria is the result of an interaction between biological factors and family dynamics. From interviews with the families of 14 transsexuals, they found that parents were not initially worried about their children's gender-inappropriate behaviour and in some cases encouraged it. However, they later discouraged it and the children then became more desperate in their attempts to manage the transsexual feelings, in some cases even attempting suicide. This suggests that while the causes may be primarily biological, psychological factors and in particular how parents respond, may play a role in the development of the disorder.

Summary

- Gender dysphoria refers to a strong and continuing belief that one has been born into the 'wrong body'. The condition can be managed with hormone treatment and in some cases gender reassignment surgery.
- Evidence for a **biological basis** for the disorder comes from the early appearance of cross-sex typed behaviour. It has been suggested that it is at least in part **genetic**.
- It may be linked to the development of the preoptic area of the **hypothalamus**. There is evidence of abnormal levels of the **H-Y antigen** in transsexuals.
- It is likely that there is a biological basis to the disorder, which interacts with **social experience**.

Biological influences on gender

The role of hormones and genes

Humans have 23 pairs of **chromosomes** in the nucleus of each cell of their bodies. These are thread-like structures that contain our genetic material (**DNA**). Males have pairs of one Y chromosome and one X chromosome, while females have two X chromosomes. The exception is egg cells (ova) and sperm cells, known as **gametes**, which contain 23 unpaired chromosomes. A gamete carries half the genetic information of an individual, one chromosome of each type. An ovum can only carry an X chromosome whereas a sperm can carry either an X or a Y chromosome. Both males and females start as an ovum bearing an X chromosome. At the time of conception, an ovum fertilised by a sperm carrying an X chromosome will develop into a female, while if the sperm carries a Y chromosome, a male will develop. The **Y chromosome** therefore determines sex.

For the first 40 days after conception, all human embryos develop in much the same way and have both male and female interior anatomy. If the ovum has been fertilised by a sperm carrying another X chromosome, development will follow the female route and the gonads will develop into ovaries. The male elements of the interior anatomy spontaneously disintegrate, while the female ones thicken and grow into a womb. At the same time, the exterior anatomy, which has up till now been similar for both sexes, develops into female genitalia. The natural route of development is therefore the female route. If the ovum has been fertilised by a sperm carrying a Y chromosome, this natural route of development must be interrupted. The **SRY gene** on the Y chromosome (mentioned in the previous section) converts the gonad cells of the embryo into testes. These secrete the hormone **testosterone**, which induces the development of male internal organs and causes female characteristics to be absorbed. The external genitalia are

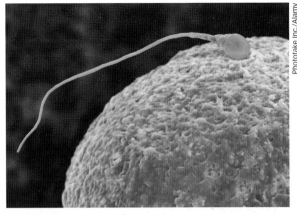

The sperm can carry either an X or Y chromosome; an ovum can only carry an X chromosome

switched away from the female route and male organs develop. If the expression of SRY is blocked in a male embryo, the person will have the appearance of a female but will not have some of the internal characteristics of most females, since the gonads will not develop into ovaries and the uterus will usually be 'blind'. In other words, all human embryos will develop into females unless they are masculinised by the product of the SRY gene. At puberty, under the influence of hypothalamic and pituitary hormones, the gonads produce hormones — testosterone in the male and oestrogen and progesterone in the female — that stimulate the development of secondary sexual characteristics such as breasts and pubic hair.

A biological account of gender differences argues that innate genetic and hormonal differences between males and females are responsible for their different psychological characteristics. It should be noted that both males and females produce androgens, i.e. male hormones, the most important of which is testosterone and the female hormones, oestrogen and progesterone. However, males produce much more of the male hormones than females and vice versa, so **hormone levels** can be taken as a measure of masculinisation and feminisation.

Another measure is the **2D:4D ratio**, the ratio of the length of the second finger to the fourth finger. This is lower in men than in women and has been found to correlate negatively with testosterone level.

Both these measures have been used to test the biological account of gender differences. For example, Sanders et al. (2005) found a negative correlation between the 2D:4D ratio and spatial ability. Since finger length is determined before birth, they argue that testosterone exposure during prenatal development influences brain development, leading to better performance by males on spatial tasks.

Eating disorders such as anorexia nervosa and bulimia nervosa are far more likely to affect women than men, and this topic is explored in more detail in Chapter 5. It is possible that sex hormones have a role in bringing about an eating disorder (see Box 6.6).

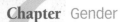

Box 6.6   Klump et al. (2006)

Aim: To investigate the relationship between eating disorder symptoms in women and prenatal testosterone exposure and adult levels of oestrogen.

Procedure: Participants were 113 adult females. Prenatal testosterone exposure was measured using the 2D:4D ratio. Current levels of oestrogen were also measured. Degree of disordered eating was measured using scores on the Minnesota Eating Behavior Survey (MEBS). Relationships between the measures were calculated.

Results: Lower levels of prenatal testosterone exposure and higher adult levels of oestrogen were both significantly correlated with eating disorder symptoms.

Conclusion: Pre- and postnatal hormone levels are associated with the development of eating disorders.

This does not imply that eating disorders have a purely biological cause, but rather that there is some biological contribution to their development. Klump et al. suggest that the relatively low levels of testosterone before birth in females permits their brains to respond to oestrogens at puberty when these hormones activate the genes that contribute to the development of eating disorders in vulnerable girls.

Further research has investigated a possible biological basis to rough-and-tumble play, which many studies (for example Smith 1982) have shown to occur at higher levels in boys than in girls. Studies have often focused on girls with **congenital adrenal hyperplasia (CAH)**, a clinical condition in which they have been exposed to high levels of prenatal androgens. Money and Ehrhardt (1972) found that these girls were tomboys; compared with a control group they played more energetically, were more athletic and interested in sports and preferred playing with boys. However, Archer and Lloyd (2002) suggest that there are other possible interpretations. For example, they may have been treated differently by their parents, who already knew that they had been exposed to a masculinising hormone, with many having undergone corrective surgery to their masculinised genitals. Moreover, a further study of children with CAH carried out by Slijper (2007) came to the conclusion that psychosocial factors, such as the child being sick and parents' doubts about the sex of the child, seemed to have more influence on behaviour than hormones.

Brüggemann et al. (2005) point out that gender differences in behaviour cannot be attributed solely to hormones, since brain development and physiology are also affected by psychological factors and social experience. It makes sense to consider the interaction of biological, social and psychological factors in development. This view is reflected in the **biosocial approach**, which will be looked at later.

Summary

- Male and female development is differentiated by the presence or absence of the **Y chromosome**.
- Development in boys is influenced by the hormone **testosterone** and female development by **oestrogen** and **progesterone**.
- There is some evidence that **biological influences** affect gender-typed behaviour, but it is likely that these interact with **psychological and social factors**.

Evolutionary explanations of gender roles

Evolutionary psychologists offer explanations of behaviour in terms of mechanisms that were laid down in the distant past, known as the **environment of evolutionary adaptation (EEA)**, thought to be the Pleistocene period, dating from between 1.8 million years ago to 10,000 years ago. They suggest that certain behaviours might have been **adaptive**, in that they promoted survival long enough for successful reproduction to take place, so the genes of individuals showing this adaptive behaviour were passed to the next generation. Human adaptations are therefore solutions to the problems of survival and reproduction that our ancestors faced over evolutionary history, for example finding food and choosing a mate. Some behaviours that were adaptive at that time may no longer be so, but this approach assumes that we are adapted to the hunter-gatherer period towards the end of that time.

Some studies have looked at differences in gender role from an evolutionary point of view. Shields (1975) proposed that men and women have evolved differently to fulfil their different and complementary functions, which are necessary for survival. One major area is behaviour related to reproduction, for example mate choice and parental investment. Buss (1989) suggests that behavioural differences in this area between men and women arise from different sexual and reproductive strategies that have evolved to ensure that men and women are able to reproduce efficiently and pass on their genes. You can read about this aspect of gender roles in the section on Human Reproductive Behaviour in Chapter 3. We will look here at other ways in which gender roles may differ. Traits such as aggression, competitiveness and dominance, generally more associated with men than with women, are relevant to reproductive success, in that they would have been adaptive in terms of securing good quality mates and controlling access to them, but can also be explored more broadly.

In modern-day hunter-gatherer societies, such as the San people in the Kalahari Desert of southern Africa, collecting food is shared by men and women who carry out different tasks. Men hunt and women gather readily available plant and animal foods. Across many cultures, men tend to be more aggressive, competitive and dominant than women; cross-cultural research on gender role will be discussed at the end of the chapter. These general differences between men and women can be applied to their different roles in acquiring food.

In our evolutionary past, men would have had to compete for food resources and therefore competitiveness would have been an adaptive trait in terms of acquiring food, while aggression would have been adaptive in making them successful hunters. Both these traits would therefore be adaptive in terms of promoting survival. Anderson (1997) reports research findings that suggest that males are more aggressive towards other men than towards women, and this makes sense in evolutionary terms, since they would have been competing for resources with other men. Other aspects of gender differences also support the role of the successful hunter. For example, the greater size, strength and musculature of men in general compared with women would promote the ability to hunt effectively. There is also a wealth of evidence that men are in general better at visuo-spatial tasks than women. Kolakowski and Malina (1974) have suggested that this ability might be adaptive for a hunting way of life.

There is also evidence that men are in general more dominant than women. For example, in an observational study of the verbal and non-verbal interaction of men and women attending job interviews, Luxen (2005) found that men showed more dominant behaviour, such as head shaking, sitting in a closed posture and using closed questions and directive remarks, while women showed more affiliation, for example in frequency of laughing, sitting in an open posture and asking open questions. It has been suggested that dominance would also be adaptive in promoting successful hunting. This has been supported by research carried out by Wynn et al. (1996), which links these characteristics with the influence of prenatal hormones, for example on spatial ability.

Silverman and Eals (1992) suggest that evolutionary theory would predict that spatial memory would be the kind of spatial specialisation required for successful foraging and that women should therefore be better than men at tasks involving this skill. Silverman and Phillips (1998) found that women indeed outperformed men on this kind of task, a characteristic that would have supported their role in gathering food.

However, this kind of approach to gender roles can be criticised. Although there are, in general, differences between males and females in different cultures in areas such as aggression and dominance, this is by no means true of all cultures, as will be shown in the final section of this chapter. The link to the hunting ability of our ancestors is also questionable, as Archer and Lloyd (2002) report there are non-hunting species where these same differences exist. There may also be implications in terms of how gender differences are interpreted. For example, differences may be seen as 'natural', and therefore individuals who do not conform may be seen as deviant.

Summary

- Evolutionary psychologists see differences in gender role as reflecting **adaptive** differences in our evolutionary past.
- Differences in gender role in sexual behaviour are explained in terms of optimising **successful reproduction**.
- Gender differences have been related to **hunting and foraging** strategies in our evolutionary past.
- There is some support for these ideas, but there is evidence that does not fit well with this interpretation.

The biosocial approach to gender development

As seen earlier, a purely biological account of gender differences is somewhat incomplete, as it gives little weight to the influence of psychological and social factors.

The biosocial account seeks to bring these two kinds of explanation together. It stresses the importance of biological factors, but at the same time claims that it is the interaction of biological and social factors that is important. The focus is the idea that different physical characteristics of individuals, such as their sex, influence how people interact with them. This has been demonstrated in studies of interaction with babies (see Box 6.7).

| Box 6.7 | Smith and Lloyd (1978) |

Aim: To investigate the effect of a baby's sex on the way an adult responds.

Procedure: Participants were 32 mothers, who were asked to play with a 6-month-old baby whom they had not met before. A baby was dressed either in pink or in blue clothing and was introduced to the mother using either a boy's or a girl's name. The same baby was presented to different participants as either a boy or a girl. Sex-typed and sex-neutral toys were available. The ways in which the mother interacted with the baby were analysed.

Results: Mothers tended to interact more vigorously with a 'boy' than with a 'girl', for example by bouncing or jiggling 'him' and responded more to motor activity of a baby presented as a boy. The toys offered to the baby were also sex-typed, with 'boys' being offered a toy hammer or a truck and 'girls' a soft toy.

Conclusion: The sex of a baby influences the way in which parents interact with them, in line with the masculine stereotype of activity and physical prowess.

This suggests that how an infant is labelled sexually determines how it is socialised and so its gender identity, from which gender role develops. There is support for this in a case study of a hermaphrodite, a rare condition where a proportion of an individual's cells are XY and the others are XX (see Box 6.8).

| Box 6.8 | Goldwyn (1979): The case of Mr Blackwell |

Mr Blackwell was a hermaphrodite, so that his body had both male and female characteristics, which were fully functional. He had an active testicle on one side and an active ovary on the other and both a vagina and a penis. At 14 he developed breasts and began to ovulate and menstruate. Tests revealed that his brain biochemistry was female in the way that his sex hormones were regulated.

He had been brought up as a boy and was quite certain that he was a male. His female parts were surgically removed and he went on to function as a male.

In this case, it appears that the way Mr Blackwell had been raised determined his gender identity and thus his gender role, even though from a biochemical point of view he was female.

On the basis of biosocial theory, Money and Earhardt (1972) claimed that it would be possible to change the sex in which a child is raised without any psychological harm being done. There is some support for this claim. Mazur et al. (2004) carried out a case study of five individuals who, although genetically male, had been raised as females because their external genitalia were ambiguous. Data were gathered through the use of interviews and questionnaires. Although their gender role behaviour was somewhat masculine in comparison to norms for women, all five participants reported a female gender identity and four of the five were judged to be well adjusted. Similarly, Bradley et al. (1998) report a case where gender reassignment as a female was carried out at 7 months. The patient was interviewed at 16 and again at 26, when she was in the hospital for further reconstruction surgery. She was firm in her identification of herself as female. However, the outcome is not always so positive (see Box 6.9).

Box 6.9	Money (1974): Accidental penectomy: the John/Joan case

A baby, one of twins, lost his penis at 8 months following a botched circumcision. On Money's recommendation and under his supervision, it was decided to raise him as a female. His male sex organs were removed and an artificial vagina constructed. He was given female hormones and was always treated as a girl.

At first all seemed well and offered support for the claim made by Money and Earhardt. As a 4/5-year-old, Joan preferred to wear dresses and was neater and tidier than her twin. However, she did show some tomboyish behaviour, such as a liking for rough-and-tumble play and preferred toy guns to Barbie dolls.

When Joan reached her teens, a follow-up study by Diamond (1982) found Joan to be generally unhappy, with few friends. She refused further hormone treatment and at 14 would no longer continue living as a girl. When she was told the story of what had happened to her, she was relieved and claimed that finally everything made sense. She started taking male hormones and underwent gender reassignment surgery to become a male, John. He married a woman and adopted her three children and apparently adapted well to a life as a man. However, his life began to unravel and he committed suicide at the age of 38.

This case seems to suggest that nature is stronger than nurture; biological factors here were stronger than social ones. This view is also supported by a further case study (see Box 6.10).

Box 6.10	Imperato-McGinley (1974): The Batista family

In some members of the Batista family in the Dominican Republic, development does not follow the normal course. Where both parents carry a particular mutant gene, some children have a normal female body shape and genitalia and are raised as girls. However, at about 10, the vagina heals over and they develop a penis and testicles. They all adapt well to being male and go on to marry women and have children.

These boys are genetically male, i.e. the fertilising sperm carries a Y chromosome and enough testosterone is produced prenatally to preserve the male parts of their anatomy. However, they lack a chemical called dihydrotestosterone, which means their male genitalia do not develop at this stage. It is only at puberty that the production of testosterone stimulates dihydrotestosterone production, leading to the development of male external genitalia.

Here too, nature seems stronger than nurture. However, the children are well aware of the anomalous development of some children in their family, so may well see the sex they have been assigned in their early years as provisional, making it easier to adjust to changing sex at puberty. The evidence concerning the role of biological and social-psychological factors is therefore mixed. However, it seems clear that both are important.

Summary

- The **biosocial approach** to gender development claims that whether children are labelled as boys or girls determines **how others respond** to them. This in turn determines a child's **gender identity** and hence their **gender role**.
- In its extreme form, it claims that it would be possible to **change the sex** in which a child is raised without psychological harm.
- The **evidence** for this viewpoint is **mixed**. However, it is clear that **both biological and social-psychological factors** are important in the development of gender identity and gender role.

Social contexts of gender role

We have seen that both biological and social psychological factors influence the development of gender identity and gender role. In this section, social factors will be looked at in more detail, and in particular the influence of others in this area of development. We will then consider similarities and differences across cultures.

The influence of parents, peers and the media

There is quite a lot of evidence that children learn about gender identity and therefore gender role from the environment. **Social Learning Theory (SLT)** suggests that this comes about through observational learning, as children take in relevant information from the environment. They learn to behave in particular ways through reinforcement; some behaviours are reinforced by others, for example by approval, and so are likely to be repeated, while behaviours that are not reinforced or are punished are less likely to be repeated. It follows that gender identity and gender roles emerge as a result of the child learning in this way what is appropriate for boys and for girls. Observational learning leads to the modelling of different behaviours and Bandura (1963) suggests that there are three sources of models: the family, the subculture and the media. Evidence relating to these ideas is looked at here.

Parents

From birth, children are exposed to ideas about what it means to be male or female, and they are perceived differently from birth by their parents (see Box 6.11).

Box 6.11 | Rubin et al. (1974)

Aim: To investigate the effect of a child's sex on parents' perceptions of newborns.

Procedure: Parents were asked to describe their newborn infants. The infants who took part were matched on size, weight and muscle tone to eliminate as far as possible individual differences as a possible confounding variable.

Results: Sons were more likely to be described as strong, active and well coordinated. Daughters were more likely to be described as beautiful, little, delicate and weak.

Conclusion: From birth, parents have different expectations of children, based on their sex.

The physical environment parents provide for children also differs in sex-typed ways. Pomerlau et al. (1990) found that boys' rooms were more likely to contain vehicles and action-oriented toys and to be blue and girls' rooms to contain dolls and be pink and decorated in a floral style.

Parents tend to promote sex-typed behaviour and environments for their children: studies show that girls' rooms were inclined to be pink and boys' blue

As children get older, parents promote sex-typing. Eccles et al. (1990) found that they encouraged their sons and daughters to participate in sex-typed activities. These included playing with dolls and housekeeping activities for girls and playing with trucks and sporting activities for boys. Etaugh and Liss (1992) asked children aged 9–14 what presents they hoped to get for Christmas and what they actually received. Both their choices and what they received were sex-typed; children's toy preferences were significantly related to parental sex-typing.

Parents also use reinforcement and punishment in response to children's spontaneous play (see Box 6.12).

Box 6.12 | Langlois and Downs (1980)

Aim: To analyse parents' response to sex-appropriate and sex-inappropriate play.

Procedure: Participants were 96 children aged either 3 or 5; the sample included both boys and girls. Mothers and fathers were tested individually and their reactions to sex-appropriate and sex-inappropriate play were observed.

Results: Both mothers and fathers rewarded play with same-sex toys for both boys and girls, for example through attention and interest and punished play with cross-sex toys, for example through teasing. Fathers were more punishing towards older boys than to girls or younger children.

Conclusion: As SLT predicts, parents use reinforcement and punishment in response to children's choice of toys.

Research carried out by Ruble (1988) also supports the difference between mothers and fathers in their response to sex-inappropriate play, with fathers reinforcing gender stereotypes.

In addition to play, gender roles are reinforced in other ways. For example, Basow (1992) investigated ways in which children were asked to help around the house. Boys were more likely to be asked to carry out maintenance tasks, such as painting and mowing the lawn, and girls to carry out domestic chores, such as cooking and helping with the laundry. This assignment of particular tasks along gender lines is likely to lead children to link different kinds of work with gender. Similarly, Cunningham (2001) interviewed young women about their attitudes to gender roles and housework and later interviewed their 18-year-old daughters in the same way. He found that the mothers' attitudes, together with how household tasks were allocated during the daughters' adolescence, predicted the daughters' attitudes to housework, suggesting that both parental attitudes and modelling influenced the daughters' gender role.

However, support for the idea that the way parents react to a child's gender-relevant behaviour shapes that behaviour is not always forthcoming. Lytton and Romney (1991) carried out a meta-analysis of 172 studies and found that the only significant effect was the encouragement of sex-typed activities, and even here the effect was not particularly strong. The size of this study makes the findings all the more impressive.

Peers and school

Children's gender roles are also influenced by their peers. The Langlois and Downs (1980) study (Box 6.12) also looked at how other children responded to sex-inappropriate behaviour. They found that girls rewarded sex-appropriate behaviour and punished sex-inappropriate behaviour in other girls, while boys punished sex-inappropriate behaviour in boys.

Another approach has been to investigate the willingness of children to act in ways that run counter to gender stereotypes (see Box 6.13).

Box 6.13   Reed (1998)

Aim: To investigate willingness to transgress gender roles when encouraged to do so by same-sex peers.

Procedure: Participants in three age groups, 40 9-year-olds, 41 13-year-olds and 48 18-year-olds replied to audiotape questions about how willing they were to take part in gender-inconsistent activities. In some cases, hypothetical same-sex peers endorsed these activities and in some cases no endorsement was given.

Results: At all ages, participants were more willing to take part in these activities in the 'endorsed' condition. In both conditions, females were significantly more ready to transgress gender roles than males.

Conclusion: Peers may influence gender roles across age groups. Boys are less willing to transgress gender roles than girls.

Topics in psychology

The finding in this study that boys have relatively rigid gender roles compared with girls bears out the importance both fathers and peers place on adhering to gender roles in boys, demonstrated in the Langlois and Downs (1980) study.

Many children grow up with **siblings** who may model gender-appropriate behaviour. McHale et al. (2001) investigated the effect of siblings on the development of children's gender roles. Over a period of 3 years, they found that while the influence of parents was obvious on firstborn children, the qualities of firstborns in the first year of the study predicted the qualities of second-born children in the third year, when qualities of the parents were controlled for.

The influence of **school** has also been investigated, given that children spend a lot of time with peers once they enter education. Baker-Sperry (2007) investigated primary school children's interpretation of the Cinderella story in a reading book and found that the boys and girls fell into two distinct groups, with the book being seen as a 'girls' book' and the children interpreting it along traditional lines and reacting negatively to alternative interpretations relating to gender. Chan (2007) found that even in kindergartens, traditional gender role stereotypes were held and acted on both by children and their teachers.

These influences persist as children get older. Etaugh and Liss (1992) found evidence of gender-typing of occupational choice in girls (though not in boys), related to school subject preferences. Dewitt (2004) carried out a survey of 116 middle-school girls, aged 11–14, and found evidence that girls were under pressure from their peers to conform to traditional gender roles, in particular in relation to their looks, as well as the traditionally negative view of maths and science subjects as being unsuitable for girls.

The media

A considerable amount of research has been carried out into the effects of the media, particularly television, on children's attitudes and behaviour. There is a lot of evidence of gender stereotyping in television. For example, in an analysis of children's programmes, Aubrey and Harrison (2004) found that although some characters were gender-neutral, male characters were still significantly more likely than female characters to answer questions, give orders, show ingenuity in solving problems and achieve a goal.

Similarly, in a study of television adverts, Kim and Lowry (2005) found that women were much more likely to be shown as dependent on others, nurturing children and to be at home. Television characters may provide models with whom children identify and that influence their understanding of gender roles (see Box 6.14).

Box 6.14 Hoffner (1996)

Aim: To identify children's favourite television characters and 'wishful identification', i.e. the traits of these characters they would like to share.

Procedure: A sample of 155 children aged 7–12, including both boys and girls, was interviewed. They were asked about their favourite television characters. Wishful identification was also investigated.

Results: Both sexes preferred same-sex characters. In terms of wishful identification, boys focused on the strength of male characters and girls on the physical attractiveness of female characters.

Conclusion: Children tend to prefer same-sex television characters and identify with them along gender-stereotypical lines.

A further study in America of the effects of television on the understanding of the gender role of boys aged 13–14 was carried out by Hust (2006). The boys linked what they saw as essential masculine characteristics with specific programmes. For example, being physically strong was linked with the daily sport show *SportCenter*; sexual prowess was linked with *Sex and the City*; having a stoic personality was linked with the *Rocky* films; and taking risks was linked to the series *Jackass*, in which people perform a variety of dangerous stunts that often lead to injury.

Counter-stereotyping can also reinforce traditional roles. In an analysis of television adverts, Scharrer et al. (2006) found that male characters carrying out the kinds of household chores traditionally carried out by women were usually portrayed in a humorous way as inept, in terms of negative responses from others, lack of success and unsatisfactory outcomes.

Television programmes may also influence gender roles in dating behaviour. In a study of 215 15-year-olds, Rivadeneyra and Lebo (2008) found those who watched 'romantic' television programmes were likely to have traditional gender role attitudes towards dating, while those who watched non-romantic television dramas were more likely to have less traditional views. However, this is a correlational study, so the findings could be explained in terms of those with more traditional attitudes preferring to watch programmes that reflected their views.

Recent studies have also investigated a possible role for video games in influencing gender roles. In an analysis of video gaming magazines, Dill and Thill (2007) found that male characters were significantly more likely to be portrayed as aggressive and female characters to be defined by their sexuality. There were similar findings in a study by Miller and Summers (2007), who found in addition that male characters were more likely to be powerful, more able and to be the main character.

It seems that to a large extent children's gender role develops as a result of the attitudes and behaviours to which they are exposed. This information comes from parent-child interactions, their peer group and the media. Through all these means of socialisation, children learn gender-stereotyped behaviour, which continues through childhood and into adolescence and so leads to their sense of appropriate gender roles.

Summary

- **Parents** respond differently to boys and girls at birth and **encourage sex-typed activities**. They **discourage counter-stereotypical play**, particularly in boys, and reinforce stereotypes in the **allocation of household chores**.
- However, the **effects** of the way parents interact with children are **often small**.
- **Peers** respond negatively to counter-stereotypical behaviour. Older **siblings** model appropriate behaviour. Peers are a major source of influence in **school**.
- There is evidence that children and adolescents are influenced by the ways in which gender roles are portrayed in the media on **television**. There may also be a similar influence from **video games**.

Cross-cultural studies of gender role

Much of what has been covered so far in relation to gender role has focused on Western cultures and may not necessarily be applicable more generally. Within many cultures, there is a broad tradition of males being seen as more assertive and dominant and women more submissive. Men work to provide for their families and women nurture children and care for the home. According to evolutionary psychologists, this broad distinction between male and female roles can be traced back to the EEA, to our hunter-gatherer ancestors. Men and women are believed to have evolved differently, based on biological factors, to fulfil their different and complementary functions, which were necessary for survival.

However, culture differs in different societies, over periods of time and indeed between subcultures within a culture. Cultures are shaped by a wide variety of factors, such as climate, geographical features, political systems, migration, invasion and patterns of trade, any of which may have psychological implications, for example on gender role.

An early study of cultural variation in gender role was carried out by the anthropologist Margaret Mead (1935), who studied three cultures in Papua New Guinea. The Arapesh were cooperative, gentle people, with little distinction between males and females. Both sexes shared domestic responsibilities such as raising children, i.e. adopting a traditionally 'female' role. However, some work was carried out by women, who were believed to have naturally strong foreheads to allow them to carry heavy weights, a task more associated in Western culture with males. The Mundugamor people also made little distinction between males and females, with both sexes being hostile and aggressive, i.e. traditionally 'male' characteristics. Children were largely disregarded by both sexes and infanticide was common. In the Tchambuli tribe, the women were aggressive and were responsible for carrying on trade and supporting their families, thus taking on the traditionally 'male' role, while the men spent their time dressing up, gossiping and shopping. Interestingly, people in all three cultures believed that their culture was structured that way naturally, i.e. determined by biology. It is clear from this research that there is more variety in gender role than can be accounted for from an evolutionary perspective.

More recent psychological research has compared perceived gender roles across cultures and attempted to explain any differences in terms of broader differences between cultures (see Box 6.15).

Box 6.15 Tiggemann and Rüütel (2004)

Aim: To compare gender roles in Australia (a Westernised culture) and Estonia, which had until recently been part of the Communist bloc.

Procedure: Participants were 394 Australian and 415 Estonian students; the samples included both men and women. They completed the Sex Role Concerns Inventory, which includes scales measuring nine attributes as to how important they are 'for a woman to achieve satisfaction'. Three are concerned with physical appearance, two with achievement, one with popularity and three with traditional family values.

Results: There were significant national differences on all the traditional gender role aspirations. For example, Estonians rated being a mother, being a good homemaker and tending to the needs of others significantly higher than Australians, though there were no significant differences in ratings for professional success.

Conclusion: There are significant differences in gender role between the two cultures.

The researchers explain these differences in sociopolitical terms. There is evidence that the status of women in the Baltic countries has declined since their independence from the former Soviet Union, with a return to conservative family values and traditional gender role aspirations for both women and men, and this could explain the difference in gender roles. At the same time, the lack of difference in relation to professional success suggests that in this area Western values have been speedily adopted. Another study has looked at cultural and subcultural differences in male gender role (see Box 6.16).

Box 6.16 Tager and Good (2005)

Aim: To compare gender roles of American and Italian males and Italians in north/central Italy and those in the south.

Procedure: Italian and American male students completed the Conformity to Masculine Norms Inventory, which includes 11 scales to assess traditional masculine norms, such as dominance, primacy of work and pursuit of status.

Results: The Italians scored significantly lower on 9 of the 11 scales, i.e. conformed less to traditional masculine norms. Participants from north/central Italy scored significantly lower than those from the south, but the southerners nonetheless scored significantly lower than the Americans.

Conclusion: There are significant differences in gender roles both between and within cultures.

Interestingly, these findings are in direct contrast to the stereotype of a man of Italian descent as patriarchal, macho, violent and domineering, as presented in television programmes such as *The Sopranos* and *The Godfather* films. The researchers explain the difference in gender roles between Americans and Italians in relation to Italian history; they cite the power of the Communist party, with its emphasis on equality and tradition, for example the traditional importance of women within the family. The north/south difference is explained in relation to northern Italians seeing themselves as different from southern Italians, who are seen as having a background more in line with traditional masculine norms. However, they also suggest that further research is needed; it may be that the differences found in this study relate to differences in what is considered traditional in the cultures studied.

Research has also looked at changes in gender norms when people move to another country with a different culture. For example, van der Vijver (2007) investigated gender role in immigrants to the Netherlands. They found that first-generation immigrants from Turkey, Morocco and Surinam held more traditional gender-role beliefs than second-generation immigrants, for example in relation to sharing household tasks and childcare. Those from the second generation had moved towards the norms of the host country, a process known as **acculturation**. However, the pattern of acculturation increasing with the length of time spent in a country is not always followed. Enrile and Agbayani (2007) compared beliefs about gender role in native Filipinos, Filipinos who had immigrated to the USA and Filipino Americans who had been born in the USA. They found that although, as expected, native Filipinos did have the most conservative attitudes towards women, Filipino Americans had more traditional values than immigrants. This is an area where more research is needed to reach a clear explanation.

Summary

- While many cultures share beliefs about gender roles, there is considerable **variation across cultures** and **between subcultures**.
- Mead's early study of cultures in the same geographical area showed that there are cultures where there is **little gender distinction** and where **traditional roles may be reversed**.
- Later research has shown variations in gender role that can be explained in terms of **sociopolitical and historical factors**.
- **Immigrants** to a country may go through the process of **acculturation**, where they adopt the gender role beliefs of the host country. The reasons why this does not always happen are unclear.

Chapter

Intelligence and learning

7

In this chapter, we will be looking at:
- theories of intelligence
  - the psychometric approach
  - the information-processing approach
  - Gardner's theory of multiple intelligences
- animal learning and intelligence
  - conditioning in non-human animals
  - intelligence in non-human animals
- evolution of intelligence
  - evolutionary factors in the development of human intelligence
  - factors in intelligence test performance

Theories of intelligence

Intelligence is difficult to define; there are almost as many definitions as there are people defining the term. Definitions include:
- the ability to carry out abstract thinking (Terman 1921)
- to judge well, to comprehend well, to reason well (Binet and Simon 1905)
- a general factor that runs through all types of performance (Jensen)
- an individual's ability to act purposefully, think rationally and deal effectively with the environment (Wechsler)
- the ability to solve problems, or to create products, that are valued within one or more cultural settings (Gardner)
- innate, general cognitive ability (Burt)
- what is measured by intelligence tests (Boring 1923)

While most are in general agreement that cognitive processes such as thinking and reasoning are involved, the definitions vary in relation to the theoretical standpoint of the person providing the definition. Some assume intelligence is an innate capacity, while others believe it to be something that can be developed. Some see it as a general ability, while others see it as a set of independent abilities. Some see it as universally applicable, while others see it as dependent on the culture within which the individual develops. Given the differing views of what constitutes intelligence, Boring's definition is an operational one, i.e. in terms of how intelligence may be measured, which he saw as 'a point of departure for a rigorous discussion...until further discussion allows us to extend [our understanding]'. The first part of this chapter will look at some of the different ways in which the concept of intelligence has been approached.

The psychometric approach

The most influential approach to understanding intelligence in terms of generating the most systematic research is based on psychometric testing. The aim of this approach is to measure differences in individuals' abilities to answer questions and solve problems. Pioneer work taking this approach was carried out by Binet and Simon (1905). With the help of teachers, Binet developed questions that teachers believed a child with 'average' ability at a particular age should be able to answer, those that only 'brighter' children of the same age might be expected to be able to answer and those suitable for the 'dullest' children. Items that discriminated between children of different abilities were retained. Revisions of the test in 1908 and 1911 allowed the 'mental age' of a child to be calculated, to provide an **intelligence quotient (IQ)**:

US National Library of Medicine/SPL

Binet developed questions that enabled the measuring of intelligence to provide an intelligence quotient (IQ)

$$IQ = \frac{\text{mental age}}{\text{chronological age}} \times 100$$

A 6-year-old child who scored at the 6-year-old level would therefore have an IQ of 100, while an 8-year-old child scoring at this level would have an IQ of 75 and a 5-year-old child scoring at this level would have an IQ of 120. However, this formula is seldom used today, since it would make no sense when applied to the results of tests on adults. Instead, norms have been worked out using large samples in each age group of the population for whom a test is intended, and individual performance is compared with these norms. When a large number of people take the test, their results form a normal distribution (see Figure 7.1) and the scores are converted to give a mean score of 100 with a standard deviation of 15.

Figure The normal distribution of IQ scores
7.1

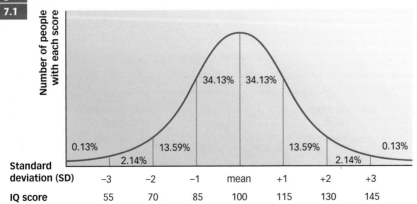

Binet's test was later adapted in 1916 as the Stanford-Binet Scale for use in the USA. Both these tests were carried out by a psychologist with individual children, but were time-consuming. When the Americans became involved in the First World War, a quick method of selecting and classifying recruits was necessary, and pencil-and-paper group tests were developed. This made possible large-scale investigations of the relationships of performance on different kinds of subtests, characteristic of the aims of the psychometric approach. This kind of comparison analyses correlations between test scores using **factor analysis**.

Factor analysis has been the main method of investigating what psychometricians refer to as the 'structure' of intelligence. After analysing children's performance on a number of tests, Spearman (1863–1945) found strong correlations between all of them and so proposed that all tests were measuring a common factor, which he called **general intelligence (g)**. However, there was not an exact match between a person's score on, say, a test of verbal ability and that same individual's score on a test of, say, mathematical ability, so he suggested there were other factors specific to each test, which he labelled **specific factors (s)**.

He thus saw measured intelligence as consisting largely of g, which he defined roughly as the ability to see relationships between things, of which 'bright' people would have a lot and 'dull' people a little, plus specific abilities. This model is therefore known as the **two-factor theory**. Spearmen believed that g was inherited and so not open to change, while scores on specific factors resulted from training.

Figure Spearman's model of intelligence
7.2

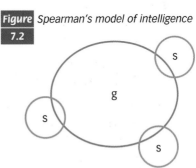

Vernon (1950) developed the model further and, on the basis of more detailed factor analysis, suggested there needed to be an additional level between g and s. He made a distinction between verbal/educational abilities (**v:ed**), such as reading, spelling and some mathematical abilities, and spatial/mechanical abilities (**k:m**), including more practical spatial, mechanical and some mathematical abilities. This is known as the **hierarchical model**:

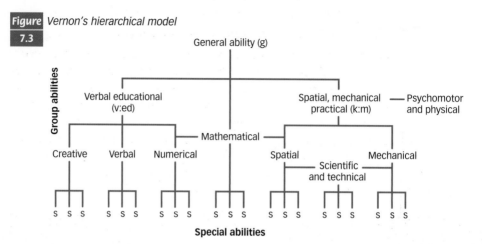

Figure 7.3 Vernon's hierarchical model

Like Spearman, Vernon believed g was inherited, but that the group factors v:ed and k:m as well as s were the result of education.

Many other psychometric tests of intelligence have since been developed, including the Wechsler scales, such as the **Wechsler Intelligence Scale for Children (WISC)**, the British Ability Scales and non-verbal tests such as Raven's Progressive Matrices. Alice Heim has also developed a series of tests such as AH7, which aim to measure higher levels of intelligence. The most popular tests are pencil-and-paper, multiple-choice, group tests, which can be completed by a large number of people at the same time and are quick to analyse. They include items such as analogies (for example 'kitten is to cat as puppy is to...'), odd-one out, number sequences, vocabulary and pattern matching.

These kinds of tests continue to be widely used. Binet originally developed his test to identify the kinds of problems with which children had difficulty, so that remedial help could be offered, and they may still be used in this way. However, they are often used as a basis for selection. For example, until fairly recently children in their last year at primary school took a test called the 11+ to identify those children who it was thought would benefit from an academic education and so should attend a grammar school, while children who 'failed' the 11+ had a less academically-oriented education at secondary modern schools. There are still parts of England, such as Kent, where this system continues. The assumption underlying the use of tests in this way is that they have **predictive validity**, i.e. that they can predict performance both within education and in related areas such as performance at different kinds of jobs. This idea in turn rests on the assumption that at least by the age of 11, intelligence is relatively fixed and indeed is largely genetically determined, a view held by Cyril Burt, who was instrumental in the introduction of the 11+ system in the UK. Jensen (1980), who shared Burt's view of the largely genetic basis of intelligence, quoted typical correlation coefficients for the relationship between IQ scores and educational performance of between 0.5 and 0.8 — significant, but far from perfect. The issues such as the possible biological basis of intelligence and other factors that may influence test performance will be returned to at the end of this chapter.

A major problem with the psychometric approach to intelligence is the lack of any adequate definition of what constitutes intelligence, so the kinds of items included in tests reflect the theoretical assumptions of the person developing the test. However, there is usually a high degree of correlation between results on the different tests, with people who score highly on one test tending to score well on others. A further and related issue is the use of factor analysis. There are various ways in which this can be carried out, which are likely to produce different relationships between the different factors the test measures and so cannot give a clear picture of the nature of intelligence, in particular whether it is largely a general factor, as Spearman suggested, or a set of largely independent factors.

Summary

- There is little agreement on a **definition** of intelligence.
- The psychometric approach is interested in measuring **differences between individuals**. There are tests for different **age groups**. Some tests are taken **individually** while others are **group** tests that are used to test people en masse.
- Tests are constructed so that results show a **normal distribution**. Relationships between subtests are compared using **factor analysis**. Different kinds of analysis can support the idea of **general intelligence** or more **independent factors**.
- Theorists' opinions differ in terms of the size of the **genetic component** of intelligence and the degree to which it is **influenced by other factors**.
- Tests can be used as a basis for **remediation** or more often for **selection**.

The information-processing approach

The psychometric approach looks at the products of cognitive processing, such as the number of problems correctly solved, but has largely ignored the processes underlying intelligent behaviour. The information-processing approach focuses on these processes: the human mind can be seen as a computer, where information is put in and then processed in some way, leading to an output. The physiology of the brain is seen as the hardware of cognition and the processes taking place during processing the software or programs. Researchers in this area often use **computer simulation** techniques, to attempt to replicate human thinking. More generally, they carry out **task analysis**, breaking down the steps involved in carrying out a task. The general aims of this approach are to understand how individuals interpret, store, retrieve and evaluate information by looking at perception, memory and the use of rules and strategies.

This approach to intelligence follows two main lines of inquiry:
- The **developmental approach** looks at age-related changes in information processing.

7

● The **study of individual differences** compares the information-processing strategies of individuals.

Within the developmental approach, Case (1978) makes the proposition of **sequential development**, that there is a clear sequence in the development of the way children think, with information processing becoming increasingly proficient. Another of Case's propositions relates to **working memory (WM)**. Development is explained in terms of **mental space (M-space)**, the increasing size of WM as children develop. Case suggests that M-space is freed up as a result of brain maturation and schemas becoming more automatic. However, Meadows (1995) argues that children's increasing ability to solve problems efficiently has less to do with an increase in WM and more to do with increasing knowledge and experience in handling cognitive tasks.

There is a lot of research evidence that shows children become more efficient at processing information as they get older. For example, Lloyd (1995) found that memory for a string of digits increases with age. Kail and Park (1992) investigated children's performance on a range of tasks, such as simple addition and reaction time, where they were asked to press a button as quickly as possible when a light appeared. As children got older, they were able to carry out these tasks more quickly. This increase in speed of processing is thought to be largely due to changes in the brain, in particular **myelination**, in which an insulating sheet develops over nerve fibres and speeds up their electrical impulses.

Children also develop a set of rules to use to solve problems, which develop with age and experience (see Box 7.1)

Box 7.1 Siegler (1991)

Aim: To investigate children's development of rules to use in problem solving.

Procedure: Children aged 3–7 were shown a balance scale with pegs on which weights could be placed. They were asked to predict which way the balance would tip depending on the number and position of the weights.

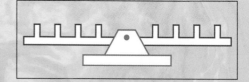

Results: Children's answers seemed to depend on one of four rules:

1 Attention was paid to the number of weights, with their position being ignored.

2 As above, unless the number of weights was equal, when the position of the weights was also taken into account.

3 Children took into account both number and position of weights, but not systematically. They often ended up guessing.

4 Children systematically considered both distance and weights on both sides.

The older the child, the more sophisticated the rule-based behaviour.

Conclusion: Children develop rules in an orderly sequence and become increasingly more proficient at applying them.

Siegler saw this developmental sequence not so much as a maturational sequence related to age, but rather as dependent on experience and practice.

The information-processing approach also looks at the role of **metacognition** in the development of intelligent behaviour. This is awareness of one's own cognitive processes and the ability to reflect on them. It is one of the skills that theorists refer to as **executive processes**, which also include considering different strategies and planning how to solve a problem. These skills also develop as children gain in experience, and it is thought that education plays a large part.

Within this approach, the other line of inquiry focuses on individual differences, suggesting that the ways in which processing differs between individuals underlie differences in intelligence. There are individual differences as well as developmental differences in the speed of information-processing, and there has been some interest in a possible link with IQ, as measured on intelligence tests. Vernon and Mori (1992) found a positive correlation between the speed of conduction of neural impulses and measured IQ. There are also differences in the strategies used (see Box 7.2).

Box 7.2	DeLoache and Brown (1987)

Aim: To investigate differences in strategies in a problem-solving task.

Procedure: The searching strategies of normally developing and developmentally delayed 2-year-old children were compared. The children were asked to search for a toy hidden in a room. Without the children knowing, the toy was removed before they were asked to search for it again.

Results: For the initial search, there was no difference in the strategies used by the two groups. Once it had been removed, the normally developing children searched for it in places other than where it had been hidden before, while the developmentally delayed children continued to search in the same place.

Conclusion: Flexibility in the use of strategies may contribute to individual differences in cognitive ability.

The information-processing approach has practical applications, in that tests can be used as a diagnostic tool to identify children who are not developing normally. This would allow strategies to be put in place to foster their development. For example, which of the four rules a child is using to solve a problem such as that in Box 7.1 could be identified and children could be shown how to use a more helpful rule. This approach has the advantage of complementing the 'product' approach of psychometric testing, giving a detailed account of cognitive processes in intelligent behaviour. However, research is still in its early days and the findings are often task-specific, so it is difficult to generalise the principles more widely. Furthermore, it does not yet provide a credible alternative to intelligence tests.

Summary

- In contrast to the psychometric approach, the information-processing approach looks at the **processes** involved in intelligent behaviour, using a **computer** metaphor, rather than its **products**.
- One line of inquiry investigates the **development** of intelligent behaviour in children. Working memory (**M-space**) is thought to be important, together with the development of **rules** and **metacognition**.
- This approach is also interested in **individual differences**, which may be linked to **processing speed** and the use of **strategies**.
- This approach emphasises the importance of **experience and education**. It could be used to **support children's development**.

In the two approaches looked at, one of the issues to emerge strongly is the relative importance of **nature and nurture**, and this will be returned to towards the end of the chapter. This issue is made more complicated by the lack of any agreed definition of what exactly intelligence is.

Binet pioneered work within the **psychometric** tradition, but did not regard intelligence as genetically fixed, but rather as something that could be developed, since his tests were intended to be used for diagnosis and remediation. However, most theorists working within this tradition have ascribed a major role to genetic factors, with little scope for development and change. This assumption underlies the use of tests for selection purposes.

The balance between nature and nurture is reversed in the **information-processing** approach. There is still a place for innate and in particular maturational factors, such as the speeding up of processing as myelination takes place. However, it makes a distinction between intelligence as something people have more or less of and focuses rather on intelligent behaviour. A parallel can be drawn here with Piaget's theory of cognitive development (Chapter 8), which in this sense is also a theory of intelligence. The information-processing approach takes the view that individuals can learn to behave intelligently, as a result of experience and practice.

Gardner's theory of multiple intelligences

While many theorists have assumed that intelligence is a single entity that underlies a range of abilities, others believe that we should instead talk of plural intelligences, a number of skills that operate independently. Based on the belief that the mind consists of distinct modules, Gardner (1983) proposed that 'intelligence' is what we call the results of the activities of these modules taken together, but they are better thought of separately than as parts of a whole. He suggested that there are seven different intelligences, each with its own biological source in the brain:

Gardner's seven types of intelligence

Linguistic intelligence: used when reading, writing or understanding speech; the ability to use language to achieve certain goals.

Mathematical-logical intelligence: used in arithmetic, mathematical calculation and logical reasoning; the ability to investigate issues scientifically.

Musical intelligence: used in appreciating, composing and performing music.

Spatial intelligence: used in finding one's way around and in visual art.

Bodily-kinaesthetic intelligence: used in dancing, sport and everyday movement and dexterity.

Interpersonal intelligence: used in relating to other people, understanding their intentions, motivation and desires; the ability to work effectively with others.

Intrapersonal intelligence: used in understanding one's own feelings and motivations; having a good working model of ourselves; being able to use this model to organise our lives effectively.

The first two are those abilities that are valued in education. The next three are associated with the arts and the final two are what he referred to as 'personal intelligences'. He later suggested further kinds of intelligence that might be added, including naturalist, spiritualist, existentialist and moral intelligences (Gardner 1999). Naturalist intelligence is often incorporated into the theory and relates to the ability to recognise and categorise features of the environment.

Gardner's argument was based on four different kinds of evidence:
- First, aptitudes develop unevenly, with particular kinds developing at different times as the individual gets older. For example, a child may at any one time be at different stages in terms of number development and spatial ability.
- Second, we know that brain damage affects specific areas of functioning, rather than having a global effect, so affects some abilities while leaving others intact.
- A third kind of evidence comes from studies of autistic children, whose general level of ability is low, but who may show what are known as **islets of ability** and so be extremely gifted in one particular area, such as music or art. An example is a case study reported by Selfe (1977); a child called Nadia had been diagnosed as mentally retarded, with autistic features, but her general retardation was in stark contrast to her drawing ability. At the age of 6, when most children's drawings are relatively primitive, Nadia was drawing from memory lively pictures of horses in motion, foreshortened and from a three-quarters viewpoint.
- Finally, Gardner drew on evolutionary theory, which suggests how a particular aptitude or ability might have evolved.

There are some advantages to Gardner's theory, in particular its ability to explain the disparity some people show in abilities usually associated with intelligence. While the theory has not found wide acceptance within academic psychology, it has been taken up within the education system, particularly in the USA and applied as one way of addressing problems in education. In particular, it has been influential in suggesting that students learn in many different ways, a view supported in a study of college students, carried out by Parker (2008), which found gender and ethnic differences in terms of students' intelligence preferences, suggesting that using the same teaching techniques with all students may not be ideal. This has led teachers to develop new approaches that might better meet the differing needs of learners, using a variety of methods to present their lessons. There is some evidence that this approach can be effective. For example, Brand (2006) found that a variety of story-telling methods and related activities, linked to children's abilities and interests, was effective in promoting literacy. Booth and O'Brien (2008) suggested that this kind of approach might also be useful in counselling children with problems.

However, Gardner's theory has also been criticised on several grounds. The criteria he used to define intelligences are (as he acknowledges) somewhat subjective and not based on empirical research. There are as yet no standardised tests to measure the strength of the kinds of intelligence he proposes, though the Multiple Intelligence Inventory assesses preferences among them. There is also a lot of research that has demonstrated an overlap between the different aspects of intelligence and intelligence measured by IQ tests. For example, Visser et al. (2006) found that there was a strong correlation between general intelligence and Gardner's linguistic, mathematical-logical, spatial, naturalistic and interpersonal intelligences, challenging Gardner's idea that his intelligences are entirely independent. It can be argued that musical and bodily-kinaesthetic intelligences might better be regarded as talents rather than forms of intelligence, since unlike the more commonly accepted forms of intelligence, they do not need to adapt to the demands life makes on us.

Summary

- Gardner suggests that there are several **different kinds of intelligence**, independent of each other.
- This idea has been **influential** in education, but has been criticised for its **lack of empirical basis** and support.

Animal learning and intelligence

Behaviourism has been a major perspective in psychology and has focused on learning, in particular classical and operant conditioning. This perspective was developed by Watson (1913), who believed that psychological research should aim to be objective and scientific and therefore psychological data should be observable, measurable behaviour and associated with environmental events. Much of the early research was carried out on animals, on the principle that humans are similar in many ways to non-human animals, and therefore general psychological principles that apply to both human and non-human animals can be developed as the result of animal research.

While conditioning theory uses laboratory studies, other approaches to animal intelligence have made use both of this kind of method and more naturalistic observations of animal behaviour to try to establish animals' understanding, rather than how behaviour is acquired.

Conditioning in non-human animals

Classical conditioning

Watson was greatly influenced by the work of Pavlov (1849–1936), a physiologist carrying out research into **reflexes** — fixed, automatic and uncontrolled responses to particular stimuli — and in particular the salivation reflex. Pavlov developed a method of collecting the saliva automatically secreted by hungry dogs when presented with food, allowing measurement of the strength of the response. He noticed that dogs would not only salivate when they could see or taste the food, but also when they saw the researcher who fed them. On the basis of this observation, he carried out experiments to demonstrate the phenomenon of classical conditioning, in which an animal learns to make a novel stimulus-response association, in this case the response of salivation to the stimulus of a bell (see Box 7.3).

Box 7.3	Pavlov (1927)

Aim: To demonstrate learning of a behaviour through classical conditioning.

Procedure: A dog was held still in a harness and a bell was rung to check that the sound did not produce the reflex response of salivation. Pavlov called the bell a neutral stimulus since it did not provoke an automatic response. The bell was then rung and food presented immediately afterwards. Pavlov called the food an unconditional stimulus (UCS), because no conditions need to be met for salivation to occur. This pairing of bell and food was repeated several times. Finally, the bell was rung on its own.

Results: The dog salivated when the bell was rung at the same time as food was presented. As this was an automatic response to the food, Pavlov called it an unconditioned response. When the bell was finally rung on its own, the dog salivated. This was called a conditioned response (CR), because it only occurred on condition that the bell-food pairings had taken place. At this stage, the bell had become a conditioned stimulus (CS), as it elicited salivation only on condition that it had previously been paired with the bell.

Conclusion: Animals can learn a new stimulus-response (SR) association through pairing a new stimulus with a stimulus that produces a reflex response.

Figure 7.4	*Classical conditioning*

Neutral stimulus (NS): bell   ⟶   No specific response

Unconditioned stimulus (UCS): food   ⟶   Unconditioned response (UCR): salivation

Neutral stimulus (NS): bell
Unconditioned stimulus (UCS): food   ⟶   Unconditioned response (UCR): salivation

Conditioned stimulus (CS): bell   ⟶   Conditioned response (CR): salivation

The dog salivating to the sound of the bell provides an objectively measurable change in behaviour, which Watson called an **index of learning**; the dog can be said to have learned to salivate to the sound of the bell. A further term here is **contingency**; this refers to the sequence of events to which an animal is exposed, when one event depends on another event. Here, conditioning occurs when the presentation of food is contingent on the ringing of the bell.

For conditioning to take place, the ringing of the bell and the presentation of food need to occur close together in time, ideally less than one second; this is known as **temporal contiguity**. Conditioning is weak if the time lapse is any longer and cannot take place if the food is presented before the bell is rung; in this case the bell cannot signal the presentation of the food.

Pavlov found there was a weaker response if the bell was rung a few times on its own with no food being presented. After about 20 such trials, the CR disappeared; this is known as **extinction**. Sometimes, if there has been a break, the CR can return, even though the bell has not been paired with food again; this is known as **spontaneous recovery**. This shows that extinction does not wipe out the original learning, but merely suppresses it, a process known as **inhibition**.

Another phenomenon demonstrated in this series of experiments is **generalisation**. This refers to a CR being given to a stimulus that is similar but not identical to the CS, for example a bell with a slightly different sound. However, as the difference between the original CS and the new stimulus increases, the CR becomes weaker. At some point the stimuli become too dissimilar for a CR to occur. This lack of a CR to the new stimulus demonstrates **discrimination**; the animal is responding to the difference between the two stimuli. Pavlov trained dogs to salivate to a circle but not an ellipse and then gradually made the ellipse more circular. When it was almost completely circular, the dogs responded by whining and trembling. Pavlov termed this behaviour **experimental neurosis**; it comes about when the limit of the dogs' ability to discriminate is reached.

It is possible to use a CS as a new UCS, i.e. **second-order conditioning**. For example, if a dog has been conditioned to salivate to the sound of a bell, the bell can be used as a UCS for learning salivation to a buzzer.

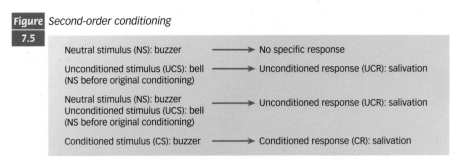

Figure 7.5 *Second-order conditioning*

By repeating this process, third-order and even fourth-order conditioning is possible, though the effect is weaker. **Higher-order conditioning** refers to second-, third- and fourth-order conditioning.

Watson explained the learning showed in classical conditioning in terms of links being established in the brain and considered reference to mental processes to be unnecessary. However, there are some problems with this account of learning (see Box 7.4).

Epstein et al. (1984) carried out a similar experiment with pigeons, with the same results. These experiments challenge the idea that learning takes place through the gradual formation of an association. They also suggest that for a full account of learning, it is necessary to refer to mental processes.

A further classic study, demonstrating the **Garcia effect**, also challenges the premises of classical conditioning (see Box 7.5).

Box 7.5 **Garcia and Koelling (1966)**

Aim: To investigate the principles of classical conditioning.

Procedure: Before the experimental procedure, rats were tested with a saccharin solution to check that they had no inbuilt dislike for the taste. The saccharin solution was then paired with a noise and a flashing light, both triggered automatically when the animal touched the drinking spout. Some time later — up to 12 hours in some cases — the rats were given a single injection, which made them nauseous and ill. They were then tested on (a) saccharin solution and (b) water, paired with the noise and light.

Results: The rat refused the saccharin solution, but drank the water.

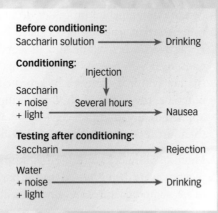

Figure 7.6 *Principles of classical conditioning (Garcia and Koelling 1966)*

Before conditioning:
Saccharin solution ⟶ Drinking

Conditioning:
Injection
Saccharin + noise + light ⟶ (Several hours) ⟶ Nausea

Testing after conditioning:
Saccharin ⟶ Rejection

Water + noise + light ⟶ Drinking

Conclusion: The rats had learned to associate the saccharin solution with nausea, but made no association with the noise and the light.

This study also challenges the idea that learning is a gradual process, since the rats formed the association between saccharin and nausea after only one experience of nausea. It also presents further difficulties for classical conditioning in terms of temporal contiguity, in that there was a gap of several hours between drinking the saccharin solution and nausea. Moreover, saccharin was paired with noise and light, so theoretically the rats should have learned an association between noise/light and nausea and refused the water when it was paired with them, but did not do so. This is best explained in terms of biological constraints on learning. In the wild, rats might well be exposed to food or drink that makes them ill and would need to make a rapid association with illness in order to survive, so forming this kind of association would be adaptive. However, light and noise are not usually associated with food or drink in the wild. Seligman (1970) used the term **preparedness** to describe what is happening here: animals are born better prepared to make some associations — those linked with survival — than others.

Summary

- Classical conditioning proposes that animals learn **stimulus-response associations**, based on **reflexes**. Associations are formed when events occur **close together in time**. It is not necessary to refer to **mental processes**.
- While learning can take place in this way, **insight learning** suggests that mental processes should be taken into account.
- The **Garcia effect** demonstrates **preparedness**, since some associations, which are **adaptive** in terms of survival, are formed more readily than others.

Operant conditioning

Operant conditioning theory was developed by Skinner (1904–90). As in classical conditioning, mental processes do not come into the account. Similarly, this theory proposes that learning takes place by association, but in this case the association is between a behaviour and its consequences, and this sequence constitutes the contingency in operant conditioning. If there is a positive outcome to a behaviour, the behaviour is likely to be repeated, while if there is no outcome, or a negative outcome, this is less likely. It also differs from classical conditioning in that it can be applied to any kind of behaviour an animal produces, i.e. **emitted behaviour**, rather than just reflexes, i.e. **elicited behaviour**.

Much of Skinner's work used a Skinner Box (Figure 7.7), with a key to peck when pigeons were being tested and a bar to press for rats; these were the behaviours to be acquired and were automatically registered on a chart. Food could also be presented automatically, as food pellets to a food tray. In a typical study, a rat would be put in the box and would emit some sort of behaviour. When the behaviour began to move towards the desired behaviour, for example if the rat moved towards the part of the box where the bar was, it would be given food. Once this behaviour was established, the rat's behaviour would need to become closer to the desired behaviour, for example touching the bar, for food to be delivered. Finally, the rat would receive food only when it emitted the desired behaviour of bar pressing. For a hungry rat, the food strengthens a particular behaviour; this is known as **reinforcement.** Moving the behaviour gradually towards what is required is known as **shaping.** Food is thus used to reinforce successive approximations of the desired behaviour.

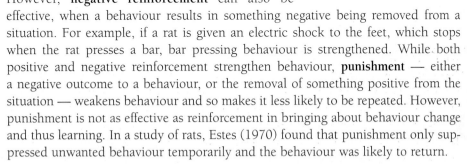
Figure 7.7 *A Skinner Box for rats*

Light
Dispenser
Lever
Food tray

Reinforcement can take two forms. **Positive reinforcement** refers to a positive outcome to a behaviour, as in food for a hungry animal. However, **negative reinforcement** can also be effective, when a behaviour results in something negative being removed from a situation. For example, if a rat is given an electric shock to the feet, which stops when the rat presses a bar, bar pressing behaviour is strengthened. While both positive and negative reinforcement strengthen behaviour, **punishment** — either a negative outcome to a behaviour, or the removal of something positive from the situation — weakens behaviour and so makes it less likely to be repeated. However, punishment is not as effective as reinforcement in bringing about behaviour change and thus learning. In a study of rats, Estes (1970) found that punishment only suppressed unwanted behaviour temporarily and the behaviour was likely to return.

There are different **schedules of reinforcement,** i.e. the patterns of reinforcement applied to behaviour. In **continuous reinforcement (CRF)**, a behaviour is reinforced every time it occurs, and Skinner found that this is the best schedule for establishing a behaviour. Once this has been achieved, behaviour can be maintained by **partial reinforcement**, where not every response is reinforced. This can take several forms:

Schedules of reinforcement

Fixed interval (FI): behaviour is reinforced at regular intervals, for example once every 20 seconds, provided there has been at least one appropriate behaviour since the previous reinforcement.

Variable interval (VI): as above, but reinforcement is given every 20 seconds on average, for example after 17 seconds, 23 seconds, 19 seconds, 21 seconds and so on.

Fixed ratio (FR): reinforcement is given after a set number of responses, for example after every tenth response.

Variable ratio (VR): as above, but reinforcement is given after every tenth response on average, for example after 9 responses, 12 responses, 10 responses, 11 responses and so on.

As with classical conditioning, the concept of **extinction** applies and occurs when a behaviour is not reinforced. Both FI and FR schedules are relatively easy to extinguish and a CRF schedule is the easiest. VR is the most effective schedule for maintaining a behaviour, so behaviour on this schedule is the hardest to extinguish. **Generalisation** and **discrimination** are also relevant to operant conditioning. A response that has been reinforced in one situation may be repeated in a similar situation, i.e. generalisation, but if the two situations are sufficiently dissimilar, discrimination will occur and this will not happen.

While there is evidence to support the concepts of operant conditioning, there is also research evidence that does not easily fit the theory (see Box 7.6).

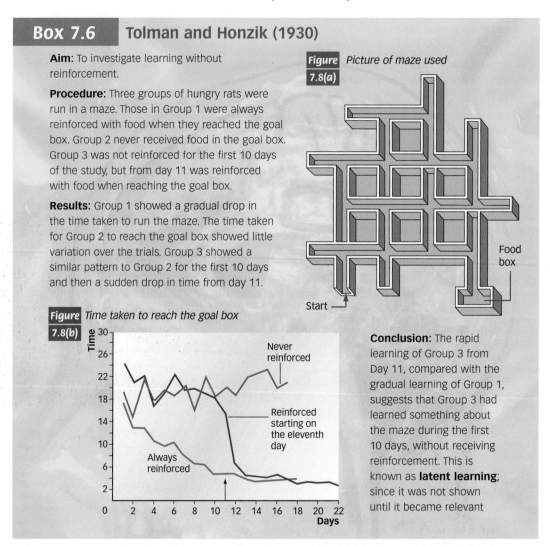

Box 7.6   Tolman and Honzik (1930)

Aim: To investigate learning without reinforcement.

Procedure: Three groups of hungry rats were run in a maze. Those in Group 1 were always reinforced with food when they reached the goal box. Group 2 never received food in the goal box. Group 3 was not reinforced for the first 10 days of the study, but from day 11 was reinforced with food when reaching the goal box.

Results: Group 1 showed a gradual drop in the time taken to run the maze. The time taken for Group 2 to reach the goal box showed little variation over the trials. Group 3 showed a similar pattern to Group 2 for the first 10 days and then a sudden drop in time from day 11.

Figure 7.8(a) Picture of maze used

Food box

Start

Figure 7.8(b) Time taken to reach the goal box

Time

Never reinforced

Reinforced starting on the eleventh day

Always reinforced

Days

Conclusion: The rapid learning of Group 3 from Day 11, compared with the gradual learning of Group 1, suggests that Group 3 had learned something about the maze during the first 10 days, without receiving reinforcement. This is known as **latent learning**; since it was not shown until it became relevant

On the basis of this and similar studies, Tolman claimed that it was necessary to include an element of cognition in the behaviourist account and so was a major exponent of **cognitive behaviourism**. What animals are learning is not fixed behaviours but information, and Tolman referred to the information about the maze in studies such as the one above as a **cognitive map**. What is being learned is a stimulus-stimulus (S-S) association, i.e. the expectancy that one stimulus will be followed by another. Here the rats had learned something about the maze during the first 10 days that they were then able to apply when it was appropriate, i.e. when food was present in the goal box. Learning this kind of information would be adaptive behaviour in the wild, since information about the environment would enable the animal to escape predators, perhaps using a route that had not been used before.

According to operant conditioning, it should be possible to use its principles to teach an animal any behaviour of which it is physically capable. However, this does not always hold true. Breland and Breland ran a business in which they trained animals to take part in films and commercials. They used the techniques of shaping and reinforcement, but things did not always go according to plan. In 1961, they published a paper called *The Misbehaviour of Organisms* (a play on words of Skinner's book *The Behaviour of Organisms*), in which they described some of the problems they had come across in their work.

For one job, they needed to train pigs to drop two coins into a piggy bank. The pigs were hungry and food was used as reinforcement. At first, all went well, with shaping and reinforcement being effective up until the time when the pig had to drop the second coin into the piggy bank. At this stage, the pig would pick up the

coin, but would also toss it in the air, root it with its snout, pick it up, drop it, root it again and so on, but not put it into the piggy bank. Breland and Breland explained this behaviour in terms of what they called **instinctive drift**, i.e. the tendency of an animal to revert to behaviour typical of its species. Pigs root for food and this behaviour is an example of a **fixed action pattern (FAP)**, a genetically preprogrammed sequence of behaviour released by the presence of food. The pigs were therefore responding to the coins as if they were food. It seems that, as with classical conditioning, there are biological constraints on what can be learned by operant conditioning.

Charles LUPICA/Alamy

Breland and Breland explained their pigs' inability to learn a task in terms of what they called instinctive drift — the animals reverted to typical behaviour for their species

Summary

- Operant conditioning proposes that learning comes about through **shaping** and **reinforcement**, with an association being formed between a **behaviour** and its **consequences**.
- Tolman's research suggested that animals can learn **information** without reinforcement; they form a **cognitive map** of a maze. Animals can use this information when it becomes relevant. What is formed is therefore an **expectancy**.
- As a result of **instinctive drift**, there are constraints on what can be learned through operant conditioning.

Intelligence in non-human animals

In this section, we will discuss a different way of studying animal intelligence, looking at the extent of their understanding of themselves and their social world. Three areas where research of this kind has been carried out are **self-recognition**, **social learning** and **Machiavellian intelligence**.

Self-recognition

A basic social concept is the understanding that each individual is a self, in a world consisting of this self and other selves. This concept depends on the ability to recognise oneself and research has investigated this ability in non-human animals using mirrors. When a chimpanzee first sees itself in a mirror, it responds to the image as though it were another chimpanzee, either making threatening or conciliatory gestures. However, after a few days it learns to use the mirror to explore parts of its body that it is usually unable to see; for example, it picks its teeth and removes mucus from its eyes and nose. This suggests that chimpanzees have some ability to recognise the image in the mirror as their own body.

However, these kinds of self-directed behaviour could be explained as coincidence, in that the animals just happened to carry out frequently occurring behaviours when they were in front of the mirror. To discount this possibility, Gallup developed the 'red mark' technique (see Box 7.7).

Box 7.7 **Gallup (1970)**

Aim: To investigate self-recognition in chimpanzees.

Procedure: Young wild-reared chimpanzees were put into individual cages for 10 days with a full-length mirror. They were then anaesthetised and a red mark was put on one ear and one eyebrow. They were returned to their cages with no mirror, to establish a baseline record of how often they touched the parts that had been dyed red. The mirrors were then put back in the cages and the number of times the red-dyed parts were touched was compared with the baseline measure.

Results: Over the first few days, the chimpanzees showed typical self-directed behaviours towards their reflection. Each chimpanzee immediately began to explore the red marks on its body and touched the dyed areas 25 times more often than during the baseline period.

Conclusion: Chimpanzees are capable of self-recognition.

This technique has been used to investigate self-recognition in other animals. Lethmate and Ducker (1973) found that orangutans also have this ability. Patterson and Cohn (1994) claimed that this is also true of gorillas, although research by Shillito et al. (1999) failed to support it. Tests with other animals have been unsuccessful, for example gibbons (Gallup 1983), elephants (Povinelli 1989) and parrots (Pepperburg et al. 1995). Self-recognition appears to be limited to the great apes. It has been suggested that this ability may be limited to animals that are able to make use of information provided by mirrors, but this has been discounted. Povinelli (1989) found that although they did not demonstrate self-recognition and always responded to their mirror image as though it were another elephant, the four elephants he tested were nonetheless able to use a mirror to retrieve a carrot from a place where it could only be seen in the mirror.

Gallup suggested that self-recognition demonstrates self-awareness, drawing on the work of Cooley (1902), who was interested in the development of the self-concept in humans. Cooley used the term **looking-glass self** to express the idea that our self-concept develops as a result of how others respond to us and so is essentially a social process. If the same is true of chimpanzees, it would follow that chimpanzees raised in isolation would fail to show self-recognition. In a replication of his study with chimpanzees raised in isolation, Gallup (1977) found that they always responded to their mirror image as though it were another chimpanzee and did not touch the red-dyed areas of their faces more often than they had done before they were marked. This provides some support for the idea that self-recognition is a social process.

Social learning

Many animals live in groups, so it is possible that younger members of the group can learn from more experienced animals. For example, copying the diet of older members of the group would protect an animal from ingesting poisonous substances without having to test them itself. Similarly, if one member of the group had learned how to solve a particular problem, other members of the group would benefit from copying this behaviour. An animal might also learn how to avoid predators by observing how other members of the group respond to them. These areas of social learning will be looked at later in this section.

Rats are neophobic, i.e. unwilling to eat anything new. When they come across a novel food, they take a trial-and-error approach and typically try only a little and will not touch the food again if there are any ill effects. This is adaptive behaviour, in that being wary of new foods that might be poisonous would promote survival. They are also influenced in what they eat by other members of the social group (see Box 7.8).

Box 7.8	Galef (1988)

Aim: To investigate the influence of other animals on food choice.

Procedure: A 'demonstrator' rat ate food with a distinctive flavour, either cocoa or cinnamon. A test rat was then put with the demonstrator for 30 minutes, with no food present, and was then offered cocoa-flavoured and cinnamon-flavoured food. It was tested again 12 hours later.

Results: Tests rats preferred the food associated with the demonstrator rat. This was still the case 12 hours after it had made its initial choice.

Conclusion: Interacting with a rat that has just eaten a particular food creates a preference in another rat for that food.

The factors that influence this choice have also been investigated (see Box 7.9).

Box 7.9 **Galef et al. (1998)**

Aim: To identify the factors that influence animals' food choice.

Procedure: A test rat was placed inside a bucket that had a wire mesh basket in the side. An anaesthetised 'demonstrator' rat was placed in the basket, in one of three conditions: (a) with a new food dusted on its face, (b) with this food placed directly into its stomach via a tube, or (c) with the rat being inserted backwards into the basket, with its rear end dusted with the food. In a fourth condition, cotton wool dusted with the food was put into the basket. Test rats were then offered a choice of foods to find out under which circumstances they would prefer the food associated with the demonstrator.

Results: A food preference was shown in conditions (a) and (b) and a slight preference in (c). There was no preference in the cotton wool condition.

Figure 7.9 *Apparatus used by Galef et al. (1988)*

Conclusion: For a rat to demonstrate a food preference through exposure to a demonstrator, the demonstrator does not need to be conscious, but does need to be a rat. Interaction with the front end of the rat is preferable. The rat needs to be able to smell food at the same time as it smells the demonstrator's breath.

Animals can also learn foraging behaviours through **observational learning** and imitation. Chimpanzees eat termites, but there is a problem in reaching them inside their nests. Lawick-Goodall (1970) reported that young chimpanzees learn 'termiting' from watching their parents. This involves pushing a stick into a termite nest and eating the termites that cling to it when it is pulled out.

This kind of learning has also been shown in other situations, such as the response to predators (see Box 7.10).

Box 7.10 **Mineka and Cook (1988)**

Aim: To investigate observational learning of a fear response to predators.

Procedure: When an adult monkey comes across a snake, it shows fear, makes a specific alarm call and attempts to flee. Laboratory-reared monkeys who had never seen a snake watched this fear response to a snake in a wild-reared monkey. The observer monkeys were then exposed individually to a snake. Their reactions were compared with those of laboratory-reared monkeys who had not seen the fear response of the wild-reared monkey but had observed a model that was not afraid of snakes.

Results: The monkeys who had observed the reactions of the wild-reared monkey responded with a similar fear response. The monkeys who had not seen this response showed no fear of the snake.

Conclusion: Fear of the snake was acquired through observational learning.

There is evidence too that the use of alarm calls to warn other members of the group of possible predators and to understand their meaning when given by others, is to some extent acquired through social learning. Seyfarth and Cheney (1980) found that Vervet monkeys have a range of alarm calls, each of which refers to a different kind of predator. When the predator is an eagle, the alarm call resembles a chuckle and the group responds to it by looking up and fleeing into the bushes. For a leopard, the alarm call is a bark and the monkeys' response is to climb up trees. For a snake, the call is a high-pitched chattering and the monkeys search the ground and may attack the snake. Young monkeys produce the full repertoire of calls at a very early age, suggesting that the physical characteristics of these calls are genetically determined.

Vervet monkeys have acquired through social learning the ability to give a range of alarm calls to warn of approaching predators

However, there is also an element of learning, both in the response to calls made by others and in the production of the calls themselves. Seyfarth and Cheney (1986) played a recording of an eagle alarm call to young monkeys who had wandered away from their mothers. At first, an infant appeared confused and then watched its mother and copied her reaction of looking up at the sky. Young monkeys also occasionally made inappropriate calls, such as giving the 'eagle' call when it saw a pigeon. Adults responded to appropriate calls by looking up and repeating the call, but ignored inappropriate ones such as this. This could be explained in terms of reinforcement and discrimination, mentioned in the section on conditioning. The behaviour of the monkeys in response to appropriate calls reinforced their use by young monkeys, while their lack of response to inappropriate calls did not reinforce their use and led to discrimination.

Machiavellian intelligence

Evolutionary theory suggests that primates possess a number of specialised mental abilities that provide an advantage in coping with the environment in terms of promoting higher social and reproductive success. One of these abilities is Machiavellian intelligence, named after the fifteenth century Italian politician and author Niccolo Machiavelli, whose work described the cunning manipulation of others in political life. This kind of social manipulation depends on having a **theory of mind**, the ability to represent the mental states of others — their beliefs, intentions and desires — and so to understand how they think and feel. This topic is discussed in relation to humans in Chapter 8. In their **Machiavellian intelligence hypothesis**,

Byrne and Whiten (1988) proposed that primates are able to predict and manipulate the behaviour of others in their social group in ways that serve their own interests. For this reason it is also known as the **social brain hypothesis**; primates have unusually large brains for their body size and it is suggested that this can be explained by the demands of living in social groups. The use of deceit allows individuals or groups to negotiate and benefit from group living and so intelligence is primarily an adaptation to the complexities of primate social life. It suggests that intelligence is by its nature social, in contrast to the idea of the general cognitive ability proposed by the theories at the start of this chapter.

Maestripieri (2007) has supported this viewpoint with naturalistic studies made of Rhesus macaques, monkeys who live in groups of about 50 individuals. There is a strong dominance hierarchy and fierce competition for social status and power. Alpha males use threats and violence to obtain the best sleeping places, food and females. They use frequent, unpredictable aggression to intimidate less powerful members of the group, who must wait for others to eat first and then have what is left and can mate only when the dominant monkeys are not looking.

Females act in Machiavellian ways when it comes to reproduction. They mate often with the alpha male to increase the chances that he will protect their infant from being killed by other monkeys, but also mate with all the other males in the group when he is not around, in case the alpha male is sterile or he dies or loses his power before the baby is born. Whiten and Byrne (1988) give an example of this kind of behaviour in relation to baboons, who live in similar social groups with a strong dominance hierarchy (see Box 7.11).

Box 7.11

Whiten and Byrne (1988)

An adult female baboon was seen edging towards a rock where she began to groom a junior male. The leader of the troop was not far away, but was prevented from seeing the young male behind the rock.

Figure 7.10 *How baboon A might see herself from the point of view of the dominant member of the troop, baboon T.*

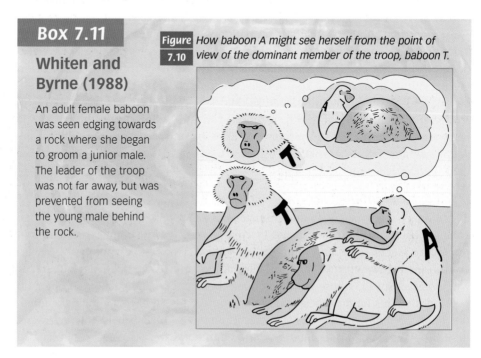

Whiten and Byrne argue that this behaviour suggests that the female baboon was able to appreciate the point of view of the dominant male and position herself in such a way that he would not be able to see the young male.

A similar example of social manipulation is given by Byrne (1995). A young male baboon came across a female who had just dug up a nutritious corm, a desirable foodstuff but difficult to get because of the hard ground in which they grew. He looked around as though to check that no other members of the troop were watching and then screamed. His mother arrived and chased away the lower-ranking female who had dug up the corm, which the young male then ate. Byrne suggests that the male pretended to have been attacked by the female so that his mother would chase her away and he could get the corm.

These are observations of naturally occurring behaviour and so have high ecological validity, and the interpretations put on them are consistent with what was observed. However, other interpretations are possible. In the first example, it may have been coincidence that the female positioned herself in such a way that the young male could not be seen by the dominant male. In the second example, screaming may have been intended to frighten away the female.

The Machiavellian hypothesis is an interesting idea. It has been suggested by Connor and Mann (2006) that this kind of social manipulation may also apply to dolphins, who also have relatively large brains and live in complex social groups. It has been put forward as an explanation of increased brain size in humans, as discussed in the next section and given the genetic similarity of humans and other primates such as chimpanzees, it is plausible that non-human primates share this kind of intelligence. However, Tomasello and Call (1997) conclude that 'there is no solid evidence that non-human primates understand the intentionality or mental states of others'. This appears to be an area where more research is required to test the accuracy of the interpretations put on observations of animals' behaviour.

Summary

- Mirror studies have shown that great apes are capable of **self-recognition** and so have a **sense of self**. There is some support for the claim that self-recognition is a **social process**.
- **Social learning** plays a part in animals' response to **novel foods** and developing **foraging behaviours**. Although there is an innate component in the **response to predators**, this response is refined through social learning.
- **Machiavellian intelligence** refers to **social manipulation** of others for one's own ends. Observation of naturally occurring behaviour suggests that **primates** have this ability. However, the **interpretation** of this behaviour is open to question.

Evolution of intelligence

Using a general definition of intelligence as the ability to function well in a particular environment, this section will initially look at evolutionary factors that have affected its development and then consider factors that affect intelligence in terms of its expression in intelligence tests.

Evolutionary factors in the development of human intelligence

Banks and Flora (1977) asked students to rank a list of animals, including humans, in order of intelligence. The results showed a strong positive correlation between rankings of intelligence and **brain size**, in line with the widely held assumption that brain size is related to intelligence. One problem with this is that elephants have much larger brains than humans, but few people would claim that elephants are more intelligent. A more plausible suggestion is that we should look at the ratio of brain size to body size, but using this measure, humans, with a relative brain size of 2%, are now outclassed by the mouse lemur, with a relative brain size of 3%. However, if brain weight is plotted against body size for mammals, using a logarithmic scale to produce a straight line graph, the weight of the human brain is much greater than expected for a mammal of our size and quite a lot greater than expected for a primate of our size.

Elephants have larger brains than humans but few would claim that elephants are more intelligent

TopFoto

The relationship between brain size and intelligence is not a simple one. The size of the human brain has tripled over the past 2 million years, and human brains also continue to increase in size after birth to make them larger than would be expected. Brains take a great deal of energy to produce and run; a brain takes up about 2% of body mass, but uses up about 20% of the energy we take in as food. A big brain must therefore confer some adaptive advantage in terms of intelligent behaviour.

One suggestion has to do with **food and foraging**. Herbivores such as cows need to spend a lot of time eating in order to take in enough calories, and this kind of foraging does not require a large brain. However, most primates are not able to deal with the large amounts of cellulose in a herbivorous diet and so have a more varied although still largely vegetarian diet. This involves travelling around to find suitable food, locating food using a highly developed perceptual system and extracting food from its source, for example extracting nuts from their shells and eating fruits while avoiding prickles, which are often part of the plant. This requires more intelligence than grazing.

Figure 7.11 *Brain weight and body weight from Young (1981)*

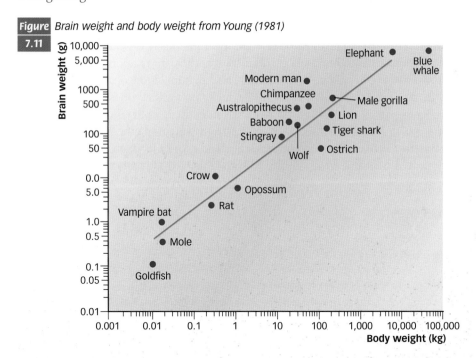

It has been suggested that the increased brain size of humans is related to the use of **tools** in extracting food from its source. For example, as we saw earlier, chimpanzees use sticks to extract termites from their nest and they use stones to crack nuts. However, Byrne (1995) pointed out that the available evidence suggests that tools used by early man — Neanderthals and Homo erectus — were only slightly more sophisticated than those used by chimpanzees today. It seems unlikely that the driving force behind human development and therefore increased intelligence was simply the search for food.

7

A more convincing explanation relates to **social factors**. Humphrey (1976) makes a distinction between low-level and high-level intelligence. Low-level intelligence is the ability to infer that something is likely to happen simply because it has happened in the past, for example a cat coming to be fed when it hears the sound of a tin opener. This kind of intelligence is widespread in the animal kingdom and can be related to conditioning theory, discussed previously. High-level intelligence, also called creative intelligence, is more complex in that it is the ability to infer in a novel situation that something is likely to happen because it is implied by a particular combination of events. He proposed that most practical problems encountered by our hunter-gatherer ancestors (and most primates today) were solved by simple trial-and-error learning, i.e. low-level intelligence. However, high-level intelligence would be needed to function effectively within a social group, where knowledge can be shared and applied cooperatively for the benefit both of the individual and the group.

Living in groups is a good defensive strategy; there is safety in numbers, which also benefits the individual and offers access to resources and potential mates. At the same time, the larger the group becomes, the more opportunities there are for conflict between group members. High-level intelligence would therefore also include Machiavellian intelligence, discussed earlier in relation to non-human primates. This would allow the prediction and manipulation of the behaviour of others for an individual's own ends, while maintaining the cohesion of the social group. Being part of a social group requires individuals both to cooperate and to compete. To decide which option is best in any situation, the individual needs to be able to calculate the consequences of their own behaviour, assess the likely behaviour of others and weigh up the advantages and disadvantages of a particular course of action.

Summary

- The **size of the human brain** has tripled over the past 2 million years and is greater than expected for a mammal of our size. This must carry some **adaptive advantage** in terms of intelligent behaviour.
- It has been suggested that this was related to **foraging**, but there is little support for this idea.
- A more likely explanation relates to **social factors** in terms of the skills required to function well within a social group.

Factors in intelligence test performance

Intelligence tests aim to compare individuals' (and more controversially groups') performance on a range of skills assumed to underlie intelligence. As discussed, there are issues in terms of how intelligence should be defined, but intelligence tests do discriminate between people, so these differences need to be explained. There has been much debate in this area about the relative contributions of genetic and environmental factors. This is an important political and social issue. For example in education, if the differences are largely genetic, it makes little sense to put resources into measures to increase intelligence.

Genetic factors

It is possible — as Spearman and Burt claimed — that there are genetic reasons for differences in performance on IQ tests. Research investigating this possibility is based on the assumption that if there is a strong genetic element, individuals who are genetically closer should be more similar in IQ than those who are less closely related. The major ways in which research in this area has been carried out are twin, family and adoption/fostering studies.

Twin studies compare monozygotic (MZ) twins with dizygotic (DZ) twins. MZ (identical) twins share 100% of their genes, while DZ (fraternal) twins share only about 50% of their genes. Studies have also compared twins reared together in the same environment with twins reared apart in different environments, to gauge the influence of the environment:

Table 7.1 Correlations in twin studies

Researchers	MZ twins	MZ twins	DZ twins
	Reared together	Reared apart	Reared together
Newman et al. (1937)	0.91	0.67	0.64
Shields (1962)	0.76	0.77	0.51
Burt (1966)	0.94	0.77	0.55
Bouchard and McGue (1981)	0.86	0.72	0.60

In all cases, there are higher correlations between MZ than DZ twins, suggesting a strong genetic component. This is also supported by the strong correlation between MZ twins even when they are reared in different environments. The most important of these studies is that carried out by Bouchard and McGue, since this analysed the data of 111 studies of related people and so was a large-scale study. The overall conclusion that they reached is that there is a strong genetic component in measured intelligence, but the environment also plays a part. However, Kamin (1974) pointed out that there are various issues with these kinds of studies that might make it unwise to accept this conclusion.

The data from MZ twins reared apart come from a small number of studies, since suitable cases are extremely hard to find. It is also the case that only 13 of the 37 'raised apart' MZ twins in the Shields study lived in unrelated families. Most were raised by members of the same family, went to the same schools and played together, so the high correlation might be due to the similar environment rather than genes. There is a similar problem with the Newman et al. study. In one of his pairs, who were raised in quite different environments, the IQ difference between them was 24 points. The only study of 'reared apart' MZ twins that claimed that the environments in which the twins were raised were quite different is that carried out by Burt and his data are open to doubt, since the results of some of his studies are thought to have been faked; for this reason, they were not included in the Bouchard and McGue review. Even when twins are truly separated, they may well be raised in similar environments, as a result of **selective placement**, where adoption agencies attempt to match the adoptive mother to the birth mother, resulting in an underestimation of the effect of the environment.

At the time these studies were carried out, there was no way of differentiating reliably between MZ and DZ twins. For example, Newman et al. simply based their assessment on how similar the twins looked and did not include in the sample any who differed in appearance or behaviour. They also excluded, on the grounds of cost, twin pairs separated by long distances, so overall there is a possibility that the sample may have been skewed. Researcher bias is also a possibility in the Shields and Newman et al. studies, since IQ testing was carried out by a researcher who knew which twins were MZ and which DZ. Kamin (1974) found that twins tested by Shields showed an IQ difference of 8.5 points (leading to a correlation of 0.84), whereas pairs in this study tested by other researchers showed a mean difference of 22.4 points (giving a correlation of 0.11). All the studies used volunteers, with a large financial incentive to take part in the Newman et al. study, which might have encouraged some twins to lie about their upbringing.

The measurement of IQ in these studies is also an issue. Different studies used different intelligence tests, which makes valid comparison difficult. There is also the issue of generalisability, since, as Herman (1984) pointed out, families who produce twins may not be typical of the general population. It could also be argued that MZ twins may be treated more similarly than DZ twins. For example, they may be dressed the same and in other ways treated as though they were the same person, so similarities may arise from this environmental factor rather than genetics.

For these reasons, information about the contribution of genes to intelligence produced by these studies may be unreliable. Moreover, some studies have not been able to show differences in IQ between MZ and DZ twins. Scarr-Salapatek (1971) studied a sample of 779 twins and found non-significant results. In an interesting meta-analysis of data from previously published studies — omitting those of Burt — Taylor (1980) removed cases affected by some of the confounding variables identified above. Only five pairs of twins were found who had dissimilar educational and socioeconomic environments, had not been reunited after separation and had lived with unrelated families. The correlation of IQ scores for these pairs — admittedly a small sample — was only 0.24.

Table 7.2 IQ correlations from family studies (Bouchard and McGue 1981)

Parent/child reared together	0.42
Parent/child reared apart)	0.22
Siblings reared together	0.47
Siblings reared apart	0.24
Cousins	0.15

Family studies have been carried out on the same principle of genetic relatedness, as shown in Table 7.2. These figures suggest the influence of genes, since there are higher correlations between parent and child, who share more of their genes, than between cousins. However, there is also evidence of an environmental effect, since there are higher correlations for siblings reared together than those reared apart. A major difficulty with this kind of study is that the environment is usually more similar for close relatives, so it is difficult to separate the effects of genes and environment.

Adoption studies are based on the principle that if genes are more important than environment as a determinant of intelligence, an adopted child's IQ should be more similar to that of the birth parents than that of the adoptive parents. A number of studies have tested this idea:

Table 7.3	IQ correlations from adoption/fostering studies	
	Parents/natural child	**Parents/adopted child**
Burks (1928)	0.52	0.20
Leahy (1935)	0.60	0.18
	Child/natural parent	**Child/adoptive parent**
Skodak and Skeels (1949)	0.44	0.02
Horn et al. (1979)	0.28	0.15

In both the Burks and Leahy studies, data from two separate sets of families produced these correlations. IQ was not directly measured for the adoptive parent in the Skodak and Skeels study, but was based on the parent's educational level. From these figures, it appears that genes play an important part in intelligence, since the correlations are higher between the child and the birth parent than the child and the adoptive parent.

However, not all studies have produced similar results. For example, Snygg (1938) found a correlation of only 0.13 between adopted children and their birth mothers. This correlation in the Horn et al. study is also low, given the proportion of their genes that are shared. Selective placement, mentioned above, is also an issue here.

In the Skodak and Skeels study, the average IQ of the adopted children was 117, while that of their birth mothers was 86. Since half the adoptive mothers (unlike the birth mothers) had been to college, it could be argued that they had increased the IQ of their children beyond what would be expected on a genetic basis. McGurk (1975) has shown that the IQ of adopted children tends to move towards that of their adoptive parents and increasingly so as time goes on, therefore the adoptive environment appears to raise IQ.

Another approach to investigating the role of genes in measured intelligence is to carry out **longitudinal studies** to look at the stability of IQ across the lifespan, on the principle that stability should be high if there is a strong genetic influence. Honzik et al. (1948) found a high degree of stability through childhood. However other studies, for example McCall et al. (1973), have found considerable variation over time. This method is problematic in that it is difficult to measure IQ in very young children. Moreover, a high level of stability could simply indicate a tendency for environmental factors to remain constant across time.

More recently, research has attempted to locate the particular **genes** involved in intelligence, with some success. In a study of 102 children aged 6–15, Chorney et al. (1998) found that those with a high IQ were more likely to have a particular gene on chromosome 6 than those with an average IQ. However, this kind of research is still in its infancy.

A controversial issue relating to genetic differences in intelligence centres on **race**. There is evidence, for example Shuey (1966), that black Americans score on average 15 points lower on IQ tests than white Americans. On the basis of this kind of research and studies of the white population indicating that variability in IQ is 80% due to inherited differences, Jensen (1969) argued that the difference between the scores of black people and white people was due to genetic differences between races. Eysenck (1971) also took this view, supported by the finding that in Britain, West Indian immigrants had been shown to have lower IQ scores than the white population, though the difference — from 5 to 13 points — was less than that reported by Jensen in America.

One problem with this is that the differences found are between averages for groups, with a lot of individual variation within each group, and there is in fact a lot of overlap between the groups. For example, Shuey (1966) showed that 15–25% of blacks scored higher than 50% of whites. Variations within groups are larger than those between groups. Given the lack of a generally accepted definition of what is meant by intelligence, it can really only be said that the research shows differences in intelligence test scores, rather than intelligence, and there are strong arguments for accounting for racial differences in measured intelligence in terms of environmental factors.

According to the US Bureau of the Census (1994), more than 25% of African-Americans lived below the poverty line, compared with fewer than 8% of white Americans. Poverty, malnutrition, prejudice and discrimination and lack of educational opportunities could well have an effect on test performance. This is supported by Tyler (1965), who found that African-Americans living in the north, where conditions were better, did better on IQ tests than those living in the southern states. Moreover, Bayley (1955) found no IQ differences between young black and white children, suggesting that later differences are better explained in terms of environmental than genetic differences.

A further point to bear in mind is that black and white people do not constitute distinct biological groups. It has been estimated that 75% of Afro-Caribbeans have at least one white ancestor. Neither were the African slaves who formed the bulk of the black American population all from one race. They came from several different countries and are generally considered to be at least as varied genetically as modern Europeans.

A key issue here is how measured intelligence may be influenced by culture and we will return to this at the end of the chapter.

Summary

- The importance of genes in intelligence has been explored through **twin studies, family studies** and **adoption/fostering studies**.
- There are **methodological issues** with all these kinds of studies, which make interpretation of the data difficult.
- **Longitudinal studies** have produced mixed results.
- A recent approach has tried to identify particular **genes** associated with intelligence.
- It has been suggested that differences in IQ test scores between black and white people reflect genetic differences between **races**. However, there is wide **variation** within races. An **environmental explanation** may be more appropriate.

Environmental factors

Research has identified a range of factors that may affect test performance, one of which is **family background** (see Box 7.12).

Box 7.12   Sameroff and Seifer (1983)

Aim: To identify environmental factors that affect intelligence test performance.

Procedure: Starting in the 1970s, several hundred children were studied from birth to adolescence.

Results: Ten factors associated with lower measured IQ were identified:
- mother having a history of mental illness
- an overly anxious mother
- a mother with rigid beliefs and attitudes about the child's development
- little positive mother-child interaction
- the main family earner having a semi-skilled job
- poor educational standard of the mother
- the child being from an ethnic minority
- the child living in a single parent family
- family experience of more than 20 stressful events before the child was 4
- the family having more than four children

Conclusion: There is a strong association between measured IQ and a range of environmental and in particular family factors.

This is correlational research, so it cannot be assumed that these factors *cause* poor performance on IQ tests. For example, it could be that people are in semi-skilled jobs because they are less intelligent and so the reason for their children being less intelligent, as measured by tests, could be genetic. However, other research has found that early home experience is a good predictor of later test performance. Caldwell and Bradley (1978) developed a checklist to assess the quality of children's early home experience, the **Home Observation for Measurement of the Environment (HOME)** and found it a good predictor of later IQ scores. Yeates et al. (1979) found that mother's IQ was the best predictor of a child's IQ score at 2, supporting the idea of a genetic contribution to intelligence, but by the age of 4, HOME scores were the best predictors. Bradley and Caldwell (1984) found that children who score well on IQ tests are usually those from families who are emotionally responsive to the child, provide appropriate opportunities to play and learn and expect their child to learn and achieve. Another factor is **diet** (see Box 7.13).

Box 7.13   Benton and Cook (1991)

Aim: To assess the influence of vitamins on IQ scores.

Procedure: Participants were 47 6-year-old children who took either tablets containing high levels of vitamins and minerals or a placebo. Before taking the tablets, they completed some of the subscales of the British Ability Scales and a similar test several weeks later. Neither the children nor the researchers running the experiment knew which kind of tablet a child was taking.

Results: The IQ scores of those taking the supplement tablets increased by an average of 7.6 points, while the average for those in the placebo group declined by 1.7 points with a decline particularly on non-verbal measures. The 'supplement' group also showed better concentration.

Conclusion: Children's performance on IQ tests is affected by the quality of the diet.

Other factors in test performance relate to the **test situation**. One aspect of this is familiarity with the kinds of materials used. Dirks (1982) found that children performed better on a test that asked them to copy a pattern using wooden blocks when they had had experience of a game using a similar procedure. Children also do better if steps are taken to make them feel comfortable in the test situation (Zigler et al. 1973).

A final but extremely important issue in considering environmental influences on measured intelligence is **culture**. Given the lack of agreement on how intelligence may be defined, tests are almost inevitably culturally biased because they are created on the basis of the test constructor's conception of what constitutes intelligence. They may assume cultural knowledge and attitudes that are not necessarily shared by those taking the test. Some IQ tests are timed, and Smith (1948) has pointed out that some cultures do not appreciate the need to work quickly. Others may not be familiar with the pictorial representation of objects (Warburton 1951). Some groups taking the test may not be familiar with the kind of language the test uses, or with the objects they are being asked about. An early use of IQ tests was to limit immigration into the USA. Goddard (1929) reported that more than three-quarters of the Italians, Jews and Russians tested were feeble-minded. The tests used required knowledge of American culture that would-be immigrants lacked.

This kind of argument could also help to explain the differences between average scores for white and black Americans, mentioned previously. Some tests include tests of vocabulary and general knowledge, which would be impossible for a black child from an impoverished background and with poor educational opportunities to answer. They also fail to take into account black cultural knowledge. This is illustrated graphically by Williams (1972), who produced the **Black Intelligence Test of Cultural Homogeneity (BITCH)**. This uses the dialect of black English vernacular and information familiar to African-Americans. Not surprisingly, white children tend to do badly on this test:

BITCH

1 **'Do rag'** refers to: (a) the hair (b) the shoes (c) washing (d) tablecloth

2 **'Four corners'** refers to: (a) rapping (b) singing (c) the streets (d) dancing

3 **Who wrote the Negro National Anthem?** (a) Langston Hughes (b) Paul Lawrence Dunbar (c) James Weldon Johnson (d) Frederick Douglass

To address the problem of cultural bias, psychologists have attempted to produce **culture-fair tests**. The best known of these is **Raven's Progressive Matrices**, which uses non-verbal material in the form of geometric shapes:

Figure 7.12 *Sample item from Raven's Progressive Matrices. Which pattern fits into the space?*

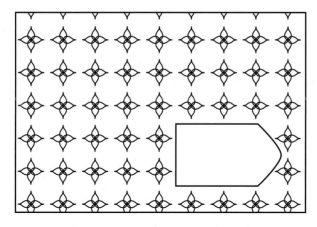

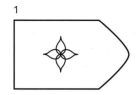

1

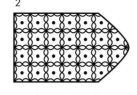

2

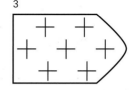

3

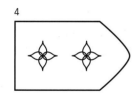

4

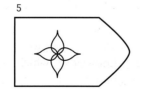

5

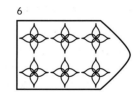

6

However, Mackintosh and Mascie-Taylor (1985) have shown that Asian children who are recent immigrants to Britain score poorly on these tests compared to white children, while Asian children who have lived in Britain for several years perform better, suggesting that such tests are not actually culture fair. It appears that people from diverse cultural backgrounds are at a disadvantage when taking these tests until they become enculturated.

We have looked in this section at the evidence for a possible genetic basis of intelligence and at environmental factors that affect its expression in the context of IQ tests. However, establishing the relative importance of these factors is limited by the issue of defining what is meant by intelligence, unless we accept Boring's operational definition, given at the start of the chapter. It should also be borne in mind that genetic and environmental factors always interact in development. Anastasi (1958) has argued that it would be more fruitful for psychologists to investigate how the two interact and to assess how changes in one may affect the influence of the other, rather than attempt to assess the relative importance of each.

Summary

- IQ test performance is related to **family background**. There is some evidence that it can be increased by **diet**. It may be affected by aspects of the **test situation**.
- IQ tests may be **culturally biased** in terms of making assumptions about cultural knowledge and attitudes. **Culture-fair tests** have met with little success.
- **Genetic** and **environmental** factors interact. It has been suggested that research should investigate the nature of this **interaction**.

Chapter

Cognition and development

Unit 3

Cognitive development

Cognition refers to information processing, including topics such as thinking, understanding, reasoning and beliefs. Theorists have been interested in the nature of children's cognitive processes, how these differ from those of an adult and how they develop as children get older. In this first section, the work of some of the most influential theorists in this area will be looked at.

Piaget's theory

Jean Piaget (1896–1980) was the first theorist to investigate systematically the development of children's thinking. Many of his early ideas came from observing his own children, but over a long career his research also involved a great number of other children. He used a technique called the **clinical interview**, in which he set children

8

tasks and problems to solve, observing their behaviour and questioning them about what they were doing and thinking. He was a **constructivist** theorist, in that he believed children played an active part in constructing their own understanding of the world and that they were **intrinsically motivated** to do so. Children's thinking cannot be modified by instruction but comes about only through their own experience.

A key term in Piaget's theory is **schema**, a mental representation of an action, which develops as a result of knowledge acquired through experience. Initially schemas are simple reflexes; for example, a baby has a sucking schema, which it applies to anything it puts in its mouth. Applying this schema to other objects without adapting it in any way is called **assimilation**; the schema just expands in terms of what it can be applied to. When the schema can be readily applied to new objects, the baby is in a state of **equilibrium**, i.e. the application of the schema is unproblematic. However, for some objects —

According to Piaget's theory, every baby has a sucking schema, which it applies to anything it puts in its mouth

such as a toy brick — the simple schema for sucking a nipple may be a poor fit. This creates what Piaget calls **disequilibrium**, an uncomfortable state of imbalance that motivates the child to adapt the schema, a process he called **accommodation**. The movement from disequilibrium to equilibrium that accommodation brings about is called **equilibration**. These same processes can be applied more generally to the way we take in and process information about the environment.

Piaget was a **stage theorist** and believed that children went through a series of four stages, in the same order, on the way to developing adult thinking. Each stage, with an approximate age range, is characterised by qualitatively different ways of thinking. Children must complete each stage before moving on to the next and the move to the next stage is brought about by their interactions with the environment.

The first stage is the **sensori-motor stage** (0–2 years). At this stage children's thinking is on a physical level, resulting from their own actions on the environment and the physical feedback received. During this stage, children practise reflex behaviour and adapt their schemas as a result of new experiences. A key characteristic of this stage is **egocentrism**, where children's thinking focuses on themselves. Piaget believed this was so extreme at birth that children make no distinction between self and not self. It gradually diminishes as children develop through the four stages, until in the fourth stage they become more capable of the detached and objective thinking of adults.

In this first stage, Piaget believed that egocentrism is shown by a lack of a concept of **object permanence**; if children cannot see an object, for them it no longer exists. Piaget gives an example of an observation he made (see Box 8.1).

TopFoto

Box 8.1 Piaget (1963)

Piaget observed his 7-month-old daughter Jacqueline playing with a plastic duck. The duck slipped out of view behind a blanket and she seemed to lose interest in it. Piaget picked up the duck and showed it to her, then obviously hid it under the blanket. Again she lost interest. This was repeated several times with the same results. Piaget concluded that for Jacqueline, the duck ceased to exist when she could no longer see it.

Piaget spent many years observing and studying children, including his daughter Jacqueline

Object permanence gradually develops in the sensori-motor stage. By 7 months, a child will reach for an object if it is only partly hidden, but not if it is completely hidden. By around 9 months, the child will search for a completely hidden object, but still does not have a complete understanding of the situation. This is shown in Piaget's **A-not-B error** studies (see Figure 8.1), in which children are shown a small toy hidden under cloth A; the child lifts the cloth and retrieves the toy. This is repeated several times. The toy is then hidden, in full view of the child, under cloth B. The child tries to retrieve it by lifting cloth A. According to Piaget, this is because of the child's egocentrism; children are unable to make a distinction between objects and their own actions on them, so connect the rediscovery of the toy with their own action of raising cloth A.

Figure 8.1 *Piaget's A-not-B error*

By around 18 months to 2 years, the child has developed the **general symbolic function**, the ability to represent things mentally even when they cannot be seen. This is shown by the child's use of language, drawing and pretend play and marks the move into the second **preoperational stage** (2–7 years). It is called this because the child is not yet able to carry out **operations**, such as internalised mental actions, but is still tied to the concrete physical world. In this stage, the child is not yet capable of **conservation**, i.e. understanding that there are things that do not change even when their physical appearance changes. Piaget carried out a series of experiments to test this idea (see Box 8.2).

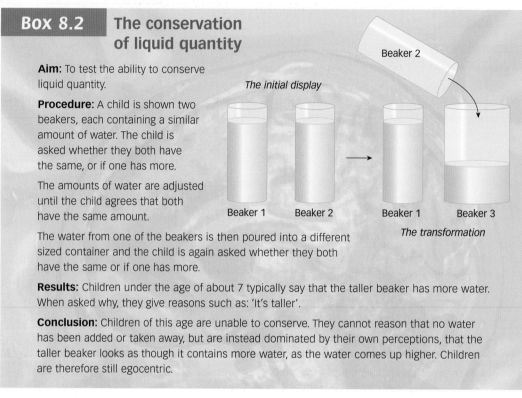

Box 8.2 **The conservation of liquid quantity**

Aim: To test the ability to conserve liquid quantity.

Procedure: A child is shown two beakers, each containing a similar amount of water. The child is asked whether they both have the same, or if one has more.

The amounts of water are adjusted until the child agrees that both have the same amount.

The initial display

Beaker 1   Beaker 2

Beaker 2

Beaker 1   Beaker 3

The transformation

The water from one of the beakers is then poured into a different sized container and the child is again asked whether they both have the same or if one has more.

Results: Children under the age of about 7 typically say that the taller beaker has more water. When asked why, they give reasons such as: 'It's taller'.

Conclusion: Children of this age are unable to conserve. They cannot reason that no water has been added or taken away, but are instead dominated by their own perceptions, that the taller beaker looks as though it contains more water, as the water comes up higher. Children are therefore still egocentric.

A similar study tests conservation of number (Box 8.3):

Box 8.3 **The conservation of number**

Aim: To test the ability to conserve number.

Procedure: A child is shown two rows of counters, with equal numbers in each row and lined up so that each counter in one row is opposite a counter in the other. The child is asked whether each row has the same amount of counters, or whether one has more. Children are usually happy to agree that both rows are the same.

○ ○ ○ ○ ○ ○ ○
● ● ● ● ● ● ●

The original display

The counters in one row are then spread out.

○ ○ ○ ○ ○ ○ ○
● ● ● ● ● ● ●

The transformed display

The child is then asked again whether each row has the same amount of counters, or whether one has more.

Results: Children under the age of about 7 usually say that the spread-out row has more counters.

Conclusion: Egocentrism means that children of this age are unable to conserve number,

Conservation studies like these demonstrate children's lack of **operations**; they do not understand **reversibility**, i.e. they cannot mentally pour the water back into the original beaker (Box 8.2), or mentally move back the spread-out counters (Box 8.3). Nor do they understand the principles of **compensation**, for example that the height of the liquid is compensated for by its width, and of **identity**, i.e. that in both cases nothing has been added or taken away. A further study carried out by Piaget relating to this stage investigated egocentrism in terms of an inability to put oneself mentally in someone else's position (see Box 8.4).

Box 8.4	Piaget and Inhelder (1956)

Aim: To test egocentrism in preoperational children.

Procedure: Children sat in front of a model of three mountains, one with snow on top, one with a cross and one with a house. They were asked to pick from a set of ten pictures the view they could see. A doll was then placed in front of the mountains, in a position giving a different viewpoint. Children were asked to pick the view the doll could see.

Results: Children could generally pick out the view they could see. Most children under 7 were unable to identify the picture that represented what the doll could see. They often picked their own view again.

Conclusion: Preoperational children are still egocentric in that they are unable to understand the viewpoint of someone in a different position from themselves.

Figure 8.2 *The three mountains study*

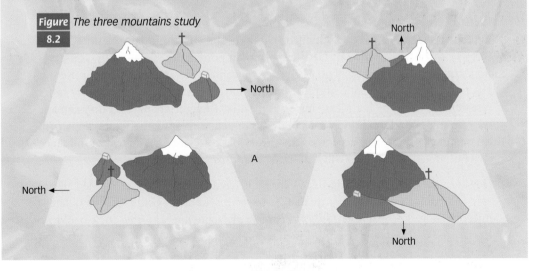

When the child enters the third **concrete operational stage** (7–11), egocentrism is much reduced. The child can now perform **operations** — they have the ability to carry out actions in their heads. They can carry out conservation tasks because they

can mentally pour the liquid back into the original beaker (Box 8.2) and move the counters back to their original position (Box 8.3). However, mental manipulation still involves concrete objects, so they are not yet capable of adult thought. This is demonstrated by their difficulty with transitivity tasks, for example Flora is taller than Kaya. Kaya is taller than Molly. Who is taller, Flora or Molly?

If they are able to use real objects such as dolls to represent this problem, concrete operational children can solve it. It is not until they reach the final **formal operational stage** (11–15 and onwards) that they can solve it as an abstract problem. While the concrete operational child manipulates things (even if this happens mentally), the formal operational child can manipulate ideas. Children can now think abstractly, hypothetically and systematically. This is demonstrated by the beaker task (see Box 8.5).

Box 8.5   **Inhelder and Piaget (1958)**

Aim: To test concrete vs formal operational thinking.

Procedure: Children are shown four beakers, each containing a colourless, odourless liquid and a small bottle, also containing a colourless, odourless liquid. They are asked to work out which liquid or combination of liquids from the beakers will turn yellow when a few drops of the liquid from the bottle are added.

Results: Children in the concrete operational stage tend to try various combinations at random, while formal operational children will try each liquid alone, then A + B, A + C, A + D, B + C and so on.

Conclusion: The move into the formal operational stage is characterised by systematic thinking.

Piaget's theory is impressive, in that it presents a comprehensive theory to account for the differences in the thinking of children and of adults. His claim that the theory can be universally applied has been supported, for example by conservation studies carried out by Nyiti (1976) in Tanzania and Kiminyo (1977) in Kenya. His research was systematic and his findings have been widely replicated by other researchers. Many of his ideas, for example that thought changes in a systematic way through childhood and that children are active in bringing about their own development, are widely accepted. His theory has also had a great deal of influence on educational practice, as will be seen later in this section.

However, the conclusions Piaget drew from his research have been questioned. There are methodological problems, in that some of his findings could bear a different interpretation. For example, the observation of Jacqueline and the duck could be interpreted as Jacqueline having lost interest in the duck, or her attention having been caught by something else until Piaget drew it back again, or in terms of the fragility of an infant's memory, rather than it ceasing to exist for her. The concept of object permanence has been tested using a simple but effective method (see Box 8.6).

Box 8.6 — Hood and Willats (1986)

Aim: To test object permanence in infants.

Procedure: Five-month-old infants were shown an interesting object either to their left or to their right. Their arms were held down so that they could not reach it. The lights were then switched off so that the infant could no longer see the object but their behaviour could still be observed and their arms were freed.

Results: Infants reached out significantly more often in the direction in which the object had been seen, rather than the other direction.

Conclusion: Children have some degree of object permanence much earlier than Piaget proposed.

This was a small-scale study and there was considerable variation in the infants' behaviour. It nonetheless suggests that Piaget may have underestimated the degree of object permanence in infants.

More generally, some of the tasks Piaget used are extremely complex and so may not allow children to demonstrate their capabilities. For example, the three mountains task involves right-left reversals, something that even many adults find difficult, and is not a necessary part of a test of egocentrism. A simplified version of the three mountains task to test a child's ability to take someone else's viewpoint has been carried out (see Box 8.7).

Box 8.7 — Hughes (1975)

Aim: To investigate egocentrism in pre-operational children.

Procedure: Children aged 3½–5 were shown a display of two walls intersecting to form a cross. Children were asked to hide a boy doll from a policeman doll. A second policeman doll was then introduced and children were asked to hide the boy doll so that neither policeman could see him.

Results: Even the youngest children were able to do this successfully around 90% of the time.

Conclusion: Children in the preoperational stage are not as egocentric as Piaget suggested

Figure 8.3 The hiding from the policeman task

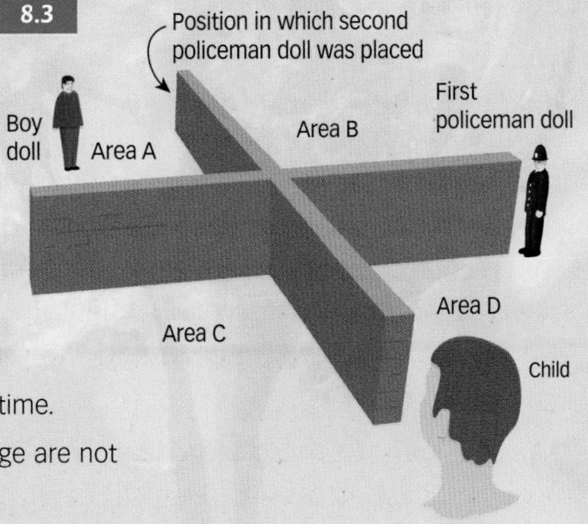

Position in which second policeman doll was placed

Boy doll — Area A

Area B

First policeman doll

Area C

Area D

Child

The complexity of the original task is one way in which the marked difference in the findings of Piaget's three mountains task and Hughes' policeman task can be accounted for. Donaldson (1978) has suggested that the policeman task related better to what she called **human sense** than the three mountains task, i.e. it was

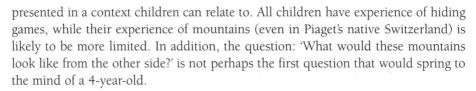

presented in a context children can relate to. All children have experience of hiding games, while their experience of mountains (even in Piaget's native Switzerland) is likely to be more limited. In addition, the question: 'What would these mountains look like from the other side?' is not perhaps the first question that would spring to the mind of a 4-year-old.

This is one aspect of Donaldson's more general criticism, that Piaget does not take into account the **social context** within which testing takes place. In conservation experiments, the child is asked the same question on two occasions. If you are asked a question and then the question is repeated, it is usually because the answer was wrong the first time. Children may therefore interpret the situation as one in which they are expected to give a different response and so should focus on the transformation in the display, which influences their response to the second question. Studies have therefore been carried out that manipulate the circumstances in which a second question is asked (see Box 8.8).

Box 8.8 McGarrigle and Donaldson (1974)

Aim: To investigate a conservation of number task when the transformation is seen as accidental rather than deliberate.

Procedure: Two rows of counters were used (see Box 8.3) and the child agreed that there was the same number of counters in each row. At this point a Naughty Teddy glove puppet appeared out of his box, pushed one of the rows of counters closer together and returned to his box. The question was then repeated.

Results: Children were much more likely to show conservation and say that both rows still had the same number of counters.

Conclusion: If there is a good reason for asking the second question in a conservation task, children are much more likely to respond correctly.

McGarrigle and Donaldson suggested that if a transformation is seen as accidental, a child is less likely to see it as an important factor that should change the second answer. However, Light et al. pointed out that children are quite aware that the teddy is being manipulated by the experimenter, so it cannot be assumed that the intervention is seen as accidental. They therefore carried out a further study to investigate the effect on conservation of a reason being given for the transformation (see Box 8.9).

Box 8.9 Light et al. (1979)

Aim: To investigate the effect on a conservation task of a reason being given for the transformation.

Procedure: A child was shown some pasta shells and told they would be using them for a game in a minute, so it was important that both players had the same amount. The shells were put into two identical beakers and the child agreed they had the same amount. The experimenter then 'noticed' that one of the beakers was dangerously chipped. Another

---

differently shaped container was then found and the contents of the chipped beaker transferred. The child was then asked if the beakers both had the same amount or if one had more.

Results: Children were much more likely to conserve and say that both beakers had the same amount of shells than in a standard conservation task.

Conclusion: When reasons for the task and the transformation are given, the task makes human sense and children are much more likely to conserve

A further issue in relation to conservation is the child's use of **language**. For example, as adults, we may take it for granted that 'more' in the counters task means 'a greater number' but children may not necessarily use it in this way. Berko and Brown (1960) found that some young children use 'more' less precisely than adults, for example to mean 'longer' or 'taller'. Language has no particular status in Piaget's theory; it merely reflects the child's thinking. As a result, he may have underestimated the role it plays in a child's thinking. When we come to look at the ideas of Vygotsky and Bruner, we will see that the role of language is much more central in their theories.

These studies challenge Piaget's theory, but do not necessarily mean that his ideas are wrong. For example, it is worth noting that in the studies we have looked at that modified Piaget's methods, some of the children nonetheless continued to respond in the ways Piaget suggested. Rather, the methods he used may have led him to underestimate young children's abilities.

Summary

- Piaget's theory of cognitive development saw children moving through four **stages**, in which they played an **active** part.
- His findings have been **replicated** many times and there is evidence that the theory can be **universally applied**. It has been **influential**.
- His **methods** have been criticised for not taking into account the **social context** of his research. The tasks do not always take into account the child's interpretation of a situation, or their use of **language**. They may lack **human sense**.
- Piaget may have **underestimated young children's abilities**.

Vygotsky's theory

Lev Vygotsky (1896–1934) was a Russian psychologist, born in the same year as Piaget and also with an interest in the development of children's thinking. His work was not readily available in translation until the 1960s, so he has been a less prominent figure in Western developmental psychology than Piaget.

Both Piaget and Vygotsky were stage theorists and both took a constructivist view of development. However, while Piaget thought of children as 'lone scientists', constructing their own development, with little emphasis given to the role of other people,

8

Vygotsky saw all development as rooted in social interaction; he is therefore a **social constructivist** theorist. Even more broadly, he proposed that any account of development must consider the **culture** within which a child is growing up. Cognitive skills change and develop in relation to the culture in which they need to be used.

Vygotsky talked of children acquiring **cultural tools**, i.e. ways of functioning in response to the demands of a particular culture. These tools can be physical, for example computers, or psychological, for example language. They are acquired through **interpersonal** processes (i.e. interaction with others) and children then adopt them as their own, a process he called **appropriation**. What was an interpersonal behaviour pattern becomes an **intrapersonal** cognitive process (i.e. within the person). For example, a child going to nursery school will want to play with the toys and use the equipment, but is in a situation where other children also want to do so. This is solved by rules, such as taking your turn, which the child comes to accept. Fitting in with these rules is the interpersonal stage. The child may internalise these rules, making them part of his or her behaviour repertoire and apply them to other situations; they have become intrapersonal.

A child in nursery school will learn to accept rules and learn to share and take turns

Another major way in which Vygotsky's theory differs from that of Piaget is the emphasis he put on **instruction**, which he believed was necessary to attain the higher levels of thinking. He claimed that purely abstract thinking is found only in highly technologically developed societies, which have a heavy emphasis on formal instruction. A key concept here is the **zone of proximal development (ZPD)**. Some things children can achieve alone and some things they are incapable of achieving. The ZPD refers to the difference between these two extremes, i.e. what a child is unable to achieve alone, but can achieve with the support of an adult or a more competent peer. An example can illustrate this (see Box 8.10).

For Vygotsky, **language** — as an important cultural tool — is crucial to development, and his stages focus on the changing relationship between language and thought. Initially, language and thought are quite separate. A young child can think without language, for example in manipulating toys.

Box 8.10

Childs and Greenfield (1982)

This study looked at children learning to weave among the Zinacantecon people of Mexico. Weaving involves six main processes, starting with setting up the loom and finally finishing a garment. The first time a child tackles these tasks, the adult instructing her needs to intervene frequently. However, very quickly the amount of help required drops off as the child achieves stand-alone competence.

Vygotsky saw a child's first attempts to communicate, for example by smiling or crying, as having a purely social function and suggested that in this way, language occurs without thought. Gradually language and thinking merge, so that language can influence thinking and thinking can be expressed in language.

As the child develops, language serves different purposes:

- In the first stage, the **social stage (0–3 years)**, language is used to express simple thoughts or feelings and to manipulate the behaviour of others, for example asking for milk.
- This is followed by the **egocentric stage (3–7 years)**, when language starts to be used to control the child's own behaviour. At this stage, it is still external speech, i.e. spoken aloud.
- It is only in the final **inner stage (7 onwards)** that the child uses inner speech, when language and thought fuse together into a tool that can then be used to shape and direct thinking.

Vygotsky was a theorist rather than a researcher, but, like Piaget, his ideas have been extremely influential in education, as we shall see at the end of this section.

Summary

- Vygotsky is a **social constructivist** and saw all development as fundamentally social.
- He emphasised the importance of **culture**; development involves the acquisition of **cultural tools**.
- Children's development can be promoted through working within the child's **zone of proximal development**. **Instruction** also plays an important part.
- Children's development goes through **stages** in which **language** and thinking progressively come together.

Bruner's theory

The theory of cognitive development proposed by Jerome Bruner (1915–) has much in common with the theories of both Piaget and Vygotsky. Like them, he believes that children's thinking differs from that of an adult, that they are active participants in their own development and that they are intrinsically motivated to change and develop. Like Vygotsky, he is a **social constructivist**, emphasising the importance of social interaction, but he does not share Vygotsky's focus on culture. He also sees **language** as playing an important part in cognitive development. His theory does not include stages, but does talk about different modes of thinking as children develop, i.e. different ways of making sense of the environment.

Bruner's theory takes an **information-processing approach**. Thinking is to do with organising information and Bruner believes the motivation to do this is innate. He uses three terms to describe how information is organised; each comes into play as thinking becomes more complex. Initially, thinking consists of **categories**. Relationships between different pieces of information are recognised, so that this information can be grouped. For example, a child will come to realise that the family dog, the squirrels in the garden and the cows in the field have something in common; putting them together as a concept under the general heading of 'animals' helps to simplify the storage of information. As thinking becomes more complex, these concepts become interrelated and organised in **hierarchies**, with more general categories at the top, moving down through more specific category levels. For example, 'animal' could be at the top of the hierarchy, the next level could be 'pet', 'farm' and 'wild' and at the next level 'pet' could branch out into 'dog' and 'goldfish', 'farm' into 'cow' and 'pig' and so on. Finally, complex interrelationships between different hierarchies develop. At this stage, the information we have is referred to as **knowledge**.

Bruner suggests that there are three **modes of thinking**: the enactive mode, the iconic mode and the symbolic mode. As with Piaget's stages, the child comes to acquire the different modes in this unvarying order and each mode has approximate ages attached to it. However, unlike Piaget's stages, each successive mode does not replace the previous one, but adds to it. In the **enactive mode (0–1 year)**, babies act on the world and their way of representing the world to themselves is related to their actions. This is similar to Piaget's sensori-motor stage, but because early ways of thinking are not lost, we continue to use this mode as adults, for example when we think about physical activities such as tying shoelaces or swimming; our knowledge is represented as muscle movements rather than verbal descriptions.

At around the age of 18 months, our perceptions — not only visual but also from other senses — become increasingly important, signalling the development of the **iconic mode (1–6/7 years)**. Children of this age build up mental images of objects and events that they have experienced, and it is on such images that thinking is based. Again, there is some similarity with Piaget's preoperational stage; for example, difficulties with conservation of number are explained in terms of children focusing on their perception of the length of the lines of counters, without taking into account the spaces in between the counters. One particular perception dominates and this sounds similar to what Bruner is describing. The iconic mode comes into play slightly earlier than Piaget's preoperational stage and this fits well with the idea that Piaget tended to underestimate the abilities of very young children.

Like Piaget, Bruner believes that there is an important change in the way that children think at around the age of seven, when the **symbolic mode (6/7 years onwards)** develops. Unlike Piaget, Bruner believes this change is strongly related to language; at this age, children can use language to guide their thinking, a similar idea to Vygotsky's **inner stage**. This has been demonstrated by research (see Box 8.11).

Box 8.11 **Bruner and Kenney (1966)**

Aim: To investigate the age at which the symbolic mode of thinking can aid problem solving.

Procedure: Children aged between 3 and 7 were shown a 3 X 3 matrix of glasses of three different heights, getting taller in each row from front to back. The glasses were of three different widths, getting wider from right to left. They were then muddled up and the children were asked to put them back the way they were to start with (the reproduction task).

They were then shown the matrix again, with all the glasses except one removed. The one from the bottom right-hand corner was put in the bottom left-hand corner and the children were asked to rebuild the matrix as the mirror-image of the way it was before (the transposition task).

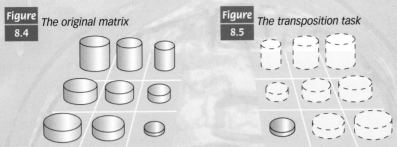

Figure 8.4 The original matrix

Figure 8.5 The transposition task

Results: A few of the younger children could do the reproduction task, and this improved with age; of the 5-year-olds, 60% were successful on the reproduction task, but none could carry out the transposition task. Of the 7-year-olds, around 80% could do both tasks, with little difference in the success rate.

Conclusion: The younger children used the iconic mode of thinking. This created an image that helped them with the reproduction task, but not with the transposition task. The older children used both the iconic and symbolic modes. In the transposition task, they could use verbal prompts, such as: 'It gets taller going this way.'

This study appears to support the importance of language in the development of thinking. However, the results could also be explained by Piaget's theory. The older children may be able to do better in the transposition task because they have entered the concrete operational stage and so are no longer as dominated by their perceptions as the younger preoperational children. They are able to carry out operations (mental actions), provided there is some support from actual objects, and so can carry out the mental reversals necessary for the transposition task. A further study has attempted to differentiate between these two explanations (see Box 8.12).

Box 8.12 Frank (1966)

Aim: To compare the explanations of Piaget and Bruner of the results of Bruner's transposition task.

Procedure: A study of conservation of liquid quantity was carried out with children aged 4–7. They were tested first using the standard procedure (see Box 8.2).

They were then tested using the same technique, but with a screen in front of the beakers so the level of the liquid could not be seen during and after the transformation.

A final test repeated the standard Piagetian technique.

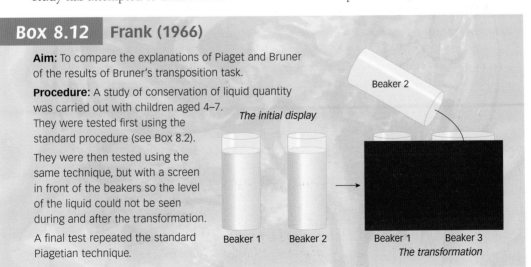

The initial display

Beaker 2

Beaker 1   Beaker 2

Beaker 1   Beaker 3

The transformation

Results: Most children failed to conserve on the first test. In the second test, most of the older children did conserve and about half the younger children. The final test showed an improvement over the first test for the older children, for example from 50% to 90% conserving answers for the 7-year-olds, although all the 4-year-olds went back to non-conserving answers.

Conclusion: The use of the screen on the second test helped to make the iconic mode less dominant, i.e. children were not so dominated by their perceptions. It also encouraged them to use the symbolic mode of thinking, by giving aloud their judgement when the screen was in place. This helped older children to make a correct judgement on the final test.

There seems to be some evidence therefore to support Bruner's belief in the importance of language in the development of thinking. This study also seems to suggest — in contrast to Piaget's theory — which children can be taught to develop the way they think, a view that Bruner shares with Vygotsky. The training that the second test provided did not benefit the younger children, as they were not yet ready to use the symbolic mode, but at the same time, children as young as 5 did benefit.

In relation to the importance of social interaction for development, Bruner uses the term **scaffolding**; in the same way that scaffolding supports a building while it is being constructed and is then taken away when no longer needed, children can be helped beyond their level of competence until they are competent without support. This can be seen as similar to Vygotsky's idea of the **ZPD**; this refers to the difference between what a child can do alone and what it is not able to achieve, while scaffolding refers to the nature of the intervention provided.

Another term in Bruner's theory is **contingency**, i.e. the adjustment in behaviour a mother makes in response to the behaviour of the child; her behaviour depends on and is influenced by what the child does. Research has demonstrated the role of contingent behaviour and scaffolding in interactions with a child (see Box 8.13).

Box 8.13 Wood and Middleton (1975)

Aim: To observe the role of scaffolding and contingent behaviour in a mother–child interaction.

Procedure: Mothers were asked to teach their 4-year-old children to assemble a 3D puzzle. Their interactions with the children were categorised at one of 5 levels, from less controlling, for example giving general verbal prompts such as: 'Now you make something' to more controlling, for example demonstrating what to do. The child then attempted to assemble the puzzle alone.

Results: Success was related to how the mother moved between control categories. Children were most successful on their own when mothers had moved to a less controlling interaction when the child responded successfully and to a more controlling interaction when the child had a problem.

Conclusion: Children can be successfully scaffolded to help them achieve success in a task that they would not be able to carry out on their own. Scaffolding is most successful when a mother's behaviour is highly contingent on the behaviour of the child.

Summary

- Bruner is a **social constructivist**, who sees **language** as crucial to cognitive development. He takes an **information-processing approach** to the development of thinking.
- Children develop different **modes of thinking** as they get older, each of which is added to the previous mode.
- Children's thinking can be promoted by a more experienced person through **scaffolding** and **contingent behaviour**.

Applications of theories in education

All three of the theories we have looked at have educational applications. Piaget's ideas had a great deal of influence on the **Plowden Report** (1967) on primary education, which brought the idea of **child-centred learning** to the attention of the public. This report placed emphasis on the use of activity methods that allow children to foster their own understanding, known as **discovery learning**. Piaget believed that children's thinking cannot be developed by instruction — indeed, he claimed that direct instruction can get in the way of children's learning if it inhibits their own exploration — so the role of the teacher is to provide opportunities for children to find things out for themselves. The report also supported the idea of **readiness**, i.e. matching learning to the child's stage of development. Teachers need to be aware of the stage a child has reached and to adapt their interaction with them accordingly. In particular, they need to be aware that young children do not think abstractly, so they should relate learning to concrete examples. They also need to be aware that children do not all reason in the same way, so a teacher will need to interact with them as individuals, with an emphasis on **individualised learning**. However, there is also a role for group work, on the principle that members of the group may have different approaches to a task, which may in turn challenge the thinking of other members of the group. This is known as **socio-cognitive conflict** (see Box 8.14).

Box 8.14   Doise and Mugny (1984)

Aim: To investigate the contribution to learning of socio-cognitive conflict.

Procedure: Participants were 100 children aged 5–7. An adapted version of the three mountains task, a layout of a pond and buildings, was used. In order to expose children to conflicting ideas, children worked either alone (the control group) or in pairs. The least able (Level 1) children worked either with slightly more advanced children (Level 2) or with much more advanced children (Level 3). Each child was later assessed individually.

Results: Level 1 children who had worked with Level 2 children showed the most gains. Those who had worked with Level 3 children showed little gain, as Level 3 children tended to impose their solution, rather than discuss possibilities.

Conclusion: In working with peers, a difference of views and a social need to reconcile them can help preoperational children progress towards higher-level operational thinking.

Doise and Mugny noted that in working together, it was not necessary for the ideas of either child to be correct — it is the conflict between ideas that promotes development. Most of these ideas relate to what is now standard practice in primary school classrooms and have influenced educational materials and courses. For example, the Nuffield Science programme uses a hands-on approach to the teaching of science to younger children. With classes in primary schools still being relatively large, the kind of individualised learning that Piaget recommends is not always practicable, but at the same time classroom practice has been positively influenced by Piaget's ideas.

For Vygotsky, all learning is social; interaction with others, both teachers and more able peers, underlies the learning process. Learning can be seen as a kind of apprenticeship, through which cultural tools become part of the child's mental resources and in which language plays a crucial part. One way in which his ideas have been applied to education has involved research in exploring how, by skilfully guiding classroom discussion, teachers can establish and maintain a shared focus of attention, provide children with a language in which to describe their own experiences and use that language to build up a common body of knowledge. Mercer (2000) calls this the **guided construction of knowledge**. On the basis of analysis of the talk of children working together, Mercer identified three kinds of talk:
- **disputational:** disagreement, with individual decision-making
- **cumulative:** positive but uncritical comment
- **exploratory:** constructive criticism of others' ideas, with new ideas being offered and justified

Mercer believed exploratory talk to be the most productive and developed the Thinking Together programme to foster this kind of talk and so enable children's participation in ongoing learning conversations. In this way, the emphasis in a Vygotskyan classroom is on processes rather than products and always on shared activity that is adult-led. There has been some criticism of this approach. For example, Hoogsteder et al. (1998) have criticised its emphasis on the one-way transmission of knowledge and skills. Children can be seen as relatively passive, with their contributions to their own learning downplayed.

Bruner too stresses the importance of social context in learning, in which the teacher plays a crucial part. The notion of scaffolding suggests that the teacher can guide and support children and so help them to extend and develop their understanding. The teacher needs to make the help offered contingent on the behaviour of the child. Given Bruner's emphasis on language, teachers need to be sensitive to the differences between the child's and adult's use of language and adjust their use of language when communicating with young children. The classroom needs to be a place in which language is used to promote understanding. Children also organise information in different ways as they develop, moving from categories, to hierarchies, to a knowledge system; this has led to the idea of the **spiral curriculum**. Children will come back to the same topic at varying stages in their schooling (hence 'spiral') and will be able to handle it in increasingly sophisticated ways as their understanding develops.

Some of these ideas can be recognised in classroom practice, but may not always be easy to apply. For example, Bliss et al. (1996) were unable to find any evidence of scaffolding by teachers. Wood et al. (1978) found that even a teacher who had been trained to teach contingently only did so for 85% of the time.

Summary

- Many of the ideas put forward by theorists have been applied in the classroom. The **Plowden report** was much influenced by **Piaget**. The emphasis put on **language** by both **Vygotsky** and **Bruner** has also influenced classroom practice.
- There are sometimes **practical difficulties** in the application of theoretical ideas.

The development of moral understanding

As children grow, they develop a sense of what is right and wrong, and how this happens has been of interest to psychologists. However, knowing what we ought or ought not to do is only the cognitive aspect of moral development. There is also the behavioural aspect, how people respond when faced with a moral dilemma, and an affective aspect, related to feelings of guilt and shame.

Kohlberg's theory

Piaget developed a theory that saw children's moral development as moving through a series of stages related to their more general cognitive development, and in particular to decreasing egocentrism. Kohlberg's (1963) theory built on Piaget's theory, in that it also takes a cognitive approach and proposed that moral development goes through a series of stages in an invariant order. However, it differed from Piaget's theory in that Kohlberg saw moral understanding continuing beyond childhood into middle age.

The method he used to test his ideas was to present participants with stories involving a moral dilemma and asking them to comment on the moral aspects of the story, giving reasons for their views. His most famous is the Heinz dilemma:

The Heinz dilemma

Heinz's wife was close to death from a particular kind of cancer. There was only one drug that doctors thought might save her, a form of radium discovered by a chemist living in the same town as Heinz. The drug was expensive to make, but the chemist bought the radium for $200 and charged $2,000 for a small dose. Heinz tried everything he knew to raise enough money, but only managed to scrape together $1,000. He begged the chemist to sell it to him cheaper, or let him pay off the balance later. But the chemist said: 'I discovered the drug and I'm going to make money from it.' Heinz broke into the man's store to steal the drug for his wife.

8

Participants were asked whether it was morally right or wrong for Heinz to steal the drug and why. The key issue here is not whether or not people think the individual faced with the dilemma should or should not act in a particular way, but the reasoning underlying their decision. On the basis of data collected using these dilemmas, Kohlberg was able to identify the stage of moral reasoning an individual had reached. He defined three levels of moral reasoning, each linked to approximate ages and with two stages in each:

Table 8.1 *Kohlberg's stages of moral reasoning*

Level	Age	Stage
Pre-conventional	6–13	1 obedience to avoid punishment
		2 obedience to obtain rewards
Conventional	13–16	3 seeking the approval of others
		4 respect for authority and maintaining the social order
Post-conventional	16–20 onwards	5 obedience to democratically accepted laws; individual rights can sometimes supersede laws
		6 morality of the individual conscience in line with universal moral principles

At the **pre-conventional level**, moral reasoning focuses on the consequences of a particular action for ourselves; we seek to avoid punishment and obtain rewards. Morality is determined by the standards of the adults in our lives, i.e. the consequences of breaking their rules (stage 1) or following them (stage 2). For example, in the Heinz dilemma, a stage 1 response might be: 'He shouldn't steal the drug as he could get caught and sent to jail.'

The **conventional level** develops in later childhood, with a broader focus as we start to internalise the moral standards of others, in particular those who act as role models. We aim to comply with the rules and values of society, either to gain the approval of others (stage 3) or to show respect for society's values (stage 4). A stage 3 response to the Heinz dilemma might be: 'His family would think him a terrible husband if he didn't steal the drug. If he let his wife die, he could never look anyone in the face again', while a stage 4 response might be: 'He should not steal the drug, because whatever the reason, people should not take the law into their own hands.'

From 16 onwards, we may move to the **post-conventional level**, where morality is a matter of individual conscience. At stage 5, we recognise that we should act in line with the law, but that sometimes conscience may tell us to act outside the law. At stage 6, we recognise universal moral rules that we may need to follow where they are in conflict with the rules of society. 'If he doesn't steal the drug, he will always blame himself for his wife's death. He must do what his conscience tells him' would be a stage 6 response.

In a later revision of the theory, Kohlberg (1978) suggested that only about 10% of people move to the third level. He also proposed (Kohlberg 1981) that for a few exceptional people, whose lives are dedicated to a humanitarian cause, such as Mother Teresa, there may be a stage 7, moving beyond moral reasoning to religious faith. Kohlberg supported his theory with research (see Box 8.15).

Box 8.15 **Kohlberg (1963)**

Aim: To assess moral reasoning on a range of dilemmas.

Procedure: A sample of 58 boys, aged 7–16, was tested on ten dilemmas and their responses analysed.

Results: There was reasonable consistency for each boy across the dilemmas. The younger ones tended to reason at stage 1 or 2 and the older ones at stage 3 or 4.

Conclusion: Individuals tend to reason at the same stage across dilemmas. Moral reasoning develops with age, in line with the theory.

Other studies have found similar results. In a review of 12 studies, Rest (1983) found that in general participants did develop moral reasoning in the sequence Kohlberg suggested. However, some participants did not show this progression, and a few actually moved back to an earlier stage over time; in stage theories, this should not happen.

Kohlberg (1969) claimed that his theory of moral development applied to all cultures and found the same pattern of development in children across different cultures, i.e. the UK, the USA, Mexico, Taiwan and Turkey. Snarey (1985) also found support for the universality of Kohlberg's theory in a meta-analysis of 44 studies covering 26 different cultures. However, it has also been suggested that the third level of development applies more to individualist societies than to collectivist cultures such as India, where the good of the community is more valued than that of the individual. It may therefore be that the theory is, to an extent, culture specific.

The methodology of studies carried out to investigate the theory has sometimes been criticised. It has been argued that the dilemmas Kohlberg used are artificial and bear little resemblance to the complex problems people face in real-life situations. In the Heinz dilemma, the information provided is fairly limited. Rosen (1980) has suggested different slants to the story. What if Heinz's wife has been contemplating suicide for some time and now wants to die with dignity? What if the chemist is her brother and respects her wishes and so has priced the drug so that Heinz cannot afford it? What if Heinz wants to keep his wife alive so that they can both live off her trust fund, which will stop paying out if she dies? Kohlberg's theory assumes that we apply general moral rules to identify relevant facts in the situations we are presented with; it is an **ethical rule theory**. In contrast, **ethical act theory** (Munsey 1980) suggests that information specific to the situation may be more important than general principles. The dilemmas are also artificial in that the only options are to steal or not to steal the drug. In real life, there is usually a range of options. For example, Heinz could see if he could take out a loan, or approach a charity, or set up a fundraising event and so on.

Gilligan (1977) has criticised Kohlberg on the grounds of **gender bias**, since much of his research (see Box 8.15) was carried out with only male participants and most of the main characters in his dilemmas are men, making it easier for men to relate to them than females. She argues that men are socialised differently from women, with males being encouraged to use abstract reasoning in resolving problems (the **justice perspective**) and females encouraged to be caring towards others (the **care perspective**). On this basis, women could be expected to use stage 3 and 4 reasoning, which in Kohlberg's theory would mean that women are less morally developed than men. She argued that men and women have separate-but-equal developmental pathways. She carried out her own research with female participants, using a real-life situation (see Box 8.16).

Box 8.16 **Gilligan (1982)**

Aim: To investigate the moral reasoning of women.

Procedure: Interviews were carried out with 29 women, aged 15–33, all of whom were facing the dilemma of whether or not to terminate a pregnancy. The conflict they faced was between personal choice and the traditional role of caring for others.

Results: Participants focused less on moral justice, the issue in Kohlberg's theory, and more on responsibility. Their moral reasoning was at one of three levels: (1) self-interest, (2) self-sacrifice and (3) a balance between self-interest and sensitivity to the needs of others.

Conclusion: There is a parallel between the three levels proposed by Kohlberg and Gilligan's three levels. However, at the highest (post-conventional) level, women tend to maintain their focus on personal concern for the needs of both themselves and others, rather than the more abstract concerns of Kohlberg's system.

There is some support for the gender differences in moral reasoning proposed by Gilligan. Skoe et al. (2002) compared the responses of men and women to real-life moral dilemmas and found that overall men scored higher than women on justice reasoning, while women scored higher than men on care reasoning. However, there was also a lot of individual variation so it would be unwise to generalise along gender lines. Further research by Gilligan and Attanucci (1988) found that while women are more likely than men to take a care perspective in moral reasoning, both men and women use both care and justice perspectives to some extent.

There are also other criticisms of Kohlberg's theory. The **age range** starts at 6, but some studies, including an observational study carried out by Dunn and Brown (1994), have shown that children show some moral understanding towards the end of their second year, much earlier than Kohlberg suggested. Another important criticism relates to the relationship between moral reasoning and **moral behaviour**. Kohlberg's theory focuses only on moral reasoning. While some studies have found a link between the two, Kutnik (1986) claims that this is rarely strong. A further issue is that Kohlberg's theory confines itself to dilemmas that involve misdeeds and breaking the law. This has been addressed by Eisenberg, whose work is discussed in the next section.

Eisenberg's theory

Eisenberg (1986) has suggested that Kohlberg's theory is limited in its definition of morality and for a more complete view, **prosocial moral reasoning**, i.e. the intention to benefit another person, should also be investigated. Her approach is similar to that of Kohlberg in that she asked children to respond to stories, but in this case the choice to be made was between helping someone else or acting out of self-interest.

Eisenberg's birthday party dilemma

Mary was going to a friend's birthday party. On the way, she saw a girl who had fallen over and hurt her leg. The girl asked Mary to fetch her parents, so that they could take her to the doctor. But this would mean that Mary would be late for the party and miss all the birthday food and games. What should Mary do? Why?

On the basis of her research, Eisenberg found a clear developmental sequence, with children moving in stages from focusing on their own needs to a focus on the needs of others. Children's answers are at first related to approval from others and later to internalised values, similar in nature to Kohlberg's levels. She also found (Eisenberg et al. 1987) that the stage of moral reasoning achieved reflected helping behaviour in real situations, although this varied with the situation and the costs involved in helping. Eisenberg's theory does not challenge the broad principles of Kohlberg's theory, but it has provided a more complete view of the development of children's moral reasoning.

Summary

- Kohlberg's theory of moral development takes a **cognitive approach**, with moral reasoning developing through a series of **stages**. It is claimed to be **universally applicable**. It is tested by asking people to respond to dilemmas, making clear their **moral reasoning**.
- The **methodology** has been criticised as **artificial**.
- Gilligan suggests that the theory shows **gender bias**.
- The theory has also been criticised for underestimating the moral capability of **younger children**. There are also only weak links between moral reasoning and **moral behaviour**.
- Eisenberg has extended Kohlberg's theory with research into **prosocial moral reasoning**.

The development of social cognition

Social cognition refers to the processing of social knowledge. Broadly, it investigates how the social context affects the way we think and in turn how our thoughts affect our social behaviour. This covers a wide range of topics, but we will look here at the two areas of theory of mind and perspective taking, together with research into possible biological factors that underlie social processing and social behaviour.

The sense of self and others: theory of mind

Theory of mind (TOM) can be defined as the understanding that others have information and mental states — hopes, beliefs, desires and intentions — that are different from our own and that shape their behaviour. There is a parallel between TOM skills and Piaget's concept of **egocentrism**, discussed earlier. Piaget explained children's problems in the preoperational stage with tasks such as the three mountains task (see Box 8.4) in terms of their inability to detach themselves from their own perspective before the age of 6 or 7, demonstrating a lack of TOM.

There are several ways in which TOM is tested. One of the most commonly used is the Sally/Anne or unexpected transfer task, in which children are shown Sally hiding a ball and then leaving the room. Anne then hides the ball in a different place. Children are asked where Sally will look for the ball when she returns, on the basis that a child who has developed TOM will realise that Sally will not know that Anne has moved it, so will look in the place where she originally hid it.

Figure 8.6 *The unexpected transfer task*

This is Sally — This is Anne

Sally puts her marble in the basket

Sally goes away

Anne moves the marble to her box

Where will Sally look for her marble?

An early experiment investigated how TOM relates to age (see Box 8.17).

Other studies have produced similar findings about the age at which TOM develops. To return briefly to Piaget, you will remember that later research suggested that Piaget may have underestimated young children's abilities and that egocentrism may decrease earlier than Piaget believed. This general finding that many children have developed TOM by around the age of four supports this claim. As with Piaget's claim that his theory is universally applicable, there is also evidence that the same is true of TOM. For example, Avis and Harris (1991) had similar results when they tested children of the Baka tribe, living in the rainforests of Cameroon.

Research has also investigated children's understanding of their own inaccurate beliefs, using the Smarties task or **deceptive box test**. Children are shown a Smarties tube and asked what they think is in it; they usually say 'sweets'. They are then shown that it contains a pencil. Then they are asked what a Sooty puppet would think is in the tube. Gopnik and Astington (1998) found that 3-year-olds usually say 'a pencil', while most 5-year-olds say 'sweets'. This suggests that the understanding of others' minds and one's own mind both develop around the age of four and so run in parallel.

There is some evidence that TOM shows gradual development. Wellman and Bartsch (1994) carried out a longitudinal study in which they analysed children's talk. They found that 2-year-olds refer to others' desires, but not yet to their beliefs. There is also evidence that there is some understanding of others' desires as early as 18 months (see Box 8.18).

Topics in psychology

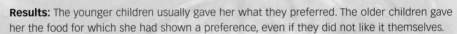

Results: The younger children usually gave her what they preferred. The older children gave her the food for which she had shown a preference, even if they did not like it themselves.

Conclusion: Children of 18 months show some understanding of the desires of others when they are different from their own. They can recognise how desires are related to emotions and their expression.

TOM development may be facilitated by particular kinds of interaction with others. Charman et al. (2000) looked at **joint attention** in infants, i.e. when a child and an adult are the focus of each other's attention, taking turns in exchanges of looks, mouth movements and so on. Toys or other objects can also be introduced into these exchanges. They found that measures of joint attention at 20 months were associated with measures of TOM at 3 years 8 months. However, it does not follow that joint attention necessarily promotes TOM. It may be that both poor joint attention and lack of TOM are the result of some underlying neurological problem.

Baron-Cohen et al. (1985) have suggested that **autism** can be linked to deficiencies in TOM. Autism is a developmental disorder, whose characteristics include difficulty with social relationships and communication and a lack of empathy with others. Children with autism also have difficulties with imaginative, pretend play. Baron-Cohen et al. proposed that they do not understand that other people have mental states and that these mental states may be different from their own. They supported this with a study using the Sally/Anne task, mentioned above. Other research evidence also supports this view (see Box 8.19).

Box 8.19 Perner et al. (1989)

Aim: To assess TOM in autistic children.

Procedure: A variation of the Smarties task (deceptive box test) was carried out with 12 autistic children and an age-matched control group.

Results: The controls all correctly said that a person who had not been shown the pencil in the Smarties tube would think the tube contained Smarties. The autistic children all answered 'a pencil' to this question.

Conclusion: The autistic children could not take into account the fact that someone else's mental state or knowledge could be different from what they themselves knew to be the case.

Leslie (1987) points out that the ability to interpret behaviour from another person's point of view starts to develop at around the age of 2 (though as we have seen from the Repacholi and Gopnik study, see Box 8.18, there are signs of TOM slightly earlier than this) and children's ability to take part in pretend play develops at around the same time. As both TOM and pretend play are lacking in children with autism, he proposes that there is some brain mechanism that underlies both and which is absent or dysfunctional in autistic children. As we will see later in this section, one suggestion is that deficiencies in mirror neurons may provide an explanation.

Summary

- **Theory of mind** (TOM) can be linked to Piaget's concept of **egocentrism**.
- Understanding of one's own and others' minds has developed by around the **age of 4**, though there are some signs of it earlier than this.
- Its development has been linked to **joint attention** in infancy.
- Children with **autism** lack TOM. It has been suggested that this is the result of a deficient **brain mechanism**.

Understanding of others: perspective-taking

The perspective-taking theory of **Selman** (1980) was influenced by Piaget's theory of cognitive development. It has something in common with Piaget's concept of egocentrism, in that it is concerned with the ability to see from someone else's perspective. However, while Piaget is concerned with cognition, Selman focuses also on understanding people's feelings. Perspective-taking is related to theory of mind but its focus is on the implications of understanding the mental state of others, for example for the development of relationships with others and their sense of morality. Selman (1971) found that there was an association between perspective-taking ability and morality, so there are links between Selman's approach and Kohlberg's theory of moral development.

Selman's methodology was also influenced by Kohlberg, in that he made use of stories and asked children questions about them, as shown in the study below.

Holly's tree-climbing dilemma

Holly is an 8-year-old girl who likes to climb trees. She is the best tree climber in the neighbourhood. One day while climbing a tree she falls off the bottom branch but does not hurt herself. Her father sees her fall and is upset. He asks her to promise not to climb trees any more and Holly promises.

Later that day, Holly and her friends meet Sean. Sean's kitten is caught up in a tree and cannot get down. Something has to be done right away or the kitten may fall. Holly is the only one who climbs trees well enough to reach the kitten and get it down, but she remembers her promise to her father.

Holly's tree-climbing dilemma is one of Selman's stories created to study the moral development of children

TopFoto

Children are asked questions such as: 'If Holly climbs the tree, should she be punished?' 'Will her father understand if she climbs the tree?' 'Will Sean understand why Holly has trouble deciding what to do?'

On the basis of his research, Selman suggested that development takes place in five stages. There is considerable overlap in the ages given since Selman believed that children could be at different stages of development in relation to the different domains of social experience that he investigated, such as friendship, peer relationships and relationships with parents.

Stages in Selman's theory

Undifferentiated perspective-taking (age 3–6): The perspective of the character in the story or the child's own perspective is attributed to everyone else. In relation to the Holly scenario, a child is likely to predict that Holly will save the kitten because she does not want it to get hurt and that her father will feel the same way.

Social-informational perspective-taking (age 5–9): A child realises that perspectives may differ, but while different views are valid, they differ because of lack of information. A child is likely to say that Holly's father would be angry, but would change his mind if he knew about the kitten.

Self-reflective perspective-taking (age 7–12): A child is able to view their own thoughts, feelings and behaviour from someone else's point of view and realises that others can do the same. When asked whether Holly thinks she will be punished for climbing the tree, the child might say that Holly does not think she will be punished because she knows that her father will understand why she did it.

Third-party perspective-taking (age 10–15): An individual can step outside the two-person situation and see it from the point of view of a third party, viewing the perspectives of Holly and her father simultaneously. They might say that Holly should not be punished because she thought it important to save the kitten, but she also knows that her father told her not to climb trees. Holly would only think she should not be punished if she could get her father to understand why she had disobeyed him.

Societal perspective-taking (age 14–adult): An individual understands that the third-party perspective can be influenced by the values of society. They might suggest that Holly should not be punished because her behaviour is justified by society valuing the humane treatment of animals. Holly's father's appreciation of this value will lead him not to punish her.

This theory suggests that as children get older, they are able to take more information into account, become better able to analyse the perspectives of others and finally to make links with social values. There are clear links with Kohlberg's theory of moral development. For example, the first two of Selman's stages are similar to Kohlberg's Level 1 moral reasoning, with the focus on self and adults who are important in a child's life. As in Kohlberg's theory, the focus gradually extends to take in broader social values.

Selman's theory is useful in that it emphasises the social nature of development, which is given little weight in the theories of Piaget and Kohlberg. The method used could perhaps be criticised, in that children's responses to questioning are open to interpretation. However, Selman's ideas have led to practical applications, in terms of interventions to promote children's perspective-taking abilities and thus help them to improve their relationships with others (Yeates and Selman 1989).

Summary

- **Selman's** theory is concerned with the development of **social perspective-taking**. There are links to the theories of **Piaget** and **Kohlberg**.
- Development takes place in **stages**, with approximate and overlapping **ages**.
- The theory emphasises the importance of **social factors** in development. It has **applications** in terms of intervention to improve children's social experiences.

Biological explanations of social cognition

While theory of mind and perspective taking are concerned with social processes, another line of inquiry within social cognition has been to investigate a possible biological basis for these processes. One recent suggestion has been mirror neurons.

A **mirror neuron** is a particular class of nerve cell that fires both when an animal acts and when the animal observes the same action performed by another animal, especially one of the same species. This occurs only in response to an **object-directed action**, so not to the movement of an object on its own, nor to a mimed action. Mirror neurons were first reported by Rizzolatti (1995); he and his colleagues carried out a series of studies measuring electrical activity in the brains of macaque monkeys, in the F5 area in a premotor part of the brain. Activity in a premotor area correlates with an animal's action; for example, when a monkey picks up a nut, neurons in F5 fire.

During each experiment, they recorded from a single neuron in the monkey's brain while the monkey was allowed to reach for pieces of food, so the researchers could measure the neuron's response to certain movements. They found that some of the neurons they recorded from would respond not only when the monkey itself picked up the food, but also when the monkey saw a person or another monkey pick up the food. In other words, the neuron was 'mirroring' the behaviour of another animal, as though the observer were personally carrying out the action. These findings have been replicated many times since, and additional areas of the brain containing mirror neurons have been identified. This has triggered research into whether humans might have a similar mirror neuron system.

8

It has been known in broad terms for many years that when people observe actions carried out by others, their motor cortex becomes active, even when they do not carry out any actions themselves, so more recent research has built on this. Studying single neurons in the human brain is not possible, since this would involve inserting a microelectrode through brain tissue and leaving it poking into a neuron. However, brain-scanning techniques have suggested that humans may also have mirror neurons. For example, in a study using **functional magnetic resonance imaging (fMRI)**, Iacoboni et al. (1999) identified areas of the human brain that are active when a person performs an action and also when the person sees someone else performing the same action. As studying single neurons is not possible, it cannot be certain that humans have mirror neurons, in the sense of single neurons responding as they did in the experiments with monkeys, so researchers sometimes prefer to talk about a **mirror neuron system** rather than mirror neurons.

Mirror neurons are specialised to code for actions, but it has been suggested that they play a wider role, in terms of understanding the **intentions** of others. Actions — gestures, facial expressions and so on — are one way in which we communicate our intentions and emotions to other people. It has been suggested that mirror neurons help us to understand others by providing an inner imitation of their actions, leading to an awareness of the intentions and emotions associated with the actions. They would thus play an important role in social cognition. There is some support for the claim that mirror neurons provide information about intentions. One source of information comes from research demonstrating that monkeys show slightly different levels of neuron activity to the same action in different contexts, for example grasping a cup to drink or grasping a cup to clear the table. This suggests it is not just the action that is coded, but also the intention behind it. There is further evidence of this (see Box 8.20).

> ### Box 8.20   Umiltà et al. (2006)
>
> **Aim:** To assess processing of information in mirror neurons.
>
> **Procedure:** A monkey's mirror neuron activity was recorded when watching a person-object interaction under different conditions: (a) the person was observed to reach for and grasp a piece of food; (b) the same procedure, but with a screen preventing the monkey from seeing the final grasping movement; (c) the same screened procedure, but with the monkey being shown that there was no food behind the screen.
>
> **Results:** The neuron responded in the first two conditions, but not when there was no food behind the screen.
>
> **Conclusion:** Since the final two conditions are identical in terms of what the monkey actually saw, but the outcome in terms of mirror neuron activity was different, the activity in (b) and lack of it in (c) must be linked to the intention of the person being observed.

It has been suggested that the mirror neuron system can explain the difficulties of people with **autism**. As we saw earlier, one of the main characteristics of autism is a lack of **theory of mind**. Inadequate functioning of the mirror neuron system in autistic people would weaken their ability to experience immediately what other people are experiencing, thus making social interactions particularly difficult for them. There is evidence that the lack of **empathy** of people with autism may also be connected to problems with the mirror neuron system (see Box 8.21).

Box 8.21 Dapretto et al. (2006)

Aim: To investigate brain activity in response to emotional expression in autistic children.

Procedure: Brain scans using fMRI were used to monitor the brain activity of 10 autistic children and 10 normally developing children. The children were asked to watch and imitate 80 different faces showing anger, fear, happiness, sadness or no emotion.

Results: Compared to controls, the autistic children showed reduced blood flow to the inferior frontal gyrus, an area of the brain near the temple that has been shown to be part of the mirror neuron system. There was less activity in this area in the autistic children than in the controls.

Conclusion: Dysfunction in the mirror neuron system may explain the lack of empathy typical of autistic children.

The claim that a defective mirror neuron system could account for autism is strengthened by the ability of a dysfunctional mirror neuron system to explain some of the other major characteristics of people with autism; they often have motor and language problems. Mirror neurons are just special types of premotor neurons, brain cells essential for planning and selecting actions, so this could explain the motor deficits. A human brain area that is likely to contain mirror neurons overlaps with a major language area, Broca's area, which could account for language problems.

Some researchers consider mirror neurons to be one of the most important advances in neuroscience in recent years. For example, Ramachandran (2000) suggests they may help to explain many mental abilities that up to now have puzzled psychologists and have not been open to empirical research, and in particular areas such as theory of mind, empathy and language acquisition. However, others have argued that the evidence for mirror neurons in humans is weak. As human mirror neurons cannot be observed directly, most studies have instead looked for them by taking fMRI scans of people carrying out and observing various activities and then identifying the regions of the brain that are active in both situations. Dinstein (2008) claims that research has not examined these regions in fine enough detail and has produced evidence that some areas, such as the intraparietal sulcus (IPS) — a region claimed by previous research to be full of mirror neurons — in fact contains a mixture of motor and visual neurons. Some previous research does not therefore appear to have been measuring the activity of mirror neurons. A further point to bear in mind is that individual brain cells and neural systems do not operate completely independently of other brain activity. Everything in the brain is interconnected, so that the activity of each cell reflects the dynamic interactions with other

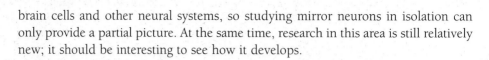

brain cells and other neural systems, so studying mirror neurons in isolation can only provide a partial picture. At the same time, research in this area is still relatively new; it should be interesting to see how it develops.

Summary

- In **monkeys**, mirror neurons fire when an animal carries out an action and when it sees another animal do so.
- There is some evidence that **humans** also possess mirror neurons and that they may explain aspects of **social cognition**.
- It has been suggested that a dysfunction of the human mirror neuron system could account for **autism**.
- There is some **controversy** over the existence and influence of mirror neurons in humans.

AQA(A)
A2 Psychology

Unit 4

Psychopathology, psychology in action and research methods

Chapter

Psychopathology

Ψ Unit 4

In this chapter, we will be looking at:
- schizophrenia
  - clinical characteristics
  - issues of classification and diagnosis
  - biological explanations
  - psychological explanations
  - the diathesis-stress model
  - biological therapies
  - psychological therapies

Psychopathology is the study of the nature and development of mental disorders, and we will be looking in this chapter at just one of the many disorders described in the classification systems DSM-IV and ICD-10; the classification systems will be considered later in this chapter. For any disorder, there are several explanations — some focus on biological factors, while others suggest that the origins of a disorder may be psychological. None of the explanations offers a complete and definitive answer, but they are not necessarily mutually exclusive. As we will see, the **diathesis-stress model** suggests that a person may be genetically predisposed to develop a disorder, but whether or not he or she goes on to do so depends on a broad range of environmental factors.

One area of focus in **biological explanations** is the contribution of genetic factors. This has been tested using twin, family and adoption studies, on the basis that if the underlying cause of the disorder is genetic, people who are genetically similar would be more likely to share a particular disorder, i.e. show a high **concordance** for the disorder. Other biological theories explain disorders in terms of an imbalance of neurotransmitters or hormones, with the suggested treatment being medication to return these to normal functioning, or physical damage.

There is also a range of **psychological explanations**. **Behaviourists** see mental disorders as learned, maladaptive behaviours, and treatment aims to change the behaviour. **Cognitive theorists** suggest that disorders are the result of faulty thought processes, which a therapist aims to change. Treatment based on these two approaches can be combined in **cognitive-behavioural therapy**.

Psychodynamic explanations focus on childhood experiences and unconscious conflict, for which the treatment is psychoanalysis or a related approach, while **humanistic psychologists** offer explanations in terms of blocked personal development, including the effects of relationships with others. In this case, a form of counselling would be the appropriate treatment. Under this heading, a wide range of social factors is also considered.

We will be looking at issues surrounding the **diagnosis** of mental disorders, and schizophrenia in particular, which can often be problematic. For example, Youngson and Schott (1996) report a study carried out at the University of Ottawa, which suggested that 43% of psychiatric patients had one or more physical disorders, the symptoms of which were seen as being related to a psychiatric problem, or were in fact caused by psychiatric drugs; in 20% of these cases, physical illness alone was the cause of the supposed psychiatric disorder.

Schizophrenia

Schizophrenia was first described by Kraepelin, who believed it was an early form of dementia, calling it **dementia praecox** (early senility). Bleuler was the first to use the term 'the schizophrenias' to describe what he believed to be a set of related disorders, because it had become clear that these conditions were not a physical degenerative condition as implied by Kraepelin's term.

Schizophrenia literally means 'split mind', and this is probably the reason why some people think (incorrectly) that people with schizophrenia have split personalities. This refers to a quite different disorder, called **dissociative identity disorder (DID)**. The split in schizophrenia is between the person and reality. It is also worth mentioning that schizophrenics do not have visual hallucinations, another popular misconception.

Schizophrenia is an extremely disabling disorder. It affects around 1% of people across a wide range of cultures; males and females are equally vulnerable. The first episode most commonly occurs in the late teens or early twenties.

Summary

- There are **biological** and **psychological** explanations of mental disorders.
- The **diathesis-stress model** suggests that these may interact.
- **Diagnosis** of mental disorders is problematic.

Clinical characteristics

Schizophrenia is a **psychotic disorder**, in that the whole of the personality is affected; contact with reality is lost, and the person does not realise that he or she has a problem. Psychotic behaviour is unlike normal behaviour and differs qualitatively from the person's behaviour before he or she developed the disorder. It is by far the most common of the psychotic disorders.

The range of symptoms shown by people who have been diagnosed as suffering from schizophrenia is extremely variable. Some theorists believe that it is one underlying condition, where psychological and behavioural manifestations can vary from person to person. Others agree that it is one underlying condition but suggest that the variation in symptoms can be explained by different parts of the brain being affected in different patients. A third view is that schizophrenia is a group of disorders, with different symptoms related to different kinds of schizophrenia.

Some theorists distinguish between reactive and process schizophrenia. **Reactive schizophrenia** is characterised by emotional symptoms, with relatively little disturbance of thought processes. Typically, the person's personality before the onset will have been stable, and he or she is likely to have had good relationships with family and peers. Reactive schizophrenia appears to be precipitated by a life crisis, so is a reaction to that event. This tends to occur in younger people and the prognosis is usually good, in that they respond well to drug treatment. In contrast, **process schizophrenia** develops gradually, usually in people with an early history of instability and difficult social relationships. Here, the prognosis is relatively poor.

In Britain, the diagnosis of schizophrenia relates to what Schneider (1959) called **first-rank symptoms**. Although they are used less for diagnosis now than formerly, his division into first-rank and other symptoms still provides a useful summary of the kinds of symptoms that may be experienced:

First-rank symptoms of schizophrenia

Passivity experiences and thought disorders

- Thought insertion: the belief that thoughts are being put into your head by outside forces.
- Thought withdrawal: the belief that thoughts are being withdrawn from your head.
- Thought broadcasting: the belief that your thoughts are being made known in some way to other people, such as the government or aliens and often via a radio transmitter.

Hallucinations

- Auditory hallucinations: these are the most common and often take the form of a voice in your head, commenting on your behaviour or telling you what to do. When schizophrenics appear to be talking to themselves, they may actually be carrying on a conversation with the voice in their head, which seems to them quite real.

Primary delusions

The main delusions are:
- delusions of grandeur (the belief that you are someone important, like the queen, Napoleon or Jesus Christ)

- delusions of persecution (the belief that people are spying on you or plotting against you)
- delusions of control (for example, the belief that your thoughts can control the movement of the clouds)

If one or more of these symptoms is present, usually for a period of at least 6 months, a diagnosis of schizophrenia is likely. Other symptoms may also indicate schizophrenia:

Additional symptoms of schizophrenia

Disturbances of thought processes
- Thought disturbances: difficulty in focusing thoughts and thought blocking, for example a person may stop speaking mid-sentence.
- Language disturbances: examples include 'word salad', when associations between words become too loose to make any sense, and neologisms, where new words are invented.

Disturbances of affect
- Blunting of emotions: for example, there may be no emotional response when a person is told that a close friend has died.
- Inappropriate emotions: for example, the response to this kind of news may be laughter.
- Flattened affect: the absence of emotional expression.

Psychomotor disturbances
- Catatonia: unusual and even uncomfortable bodily postures are held for lengthy periods of time, in some cases weeks.
- Stereotypy: characterised by repeated movements, such as rocking.
- Lack of volition: this refers to apathy, lack of motivation and social withdrawal.

There are two categories of symptoms in schizophrenia:
- **Positive symptoms** — also referred to as **Type I** symptoms — are those that are not usually present in normal people, such as delusions.
- **Negative symptoms** — also referred to as **Type II** symptoms — are those that are usually present in normal people but not experienced by schizophrenics, such as lack of motivation.

In many respects, the Type I characteristics of schizophrenia relate quite closely to reactive schizophrenia, and the Type II symptoms to process schizophrenia.

According to the classification system DSM-IV, there are five types of schizophrenia, each with different characteristics:

Characteristics of the five types of schizophrenia (DSM-IV)

Paranoid schizophrenia: delusions of persecution or grandeur; hallucinations; relatively normal language; a tendency to be argumentative and occasionally violent; often has a later onset than other types.

Disorganised schizophrenia (or hebephrenic schizophrenia, from the Greek word 'hebe' — youth): hallucinations; disturbances of thought, language and affect; social withdrawal; usually diagnosed in adolescence or young adulthood.

Catatonic schizophrenia: motor disturbances, including catatonic immobility, during which the patient's limbs can be moved to a new position in which they will be held, known as waxy flexibility; agitated catatonia, i.e. wild and unpredictable movements; mutism, where the patient is unresponsive; negativism, resisting or doing the opposite of what has been asked.

Undifferentiated schizophrenia: people show symptoms of schizophrenia, but the pattern does not correspond with any of the previous three categories.

Residual schizophrenia: people have had a schizophrenic episode within the past 6 months and still have some symptoms, but not to such a degree that they can be put into one of the first three categories.

The classification system ICD-10 uses the category **simple schizophrenia**, and this is still used in some countries. This describes the disorder when its onset is early, usually in the late teens. It is characterised by social withdrawal, loss of motivation and a loss of touch with reality.

There are other related disorders, such as **schizophreniform disorder**, where psychotic symptoms such as delusions last for less than 6 months. The diagnosis of **schizoaffective disorder** is used when the clinician cannot decide on a definite diagnosis; the problem may be schizophrenia or alternatively an affective (mood) disorder. This again has a relatively short duration. In **delusional disorder**, the patient has one or more delusional symptoms but none of the other symptoms that would lead to a diagnosis of schizophrenia.

Social withdrawal and a lack of motivation are characteristics of simple schizophrenia

Liddle (1987) proposed that the symptoms of patients with chronic schizophrenia can be classified in terms of three syndromes:

- **Psychomotor poverty** — poverty of speech, flatness of affect, decreased spontaneous movement.
- **Disorganisation** — disorders of form of thought, inappropriate affect.
- **Reality distortion** — delusions and hallucinations.

There is some support for this three-syndrome approach. For example, in a study of 329 patients with schizophrenia, Johnstone and Frith (1996) found that these different clusters of symptoms were clearly apparent and suggest that they may reflect distinct underlying pathologies.

There are three phases in the development of schizophrenia:

- In the **prodromal phase**, symptoms start to appear.
- Major symptoms become clearly apparent in the **active phase**.
- The final phase is the **residual phase**, when the disorder becomes less acute, for example as the result of treatment.

Harrison (1995) claims that in Western cultures approximately a third of patients regain the ability to function normally, a third are permanently in the active phase, while a third move between the active and residual phases.

Summary

- Schizophrenia is a **psychotic** disorder, where the individual is out of touch with reality.
- **Symptoms** are variable and may be positive or negative.
- DSM-IV categorises **five types of schizophrenia**, each with its own characteristics.
- There are several other **related disorders**.
- Schizophrenia moves through a series of **three phases**.

Issues of classification and diagnosis

The term 'diagnosis' is used in the medical model of illness, which proposes that symptoms are caused by an organic lesion, i.e. a change in the structure of body tissue caused by disease or injury. The term 'classification' is used in the medical model of mental illness, where abnormal behaviour is considered to be a symptom caused either by a hypothetical lesion, or by a physical lesion that has not yet been identified.

While the classification of mental disorders can be traced back to the Ancient Greeks, the first classification of modern times was produced by Kraepelin (1913). He suggested that there were 18 different disorders, each with its own:

- characteristic pattern of symptoms, called a **syndrome**
- causes or **aetiology**, or cause, with a common biological basis
- typical pattern of development and outcome, i.e. **prognosis**

While there is no evidence to support the details of Kraepelin's approach, the general principles have been applied in the two best-known classification systems: **International Classification of Diseases (ICD)** and **Diagnostic and Statistical Manual of Mental Disorders (DSM)**. Shortly after the World Health Organization (WHO) was formed in 1948, it published ICD, while DSM was first published by the American Psychological Association in 1952. ICD is used in Britain and in most other parts of the world. DSM is used in North America but has become more widely utilised around the world. Both systems are regularly revised. DSM is now in its fourth edition and is therefore known as **DSM-IV**, with a new revision planned for 2012. ICD is now in its tenth edition, so is known as **ICD-10**. The revision of the systems aims to improve their reliability and validity, which are issues we will be looking at later in this section.

In relation to schizophrenia, ICD-10 uses a category that covers schizophrenia, schizotypal and delusional disorders, while DSM-IV uses a category that covers schizophrenia and other psychotic disorders, i.e. where the patient is out of touch with reality. As well as categorising mental disorders, DSM-IV also has a system of **multiaxial classification**, which allows the clinician to make a broad assessment of the individual's level of functioning. A person is assessed on five separate axes, aiming to help the clinician to consider as much information as possible. This system is based on the idea that disorders must be due to both the physical and psychological states of the individual, as well as environmental factors:

The five axes in DSM-IV

Axis I — clinical syndromes and other factors that may be a focus of clinical attention: the disorder(s) from which the person is suffering are listed together with other problems such as a history of abuse and factors related to the stage of a person's life, for example the menopause.

Axis II — personality disorders: traits or behaviours generally typical of the person over and above those related to the particular disorder are identified.

Axis III — medical disorders: medical conditions are noted, for example a heart condition, which might be relevant.

Axis IV — psychosocial and environmental problems: stressful events in the person's life are recorded, such as a recent bereavement or poor housing conditions, which could be relevant. These are rated on a scale of 0 (none) to 7 (catastrophic).

Axis V — global assessment of functioning: an assessment is made of the person's current level of functioning, using the Global Assessment of Functioning Scale, from 0 (persistent danger) to 100 (superior functioning).

The first three axes always need to be used when making a classification, while axes IV and V may be used to give a broader basis for clinical assessment.

Mental health professionals using ICD-10 use a similar range of information to make a classification. They will need to find out about the psychiatric, medical, personal and family history of the patient, their social circumstances and their personality. They will make a cognitive assessment, for example of memory and IQ, test the functioning of the central nervous system (CNS) and perform a physical examination. This information can then be summarised in the grid in Figure 9.1.

Figure 9.1 *Assessment grid for ICD-10*

	Biological	Social	Psychological
Precipitating			
Predisposing			
Perpetuating			

This will show the factors that are the immediate or precipitating cause of the disorder, factors that have predisposed the person to develop a particular disorder and factors that serve to maintain or perpetuate it.

Goldstein and Anthony (1988) suggested that a good and valid classification system has to have three uses:

- to allow a **prognosis** to be made, i.e. to predict the future development of the disorder
- to develop **treatment** plans
- to study the **aetiology** of specific disorders

One reason that classification is useful is that mental health professionals may then have a better idea of what treatments will be suitable for an individual, although this will often involve an element of trial and error. Classification may also help patients to come to terms with their disorder by being able to give their problems a label. Classification systems are useful for researchers, as their structure can guide research. Similarities between patients can help to identify the cause of a disorder, facilitate communication between health professionals and be of help in assessing the effectiveness of treatment.

However, there are a number of problems with the use of classification systems in terms of their reliability and validity, particularly in relation to schizophrenia; these will be discussed in the next section.

Summary

- The classification systems of **DSM-IV** and **ICD-10** both include a category covering schizophrenia and related disorders.
- In both systems, **additional information** is used to make a diagnosis.
- A good classification system should allow a **prognosis** to be made, a **treatment plan** to be developed and the **aetiology** of the disorder to be studied.
- The systems have problems in terms of **reliability** and **validity**.

Reliability

For a classification system to be useful, it needs to be reliable; in other words, it must produce consistent results, so that the professionals using it can agree on a classification for a particular patient. One problem is that of **differential diagnosis**, in this case differentiating the symptoms of schizophrenia from those of organic illnesses and other psychiatric illnesses. Bhui et al. (1998) list a range of physical disorders in which patients may exhibit some of the symptoms of schizophrenia, including Huntingdon's chorea, tumours in the temporal or frontal lobes of the brain, temporal lobe epilepsy, early multiple sclerosis and substance abuse, especially LSD, ecstasy, amphetamines and cocaine/crack. They also report that there may be difficulties in differentiating schizophrenia from mania and depression, both of which may share symptoms.

However, reliability alone is not a guarantee that a system is valid. This may be a particular problem with schizophrenia, since as we have seen the range of symptoms shown by people whose disorder has been classified as schizophrenia is extremely variable (see Box 9.1).

Box 9.1   Beck (1967)

Aim: To assess the reliability of a classification of schizophrenia using DSM.

Procedure: Four experienced psychiatrists met and discussed the classification system (DSM) they were to use in the study, to ensure that they agreed as to how it was to be applied. They then made a diagnosis for 153 patients during their first week in a psychiatric hospital. Each patient was interviewed separately by two different psychiatrists.

Results: The psychiatrists agreed on a classification of schizophrenia in only 54% of cases. There was even less agreement on subcategories of the disorder. Discussion about why the classifications differed showed that some disagreements were due to inconsistencies in the information given by the patients and some were due to inconsistencies on the part of the psychiatrist, such as differences in judging the importance of particular symptoms. However, most of the disagreements were considered to be the result of inadequacies of the classification system.

Conclusion: Classification systems such as DSM can lead to unreliable diagnosis.

However, this is an old study and a great deal of work has since been carried out to make classification more consistent. At the same time, the initial discussion between the psychiatrists is artificial and would be expected to produce a higher-than-real-world reliability score.

A further study also questions the reliability of classification in relation to psychosis (see Box 9.2).

Box 9.2   Temerline (1970)

Aim: To assess the reliability of classification.

Procedure: An interview was recorded with an actor playing the role of someone enjoying good mental health. The actor gave as his reason for coming to the clinic that he had just read a book about psychotherapy and wanted to talk about it.

Several groups of people, including psychiatrists, clinical psychologists and graduate students in clinical psychology, were asked to assess the man. These groups had heard a famous psychiatrist, a well-known expert in his field, make the suggestion: 'I know the man being interviewed today; he is an interesting man because he looks neurotic but is actually quite psychotic.'

After hearing the interview, participants were asked to make a classification by ticking items on a data sheet that listed various psychotic, neurotic and personality disorders, plus a 'healthy' category.

Results: Of the psychiatrists, 60% made a classification of psychosis. Only 28% of the clinical psychologists and 11% of the graduate students made a similar classification. None of the

---

psychiatrists but 12% of the clinical psychologists and 12% of the graduate students made a 'healthy' diagnosis.

Conclusion: As classification is not objective, it may be unreliable. It may be affected by preconceptions, in this case the expert opinion participants heard.

A classic study in this area is *On Being Sane in Insane Places* (see Box 9.3).

Box 9.3   Rosenhan (1973)

Aim: To assess the reliability of a classification of schizophrenia.

Procedure: Eight people with no history of mental illness were asked to turn up at different psychiatric hospitals, complaining of auditory hallucinations — indistinct voices saying 'empty', 'hollow' and 'thud'. This was the only symptom they claimed to have and apart from this they answered honestly any questions they were asked. All were admitted to hospital and from that point on behaved normally.

Results: Seven of the eight people were classified as having schizophrenia in remission, although there was some disagreement among psychiatrists. Even though they said they now felt fine and no longer had any symptoms, it took an average of 19 days for them to be discharged. They noticed that staff at the hospital treated them in an offhand way, either giving inappropriate answers when asked about discharge or ignoring them completely. Many of their normal behaviours were reported on their notes as symptoms of the disorder. For example, writing a diary — required for the research — was reported as 'excessive note-taking'. Although many of the genuine patients in the psychiatric hospitals quickly recognised that they did not have a mental disorder, not one of the mental health professionals detected any of the pseudo-patients.

Conclusion: If people are classified with a disorder, everything they say and do may be taken as a symptom of the disorder. Psychiatrists may not be able to distinguish people with a mental disorder from those with no such disorder.

In a follow-up study carried out by Rosenhan, a hospital was told about the original study and staff were warned that more pseudo-patients would seek admission over the next 3 months. Although no pseudo-patients were in fact sent, of the 193 people who were admitted to the hospital during this period, one member of staff spotted that 43 of them were pseudo-patients. Admission statistics for schizophrenia at this hospital were also lower during this period. The results of his research led Rosenhan to conclude that 'it is clear that we cannot distinguish the sane from the insane in psychiatric hospitals'.

However, there are a number of criticisms of Rosenhan's research in terms of what the study claims to show about the reliability of classification. Perhaps the study really shows that psychiatrists cannot tell the difference between someone with a mental disorder and someone pretending to have a mental disorder, rather than an inability to distinguish between a person with a mental disorder and someone with no such disorder. It is also worth noting that the pseudo-patients insisted on being admitted, which is, in itself, a sign of serious mental disturbance, and that they

claimed to hear voices, a symptom for which there is no possibility of independent confirmation. It may also be that the psychiatrists involved in the study were more likely to diagnose a healthy person as being ill rather than an ill person as being healthy, erring on the side of caution, given that it would be potentially dangerous to leave an ill person untreated.

There are clearly ethical problems here in that mental health staff were deliberately deceived about the mental health status of patients, although it could be argued that deception was necessary for the study to be viable. Perhaps more importantly, it is possible that in the follow-up study, people with genuine mental health problems who were identified as pseudo-patients did not receive the treatment they needed.

It has been claimed that if the same study were carried out today, the pseudo-patients would not be able to gain admission, as DSM-IV would not now diagnose them as schizophrenic. The diagnostic criteria used in both DSM-IV and ICD-10 are much more detailed and precise than the versions of the classification systems at the time when Rosenhan carried out his research. Wing et al. (1974) claimed that with DSM-IV the reliability of classification is improved when a structured interviewing technique is used, which involves a standardised diagnostic procedure with specific criteria and a computerised scoring program. There is more recent evidence that correlations for the classification of schizophrenia, when different psychiatrists make assessments, are now in the region of 0.8, suggesting high reliability. Miller et al. (2002) reported 93% interrater reliability; however, their study was small, as only 18 participants were involved.

Summary

- A reliable classification of schizophrenia is difficult given the **range of possible symptoms**.
- Some studies have shown that classification of schizophrenia is **unreliable**.
- Reliability has **improved** with the techniques used in the latest version of DSM-IV

Validity

In this context, validity refers to the meaningfulness and usefulness of the categories used. A valid system should use categories that refer to a consistent pattern of symptoms, a single aetiology, an indication of treatment and provide guidance as to the expected outcome. It should be borne in mind that even if a classification is reliable, in that clinicians agree on it, the classification itself is not necessarily valid.

Mental disorders are by their nature harder to classify than physical illnesses. One reason is that there is often considerable overlap between conditions and it cannot be assumed that conditions are discrete. Moreover, many of the symptoms patients report are subjective, and the clinician is likely to lack the detailed and objective information, such as the results of blood tests and X-rays, available to doctors diagnosing a physical illness; classification depends entirely on symptoms. Another difference between diagnosing a physical illness and a psychiatric one is that for most physical illnesses the causes are known, making it relatively easy to check that a diagnosis is correct. However, the causes of mental disorders are largely unknown.

If a classification is valid, it should be possible to make accurate statements about the nature of the disorder and predictions about the course it will run. In simple terms, this may be particularly problematic in relation to schizophrenia, since several patients — all classified as schizophrenic — may not have a single symptom in common. However, within the area of mental illness, classification can have three forms of validity:

Validity in the classification of mental disorders

Aetiological validity: the same factors have caused the disorder in the diagnostic group. For example, if a disorder is thought to be genetic, there should be a family history of the disorder in everyone who is classified as having it.

Concurrent validity: other symptoms, not part of the classification itself, should be characteristic of those diagnosed. For example, most people classified with schizophrenia also have problems in personal relationships.

Predictive validity: there should be similarities in the course of the disorder, with patients suffering from it showing similar behaviour. In other words, a specific prognosis can be made and the effects of treatment should be predictable.

In relation to schizophrenia, these aspects of validity are not without their problems. In relation to aetiological validity, there are no clear causes for schizophrenia, so a classification tends to be symptom based rather than aetiology based. Patients do not come with symptoms that conform to tidy diagnostic categories, so a decision has to be made in terms of which category provides the best fit. In terms of concurrent validity, as Costello (1992) points out, there is a lot of variation between individuals given the same classification, particularly in the case of schizophrenia. As there is often little in the way of a pathological basis for most psychiatric illnesses, predictive validity is established through follow-up studies, but this is made difficult by the inability to measure mental states accurately.

There is also some disagreement between the different systems used by DSM and ICD. For example, Cooper et al. (1972) found that a classification of schizophrenia was twice as likely to be made by New York psychiatrists, using DSM, than by psychiatrists in London, using ICD, leading to the ironic suggestion that the easiest way for a New Yorker to be cured of schizophrenia would be to cross the Atlantic. However, the more recent versions of the two systems are much closer than previously, so later research is less prone to contamination as a result of schizophrenia being described in widely disparate ways.

The main aim of making a classification is as a guide to the appropriate therapy, so perhaps the question we should be asking is whether or not the classification systems are useful in terms of suggesting treatments. Heather (1976) argued that there is only a 50% chance of predicting what treatment a patient will receive on the basis of the classification he or she has been given. However, our knowledge in this area has expanded greatly since then, so perhaps the picture is no longer as bleak as Heather suggested.

The system may also work in reverse, with the response to treatment guiding diagnosis. For example, a patient may be classified as schizophrenic but not respond to the drugs used to treat schizophrenia. If, on the other hand, he or she responds to drugs used to treat bipolar disorder (manic depression), the classification can be changed to bipolar disorder. As treatment is usually based on individual symptoms rather than overall classification, the category of schizophrenia in particular seems to be of little use.

Given the difficulties in this area, it seems that problems of validity are inevitable in the classification of mental disorders. Classification may be illusory, giving the impression of the precision of a medical diagnosis, but resting heavily on interpretation and inference. This has been demonstrated in bias shown when providing a classification for different ethnic groups. For example, Mukherjee (1983) found that African-Americans were far more likely than white Americans to be classified as schizophrenic, even when both groups presented with similar symptoms. The classification systems have not been rigorously tested on a UK African-Caribbean population and so may not be accurate for this group. This kind of bias can also work the other way. For example, Lopez and Hernandez (1986) reported a clinician as believing that blacks were more likely than whites to suffer from hallucinations, so did not consider a classification of schizophrenia for a black person with hallucinations. A further difficulty of this kind in making a valid classification may arise as a result of communication difficulties between clinician and patient (see Box 9.4).

Similarly, in an American study, Heurtin-Roberts et al. (1997) found that the language used by African-Americans when talking about mental health differs greatly from that on which structured classifications for DSM-IV are based.

Box 9.4	Howes et al. (2007)

The researchers carried out a case study of a 26-year-old man who presented with low mood and lack of motivation. He complained of feeling less sociable and finding it harder to think. He was otherwise fit and healthy and there was no history of a recent stressor that might have brought on his symptoms. He also used words in an unusual way, which he claimed was street slang, although it was not clear whether this was indeed the case; it could instead have been a symptom of thought disorder, one of the diagnostic criteria for schizophrenia. In this kind of situation, it may be difficult for a clinician, unfamiliar with street slang, to make a valid classification.

Summary

- Valid classification of mental disorders is difficult, as there is a **lack of objective information**.
- Identifying a valid category of schizophrenia is difficult, as the **symptoms can overlap** with the symptoms of organic or other psychiatric disorders.
- **Aetiological, predictive and concurrent validity** are all problematic in a classification of schizophrenia.
- In the past, differences between **DSM-IV** and **ICD-10** have also made classification problematic.
- Classification may be difficult where doctor and patient have **different backgrounds**, and with patients from a group on which the **classification systems have not been standardised**.

Biological explanations

Genetic explanations

A convincing amount of research suggests that at least a predisposition to develop schizophrenia is **genetic**. As we saw earlier, the likelihood of someone developing schizophrenia is 1 in 100. However, on the basis of evidence collated from 40 **family studies**, carried out in a number of different countries between 1920 and 1987, Gottesman (1991) found a clear relationship between the closeness of a person's blood relationship to a schizophrenic patient and the risk of developing the disorder, suggesting a genetic component (see Box 9.5).

Box 9.5	Gottesman (1991)

Relationship to a person suffering from schizophrenia	Risk of developoing schizophrenia
Grandchild	5
Half-sibling	6
Sibling	9
Child of one schizophrenic parent	13
Child of two schizophrenic parents	46
Fraternal (DZ) twin of a schizophrenic patient	17
Identical (MZ) twin of a schizophrenic patient	48

Although the effect of family relationships seems clear, Gottesman found that most schizophrenic patients did not have a schizophrenic parent, and that two-thirds did not have a first- or second-degree relative with the disorder. At the same time, many relatives of schizophrenic patients, who are not diagnosed with schizophrenia, suffer from a range of psychiatric disorders, some of which are related to schizophrenia, such as schizophreniform disorder. It should be remembered that some of the data Gottesman used were old, when classification of both schizophrenia and assessment of zygosity were carried out in a different and less precise manner than today.

A number of **twin studies** have also been carried out to investigate a possible genetic basis of schizophrenia, on the basis that if there is a strong genetic component, MZ twins, who have 100% of their genes in common, should show higher concordance (i.e. be more likely to both have the disorder) than DZ twins, who only have around 50% of their genes in common (see Box 9.6).

Box 9.6 Gottesman and Shields (1972)

Aim: To compare the concordance for schizophrenia between MZ and DZ twins.

Procedure: Over 26 years, data were collected on twin pairs where one had been diagnosed with schizophrenia. Of 57 twin pairs, 24 were determined to be MZ and 33 DZ. Where concordance could not be established on the basis of the co-twin's psychiatric history, the co-twin was monitored for up to 16 years to assess whether schizophrenia developed.

Results: The concordance for MZ twins was 42%, but only 9% for DZ twins. In cases where the original schizophrenic twin was judged to be severely ill, on the basis of length of hospitalisation, the concordance rate for MZ twins was considerably higher at 77%.

Conclusion: There is higher concordance for schizophrenia in MZ twins than in DZ twins, providing evidence of a genetic basis to the disorder.

9

This study tested a relatively large sample of twin pairs, and so provides convincing evidence of genetic vulnerability to schizophrenia. Later studies have also confirmed this degree of difference. For example, the Gottesman (1991) study (see Box 9.5) found a concordance rate of 48% for MZ twins and 17% for DZ twins. However, these studies also show that many MZ twin pairs are discordant for schizophrenia, even though the twins are genetically identical. It is possible that this discrepancy can be explained by environmental factors, for example exposure to prenatal and postnatal stressors, infection, physical trauma or differences in diet. Nonetheless, Gottesman (1991) reported that of 14 twin pairs reared apart and who therefore had different environmental experiences, no fewer than nine pairs were concordant for schizophrenia. More generally, a problem with twin studies is that they assume that the degree of similarity between MZ environments and DZ environments is comparable, so differences in concordance must be due to genetic factors, and this may not be true.

Further evidence for a strong genetic component in schizophrenia comes from studies of twins who are discordant for schizophrenia. Since MZ twins are genetically identical, they will both have a similar risk of passing on genes relevant to the development of schizophrenia, whether or not they have developed it themselves (see Box 9.7).

Box 9.7 Gottesman and Bertelson (1989)

Aim: To assess the concordance for schizophrenia in the offspring of MZ and DZ twins who were themselves discordant for the disorder.

Procedure: In a Danish study, the proportion of the offspring of 21 MZ and 41 DZ twin pairs (discordant for schizophrenia) who went on to develop the disorder was assessed.

Results: For MZ twins, the percentage of offspring who developed schizophrenia was identical whether or not the parent was schizophrenic, i.e. 17% in both cases. For DZ twins, 17% of the offspring with a schizophrenic parent went on to develop the disorder, but the rate was only 2% for offspring of the non-schizophrenic twin.

Conclusion: There is a strong genetic component in schizophrenia.

Adoption studies have been carried out with the same aim, on the basis that if the disorder develops when environments differ, then this must be the result of genetic factors. These studies again suggest a strong genetic element in the development of schizophrenia. In a classic study, Heston (1966) examined 47 adult children of mothers who had been diagnosed as schizophrenic. They had been raised either by relatives or in institutions. These participants were compared with a control group who had been raised in institutions, so that being raised in an institution would not be a confounding variable. Heston found that five of the children with schizophrenic mothers, but none of the controls, had been diagnosed as schizophrenic.

Prospective studies in this area are also being carried out, a method where suitable participants are selected and followed over an extended period of time, with assessment taking place at regular intervals. In relation to schizophrenia, high-risk children, those where one or both parents have been diagnosed with schizophrenia, are followed up to see if they develop the disorder. A control group of similar children, where neither parent has been diagnosed as schizophrenic, is followed at the same time, so that comparisons can be made. This method has the advantage of allowing the researcher to look at the incidence of the development of the disorder over many years in the person's lifetime. The Finnish Adoption Study was started in 1969 (see Box 9.8).

Box 9.8   Tienari et al. (2006)

Aim: To carry out a prospective study to assess the importance of genes in the development of schizophrenia.

Procedure: A group of 190 adopted-away children of birth mothers who had been diagnosed with schizophrenia or a related disorder was compared with a group of 190 adoptees whose mothers had either been diagnosed with a psychiatric disorder unrelated to schizophrenia or who had no history of psychiatric illness. The age range of the children at the start of the study was between 5 and 7, and all the children had been separated from their mothers before the age of 4.

Results: For those children whose mothers had been diagnosed with schizophrenia, the risk of developing schizophrenia over the course of the study was 5.34%, compared to 1.74% for controls. For adopted children whose mothers had been diagnosed with a schizophrenia-related disorder, the risk of developing a schizophrenia spectrum disorder was 22.46% compared to 4.36% for controls.

Conclusion: There is a strong genetic component in the development of schizophrenia and related disorders.

All these studies suggest that genes play an important part in the development of schizophrenia. Crespi et al. (2007) report that 76 genes have been identified that mediate a vulnerability to the disorder, and research is currently in progress, for example Pedrosa et al. (2009), to identify the alleles — the particular form of these genes — related to the development of the disorder.

However, it should be noted that Tienari et al. (see Box 9.8) found that the risk of developing schizophrenia was also strongly related to family factors, with children raised in dysfunctional families being considerably more vulnerable than those in families that functioned well. While genes may predispose an individual to develop schizophrenia, other factors determine whether or not he or she will do so.

Neurochemical explanations

The development of schizophrenia has also been linked to neurochemical factors. Years before technology enabled scientists to isolate and analyse chemicals, Jung suggested that schizophrenia was

Summary

- **Family, twin** and **adoption** studies all suggest that there is a strong **genetic component** to schizophrenia.
- There are **other factors** that affect its development.

caused by the presence of a chemical he called Toxin X, which he thought would be identified in years to come. It is now thought that an excess of the neurotransmitter dopamine may play a part in causing schizophrenia. This is known as the **dopamine hypothesis**.

There is some evidence to support this idea. The phenothiazines are a type of drug used to treat schizophrenia, but a side effect of these drugs is that they can produce symptoms similar to that of Parkinson's disease, such as trembling. Parkinson's disease appears to be caused partly by insufficient dopamine in parts of the brain. It might therefore be concluded that phenothiazines work in the treatment of schizophrenia by interfering with dopamine activity in the brain, i.e. by blocking dopamine receptors. However, drawing the conclusion that their effectiveness is an indication that the symptoms they suppress are caused by high levels of dopamine is an example of the **treatment aetiology fallacy**. For example, this would be like arguing that shyness is caused by low levels of alcohol in the brain, since shyness is reduced by drinking alcohol.

Further evidence is provided by the fact that if non-schizophrenic people take amphetamines in large doses, they show symptoms similar to schizophrenia, such as hallucinations and delusions. It is known that amphetamines increase dopamine levels, so this in turn suggests that excess dopamine could cause schizophrenia. However, the findings are not clear-cut. Van Kammen et al. (1977) reported that taking amphetamines can actually lead to a reduction in the symptoms of schizophrenia.

Brain-scanning techniques such as **positron emission tomography (PET)** and **magnetic resonance imaging (MRI)** allow us to study the characteristics of living brains. Early research by Iverson (1979), who carried out postmortems on schizophrenics, found higher than normal concentrations of dopamine in the brain, and there have been similar findings using PET scans. However, a review carried out by Haracz (1982) found that the majority of such studies tested schizophrenics who had been on antipsychotic medication for a long period of time; this would be expected to produce just such a compensation reaction within the brain. Wong et al. (1986) have shown that people suffering from schizophrenia have a greater density of dopamine receptors on cells in various parts of the brain, although these findings have not always been replicated. It may be that the symptoms of schizophrenia are due not so much to an excess of dopamine, but a more complex dysregulation of the dopamine system, with schizophrenics having an excess of dopamine in some parts of the brain and low levels in others. For example, Davis et al. (1991) have suggested that an abnormally low level of dopamine activity in the prefrontal regions of the brain may lead to excessive dopamine activity in the limbic system.

If the neurochemical theory regarding the cause of schizophrenia does indeed hold true, then it follows that treatment for the disorder should involve the use of drugs in an attempt to regulate the imbalance of chemicals. Crow (1982) has suggested that drugs are only useful in treating the positive (Type I) symptoms of schizophrenia and are ineffective in treating negative (Type II) symptoms. This could suggest that the link between dopamine and schizophrenia may only be relevant in helping to explain the disorder in some patients, or (and more likely) that schizophrenia is not a single disorder in the first place, an issue of the validity of a diagnosis of schizophrenia. However, this approach is another example of the treatment aetiology fallacy, mentioned earlier. It is also possible that the interaction of dopamine with other neurochemicals may be an important factor; suggestions have been made that serotonin, acetylcholine, GABA, neuropeptides and prostaglandins may be implicated.

There may be confounding variables in this type of research. It is possible that schizophrenics have different lifestyles than other groups of people; perhaps they smoke more or have a poorer diet. There could therefore be factors that produce a neurochemical difference but that do not explain the cause of the disorder. A further problem is that neurochemical abnormalities may be the result rather than the cause of schizophrenia, and in particular are caused by the drugs used to treat schizophrenics.

Summary

- There is considerable evidence that a malfunctioning **dopaminergic system** is implicated in schizophrenia.
- However, **drugs** that regulate dopamine are only successful in treating **some of the symptoms** of schizophrenia.

Differences in the anatomy and functioning of the brain

Research has shown structural differences between the brains of schizophrenics and those of controls. MRI studies, such as Brown (1986), have shown that many schizophrenics have **lighter brains** with **enlarged ventricles**, cavities holding cerebrospinal fluid. However, some studies, for example Pearlson et al. (1989), have failed to replicate this finding. Again, it may be that ventricular enlargement is the result rather than the cause of the disorder; antipsychotic drugs are a known cause of ventricular enlargement. Moreover, Copolov and Crook (2000) point out that ventricular enlargement is not specific to schizophrenics but is also found in alcoholics and depressives. They also found that there is a 60% overlap in ventricular size between schizophrenics and controls.

Birchwood et al. (1988) found that the balance of activity between the two hemispheres of the brain was disturbed in some schizophrenic patients. Some studies have identified a dysfunction in the **frontal lobes** of schizophrenics, while Roberts (1991) suggested that there may be abnormal functioning in the **medial temporal lobe**. Since this part of the brain is involved in integrating information, a dysfunction in this area could account for some of the typical symptoms of schizophrenia.

Abnormalities have also been found in the **corpus callosum**, the bundle of nerve fibres that allow communication between the hemispheres of the brain. Some studies have found this structure to be enlarged in schizophrenics, while others have found it to be abnormally thin. Coger and Serafetinides (1990) suggested that enlargement is associated with early-onset schizophrenia and negative symptoms, while a thin corpus callosum is associated with late-onset schizophrenia and positive symptoms. There is some empirical support for this idea.

David and Cutting (1993) reported that in the brains of schizophrenics, neural connections in the **hippocampus** are disorganised compared with the regularly arrayed connections in non-schizophrenics. However, as with all the studies in this area, this research is correlational, so some caution needs to be applied in interpreting the findings.

One possibility that has been investigated is that neurological abnormalities and schizophrenia both come about as the result of infection by a **virus** during foetal development (see Box 9.9).

Box 9.9   **Mednick et al. (1988)**

Aim: To investigate the possibility of a viral infection during foetal development being a cause of schizophrenia.

Procedure: In 1957, there was a 5-week influenza epidemic in Helsinki. The incidence of schizophrenia in people who had been exposed to this virus during their mother's pregnancy was investigated.

Results: Those exposed during the second trimester of pregnancy were significantly more likely to be schizophrenic than those exposed during the first or third trimesters, or controls.

Conclusion: The second trimester is a crucial time for cortical development. Exposure to the virus at this time could therefore have led to the neurological abnormalities associated with schizophrenia.

Similarly, Sham et al. (1993) have shown that people born some months after an influenza epidemic have an increased risk of developing schizophrenia, suggesting that a prenatal infection might affect the brain development of the foetus and so predispose the individual to develop schizophrenia some years later. Postnatal infection could also be a factor and would account for the fact that more schizophrenics are born in the winter months, when they would be more susceptible to infection, than in the summer.

There is also some evidence that **birth complications** may interact with a genetic predisposition to bring about the development of the disorder. In a review of evidence in this area, McNeil and Kaij (1978) reported that in MZ twins who were discordant for schizophrenia, the twin with schizophrenia was the one for whom there were more obstetrical complications, while if they were concordant, the one for whom birth complications were more severe was likely to have more severe symptoms and a worse prognosis.

However, Seidman (1983) has estimated that only about a quarter of schizophrenics have any forms of gross brain abnormality. It is also possible that where such abnormality has been found it may be the result of antipsychotic drugs used to treat the disorder, or other as yet unidentified factors.

Summary

- There are **structural differences in the brains** of some schizophrenics compared with normal brains.
- There is some evidence linking schizophrenia with a **viral infection**.
- It may also be linked to **birth complications**.

Psychological explanations

While there is good evidence for genetic factors playing an important role in the development of schizophrenia, some psychologists have tried to explain the disorder in terms of **dysfunctional families**. The Finnish Adoption Study (see Box 9.8) found that family factors of this kind were indeed a factor in its development. As early as 1956, Bateson et al. suggested that some parents may predispose their children to schizophrenia by giving them conflicting messages. For example, a mother might ask her child to give her a hug, while at the same time telling the child when it does so that it is too old to show affection in that way. Bateson argued that as a result of this type of interaction, for which he used the term **'double bind'**, children may start to doubt their own understanding and lose their grip on reality.

R. D. Laing described 11 case studies of families in his book *Sanity, Madness and the Family* (1964). In each family history, one member of the family was diagnosed as schizophrenic, and Laing suggested that the cause of the schizophrenia was the way in which the family relationships worked. This **family interaction model** suggests that family members communicating in pathological ways is the cause of schizophrenia. More recently, Norton (1982) found that if parents were communicating poorly, this was a good predictor of the later onset of schizophrenia in their offspring.

However, there is no convincing evidence that families are in fact responsible for the development of schizophrenia. There is also the problem of cause and effect when trying to establish a link between the ways in which families function and the development of schizophrenia. For example, the kinds of behaviour that families show to an affected family member may well be a reasonable response to an unusual child.

Poor parental communication has been shown to be a predictor of later onset schizophrenia

9

In his book *The Divided Self* (1965), Laing put forward an **existential explanation** of schizophrenia. According to Laing, schizophrenia should not be seen as a disorder; what schizophrenics say and do makes sense if related to what he refers to as their 'being-in-the-world'. Their problems lie in their relationship with the world and with the self. The schizophrenic experiences what Laing called '**ontological insecurity**'. Ontologically secure people meet all that life has to offer with a firm sense of their own and other people's reality and identity; this is missing in the schizophrenic. Laing suggested that there are three forms of anxiety experienced by the schizophrenic:

Laing's three forms of anxiety

Implosion: the terror associated with the possibility that the world may crash in and obliterate identity.

Engulfment: the possibility of any kind of relationship with another person threatens to be overwhelming.

Petrification: the fear of being depersonalised by and depersonalising others.

Laing believed that many of the things schizophrenics say and do make sense when seen against this background. However, these kinds of explanation are speculative and fell into disfavour when evidence for a genetic cause of schizophrenia began to emerge in the 1970s.

Interest in this area has tended to shift from seeing families as the cause of the disorder to investigating the role they might play in maintaining it. Brown (1972) looked at the effect of **high expressed emotion (high EE)** in the homes of schizophrenics returning from hospital. By this he meant homes where there were high levels of negative emotions such as hostility, anger and criticism. He found that schizophrenics returning to high-EE homes were more likely to relapse than those returning to low-EE homes. This idea was explored in later research (see Box 9.10).

Box 9.10 Vaughn and Leff (1976)

Aim: To investigate the effect of high-EE homes on the relapse of schizophrenics.

Procedure: Patients returning from hospital to high-EE homes were compared with those returning to low-EE homes. Data were also collected on the amount of time spent in direct contact with relatives during the period at home, as well as whether the patient was on medication.

Results: Patients in high-EE homes showed a 51% relapse rate, significantly higher than the rates for those in low-EE homes: 12% when patients were on medication and 15% when they were not on medication. The effect of medication on low-EE homes was non-significant. In high-EE homes, the relapse rate increased with the amount of time spent in contact with relatives. If patients in high-EE homes with high contact were also not taking medication, relapse rates rose to 92%.

Conclusion: In high-EE families, the nature of communication within the family plays a part in whether treated patients relapse.

The belief that high EE maintains schizophrenia is well established. Other studies have provided support for it, across a range of cultures.

Other psychological explanations of schizophrenia have focused on the social context beyond the family. Research has shown significant correlations between **social class** and the diagnosis of schizophrenia. For example, Hollingshead and Redlich (1958) conducted a 10-year study of schizophrenia and social class in Connecticut. They found that the diagnosis of schizophrenia was twice as likely to be made in people from the lowest social class as in those from a higher class, particularly those living in densely populated inner-city areas.

This has led to the **social causation hypothesis**, that schizophrenia is caused by factors related to social class. However, this research was again correlational, so it would be unwise to draw this conclusion. It could be that the poor education received by those in the lower social classes in Connecticut, together with their lack of access to social opportunities and rewards, could be so stressful that they led to the development of schizophrenia. Alternatively, it could be that the development of schizophrenia, and the difficulties a schizophrenic experiences in earning a living, might lead to the individual 'drifting' into the poorer areas of the city. This **social-drift hypothesis** suggests that the cognitive and motivational problems a schizophrenic experiences can lead to him or her living in deprived areas, unable to obtain employment and unable to afford to move out of the area. Dauncey et al. (1993) report that some degree of drift may occur even before there are clear signs of schizophrenia. In interpreting the relationship between schizophrenia and social class, there is also the confounding variable that schizophrenics in the upper classes may be less likely to come to the attention of the authorities, since they may be sheltered and protected by their families.

Frith (1997) has suggested that delusions of alien control in schizophrenia should be seen in **information processing** terms, as a result of faulty monitoring of intentions and plans; schizophrenics do not recognise thoughts and behaviours as being self-generated. A similarly cognitive explanation comes from McGhie and Chapman (1961), who suggested that attentional processes may not function appropriately; schizophrenics are unable to filter out irrelevant information that reaches their senses and so are bombarded by excessive stimulation. Knight (1984) suggests that schizophrenics' poor performance on tasks that require perceptual processing may be the result of an inability to differentiate between meaningful and meaningless information.

Summary

- It has been suggested that **family dysfunction** may contribute to the development of schizophrenia.
- The perceived importance of the family lost ground as a result of **genetic evidence**, although the family is seen to be important in **maintaining schizophrenia**, in particular in **high-EE** families.

- The **social context** may also have a part to play.
- It has been suggested that **cognitive factors** are involved.

The diathesis-stress model

There is good evidence that the development of schizophrenia is related to biological factors, in that genetic features can lead to the disruption of neurochemical activity, which in turn leads to the cognitive defects and other symptoms shown in schizophrenics. At the same time, social and psychological factors, such as how well a family functions, are also involved. The diathesis-stress model — suggesting that schizophrenia is probably the result of an interaction between genetic vulnerability and environmental stress — may have something to offer. A person may inherit a predisposition to develop schizophrenia, but will not go on to do so unless stressors in the environment activate that predisposition. Among other things, this would help to explain why middle-class people living in a supportive family and with a rewarding job are less likely to be diagnosed as suffering from schizophrenia than those who do not enjoy these advantages.

Summary

- The **diathesis-stress** model suggests that there may be an **interaction** of different factors in causing schizophrenia.

Biological therapies

Treatment for schizophrenia can help to manage the symptoms and help patients who are in remission to avoid another acute episode. Before the 1950s, a patient diagnosed with schizophrenia was likely to remain in a mental hospital for life. Biological treatments used included psychosurgery and electro-convulsive therapy (ECT), but these had little, if any, effect on the condition. Otherwise the 'treatment' was simply long-term care within a hospital, now known as 'patient warehousing'. However, with the finding that phenothiazines — a class of drug that was used to slow metabolic rates in major surgery — could be effective in reducing some symptoms in schizophrenics, the main form of treatment is now medication, in particular a class of drugs known as **antipsychotics** or **major tranquillisers**, used to treat psychotic conditions and in particular schizophrenia.

Phenothiazines block dopamine receptors, and Leff (1992) reports that they are extremely effective in treating the positive symptoms of schizophrenia but have little effect on negative symptoms. The beneficial effects last as long as the drug is taken, but if the patient fails to continue with the medication, relapse — although relatively rare in a low-EE environment — may follow. It should also be noted that relapse, following withdrawal from medication, is likely to be a response to withdrawal and not a response to being in a drug-free state.

Unfortunately these drugs can have adverse **side effects**, including weight gain, diabetes, sexual dysfunction, neuroleptic dysphoria (drug-induced depression), increased sensitivity to sunlight, insomnia, muscle tremors, drowsiness and visual disturbances, all or any of which may make it more likely that the patient will not continue with the medication and thus experience a relapse. Most side effects can be controlled with appropriate medication.

There is one serious side effect known as **tardive dyskinesia**, that cannot be controlled in this way. Around 60% of people prescribed antipsychotics develop the disorder within 3 years, and 75% of cases are irreversible; the only way of controlling symptoms is to remain on antipsychotic medication. Tardive dyskinesia is a neurological disorder. 'Dyskinesia' refers to the involuntary jerky movements of the mouth, face and tongue and sometimes impaired movement of the fingers that characterise the disorder; 'tardive' relates to the dyskinesia sometimes continuing or appearing even after the drugs are no longer taken. This disorder can be embarrassing for patients and can impair their ability to speak and to eat and in extreme cases may affect their breathing. It appears to come about as a result of sensitivity to dopamine. Hill (1992) estimated that there were 86 million sufferers worldwide.

The limitations associated with early antipsychotic drugs such as chlorpromazine, for example Largactil, has resulted in a new generation of antipsychotics — known as **atypical antipsychotics** — being developed. These include risperidone, for example Risperdal, and clozapine, for example Clozaril. These were marketed as being more effective at treating individuals with schizophrenia. However, a meta-analysis of studies carried out by Leucht et al. (1999) found two of the four new drugs to be only 'slightly more effective' than conventional antipsychotics and claimed that 'it is questionable whether the superiorities...are clinically relevant'; the other two were found to be no more effective than conventional antipsychotics. They are also more likely than conventional antipsychotics to cause obesity and diabetes. They do appear to be less likely to cause tardive dyskinesia, although many of the studies used to make this comparison have compared atypical antipsychotics with haloperidol, a drug that is particularly likely to cause tardive dyskinesia.

Risperidone has been available since the 1990s. A large-scale double-blind study carried out by Marder et al. (1997) found that it was significantly more effective than older antipsychotic drugs in controlling not only the positive symptoms but also the negative symptoms of schizophrenia, and also reduced patients' drop-out rate. Unfortunately, this drug too has side effects. It can result in insomnia, low blood pressure and stiffness and pain in the muscles. It can cause weight gain, sexual dysfunction and (rarely) a mild form of tardive dyskinesia called 'rabbit syndrome'.

Clozapine is also effective for both the positive and the negative symptoms of schizophrenia, although the extent to which patients respond to it is variable. It has a lower risk of tardive dyskinesia than older antipsychotics. However, its use has been greatly limited because of the risk of **agranulocytosis**, a rare disorder that affects the bone marrow and can cause death. However, less than 1% of patients develop the disorder, and if blood is monitored periodically, the risk drops considerably lower than this. Clozapine is expensive and the effects may not be apparent for several months.

Chris Gallagher/SPL

Risperidone is significantly more effective than older antipsychotic drugs in controlling both positive and negative symptoms of schizophrenia

When considering the use of drugs, risks need to be assessed against benefits. For example, Walker et al. (1997) found that the mortality rate through suicide among patients not treated with clozapine was much higher than the mortality rate from agranulocytosis. Studies have been carried out to compare the effectiveness of different drugs (see Box 9.11).

Box 9.11 **Sharif et al. (2000)**

Aim: To compare the effectiveness of risperidone and clozapine.

Procedure: A total of 24 patients, who at different time periods had been medicated with risperidone and clozapine, took part in the study.

Using information from the patients' charts, two psychiatrists made a 'blind' rating of the patients' overall clinical state, as well as in relation to positive symptoms, negative symptoms and aggressive behaviour.

Results: For clozapine, 58% of patients were classified as having responded to the drug, compared with 25% to risperidone. For clozapine, the response rate was 38% for positive symptoms, 29% for negative symptoms and 71% for aggressive behaviour. For risperidone, the corresponding response rates were 17%, 8% and 41%.

Conclusion: Clozapine is more effective in managing the symptoms of schizophrenia than risperidone.

Although clozapine was withdrawn by the manufacturer because of the risk of agranulocytosis, it was later made available again because the results of studies like that of Sharif et al. demonstrated its effectiveness. However, it is only used when other antipsychotic drugs — at least two — have failed to bring about an improvement.

Summary

- **Antipsychotic drugs** are the main biological treatment of schizophrenia.
- They can be **effective**, but can have serious **side effects**.

A general criticism of the use of drugs is that they tend to create in patients a passive attitude to their disorder and play down the idea that the difficulties schizophrenics experience may be related to their life history or current circumstances. This in turn is likely to reduce their motivation to attempt to take effective action to improve their circumstances.

Psychological therapies

Some psychological treatments are inappropriate for dealing with schizophrenia, for example Freud did not consider psychoanalysis to be useful in treating this disorder. However, there are several psychological interventions that can be used successfully with schizophrenic patients. One is **milieu therapy**. In dreary surroundings, a patient may adopt the role of a sick person, so milieu therapy involves changing the physical and social environment, particularly in hospitals, to encourage appropriate behaviour and social interaction. It has been shown to be effective (see Box 9.12).

Box 9.12   Paul and Lentz (1977)

Aim: To evaluate the effects of milieu therapy for schizophrenic patients.

Procedure: The study was carried out with a group of long-term schizophrenic patients. Their symptoms included incontinence, long periods of screaming and assaults on staff. The patients were divided into groups, matched on variables such as age, gender, symptoms and the length of time they had spent in the institution.

On the control ward, patients received their normal treatment of antipsychotic drugs and little else in the way of therapy.

On the milieu therapy ward, staff treated the patients as normal individuals and not as mentally ill people. They praised patients for good behaviour and expected them to be active rather than passive, for example by participating in decisions about how the ward was to function.

The patients were evaluated over the 4 and a half years of the research and for 18 months after that as part of a follow-up study.

Results: The milieu therapy patients showed a significant reduction in maladaptive behaviour compared with the controls, with 7% able to leave the ward to live independently; none of the controls were able to do so.

Conclusion: Milieu therapy can have a positive effect even on the behaviour of chronically institutionalised patients with severe schizophrenia.

However, while several more recent studies have supported the effectiveness of this kind of therapy, some patients do not respond well to these kinds of changes.

There is also some evidence that cognitive-behavioural therapy (CBT), in conjunction with antipsychotic medication, can be effective (see Box 9.13).

Box 9.13   Startup et al. (2004)

Aim: To assess the value of CBT in the treatment of schizophrenics.

Procedure: This study recruited 90 patients with schizophrenia, who had been admitted to hospital suffering from an acute episode of psychosis. Of these, 43 were given the standard treatment of antipsychotic drugs and nursing care, while the remaining 47 were given — in addition to the standard treatment — up to 25 90-minute sessions of CBT provided by one of three clinical psychologists. They were assessed for symptoms and social functioning on admission to hospital, then 6 months later, and again a year after admission.

Results: Of the CBT group, 60% showed reliable and clinically important change, with fewer positive symptoms, such as hallucinations and delusions, and fewer negative symptoms, such as apathy and lack of emotion. Only 40% of the control group showed significant improvement. When assessed after 6 months and a year, none of the CBT group showed deterioration from their admission assessment, compared with 17% of the controls.

Conclusion: CBT can produce significant and lasting benefits in the treatment of schizophrenics suffering from acute psychotic episodes.

A year later, Startup et al. (2005) tested 73% of the original sample, 2 years after their original hospital admission. They found that the CBT group still had an

9

advantage over controls in terms of the reduction of negative symptoms and social functioning. However, the difference from controls in terms of positive symptoms had not been maintained. They suggested that after the end of regular treatment, patients should be given CBT when early signs of relapse appear in order to target positive symptoms. They also point out that although offering patients CBT is an extra expense, this is offset by money saved from patients spending less time in hospital.

Taking the same general approach, some patients can be taught **self-control of symptoms**. Those who have enough insight to understand their condition may be able to develop coping strategies, such as avoiding people whom they perceive as threatening and staying close to those they see as friendly and supportive. They may realise how their behaviour appears to other people and find ways of keeping it in check, for example learning to remind themselves not to reply to disembodied voices (see Box 9.14).

Box 9.14	**Meyers et al. (1976)**

In this case study, a schizophrenic patient was taught to monitor his social behaviour and to control his speech so that it became more coherent and normal. He learned a series of self-instruction phrases which he was able to say to himself, such as 'I mustn't talk sick'; 'I must talk slowly'; 'I mustn't ramble on'. Through these means, his behaviour improved considerably; he was glad that the method had 'stopped me talking like a crazy man'.

Typically, a schizophrenic's life is marked by several relapses and remissions. An important factor in avoiding relapse is that the patient should continue to take his or her prescribed medication. However, another psychological intervention that can improve the lives of schizophrenics and help to avoid relapse is helping the patient and his or her family to **recognise symptoms** in the prodromal phase that may signal an imminent episode, usually a week or so later.

Birchwood et al. (1989) found that interviews with patients and their families helped them to identify signs that warn of an imminent relapse, such as loss of interest, problems with concentration and social withdrawal. If they can spot these signs, they may be able to take steps to avoid the relapse occurring. For example, the level of medication could be raised, or the family given psychological support and counselling.

Patients themselves may be able to use strategies to avoid relapse, such as relaxation techniques and the use of self-statements, as described previously. It is important that the patient does not become too stressed in the prodromal phase, as this in itself may trigger a relapse. Smith et al. (1992) suggest that patients need to be helped to avoid catastrophic thinking and to appreciate the extent to which prodromal symptoms can be controlled.

As detailed earlier, relapse is more likely when the schizophrenic lives in a family with high EE. Patients' families therefore need to be encouraged to provide an environment where there is no undue criticism of the patient or hostility. This may not always be possible, and alternative accommodation may be needed for the patient (or at least a form of daycare) to reduce the amount of contact between patients and their high-EE families. However, several **family intervention programmes** have been developed to try to lower the degree of EE in families (see Box 9.15).

Box 9.15   Leff et al. (1982)

Aim: To develop and test the effectiveness of a family intervention programme aimed at modifying the behaviour of families seen as overly critical and controlling of a schizophrenic family member.

Procedure: A programme was developed that involved:
- educational sessions, which dealt with the nature of schizophrenia and its symptoms and the best ways of dealing with difficult behaviour
- group meetings, which took place with families who coped well with their schizophrenic member
- family sessions, where social workers and other professionals met the whole family at home to discuss the family's particular problems

The effects of the intervention were evaluated during the following 2 years. Families who did not take part in the programme acted as a control group. Patients in both groups were taking antipsychotic medication throughout.

Results: The families who had been through the programme showed a significant decrease in the number of critical comments made about the patient and in emotional over-involvement, both major characteristics of high EE. Moreover, while 78% of the patients in the control group had been readmitted to hospital on at least one occasion during this period, this was true of only 14% of the programme group.

Conclusion: The family intervention programme made a significant difference to the interactions within the families of schizophrenics and was also effective in helping schizophrenics avoid a relapse.

More limited interventions of this kind can be helpful in the management of schizophrenia. Smith and Birchwood (1987) carried out a brief educational programme, similar to the educational aspect of the programme in the Leff et al. study (Box 9.15), and found that the involvement of the family was of value to patients.

Summary

- **Milieu therapy** can help to improve the quality of a schizophrenic's life.
- **CBT** may also produce significant and lasting benefits.
- Some patients can be taught **self-control of symptoms**.
- Patients and their families can be taught to **recognise the symptoms that signal a relapse** and so take steps to avoid it.
- **Family intervention programmes** have been shown to be effective in improving communication when there is **high EE** within the family and so make a relapse less likely.

Media psychology

In this chapter, we will be looking at:
- media influences on social behaviour
  - explanations of media influences on pro- and antisocial behaviour
  - the effects of video games and computers
- persuasion, attitude and change
  - models of persuasion and attitude change
  - the influence of attitudes on decision making
  - explanations for the effect of television in persuasion
- the psychology of celebrity
  - the attraction of celebrity
  - research into fandom

Media influences on social behaviour

The term 'media' refers to any method of communication, such as books, newspapers, films, television, video games and the internet. There is a long tradition of concern about the negative effects that the media might have on behaviour, and in particular on the behaviour of young people. For example, in Victorian times, 'penny dreadfuls' were cheap, sensational fiction published in serial form, each part costing a penny, and there was concern about the effects that they might have on the working-class adolescents at which they were aimed. The main concern in this area has been that the media might stimulate antisocial behaviour, i.e. behaviour that harms other people or society as a whole. However, the effects could also be prosocial, leading to behaviour that benefits others or society more generally.

Until fairly recently, much of the psychological research into the effects of the media has focused on television. However, with the increasing widespread use of video games, many of which have extremely violent content, and more importantly the rise in internet use, research has looked at the effects on young people of these relatively new media.

In this first section, we will look briefly at the different psychological explanations that suggest how the media might exert an influence on people's behaviour. We will then look specifically at research into the effects of video games and the internet on young people.

Explanations of media influences on pro- and antisocial behaviour

A major theory in this area is **social learning theory (SLT)**, put forward by Bandura in the 1960s. SLT is a development of operant conditioning theory. It proposes that we learn to produce certain behaviours not only as a result of the consequences of our own behaviour (as operant conditioning theory suggests) but also through **observational learning** and **modelling**, when we observe the behaviour of others and its consequences. If we perceive there to be a positive outcome, we may then model this behaviour. SLT also differs from operant conditioning in that there is a **cognitive** element in observational learning and modelling. A person does not simply model behaviour that he or she has seen reinforced, but processes this information in terms of whether the behaviour is appropriate for him or her, and in what circumstances.

Bandura suggested that there are three sources of models: the family, subculture and the media. He believed that there are several factors that make it more likely that a person will model the behaviour he or she has observed, such as:

- The model being similar to the person, for example being the same gender or age.
- The individual having low self-esteem.
- Observation being direct, for example, when the model is seen in action rather than on film.
- The model being seen as having desirable characteristics, for example being warm and friendly, or an admired celebrity.

We will be looking in more detail at celebrity in the final section of this chapter.

It has been suggested that some films have inspired copycat crimes. For example, *A Clockwork Orange* showed scenes in which an old man was kicked to death. After the film was released, a young man pleaded guilty to a similar killing, implicating the film. It also appeared that there was a copycat rape from the same film; the perpetrators sang 'Singing in the Rain' as they carried out the assault, just as the attackers had done on screen.

There is a lot of research evidence to support Bandura's ideas, and there are further examples in relation to the effects of antisocial behaviour in the media in Chapter 4. While much of the research in relation to this theory has focused on the modelling

10

of antisocial behaviour, there are also examples of prosocial behaviour being modelled (see Box 10.1).

| **Box 10.1** | **Sprafkin et al. (1975)** |

Aim: To investigate whether watching a film showing prosocial behaviour can make behaving in a similar way more likely.

Procedure: Children aged 5 and 6 watched one of three films:
- Group A saw a film of *Lassie*, in which a boy risked his life to save a puppy.
- Group B watched an episode of *Lassie* that carried a positive message about dogs but with no incident of a human helping a dog.
- Group C watched an episode of *The Brady Bunch*, a family-based situation comedy.

All the children then took part in a button-pressing game in which they could win prizes. At the same time, they wore headphones through which they could (supposedly) hear a kennel and were asked to press a button if they heard the barking of a puppy in distress. This would mean breaking off from the prize game, so they needed to make a choice between the prize game and helping the puppy.

Results: Children in Group A chose to help the puppy more quickly and for longer periods than children in the other two groups.

Conclusion: Programmes showing children behaving in a prosocial way can encourage children to behave in a similar way.

This study has the advantage of showing children behaving in a similar way to the behaviour they saw in the film, and so supports the idea of their behaviour being the result of modelling.

Zillmann (1999) put forward the **exemplification theory** of media influence. We extract information from our experiences (exemplars) and selectively store it, chunking similar events together. We can then use this information when we encounter similar events. In evolutionary terms, this would be adaptive in terms of promoting survival, as it would help us to act and react quickly and appropriately in particular situations. Information received through the media has the benefit of providing additional information beyond our own immediate experience, which we can use to help determine how to behave in similar circumstances. This theory has the advantage of focusing more specifically on the circumstances in which behaviour is likely to be influenced by the media. For example, Aust and Zillman (1996) found that the effects of the media are stronger when information is presented in an emotional manner. The theory also proposes that the effects are influenced by personal factors, for example the age, gender and personality characteristics of the individual.

A further explanation is the **disinhibition effect**. For example, we generally exert conscious control over (inhibit) aggressive impulses, but observing these kinds of behaviour on television programmes may remove these constraints and we may come to see aggression as a legitimate way of dealing with problems. This theory is generally used as a way of explaining the effect of the media on antisocial behaviour, but there is no reason why it should not apply equally to prosocial behaviour. Observing a person in the media intervening in a quarrel and successfully defusing the situation may reduce our inhibitions about behaving in this way and lead to us seeing it as an appropriate response.

Cognitive priming may also play a role; this too relates largely to antisocial behaviour. The idea here is that aggressive cues in films or television programmes lead to aggressive thoughts and feelings, which may then be expressed in aggressive behaviour. There is research evidence to support this idea (see Box 10.2).

Box 10.2	Josephson (1987)

Aim: To assess the effect of cognitive priming on aggressive behaviour.

Procedure: Boys watched a television programme of a gun battle, in which the snipers communicated using walkie-talkies. A control group watched a non-violent programme about a motocross team. Both groups then played a game of floor hockey and were given instructions beforehand either by walkie-talkie or a tape recorder.

Results: The boys who had watched the violent television programme and had received instructions by walkie-talkie were more aggressive than the control group and than those who had watched the same programme but received instructions by tape recorder.

Conclusion: The walkie-talkie acted as a cognitive prime to aggression.

There is also evidence to support the idea of cognitive priming for prosocial behaviour. Participants in a study by Hertel and Fiedler (1993) carried out a verbal learning task, in which for some participants the positive aspects of cooperation and negative aspects of competition were highlighted. Compared with controls, these participants showed greater cooperation in a game they took part in afterwards.

The influence of the media on aggressive behaviour has also been explained in terms of **desensitisation**. If we are continually exposed to violence, we become less sensitive to it and it has less effect on us. Cline et al. (1973) looked at physiological responses to violence, for example increased heart rate and raised blood pressure. They found that children who watched a lot of television with a violent content showed less physiological response when shown a violent film, suggesting that they were less sensitive than controls to what they were seeing. However, this was a correlational study, so the results could equally be explained in terms of children with low levels of physiological response tending to prefer violent television.

Summary

- There is a history of considerable concern about possible **negative effects** of the media. Research is also interested in **positive effects**.
- Explanations of the effects of the media include **SLT**, **exemplification theory**, the **disinhibition effect**, **cognitive priming** and **desensitisation**, each of which has a slightly different focus.

The effects of video games and computers

As video games are one of the newer media forms, their use has been a focus of recent research, particularly in relation to the possible negative effects on young people of some of the violent games available. Smallwood (2008) has pointed out that every year interactive video-game technology has become ever more advanced, so the violent content in these games has become increasingly realistic and graphic. Moreover, the video-game industry has grown over 200% in revenue in less than 10 years, so use of these games has become increasingly widespread.

To restrict the kind of material available to children and young people, the British Board of Film Censors (BBFC) uses the same classification system for video games as it uses for films. However, the BBFC recognises that the active experience of playing video games is different from that of watching films and this is taken into account when classifying games. The role of active involvement has also been shown by research (see Box 10.3).

Box 10.3   Polman et al. (2008)

Aim: To compare the effects on aggression of playing and watching video games.

Procedure: A sample of 57 children aged between 10 and 13 either played a violent video game, watched the same game, or played a non-violent video game. Aggression was assessed by asking their friends about aggressive incidents involving the participants during a free-play session at school.

Results: Boys who had played the violent game were more aggressive than those who had passively watched it. In girls, the game condition was not related to aggression.

Conclusion: For boys, playing a violent video game is likely to lead to more aggression than watching a violent television programme.

This study has the advantage of using a measure of aggression with quite high mundane realism, in that it looked at spontaneously occurring behaviour in a real-world situation. Many studies in this area have also established a link between playing violent video games and aggression (see Box 10.4).

Box 10.4   Cohn (1996)

Aim: To test the effect of playing violent video games on children's aggression.

Procedure: A sample of 124 children aged 12–14 were randomly assigned to one of three conditions. They either played a violent video game, played a non-violent video game, or worked on a simple puzzle. Baseline levels of aggression were compared with aggression shown after the game, measured by the intensity of unpleasant noise delivered to an opponent in a competitive game.

Results: There was a significantly greater rise in aggression in those children who had played the violent video game than in those in the other two groups.

Conclusion: Violent video games are a cause of increased aggression.

There is a considerable amount of evidence of this kind linking the use of violent video games and aggressive behaviour. Bartholow et al. (2006) have shown that the concept of **desensitisation**, mentioned earlier, can in part account for this effect and have demonstrated a physiological basis for it. They found that in players of violent video games there was reduced activity in an area of the brain associated with aversive motivation, compared to non-violent video-game players. This reduced brain response was also a predictor of increased aggressive behaviour in a later task.

Polman et al. (2008) suggested that there are gender differences in relation to the effects of playing violent video games (see Box 10.3). A number of studies have shown this, together with a number of other individual differences in the effects of violent video games (see Box 10.5).

Box 10.5	Wiegman and van Schie (1998)

Aim: To investigate the relationship between the amount of time children spent playing video games and levels of aggressive and prosocial behaviour, and to establish other factors that influenced any relationships found.

Procedure: In this Dutch study, there were 278 participants aged 10–14. Measures were taken of the amount of time they spent playing aggressive video games and levels of aggressive and prosocial behaviour. Boys, but not girls, who preferred aggressive video games were more aggressive and showed less prosocial behaviour. Children who preferred playing aggressive video games tended to be less intelligent.

Conclusion: Video-game use is associated with low levels of prosocial behaviour. There are gender differences and differences in intelligence in relation to a preference for aggressive video games.

A drawback with this study is that the evidence is correlational. For example, it cannot tell us anything conclusive about whether the differences noted are the result of playing violent video games, or causes of a preference for video gaming, or neither.

There is a great deal of concern that playing violent video games could lead to violent behaviour. However, there is evidence that these games are not the most important factor in aggression. Ferguson et al. (2008) found that trait aggression (i.e. being innately aggressive), being male and family violence were better predictors of violent crime than exposure to video-game violence.

Young gamers see these games as having a positive effect. Olson et al. (2008) conducted focus groups with 42 boys aged 12–14. The boys felt that the games were exciting and that they had not been harmed by violent games. They believed these games helped them to work through angry feelings and relieve stress and thus had a prosocial effect. However, they were concerned that younger children might imitate game behaviour, especially swearing.

There is some evidence that video games can be used effectively with a prosocial purpose. Fontana et al. (2004) used game technology to develop video games that would teach skills to 8-year-olds to help them avoid violence. Their data, collected pre-test and post-test, indicated that the games had produced a positive change in the children's prosocial knowledge, attitudes and beliefs.

Research commissioned by the BBFC and published in 2007 has also suggested that there are significant social benefits to playing some kinds of video game. They highlight in particular games such as *SingStar* and dance-mat games, designed to be played among family and friends. Games can also generate conversation and social interaction, particularly among boys. Although they often play on their own, they also talk about games and share them. Games that require two or more players provide a ready-made social situation and a focus for social activity.

Both pro- and antisocial behaviour are associated with playing video games

This area of study raises ethical and methodological issues. In designing controlled laboratory experiments, there are ethical problems in terms of the kinds of video-game material to which young people can be exposed; experimental studies frequently use relatively trivial violence, with the result that such studies may have limited ecological validity. On the other hand, field studies are open to inaccurate reporting by young people in their degree of experience of video games and the nature of those games. Moreover, the design of many of the studies in this area is correlational and so cannot provide any information about causation. Anderson (2002) also highlighted the need for researchers to pay more attention to variability among violent video games when comparing their effects with non-violent games. Sample sizes should be large, in order to minimise the effects of individual differences, and detailed data should be provided, so that the size of any effects can be calculated. Appropriate measures should be used to provide quantitative data about the amount of exposure to violent video games.

Concerns have also been raised in relation to young people's use of computers, and in particular about the effects of internet use, given that most children in the Western world have access to the internet and many are able to use it in the privacy of their rooms without supervision.

Some psychologists have suggested that internet use may be socially isolating and might affect young people's ability to interact face-to-face with others, for example Kraut et al. (1998). In contrast, others, for example Katz and Aspden (1997), argue that the internet could lead to more and better social relationships, especially for shy people, since its anonymity reduces feelings of shyness and embarrassment. From this point of view, Shapiro (1999) has suggested that social isolation might lead to greater internet use, rather than being caused by it and so could be seen as beneficial for those who have difficulty with face-to-face relationships. However, in the long term this could have more negative effects. The attraction of the internet for those who experience social difficulties could lead to excessive internet use, which could in turn increase their social isolation and damage real-world relationships. The short-term benefits may therefore lead to long-term costs.

A further concern is that on the internet, children may be able to access unsuitable content. For example, Davies and Lipsey (2003) have highlighted the prevalence of pro-anorexia — or 'Ana' — websites, written by anorexics and promoting anorexia as a lifestyle choice. Although such websites are taken down as soon as possible after they appear, it is not possible to prevent them from appearing at all. They usually contain tips on how to fool parents and professionals into not seeing the effects of anorexic eating habits and to simulate normal eating, for example by dirtying crockery while nobody is looking. These websites allow relationships to be formed within groups of like-minded friends who support and reinforce each other in the idea of anorexia not only as acceptable, but as a way of life to be positively pursued.

However, the internet has the advantage of offering instant access to a huge amount of information. More generally, there is evidence that computer use can be beneficial in an educational context (see Box 10.6).

Box 10.6 Mevarech et al. (1991)

Aim: To assess the effect of cooperative working on an academic task.

Procedure: Twelve-year-old children worked on a computer program aimed at improving arithmetic skills. They worked either individually or in pairs, and the task was set up so that of those working in pairs, both children had to play an active role. They were then tested individually 4 months later, and again after another 2 months, on the kinds of problems they had been working on.

Results: On both sets of tests, those who had worked in pairs showed significantly greater achievement gains than those working alone.

Conclusion: Educational computer programmes that allow cooperative learning can enhance children's educational experience and progress.

Computers can have educational benefits, as they can provide an effective environment for supporting productive interaction between children.

Summary

- There is some evidence that playing violent video games can **increase aggression** and **reduce prosocial behaviour**.
- There are **gender** and other **individual differences** in the effects of video games on children.
- Factors other than violent video games may be more important in promoting aggression.
- Video games can also have a **prosocial effect**.
- Research in this area raises **ethical** and **methodological issues**.

- There is disagreement about whether **internet** use promotes or damages **social interaction**.
- There is concern about the **content** of some internet sites.
- Computer use may offer **educational benefits**.

Persuasion, attitude and change

Attitudes are described in terms of three components: cognitive, affective and behavioural. The **cognitive** component includes the knowledge, ideas and beliefs associated with a particular opinion. The **affective** component is to do with emotions and values. The **behavioural** component refers to how a person acts towards people or things about which they have an attitude. These three components of an attitude usually coincide, although the cognitive and affective aspects do not necessarily lead to consistent behaviour, but rather make it more likely that a person will behave in a particular way. For this reason, some psychologists believe that attitudes should only be defined by the cognitive and affective components:

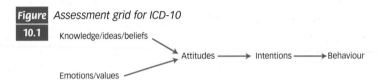

Figure 10.1 *Assessment grid for ICD-10*

Attitudes may serve several functions:

Summary

- Attitudes have **cognitive, affective** and **behavioural** components.
- They may serve **different functions**.

- They can be **socially adaptive**, in that if we demonstrate socially acceptable attitudes, we will be rewarded by approval and acceptance.
- They relate to our need for **knowledge**, as they help us to organise and structure our experiences.
- Their **self-expressive** function relates to our self-concept, as they are part of our identity.

Knowing the function an attitude serves is important in attitude change. For example, if the attitude serves the knowledge function, providing new information is the most likely way in which the attitude can be changed.

Models of persuasion and attitude change

The Hovland-Yale model

We will look in this section at two models of persuasion and attitude change, starting with the **Hovland-Yale model**. Hovland's ideas arose from an interest in wartime propaganda. Working with others at Yale University in the 1950s, his research focused on isolating and testing systematically the effects of the component parts of the communication process. These include the communicator, the content of the message, the type of medium employed (for example spoken or written communication) and the receiver of the message. Most of the research in this area has focused on the first two aspects; we will look at some of the research in these areas and briefly at the influence of characteristics of the receiver.

Communicator

The most crucial factor here is **credibility**, i.e. the expertise and trustworthiness of the person delivering the message, as perceived by those who receive the message. In general, the more knowledgeable a communicator appears to be, the more likely it is that attitude change will be brought about (see Box 10.7).

Box 10.7 **Kelman and Hovland (1953)**

Aim: To assess the importance of the credibility of the communicator on the effect of a message.

Procedure: Participants heard a talk on juvenile delinquency, suggesting that young offenders should be treated leniently. They believed the talk to be given either by a juvenile court judge, a drug dealer or a randomly chosen member of the public. The effect of the talk on participants' attitudes to juvenile crime was assessed.

Results: On immediate testing, participants were more likely to be influenced by the judge (a high credibility source) and least likely to be influenced by the drug dealer (a low credibility source). However, there was a 'sleeper effect', as the differences between the effects of the different sources had disappeared after 4 weeks.

Conclusion: In the short term, the credibility of the communicator influences the effectiveness of a message, but over time the content of the message may become more important.

Communicators are also seen as more trustworthy when they are perceived to be arguing against their own interests. For example, Walster et al. (1966) found that adolescents were more influenced by a newspaper article arguing for greater power for the courts when they believed it to have been written by a man serving a prison sentence rather than a public prosecutor. Similarly, they were more influenced by an article arguing that the courts should have less power when they thought it had been written by a public prosecutor rather than a convicted criminal.

The perceived **attractiveness** of a communicator can also be important. Someone who is witty and charming is, unsurprisingly, likely to have more effect than someone who is not. This is an example of the **halo effect**, where someone who is attractive is seen to have other positive characteristics, for example to be wise and knowledgeable. However, Benoit (1987) found that an attractive communicator did not

The perceived credibility and attractiveness of a communicator are important factors

10

produce significant attitude change on a topic that was of high personal importance to the receiver, so the effects of attractiveness are limited.

Message

As a general point, organised messages are more effective than disorganised ones. **Organisation** not only makes a message more readily comprehensible, but may also encourage attention to it. One aspect of organisation is whether presenting one or both sides of an argument is more effective. Two-sided here does not mean putting forward both sides of the argument and then allowing the audience members to make up their own minds, but briefly presenting opposing viewpoints and then refuting them, together with arguments supporting the communicator's own viewpoint. A one-sided approach just gives arguments for the point of view being advocated, without acknowledging that some people disagree with that point of view. This was explored in an early study by Hovland (see Box 10.8).

Box 10.8   Hovland et al. (1949)

Aim: To assess the relative effects of one- and two-sided presentations.

Procedure: During the Second World War, soldiers were given articles to read that suggested it would take at least 2 years to end the war with Japan. One group was given a one-sided message, while for the other group both sides of the argument were covered.

Results: There was no overall difference between the two groups in terms of attitude change. However, those who were less educated were influenced more by the one-sided argument, while the better educated were influenced more when the argument was two-sided. Education level apart, participants whose initial attitude was similar to the article were influenced more by the one-sided presentation, and the two-sided presentation was more effective for participants who already knew quite a lot about what was being discussed.

Conclusion: Education, existing attitude and prior knowledge all influence whether a one-sided or two-sided presentation is more effective in changing attitudes.

A further issue is whether a persuader should make explicit the conclusion he or she wishes the audience to draw. Cruz (1998) reports that explicit conclusions may help both with the comprehension of a message and how well it is remembered.

The order in which arguments should be presented to achieve the optimum effect has also been investigated. Several studies have found a **primacy effect**, when the first argument heard has the most effect. For example, McGuire (1957) tried to persuade his participants to take an educational course. His efforts were more effective if the positive aspects of taking the course were given first and more negative aspects afterwards. It is possible that more attention is given to what comes first, or that once one side of the argument has been heard, a decision is reached that is then hard to shift. O'Keefe (1990) found that there is a slight primacy effect when topics are controversial, interesting and familiar.

Other research has found a **recency effect**, when the last argument heard has the most effect. In an experiment conducted by the television programme *Tomorrow's World* on 25 March 1995, viewers were shown a man being interviewed for an ambulance driver's job. Without the viewers' knowledge, two different versions of the interview were shown. In the east of England, the interviewee began by making positive points, for example that he had been in the army medical corps where he had learned various skills. This was followed by more negative points, for example that since leaving the army he had been unable to hold down a job for long. In the west, exactly the same information was given, but with the negative points first. Viewers were asked if they would have given him the job. In the east 45% of viewers would have given him the job; in the west 54% would have given him the job, suggesting a recency effect. However, it cannot be assumed that people living in eastern England are necessarily similar to those in western England. For example, it may be that those in the west, being further away from London, have lower criteria for employment acceptability.

The **timing** of the presentation of the two sides of an argument may be important in helping to reconcile these contradictory findings. Miller and Campbell (1959) investigated primacy and recency effects in a simulated courtroom situation. If there was an interval between hearing the arguments and coming to a decision, a primacy effect was likely, while if there was a delay between argument and counter-argument and then a decision was made immediately, there was likely to be a recency effect. A study carried out by Petty and Cacioppo (1996) had similar findings and established that if there is no delay, or two delays (between the messages and between the second message and the action), primacy and recency effects virtually disappear.

There is a good deal of evidence to show that the stronger the arguments presented, the more likely the message is to bring about attitude change. Messages with more arguments are potentially more persuasive than those with fewer arguments, for example Calder et al. (1974). The more arguments in a message, the more likely that it will seem to be true and that it will include at least one argument that appeals to the audience. One factor in the influence of a message is the use of **fear** (see Box 10.9).

Box 10.9	Janis and Feshbach (1953)

Aim: To investigate the use of fear to bring about changes in attitudes and behaviour.

Procedure: Participants were given a presentation with colour slides about caring for teeth and the effects of tooth decay. A 'high-fear' group heard 71 references to the unpleasant effects of not looking after your teeth, including toothache, painful dental treatment and the possible secondary effects of blindness and cancer. A 'moderate-fear' group heard 49 references, and a 'low-fear' group heard 17. A control group heard a talk about the eye. Attitudes to dental health were assessed a week later.

Results: Members of the 'high-fear' group were the most worried about their teeth, but of the experimental groups, this condition was the least effective in changing behaviour.

Conclusion: Extreme fear may help to focus attention on a message, but is less effective in changing behaviour.

McGuire (1969) has suggested that low fear arousal is ineffective because the message is not attended to, while messages using high fear arousal may trigger defence mechanisms such as denial ('this could not happen to me') or repression, where the message is pushed into the unconscious. However, it has been found that if a frightening message is accompanied by information about how the dangers described can be avoided, fear may be effective in changing behaviour.

Roger (1983) identified four key elements to an effective fear appeal:

- The threat in the fear appeal must be serious. For example, smokers must believe that cigarettes really can damage their health.
- The audience members must believe that the problem could affect them, for example they must accept that smoking could lead to them developing lung cancer or heart disease.
- The message should offer an effective way of coping with the threat, for example smokers need to believe they can stop.
- The audience members must believe that they are able to apply the solution, for example if there is an effective treatment for smoking but it is too expensive, the appeal is likely to fail.

The use of evidence has a strong effect on persuasion. Taylor and Thompson (1982) found that evidence using **examples** was more effective than statistics, and they seem to be particularly useful in increasing understanding.

Receiver

Some of the research already discussed has demonstrated that the characteristics of the receiver are important in attitude change, in that different kinds of people may respond to the same message in different ways. For example, the Walster et al. study (mentioned previously) showed that whether or not the communication was seen to be for or against the interests of the communicator affects the impact of the message, suggesting that **cognitive factors** are important, i.e. how the receiver perceives the situation. The Janis and Feshbach study (see Box 10.9) suggests that **personality factors**, in this case anxiety levels, are important. McGuire (1968) goes beyond this to suggest that **persuasibility** may itself be a personality characteristic, so that some people are much easier to influence than others. Some early studies suggested that there might be **gender** differences, with women being easier to influence than men. However, there is little recent support for this idea and differences found in earlier research are likely to have come about as a result of the research topics chosen.

Evaluation of the model

You will remember from the start of this section that attitudes serve different functions for different people. The Hovland-Yale approach has been useful in that it identified different kinds of factors involved in attitudes and attitude change and so provided a framework within which research could take place. It allowed the gathering of useful data about the effectiveness of different kinds of communication, which could have practical applications, for example, putting across health messages in a way that people would find acceptable and on which they might act.

However, in some ways it could be seen as limited in its scope. For example, Kenton (1989) points out the importance of the communicator in terms of trustworthiness and expertise, but even when men and women are objectively equal on these dimensions, receivers perceive men as being more persuasive than women. More broadly, the Hovland-Yale model is a transmission model, where communication is reduced to a question of transmitting information: ideas are put into words and sent to the receiver, who receives the ideas. This is a somewhat mechanical view of human communication and is limited in that it does not deal with meaning, in terms of how a communicator succeeds in putting meanings into words and how the receiver succeeds in accessing the meaning. It tends to assume that attitude change comes from learning the ideas of a message, and while this can lead to persuasion, it does not guarantee it. For example, an advertisement can be so annoying that we cannot forget it, but we are not persuaded to buy the product or service.

Summary

- The **Hovland-Yale model** of persuasion and attitude change looks at the component parts of communication: **communicator**, **message content**, **medium** and **receiver**.
- It has identified factors in these areas that influence attitudes and could have **practical applications**.
- It can be seen as **mechanical**, with little emphasis on the **meaning** of a communication.

The Elaboration Likelihood Model (ELM)

An alternative type of model takes a **cognitive response** approach. Persuasion is not directly caused by messages; we are only persuaded if we have thoughts that agree with the message, so attitude change only comes about if a message encourages the receiver to have positive thoughts about possible change. There are two main versions of this kind of model. The **Heuristic and Systematic Processing Theory** was developed by Chaiken (1980). This model suggests that we have two ways of processing information:

- **Systematic processing** is active, conscious and cognitively demanding, and is only likely to be used when a person is highly motivated.
- **Heuristic processing** involves short cuts in processing information, using non-content cues; for example, if in the past a person has learned to trust people that they like, they will apply a 'liking-agreement' heuristic, such as 'People I like usually have correct opinions'.

The **Elaboration Likelihood Model (ELM)** proposed by Petty and Cacioppo (1981) is similar, but there has been more research associated with it than with Chaiken's model. Again, the ELM suggests that there are two ways of processing information:

- **Central processing** involves focusing on arguments, i.e. thinking carefully about information, weighing up facts and using logical reasoning.
- However, where recipients are unwilling or unable to spend the time and make the effort to carry out this kind of extensive processing, then **peripheral processing** may be used. This involves only shallow processing of information and focuses on cues, with attention given to features that are less relevant to the message being put across, for example the attractiveness or perceived expertise of the source of information.

Central processing is thus similar to the systematic processing of Chaiken's theory, and peripheral processing is similar to the theory's concept of heuristic processing.

10

Over a period of time, a person is likely to use both central and peripheral processing, although there is some evidence that individuals have a preference for one over the other.

Elaboration likelihood refers to the probability of a person critically evaluating the arguments put forward in a communication. The extent to which they will do so depends on both motivation and ability. Motivation is important because of the amount of time and effort involved in central processing, while ability is determined by such factors as previous knowledge, whether or not the receiver is tired and how the message is put across. For example, ability would be affected if the communicator was to speak fast, and in this case it is likely that peripheral processing would be used.

While both kinds of processing can lead to attitude change, the factors that influence this change vary in each case. For example, a person is more likely to be motivated to think carefully about something and use central processing if the message has **personal relevance**. When this is low, motivation is also low and peripheral processing is used (see Box 10.10).

Box 10.10 Petty et al. (1981)

Aim: To investigate the effects of expertise and strength of argument on attitude change, in relation to routes of processing.

Procedure: Student participants received a persuasive communication, contrary to their previously expressed opinion, in support of a major change to the university exam system. Three factors were manipulated:
- the strength of the arguments
- the expertise of the speaker
- personal relevance to the students — either high (the new exam system would be brought in the following year) or low (the changes would take place in 10 years time)

Results: When the topic was of high personal relevance, agreement with the communication was predicted by the strength of the arguments, i.e. central processing. Where personal relevance was low, it was predicted by the expertise of the speaker, i.e. peripheral processing.

Conclusion: There is an association between personal relevance and the route used to process information.

As we saw earlier, **attractiveness** of the source — a peripheral cue — can have an effect on attitude change, although only when there is little personal involvement.

Mood is also a factor in the route that processing takes. Bless et al. (1990) found that people in a bad mood were more affected by the quality of the argument presented, suggesting they were using central processing, while those in a good mood were more likely to use peripheral processing.

There are also **individual differences** in terms of which route is generally preferred. Cacioppo and Petty (1982) developed the **Need for Cognition scale (NFC)**, which measures the extent to which people enjoy thinking, and predicted that high scorers would be more likely to use central processing than low scorers. This prediction has been generally supported by research; for example, Bakker (1999) presented messages about safe sex to a sample of 119 adolescents. For high-NFC participants, a written message was more effective in bringing about attitude change than the message in cartoon form. The opposite was true of low-NFC participants.

Petty and Cacioppo claim that attitude change resulting mostly from central processing is likely to last longer, to be a better predictor of behaviour and to show greater resistance to counter-persuasion than change that is based on peripheral processing. There is some support for this claim (see Box 10.11).

Box 10.11 Chaiken (1980)

Aim: To compare the effects of systematic (central) and heuristic (peripheral) processing.

Procedure: Participants were given a message containing either two or six arguments in favour of a particular issue. In condition 1 (systematic processing), they were told that they would later be interviewed about the issue. In condition 2 (heuristic processing), they were told they would be interviewed about a different topic. The two groups were compared for amount of attitude change, factors involved in that change and how stable the change was.

Results: Participants in condition 1 were more affected by six arguments than two. Their attitudes remained stable when they were tested again 10 days later. Those in condition 2 were not affected by the number of arguments, but they were affected (unlike those in condition 1) by whether or not they had liked the speaker. Their attitude change was less stable.

Conclusion: Systematic processing is likely to provide more stable attitude change than heuristic processing.

This kind of model does not discount the possibility that both kinds of processing can take place at the same time. For example, when close attention to the arguments of a message does not lead to a clear-cut conclusion, we may then use heuristic cues. This idea was supported by Chaiken and Maheswaran (1994), who found that when the arguments in a message were ambiguous, the credibility of the source (a peripheral cue) influenced attitudes, even when the issue was of high personal relevance.

As with the Hovland-Yale model, **perceived expertise** can influence the effectiveness of a message, but only if the receiver is told in advance that the communicator is an expert. ELM suggests that believing the communicator to be an expert reduces the number of unfavourable thoughts we may have; once the message has been delivered, we have already made our cognitive responses to it, so this information comes too late to make a difference. However, believing that the communicator is not an expert increases our motivation to use central processing, as we may be suspicious of the contents of the message.

Much of the time we make use of peripheral/heuristic processing. We are motivated to make sense of our world, but we act as 'cognitive misers', simplifying the task as much as possible to minimise cognitive effort. We therefore think only enough to meet the minimum demands of the situation.

One strength of the ELM theory is that it recognises that sometimes audiences actively think about messages and the arguments presented, while at the same time acknowledging that sometimes receivers are passive and so can be persuaded by the peripheral route. It identifies motivation and ability as important in determining the kind of processing used and has established several factors, for example personal involvement and mood, which influence the thoughts of the receiver of a message. There is a lot of research evidence that supports these ideas.

However, it could perhaps be criticised for seeing central and peripheral processing as a dichotomy. They may perhaps be better seen as a continuum, since even peripheral processing requires some thinking to take place.

Summary

- The ELM suggests that there are two ways of processing information: **central** and **peripheral**. It focuses on **motivation** and **ability**.
- Central processing is used when an issue has **personal relevance**, and attitude change is likely to be more stable than that produced by peripheral processing.
- The type of processing used depends on **mood**. There are individual differences in which it is more likely to be used. We often use less effortful peripheral processing.
- ELM acknowledges that the audience can be **active** or **passive**.
- Central and peripheral processing may be seen as ends of a **continuum** rather than distinct.

The influence of attitudes on decision making

Attitudes also affect decision making. In this section, we will look at the roles of cognitive consistency/dissonance and self-perception in decision making.

The theory of **cognitive dissonance**, proposed by Festinger (1957), starts from the idea that we seek consistency in our attitudes, beliefs and behaviour in any situation. For example, if someone who smokes believes that smoking damages health, his or her behaviour is inconsistent with this belief. Festinger suggests that this kind of inconsistency creates dissonance, a state of psychological discomfort. In these circumstances, we are motivated to reduce or eliminate the inconsistency and achieve **cognitive consonance**. In his research, Festinger found that cognitive dissonance can provide a serious hindrance to decision making, and reducing dissonance may significantly improve decision-making skills. Festinger demonstrated his ideas in a classic study (see Box 10.12).

Box 10.12   Festinger and Carlsmith (1959)

Aim: To investigate the role of cognitive dissonance in explaining behaviour.

Procedure: Participants were given the extremely boring task of turning pegs in a pegboard for an hour. They were then asked to tell the next participant that the task was really good fun to do and were paid either $1 or $20 to do so. They were later asked to rate how interesting they had found the task.

Results: Participants who had been paid $1 rated the task as more interesting than those who had been paid $20.

Conclusion: For participants paid $20, the payment justified the lie they had told the next participant. However, for those who were paid $1, the money was too little to justify the deception. They therefore experienced dissonance between the lie they had told and their experience of the task. This was reduced by modifying their view of how interesting the task was, expressed in their more positive ratings.

In a similar study, Chatzisarantis et al. (2008) found that participants who had chosen to carry out the boring exercise of stepping up and down on a bench reported the exercise as having been more pleasurable than those who were simply instructed to carry it out. The dissonance between the choice they had made and the boring nature of the exercise was resolved by seeing the exercise as more pleasurable and thus provided a satisfactory reason for their decision. Festinger distinguished between three types of decisions:

- **Preference:** one option is clearly preferable to the other.
- **Conflict:** alternatives are similar in attractiveness. The decision is likely to take time and the individual may later wish that the other option had been chosen.
- **Indifference:** the decision is not important to the individual.

Dissonance arises in a conflict situation and is greatest when the decision has important consequences and the individual will be held responsible for those consequences. In order to reduce dissonance, a person will find (or distort) information to support his or her decision, downgrade the options not chosen, or play down the negative aspects of the decision and exaggerate the importance of its positive aspects, as the $1 participants in the Festinger and Carlsmith study did. Research carried out by Elliot and Devine (1994) supported the idea that dissonance is experienced as psychological discomfort and that this is reduced when these kinds of strategies are used.

Festinger claimed that more dissonance is experienced when the inconsistency between belief and behaviour matters to us. The theory assumes that people like to think of themselves as basically decent and honest; for example, if lying in the Festinger and Carlsmith study was not seen as a problem, then no dissonance would be experienced. In the light of this, Aronson (1968) proposed that the definition of dissonance should be narrowed down in terms of inconsistency between a person's self-concept and cognition about their behaviour. This can be related to self-perception theory, which we will be looking at next.

Cognitive dissonance theory has been widely applied to people's experience *after* a decision has been made. However, there is also research evidence for the effects of cognitive dissonance on decision making (see Box 10.13).

Box 10.13   Stellefson et al. (2006)

Aim: To investigate whether cognitive dissonance about diet and exercise behaviours will lead to the intention to change these behaviours.

Procedure: A sample of 126 college students, aged 18–23, provided information about their diet and exercise behaviours. Their risk perceptions of the negative consequences for appearance and health as a result of poor diet and inadequate exercise were assessed. They were asked to write either about why high-quality diet and exercise promote health, or how they improve physical appearance. A control group wrote about an unrelated topic. All participants then indicated whether they intended to change their diet or exercise behaviours, for the better, during the next 6 months.

Results: Those in the 'physical appearance' group were significantly more likely than controls to express an intention to change their diet and exercise behaviour. However, the results for those in the 'health' group were not significant.

Conclusion: Introducing cognitive dissonance between desired consequences and behaviour can lead to an appropriate decision.

It is interesting that health concerns were not affected in this study. However, this may be explained by the relative importance of appearance compared with health in the age group tested.

Festinger suggested that if a clear preference already exists, then dissonance must be introduced if the decision is to be influenced, for example, by providing information that makes the less-preferred option more attractive. However, when a decision has been made, even if it has not yet been expressed in behaviour, introducing cognitive dissonance may be unlikely to change the decision (see Box 10.14).

Box 10.14 Kiss et al. (2004)

Aim: To assess the effect on a medical decision of explaining the risk factors involved.

Procedure: A sample of 70 cataract patients awaiting surgery participated in the study. Around 40% had been given no information about the surgery, a quarter believed that surgery could be without risks and three quarters believed that there was no risk in their surgery. On the day before the scheduled surgery, they were given detailed information about the procedure, including the risks involved. They were then asked about their decision to have the surgery.

Results: Three quarters said that the information had not affected their decision to go ahead with the surgery, while the remainder said it had confirmed their decision.

Conclusion: Introducing dissonance does not affect a decision once it has been made.

There is quite a lot of research evidence that supports cognitive dissonance theory. However, a limitation is that attitude change can come about when no dissonance is experienced and so must be explained in other ways.

The effect of attitudes on decision making can also be explained in terms of **self-perception theory**, proposed by Bem (1967). This theory suggests that people observe their own behaviour in the same way as they observe the behaviour of others and infer their attitudes from their behaviour, just as an outside observer might do — to use one of Bem's examples, 'Since I eat brown bread, I must like brown bread'.

Bem ran his own version of the Festinger and Carlsmith experiment. Participants listened to a recording of a man enthusiastically describing a tedious peg-turning task. Some were told that the man had been paid $20 to recommend it; others were told that he was paid $1. Those in the $1 condition thought that the man must have enjoyed the task more than those in the $20 condition. Bem pointed out that the participants judged the man's attitude without needing to bring in the idea of cognitive dissonance and so the man could have explained his behaviour in the same way.

As with cognitive dissonance theory, self-perception theory has been largely applied to attitude change after a decision has been made. However, it can be used to explain how self-perception can influence decision making, in particular in the context of **self-efficacy**, i.e. a person's belief that he or she is capable of behaving in ways that will enable him or her to achieve his or her goals (see Box 10.15).

Box 10.15 Maddux and Rogers (1983)

Aim: To investigate the role of self-efficacy in decision making.

Procedure: A sample of 153 undergraduate smokers read a series of articles about the probability and seriousness of smoking-related health consequences, the effectiveness of stopping smoking in reducing the risks and how this could be achieved.

Results: Participants with high self-efficacy, who believed they were capable of following the advice in the articles, were more likely than those with lower self-efficacy to decide to stop smoking, with the expectation that they would be successful.

Conclusion: Self-perception, and in particular high self-efficacy, can influence decision making.

Similarly, Hauck et al. (2007) found that self-efficacy was related to women's decision to breastfeed their babies, and Dilorio et al. (2009) found that it was a good predictor of people with AIDS deciding to continue taking antiretroviral medication.

Cognitive dissonance theory and self-perception theory vary only in their assumptions about the processes that bring about attitude change, so assessing their relative validity is not easy. However, a study was carried out to evaluate their relative merits (see Box 10.16).

Box 10.16 Zanna and Cooper (1974)

Aim: To compare the cognitive dissonance and self-perception theories of attitude change.

Procedure: Participants were given a placebo pill. They were either told (accurately) that it would have no effect, or that it would lead to unpleasant arousal. They were then asked to write an essay, putting forward attitudes that they did not share, under conditions of either high choice (participation was voluntary and there was an opportunity to refuse) or low choice (they were asked to write the essay, with the assumption that they would comply).

According to cognitive dissonance theory, writing the essay should lead to unpleasant arousal, which would normally be attributed to expressing views contrary to those actually held in the essay. However, those who had been told that the pill they had taken would lead to unpleasant arousal should misattribute these feelings to the pill. If cognitive dissonance theory is correct,

10

positive attitude change about the views expressed in the essay would therefore be expected only in high-choice participants in the placebo condition. If self-perception theory is correct, it could occur in any condition.

Results: Participants in the high-choice placebo condition were significantly more likely to show attitude change than those in the other conditions.

Conclusion: Cognitive dissonance theory offers a better explanation of attitude change than self-perception theory.

Yet another way of explaining the relationship between attitudes and decision-making has been put forward by Tedeschi et al. (1971) in **impression management theory**. They suggested that our behaviour is aimed at making us *appear* consistent, rather than from any need to *be* consistent. For example, in the Festinger and Carlsmith study (see Box 10.12), participants could have been pretending that they thought the task was interesting, so that it would not seem that they had let themselves be bribed.

Summary

- **Cognitive dissonance theory** suggests that when attitudes and behaviours are inconsistent, we are motivated to reduce the resultant unpleasant feeling by changing our attitudes.
- While there is research evidence to support this interpretation, results can also be explained by **self-perception theory**; we infer our attitudes from our behaviour.
- There is support for self-perception theory, particularly in relation to **self-efficacy**. There is some support for cognitive dissonance providing a better explanation.
- **Impression management theory** suggests that it may be more important to *appear* consistent, rather than to *be* consistent.

Explanations for the effect of television in persuasion

In the Western world, most people have a television and may spend a large number of hours a week watching it. Psychologists have been interested in the persuasive effects of television in three areas:

- commercial advertising
- public information advertising, for example in health campaigns
- television programmes

It is these last two areas that we will be looking at in this section.

Given the emphasis on the media in Bandura's **SLT**, discussed at the start of this chapter, this theory could be used to explain the effectiveness of television in changing attitudes and behaviour. His later development of SLT as **social cognitive theory** (1986), which emphasises the active role people play in selecting what they attend to, organising observed behaviour, deciding if and when to carry it out and monitoring the outcome, is also relevant here.

The influence television programmes have may not always be intended by the makers, but some are specifically designed to influence viewers, as they can be a cost-effective way of reaching a large number of people. **Entertainment-education (E-E)** refers to such programmes, which can use a variety of formats, such as soap operas and sitcoms, either specially written for the purpose or with messages incorporated into mainstream television programmes. They are often used to provide health-related information, with suggestions as to how viewers might act to address the problems identified in the programme (see Box 10.17).

Box 10.17 Valente et al. (2007)

Aim: To assess the effectiveness of E-E in a mainstream television programme in relation to teenage obesity, hypertension and 5-a-day fruit and vegetables.

Procedure: A minor storyline was included in *ER* in 2004 over three episodes, in which an African-American male teenager presented at the emergency room with burns from a workplace injury. He was discovered to have hypertension and advised to eat more fruit and vegetables and to take more exercise. Data were collected from a sample of viewers before and after the programmes were shown.

Results: The story had a small but significant effect on self-reported behaviour change and some impact on knowledge, attitudes and practices related to the topics discussed.

Conclusion: E-E can be effective in changing attitudes and behaviour.

This study was somewhat limited in that only a relatively small sample was tested and, in particular, few African-American males; given that Bandura suggests that we are more likely to model the behaviour of someone who is similar to ourselves, there is scope for further research in this area in which the sample of participants better represents the models shown. There is also no guarantee that participants reported accurately the changes in their behaviour. However, other studies have shown similar effects. For example, Kennedy et al. (2004) found there was a dramatic surge in calls to an information hotline after a storyline in a soap opera about HIV infection and its prevention. Specially written stories can also be effective (see Box 10.18).

Box 10.18 Moyer-Guse (2008)

Aim: To compare the effectiveness of E-E in specially produced television programmes with education and entertainment alone.

Procedure: A sample of 437 undergraduates watched one of three versions of a story about unplanned teenage pregnancy:
- an E-E programme with a negative outcome
- an educational program about the same topic
- an entertainment drama about a teenage pregnancy with a positive outcome

Safe-sex attitudes, intentions and behaviours were measured 2 days before and then immediately following the programme, and also 2 weeks later.

10

Results: The first two versions increased positive attitudes toward safe sex, but only in the short term. The E-E version was the most effective in changing behaviour.

Conclusion: E-E can be effective in changing behaviour.

E-E programmes can also be effective in changing attitudes and behaviour towards minorities. For example, Strong (2008) discussed the effect of a children's television series in Nepal, designed specifically to influence attitudes and actions toward people with disabilities. The series was successful in its aim, with the children's ability to relate to the characters being identified as a key issue in its success, in line with SLT.

However, theories other than SLT may be relevant in explaining the effectiveness of television in persuasion. Skumanich and Kintsfather (1996) found that students' response to an organ donor card appeal was related to values, empathy and their involvement with the issue, and suggested that the **ELM**, discussed earlier, might be used to explain these findings. They found that involvement with the issue directly influenced attitudes. Personal involvement is one of the factors that make it more likely that central processing will be used; Petty and Cacioppo found that this was a better predictor of behaviour than peripheral processing. The empathy the students experienced would also motivate them to carry out central processing.

Factors other than those identified in SLT and ELM also play a part in the success of television in changing attitudes and behaviour. For example, Goldstein (1993) carried out a review of the role of **humour** in children's educational television programmes and concluded that one of the reasons humour is effective is because it can increase attention and interest and so allow more information to be absorbed.

Summary

- **SLT** and **social cognitive theory** have been used to explain the effectiveness of television in persuasion.
- **Entertainment-education (E-E)** programmes have been used successfully to influence viewers, particularly in the area of **health education**.
- The **Elaboration Likelihood Model** can also be used to explain the effectiveness of television.
- **Humour** can increase attention and so make E-E programmes more effective.

The psychology of celebrity

Increasingly, we live in a celebrity-oriented culture. The term 'celebrities' refers to people who are well known in some way, for example sportspeople, rock musicians, film actors, models, people who have appeared on reality television programmes and in some cases people who are famous just for being famous. They are the mainstay of magazines such as *Hello!* and are widely used in advertisements, in the expectation that their endorsement will help to sell products and services.

The attraction of celebrity

For some people, celebrities or one particular celebrity can play an important part in their lives. The relationship between celebrity and fan is known as a **parasocial relationship**, i.e. one in which one person knows a lot about the other, but the other does not. For a few people, the relationship may be intense, to the point of obsession. McCutcheon et al. (2002) developed the **Celebrity Attitude Scale (CAS)**, on the basis of which three distinct dimensions of fandom have emerged, which vary in terms of the parasocial interaction between fans and celebrities and the purpose they serve:

Dimensions of fandom (McCutcheon et al. 2005)

Entertainment-social: fans are attracted to a celebrity because they find him or her entertaining and a source of social interaction and gossip.

Intense-personal: there is a strongly personal aspect of attraction to a celebrity; a person may feel something bad happening to a celebrity as though he or she were experiencing it personally.

Borderline-pathological: this is characterised by obessional behaviour and fantasies about the celebrities; people may imagine that they have a special relationship with the celebrity.

Giles (2000) explains 'celebrity' and the widespread nature of celebrity worship in modern societies as direct products of the mass media. Films, radio, television, magazines and the internet have filled our sensory worlds with faces, voices, bodies and personal histories that bring us into contact with people outside our social circle in a way that would earlier not have been possible.

Several theories have been put forward to explain this kind of parasocial relationship. One basic evolutionary explanation suggests that in our evolutionary past, it would have been highly adaptive to form relationships with people with whom we feel safe, rather than with people who make us feel anxious or in danger. We may have positive feelings towards actors in particular because of the characters they play on screen. For example, Tom Hanks invariably plays a sympathetic character, for example an AIDS victim in *Philadelphia* and a plane-crash survivor in *Cast Away*. We may unconsciously confuse the screen persona and the actor.

Parasocial relationships between a celebrity and a fan can become dangerously obsessive

TopFoto

Kanasawa (2002) takes this further, pointing out that when the human brain evolved around 100,000 years ago, the only realistic images of people we saw were of a limited number of other real people. There is no brain module to recognise that we have a different relationship, or no relationship, with people whom we now come across in the media. Our brain has not adapted to this new environment and responds as though the celebrities we come across in the media are trusted friends. There is support for Kanasawa's theory, from his research showing that people who watch a lot of television report having a wider circle of friends than they actually have. They also report being happier than others who do not have parasocial relationships with television actors. People become happier when they see their friends more often and the same thing happens with watching television.

Research into fandom

The different dimensions of fandom have also been explained in terms of **personality**, and in particular **Eysenck's personality theory**. This theory describes personality in terms of three dimensions:

- extraversion-introversion
- neuroticism-stability
- psychoticism

Maltby et al. (2003) found a positive correlation between:

- the entertainment-social factor of the CAS and aspects of extraversion (sociable, lively, active, venturesome)
- the intense-personal factor and neuroticism traits (tense, emotional, moody)
- (to a limited degree) borderline-pathological and psychoticism (impulsive, anti-social, egocentric)

In a later study, Maltby et al. (2006) found that celebrity worship for intense-personal reasons was significantly correlated with fantasy proneness, and for borderline-pathological reasons was significantly correlated with both fantasy proneness and dissociation, i.e. a loss of the sense of self. Evans and Claycomb (1999) found that dissociation can lead to episodes of violence, and this might explain why some fanatical celebrity worshippers become dangerous in relation to a particular celebrity. Celebrity worship has also been explained in **cognitive** terms (see Box 10.19).

Box 10.19　McCutcheon et al. (2003)

Aim: To examine the relationship between celebrity worship and cognitive measures.

Procedure: A sample of participants completed the CAS and were also assessed on measures of cognitive ability:

- verbal creativity
- crystallised intelligence (the kind of intelligence based on knowledge and skills gained through experience)
- critical thinking

- spatial ability
- need for cognition (the extent to which people enjoy the challenge posed by intellectual problems)

The scores on the CAS and the cognitive measures were compared.

Results: There were consistently high negative correlations between scores on the CAS and scores on the tests measuring cognitive ability, with the exception of the creativity scores, which showed a small but significant positive correlation with scores on the borderline-pathological subscales of the CAS.

Conclusion: Celebrity worship is associated with poor cognitive functioning.

McCutcheon et al. (2002) proposed the **absorption-addiction model** to explain this relationship. According to this model, individuals may have a poor sense of their own identity, which brings about psychological absorption with a celebrity to try to establish an identity and achieve a sense of fulfillment. This could in turn become addictive, leading to more extreme behaviours such as seeking contact or stalking to raise the individual's satisfaction with the parasocial relationship. Other studies, for example Maltby et al. (2004), have offered support to these ideas, suggesting that individuals who engage in celebrity worship for intense, personal reasons have difficulty in dealing with novel or unusual situations.

Parasocial relationships are more common in adolescence than later in life, so celebrity worship has also been related to **attachment**. Giles and Maltby (2004) suggested that celebrity attachments reflect the transition at adolescence from attachment to parents to attachment to peers, as a part of the process of attaining emotional autonomy. They found that high emotional autonomy was a significant predictor of celebrity worship and that entertainment-social aspects were related to high attachment to peers and low attachment to parents. The main function of celebrity attachments in adolescence may therefore serve an emotional-social end as part of an extended social network — a group of 'pseudo-friends' who form the subject of peer gossip and discussion. The more intense dimensions of celebrity worship may then arise from difficulty in making the attachment transition from parents to friends.

There is also good evidence that attachment in early childhood is a good predictor of later adult relationships. For example, Hazan and Shaver (1987) found that people who recalled having secure attachments with their parents tended to form secure attachments with their adult partners; those who recalled their parents as inconsistent or rejecting were less likely to be securely attached to their adult partners. If insecurely attached children are more likely to have relationship difficulties as adults, they might be tempted to form parasocial relationships, as this does not involve a real relationship with a celebrity; there is no risk of criticism or rejection unless the person seeks contact with the celebrity.

As we saw earlier, there are three stages in attraction to a celebrity; in many, if not most cases, this does not go beyond admiration for celebrities because of their

10

social or entertainment value. However, it may develop to include a firm belief by the person that he or she has a real relationship with the celebrity and that they are destined to be together.

Active attempts may be made to contact the celebrity, leading to **stalking**. The term 'stalking' came into use in the late 1980s and is defined as persistent attempts to impose on another person unwanted contact or communications, for example by phone or letter. This may also involve following and surveillance. Stalking behaviours include sending unsolicited gifts and ordering or cancelling services on the victim's behalf. It may also involve threats, which can lead to violence. Stalking is a criminal offence. While there has been a lot of publicity about people who have stalked celebrities and harmed them, Logan et al. (2000) report that celebrity worshippers are more likely to harm people with whom they have a real rather than a parasocial relationship. The effects of stalking on victims can be extremely serious (see Box 10.20).

Box 10.20 **Pathe and Mullen (1997)**

Aim: To investigate the effects of stalking on victims.

Procedure: A hundred victims who had been stalked for periods of between 1 month and 20 years completed a 50-item questionnaire to assess its psychological impact, its effects on their social functioning and the risk of assault.

Results: Most had experienced a variety of forms of harassment. Over half had received threats and a third had been assaulted. Half had changed their jobs and 39 had moved home. A third of the victims met the criteria for a diagnosis of post-traumatic stress disorder (PTSD), with most participants experiencing symptoms that included anxiety, flashbacks, nightmares, sleep disturbance, depression and thoughts of suicide.

Conclusion: Being the victim of a stalker has extremely serious psychological and social effects.

Stalkers appear to be obsessed with thoughts about their victims and often engage in behaviours designed to attract their attention. It seems reasonable to suppose that stalkers of celebrities would be people who score high on the borderline-pathological subscales of the CAS and that high scorers on this subscale would be more likely than low scorers to hold pro-stalking attitudes. This was confirmed in a study of 299 college students, carried out by McCutcheon et al. (2006). They also related stalking to **attachment**, finding that people who were insecurely attached as children were more likely than those who had been securely attached to condone behaviours associated with celebrity stalking.

Kienlen (1998) suggested that the motivation of people who stalk celebrities may vary in terms of their type of insecure attachment. Those who are anxious/ambivalent tend to have a weak sense of self-worth and are anxious about social rejection. This suggests they would be motivated to seek the approval of the person they are stalking. Those who are anxious-avoidant try to maintain an emotional distance from others and so might be expected to stalk a celebrity as a form of retaliation against a perceived wrongdoing. Roberts (2007) found a significant positive relationship between scores on a scale measuring the frequency of self-reported attempts to contact a favourite celebrity and anxious/ambivalent insecurity. However, there was a small negative relationship with anxious-avoidant insecurity.

Stokes et al. (2007) also report that stalking is more common in people with **autistic spectrum disorder (ASD)**. People with this disorder have difficulty in forming social relationships with others, and so may be more likely to form the kind of parasocial relationship with a celebrity that could lead to stalking.

While stalking is punishable by law, it is also pathological, raising questions about how it should be treated. Mullen et al. (2000) report that for some stalkers, the reality of fines and imprisonment may be enough to stop the behaviour, but for most, therapy should be attempted to try to address the underlying issues, for example, helping stalkers to develop appropriate social skills and to deal with the underlying depression

John Lennon (top) was murdered in 1980 by obsessed fan, Mark Chapman

and substance abuse that are sometimes associated with it. Delgado (2005) reports that the **Child and Adolescent Stalker Prevention Program (CASPP)** can be useful in helping young people. This uses cognitive behavioural and psychodynamic techniques to try to bring about appropriate development of interpersonal relationships and prevent future stalking behaviours.

Summary

- The relationship between fan and celebrity is **parasocial**. Being a fan can serve a **social** purpose, but in some cases can lead to **pathological** behaviour.
- **Evolutionary psychologists** suggest that our brains have not caught up with widespread coverage of celebrities in the **media**, so we respond to them as people we know.
- Different dimensions of fandom can be related to **personality** differences. It can also be explained in **cognitive** terms, as in the **absorption-addiction model**, and has also been linked to **attachment theory**.
- In extreme cases, fandom can lead to **stalking**, which has serious **social and psychological effects** on victims. This has also been explained in terms of **attachment theory** and is more common in people with **ASD**.
- Programmes are being developed as **therapy** for stalkers.

The psychology of addictive behaviour

In this chapter, we will be looking at:
- models of addictive behaviour
  - biological models
  - cognitive and learning models
  - explanations for smoking and gambling
- factors affecting addictive behaviour
  - vulnerability to addiction
  - the role of the media
- reducing addictive behaviour
  - models of prevention
  - types of intervention

Models of addictive behaviour

Traditionally, the concept of addiction was only applied to substance abuse, such as addiction to alcohol, nicotine or heroin. Addiction in this context refers to a state in which the body relies on a substance for normal functioning. The addict develops a strong craving for and a physical dependence on the substance, so that deprivation causes a characteristic set of withdrawal symptoms. However, the concept has now been extended to cover other forms of compulsive behaviour, for example addiction to gambling, sex or shopping.

We will look in this first section at some of the models, both biological and psychological, which have set out to explain the initiation and maintenance of addictive behaviours. Initiation and maintenance need to be looked at separately, since many people experiment with different kinds of drugs or use them occasionally, but only for some will this initial use become an addiction. These models also look at reasons for relapse once an addiction has apparently been successfully overcome. We will then look in more detail at the specific addictions of smoking and gambling.

Biological models

In a study of 1,214 twin pairs, Fowler et al. (2007) found that for alcohol, nicotine and cannabis, environmental influences were more important for initiation than genetic factors, while genetic influences played a greater role in progression to heavier use and addiction. Similarly, in a large-scale longitudinal twin study, Rose and Dick (2004–05) found that initial alcohol use was primarily the result of environmental influences, while the development to habitual use was mostly influenced by genetic factors. We will therefore focus in particular on the role of biological factors in habitual use.

The move from initial use to drug dependency can be explained in terms of a drug's physiological effects. Substance addiction is the result of changes in the structure and function of parts of the brain, which is one of the reasons why it is difficult to stop taking drugs and why later relapse can happen even when a person has apparently succeeded in doing so. Drugs are chemicals that can disrupt the way nerve cells send, receive and process information. One way they do this is by imitating the brain's neurotransmitters. Marijuana and heroin are similar in structure to the neurotransmitters that are naturally produced by the brain. As a result, they can fool the brain's receptors and activate nerve cells to send abnormal messages. Cocaine can cause the nerve cells to release abnormally large amounts of natural neurotransmitters, or prevent the normal recycling of them, which terminates the signal between neurons. This produces a greatly amplified message that disrupts normal communication patterns.

The chemicals in marijuana cause abnormal brain messages

The rewarding effects of substances such as alcohol, cocaine and heroin are strongly linked with the **mesolimbic system**, the 'reward circuit' of the brain, which is the central part of the limbic system involved with emotion, pleasure and memory. The neurotransmitter **dopamine** plays an important part within this system. Nearly all drugs overstimulate the brain, by flooding it with dopamine, a neurotransmitter associated with, among other things, feelings of pleasure. The overstimulation of the dopaminergic system creates feelings of euphoria in response to the drug, which motivates people to take it again.

However, with continued drug use, the brain adapts to the surges in dopamine by producing less of it, or by reducing the number of dopamine receptors in the reward circuit. Dopamine therefore now has less impact on the reward circuit and so reduces a person's ability to experience pleasure. In response, he or she must keep taking the drug in an attempt to bring his or her dopamine function back to normal. To do this, he or she needs more of the drug than at first to achieve the dopamine high, an effect known as **tolerance**, a characteristic of addiction.

One suggestion has been that there is a **genetic basis** for the likelihood of an individual developing an addiction, with studies in this area attempting to assess the relative contribution of genes and environmental factors. These include family, twin and adoption studies, on the basis that if the main underlying cause of addiction is genetic, people who are more similar genetically would be more likely to share a particular disorder, i.e. show a high **concordance** for it.

In a family study, Sarafino (1990) found that alcohol addiction was four times as likely in children with an alcoholic parent, and that this was the case even when children had been adopted. Agrawal and Lynskey (2008) carried out a survey of studies of the heritability of addiction to alcohol, nicotine, cannabis and other drugs that had used these methods, and in particular those comparing MZ and DZ twins.

Janine Wiedel Photolibrary/Alamy

Alcohol addiction is more likely in children with an alcoholic parent

They concluded that there was a moderate to high genetic influence in addiction, with concordance estimates ranging from 0.30 to 0.70. However, they also pointed out that gender, age and cultural characteristics must be taken into account and emphasised the importance of the interaction between genes and the environment in relation to the risk of addiction.

Some studies have also attempted to identify the genes responsible for the heritable component of addiction. For example, in a large study of over 2,000 families, Agrawal et al. (2008) found evidence of a link between chromosomes 18 and 19 and cannabis use. In a review of studies on alcohol addiction, Higuchi et al. (2006) reported that animal studies have shown that the Mpdz gene predisposes to alcohol dependence. This finding must be treated with caution, as it is unwise to extrapolate directly from non-human animals to humans. However, the review also reported that two gene complexes, ADH and ALDH2, have been identified as predisposing to alcohol addiction in humans. According to Devaux and Krebs (2004), research has suggested that heroin dependence may be the most genetically influenced addiction and is probably influenced by a number of genes that make an individual vulnerable. More detailed information about specific genes relating to all these kinds of substance addiction is likely to emerge from ongoing research in this area.

Along with emotions, the **limbic system** — of which the mesolimbic system is a part — is involved with many aspects of cognitive functioning, in particular the ability to learn, linking thought and action and memory. Drug use can cause changes in the functioning of the neurotransmitter **glutamate**, which influences the reward circuit. When this is altered by drug use, cognitive functioning can be impaired. We will look next at a theoretical explanation for addiction, which focuses in particular on cognition.

Summary

- Environmental factors have more influence on **initiation** than **maintenance** of substance abuse.
- Drugs alter the **structure** and **function** of parts of the brain.
- The neurotransmitter **dopamine** plays an important part in addiction.
- There is some evidence for a **genetic** component in addiction, although the contribution of genes varies with different substances. Research has identified some of the genes involved.

Cognitive and learning models

In contrast to biological models, Beck et al. (1993) explain addiction and relapse in terms of dysfunctional thinking, rather than the result of physical characteristics. A person's underlying beliefs shape the physiological sensations linked to craving and drug use:

Figure 11.1 *Addiction as dysfunctional thinking (Beck et al. 1990)*

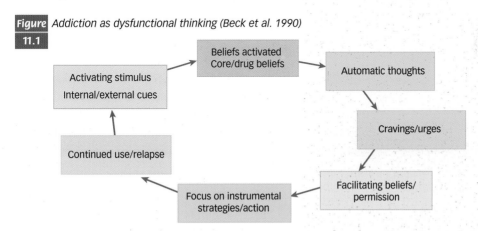

Beliefs and desires are typically activated in specific and often predictable circumstances, which provide cues that are either external (such as being with people who are using cocaine) or internal (such as feeling bored or depressed). This leads to the activation of core beliefs (for example, 'I am a powerless person') and beliefs about drugs (for example, 'I feel better about myself when I take cocaine'). These in turn lead to associated automatic thoughts ('I will get some cocaine') and then to craving for the drug. This craving activates facilitating/permissive beliefs about drug use ('A lot of people use it, so why not me?'), leading to strategies for getting the drug and its use. At this point, drug use itself can trigger other drug-related beliefs (for example, 'Since I have taken cocaine, I might as well go on with it'), resulting in a vicious cycle. Beck proposes that there are three major categories of dysfunctional beliefs associated with substance abuse:

Categories of dysfunctional beliefs (Beck et al. 1990)

- Anticipatory beliefs: expectations of drug use, for example 'I feel good when I take drugs'.
- Relief-oriented beliefs: assumptions that taking drugs will change an uncomfortable state, for example 'The craving will not go away unless I take the drug'.
- Facilitative or permissive beliefs: considering drug use acceptable in spite of potential consequences, for example 'There is nothing wrong with taking risks'.

Tison and Hautekeete (1998) developed a questionnaire to assess the categories of dysfunctional thinking that Beck suggested and found it differentiated well between drug users and controls, offering some support to Beck's theory. Similarly, Chabrol et al. (2001) found that the questionnaire successfully discriminated between cannabis users and non-users, and those who were dependent on the drug and those who were not. There was a correlation between the strength of dysfunctional beliefs and the frequency of cannabis use. In a further study, Chabrol et al. (2004) found that permissive beliefs were the main predictor for cannabis use and only relief-oriented beliefs predicted cannabis dependence. There is additional research support for the role of cognition in alcohol addiction (see Box 11.1).

Box 11.1   Marlatt et al. (1973)

Aim: To investigate beliefs about the alcohol content of drinks on drinking behaviour.

Procedure: Participants were 64 males, aged 23–65, half of whom were alcoholics and half social drinkers. They were given a series of either alcoholic drinks (vodka and tonic) or non-alcoholic drinks (tonic water) and were asked to rate them for taste in a number of ways, for example strength and bitterness. Some in each group were told that the drinks to be rated contained alcohol, while others were told they did not. They were told they could sample as much of each drink as they liked in order to make their ratings. The amount each group drank was measured.

Results: Regardless of whether they were alcoholics or social drinkers, participants drank 9 ounces if they had been told the drinks were non-alcoholic and almost double that if they were told the drinks were alcoholic.

Conclusion: The amount drunk was determined by participants' beliefs about what they were drinking. As this was true of both alcoholics and social drinkers, it challenges the claim that the effects of alcohol alone are responsible for increases in an alcoholic's drinking behaviour.

This study offers support for Beck's theory, in that it highlights the influence of cognitive as well as physiological factors in addictive behaviour. Further support comes from the effectiveness of the therapy that is based on it, and we will be looking at this towards the end of the chapter.

Other theories have linked addiction to learning. **Conditioning theory** suggests that addiction is the result of **reinforcement**; addiction comes about because of the reinforcing power of the pleasure associated with it. It follows that anyone can become addicted given appropriate reinforcement, regardless of whether or not they have a genetic predisposition to develop an addiction. One advantage of this theory is that it allows us to consider all compulsive activities, along with drug abuse, within a single framework. In relation to drugs, this theory can explain addiction in two ways. The first is that the drug provides a biological reward, in that it prevents the pain of withdrawal, while the second is that the drugs create a high degree of pleasure. These mechanisms could act independently or together, but in either case, the primary motivation is the reinforcement of the behaviour.

Wikler (1948) was one of the first psychologists interested in this kind of explanation, and in particular reasons for relapse after treatment, with his interest originally sparked by reports from relapsed heroin addicts. They claimed that although they normally had no symptoms after treatment, they experienced withdrawal symptoms and craving when they returned to the environments where they had previously used drugs and that these feelings were responsible for their relapse. Wikler proposed that events that reliably signal drug self-administration or drug withdrawal elicit the conditioned responses of withdrawal and craving. This motivates further drug use, which acts as negative reinforcement, as it eliminates the negative withdrawal symptoms and so creates a vicious spiral. This account therefore uses ideas from both classical and operant conditioning.

Shiffman (1996) tested the importance of environmental cues by asking smokers who had just quit smoking to record on a palmtop the situations in which they lapsed to smoking. Almost all lapses occurred in situations in which cigarettes were readily available, smoking was allowed and in the presence of other smokers. This suggests that situational cues for drug availability/acceptability can play a critical role in maintaining drug use in addicts who would otherwise quit. This kind of explanation could account for the findings of Robins et al. (1974), who found that of American soldiers who had become addicted to illicit drugs while fighting in Vietnam, those who most often relapsed were those who had abused drugs or narcotics before going away to fight; they were returning to a familiar drug-taking environment.

However, a number of studies have failed to support the role of environmental cues. For example, McAuliffe and Gordon (1974) interviewed 60 relapsed addicts; in only one case could relapse be linked to a response to conditioned withdrawal symptoms. Marlatt and Gordon (1980) found that in the interviews they carried out, none of the cigarette smokers or alcoholics and few heroin addicts reported withdrawal symptoms to be the reason they relapsed.

It is also possible to explain both the initiation and maintenance of addiction in terms of **social learning theory (SLT)**, put forward by Bandura in the 1960s, which proposes that we learn to produce certain behaviours through **observational learning** and **modelling**; we observe the behaviour of others and its consequences, and if these are perceived as positive, we may model the behaviour. Sources of models include the family and subculture, for example peers, and the media. There is a **cognitive** element in observational learning and modelling. A person does not simply model behaviour that he or she has seen reinforced, but processes this information in terms of whether the behaviour is appropriate for him or her and in what circumstances. In support of SLT, Durkin et al. (2005) found that in a sample of 1,500 college students, by far the best predictor of binge drinking was the drinking behaviour of an individual's peer group. However, this is correlational evidence and could be explained in terms of choosing friends on the basis of them having the same ideas about how best to spend an evening.

Marlatt and Gordon (1985) emphasised the cognitive aspect of SLT in their development of a **cognitive social learning theory (CSLT)**, relevant particularly to relapse in addicts. In a given 'high-risk situation', for example where an abstinent drinker is faced with the choice of drinking or not drinking, the likelihood of relapse will depend on his or her expectations. This falls into two groups: **efficacy expectations** refer to a person's confidence that he or she will be able to resist the temptation to drink. **Outcome expectations** are the person's beliefs about the consequences of drinking or not drinking. For example, a positive outcome expectancy could be the belief that alcohol would lead to pleasure and a negative expectancy could be that it would lead to a hangover. Whether or not a person drinks will depend on an interaction between these factors. For example, with positive outcome expectations and low self-efficacy, relapse is more likely. A study of relapse among problematic gamblers, carried out by Holub (2005), found support for these proposals.

Summary

- The **cognitive** approach sees addiction as the result of **dysfunctional thinking**.
- There is research support for the three kinds of inappropriate beliefs identified by **Beck** and the role of beliefs in addiction.
- Addiction has also been explained in terms of **conditioning** and **reinforcement**, although research into reasons for **relapse** has challenged the role of conditioning.
- **SLT** suggests that addiction develops through **observational learning** and **modelling**. CSLT developed from this suggests that relapse results from **positive expectations** of an addictive behaviour and low **self-efficacy**.

Explanations for smoking and gambling

Smoking

Most people who have ever smoked start smoking during their adolescent years. Research has shown that the younger people are when they begin smoking, the more likely they are to become regular smokers and the less likely they are to quit.

As we saw earlier, it has been suggested that starting to smoke is more influenced by environmental than genetic factors, and there is considerable research evidence to support this idea.

The environment in which a young person is growing up has been found to be associated with starting to smoke. For example, McCaffery et al. (2008) found that smoking initiation was strongly associated with low socioeconomic status and poor education, a finding replicated in an Indian sample of young people carried out by Mathur et al. (2008) and in an Estonian sample by Leinsalu et al. (2008). Bush (2008) found that young people who lived in poor and dangerous urban areas, whose residents were of low socioeconomic status, were more likely to start smoking than those in better neighbourhoods. However, these studies only show an association between environmental factors and not the precise triggers that lead young people to start smoking.

SLT, mentioned earlier, suggests that we observe the behaviour of others and may model that behaviour. Sources of models include the family and subculture, and there is quite a lot of research that has demonstrated these influences on smoking initiation (see Box 11.2).

Box 11.2	Harakeh et al. (2007)

Aim: To investigate the influence of peers and siblings on smoking initiation.

Procedure: Data on 428 families with two adolescent children between the ages of 13 and 17 years were analysed. This information was taken from a previous large-scale study that had collected information on a variety of health issues over a period of time.

Results: Non-smoking adolescents with older siblings who smoked and those with a smoking best friend were more likely to have started to smoke 1 year later. However, older adolescents were not affected by smoking by their younger siblings.

Conclusion: Friends and older siblings influence the initiation of smoking in adolescents.

In a qualitative study, Milton et al. (2008) found that young smokers identified peer influence as an important factor in smoking initiation. On the basis of interviews carried out with young smokers, Gilbert (2007) found that fear of rejection by their peer group was one motivation to start smoking. However, Arnett (2007) suggests that a direct link between peer influence and smoking initiation is an oversimplification and proposes that an individual's personal characteristics influence their choice of friends, who then provide a peer context that may or may not encourage smoking. There is also evidence that parents and step-parents can act as models in smoking initiation (see Box 11.3).

Box 11.3	Fidler et al. (2008)

Aim: To investigate the extent to which smoking by step-parents and biological parents predicts adolescent smoking.

Procedure: In a 5-year study, 650 students were assessed annually between ages 11–12 and 15–16. They reported whether or not they smoked, whether their parents smoked and, if they lived with a step-parent, whether that step-parent smoked.

Results: Students who reported at 11–12 that just their step-parent smoked were significantly more likely to report current smoking at some time in the study than those who reported having neither biological parents nor a step-parent who smoked. The same was true of those with both a parent and a step-parent who smoked. Students with a parent who smoked were neither more nor less likely to smoke than those with just a step-parent who smoked.

Conclusion: Smoking by a non-biological parent appears at least as influential as smoking by biological parents. There is a strong social influence on smoking initiation.

However, there is also evidence of a genetic component in smoking once it has been initiated. For example, Li et al. (2003) report that heritability for nicotine addiction is high, ranging from 39–80%. As with some of the other addictions discussed earlier, Goldman et al. (2005) have shown that genes that affect drug metabolism and the dopaminergic system are likely to be involved in nicotine addiction. However, Hall et al. (2008) claim that research to date has not managed to identify commonly occurring alleles, i.e. alternative forms of genes, that contribute to addiction susceptibility and are strong predictors of developing nicotine addiction. They suggest that nicotine addiction is likely to involve multiple alleles, each having a small effect, which interact with each other and with environmental factors. However, the idea that adverse environmental factors interact with genetic factors to increase the likelihood of nicotine addiction has not always been supported (see Box 11.4).

Box 11.4   Kendler et al. (2004)

Aim: To investigate the effect of an interaction between genetic risk factors for nicotine addiction and family conflict.

Procedure: The number of cigarettes smoked over their lifetime was calculated for a sample of 1,676 twins, consisting of both MZ and DZ female pairs. Their degree of family dysfunction, based on interviews with the participants, their co-twins and their parents, was also assessed.

Results: With increasing levels of family dysfunction, levels of cigarette smoking increased substantially. However, correlations for cigarette smoking in both MZ and DZ twins showed a slight decrease. The results indicated high levels of heritability for cigarette smoking and no evidence for a role of shared environment. With increasing levels of family dysfunction, the influence of genetic factors decreased.

Conclusion: The findings do not support the idea that adverse environments interact with genetic factors to increase the likelihood of addiction.

As we saw in the previous section, Shiffman (1996) found that relapses after stopping smoking occurred most frequently in situations in which smoking was allowed and when other people were smoking. In a study of women who had stopped smoking while pregnant, but had started again after their babies were born, Letourneau et al. (2007) found that the main reasons given were being around others who smoked, but also in response to the stress they experienced as new mothers. We will be looking at the role of stress in addiction in the next section.

Summary

- **Smoking initiation** has been associated with low socioeconomic status and poor education.
- There is evidence that it may be influenced by **peers, older siblings** and **parents**.
- Progression to **habitual smoking** appears to be influenced by genes. The idea that it is brought about by the interaction of genes and the environment has not always been supported.
- Environmental factors and stress influence **relapse**.

Gambling

Problem gambling usually begins in early adolescence in males and at a somewhat later age for females. Griffiths and Wood (2000) report that adolescents appear to be more susceptible to developing pathological gambling, and that this is often related to activities such as alcohol abuse and drug taking. Rush et al. (2008) also found that problem gambling in this age group was often associated with substance abuse. Griffiths and Wood highlight the availability of internet gambling, suggesting that the technology involved may be particularly appealing to young people.

Pathological gambling does not involve substance abuse, and there has been some discussion as to whether it should be classed as an addiction. However, there is evidence to suggest that it should be seen in the same light as addiction to nicotine or alcohol. For example, as in substance addiction, Rosenthal and Lesieur (1992) found that at least 65% of pathological gamblers reported at least one physical side effect during withdrawal. Indeed, they found that people experienced more physical withdrawal effects when attempting to stop gambling than people who were substance dependent.

Another parallel is that there is some evidence that the **dopamine** system is involved. There have been several case studies of patients with Parkinson's disease, a disorder characterised by low levels of dopamine that is treated by drugs such as L-dopa, which are used to raise available dopamine levels. For example, Gschwandtner et al. (2001) report a case study of two Parkinson's patients who had become addicted to the drugs used to treat this disorder, both of whom developed pathological gambling. However, when the drugs were reduced, the gambling stopped within a few months. This suggests that the gambling developed as a result of the over-stimulation of dopamine receptors in the mesolimbic areas of the brain as a result of addiction to dopaminergic drugs, affecting the reward circuit and resulting in behavioural disturbances, in these cases gambling. Evidence from a study carried out by Marazziti et al. (2008) suggested that the serotonergic neurotransmitter system may also be involved.

Cognitive explanations have been put forward to explain why some people progress from social gambling to problem gambling. In an overview of research into cognitive factors associated with problem gambling, Jacobsen et al. (2007) found that problem

Psychopathology, psychology in action and research methods

gamblers typically have irrational beliefs, for example that they are able to influence or predict the outcome of a chance event. This kind of factor appears to be particularly important in the move from social to problem gambling. As we saw earlier, addiction has also been explained in terms of **cue reactivity**, i.e. responsiveness to cues in the environment; this has been shown to play a role in gambling addiction. For example, Kushner et al. (2008) found that problem gamblers experienced a stronger urge to gamble in a simulated casino environment than a neutral environment, particularly if they had gambled there before. Cues may also be relevant to relapse. Gruesser et al. (2005) found that pathological gamblers still had a physical response to cues even after abstinence for more than a year.

Explanations have also been offered in terms of **life experiences**, both gambling-related and more generally. On the basis of a series of questionnaires, Turner et al. (2006) found that compared to controls, pathological gamblers were more likely to have had big wins early in their gambling career, to have experienced stressful life events and depression, and to use gambling as an escape to cope with problems. They also found that problem gamblers were more impulsive, and we will be looking at **individual differences** in the next section.

Conditioning theory suggests that **reinforcement** plays a major role in gambling. In studies of operant conditioning, it has been found that the best way to establish a behaviour is through continuous reinforcement, i.e. reinforcing a correct response every time it occurs. However, once a behaviour is well established, **variable ratio reinforcement** is the most effective schedule to maintain it, where reinforcement varies on average around a pre-set number of correct responses. This is the basis on which slot machines are set up, creating the belief that as a win has not happened for a while, one is about due and could come at any time, encouraging the person to continue gambling.

Parke and Griffiths (2004) point out that apart from the reinforcement of winning money, a number of other reinforcements may be involved: the 'buzz' of gambling, the arousal created by the flashing lights of a slot machine, the excitement generated by pre-race betting and the company of like-minded people. They also suggest that gamblers experiencing 'near misses' may find them reinforcing and take them as encouraging signs for future success.

As with any other addiction, many people who have given up gambling may relapse. Grant et al. (2004) found that of those who relapsed, over 40% said they did so because they missed the thrill of gambling, supporting the idea of reinforcement as an important factor. Over 20% said they felt certain they could win and relieve their financial problems, suggesting that cognitive factors also play a role in relapse.

Summary

- There is evidence that pathological gambling is similar to substance addiction. There are **withdrawal effects** and the **dopamine** system is involved.
- **Cognitive factors**, such as **cue reactivity** and **life experiences**, play a part.
- **Reinforcement** appears to be important both in the **maintenance** of addiction to gambling and in **relapse**.

Factors affecting addictive behaviour

We have already seen some of the factors that are associated with developing an addiction, for example low socioeconomic status, the influence of family and friends, and the role of inappropriate thinking and conditioning. In this section, we will look at some of the other factors associated with addiction, and the role of the media.

Vulnerability to addiction

There is some evidence that addiction is linked with **low self-esteem**. In a large-scale study of teenagers, Veselska et al. (2009) found that cigarette smoking and cannabis use was related with low self-esteem, but only in boys. However, this study was correlational, so it cannot tell us whether low self-esteem is likely to lead to drug abuse, or whether drug abuse leads to low self-esteem, or whether both are caused by a third factor. However, there is evidence that low self-esteem leads to drug abuse (see Box 11.5).

Box 11.5 **Kaufman and Augustson (2008)**

Aim: To investigate factors that predispose girls to smoking behaviour.

Procedure: Participants were nearly 7,000 girls aged 13–18. They were assessed on their perceived weight, whether they were trying to lose weight, self-esteem and their smoking behaviour.

Results: The measures relating to weight significantly predicted regular smoking 1 year later. Smoking was also significantly predicted by low self-esteem.

Conclusion: In girls, low self-esteem, associated with dissatisfaction with body weight, predicts regular cigarette smoking.

The connection between body weight and smoking is supported by Bean et al. (2008), who found that the idea that smoking aids weight loss, and that stopping smoking would lead to weight gain, was widely held by teenage girls.

Kassel et al. (2007) have also produced evidence that adult **attachment type** might influence drug use indirectly through causing low self-esteem, in particular in those who were anxious-avoidant. However, Trucco et al. (2007) found that self-esteem was not a significant factor in relapse. Randarajan et al. (2006) found that within families, alcohol abuse in parents predicted low self-esteem in children, so it could be that the explanation of the vulnerability to addiction running in families could be not only genetic but also indirectly caused by the psychological effects on children of parents' addiction.

Attribution theory has also been used to explain differences between those who become addicted and those who do not. According to Heider (1944), we have a strong need to make sense of our social world and so look for the causes of our own and others' behaviour. One distinction we make is between an external locus of

11

control (a **situational attribution** — i.e. the attribution of behaviour being caused by circumstances over which the individual has no control) and an internal locus of control (a **dispositional attribution** — i.e. the belief that a person could control his or her behaviour). Differences are likely when we are attributing causes to others' behaviour and to our own; this is known as the **actor-observer effect**. We are more likely to make dispositional attributions about others' behaviour but situational attributions about our own behaviour. This idea may be relevant to addiction (see Box 11.6).

Box 11.6	**Seneviratne and Saunders (2000)**

Aim: To investigate the attributions made by people addicted to alcohol about their own relapses and those of others.

Procedure: Seventy alcoholics were asked to give reasons for their own relapses from abstinence and in relation to a set of four relapse scenarios of other people. The causes ascribed for their own relapse and those of others were compared.

Results: Their own relapses were seen as due to circumstances over which they had no control, for example an environmental cue that they were powerless to resist. Others' relapses were seen as the result of circumstances that they could control; they were seen as having made the choice to resume drinking.

Conclusion: Addicts' explanations of their relapses use situational attributions — the result of circumstances over which they have no control.

In a study with student participants, Hatgis et al. (2008) found that internal attributions about drug taking were more common among participants with no experience of drugs than among those who had taken drugs, or had a close friend who regularly used drugs. They also found that attributions for problem drug use varied with the substance, with internal attributions being more common for the use of marijuana, compared with alcohol or heroin.

In relation to smoking, Wright et al. (2007) found that attributing smoking to genetic factors was associated with lower levels of perceived control. In a study of smokers, McAllister and Davies (1992) compared attributions smokers gave about smoking before and after they were allocated to a 'heavy' or 'light' smoking group. Before allocation, there was no significant difference in the attributions made, but afterwards the 'heavy' group made more external attributions, thus absolving themselves of responsibility for the negative effects of their smoking. Eiser et al. (1978) argue that external attributions to explain addiction provide smokers with an explanation for previous failures at cessation, and attribution has implications in terms of treatment.

Self-esteem and attributions are factors that lie within the individual. However, addiction may best be understood in terms of the interaction of a range of personal and environmental factors. We have looked at some of the factors outside the individual that influence addiction, particularly in the initiation of a behaviour; these include cues in the environment, the behaviour of others, the availability of addictive substances, life experiences, socioeconomic status and level of education.

One final environmental factor we will look at is **stress**. There is quite a lot of evidence that stress is a risk factor for substance abuse. For example, King and Chassin (2008) found that experiencing stressful life events in adolescence was a factor in young people developing a dependence on drugs. Similarly, Cheung and Tse (2008) found that unhappiness at home or at school were specific risk factors for substance abuse. In a study of students, Felsher (2007) found that stress was a predictor of gambling addiction in males.

Summary

- There is some evidence to link addiction with low **self-esteem** and indirectly with **attachment type**.
- Attribution theory suggests that people are likely to make **external attributions** for **relapse** that absolve the addict from blame.
- A number of **environmental factors** influence addiction, including **stress**.

The role of the media

The final factor we will look at in this section is the influence of the media. In Bandura's **social learning theory**, discussed earlier, one of the three sources of models he identifies is the media. Advertising addictive substances that are legal to use, i.e. tobacco and alcohol, has been big business, with adverts on street hoardings, in the press and on commercial television. However, although it is still legal to advertise alcohol, all tobacco advertising and sponsorship on television has been banned within the European Union since 1991, and the ban was extended in 2005 to cover other forms of media such as the internet, print and radio.

However, young people are still exposed to images of people smoking on television, and there has been research to suggest that this might be related to people's smoking behaviour. For example, Gutschoven and van den Bulck (2005) found that there was a significant relationship between higher levels of television viewing and the age at which young people started smoking. This could be explained within the framework of social learning theory, in that actors might serve as behavioural role models. However, the relationship is correlational and it could be that those who choose to watch a lot of television do so as a result of personal characteristics that also make them more likely to smoke. However, a study carried out in Scotland by Hunt et al. (2009) found that there was no relationship between the number of occurrences of smoking estimated to have been seen in films (film smoking exposure) and current (or ever) smoking in young adults. This may be to do with the type of media, because a similar study carried out in the USA had found a significant relationship. It is possible that the results of this study may have been affected by cultural differences; at the time the study was carried out, real-life smoking was extremely common in Scotland.

Since tobacco advertising was banned, the British government, among others, has spent a great deal of money on anti-smoking campaigns, with advertisements appearing frequently on television to warn of the health risks of smoking and to promote ways of stopping smoking. Commercial firms also advertise products to help smokers quit. Research has investigated the effect of anti-smoking campaigns in the media (see Box 11.7).

Box 11.7 McVey and Stapleton (2009)

Aim: To assess the effectiveness of televised anti-smoking advertisements in motivating smokers to give up and preventing relapse.

Procedure: The research was carried out in four television regions. Two regions received televised anti-smoking advertising, one received anti-smoking advertising plus locally organised anti-tobacco campaigning, and the fourth acted as a control. The advertisements were screened over a period of 18 months. Interviews were carried out with 5,468 men and women (2,997 smokers and 2,471 ex-smokers) before the intervention, of whom 3,610 were re-interviewed 6 months later, after the first phase of the campaign. At the end of the campaign, 2,381 were interviewed again.

Results: The interviews after 6 months showed no significant effects. However after 18 months, 9.8% of smokers had stopped and 4.3% of ex-smokers had relapsed. Compared with controls, smokers in the other three conditions were significantly more likely to have stopped smoking, although the effect of the local campaign was not significant.

Conclusion: The televised anti-smoking campaign was effective in reducing smoking through encouraging smokers to stop and helping to prevent relapse in those who had already stopped. If advertising is to have an impact, a prolonged campaign is necessary.

In a longitudinal study carried out over 4 years in the USA, Siegel and Biener (2000) found that televised campaigns were effective in preventing younger smokers, aged 12–13 at the start of the study, from becoming habitual smokers. However, they had no effect on older adolescents. They also found that televised advertisements were more effective than radio and outdoor advertising.

Wolburg (2004) highlights the need to create advertisements specifically targeted at the intended audience. She found that when a campaign targeted at young teenagers was used with college students, the advertising had a negative effect and so was counterproductive.

Research has also looked at the effects of the media on alcohol consumption (see Box 11.8).

Box 11.8 Connolly et al. (1994)

Aim: To investigate a possible association between recollection of alcohol-related material in the mass media and later alcohol consumption.

Procedure: A sample of 667 students aged 13–15 were asked to recall alcohol-related media material. This was then organised into three categories: entertainment, alcohol moderation messages and commercial alcohol advertising. Their alcohol consumption was later assessed when they were 18.

Results: Televised advertising was the predominant material recalled. Among males (but not females) there was a consistent positive relationship between recalling more alcohol advertisements at 15 and drinking larger quantities of beer at 18.

Conclusion: Commercial advertising of alcohol on television may have a long-term effect on males in promoting later excessive beer drinking.

Zwarun et al. (2006) exposed college students to alcohol commercials containing images of activities that would be dangerous to undertake while drinking. They found that those exposed to these advertisements, particularly young males, were more likely than controls to believe in the social benefits of drinking and to have an increased tolerance of drink driving. This suggests that the imagery in beer commercials may contribute to beliefs about alcohol that predict drinking and to an increased acceptance of dangerous drinking behaviour.

Music videos are another source of concern. Several studies have shown that these videos often glamorise the drinking of alcohol, through both the behaviour of the performers (DuRant et al. 1997) and in pop-song lyrics (Beckley and Chalfant 1979). As music videos are aimed at young people, these findings have led to research into the drinking of alcopops, where advertising appears to be aimed at young adolescents and because of the possibility that the alcopops' sweet taste makes it easier for young people to start drinking and perhaps develop bad drinking habits. In a study of a possible relationship between watching music videos and drinking alcopops, Van den Bulck et al. (2006) found that those who watched music videos several times a week were twice as likely to drink alcopops at home as those who did not, and two and a half times as likely to drink them when going out. The amount of time spent watching music videos was a better predictor of alcopop consumption than the overall time spent watching television.

Summary

- Although the advertising of **tobacco products** is banned, **alcohol** can legally be advertised.
- People may be influenced by **smoking** behaviour demonstrated in the media.
- **Anti-smoking advertising campaigns** can be effective in persuading people to stop smoking.
- There is evidence that **alcohol advertising** can promote dangerous drinking behaviour.
- **Alcopops** are of particular concern, as they are aimed at young people.

Reducing addictive behaviour

Models of prevention

There are several theoretical models that link various factors in terms of their influence on behaviour, which can be applied to addiction and suggest ways in which it can be prevented. The **theory of reasoned action**, developed by Fishbein and Ajzen (1975), was further developed by Ajzen (1991) into the **theory of planned behaviour (TPB)** by the addition of the new factor of perceived behavioural control (see Figure 11.2).

Figure 11.2 *Theory of planned behaviour (Ajzen 1991)*

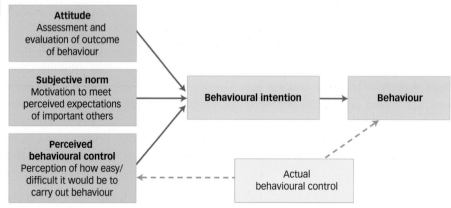

In this model, the immediate determinant of behaviour is a person's intention to carry it out, or not to do so.

Behavioural intention is determined by the person's **attitude** towards the behaviour, i.e. whether he or she sees it as positive or negative. This in turn is shaped by belief and expectation that the behaviour will lead to particular consequences, and the value the individual places on these consequences. For example, in the case of alcohol, the belief might be, 'I will feel more relaxed if I have a drink', and this outcome will be seen in a positive light, leading to a positive attitude towards drinking. For this reason, these models are described as **expectancy-value models**.

The second determinant of behavioural intention is the **subjective norm**, defined as the person's judgement that other people who are relevant — friends, partner, family and so on — expect him or her to behave in this way. This in turn is shaped by two factors: **normative beliefs** (the expectations of relevant others) and the **motivation** to comply with these expectations.

In the original theory of reasoned action, these were the only two determinants of intentions and therefore behaviour. However, this model was only effective in predicting behaviour when the individual had a high degree of voluntary control over the behaviour, so the final component of the theory, **perceived behavioural control**, was added. This is a person's perception of how easy or difficult it would be to carry out the behaviour. When this was added, Ajzen and Madden (1986) found that the model led to much better predictions of behaviour in situations where an individual felt that he or she had little control.

There is some evidence that the theory of planned behaviour can be useful in predicting the likelihood of an individual developing a habit of substance abuse and can therefore make a contribution in identifying those at risk and putting in place measures to prevent addiction and relapse. In a large study of 14 year olds,

Marcoux and Shope (1997) assessed the usefulness of the theory in predicting and explaining the use of alcohol, how often it was used and its misuse. They found that all the components of the model were useful and that it was more valuable than the theory of reasoned action. They found that peer pressure and friends' experience with alcohol were important variables in the model, along with the normative belief of parents. The use of the model led to recommendations for preventing alcohol abuse, such as reducing its availability, taking measures to reduce peer pressure and encouraging parents to discuss alcohol use with their children and get involved in prevention programmes.

A study carried out by Wall et al. (1998) assessed the usefulness of the TPB in predicting alcohol use in undergraduates. They also found the model to be a useful framework for predicting excessive drinking. However, on the basis of their findings, they suggested that in relation to alcohol, it would be improved if it included gender-specific alcohol outcome expectancies. For example, in addition to attitudes and perceived behavioural control, women's expectancies for sociability strengthened the prediction of intentions to drink too much, while assertiveness improved the prediction of excessive consumption over and above intentions and perceived behavioural control. Swaim et al. (2007) also found the TPB useful in predicting cigarette smoking.

However, in spite of being widely applied, both the theory of reasoned action and the theory of planned behaviour have been criticised. Based on a literature review, Ogden (2003) has pointed out that not all parts of the model have been consistently validated. Some studies reported no role of subjective norms, while others showed no predictive role for perceived behavioural control, and some showed no role for attitudes. However, this may be because the variables were not adequately operationalised in these studies, rather than these aspects of the theory lacking predictive potential. In reply to this criticism, Ajzen and Fishbein (2004) pointed out that the relative importance of attitudes, subjective norms and perceptions of behavioural control for the prediction of intentions will necessarily vary for different behaviours and in different populations. They argued that only one or two of the three aspects may be necessary in any particular situation.

Another point raised by Ogden is that in most studies, behaviour was measured by self-reports rather than in an objective way, so there was no guarantee that the data participants provided were accurate. In response to this criticism, Azjen and Fishbein pointed out that it is virtually impossible to measure some behaviours objectively and, even where it would be possible, measurement would be impractical, given the expense and time involved.

As a final point, Ogden noted that asking people to answer questions about the way they think may, in itself, change thinking, rather than assess the way a person was thinking originally. However, this is a general problem with any research that uses this kind of method.

In the light of some of the criticisms made of the TPB, Eagly and Chaiken (1993) proposed a somewhat more complex model. This included the basic ideas of the TPB, but also included other variables that have been suggested to be important. A study of the relationship between voting intention and behaviour, carried out by Granberg and Holmberg (1990) using data from national election surveys, found that the level of consistency between intention and behaviour was high in both Sweden and the USA. However, it was much weaker when voting intentions were not compatible with people's self-image and their previous behaviour, suggesting that self-identity is important in linking intention to behaviour. This was incorporated into the model by Eagly and Chaiken, who also suggested that habits and attitudes towards targets (and towards behaviour) should be included.

In spite of the criticisms made of it, the TPB has been widely used as a way of identifying those at risk of addiction and in shaping interventions, both to prevent potentially addictive behaviour developing and to help people avoid relapse.

Summary

- The **theory of reasoned action** proposed that attitudes and subjective norms lead to intentions, which lead to behaviour.
- From this, the **theory of planned behaviour** was developed, adding the element of **perceived behavioural control**.
- This theory can be used successfully to **predict** who is likely to develop an addiction.
- The theory has been criticised for not taking **gender** into account, for lack of **validation** of all parts of the model and for lack of **objective measurement**.
- Later theorists have built **additional factors** into the model.

Types of intervention

There are numerous types of intervention to prevent and treat addiction. These can vary with the type of addiction and include:

- direct biological and psychological interventions with addicts
- public health interventions to promote seeking help for an addiction
- legislation to make access to addictive substances more difficult

Some addictions involve medical treatment. Drug detoxification is used to reduce or relieve withdrawal symptoms while helping the addict adjust to living without drug use. It does not treat addiction, but deals with the physical dependency rather than the psychological aspects of drug addiction. It is the first step in long-term treatment, which includes counselling and therapy and often takes place in a residential centre within a wider programme that lasts several months.

Withdrawal from long-term alcohol addiction without medical management can cause severe health problems and can be fatal. Benzodiazepines or barbiturates are the drugs most commonly used. Treatment may then include medication such as Antabuse or Naltrexone. The medication causes a fast-acting and long-lasting hangover when alcohol is drunk, which discourages an alcoholic from drinking in significant amounts. Krampe et al. (2006) found that this kind of medication, used within a comprehensive treatment programme, led to an abstinence rate of over 50%.

Drug treatment is usually combined with social support, such as attending meetings of Alcoholics Anonymous, to help avoid a relapse.

For heroin addiction, methadone is likely to be used. However, there are possible side effects, including constipation, headaches, vomiting, seizures and in rare cases death, which have to be weighed against the harmful effects of heroin. Methadone Maintenance Treatment (MMT) is then used to eliminate the use of heroin. It is seen as ongoing symptom management rather than a cure. The amount of methadone used can be gradually tapered off, but many studies suggest that under these circumstances, some addicts relapse into heroin use. However, as an alternative, Symington (2008) reported that a trial of providing addicts with pharmaceutical-grade heroin under medical supervision is a safe and highly effective treatment for people with chronic heroin addiction.

Drug treatment is usually combined with social support, such as attending meetings of Alcoholics Anonymous, to help avoid a relapse

For nicotine addiction, withdrawal symptoms are not so severe as for alcohol or heroin, and nicotine is out of the system within 72 hours of stopping smoking. Nicotine replacement therapy, such as nicotine patches, gum and lozenges, deliver a therapeutic dose of nicotine in the early stages of stopping smoking.

Behavioural methods of treatment can also be used, either alone or in conjunction with medication. **Aversion therapy** uses the principles of classical conditioning in creating a new stimulus-response association; for example, changing positive emotional associations with the sight, smell and taste of alcohol to negative associations (see Box 11.9).

Box 11.9   Owen (2001)

Aim: To assess the effectiveness of aversion therapy for alcoholics.

Procedure: Participants were 82 hospitalised alcoholics. Over a 10-day period they were given five conditioning sessions of aversion therapy. They were given an emetic to make them nauseous. Shortly before this had an effect, they were given an alcoholic drink of their choice that they were instructed to smell, swish around in their mouth and then spit out. A few minutes later they were given another drink, which they were instructed to swallow, but as

11

nausea had then set in, this was quickly regurgitated. They also completed a range of question-naires to provide behavioural and cognitive measures of experience and change.

Results: Positive alcohol-related outcome expectancies were significantly reduced and confidence that drinking could be avoided in various high-risk situations for consumption was increased.

Conclusion: Aversion therapy can be effective in treating alcoholics.

This study used a chemical — the emetic — but other treatments have used electric shocks as an aversive stimulus. Another possibility is **covert aversion**, which uses the patient's imagination. Kraft and Kraft (2005) reported successful case studies of this treatment, where under hypnosis, cravings for addictive behaviours — including drinking alcohol and smoking cigarettes or cannabis — were paired with feelings of nausea and vomiting. The treatment took only four sessions, so was rapid and therefore cost-effective.

However, one problem with this approach is that it is unclear how successful it is in the long term. For example, when a person is exposed after treatment to an environment associated with drug taking, some of the physical and mental changes associated with craving are reactivated and the person may relapse (Siegel et al. 1987).

Some therapies take a cognitive behavioural approach. **Cognitive-behavioural therapy (CBT)** is based on the principle that addiction is a learned behaviour that can be modified. This approach aims to change the behaviour in one of three ways:

- by changing the faulty cognitions that serve to maintain it
- by promoting positive cognitions, for example self-efficacy (a person's belief that he or she is capable of carrying out a particular behaviour)
- by increasing motivation to change behaviour

According to Curran and Drummond (2005), CBT is the main treatment for alcohol and cannabis dependency, and addictions to stimulants such as cocaine.

In Beck's model (see Figure 11.3), dysfunctional thinking may be addressed at any stage of the progression he describes:

Figure 11.3 *Interventions in dysfunctional thinking (Beck et al. 1990)*

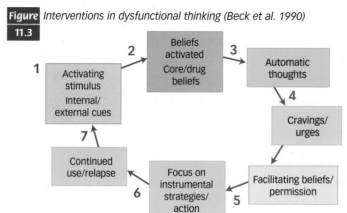

1 Recognise cues and develop plans to avoid them.
2 Distract and/or develop plan to move out of the risk situation.
3 Challenge thoughts, increase negative expectancies, enhance dissonance, enhance control over the decision-making process.
4 Experience natural process of craving, coping with craving without using.
5 Challenge facilitating beliefs, increase coping skills, exit situation, change lifestyle.
6 Exit situation, change lifestyle.
7 De-catastrophise, learning from experience

CBT involves teaching self-control strategies, identifying high-risk situations and acquiring coping skills to deal with these situations. These include communication training, problem solving, learning how not to give in to peer pressure and coping with negative mood.

Killen et al. (2008) found that for smoking cessation, extended CBT plus telephone counselling was more effective than telephone counselling alone. There are various forms of CBT, and the length and spacing of the sessions plays a role. Cavallo et al. (2007) compared weekly CBT sessions, each lasting 45 minutes, with behavioural counselling three times a week, where each session lasted 10–15 minutes. Although the content of both kinds of session was identical, the CBT sessions were more effective with adolescent smokers who wanted to stop smoking. When combined with CBT, contingency management can contribute to the success of CBT. This involves offering reinforcement, usually in the form of monetary rewards, as treatment progresses (see Box 11.10).

Box 11.10 Krishnan-Sarin et al. (2006)

Aim: To evaluate the contribution of contingency management in combination with CBT in smoking cessation.

Procedure: Twenty-eight adolescent smokers who wished to give up smoking were randomly allocated to two groups, one receiving CBT and the other receiving CBT and contingency management (CM). The programme lasted 1 month. As long as a urine sample showed that they had not smoked, those in the CBT + CM group were paid twice daily during the first 2 weeks, once a day during the first week and once every other day in the final week.

Results: After 1 week, abstinence levels were 77% in the CBT + CM group, compared with only 7% in the CBT group. At the end of the month, the percentages were 53% and 0% respectively.

Conclusion: Contingency management is a useful adjunct in the use of CBT for smoking cessation.

CBT can be used not only with substance abuse but with any addictive behaviour. It has been shown to be effective with gamblers. Jimenez-Murcia et al. (2007) treated 290 pathological gamblers with weekly outpatient CBT over a period of 16 weeks. They found that the success rate 6 months after the end of treatment was over 80%. However, they noted that dropout during the treatment, and relapse after it ended, was related to certain personality characteristics; in particular, this was more likely to happen with patients with obsessive-compulsive symptoms.

Another study has also demonstrated the role of individual differences in the usefulness of CBT (see Box 11.11).

Box 11.11 Petry et al. (2007)

Aim: To assess the usefulness of CBT with pathological gamblers and test the principle that its effectiveness depends on the acquisition of coping skills.

Procedure: A total of 127 pathological gamblers were randomly assigned to one of two groups, one group receiving a referral to Gamblers Anonymous and the other receiving CBT as well as the referral. They also completed the Coping Strategies Scale (CSS) to assess their coping skills before treatment and 2 months later. Measures of gambling behaviour were taken before treatment, after 2 months, and again after 12 months.

Results: The relationship between coping skills and gambling behaviour was fairly strong, irrespective of the treatment received. However, participants receiving CBT showed greater improvement in gambling behaviour than the control group, together with a significantly greater increase in CSS scores, which were related to the behavioural outcome at 2 months. However, there was little evidence that coping strategies mediated the outcome at 12 months.

Conclusion: The beneficial effects of CBT appear to be related in part to changes in coping responses. Improved coping responses are associated with long-term changes in gambling behaviour.

Raistrick et al. (2006) claim that CBT has the best chance of success of any of the available treatments for addiction and is cost effective. There is some support for this claim. For example, in a large systematic review of 381 studies, using a range of treatments, Miller et al. (2003) found that CBT emerged as the most effective treatment for alcohol problems.

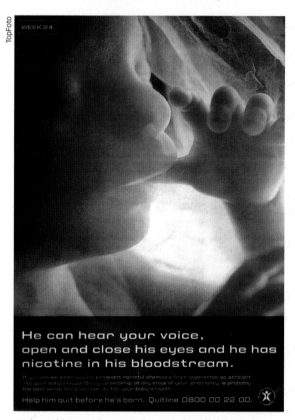

He can hear your voice, open and close his eyes and he has nicotine in his bloodstream.

Help him quit before he's born. Quitline 0800 00 22 00.

Anti-smoking media campaigns can be effective

TopFoto

Summary

- **Detoxification** may be necessary before substance abuse can be treated with **medication**. Psychological **support** is usually offered alongside medication.
- Behavioural methods include **aversion therapy**, which has been shown to be effective for treating substance abuse. However, it may not be effective in the long term.
- Cognitive behavioural therapy aims to change **faulty cognitions**. It has been shown to be effective in treating a range of addictions, particularly in combination with **contingency management**, and is cost effective.

The methods we have looked at so far all treat individuals who have developed an addiction. However, **public health campaigns** are also widely used to offer help to people who have become addicted. As we saw earlier in the McVey and Stapleton study of anti-smoking advertising (see Box 11.7), media campaigns can be effective. Most campaigns have been concerned with smoking, and quite a lot of research has been carried out into their effectiveness.

In 2004, the Health Development Agency, which works within the NHS to gather information and provide advice for policy makers, reported on aspects of anti-smoking campaigns that are effective. The points made include the need for campaigns to:

- contain a variety of messages, both threatening and supportive
- engage the emotions of the target audience, using humour, fear, sympathy or aspiration
- motivate smokers by letting them know that help is available and reminding them of the benefits of not smoking

Some of these recommendations reflect the findings of early research into the use of fear in advertisements of this kind. Janis and Feshbach (1953) found that a 'high fear' approach was not effective in changing behaviour. However, it has also been found that if a frightening message is accompanied by information about how the dangers described can be avoided (in this case where help may be found), fear may be effective in changing behaviour. The effectiveness of helplines has also been evaluated (see Box 11.12).

Box 11.12   Platt et al. (1997)

Aim: To assess the effectiveness of a smoking helpline — Smokeline — set up in Scotland.

Procedure: The number of callers over the first year was noted. The prevalence of smoking in Scotland before and after the introduction of the helpline was compared. A sample of 848 adult smokers who called Smokeline was also followed up by telephone interview 1 year after their initial call.

Results: An estimated 82,782 regular adult smokers made genuine contact with Smokeline over the year, just under 6% of all adult smokers in Scotland. After 1 year, 143 of the sample of 848 callers (nearly 24%) reported that they had stopped smoking, and 534 (88%) reported having made some change. This suggests that about 19,500 adult smokers, equivalent to 1.5% of the adult smoking population, stopped smoking with direct help from Smokeline. During the second year of the campaign, smoking prevalence among 25–65 year olds in Scotland was 6% lower than it had been before the start of the campaign.

Conclusion: The anti-smoking campaign reached a high number of adult smokers and was associated with a high cessation rate among adults given direct help through the helpline.

While these results are impressive, they rely on self-report, so there is no guarantee that the data are accurate. Extrapolating from a sample of around 10% of all the callers may not have produced accurate results. However, similar research carried out by Owen (2000) on the effects of 'Quitline', an anti-smoking helpline in England, had similar results.

As well as media campaigns, governments have introduced large printed warnings on cigarette packets. In a study in Australia, Borland (1997) found that these were more effective at stimulating thoughts about the negative effects of smoking than the previously used much smaller warnings and could influence people not to smoke the planned cigarette, a step towards giving up smoking. However, Cecil et al. (1996) reported that teenagers did not accept the truth of some of the warnings, which supports previous findings that smokers in this age group are less likely to accept the specific health risks associated with smoking than non-smokers. The findings also support the point raised by Wolburg (2004) that campaigns may need to target different sections of the population in different ways.

Legislation can also have a part to play. On 1 July 2007, legislation came into effect in England banning smoking in public places. It had been introduced in Wales and Northern Ireland earlier in the year and in Scotland in March 2006. Several studies have looked at the effect of this kind of legislation. For example, Fowkes at al. (2008) found that in Scotland, there was a steady rise in the number of people who gave up smoking in the 5 years prior to the legislation. However, in the 3 months immediately prior to the law coming into effect, the quit rate rose quite markedly. Approximately half of the 57 people who were interviewed for the study and who had given up smoking around the time the ban became law said that the legislation had helped them to quit. However, Eadie et al. (2008) reported that compliance with the ban in bars in Scotland was patchy, and it was particularly likely to be flouted in deprived communities. They suggested that smoke-free legislation could be more effective if accompanied by initiatives, planned in advance, targeting support to smokers in this kind of area.

While almost all the research into legislation is concerned with smoking, there is some indication that similar legislation in regard to drinking could be a possibility. In March 2009, the UK Chief Medical Officer, Sir Liam Donaldson, suggested that the government should also takes steps to curb excessive drinking by tightening the licensing laws and introducing minimum prices on alcohol. However, there has as yet been little support from politicians.

Summary

- **Public health campaigns**, using different types of appeal, have been shown to be effective in encouraging people to give up smoking.
- **Helplines** and **warnings** on cigarette packets may also be effective.
- **Legislation** has had some influence on the prevalence of smoking.

Chapter

Anomalistic psychology

In this chapter, we will be looking at:

- theoretical and methodological issues
  - pseudoscience and scientific fraud
  - controversy relating to Ganzfeld studies and psychokinesis
- factors underlying anomalous experience
  - cognitive, personality and biological factors
  - functions of paranormal and related beliefs
  - the psychology of deception, self-deception, superstition and coincidence
- belief in exceptional experience
  - psychic healing
  - out-of-body and near-death experience
  - psychic mediumship

Anomalistic psychology is an area of psychology concerned with behaviour and experience that are described as **paranormal**, i.e. phenomena that ostensibly cannot be explained in terms of conventional scientific theories; they are also known as **psi phenomena**. These include, among others, **extra-sensory perception (ESP)** (communication or perception by means other than the physical senses), **psychokinesis (PK)** (the ability to control the movement of objects by the power of thought), **psychic healing** and **out-of-body experiences**. The term itself is purely descriptive, neither implying that anomalous phenomena are paranormal nor suggesting anything about their underlying mechanisms. Parapsychologists accept that paranormal events occur and they try to find evidence to support this belief. Anomalistic psychologists, on the other hand, tend to be sceptical about paranormal phenomena and they work on the assumption that apparently paranormal experiences can be explained in terms of known psychological and physical factors.

Theoretical and methodological issues

Parapsychology claims to be a science, with studies providing scientific evidence for paranormal phenomena. In 1969, the Parapsychological Association was accepted as an affiliate of the American Association for the Advancement of Science. However, its scientific status has been questioned. Supporters of parapsychology claim that psi phenomena are a valid field of scientific research and that this research is scientific in nature. Anomalistic psychologists claim that it is a pseudoscience; it uses methods that in some ways appear scientific, but does not observe basic scientific principles in its research. There are also a number of instances where deliberate fraud has been practised in order to support its claims.

Pseudoscience and scientific fraud

Parapsychology causes problems for scientists because it implies the existence of powers not just unknown to science but that contradict well-established scientific laws and understanding of how the universe works. For example, the acceptance of PK as a genuine phenomenon contradicts the principle that a person's mind cannot affect the physical world without the agency of some physical force or energy. Given the huge amount of empirical evidence supporting our current scientific understanding, it is crucial that studies are carried out, applying the principles of scientific research, if ideas such as the existence of PK are to be accepted.

According to Broughton (1991), surveys typically find that over half of the population report having had a psi experience. However, closer examination of the cases suggests that only between 10–15% of the population have had experiences that appear to be possible psi phenomena. One method of carrying out research into psi is the study of specific and allegedly extraordinary individuals. In a survey of belief in the paranormal among academics, Wagner and Monnet (1979) found that this kind of study was most often cited as evidence of the paranormal. When this kind of study is carried out in controlled conditions with no significant results, it is often claimed that the presence of sceptics creates 'negative vibrations', which prevent the phenomena from appearing.

The other method is to carry out large-scale experiments. For this kind of research to be considered genuinely scientific, rather than pseudoscience, several principles must be observed. One of these is **replicability** — another person should be able to repeat the study in exactly the same way to see if he or she produces similar results; a single experiment, even if the results are statistically significant, cannot justify a claim of having established a particular cause-and-effect explanation of a phenomenon. Although they do not prove the explanation correct, successful replications that confirm existing findings make it more likely to be accepted. This is a particular issue in parapsychological research, which often demonstrates experimenter effects; some experimenters are able to elicit 'real' psychic phenomena whereas others, quite inexplicably, cannot.

In science, appropriate **controls** are important; the experiment should be designed in such a way as to eliminate confounding variables and thereby alternative inter-

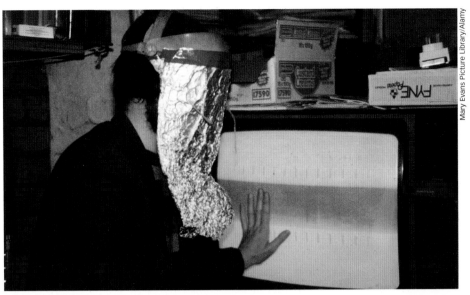

Mary Evans Picture Library/Alamy

A psychokinesis experiment: to be considered a genuine science, controlled psi research should be replicable

pretations of the findings. There have been instances of research into psi phenomena where significant results have been found, but where critics have claimed that controls have not been adequate. For example, in some early studies of ESP, where a participant was asked which one of five cards an experimenter was looking at, it was found that the cards were so thin that the participants could tell which card had been selected without being able to see its face directly. When more effective controls have been put in place, the results have generally been found to be non-significant. However, some parapsychologists explain this in terms of an active agency that prevents sustained psi effects. For example, Batcheldor (1994) wrote of psi as seeming 'to avoid those positions in space and time when we are actively looking for it' and McClenon (1994) described it as acting 'capriciously, as if…to resist complete verification'.

Another issue concerns **probability**. Within psychology, if a statistical analysis of a study's results is significant at the 5% level, the outcome is considered to be unlikely to have come about by chance. However, this means that there is still up to a 5% probability that the results *have* come about by chance, so there is the possibility of a Type 1 error, i.e. claiming that an effect exists when it does not.

There is also the possibility of selective reporting of parapsychological studies; the **'file drawer' problem** relates to the fact that as studies with non-significant results are less likely to be offered for publication, or to be accepted, it is impossible to know how many of these studies have been carried out and then abandoned in a file drawer. Blackmore points out that if 100 studies are carried out, it could be expected that, by chance, around five will produce significant results. If only those five are published, the evidence will be unfairly biased. Selective reporting could therefore account for some of the significance reported in the parapsychological literature.

However, in 1975 the Parapsychological Association Council adopted a policy opposing the selective reporting of positive outcomes and it claims that negative findings have been routinely reported at the association's meetings and in its publications since then.

A further characteristic of a scientific theory, which distinguishes it from pseudo-science, is **falsifiability**. We cannot prove a theory to be true; however many tests are carried out which suggest that this is the case, it is always possible that the results of the next test will not support the theory. Popper (1959) proposed that it is the ability to falsify a theory that makes it scientific, not the ability to verify it. A theory should be developed in such a way that it can potentially be shown to be untrue. In parapsychology, there do not appear to be any circumstances which could be seen to falsify parapsychological claims; there are always reasons — the presence of sceptics, the wrong time of day and so on — which can be used to account for test results that fail to support parapsychological claims. There is no reason why some of these explanations could not be true, for example the weakening of paranormal forces by the presence of sceptics, but at the same time parapsychologists have failed to develop experiments and make predictions that could allow their theories to be falsified. By this criterion, parapsychology is not science.

As well as claims that parapsychology does not meet the criteria of a science, it has also been shown that some of the data produced by the experimental research carried out in this field are the result of **scientific fraud**. In a move away from earlier dependence on anecdotal evidence, and in order to test psi phenomena in a scientific way (in particular ESP and PK, which he believed to share a common underlying mechanism), Rhine set up an experimental laboratory at Duke University in the USA in the 1930s. He went to considerable lengths to counter the possibility of fraud in the research carried out there, but some instances have nonetheless been uncovered. Rhine wrote a paper in 1974 discussing instances of fraud among the staff working there and how the circumstances that made fraud possible had been addressed, with rigorous security checks being put in place. Even so, some of the data produced under these conditions have nonetheless been shown to be fraudulent (see Box 12.1).

Box 12.1   Levy's studies

The director of Rhine's laboratory was Walter Levy, who carried out a series of studies of PK in the early 1970s:

(1) In one of a series of studies of PK in rodents, rats had electrodes implanted in the pleasure centre of the brain, which would stimulate that area of the brain when the rat pressed a lever. Levy was testing whether the animals could use PK to affect the mechanism that delivered the stimulation in such a way as to increase the number of stimuli received. The recording of data was completely automated and the data showed strong evidence to support psi phenomena, leading Randall (1974) to claim that: 'The fully automated experiments...have been replicated sufficiently often and yielded such clearly significant results that we are now justified in claiming this phenomenon as one of the most firmly established in parapsychology.'

However, a research assistant noticed Levy tampering with the automatic recording apparatus. He set up a parallel recording apparatus of his own and found that Levy was manipulating the data to 'improve' the results.

(2) In a similar series of studies, Levy investigated PK in chick embryos. Fertilised eggs were kept in an incubator in which the temperature was slightly lower than optimal for hatching. The studies successfully demonstrated that chick embryos could influence the heating apparatus so that the temperature was raised. Although Levy denied falsifying the data, one of the research assistants reported strong circumstantial evidence. For example, on at least one occasion, an egg in which the embryo was dead at the time of testing nonetheless showed significant scoring.

There is also evidence of fraud in some ESP studies (see Box 12.2).

Box 12.2   The Soal-Goldney experiments

Soal carried out a series of ESP studies using card guessing. Five cards were used, each with a picture of a different animal (elephant, giraffe, lion, pelican and zebra). Virtually all his results were negative, and he was for a time a harsh critic of parapsychological research. It was then suggested that he look again at his data to see if there was any evidence of displacement, i.e. where a participant's guesses corresponded to the card immediately before or following the target card. Using these criteria, the data from two participants proved to be significant. In collaboration with Goldney, Soal began a fresh series of carefully controlled tests with one of these participants, Basil Shackleton, with the highly significant results being published in 1934. Rhine (1947) described this work as 'one of the most outstanding researches yet made in the field...a milestone in ESP research'.

Soal continued his work in this area, again with Shackleton and with extremely significant results. However, Price (1955) suggested several ways in which the data could have been manipulated, which Soal (1956) refuted with outrage. Then in 1960 one of Soal's participants, Gretl Albert, claimed that she had noticed Soal altering some of the data during one of the sessions. This was confirmed by Soal and Goldney (1960) after a critic interviewing Gretl Albert threatened to reveal what she had said. The issue of fraud was finally settled by Marwick (1978), who demonstrated that Soal had manipulated the random number sequences used in the test by inserting dummy digits, which could then be altered in line with the guesses made by participants.

While these cases of fraud are worrying, it should be noted that fraud can also be a problem for more established sciences. For example in 1912, skull fragments were discovered that were thought to be the remains of an unknown form of early human. The discovery was known as the Piltdown man, but was later found to be a forgery, combining the lower jawbone of an orang-utan and the skull of a modern human. There have also been instances of fraud in the field of mainstream psychology. Perhaps the best known example is Burt's study of intelligence in twins, where there seems little doubt that the data were faked to promote Burt's belief that intelligence is largely genetic. Occasional evidence of fraud should not on its own be used to dismiss a scientific discipline as worthless.

Summary

- Paranormal or **psi phenomena** cannot be explained in terms of established scientific theories.
- Researchers in this area claim that they take a **scientific approach**. However, their research raises issues in relation to standard scientific principles, including **replicability, experimenter effects, control, probability, selective reporting** and **falsifiability**.
- There are documented cases of **fraud** in parapsychological research. However, this is also true of other disciplines.

Controversy relating to Ganzfeld studies and psychokinesis

The two main psi phenomena that have been tested experimentally are ESP and PK. In both these areas, there has been considerable controversy, with some psychologists claiming that studies have produced robust evidence to support their existence and others claiming that the research is flawed.

Rhine pioneered the original method for testing ESP in the 1930s. He used a special set of 25 cards, designed by Zener, a colleague at Duke University. One of five geometric shapes appeared five times within the pack. The pack was shuffled and the experimenter looked at each card in turn, usually in a distant room so that the possibility of cheating was eliminated. The experimenter worked through the pack one by one and the participant was asked to guess each time which of the designs the experimenter was looking at.

Figure 12.1 *Zener cards*

However, psi phenomena have historically been associated with altered states of consciousness, such as meditation or hypnosis, and there is some evidence that these altered states of consciousness do facilitate psi performance. For example, Honorton (1977) found that meditation increased performance on psi tests. Parapsychologists suggest that psi information can be masked by other stimuli, so reducing sensory input could improve an individual's detection rate. For this reason, the **Ganzfeld technique** (from German, 'total field') was developed.

This technique is the one most often used to test for telepathic communication between a sender and a receiver. The receiver sits in a reclining chair in a soundproof room. Translucent ping-pong ball halves are taped over the eyes and headphones are placed over the ears. A red light directed towards the eyes creates an undifferentiated visual field and white noise, played through the headphones, produces a similar auditory effect; this perceptual environment is the Ganzfeld. To reduce internal 'noise', the receiver typically carries out a series of relaxation exercises at the beginning of the test.

The sender is put in a separate room and a visual stimulus (a picture, photograph, or brief video clip) is randomly chosen as the target from a large pool of stimuli. While the sender concentrates on the target, the receiver reports the imagery and thoughts going through his or her mind, usually for about 30 minutes. The receiver is then presented with several stimuli (usually four) and without knowing which stimulus was the target, is asked to rate the degree to which each matches what they experienced during the Ganzfeld session. If the receiver assigns the highest rating to the target stimulus, it is scored as a 'hit', so if the experiment uses judging sets with four stimuli (the target and three control stimuli), the hit rate expected by chance is 1 in 4. Using this

The Ganzfeld technique reduces sensory input during psi tests

technique, several studies, for example Honorton and Harper (1974), have shown the receiver to pick out the relevant picture far more frequently than would be expected by chance. The ratings can also be analysed in other ways, for example they can be converted to ranks or scores within each set. Similarity ratings can be made by outside judges using transcripts of what the receiver has reported during the session.

On the basis of the findings of many studies using this technique, in 1985 the **Journal of Parapsychology** published a meta-analysis and critique by Hyman, a sceptic, and a competing meta-analysis and rejoinder by Honorton, a parapsychologist who had carried out a large number of ESP experiments. A number of controversial issues arose (see Box 12.3).

Box 12.3 Hyman (1985) and Honorton (1985)

Statistical analysis: In a meta-analysis of 42 Ganzfeld studies, there was a problem of multiple statistical analyses. Hyman suggested it was possible that researchers had tried various methods until they found one that produced favourable results. Honorton re-analysed 28 of the studies using only the hit rate and concluded that the results could not reasonably be attributed to chance.

Investigator effects: It is possible that a small number of investigators were responsible for the overall significant outcomes; half the studies were contributed by only two laboratories, one of which was Honorton's. Although the work of only ten laboratories was considered, most of them reported significant studies; the significance of the overall effect did not depend on just one or two of them.

Selective reporting: In 1975, the Parapsychological Association Council adopted a policy of opposing selective reporting and more than half the studies used in the meta-analysis had failed to reach the 5% level of statistical significance. However, Hyman pointed out a problem he called the 'retrospective study', in which an investigator would carry out a small set of exploratory trials. If the results were unpromising, they would be discarded, but if the results were positive, the exercise would then be defined as a study and submitted for publication. In support of this possibility, Hyman noted that 8 of the 42 studies with significant results had used fewer than 20 trials. However, there would need to be a large number of discarded studies with non-significant results to cancel out the overall significance found.

Methodological flaws: Some of the issues where Hyman and Honorton disagreed related to inadequate randomisation of target selection and the possibility that the data were contaminated by sensory leakage, i.e. participants receiving information through normal sensory channels, either inadvertently or through deliberate cheating.

In 1986, in the same journal, Hyman and Honorton issued a joint statement:

> We agree that there is an overall significant effect in this database that cannot reasonably be explained by selective reporting or multiple analyses. We continue to differ over the degree to which the effect constitutes evidence for psi, but we agree that the final verdict awaits the outcome of future experiments conducted by a broader range of investigators and according to more stringent standards.

A further meta-analysis of 30 Ganzfeld studies was carried out by Bem and Honorton (1994), in which strict methodological guidelines were followed. They concluded that taken together, these studies provided convincing support for the existence of ESP. However, a re-analysis of the same data carried out by Milton and Wiseman (1999) challenged this view, finding the results non-significant.

This appears to be an area of continuing controversy, and there is a similar debate surrounding PK. In the 1930s, Rhine carried out a series of PK experiments into whether it was possible to influence the fall of dice; many studies were carried out using this method. However, it was not without its problems, for example potential bias in the dice. In a meta-analysis of 148 experimental dice studies, Radin and Ferrari (1991) identified this as a possible confounding variable in many of them. The use of dice was therefore replaced in most studies by the use of random number generators (RNG), where a participant is asked to influence the output.

Radin and Nelson (1989) carried out a meta-analysis of 597 PK RNG studies, finding a small but significant effect. Bösch et al. (2006) criticised this analysis on statistical and methodological grounds. For example, many of the studies did not take what are called **moderator variables** into account, such as the distance between the participant and the target, and potential **psychological variables**, i.e. individual differences between participants. They carried out a similar meta-analysis of 380 PK studies and found overall a small positive effect. However, when the larger studies were analysed separately, there was a small, non-significant effect in the opposite direction. They suggested that this could be explained by publication bias and, given that it was the smaller studies that contributed to a significant overall result, highlighted the idea of **optional stopping**, i.e. stopping the experiment at a point of statistical significance.

If the phenomenon of PK were to exist, it would violate some well-established laws of physics, so would require a high standard of proof. Hanlon (2007) claimed that PK (and ESP) could possibly be explained in terms of quantum physics, but in general there is a broad consensus that there has been, as yet, no reliable demonstration of either phenomenon.

Summary

- **ESP** is usually tested using the **Ganzfeld technique**, under conditions of **sensory deprivation**.
- While many studies of ESP have shown significant results, there is **controversy** about the adequacy of the **methodology** used. **Meta-analyses** have produced **conflicting results**.
- There is similar controversy surrounding **PK** research.

Factors underlying anomalous experience

Several surveys have been carried out which show that belief in the paranormal is widespread. For example, Gallup and Newport (1991) found that 17% of American adults believed in 'the ability of the mind to move or bend objects using just mental energy', i.e. PK. The results of a similar Gallup poll reported by Moore (2005) found that 41% believed in ESP. When the field of paranormal experience is widened, to include belief in ghosts, astrology and clairvoyance (the power of the mind to predict the future), the same survey found that the percentage of believers in the paranormal rose to 73%. Several psychologists have therefore been interested to establish what leads people to these beliefs, focusing in particular on cognitive, personality and biological factors. There is a lot of research showing that some people outperform others on psi tasks and that this is related to whether or not they believe in psi. For example a meta-analysis by Lawrence (1992), covering 73 experiments by 37 different researchers, found that people who believe in psi, in general, obtain better results than non-believers. In this section, we will look at factors that underlie both belief in the paranormal and performance on psi tasks.

Cognitive, personality and biological factors

Cognitive factors

The **misattribution hypothesis** is concerned with factors that underlie belief in the paranormal. It suggests that people have developed beliefs in psychic ability because they have ascribed psychic causes to normal experience. This may be the result of a variety of cognitive processes.

One factor is poor general cognitive abilities; believers may be less able to judge whether apparently psychic phenomena have normal explanations because they are less intelligent. Using various measures of academic achievement, such as exam performance and highest level of educational attainment, some studies have shown that believers in the paranormal tend to have poorer cognitive abilities than non-believers (for example Gray 1987), while others have found that believers have superior cognitive abilities than non-believers (for example Emmons and Sobal 1981), so overall the findings have been inconsistent. There have been similar mixed findings in studies using intelligence tests as a measure of general cognitive ability. However, measures such as educational attainment may be crude measures of cognitive ability, since other factors such as socioeconomic status and educational opportunity are likely to be confounding variables, and there is considerable debate as to what exactly is being measured by intelligence tests.

Syllogistic reasoning

Syllogism 1
- All cheats are immoral.
- This psychic is a cheat.
- Therefore this psychic is immoral.

The conclusion follows logically from the propositions.

Syllogism 2
- If the government is engaged in a cover-up of the existence of UFOs, then it will deny that UFO landings have taken place.
- The government does deny that UFO landings have taken place.
- Therefore the government is engaged in a cover-up of the existence of UFOs.

The conclusion does not follow logically from the propositions. For example, the government may deny that UFO landings have taken place because they have not taken place.

A second possible factor is a lack of ability to think critically. For example, Gray and Mill (1990) carried out a study in which participants were asked to identify methodological problems in mock scientific papers and found that believers demonstrated significantly poorer critical-thinking skills than non-believers. However, a replication carried out by Roe (1999) found no significant differences between believers and non-believers.

It could be that people who believe in paranormal phenomena lack the ability to think logically. This has been tested using **syllogistic reasoning**, where two propositions are followed by a conclusion and the individual is asked whether the conclusion follows logically from the propositions:

Several studies have examined a possible link between belief in the paranormal and logical thinking (see Box 12.4).

Box 12.4   Wierzbicki (1985)

Aim: To test the hypothesis that belief in the paranormal is positively correlated with the number of errors on tests of logical reasoning.

Procedure: Participants were 64 psychology students. They completed the 25-item Belief in the Paranormal Scale (BPS), where each item is rated on a scale of 1–5. They were then given 16 syllogisms and were asked in each case whether the conclusion was correct.

Results: There was a significant positive relationship between degree of belief in the paranormal and the number of errors made on the syllogism task.

Conclusion: The findings support the idea that there is a relationship between belief in the paranormal and poor logical thinking.

This is a correlational study, so a simple cause-and-effect relationship cannot be inferred. There could also be an experimenter effect. Wierzbicki is a known sceptic, so the more intelligent students might not want to admit to a belief in the paranormal, with the result that their scores on the BPS were artificially low. This study is not the only one where there is evidence of an experimenter effect. Wiseman and Watt (2002) carried out a study investigating a possible link between belief in the paranormal and cognitive ability, finding a significant negative correlation with syllogistic reasoning. This result was attributable to the data collected by just one of the experimenters. Curiously, this was Watt, a researcher sympathetic to the idea of the paranormal, and so the results were the opposite of what might have been expected. This could be explained in terms of the possibility of a significant result nonetheless having come about by chance, as discussed in the first section of this chapter. However, several similar studies have been carried out into belief in the paranormal and logical reasoning, with few studies failing to find significant results.

A further possibility is **probability misjudgement**. It may be that people are poor at estimating how likely it is that an event could happen by chance, for example thinking about a friend you have not seen for a while and that friend telephoning a few moments later; the occurrence is then attributed to paranormal factors rather than coincidence. There is considerable research evidence demonstrating that people have problems with the judgement of probability. It may be that those who believe in the paranormal are less able than non-believers to make accurate judgements (see Box 12.5).

Box 12.5 Blackmore and Troscianko (1985)

Aim: To investigate whether people who believe in the paranormal are less accurate in judging probability than those who do not.

Procedure: Participants were 50 girls aged 14–18. They answered a range of questions about their belief in various paranormal phenomena such as ESP and were divided into believers and non-believers at the mid-point of the scores. They then took part in various tasks relating to probability. One of these was a coin-tossing task, where they were given statements such as: 'I toss a coin 20 times and I get heads 15 times.' They were then asked to say whether they thought the coin was biased. Over the series of questions the proportion of heads was either 50% or 75% and the number of tosses was 4, 12, 20 or 60. It was expected that non-believers would be more sensitive to the effect of sample size.

Results: While the difference between believers and non-believers on the other tasks was not significant, there was a significant difference in the predicted direction on the coin-tossing task.

Conclusion: People who believe in the paranormal are less able to make accurate judgments of probability than non-believers.

A final suggestion is that belief in paranormal phenomena may be linked to **creativity**. For example, Joesting and Joesting (1969) found a positive correlation between belief in ESP and creativity as measured on the **Torrance Creative Motivation Inventory (TCMI)**, a standardised test of creativity. However, this raises issues in relation to how creativity might best be defined. Does it relate to aspects of the person, such as imagination and originality? Wood (1981) identified practice, for example the development of expertise in musicians, as a major part of creativity, which is not assessed in creativity tests.

In relation to creativity, research has also investigated whether it might be related to performance on psi tasks and attempted to test this in a more ecologically valid way than using standardised tests (see Box 12.6).

Box 12.6 Dalton (1997)

Aim: To investigate the relationship between creativity and ESP.

Procedure: Different types of creative individuals were tested on a Ganzfeld task. The 128 participants included musicians, artists, creative writers and actors.

Results: Each group achieved significance on the task, with the musicians in particular achieving a significance level of $p < 0.0001$.

Conclusion: Creativity is strongly related to ESP performance.

Believers in psi would argue that this constitutes strong evidence for a link between creativity and ability in psi phenomena. However, each participant carried out only one trial, so the data on which the statistical calculation was based were limited. Moreover, there was no control group of non-creative people with whom the performance of these groups could be compared.

A final cognitive factor is **locus of control**, i.e. whether people believe that what happens to them is largely in their own hands (internal locus of control) or whether events in their lives are governed by factors over which they have no influence, such as luck and chance (external locus of control). Irwin (1986) found a positive relationship between belief in psi and an external locus of control in relation to both a general belief in the paranormal and a belief in ESP in particular. Schumaker (1990) has suggested that a belief in psi is the result of an illusion of mastery over uncertain events motivated by the need for control.

A considerable amount of research has been aimed at identifying cognitive factors that differentiate between those who believe in the paranormal and those who do not, and between those who do well on psi tasks and those who do not; this has yielded some positive results. However, many similar studies have produced non-significant results, so a clear picture of links between cognitive factors and belief in the paranormal and psi test performance has yet to emerge.

Personality factors

Kennedy (2005) suggested that scepticism about the paranormal is associated with materialistic, rational, pragmatic personality types, and there is some evidence that different aspects of personality are related to a belief in the paranormal.

Several studies, for example Thalbourne and Haraldsson (1980), have suggested that people who believe in ESP tend to be slightly extravert. Extraversion is a personality dimension that includes the traits of sociability, sensation seeking, impulsivity, restlessness and optimism. Tobacyk and Milford (1983) found that the sensation-seeking element of extraversion — the need for sensation and variety of experience — showed a particularly strong correlation with belief in the paranormal. However, other studies have contradicted these findings. For example, Williams et al. (2007) found no relationship between belief in the paranormal and extraversion. They did find a relationship with neuroticism, characterised by anxiety and sensitivity, but this finding has not been replicated in other research. One of the problems is methodological; for example in the study by Williams et al., belief in the paranormal was measured using a 6-point scale, which might be criticised for lacking the detail required for an accurate measurement.

Personality characteristics may also be related to performance on psi tasks. Honorton et al. (1990) found that those who scored high on extraversion tended to score well on ESP tests. However, Morris et al. (1995) found a relationship between introversion — the opposite of extraversion, characterised by caution and a withdrawal from social stimulation — and performance on psi tests, so clearly any relationship is not a simple one.

Links have also been made between belief in the paranormal and the personality dimensions on the Myers-Briggs Type Indicator:

The Myers-Briggs Type Indicator

This model uses 16 personality categories, based on the combinations of four factors:

- extraverted–introverted (E–I), relates to whether a person feels energised (E) or drained (I) in a group of people
- sensing–intuitive (S–N), relates to whether a person focuses more on the external world and prefers facts (S) or internally on the self and prefers abstract ideas (N)
- thinking–feeling (T–F) indicates whether a person tends to value rational thinking and self-control (T) or emotional expression (F)
- judging–perceiving (J–P) indicates whether a person prefers setting and achieving goals (J) or spontaneously exploring possibilities

For example, ESTJ is one personality type, and the most different type from that is INFP.

Gow et al. (2001) found that belief in paranormal phenomena is associated with the N (intuitive) and F (feeling) personality factors. There is also some evidence for a physiological basis for these differences. In a study of 129 psychology and drama students, Huot et al. (1989) found that those who scored high on N and P, and to some extent F, showed greater temporal lobe lability (i.e. the amount of spontaneous electrical activity taking place in the temporal lobes of the brain) than low scorers.

A further relevant personality construct is fantasy proneness, i.e. a tendency to fantasise a large part of the time and to be deeply absorbed in or fully experience what is being fantasised. Irwin (1990) has shown that measures of fantasy proneness correlate positively with paranormal belief.

Biological factors

It is possible, as suggested by the Huot et al. study on temporal lobe lability, that neurological differences might help to explain why some people are believers in paranormal phenomena and some are not. There is some research that suggests that the right hemisphere of the brain is associated with factors such as holistic processing of information and musicality, which have been associated with creativity, and as we saw earlier, links have been made between belief in the paranormal and superior performance on psi tests and creativity. It could be that believers might show higher levels of right-hemisphere activation and that this could be related to their belief in psychic phenomena and their performance on psi tasks. Brugger et al. (1993) compared the performance of believers and non-believers on a cognitive task presented to the left visual field (so information is processed in the right hemisphere) and the right visual field (so information is processed in the left hemisphere). Unlike the non-believers, the believers performed equally well irrespective of the visual field to which the information was presented, and the study further established that this was due to increased right-hemisphere activity in believers compared to controls.

Differences in activation of the hemispheres of the brain in believers and non-believers have been confirmed by other research. Pizzagalli et al. (2000) measured EEG activity in believers and non-believers during a 4-minute, eyes-closed, resting period. Compared with non-believers, believers showed relatively higher right-hemisphere activation.

Summary

- Research has investigated a possible relationship between **individual differences** in cognition, personality and biological characteristics and a **belief in the paranormal** and **performance on psi tests**.
- A variety of **cognitive** factors have been investigated, with generally inconsistent results.
- There is some support for **personality** differences, but again the results of studies often conflict.
- There is evidence of differences in **brain function** between believers and non-believers, but how these should be interpreted is not clear.

Overall, the inferences to be drawn from findings in studies of cognitive, personality and biological factors are not clear. There is insufficient evidence to claim that these differences lead to people either believing or not believing in the paranormal, or that they enhance performance. Moreover, they may be innate, but they may also develop as a result of experience.

Functions of paranormal and related beliefs

As noted at the start of the chapter, Broughton (1991) reported that many people claim to have had psychic experiences. The question then arises as to the role these experiences play in their lives and what functions they serve. There appear to be both individual and cultural reasons for belief in the paranormal. A number of studies have suggested that the primary effect of psi experiences is an altered worldview and an increased sense of meaning and purpose in life (see Box 12.7).

Box 12.7	Kennedy and Kanthamani (1995)

A survey was carried out of people who were interested in parapsychology and reported having paranormal or transcendent experiences, i.e. experiences beyond the material universe and our experience or knowledge of it. The survey asked whether or not they agreed with a list of statements:

- 72% agreed with the statement 'As a result of my paranormal or transcendent experience, I believe my life is guided or watched over by a higher force or being'.
- 45% agreed with the statement 'I feel like I have a purpose or mission in life as a result of my paranormal or transcendent experience(s)'.
- 25% agreed with the statement 'One or more paranormal or transcendent experiences motivated me to make a major life change that I was not previously thinking about making'.
- 38% agreed with the statement 'One or more paranormal or transcendent experiences seemed to confirm or reinforce that I was doing what I should be doing'.

Baumeister (1991) has suggested we need a sense of meaning in life, which religion can fulfil, but this need can also be met by a broader belief in the paranormal. He commented that while science is highly successful at providing efficacy (our need to be able to control the environment and to have an impact on the world), it may not provide a sense of purpose and self-worth. He noted that this makes it more difficult for a person to obtain a sense of meaning and to handle stresses and traumas. Similarly, Schumaker (2001) argued that religion and transcendence have important functions in human mental health that are not being met by the secular materialism of modern society. Declining meaning, purpose, values and spirituality are contrary to human nature, and he argues that this leads to mental-health problems.

While this is a general commentary on the functions that belief in the paranormal may serve, a more specific suggestion is that it can serve significant psychodynamic needs — the **psychodynamic functions hypothesis**. Irwin (1992) proposed that paranormal belief is the result of childhood trauma, especially physical abuse. These beliefs provide a sense of control, necessary for emotional security and psychological adjustment. Traumatic events create a threat and a sense of uncertainty, and a system of paranormal beliefs provides a cognitive framework for structuring life events and allowing them to be mastered, creating what Langer (1975) calls an '**illusion of control**'.

There is some evidence linking paranormal belief with childhood trauma and the sense of control. The study carried out by Irwin (1992) found that to some extent paranormal beliefs were generated in response to traumatic childhood events and that a function of these beliefs was to create a sense of control over the social world, while Rogers et al. (2007) also found a link between childhood trauma and paranormal belief. However, both these studies used questionnaire data, so their accuracy — particularly in relation to their reports of childhood trauma, which by definition had happened many years before — is open to question. An alternative explanation for the link between childhood trauma and a belief in the paranormal has also been offered by Wright (1999), who suggested that childhood trauma may lead to disengagement from the immediate world and thus becoming more sensitive to psychic phenomena.

Several studies have linked belief in the paranormal with a sense of control. For example, Blackmore and Troscianko (1985) asked participants to carry out a computer-controlled coin-tossing task. Those who believed in the paranormal felt that they were exercising greater control than non-believers and underestimated chance scores.

An alternative suggestion is the **social marginality hypothesis**. Bainbridge (1978) proposed that paranormal beliefs might be more likely to be found among socially marginalised groups, as a way of compensating for the shortcomings of their lives. On this basis, it might be expected that elderly people would be more likely to hold these beliefs than younger people. However, Emmons and Sobal (1981) found that belief in the paranormal was significantly stronger in young adults than in elderly people. In terms of gender differences, McGarry and Newberry (1981) found that paranormal belief is stronger among women than men, but only in some areas, such as ESP. However, Tobacyk and Milford (1983) found that men showed a relatively stronger belief in extraordinary life forms such as the Loch Ness monster. The extent to which the elderly and women are socially marginalised is open to question, but research has also looked at the extent of paranormal belief in clearly marginalised groups. In contrast to what the hypothesis would predict, Emmons and Sobal (1981) found that unemployed people showed relatively low levels of paranormal belief, and the same was true for African-Americans, who were a marginalised group at the time the study was carried out. Overall, there seems to be little support for the social marginality hypothesis.

Several cross-cultural studies have been carried out, which have shown cultural differences in the extent of belief in the paranormal and in the kinds of beliefs held. For example, Otis and Kuo (1984) found a higher level of global paranormal belief among university students in Singapore than those in Canada, and Tobacyk and Pirttila-Backman (1992) found that students in Finland had higher scores for belief in extraordinary life forms than American students but lower scores for traditional religious concepts. These differences suggest that an individual's level of paranormal belief and the nature of those beliefs is in part a function of that person's broader cultural environment. There may be some variation in the extent to which a given paranormal belief is integrated into a particular mainstream culture, and this in turn may influence the likelihood of the person holding that belief.

Arguing from an evolutionary point of view, Donald (2001) proposed that the human mind and human culture evolved together, with the mind becoming extremely plastic in order to adapt to the diversity of culture. Culture, and in particular beliefs (including paranormal beliefs), provide a framework for experiencing life and so are actively accepted by members of the culture. From this point of view, belief in psi may be motivated more by a need for a sense of interconnectedness within the culture than by an individual need for control. Paranormal beliefs may therefore be held primarily to fit into a social group. Alternatively, it could be that the beliefs reflect and reinforce the motivation for interconnectedness. Blackmore (1994) has suggested that belief in psi may be more common among women because of their greater sense that the world is interconnected; Tart (2002) has commented on the sense of interconnectedness that results from psi experiences.

However, as suggested by the research carried out by Tobacyk and Pirttila-Backman (1992), culture is not responsible for paranormal belief per se but rather for the specific forms that the beliefs might take. Cowan (1989) gives the example of the belief that the ritual insertion of small quartz crystals under the skin creates special spiritual powers, a belief held by some Australian Aboriginal tribes, but unlikely to be found by American believers in the paranormal.

Summary

- There is some evidence that belief in the paranormal is driven by a need to find **meaning** in life.
- The **psychodynamic functions hypothesis** explains individual differences in belief in the paranormal in relation to **childhood trauma** and the need for **control**. There is some evidence supporting this.
- There is little research support for the **social marginality hypothesis**.
- There are **cultural variations** in paranormal beliefs. Such beliefs may arise from a need for **social connectedness**. The form they take varies between cultures.

The psychology of deception, self-deception, superstition and coincidence

Deception and self-deception

As we have already seen, there have been cases of deliberate fraud in relation to paranormal phenomena, and further cases are discussed in the final section on psychic mediumship. A particularly famous case of deception being used to create the impression of psychic powers is that of Uri Geller, who claimed among other things to be able to bend spoons using the power of his mind, identify the face of a die that was enclosed in a metal box and reproduce a picture drawn by someone in a different room. In the 1970s, he performed frequently on television shows in Europe and the USA.

Uri Geller used 'psychic powers' to bend spoons

According to the stage magician James Randi, all these apparently paranormal phenomena could be explained using magicians' tricks. For example, in relation to spoon bending, Randi suggested that the magician could distract the audience briefly, during which time he could physically bend the spoon. The bend would then gradually be revealed, creating the illusion that the spoon was bending while it was being watched. Other ways could be to heat the spoon before the performance, weakening it so that it would be easier to bend, or to apply a corrosive chemical, so that the spoon would weaken and bend in a set period of time.

Although Geller has not always been able to reproduce his effects under controlled conditions, he has continued to claim that even though he could have used trickery, his results are achieved through psychic powers, and many people, including scientists, accepted this. He managed to convince several scientists, including Targ and Puthoff at the Stanford Research Institute, that he was producing genuinely paranormal phenomena. They tested his ability to reproduce target pictures while he was located in an electrically shielded room, and published a paper in 1974 in the prestigious scientific journal *Nature*, supporting his claims.

According to Broad and Wade (1982), successful deception depends not only on the deceiver, but also on characteristics of the people being deceived. They point out that professional magicians believe scientists to be easier to deceive than other people as a result of their confidence in their own objectivity. Broad and Wade also raise the point that we see what we expect to see; expectancy leads to self-deception, which in turn leads to a propensity to be deceived.

The power of expectancy in deception has been demonstrated in research (see Box 12.8).

Box 12.8   Wiseman et al. (2003)

Aim: To investigate the power of expectancy in deception.

Procedure: In two experiments, participants took part in a fake séance. All completed a questionnaire to establish the extent of their belief in the paranormal; they were classified as believers, uncertain or disbelievers.

In the first experiment, the experimenter suggested (wrongly) that a table was levitating. In the second, with different participants, the experimenter asked participants to try to move objects on a table using psychic powers. He claimed on one occasion that a slate that had moved had not in fact moved and on another that a hand-bell that had not moved had in fact moved. On two other occasions, no comment was made when a candlestick moved or when a tambourine failed to move. The movement was controlled by a hidden assistant.

Results: In the first experiment, about a third of participants incorrectly reported that the table had levitated, with a significantly greater proportion of believers than non-believers reporting that the table had moved. In the second experiment, although differences between believers and disbelievers failed to reach significance in reporting movement of the slate, candlestick and tambourine, participants classified as believers were significantly more likely than disbelievers to report that the hand-bell had moved. Overall, about one fifth of participants believed that the fake séance demonstrated genuine paranormal phenomena.

Conclusion: Believers are more suggestible than disbelievers for suggestions that are consistent with the existence of paranormal phenomena.

Superstition

Superstition is a belief that an object, action or circumstance not logically related to a course of events influences its outcome. Superstitions can be negative, such as the belief that breaking a mirror will cause bad luck, or positive, such as the belief that a lucky charm will bring good luck.

Some studies have suggested that superstition should be considered as separate from paranormal belief. For example, Irwin (1990) found that fantasy proneness, discussed earlier, correlated positively with global paranormal belief and with various aspects of it, such as psi and a belief in extraordinary life forms, but not with superstition. However, the findings in this area have been inconsistent.

Research has also established some of the personality factors associated with superstition. For example, Tobacyk and Shrader (1991) found that there was a relationship between superstition and self-efficacy in both men and women, in that superstitious people tended to have low self-efficacy, i.e. only a weak belief that they were capable of acting in such a way as to achieve their goals. Rudski (2004) found that superstitious people also tended to be pessimistic, Dagnall et al. (2007) found that they tended to be neurotic and Hergovich (2003) that they were more suggestible. Groth-Marnat and Pegden (1998) found that they were more sensation-seeking, a result similar to that of the Tobacyk and Milford (1983) study, mentioned in the section on extraversion in relation to belief in the paranormal.

People may be superstitious in some areas and not others. McClearn (2004) found that interest in sport was significantly correlated with a belief in superstitions related to sport, but not to superstition more generally.

Coincidence

Earlier in the chapter, a possible link between probability misjudgement and a belief in the paranormal was discussed, and this could apply equally to the understanding

12

of coincidence; people who are poor at making these judgements may see coincidences as evidence of the paranormal. However, Bressan (2002) challenged this idea, turning it on its head with an alternative explanation. In a large-scale study, she found that believers reported experiencing more coincidences than non-believers and were not as good at tasks relating to probability, and suggested that believers in the paranormal may just be more likely to connect separate events, resulting in them experiencing coincidences more often and so developing a biased understanding of probability.

Summary

- Deception depends not only on the deceiver but also on people's **willingness to be deceived**. **Expectancy** can lead to **self-deception**.
- Some psychologists suggest that **belief in the paranormal** and **superstition** should be seen as **separate**.
- Superstition has been associated with the **personal characteristics** of low self-efficacy, pessimism, neuroticism, suggestibility and sensation seeking. It may be limited in a person to **one particular area**.
- Interpreting coincidence in paranormal terms may be the result of **poor judgement of probability**, but it could also be that it might lead to it.

Belief in exceptional experience

In relation to paranormal beliefs, we have largely focused so far on ESP and PK, those aspects of psi that are most commonly investigated by parapsychologists using experimental methods. In this final section, we will consider some further aspects of paranormal experience.

Psychic healing

The followers of a number of religions believe that illnesses can be cured through non-medical means. According to Clarke (1991), there is a strong correlation between being religious and belief in psychic healing. This can take several forms, including **intercessory prayer (IP)** and '**healing intentions**', either in the presence of the person or, more commonly, in their absence, known as **distant IP**. Research results in this area have not been encouraging (see Box 12.9).

Box 12.9 Krucoff et al. (2005)

Aim: To investigate the effectiveness of prayer in the clinical outcome of coronary surgery.

Procedure: Participants were randomly assigned to one of two conditions, with 181 assigned to a 'prayer' condition, where they were prayed for by established congregations of various religions, and 192 to a control condition who received standard care. Six months after the surgery, records were compared for a recurrence of heart problems, readmission to hospital and deaths.

Results: On all measures, there was no significant difference between the two groups.

Conclusion: Prayer does not affect the outcome of medical procedures.

In a commentary on this study, Sloan and Ramakrishnan (2006) suggest that it would be unwise to discount the power of prayer because researchers cannot control for additional prayers made on behalf of the participants. The extent of this is unknown and may well be greater than the IP used for the study and is likely to vary widely from person to person. They also make the more general criticism that in this kind of study, the outcome variables are often poorly defined. They suggest that unless these problems can be addressed, studies of IP should not be carried out.

Although there is little evidence for the effectiveness of psychic healing, at least in this form, it may be that it is the belief in psychic healing that has an effect (see Box 12.10).

Box 12.10   **Lyvers et al. (2006)**

Aim: To investigate the effects of psychic healing and of belief in psychic healing, on the relief of pain.

Procedure: Twenty volunteers who suffered from chronic back pain were recruited through newspaper advertisements. Half were randomly assigned to a psychic healing treatment carried out by a well-known Australian psychic and the others to a control condition. The study used a double-blind procedure, so that neither the participants nor those running the study knew to which group a particular participant had been allocated. Participants completed the McGill Pain Questionnaire before and after treatment and a questionnaire about their beliefs in psychic healing and related phenomena before the treatment.

Results: There were no differences between conditions in terms of the ratings on the McGill Pain Questionnaire before and after treatment. However, there was a significant correlation, unrelated to whether the participants were in the psychic healing or the control condition, between scores on the 'belief' questionnaire and reported improvement on the McGill Pain Questionnaire after treatment.

Conclusion: Any effects of psychic healing are the result of belief in its effectiveness.

McClenon (2002) has proposed that belief in psychic healing promotes healing through **placebo** and **hypnotic** effects. He noted also that even if psi effects are not real, the benefits of belief will still apply. Placebo effects are basically the body healing itself, and it has been suggested, for example Hyland (2003), that expectation plays a major role. It may be that some aspects of modern medical practice, such as the requirement to give patients full information so that they can give informed consent to a procedure, may reduce expectations, so psychic healing techniques may promote healing in ways difficult to achieve in standard medical treatment.

Summary

- There is no evidence for the power of **prayer** in healing but testing it raises methodological difficulties.
- A **belief in psychic healing** may promote healing.

Out-of-body and near-death experience

An out-of-body experience (OBE) typically involves a sensation of floating outside of one's body and sometimes seeing it from a place outside the body. OBEs often occur during the borderline stage between REM sleep and waking, when the paralysis that occurs during REM sleep may persist and dream imagery may be mixed with sensory input. OBEs can be spontaneous or induced, for example by meditation and visualisation, or by electrical stimulation of the brain, particularly the temporoparietal junction, where the temporal lobe meets the parietal lobe. Blanke and Thut (2007) propose that the right temporal-parietal junction is important for the sense of spatial location of the self and that when this area malfunctions an OBE arises.

An out-of-body experience typically involves a floating sensation

The first extensive scientific study of OBEs was made by Green (1968), who collected written, first-hand accounts from a total of 400 people who had experienced an OBE, together with a questionnaire. Her aim was to collect information about these experiences, leaving open the question of whether at least some of the cases might have a paranormal explanation.

These experiences can be interpreted as paranormal or mystical. There is an occult tradition in many cultures that we have another body, an astral body separate from the physical one, which is free to roam outside our current experience of time and space. This relates to OBE experience and so OBEs may be seen as evidence of survival after death.

Several ideas have been put forward to explain why people hold these beliefs. Palmer (1978) takes a psychoanalytic view, suggesting that it relates to a fear of death. As a result of this fear, any change of body image, for example due to ageing, is seen as threatening, so an OBE is a way of re-establishing personal identity. This reduces the fear of death and increases the belief in survival after death. However, as with all psychoanalytic ideas, this proposal is difficult to test scientifically.

A physiological explanation of this experience challenges a paranormal account of OBEs. In the 1930s, Penfold operated on the brains of people with epilepsy, a procedure that required them to be conscious to make sure that the appropriate part of the brain was lesioned. When operating on one patient, he found that electrical stimulation of a part of the brain called the angular gyrus led to the patient reporting an OBE. Similarly, during an evaluation for epilepsy, Blanke et al. (2002) found that an OBE could be induced repeatedly by electrical stimulation of the right angular gyrus. However, Giesler-Petersen (2008) has pointed out that brain stimulation does not produce all the typical features of spontaneous OBEs, for example that they can take place with the eyes closed and claim to produce accurate perception of material from a remote location that is not directly visible to the eye. Greyson et al. (2008) also urge caution in drawing analogies between induced and spontaneous OBEs, pointing out that while the location of brain activation is the same in both cases, it does not necessarily follow that they can be seen as equivalent experiences; further testing is required to establish this.

Blanke et al. (2002) offer a cognitive explanation of OBEs, suggesting they are the result of the brain's failure to integrate different kinds of information. The idea of OBEs being related to information processing has been developed by Blackmore (1984). She suggests that an OBE begins when a person loses contact with sensory input from the body while remaining conscious. Drawing a parallel with dream experience, she suggests that a person may experience an OBE when he or she retains the perception of having a body, but this perception is no longer derived from the senses. The perceived world may resemble the world a person generally lives in while awake but this perception does not come from the senses. The vivid body and world is produced by the brain's ability to create convincing experiences, even in the absence of sensory information. She proposes that the cognitive system builds many models of reality at once, but at any one time, only one model is taken to represent external reality and this is the most complex, stable, or coherent, model. Normally, the chosen model is built largely from sensory input, but when there is little or no sensory information, it can break down, allowing other models to take over. The cognitive system aims to build the best model it can of the surroundings it thinks it should be seeing, based on information in memory and imagination. If this model becomes more stable than the input model, it takes over as reality, the imagined world then seems real and an OBE has occurred. This fits well with reports that an OBE can occur in conditions of sensory deprivation, described in the section on Ganzfeld studies, for example Tart (2004).

Research has also investigated whether certain people are more likely than others to have OBEs. Irwin (1985) found that this experience was most likely to occur in people who were easily hypnotised and who had a belief in the paranormal, similar to the findings in this area related to ESP. Tobacyk et al. (1987) also made a link between OBEs and belief in the paranormal but, unlike ESP research, failed to find any link with personality characteristics. Blackmore (1987) found that people who claimed to have had such experiences, when asked to describe a scene, reported clearer and more vivid images from different viewpoints than those who did not.

OBEs are often part of a **near-death experience (NDE)**. This term covers a range of sensations, including being detached from the body, feelings of levitation, extreme fear, total serenity, security or warmth, and the presence of a light. They are usually experienced when a person is close to death or has been judged to be clinically dead, i.e. showing no brainstem activity. It has been related to resuscitation after cardiac arrest, anaphylactic shock, electrocution, coma, brain haemorrhage and near-drowning or asphyxiation. The experience typically goes through a series of stages in a set order.

Stages of a NDE

- an unpleasant noise
- a sense of being dead
- a feeling of peace
- an out-of-body experience
- floating up a tunnel with a bright light at the end
- meeting dead relatives or perhaps spiritual figures
- meeting a being made of light
- experiencing your life flashing before your eyes
- reaching a boundary
- a sense of reluctantly returning to your body
- a sensation of warmth

Ring (1980) found that many people do not experience all the stages. Although many people find a NDE life-enhancing, for some the experience is unpleasant.

A clinical study of 344 patients who had been successfully resuscitated after cardiac arrest was carried out by van Lommel (2001). He found that 18% had experienced a NDE, with patients remembering details of what had happened after their heart stopped, in spite of being clinically dead. If these reports are accurate, this would seem to challenge the generally held belief that consciousness is situated entirely within the brain; this issue remains unresolved.

Some people have interpreted this kind of evidence as supporting the idea that consciousness can survive death and so see it as evidence for life after death. However, there are a number of arguments against this position. Most medical professionals see dying not as an event but as a process, of which a lack of brainstem activity is part. In no case can we therefore say that a person has died and come back to life; what we are dealing with is the process of dying, or indeed a person's belief that he or she is dying. Blackmore (1993) therefore concludes that NDEs are purely psychological phenomena, when the person facing death is experiencing hallucinations or has reached a state of depersonalisation, or they are the result of changes in brain chemistry and the nervous system.

Blackmore (1983) argues that NDEs can provide evidence of survival only if it can be shown that 'something' leaves the body during the NDE and that this 'something' could survive the death of the body. This has not been shown and it is difficult to see how anything could perform the necessary movement, perception, and information transfer. As with her account of OBEs, Blackmore goes on to suggest that these apparently mystical experiences are better explained in cognitive terms.

Blackmore (1993) also carried out a study of people in India who had had NDEs and found that their experiences — tunnels, dark places and lights — were remarkably similar to those reported in Western cultures. She argues that the fact these features appear to be independent of the person's culture supports the idea that they are a product of brain physiology. However, it could also be argued that this similarity makes a case for the idea that we all embark on a spiritual journey to an afterlife that everyone experiences.

There have been several suggestions about the possible physiological basis for NDEs. Jansen (2004) pointed out that NDEs can be reproduced by ketamine, which blocks receptors in the brain for the neurotransmitter glutamate. A flood of glutamate is also released in other conditions that are associated with NDEs, such as ischaemia and temporal lobe epilepsy, so an NDE could be the result of this kind of neurochemical action. Morse et al. (1989) put forward a similar theory, involving the serotonergic system. However, as with OBEs, this is still an area of controversy.

A near-death experience may involve the sensation of floating through a tunnel toward light

The psychodynamic ideas of Palmer (1978) in relation to OBEs apply as a possible explanation of why some people and not others see NDEs as evidence of life after death. A further psychodynamic idea has been put forward by Irwin (1993), who suggests that people who experience NDEs may have had traumatic childhood experiences to which they responded by dissociation, i.e. psychologically distancing themselves from the trauma. Although his ten participants who had experienced NDEs did indeed have a history of traumatic events in childhood, they did not have a dissociative response style.

There do not appear to be any clear differences between people who experience an NDE and those in similar circumstances who do not. For example, Locke and Shonz (1983) found no significant differences between those who had had this kind of experience and controls on measures of intelligence, extraversion, neuroticism or anxiety.

Research findings in the area of OBEs and NDEs have been interesting. However, this is a relatively new area of inquiry, and hopefully future research will help to provide a clearer picture.

Summary

- **OBEs** may be spontaneous or induced. Some people see them as evidence of life after death. There are **psychoanalytic explanations** for this belief.
- **Physiological** and **cognitive** explanations have been proposed to explain their occurrence.
- There are some **individual differences** between people who accept a paranormal explanation of OBEs and those who do not.
- **NDEs** follow a particular sequence and again raise controversy between those who believe they demonstrate that there is an **afterlife** and those who favour **physiological explanations**.

Psychic mediumship

Psychic mediumship refers to the claims of some people that they are able, under the guidance of spirits, to communicate with the spirits of the dead. Psychic mediumship started in America in 1848, when the Fox sisters, Margaret and Kate, claimed that they could receive messages from 'the spirit world beyond'. When they first heard unexplained rapping in their house, they ordered the spirit to communicate with them and answer their questions and eventually developed a system which used the number of raps to spell out the alphabet. They discovered that the spirit was a man who had been murdered in their house some years previously and was buried in the cellar. This was the start of the spiritualist movement, whose basic premise was that the human personality survived death and could communicate with our world through mediums, people who were psychically gifted.

From the start of the movement, many people who call themselves mediums have been found to be fraudulent. In 1851, a committee of medical doctors at the University of Buffalo tested the Fox sisters and attributed their raps to the cracking of their toes or knee caps against a wooden floor or bedstead. When they carried out a controlled experiment by placing the girls' feet on pillows, the rapping stopped. Late in his career, the famous magician Houdini (1874–1926) exposed several bogus mediums. By the 1920s, the spiritualist movement was thoroughly discredited because when the controls were tightened, the effects disappeared.

Nonetheless, claims of psychic mediumship have continued, fuelled in part by the media. Some mediums have popular television shows in America and have written best-selling books. There have been a number of films with psychic communication as their theme, for example *The Sixth Sense*, in which a young boy claims to see the dead and realises that communication with the dead is a gift that he can use to help the living.

A popular form of psychic mediumship is **channelling**, where mediums — now called channellers — carry out a reading in which they claim to be able to make contact with a person's dead relative or friend and to convey a message back. The only evidence that this is occurring are subjective reports based on the word of the channeller that he or she is in touch with the departed spirit. This can be done through 'hot' readings, when the channeller has found out something about the person being read, but more common are 'cold' readings, used in public performances. Hyman (1977) has shown how this may be faked. The psychic asks a general question, such as: 'Does anyone know a Jack or a Mary?' Usually this will apply to someone in the audience and the reading proceeds in a hit-and-miss fashion, with only a few lucky hits required to impress the audience. The death of someone close to us is traumatic, so we are likely to be strongly motivated to believe in his or her survival.

A study by Roe (1994) found that people realised that the psychic readings they have asked for have been given in a form that meant the information could be true for many people, but they were nonetheless convinced that some elements of the reading were especially true of them or their circumstances. This can perhaps be explained by the '**Barnum effect**', named after the American showman Phineas T. Barnum (1810–91), who famously claimed, 'There's a sucker born every minute'. In this context, Dickson and Kelly (1985) define this effect as, 'the psychological phenomenon whereby people accept general personality interpretations as accurate descriptions of their own unique personalities'. The general nature of the statements used allows clients to read their own meaning into them, as well as focusing upon characteristics of clients that may leave them especially vulnerable to this kind of deception. Clients may also underestimate the extent to which their own life experiences overlap with those of others. A further factor may be selective memory. Wilson and French (2008–09) asked participants to watch a video of a psychic giving a reading and then an interview with the client describing her reaction to the reading. The videos were scripted, and those with paranormal beliefs had less accurate recall of the reading than non-believers.

Summary

- Psychic mediums claim that they can **communicate with the dead**. **Channelling** has become popular, in part due to **media influence**.
- Many mediums have been shown to be **fraudulent**, and their methods have been explained in non-paranormal ways.
- People's **motivation to believe** is one factor in acceptance, together with **cognitive biases**.

Chapter

Psychological research and the scientific method

In this chapter, we will be looking at:

- the application of the scientific method in psychology
  - features of science and the scientific process
  - validating new knowledge and peer review
- designing psychological investigations
  - selection and application of appropriate methods
  - sampling
  - reliability
  - validity
  - ethical considerations
- data analysis and reporting research
  - graphical representations
  - probability and significance
  - statistical tests and inferential analysis
  - analysis and interpretation of qualitative data
  - conventions of reporting on psychological investigations

The application of the scientific method in psychology

There are many different ways in which research in psychology can be carried out. Many psychologists believe that the approach taken and the methods used should be scientific and should therefore be the same as those used in any other science. Whether this is the case depends to some extent on the subject matter to be studied. For example, this is the approach largely favoured by those interested in cognition.

For others, such as those working within a humanistic perspective, this is not an appropriate approach, since they are interested in exploring subjective human experience. However, we will focus in this chapter mainly on the methods used by those who aim to take a scientific approach.

Features of science and the scientific process

A major feature of science is that it aims to be objective, in that it strives to carry out research and collect data that accurately represent a phenomenon in a way that is not affected by personal or cultural biases. Objectivity is ensured by carrying out research in such a way that the results are observable and measurable. This is reflected clearly in the work of the early behaviourists, who aimed to make psychology more scientific by rejecting the idea of studying unobservable mental processes. However, it could be argued that objectivity is difficult in psychology, as psychologists who study people are people themselves, so researchers inevitably approach a study with some preconceptions, and much of what guides behaviour is internal and so not directly observable. Scientific research should also be replicable, i.e. it should be possible for someone else to repeat an experiment in exactly the same way to see if his or her findings are similar.

In order to qualify as scientific, Allport (1947) claims that theories should aim to do three things: **understand**, **predict** and **control**. One way in which they can promote understanding is by being able to provide an explanation for an observed phenomenon. However, they should also be able to organise information in a consistent way, through experimentation and observation, so that it can be used to generate general laws and principles. This is a feature of established sciences such as physics and chemistry, and one that has been adopted by psychologists who take a scientific approach to the subject. They should also aim to be **parsimonious**, i.e. to provide the greatest degree of explanation in the simplest possible way.

For a theory to be useful, it should be possible to use it to derive **predictions**, i.e. testable hypotheses that can be used either to support or to refute it. Popper (1969) suggests that research that is scientific should be constructed in such a way that hypotheses being tested are **falsifiable**, in that it should be potentially possible to test whether a hypothesis

Stockbyte/Alamy

Scientific objectivity is ensured with observable and measurable results

13

can be proved wrong. If we test the same hypothesis on many occasions and the results consistently support it, this does not prove that the hypothesis is correct. For example, to test the hypothesis that 'all swans are white', white swan after white swan could be observed, but it would always be possible that a different-coloured swan could (and indeed does) exist. Scientists should therefore aim to test a theory by creating and testing as many different hypotheses as possible. While many psychological theories meet this criterion, some do not. For example, it is hard to see how some of Freud's ideas, such as his proposal that the mind consists of id, ego and superego, could be falsified.

If theories make clear predictions, they allow us to control aspects of our environment, hopefully in ways that improve the human condition. For example, the principles of behaviourism have been used as the basis for therapies such as systematic desensitisation to help people with phobias. However, the matter of control raises ethical issues, such as who should have control over others and for what reasons.

Kuhn (1962) claimed that science is defined in terms of working within a **paradigm**, i.e. a set of assumptions, methods and terminology shared by those working within a particular scientific discipline. He suggested that there are continual revolutions in science; the contradictions inherent within a paradigm, for example challenges to it from new evidence, build up until it must be abandoned and a new paradigm takes its place, i.e. there is a **paradigm shift**. An example of this kind of shift occurred when Einsteinian physics replaced Newtonian physics.

Kuhn proposes that there are three stages in the development of a science:
- **Pre-science:** there is no generally accepted paradigm, with several different opinions about the best approach to be taken.
- **Normal science:** there is a generally accepted paradigm, which is adopted by most workers in this field. It defines how research is carried out and the findings explained.
- **Revolutionary science:** there is a paradigm shift when evidence against the old paradigm mounts up and it is replaced by a new paradigm.

Kuhn himself argued that psychology is in the pre-science stage and certainly there are different and conflicting perspectives in psychology. For example, psychodynamic, behaviourist and humanistic perspectives clearly do not support the same paradigm. Alternatively, it could be argued that psychology has gone through many paradigm shifts, for example from behaviourism to cognitive psychology, and so could be seen as a science using these criteria. Valentine (1982) has suggested that psychology has had unified paradigms in the past, in particular the behaviourist paradigm that dominated psychology in the 1940s and 1950s.

However, not everyone agrees that science progresses through the stages suggested by Kuhn. Feyerabend (1975) argues that science involves individuals, each following their own path rather than conforming to paradigms, which may only serve to stifle creativity and therefore hold back progress. This seems to reflect quite closely how psychology has developed.

There is a recognised procedure in carrying out scientific research in psychology:

Scientific procedure

- Develop a question from existing theory, research or observation of a natural phenomenon.
- Research the topic.
- Formulate a specific research question.
- Develop a research hypothesis, i.e. a prediction of what the outcome of the study is expected to be, on the basis of theory and previous research.
- Plan a study to test the research hypothesis.
- Carry out the study and collect data
- Analyse the data statistically, to see if the results support or refute the hypothesis.
- Interpret the data and draw conclusions that serve as a starting point for a new study.
- The research may then be written up as a scientific paper. Whether or not the results of the study are significant, they may raise further questions, leading to the process of inquiry starting again, in an iterative cycle. Other researchers may then replicate the study to test the findings and conclusions drawn.

Validating new knowledge and peer review

Scientists have the common aim of disseminating scientific knowledge and understanding. For this to happen, it is important that research is carried out carefully and presented appropriately. If the findings of a psychological study are submitted for publication to a reputable scientific journal, they will be subject to peer review before being published. This means that the editor of the scientific journal to whom the research has been submitted will refer it for scrutiny to other psychologists who are experts in the same field of research. There are between one and three of these referees, and the process is usually anonymous.

The referees will consider whether the research method used was suitable for the aims of the study, that adequate controls have been used to eliminate, as far as possible, the influence of extraneous variables, that scientific procedure has been followed and whether the data collected are appropriate and accurately reported. They will also look at the interpretation of the findings to see whether other interpretations are possible.

Quite a lot of research is funded by organisations, for some of whom it is in their interests not only to influence the direction research takes, but also to promote particular claims. The peer review process will ensure that any claims made are valid, based on the study under review.

The referees may or may not recommend publication, or suggest modifications before the research is published. They may also recommend publishing the research in another journal that is felt to be more suitable, where the same review process will take place before publication. The peer review process helps to cut down on obvious errors, screen out unsuitable material and generally improve the quality of the scientific literature; as a result, research published in peer-reviewed journals carries a lot of weight in the scientific community.

Another way of validating research is replication. It is possible that a researcher has made systematic errors in a piece of research or, in rare cases, has deliberately falsified the results. It is therefore common practice for other psychologists who are experts in the same field of research to repeat a study to see if they achieve similar results, i.e. to check the reliability of the data.

Editorial Image, LLC/Alamy

Peer-reviewed journals carry a lot of weight in the scientific community

Summary

- Science aims to carry out **objective** and **replicable** research.
- Theories should aim to promote **understanding**, lead to **general laws** and be **parsimonious**.
- They should lead to **predictions** that are **falsifiable** and have practical **applications**.
- Kuhn claims that a science should work within a **paradigm**. It is unclear whether psychology meets this criterion and whether it should aim to do so.
- There is a recognised **procedure** for carrying out scientific research.
- Scientific knowledge is validated by **peer review** of research and by **replication**.

Designing psychological investigations

There are numerous ways in which psychological ideas can be tested, although the choice of method used is often dictated to some extent by the topic area and the research question. There are a number of decisions relating to the design of an investigation that need to be made before carrying it out.

Selection and application of appropriate methods

The **experimental method**, the traditional method of scientific enquiry, has been the main method used by psychologists. In this method, an **independent variable (IV)** is manipulated by the experimenter, i.e. a difference is created between two or more conditions, while, as far as possible, all other variables are kept constant. The **dependent variable (DV)** is the performance of participants in the experiment, i.e. what is measured. Any difference in the DV between conditions is then seen as the effect of this manipulation.

To qualify as an experiment, there should also be an element of random allocation of participants to conditions, i.e. every participant should have an equal chance of being allocated to either condition. This method has the advantage that a cause-and-effect relationship between manipulation of the IV and a difference between conditions in the DV can be inferred, provided that any possible confounding variables — variables that could affect the outcome, but are not the IV in which the researcher is interested — are controlled.

Laboratory experiments are carried out in many areas of psychology because they give the researcher more control over the procedure; it is easier to isolate the IV and control confounding variables in laboratory conditions than elsewhere. However, laboratory experiments can sometimes lack ecological validity, i.e. they are artificial and not a good model of real life. For example, Hofling et al. (1966) were interested in whether nurses would obey instructions from a doctor who required them to break several hospital rules; this could not have been investigated in any realistic way under laboratory conditions. For this reason, field experiments may be carried out that take place in natural conditions. While field experiments have high ecological validity, they have the disadvantage of the experimenter having less control over other variables; there is more likelihood than in a laboratory experiment of confounding variables affecting the outcome. The lack of control also means that replication is more difficult. There are ethical issues; in particular, participants will not have given informed consent if they are unaware of taking part in a study.

Another type of experiment is the **natural experiment**, which takes advantage of a naturally occurring event, with a naturally occurring situational variable. For example, Williams (1985) monitored children's level of aggression in a town in Canada before and after it was able to receive television; real life provided the environmental IV of whether or not the children were exposed to television, rather than it being manipulated by the experimenter. This kind of experiment has similar advantages and disadvantages to field experiments.

The term **'quasi-experiment'** is used to describe a study that takes a broadly experimental approach but does not meet fully the criteria of an experiment, i.e. the manipulation of the IV and random allocation. For example, if a study were to compare belief in the paranormal in people of different ages, random allocation of participants to different age groups would not be possible.

With an experiment, the researcher has to decide on the design. One possibility is an **independent groups design** (also referred to as a between-groups design), where different participants take part in each condition. Participants should be randomly allocated to conditions. Since participants are only exposed to one condition, this design eliminates possible **order effects**, i.e. where carrying out a task in one condition may affect performance in the other condition(s). However, there is a problem with individual differences, since the participants in one condition may be different in some important respect from those in the other condition(s), which would bias the results.

A second possibility is a **repeated measures design** (also referred to as a within-groups design), where each participant provides data in both (or all) conditions and his or her performance in each condition is compared. An advantage of this design is that any effects of individual differences are eliminated, since the performance of each participant in one condition is compared with that same person's performance in the other condition(s). However, the main problem with this design is possible order effects, such as practice, boredom and fatigue. For example, a participant may perform less well in the second condition because he or she has become tired, not because of the experimental manipulation of the IV. It is possible to minimise these effects by **counterbalancing**, i.e. varying the order in which participants carry out conditions. If some participants start by carrying out the task in condition A, followed by condition B, while others start with B, followed by A, then any order effects should affect the results in both conditions equally. However, counterbalancing may not always be possible. For example, if the effectiveness of two teaching methods for learning were to be compared, participants could only take part in one condition and an independent groups design would need to be used. For a repeated measures design, more materials may need to be prepared. For example, in a memory study using word lists, two different lists would need to be prepared, as the experiment would be compromised if participants were asked to learn the same list again in the second condition.

One criterion of an experiment is that there should be an element of **random allocation**, to avoid the possibility of bias in the way in which the experiment is carried out. In an independent groups design, participants would be randomly allocated to a condition, i.e. all participants would have an equal chance of being placed in either condition (or any condition if there are more than two). In a repeated measures design, random allocation to conditions is not possible, as participants take part in both or all the conditions. However, the order in which they carry out each condition should be randomised, within the constraints of counterbalancing.

A final possibility is a **matched pairs design**, which aims to exploit the advantages of both independent groups and repeated measures designs, while avoiding some of the drawbacks of both. It is usually used in natural experiments, where random allocation is impossible, for example studies comparing children raised in an institution with those reared at home. Each participant is matched with another participant on characteristics that are thought to be relevant to the experiment, such as age and sex. When it is used with a laboratory or field experiment, one participant from each pair is then randomly allocated to each condition and takes part only in that condition. It is assumed that the matching process produces pairs who are so similar that they can be treated as if they were the same person and the statistical tests used to analyse the data from an experiment using a matched pairs design are the same tests that would be used for a repeated measures design. The main drawback of a matched pairs design is that the process of matching participants is time consuming, and they may not be matched on a characteristic that turns out to be important.

Summary

- **Experiments** are defined in terms of **manipulating an IV** and involving some measure of **random allocation**.
- They can be **laboratory** or **field** experiments in a natural setting. **Natural experiments** take advantage of naturally occurring events and are not true experiments. **Quasi-experiments** do not fully meet the criteria for an experiment.
- **Designs** of experiments include **independent measures**, **repeated measures** and **matched pairs**. All have advantages and drawbacks.

As well as a broadly experimental approach, a number of other methods may be used. **Correlational analysis** is a widely used technique for measuring the relationship between two variables, for example, the relationship between the experience of stress and illness. With a positive correlation, as the values of one variable increase, the values of the other variable also tend to do so. With a negative correlation, as the values of one variable increase, the values of the other variable tend to decrease.

Correlational analysis has the advantage of being able to indicate the direction, i.e. positive or negative, of the relationship between two variables and the strength of this relationship. It is often useful at the start of a research project to establish if there is a phenomenon worth investigating, which could then be explored more thoroughly using the experimental method. As we will see later, it is also used to establish the reliability and validity of tests. The main drawback is that, unlike the experimental method, it cannot establish cause-and-effect relationships. The statistical test used to analyse the data cannot show non-linear relationships. For example, the relationship between arousal and performance is initially a positive one; people are likely to carry out a task better when they are awake and alert rather than when they are half asleep. However, when arousal becomes too great, so that it can be described as stress, performance drops off. This kind of relationship is called a **curvilinear relationship** and correlational analysis would indicate no relationship between the variables.

Observational studies simply record behaviour as it occurs, either within a laboratory setting, or more usually in a natural setting (i.e. naturalistic observation), and therefore have high ecological validity. In **participant observation**, the researcher becomes part of the group being studied. The advantage of this method is that people may be more likely to be open and honest with someone whom they perceive as a member of their group. In **non-participant observation**, the researcher remains apart from the people being studied. With this method, participants are often unaware that they are being observed which, as noted earlier in relation to field experiments, can raise ethical problems. However, if carried out carefully, this method allows naturally occurring behaviour to be observed.

When observational methods are used, the researcher has no control over what is going to happen, so careful planning is necessary, i.e. what is to be observed and how observations are to be recorded. Behaviour can be filmed, so repeated viewing is possible, enabling the researcher to pick up on details that might have been missed on an earlier viewing and allowing a fuller analysis to be made of the behaviour observed. If this is not possible, the observation can be made more manageable through either **time sampling** or **event sampling**.

In time sampling, observations are made for only short periods of time within the observation period. For example, a researcher might divide the observation period into 10-minute slots and within each slot observe the behaviour for 3 minutes and use the remaining 7 minutes to make notes on his or her observations. In event sampling, a specific event is noted each time it occurs. For example, in a study investigating aggressive behaviour, a checklist of possible behaviours could be prepared, such as hitting another child, biting, verbal aggression and so on, with each category being ticked each time it occurred.

Naturalistic observation is a useful technique when the researcher is interested in something that it would be hard, if not impossible, to recreate realistically under laboratory conditions, for example driver behaviour. It can also play a part in exploratory studies to identify phenomena that could then be investigated under the more controlled conditions of a laboratory setting. One practical problem of observational studies is the **observer effect**, whereby observing a phenomenon may affect what is being observed; people may behave differently because they know they are being watched. **Observer bias** is also possible; observers may interpret what they see in line with the expectations and beliefs that they bring to the study. One way to address this problem is by creating unambiguous and objective categories and carefully training observers. To improve accurate measurement, two people can make observations of the same event(s), each collecting data independently. If their observations are similar, the data are said to have **inter-observer reliability**.

Replication is also an issue in naturalistic observational studies. It is highly unlikely that a precise replication could be carried out, as some aspects of the observation would inevitably be different if the study were to be repeated. For this reason, **generalisation**, i.e. applying the conclusions drawn from the outcome of the study more widely, is difficult.

Summary

- **Correlational analysis** describes the **relationship** between variables and can show the **direction** and **strength** of the relationship. One of its uses is to test **reliability**.
- It cannot show **cause and effect**, nor be used with **non-linear relationships**.
- **Observational techniques** record behaviour as it occurs. It can take the form of **participant** or **non-participant** observation.
- Ideally, behaviour is filmed to allow a full analysis of what is observed. If this is not possible, **time sampling** or **event sampling** may be used.

- **Naturalistic observation** is a useful technique when studying phenomena that cannot easily be created in a laboratory setting.
- **Observer effects** and **observer bias** can create problems. **Replication** and therefore **generalisation** are also difficult.

Research may use **questionnaires** and **interviews**, which involve asking people to provide information about themselves. Questionnaires have the advantage of allowing the researcher to collect a lot of data relatively easily, but one of the problems is that respondents may not be prepared to be honest in the information they give. However, this kind of issue is less likely to arise when people are completing questionnaires than when questions are asked in interviews, face-to-face. It can also be minimised by allowing people to complete questionnaires anonymously, only giving information that is relevant to the aims of the study, for example age and/or sex. Postal questionnaires allow data to be collected from a large number of people with few demands on the researcher, although the return rate of postal questionnaires is relatively low and those who choose to complete and return them may not be representative of the group of people in which the researcher is interested.

Interviews can take several forms. At its most structured, an interview can be identical to a questionnaire except that it is carried out face-to-face, with a standard set of questions and a limited number of answers from which the respondent is asked to choose. At the other end of the scale, interviews can be open-ended and unstructured. The researcher has a set number of topic areas that he or she wishes to investigate, but the respondent is encouraged to talk about the topics in any way he or she thinks appropriate, with the interviewer being free to follow up any points raised that he or she feels are interesting. This method has the advantage of producing rich and detailed data and is flexible, potentially providing information that could not easily be accessed in any other way. Conversely, analysis of the data is open to researcher bias, and because of the potentially large variation in the information given by respondents, the data are time consuming to analyse. In practice, a semi-structured interview technique is often used, to draw on the advantages of both structured and unstructured approaches. Specific questions are asked

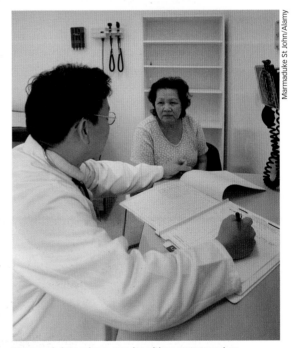

Marmaduke St John/Alamy

Research interviews can be either structured or unstructured

that require simple answers, but this information is also followed up in more detail where this is felt to be useful. One of the drawbacks of both unstructured and semi-structured interviews is that the data they provide depends on the ease with which an individual can express himself or herself, which may also be affected by the skill of the interviewer.

Case studies are in-depth investigations of an event, an individual or a small group of people who share a characteristic in which the researcher is interested. They can include interviews, detailed observation and information from others about the individual(s) being studied. While some of the data collected may be quantitative, providing precise measurements (such as test scores), at least some if not most of the data is usually qualitative, i.e. largely descriptive.

Case studies are useful for developing an understanding of a particular individual, or for investigating the characteristics of someone who is unusual in some way; for example Luria (1976) carried out a case study of a man known as 'S', who had a phenomenal memory. However, a major problem is **generalisability**, the extent to which what is true of the person or small group of people who have been studied can also be assumed to apply more widely.

Case studies rely heavily on the willingness and ability of the individual to provide accurate information. Researcher bias is also a problem.

Summary

- **Questionnaires** are widely used since they allow a lot of data to be collected relatively easily.
- There are **problems** in terms of the honesty of respondents and the return rate of postal questionnaires.
- **Interviews** can be open-ended or more tightly structured. **Semi-structured interviews** are often carried out, as they provide rich data and analysis is not as complex and time consuming as a completely unstructured approach.
- **Case studies** are in-depth studies of one or a small group of individuals who are often unusual in some way.
- They provide rich and **detailed data**, but there are problems of **generalisability, researcher bias** and **accuracy**.

Once the method to be used has been decided, other steps in the planning process need to be taken. For example, in an experiment the IV and the DV need to be **operationalised**, i.e. the IV defined in terms of how it is to be represented and the DV in terms of what is to be measured in a particular study. Similarly, a study using correlational analysis must define the **co-variables**. In an observational study, the researcher must decide what is to be observed, what data are to be collected and how data are to be recorded. If questionnaires are to be used, possible items must be generated and tested for suitability, and a similar process is necessary for the questions to be asked in interviews. The different methods to be used to collect data from a case study must also be decided.

Whatever method is chosen, the researcher is likely to carry out a **pilot study**, before the process of collecting data begins. This is a small-scale study carried out with a small number of participants, who will not take part in the main study itself. The aim is to identify any potential problems with the procedure. For example, in an experiment a pilot study is useful in making sure that any instructions given to participants are clear, and it is helpful in determining the timing and presentation of any materials. In a study using naturalistic observation, a pilot study will help to establish the possibilities and potential problems of the planned observation. For questionnaires and interviews, a pilot study can help to identify questions that are ambiguous, or that do not produce relevant material. In all cases, necessary adjustments can then be made before the study is carried out.

Summary

- A **pilot study** should be carried out before starting the main study, in order to refine the precise ways in which the study will be carried out and data collected.

Sampling

A **target population** is a set of people who share particular characteristics in which the researcher is interested. In most cases, because of limitations in terms of time and resources, it is not feasible to test every member of the population, so a sample is tested. Ideally, this should be a **representative sample**, i.e. one in which all the characteristics of the parent population are represented in appropriate proportions. If the sample is representative, it follows that any conclusions drawn from the results of testing it can be generalised to the population as a whole, since the sample will be an accurate representation. An **unrepresentative sample** is a biased sample, i.e. some characteristics of the parent population are either over- or under-represented, and it would therefore be unwise to draw general conclusions based on its data. If the sample is too small, it is likely to be biased; while a large sample is more likely to be representative, it also requires more resources. Whatever the sample size, there is likely to be **sampling error**, i.e. inaccuracies in the sample in terms of its representativeness of the parent population. This is reduced, although not necessarily eliminated, by testing a larger sample.

There are several ways of selecting a sample. In **random sampling**, every member of the population has an equal chance of being selected to be part of the sample each time a selection is made. For example, if the population from which the sample is to be drawn is students attending a particular college, all the students at the college could be given a number. A computer programme that generates random numbers could then be used to select the sample, matching the numbers given by the computer with the numbers given to the students until an appropriate sample size is reached. The strength of this method is that there is no possibility of experimenter bias in the selection of the sample, where the experimenter, consciously or not, might select participants who are likely to confirm the hypothesis being tested. On the other hand, a random sample may not be representative of the population. For example, in this case it could be that by chance the computer selects only male students, so female students would not be represented in the sample. It is also only possible when a list of every member of the population is available.

Systematic sampling may be used, where participants are selected using a structured system. Using the college example, class registers of all the students at the college could be used, with every fifth and tenth person forming the sample. This is not random, since only those students in the relevant positions on the registers are chosen. It shares the strengths and drawbacks of random sampling, but is likely to be a faster process. It is sometimes called **quasi-random sampling**.

In an **opportunity sample**, anyone who is available and willing to take part in the study becomes part of the sample. This is a straightforward way of obtaining a sample and is often used by students carrying out a psychological study. However, the sample could be affected by experimenter bias; for example, the experimenter might only approach students whom he or she knows, so the sample could be biased in terms of age and the subjects being studied.

In a **self-selecting sample**, people volunteer either directly or indirectly to be part of the sample. For example, Milgram (1963) advertised in a newspaper for people to take part in his studies of obedience. This approach might lead to a biased sample, in that only a particular kind of person might respond. People may also volunteer indirectly. For example, if a researcher were interested in possible gender differences in how people respond to someone dropping shopping in the street, the people he or she observes, who help or do not help to pick up the shopping, would be unaware that they were taking part in a study, but would be indirectly volunteering by walking along the street at that time.

Summary

- Samples aim to be **representative** of the population from which they are drawn so that the results can be **generalised**.
- Sampling methods can introduce **sampling error**, which can lead to a **biased sample**. Most methods are likely to be biased.

In **quota sampling**, the sample is selected so that particular characteristics are represented in the same proportion in which they occur in the target population. As an example, if the population were students at a college, with 40 males and 30 females in the first year and 50 males and 20 females in the second year, the sample would need to include first-year students in the proportion of 4 males to 3 females and second-year students in the proportion of 5 males to 2 females. This is the only sampling method that tries to ensure representativeness, rather than simply making it likely. The drawback is that the selection of the sample may be complex if several different characteristics of the population are to be represented in appropriate proportions.

Reliability

Reliability in psychological research refers to **consistency**. For example, to be a reliable measuring instrument, a personality test needs to give relatively consistent results if the same person takes it more than once. This is **test-retest reliability**, which assesses external reliability, i.e. the reliability of a test over time. If the test is reliable, scores on the two occasions should be similar. The timing here is important, because if the test is repeated too soon, the person taking it might remember the answers he or she had given the first time, while if there is a long gap, there might have been important changes in the person's life.

Split-half reliability refers to internal reliability, i.e. the extent to which all parts of the test contribute equally to what is being measured. A test can be split in several ways, for example the first half of the test and the second half, odd number and even number questions, or randomly. If the test is reliable, the halves should yield similar results.

Inter-rater (or inter-observer) reliability refers to the extent to which two people rating or observing the same event agree in their assessments. For example, if a rating scale is to be used to assess levels of aggression shown by children playing in a playground, two or more raters would independently rate each child and their ratings would be compared. The observations would be reliable if the ratings were similar.

All these types of reliability can be tested using **correlational analysis**. If a test or rating scale is reliable, there should be a high positive correlation. If this is not the case, the test items or rating scale will need to be adjusted and re-tested, and reliability will need to be established, before the test or scale is used in psychological research.

Validity

Validity refers to the extent to which research is measuring what it sets out to measure. A test may be reliable, but not valid. For example, a personality test could be shown to be reliable, but it could not be considered a valid test of, for example, intelligence.

Ecological validity refers to the extent to which a test situation adequately models real life and so the conclusions can be generalised from the conditions in which the research is carried out to the natural environment. A criticism frequently made of laboratory studies is that they lack ecological validity. For example, Ebbinghaus' research using meaningless, nonsense syllables was a highly artificial way of testing memory, relating poorly to the role of meaning in memory in everyday life.

External validity is the extent to which the results of a research study can be generalised to other people and other situations, and **internal validity** is the extent to which an effect found in a study can be taken to be real and brought about by the experimental situation. For example, Berkowitz and LePage (1967) were interested in whether the presence of a gun in the laboratory would make participants respond more aggressively, measured by the number of electric shocks they gave when evaluating another person's performance. However, many of the participants claimed that they had guessed that the gun was there to encourage aggressive feelings, so may have responded in an aggressive way because they believed this was expected of them, rather than because the gun acted as an aggressive cue.

One way to improve internal validity is to carry out a small-scale pilot study before the main study and ask for feedback from the participants, so that any necessary adjustments can be made.

There are two overall types of validity in research:

- **content-related validity** — is the content of the test appropriate for what the test aims to measure?
- **criterion-related validity** — does it relate well to other measures to which it is believed to be related?

A simple way of assessing content validity is to use **face validity** — does the test appear to be testing what it is setting out to test? For example, a test that asks how a person would respond to particular situations and other people seems to be testing personality and so would have face validity. A person who is an expert in that particular field might assess the content, in terms of its nature and the range of material it covers, to make this assessment. **Construct validity** refers to the extent to which test items relate to the hypothetical constructs that underlie them. For example, the **Eysenck Personality Inventory (EPI)** relates to the personality theory on which the questionnaire is based.

One way of testing for criterion-related validity is to assess its **predictive validity**; if this is high, the results of the test should be similar to the outcome of another later measure to which it is assumed to be related. For example, an individual's measured intelligence on an IQ test might be assumed to be a good predictor of his or her highest level of academic qualification. **Concurrent validity** is another way of testing criterion-related validity. For example, when a new personality test is being developed, it would be evaluated in terms of the extent to which it produces similar results to an existing personality test.

Summary

- **Reliability** refers to consistency. **Test-retest reliability** is a test of external reliability, and **split-half reliability** is a test of internal reliability.
- **Inter-rater reliability** refers to the level of agreement of ratings made by two observers of the same event.
- Reliability is tested using **correlational analysis**.
- **Validity** refers to the extent to which a study is actually testing what it sets out to test.
- A distinction can be made between **external** and **internal** validity.
- **Content-related validity** refers to whether the content of a test is appropriate for what the test aims to measure.
- **Criterion-related validity** assesses whether a test relates to other associated measures.

Ethical considerations

Ethics need to be considered before any research is carried out. This is particularly important in psychology because people and non-human animals are capable of pain and fear. People are thinking creatures and may experience participating in research as threatening, embarrassing or stressful. For this reason, the **British Psychological Society (BPS)** and similar societies in other countries have developed guidelines in relation to issues that need to be considered before research can be carried out. It is important that there is mutual confidence and respect between researcher and participants, and the guidelines help to promote this.

Ideally, potential participants should be given full information about the aims and procedures of a study before they decide whether or not they are willing to take part. They would then be able to give **fully informed consent**. However, in some circumstances, this is not possible. For example, children may be too young to understand, or below the legal age of consent. Consent must then be obtained from parents or guardians. Informed consent can also be an issue with some adults, for example those with a mental disorder or learning difficulties, where consent from a responsible adult on the person's behalf would be needed. Researchers would also need to be sensitive to any change in the participant's demeanour that might suggest that he or she was no longer happy to take part.

Sometimes full information would jeopardise the study, and some element of **deception** may be necessary. For example, if the participants in Milgram's obedience experiments had been told that the study was about obedience and that no electric shocks were given, the research could not have produced valid results. The guidelines do not state that participants should never be deceived, but only when deception is unavoidable.

Debriefing involves giving participants full information about the study, if this has not already been done before they have agreed to take part, and answering any questions they may have. It is particularly important if information has had to be withheld, or if deception has been involved. They should also be reassured about their own performance and that it was in no way unusual or shameful. This can be linked to the guideline which states that participants should be protected from physical or psychological harm, as it helps to ensure that participants leave the study in as positive a frame of mind as when they arrived. When planning a study, a researcher should consider how he or she might be able to modify what he or she plans to do to cause participants as little stress as possible.

Participants need to know at the outset that they have the **right to withdraw** from the study at any time and to have their data destroyed. This needs to be given particular emphasis when there is an existing relationship between the researcher and potential participants, particularly when the researcher is in a position of authority, for example when the researcher is a lecturer and participants are students. In this case, steps must be taken to ensure that consent is freely given, and it should be made clear that deciding not to take part will have no negative consequences.

The BPS guidelines highlight the importance of **confidentiality**, which is a legal right under the Data Protection Act. Anonymity is part of confidentiality. However, there are exceptions to the rule of confidentiality when psychologists feel they have a wider ethical duty. For example, if a psychologist became aware that a participant was contemplating suicide, he or she might not feel bound to respect the participant's confidentiality, but should make sure that help was offered.

It is a well-accepted principle of psychological research that if researchers are in any way unsure about the procedures in a study and their possible effects on participants, they should ask a colleague for advice. Ideally, this should be someone who has carried out similar research and who will not be affected by the outcome of the research and so can offer an unbiased opinion. With most university studies, researchers will need to put forward a research proposal to an **ethics committee**, who will decide whether it should go ahead, and suggest any changes that might be made to make the study more ethical. Similarly, if informed consent is not possible, one way to tackle the problem is to discuss the study with people from the population from which the sample is drawn, but who are not participating, and ask for their advice. This may be particularly useful when the participants are drawn from a population of whom the researcher has little knowledge, for example from different ethnic or national groups.

In many observational studies, participants are not aware that their behaviour is being observed. They have not consented to take part and are not debriefed afterwards; deception may also be involved. This kind of study involves what is called **involuntary participation** and may involve invasion of privacy. It could be argued that if a behaviour is taking place in a public place, when people would expect their behaviour to be seen by others, consent is implicitly being given for it to be observed. Certainly, if the behaviour observed is uncontroversial, ethical problems are relatively minimal.

Research must be carried out with sensitivity and with an awareness of the rights of participants and respect for their contribution to psychological knowledge.

Summary

- The **BPS** has produced **ethical guidelines** for psychological research. These give detailed advice about issues that researchers need to consider before embarking on research.

Data analysis and reporting research

Once data from a study have been collected, they must be analysed and the findings reported in an appropriate way, so that information gathered can be communicated to the scientific community. In this section, we will look briefly at how this is done.

Graphical representations

Descriptive statistics refers to ways in which quantitative data can be summarised or presented in an easily accessible way. One way in which this can be done is to show the data in an experiment by using charts and graphs, appropriately titled and labelled, to present a clear overview of the findings of a study.

One simple way of doing this is to use a **bar chart** (or **bar graph**). Bar charts are often used to show the **means** or **medians** for the different conditions of an experiment, or the percentages of participants who fall into different categories. They therefore allow visual comparisons to be made easily. The first chart, in Figure 13.1, shows the means for a memory experiment, comparing recall for words presented in a semantic hierarchy and presented randomly. The second compares the prosocial behaviour of males and females in terms of helping someone to pick up dropped groceries.

Figure 13.1 *Examples of bar charts*

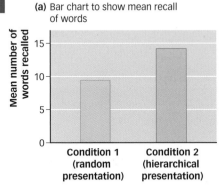

(a) Bar chart to show mean recall of words

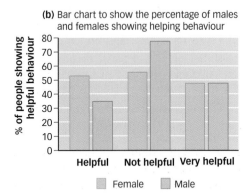

(b) Bar chart to show the percentage of males and females showing helping behaviour

Alternatively, when presenting data where the measurements are precise, in that the scale used has equal intervals between the points on the scale, such as measures of times or length, a **histogram** can be used. The bars are of equal width and are drawn touching each other. Since histograms can only be used with continuous data, i.e. where there are no gaps between scores for the categories, categories that do not contain scores must also be shown, as in the first category in Figure 13.2. The categories are shown on the *x*-axis, with the midpoint of each category identified. The frequency with which each category occurs is shown on the *y*-axis. The example in Figure 13.2 displays the results from a memory test, in which participants have been shown 30 words and are asked to write down as many as they can remember.

Figure 13.2 *Histogram to show the number of words recalled on a memory test*

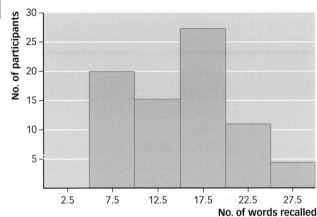

A **frequency polygon** is an alternative to a histogram (see Figure 13.3). Instead of using bars, the midpoints at the top of each bar are joined. It is a useful technique for showing the results of two or more conditions together. In a memory experiment, participants in one condition could be asked to use the method of loci to aid recall, where items are associated with a well-known place, for example mentally placed around your house, with no particular strategy suggested in the control condition.

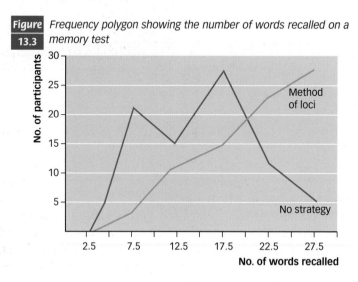

Figure 13.3 *Frequency polygon showing the number of words recalled on a memory test*

Data from correlational studies are presented using a **scattergraph**. Each of the two variables being correlated is represented on one of the axes, each labelled with one of the variables. The point where the two scores of each individual intersect is marked (see Figure 13.4).

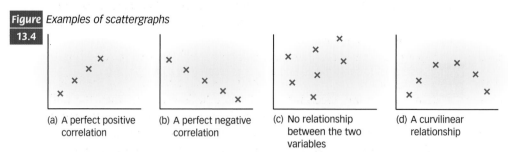

Figure 13.4 *Examples of scattergraphs*

(a) A perfect positive correlation

(b) A perfect negative correlation

(c) No relationship between the two variables

(d) A curvilinear relationship

In practice, there is rarely a perfect positive or a perfect negative correlation, so it is helpful to draw on a line of best fit, i.e. a line that is as close as possible to all the points that have been marked. This will indicate the direction of any relationship. The closeness to this line of the points marked suggest how strong that relationship is; the closer the points, the stronger the relationship. Any outliers, i.e. points well away from the line, will indicate a reduction of the size of the relationship (see Figure 13.5).

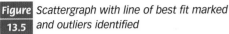

Figure 13.5 Scattergraph with line of best fit marked and outliers identified

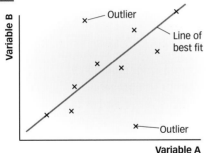

Variable B

Outlier

Line of best fit

Outlier

Variable A

Summary

- **Graphical representation** provides a visual summary of the data.
- Methods include **bar charts**, **histograms** and **frequency polygons**.
- **Scattergraphs** are used for correlational studies.

Unit 4

Probability and significance

When a study produces quantitative data, a statistical analysis can be carried out that indicates the **probability** of a particular pattern of results coming about by chance. If this is small — conventionally in psychology equal to or less than 5% — then the results are considered to be **significant**. This is usually expressed as $p \leq 0.05$. In an experiment, this is then interpreted in terms of the manipulation of the IV having caused the difference in the DV. In correlational analysis, it is accepted that there is a genuine relationship, either positive or negative, between the variables. It may be that the test will show that the results are even more significant, for example $p \leq 0.01$, where there is only a 1% or less probability of the results coming about by chance, an even more convincing result.

The interpretation of significance relates to the hypotheses generated for a study. A researcher will have generated two hypotheses:

- **The research hypothesis** (or alternative hypothesis, or in the case of an experiment, the experimental hypothesis): this states that there will be a significant difference between two conditions, or a significant relationship between variables, in the case of correlational analysis.
- **The null hypothesis:** this states that there will be no difference or relationship.

If the statistical test indicates that there is only a small probability of the difference or relationship coming about if the null hypothesis was true, then the null hypothesis can be rejected in favour of the research hypothesis. The term **alternative hypothesis** may be used to describe the research hypothesis because it is the alternative to the null hypothesis, as it is the likelihood of the null hypothesis being true that statistical analysis is actually testing.

However, there are two errors that can come about when reaching a conclusion based on the results of a statistical text:

- **Type I error:** the null hypothesis is rejected in favour of the research hypothesis when the results are actually due to chance. The probability of this happening is given by the level of statistical significance, so it is more likely if the results are significant at the 5% level than at the 1% level.

■ **Type II error:** the null hypothesis is retained, even though the research hypothesis is correct.

The likelihood of a Type I error can be reduced if a more stringent level than 5%, such as 1%, is adopted. However, this would also increase the likelihood of a Type II error. Similarly, the likelihood of a Type II error can be reduced by using a less stringent level such as 10%, although this would increase the likelihood of a Type I error. The 5% level is a compromise, which keeps the probability of either kind of error quite low. However, the more stringent 1% level is used when it is important that a Type I error is not made, for example when the effectiveness of a therapeutic treatment is being evaluated. This level may also be used when a piece of research is challenging existing findings.

Summary

- Statistical analysis shows the probability of a result coming about by chance. Conventionally in psychology, the results of a study are considered to be significant if this is **equal to or less than 5%**.
- If the result is significant, the null hypothesis can be rejected.
- The 5% level is a compromise between the likelihood of making a **Type I error** and a **Type II error**. A more stringent level is used when it is crucial to avoid a Type 1 error.

Statistical tests and inferential analysis

Quantitative data are analysed using statistical tests, which are known as **inferential statistics**. A number of possible tests can be used. Some of these, **parametric tests**, can only be used with data where particular criteria are met, but there are also **non-parametric tests**, which can be used with any kind of data. They are less sensitive than parametric tests but are quick and easy to use. Which test will be used will depend on the study.

For an experiment looking for a difference between conditions, the decision as to which test to use depends on the level of measurement used and the design of the study. The term **levels of measurement** refers to the precision of the data gathered; what this will be is decided before the study takes place. For example, to return to the study of observing people helping or not helping someone to pick up dropped groceries in the street, it would be possible to put people into categories, i.e. 'helped' or 'did not help'. This is called **category** or **nominal data**; it is not very informative, as someone who barely helped would be put in the same category as someone who helped a lot. An alternative that would bring out some of the differences between those who helped would be to rate each passer-by on a **rating scale**, for example of 1–10, where 1 would indicate little help (for example pushed an item of shopping with their foot towards the shopper), 5 would be quite helpful (several items picked up and returned to the shopper) and 10 would be extremely helpful (made sure all the items were picked up and that the shopper was happy to go on her way).

This is an example of **ordinal data**, i.e. data in the form of scores that can be put in order. The design of the study, i.e. whether it is independent groups (with different participants in each condition) or repeated measures (where each participant provides data in all conditions and his or her performance in each condition is compared) also affects the choice of test. For the purposes of choosing a test, a matched pairs design is treated as a repeated measures design.

For studies looking at a relationship between variables, the test chosen will depend on whether the data are nominal or ordinal. Figure 13.6 shows the test to be used on the basis of these criteria.

Figure 13.6 *Choosing a statistical test*

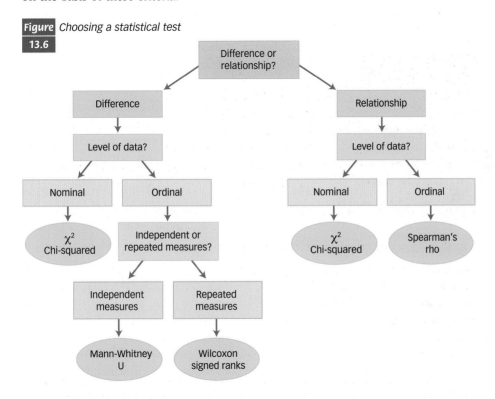

Summary

- Statistical tests are used to analyse **quantitative data**.
- In **experiments** that look for a **difference** between conditions, the choice of test depends on the **level of measurement** used and the **design** of the experiment.
- For studies that look for a **relationship** between variables, the choice of test depends on the **level of measurement** used.

Analysis and interpretation of qualitative data

As qualitative data are descriptive and not in numerical form, statistical tests cannot be used. Although the main emphasis in qualitative research is on detailed description of behaviour, many of the same principles apply as with quantitative data. Information needs to be presented in such a way to give a clear picture of what are felt to be important aspects of the findings, in a structured way and with evidence to support the analysis of the data.

Some forms of numerical presentation can be used. Data may be put into categories and percentages in each category may be given. For example, in the Strange Situation, the percentages of children falling into each of the attachment categories — secure, insecure-avoidant and insecure-ambivalent — are usually given. Graphical techniques such as bar charts can also be used to display this kind of information. The use of categorisation is widespread in qualitative research, but does not necessarily involve quantitative analysis. Another way in which the presentation of data can be structured is by the use of **thematic analysis**, where themes that emerge from the material are identified and discussed.

Summary

- In qualitative research, some forms of **numerical** and **graphical presentation** may be used.
- Material may be **analysed thematically**.
- Analysis is **subjective**, so interpretation must be supported by evidence drawn from the data.

With quantitative research, the results of statistical tests provide objective evidence that allows conclusions to be drawn, in terms of the research hypothesis that is being tested. In qualitative research, there is no such objective evidence on which conclusions can be based. Interpretation of the findings is necessarily subjective, so it is important that interpretation is supported by evidence drawn from the behaviour that is being analysed; specific examples of behaviour can be used to illustrate the main points to emerge. If a verbal interaction is being analysed, quotations can be used to highlight important points.

Conventions of reporting on psychological investigations

Careful planning of a research project and analysis of the data are only part of research. Communicating the findings to others and commenting on them is also an important part of the process and there is a conventional way in which this is done, with the report divided into sections. For **quantitative research**, reports are written in an impersonal style, for example 'Participants were read the instructions' rather than 'I read the instructions to the participants'.

The report needs to be given a suitable **title**. This should be concise, but at the same time give a clear idea of the research question that was investigated. The title often includes the IV and DV of an experiment, or the two co-variables in correlational research.

The next section is the **abstract**, a short summary of the research, with information drawn from the four main sections of the report: introduction, method, results and discussion. For this reason, it is usually written last, when the main body of the report has been completed. The aim is to give readers a clear and accessible overview of the research so that they can decide whether they would like to read about it in more detail. It should make brief reference to background theory, the aims of the study and the hypothesis being tested. It should say how the hypothesis was tested and give details of the statistical analysis. Finally, it should include brief comment on any limitations of the research and suggest how the topic could be followed up in future research.

This is followed by the **introduction**, the purpose of which is to provide a rationale for the research being carried out. It starts with an outline of background theory and related research. This should lead to the aims of the research and a statement of the hypothesis being tested.

The **method** section then gives a detailed account of how the study was carried out. It should contain enough information for full replication to be possible. It is divided into four subsections:

- **Design:** this states the method used, for example a laboratory experiment, and the design if it is an experiment, and should identify the conditions (or the variables in correlational analysis). Factors that have been controlled, i.e. that have been kept the same in different conditions, should be stated.
- **Participants:** the population from which the sample has been drawn should be identified, together with the sampling method used. The number and age range of participants and a breakdown by gender are given, along with other relevant information; for example, in a study involving colour, such as the Stroop test, it would be relevant to state that no participant was colour-blind.
- **Materials/apparatus:** apparatus could include a computer, if stimulus material has been presented in this way, or the method used to time performance if this is what is being measured. Materials such as word lists, questionnaires, tests, a list of questions asked and so on are mentioned, and samples included in numbered appendices. Scoring systems for tests and questionnaires are also included, so that full replication would be possible. If instructions given to participants are lengthy these are also referred to and included in the appendices.
- **Procedure:** this section gives a detailed account of how the study was carried out, such as including the time allowed for participants to carry out a task, again to make replication possible. Any ethical issues also need to be mentioned, together with how they were dealt with, or why they were not thought to be problematic.

For a quantitative study, the **results** section is usually quite short. It starts by restating the research hypothesis and then presents summary data, such as means and standard deviations in each condition, in an easily accessible form, i.e. a table or graph. Readers are referred to more detailed data in an appendix. The statistical test used to analyse the data is identified and the results given, together with a statement as to whether they justify rejecting the null hypothesis.

The **discussion** section does several things. It relates back to the theoretical issues and research outlined in the introduction in the light of the results and considers the implications of the findings. It may also identify any weaknesses or limitations of the methodology in the study and suggest how these might be addressed in future research. It will also discuss the direction that future research in this particular area might usefully take. It may end with a brief conclusion, which restates briefly the findings of the study, says what conclusions can be drawn from them and indicates any theoretical or methodological problems.

The report will then have a list of **references**. In the report, various theories will have been mentioned and research studies carried out by other psychologists, and these are listed in alphabetical order in a standard form at the end of a report. The aim here is to make it easy for anyone reading the report to find the original material referred to and so check its accuracy.

Finally, there will be the numbered **appendices** that have been referred to in the report. These will provide full information about the procedures, materials and the results of the statistical analysis carried out.

The system is similar for **qualitative research**. However, there are some differences. As this kind of research acknowledges the subjectivity of the researcher, it is acceptable to write in a more personal style. Instead of a hypothesis, a more general **research question** is used, as a precise prediction of the outcome is not possible and studies are often exploratory in nature. In most cases, the results section of a quantitative report is replaced by **analysis**, where the data are described, for example by identifying themes, supported with quotations. If the material is verbal, a transcript should be provided as an appendix, on the general principle that all materials related to the study should be made available to the reader. The discussion section is similar to that of a quantitative report, but a qualitative report will also include a **reflexive analysis**. This discusses how the researcher's own experiences, beliefs and expectations might influence their analysis and interpretation of the data. It may also discuss issues arising from the interpretations they have made and suggest other ways that the data might be analysed and interpreted.

Summary

- **Reports** of psychological research follow an **established format**, in which particular materials are put into specific sections.
- There are minor **differences** in reporting **quantitative** and **qualitative** research.

AQA(A)
A2 Psychology

Appendix

References

Abdel-Rahim, A. R. et al. (1988) 'Familial resemblances for cognitive abilities and personality in an Egyptian sample', *Personality and Individual Differences*, Vol. 9, pp. 155–163.

Achenbach, T. M. et al. (1987) 'Child/adolescent behavioral and emotional problems: Implications of cross-informant correlations for situational specificity', *Psychological Bulletin*, Vol. 101, No. 2, pp. 213–232.

Adam, T. C. and Epel, E. S. (2007) 'Stress, eating and the reward system', *Physiology & Behavior*, Vol. 91, No. 4, pp. 449–458.

Agrawal, A. et al. (2008) 'Autosomal linkage analysis for cannabis use behaviors in Australian adults', *Drug and Alcohol Dependence*, Vol. 98, No. 3, pp. 185–190.

Agrawal, A. and Lynskey, M. T. (2008) 'Are there genetic influences on addiction: Evidence from family, adoption and twin studies', *Addiction*, Vol. 103, No. 7, pp. 1069–1081.

Ainsworth, M. et al. (1978) *Patterns of Attachment: a Psychological Study of the Strange Situation*, Lawrence Erlbaum.

Ajzen, I. (1991) 'The theory of planned behavior', *Organizational Behavior and Human Decision Process*, Vol. 50, pp. 179–211.

Ajzen, I. and Madden, T. J. (1986) 'Prediction of goal-directed behavior: attitudes, intentions and perceived behavioral control', *Journal of Experimental Social Psychology*, Vol. 22, pp. 453–474.

Ajzen, I., and Fishbein, M. (2004) 'Questions raised by a reasoned action approach: comment on Ogden (2003)', *Health Psychology*, Vol. 23, No. 4, pp. 431–434.

Albert, D. J. et al. (1993) 'Aggression in humans: what is its biological foundation?', *Neuroscience & Biobehavioral Reviews*, Vol. 17, No. 4, pp. 405–425.

Allen, K. N. et al. (2007) 'Effectiveness of nutrition education on fast food choices in adolescents', *Journal of School Nursing*, Vol. 23, No. 6, pp. 337–341.

Allport, G. W. (1947) *The Use of Personal Documents in Psychological Science*, Holt, Rinehart and Winston.

Anand, B. K. and Brobeck, J. R. (1951) 'Hypothalamic control of food intake in rats and cats', *Yale J Biol Med*, Vol. 24, No. 2, pp.123–40.

Anastasi, A. (1958) in Lerner, R. M. (1986) *Concepts and Theories in Human Development* (2nd edn), Random House.

Anderson, C. A. (2002) 'Violent video games and aggressive thoughts, feelings, and behaviors', in Calvert, S. et al. (eds) *Children in the Digital Age: Influences of Electronic Media on Development*', Praeger Publishers/Greenwood Publishing Group.

Anderson, J. L. and Crawford, C. B. (1992) 'Modeling costs and benefits of adolescent weight control as a mechanism for reproductive suppression', *Human Nature*, Vol. 3, No. 4, p. 299–334.

Anderson, K. B. (1997) 'Cognitive and personality predictors of male-on-female aggression: an integration of theoretical perspectives', *Dissertation Abstracts International: Section B: The Sciences and Engineering*, Vol. 58, No. 6-B, p. 3365.

Annis, R. C. and Frost, B. (1973) 'Human visual ecology and orientation anisotropies in acuity', *Science*, Vol. 182, pp. 729–731.

Apostolou, M. (2008) 'Bridewealth and brideservice as instruments of parental choice', *Journal of Social, Evolutionary, and Cultural Psychology*, Vol. 2, No. 3, pp. 89–102.

Archer, J. and Lloyd, B. (2002) *Sex and Gender* (2nd edn), Cambridge University Press.

Archibald, A. B. et al. (2002) 'Parent-adolescent relationships and girls' unhealthy eating: testing reciprocal effects', *Journal of Research on Adolescence*, Vol.12, No. 4, pp. 451–461(11).

Argyle, M. (1994) *The Psychology of Interpersonal Behaviour* (5th edn.), Penguin.

Arms, R. L. et al. (1979) 'Effects on the hostility of spectators of viewing aggressive sports', *Social Psychology Quarterly*, Vol. 42, No. 3, pp. 275–279.

Arnett, J. J. (2007) 'The myth of peer influence in adolescent smoking initiation', *Health Education & Behavior*, Vol. 34, No. 4, pp. 594–607.

Aronson, E. (1968) 'Dissonance theory: progress and problems', in Abelson, R. P. et al. (eds) *Theories of Cognitive Consistency: A Sourcebook*, Rand McNally.

Asch, S. E. (1951) 'Effects of group pressure upon the modification and distortion of judgments' in Guetzkow, H. (ed.) *Groups, Leadership and Men: Research in Human Relations*, Carnegie Press.

Aubrey, J. S. and Harrison, K. (2004) 'The gender-role content of children's favorite television programs and its links to their gender-related perceptions', *Media Psychology*, Vol. 6, No. 2, pp. 111–146.

Aust, C. F. and Zillmann, D. (1996) 'Effects of victim exemplification in television news on viewer perception of social issues', *Journalism and Mass Communication Quarterly*, Vol.73, pp. 787–803.

Avis, J. and Harris, P. L. (1991) 'Belief-desire reasoning among Baka children: evidence for a universal conception of mind', *Child Development*, Vol. 62, No. 3, pp. 460–467.

Baicy, K. et al. (2007) 'Leptin replacement alters brain response to food cues in genetically leptin-deficient adults', *Proceedings of the National Academy of Sciences of the United States of America*, Vol. 104, No. 46, pp. 18276–18279.

Baillargeon, R. (1993) 'The object concept revisited: new directions in the investigation of infants' physical knowledge', in Granrud, C. (ed.) *Visual Perception and Cognition in Infancy*, Erlbaum.

Bainbridge, W. S. (1978) 'Chariots of the gullible', *Skeptical Inquirer*, Vol. 3, No. 2, pp. 33–48.

Baker-Sperry, L. (2007) 'The production of meaning through peer interaction: children and Walt Disney's Cinderella', *Sex Roles*, Vol. 56, No. 11–12, pp. 717–727.

Bakker, A. B. (1999) 'Persuasive communication about AIDS prevention: need for cognition determines the impact of message format', *AIDS Education and Prevention*, Vol. 11, No. 2, pp. 150–162.

Bandura, A. et al. (1963) 'Transmission of aggression through imitation of aggressive models', *Journal of Abnormal and Social Psychology*, Vol. 63, pp. 575–582.

Bandura, A. et al. (1963) 'Vicarious reinforcement and imitative learning', *Journal of Abnormal and Social Psychology*, Vol. 67, No. 6, pp. 601–607.

Banks, W. P. and Flora, J. (1977) 'Semantic and perceptual processes in symbolic comparisons', *Journal of Experimental Psychology*, Human Perception and Performance, Vol. 3, No. 2, pp. 278–290.

Barbarich, N. (2002) 'Is there a common mechanism of serotonin dysregulation in anorexia nervosa and obsessive compulsive disorder?', *Eat Weight Disord*, Vol. 7, No. 3, pp. 221–31.

Baron, R. A. (1977) *Human Aggression*, Plenum.

Baron, R. A. and Byrne, D. (1997) *Social Psychology* (8th edn), Allyn and Bacon.

Baron-Cohen, S. et al. (1985) 'Does the autistic child have a "theory of mind"?', *Cognition*, Vol. 21, No. 1, pp. 37–46.

Bartholow, B. et al. (2006) 'Chronic violent video game exposure and desensitization to violence: behavioral and event-related brain potential data', *Journal of Experimental Social Psychology*, Vol. 42, No. 4, pp. 532–539.

Basow, S. A. (1992) *Gender: Stereotypes and Roles* (3rd edn), Thomson Brooks/Cole Publishing Co.

Batcheldor, K. J. (1994) 'Notes on the elusiveness problem in relation to a radical view of paranormality', *Journal of the American Society for Psychical Research*, Vol. 88, pp. 90–115.

Bateson, G. et al. (1956) 'Toward a theory of schizophrenia', *Behavioral Science*, Vol. 1, pp. 251–264.

Baumeister, R. F. (1991) *Meanings of Life*, Guilford.

Bayley, N. (1955) 'On the growth of intelligence', *American Psychologist*, Vol. 10, No. 12, pp. 805–818.

Bean, M. K. et al. (2008) 'Rural adolescent attitudes toward smoking and weight loss: relationship to smoking status', *Nicotine & Tobacco Research*, Vol.10, No. 2, pp. 279–286.

Beck, A. et al. (1993) *Cognitive Therapy of Substance Abuse*, Guilford Press.

Beck, A. T. et al. (1990) *Cognitive Therapy of Cocaine Abuse*, Center for Cognitive Therapy.

Beck, A. T. (1967) *Depression: Causes and Treatments*, University of Philadelphia Press.

Beckley, R. E. and Chalfant, H. P. (1979) 'Contrasting images of alcohol and drug-use in country and rock music', *Journal of Alcohol and Drug Education*, Vol. 25, pp. 44–51.

Bem, D. J. (1967) 'Self-perception: an alternative interpretation of cognitive dissonance phenomena', *Psychological Review*, Vol. 74, pp. 183–200.

Bem, S. L. (1989) 'Genital knowledge and gender constancy in preschool children', *Child Development*, Vol. 60, pp. 649–662.

Bem, S. L. (1981) 'Gender schema theory: a cognitive account of sex typing', *Psychological Review*, Vol. 88, pp. 354–364.

Bem, S. L. (1974) 'The measurement of psychological androgyny', *Journal of Consulting and Clinical Psychology*, Vol. 42, pp. 155–162.

Bem, D. J. and Honorton, C. (1994) 'Does psi exist? Replicable evidence for an anomalous process of information transfer', *Psychological Bulletin*, Vol. 115, No. 1, pp. 4–18.

Benoit, W. L. (1987) 'Argument and credibility appeals in persuasion', *Southern Speech Communication Journal*, Vol. 52, pp. 181–197.

Benton, D. and Cook, R. (1991) 'Vitamin and mineral supplements improve the intelligence scores and concentration of six-year-old children', *Personality and Individual Differences*, Vol. 12, No. 11, pp. 1151–1158.

Berko, J. and Brown, R. (1960) 'Psycholinguistic Research Methods', in Mussen, P. (ed.) *Handbook of Research Methods in Child Development*, John Wiley.

Berkowitz, L. (1974) 'Some determinants of impulsive aggression: Role of mediated associations with reinforcements for aggression', *Psychological Review*, Vol. 81, No. 2, pp. 165–176.

Berkowitz, L. and LePage, A. (1967) 'Weapons as aggression-eliciting stimuli', *Journal of Personality and Social Psychology*, Vol. 7, No. 2.1, pp. 202–207.

Bernhardt, P. C. (1997) 'Influences of serotonin and testosterone in aggression and dominance: convergence with social psychology', *Current Directions in Psychological Science*, Vol. 6, No. 2, pp. 44–48.

Bhopal, K. (1997). 'South Asian women within households: dowries, degradation and despair', *Women's Studies International Forum*, Vol. 20, 483–492.

Bhui, K. et al. (1998) *Pocket Psychiatry*, W.H. Saunders.

Bigler, R. S. and Liben, L. S. (1990) 'The role of attitudes and interventions in gender-schematic processing', *Child Development*, Vol. 61, No. 5, pp. 1440–1452.

Birchwood, M. et al. (1988) *Schizophrenia: an Integrated Approach to Research and Treatment*, Longman.

Birchwood, M. et al. (1989) 'Predicting relapse in schizophrenia: the development and implementation of an early signs monitoring system using patients and families as observers: a preliminary investigation', *Psychological Medicine*, Vol. 19, No. 3, pp. 649–656.

Blackmore, S. J. and Troscianko, T. (1985) 'Belief in the paranormal: probability judgements, illusory control, and the "chance baseline shift."', *British Journal of Psychology*, Vol. 76, No. 4, pp. 459–468.

Blackmore, S. J. (1994) 'Are women more sheepish?', in Coly, L. and White, R. (eds) *Women and Parapsychology*, pp. 68–84, Parapsychology Foundation.

Blackmore, S. (1987) 'Where am I? Perspectives in imagery and the out-of-body experience', *Journal of Mental Imagery*, Vol. 11, No. 2, pp. 53–66.

Blackmore, S. (1983) 'Are out-of-body experiences evidence for survival?', *Journal of Near-Death Studies*, Vol. 3, No. 2, pp. 137–155.

Blackmore, S. J. (1993) 'Near-death experiences in India: they have tunnels too', *Journal of Near-Death Studies*, Vol. 11, No. 4, pp. 205–217.

Blackmore, S. J. (1984) 'A psychological theory of the out-of-body experience', *Journal of Parapsychology*, Vol. 48, pp. 201–218.

Blair, A. J. et al. (1989) 'The relative success of official and informal weight reduction techniques: retrospective correlational evidence', *Psychology & Health*, Vol. 3, No. 3, pp. 195–206.

Blakemore, C. (1988) *The Mind Machine*, BBC Publications.

Blanke, O. and Thut, G. (2007) 'Inducing out-of-body experiences', in Della Sala, S. (ed.) *Tall Tales About the Mind & Brain: Separating Fact from Fiction*, Oxford University Press.

Blanke, O. et al. (2002) 'Stimulating illusory own-body perceptions', *Nature*, Vol. 419, No. 6904, pp. 269–270.

Bless, H. et al. (1990) 'Mood and persuasion: a cognitive response analysis', *Personality and Social Psychology Bulletin*, Vol. 16, No. 2, pp. 331–345.

Bliss, J. et al. (1996) 'Effective teaching and learning: scaffolding revisited', *Oxford Review of Education*, Vol. 22, pp. 37–61.

Blos, P. (1967) 'The second individuation process of adolescence', *Psychoanalytic Study of the Child*, pp. 162–186.

Blount, G. (1986) 'Dangerousness of patients with Capgras syndrome', *Nebraska Medical Journal*, Vol. 71, pp. 207.

Boldizar, J. P. (1991) 'Assessing sex typing and androgyny in children: the children's sex role inventory', *Developmental Psychology*, Vol. 27, No. 3, pp. 505–515.

Book, A. S. et al. (2001) 'The relationship between testosterone and aggression: a meta-analysis', *Aggression and Violent Behavior*, Vol. 6, No. 6, pp. 579–599.

Booth, R. and O'Brien, P. J. (2008) 'An holistic approach for counsellors: embracing multiple intelligences', *International Journal for the Advancement of Counselling*, Vol. 30, No. 2, pp. 79–92.

Boring, E. G. (1923) 'Proceedings of the thirty-first annual meeting of the American psychological association, Cambridge, Massachusetts, December 27, 28, 29, 1922', *Psychological Bulletin*, Vol. 20, No. 2, pp. 61–108.

Borland, R. (1997) 'Tobacco health warnings and smoking-related cognitions and behaviours', *Addiction*, Vol. 92, No. 11, pp. 1427–1436.

Bösch, H. et al. (2006) 'Examining psychokinesis: the interaction of human intention with random number generators — a meta-analysis', *Psychological Bulletin*, Vol. 132, No. 4, pp. 497–523.

Bouchard, T. J. and McGue, M. (1981) 'Familial studies of intelligence: a review', *Science*, Vol. 212, No. 4498, pp.1055–1059.

Bradbury, T. N. and Fincham, F. D. (1990) 'Attributions in marriage: review and critique', *Psychological Bulletin*, Vol. 107, pp.3–33.

Bradley, R. H. and Caldwell, B. M. (1984) 'The relation of infants' home environments to achievement test performance in first grade: a follow-up study', *Child Development*, Vol. 55, No. 3, pp. 803–809.

Bradley, S. J. et al. (1998) 'Experiment of nurture: ablatio penis at 2 months, sex-reassignment at 7 months, and a psychosexual follow-up in young adulthood', *Pediatrics*, Vol. 102.

Brand, S. T. (2006) 'Facilitating emergent literacy skills: a literature-based, multiple intelligence approach', *Journal of Research in Childhood Education*, Vol. 21, No. 2, pp. 133–148.

Branscombe, N. R. and Wann, D. L. (1992) 'Physiological arousal and reactions to outgroup members during competitions that implicate an important social identity', *Aggressive Behavior*, Vol. 18, No. 2, pp. 85–93.

Breland, K. and Breland, M. (1961) 'The misbehaviour of organisms', *American Psychologist*, Vol. 16, pp. 681–684.

Breslin, F. C. et al. (1990) 'Family precursors: expected and actual consequences of dating aggression', *Journal of Interpersonal Violence*, Vol. 5, No. 2, pp. 247–258.

Bressan, P. (2002) 'The connection between random sequences, everyday coincidences, and belief in the paranormal', *Applied Cognitive Psychology*, Vol. 16, No. 1, pp. 17–34.

Brewer, S. (1978) *The Chimpanzees of Mt Asserik*, Knopf.

Broad, W. and Wade, N. (1982) *Betrayers of the Truth*, Simon & Schuster.

Broughton, R. et al. (1994) 'Homicidal somnambulism: a case report', *Sleep*, Vol. 17, No. 3, pp. 253–264.

Broughton, R. S. (1991) *Parapsychology: the Controversial Science*, Ballantine Books.

Brown, G. W. (1972) 'Influence of family life on the course of schizophrenic disorders: a replication', *British Journal of Psychiatry*, Vol. 121, pp. 241–248.

Brown, R. (1986) 'Postmortem evidence of structural brain changes in schizophrenia: differences in brain weight, temporal horn area, and parahippocampal gyrus compared with affective disorder', *Archives of General Psychiatry*, Vol. 43, No. 1, pp. 36–42.

Bruce, V. et al. (1996) *Visual Perception, Physiology, Psychology, and Ecology*, Psychology Press (3rd edn).

Bruce, V. and Valentine, T. (1988) 'When a nod's as good as a wink: the role of dynamic information in face recognition', in Gruneberg, M.et al. (eds) *Practical Aspects of Memory: Current Research and Issues*, Vol. 1, John Wiley.

Bruce, V. and Young, A. W. (1986) 'Understanding face recognition', *British Journal of Psychology*, Vol. 77, pp. 303–327.

Bruch, H. (1973) *Eating Disorders*, Basic Books.

Brugger, P. et al. (1993) 'Functional hemispheric asymmetry and belief in ESP: towards a "neuropsychology of belief"', *Percept Mot Skills*, Vol. 77, No. 3.2, pp.1299–308.

Bruner, J. S. and Minturn, A. L. (1955) 'Perceptual identification and perceptual organization', *Journal of General Psychology*, Vol. 53, pp. 21–28.

Bruner, J. S. and Kenney, H. (1966) *The Development of the Concepts of Order and Proportion in Children*, Wiley.

Brunner, H. G. et al. (1993) 'Abnormal behavior associated with a point mutation in the structural gene for monoamine oxidase A', *Science*, Vol. 262, No. 5133, pp. 578–580.

Bryant, R. and Dundes, L. (2008) 'Fast food perceptions: a pilot study of college students in Spain and the United States', *Appetite*, Vol. 51, No. 2, pp. 327–330.

Buckle, L. et al. (1996) 'Marriage as a reproductive contract: patterns of marriage, divorce, and remarriage' *Ethology & Sociobiology*, Vol. 17, No. 6, pp. 363–377.

Buckley, T. R. and Carter, R. T. (2005) 'Black adolescent girls: do gender role and racial identity impact their self-esteem?', *Sex Roles*, Vol. 53, No. 9–10, pp. 647–661.

Burks, B. S. (1928) 'The relative influence of nature and nurture upon mental development: a comparative study of foster parent–foster child resemblance', *Yearbook of the National Society for the Study of Education* (Part 1), Vol. 27, pp. 219–316.

Burt, C. (1966) 'The genetic determination of differences in intelligence: a study of monozygotic twins reared together and apart', *British Journal of Psychology*, Vol. 57, No. 1–2, pp.137–153.

Burton, A. M. and Bruce, V. (1992) 'I recognise your face but I can't remember your name: a simple explanation?', *British Journal of Psychology*, Vol. 83, pp. 45–60.

Burton, A. M. et al. (1990) 'Understanding face recognition with an interactive activation model', *British Journal of Psychology*, Vol. 81, pp. 361–380.

Bush, N. R. (2008) 'Tests of temperamental dispositions as moderators of neighborhood effects on adolescent problem behaviors: basic and two-part latent growth curve analyses', *Dissertation Abstracts International: Section B: The Sciences and Engineering*, Vol. 68, No. 11-B, pp. 7657.

Bushnell, I.W. R. (2003) 'Newborn face recognition', in Pascalis, O. and Slater, A. (eds) *The Development of Face processing in Infancy and Early Childhood: Current Perspectives*, NOVA Science.

Buss, D. M. (1989) 'Sex differences in human mate preferences: evolutionary hypotheses tested in 37 cultures', *Behavioural and Brain Sciences*, Vol. 12, pp. 1–49.

Buss, D. M. et al. 'Sex differences in jealousy: evolution, physiology, and psychology' *Psychological Science*, Vol. 3, No. 4, pp. 251–255.

Buss, D. M. (1999) *Evolutionary Psychology*, Allyn and Bacon.

Buss, D. M. (1989) 'Sex differences in human mate preferences: evolutionary hypotheses tested in 37 cultures', *Behavioural and Brain Sciences*, Vol. 12, pp. 1–49.

Bussey, K. and Bandura, A. (1999) 'Social cognitive theory of gender development and differentiation', *Psychological Review*, Vol. 106, No. 4, pp. 676–71.

Byrne, D. and Clore, G. L. (1970) 'A reinforcement model of evaluative responses', *Personality: An International Journal*, Vol. 1, pp.103–107.

Byrne, R. (1995) *The Thinking Ape*, Oxford University Press.

Byrne, R. and Whiten, A. (1988) *Machiavellian Intelligence: Social Expertise and the Evolution of Intellect in Monkeys, Apes and Humans*, Clarendon Press.

Cacioppo, J. T. and Petty, R. E. (1982) 'The need for cognition', *Journal of Personality and Social Psychology*, Vol. 42, pp. 116–131.

Calder, B. J. et al. (1974) 'The relation of cognitive and memorial processes to persuasion in a simulated jury trial', *Journal of Applied Social Psychology*, Vol. 4, pp.62–93.

Caldwell, B. M. and Bradley, R. H. (1978) 'Home Observation for Measurement of the Environment', University of Arkansas.

Campos, J. et al. (1992) 'Early experience and emotional development: the emergence of wariness of heights', *Psychological Science*, Vol. 23, pp. 61–64.

Carter, J. C. et al. (2006) 'The impact of childhood sexual abuse in anorexia nervosa', *Child Abuse & Neglect*, Vol. 30, No. 3, pp. 257–269.

Cartwright, J. (2000) *Evolution and Human Behaviour*, MacMillan.

Case, R. (1978) 'Intellectual development from birth to adulthood: a neo-Piagetian interpretation', in Siegler,

R.S. *Children's thinking: What develops?*, Lawrence Erlbaum Associates.

Cattell, R. B. and Nesselrode, J. R. (1967) 'Likeness and completeness theories examined by 16 personality factor measures on stable and unstable married couples', *Journal of Personality and Social Psychology*, Vol. 7, pp.351–361.

Cavallo, D. A. et al. (2007) 'Combining cognitive behavioral therapy with contingency management for smoking cessation in adolescent smokers: a preliminary comparison of two different CBT formats', *The American Journal on Addictions*, Vol. 16, No. 6, pp. 468–474.

Cecil, H. et al. (1996) 'Perceived believability among adolescents of health warning labels on cigarette packs', *Journal of Applied Social Psychology*, Vol. 26, No. 6, pp. 502–519.

Chabrol, H. et al. (2001) 'Study of dysfunctional beliefs in adolescent cannabis use using the Questionnaire of Anticipatory, Relief-Oriented and Permissive Beliefs for Drug Addiction', *Journal de Thérapie Comportementale et Cognitive*, Vol. 11, No. 3, pp. 105–108.

Chabrol, H. et al. (2004) 'Factor structure of cannabis related beliefs in adolescents', *Addictive Behaviors*, Vol. 29, No. 5, pp. 929–933.

Chaiken, S. (1980) 'Heuristic versus systemic information processing and the use of source versus message cues in persuasion', *Journal of Personality and Social Psychology*, Vol. 39, pp. 752–766.

Chaiken, S. and Maheswaran, D. (1994) 'Heuristic processing can bias systematic processing: Effects of source credibility, argument ambiguity, and task importance on attitude judgment', *Journal of Personality and Social Psychology*, Vol. 66, No. 3, pp. 460–473.

Chan, B. (2007) 'Preschools and gender socialization in early childhood: a comparison of Hong Kong and Japan (China)', *Dissertation Abstracts International Section A: Humanities and Social Sciences*, Vol. 67, No. 8-A, pp. 2873.

Charlton, T. et al. (1998) 'Broadcast television as a cause of aggression? Recent findings from a naturalistic study', *Emotional and Behavioural Difficulties*, Vol. 3, No. 2, pp. 5–13.

Charman, T. et al. (2000) 'Testing joint attention, imitation, and play as infancy precursors to language and theory of mind', *Cognitive Development*, Vol. 15, No. 4, pp. 481–498.

Chatzisarantis, N. et al. (2008) 'An experimental test of cognitive dissonance theory in the domain of physical exercise', *Journal of Applied Sport Psychology*, Vol. 20, No. 1, pp. 97–115.

Cheng, C. (2005) 'Processes underlying gender-role flexibility: do androgynous individuals know more or know how to cope?', *Journal of Personality*, Vol. 73, No. 3, pp. 645–673.

Cheung, C. K. and Tse, J. W. (2008) 'Hong Kong children's posited "vulnerability" to social influence on substance abuse', *Substance Use & Misuse*, Vol. 43, No. 11, pp. 1544–1558.

Childs, C. P. and Greenfield, P. M. (1982) 'Informal modes of learning and teaching: the case of Zinancanteco learning', in Warren, N. (ed.) *Advances in Cross-Cultural Psychology*, Academic Press.

Cho, K. (2001) 'Chronic "jet lag" produces temporal lobe atrophy and spatial cognitive deficits', *Nature Neuroscience*, Vol. 4, No. 6, pp. 567–568.

Cho, K. et al. (2000) 'Chronic jet lag produces cognitive deficits', *Journal of Neuroscience*, Vol. 20, No. 6, p. 66.

Choi, N. (2004) 'Sex role group differences in specific, academic, and general self-efficacy', *Journal of Psychology: Interdisciplinary and Applied*, Vol. 138, No. 2, pp. 149–159.

Chorney, M. J. et al. (1998) 'A quantitative trait locus associated with cognitive ability in children', *Psychological Science*, Vol. 9, No. 3, pp. 159–166.

Christensen, L. and Brooks, A. (2006) 'Changing food preference as a function of mood', *Journal of Psychology: Interdisciplinary and Applied*, Vol. 140, No. 4, pp. 293–306.

Clare, A. W. (1985) 'Hormones, behaviour and the menstrual cycle', *Journal of Psychosomatic Research*, Vol. 29, No. 3, pp. 225–233.

Clark, R. D. and Hatfield, E. (1989) 'Gender differences in receptivity to sexual offers', *Journal of Psychology and Human Sexuality*, Vol. 2, No. 1, pp. 39–55.

Clarke, D. (1991) 'Belief in the paranormal: a New Zealand survey', *Journal of the Society for Psychical Research*, Vol. 57, No. 823, pp. 412–425.

Clausen, J. A. (1975) 'The social meaning of differential physical and sexual maturation', in Dragastin, S. E. and Elder, G. H. (eds) *Adolescence in the Life Cycle: Psychological Change and Social Context*, Hemisphere.

Clavadetscher, J. E. et al. (1988) 'Spectral sensitivity and chromatic discriminations in 3- and 7-week-old human infants', *Journal of the Optical Society of America, A, Optics, Image & Science*, Vol. 5, No. 12, pp. 2093–2105.

Cline, V. et al. (1973) 'Desensitization of children to television violence', *Journal of Personality and Social Psychology*, Vol. 27, No. 3, pp. 360–365.

Cochrane, R. (1996) 'Marriage and madness', *Psychology Review*, Vol. 3, No. 1, pp. 2–5.

Coger, R. W. and Serafetinides, E. A. (1980) 'Schizophrenia, corpus callosum, and interhemispheric communication: a review', *Psychiatry Res.*, Vol. 34, No. 2, pp.163–84.

Cohn, L. B. (1996) 'Violent video games: aggression, arousal, and desensitization in young adolescent boys', *Dissertation Abstracts International: Section B: The Sciences and Engineering*, Vol. 57, No. 2-B, pp. 1463.

Cohen-Kettenis, P. T. and Gooren, L. J. G. (1999) 'Transsexualism: a review of etiology, diagnosis, and treatment', *Journal of Psychosomatic Research*, Vol. 46, No. 4, pp. 315–333.

Collins, N. L. and Read, S. J. (1990) 'Adult attachment, working models, and relationship quality in dating couples', *Journal of Personality and Social Psychology*, Vol. 58, No. 4, pp. 644–663.

Connolly, G. M. et al. (1994) 'Alcohol in the mass media and drinking by adolescents: A longitudinal study', *Addiction*, Vol. 89, No. 10, pp. 1255–1263.

Connor, R. and Mann, J. (2006) 'Social cognition in the wild: Machiavellian dolphins?', in Hurley, S. and Nudds, M. (eds) *Rational Animals?*, Oxford University Press.

Cooley, C. H. (1902) *Human Nature and the Social Order*, Charles Scribner's Sons.

Cooper, J. E. et al. (1972) *Psychiatric Diagnosis in New York and London*, Oxford University Press.

Copolov, D. and Crook, J. (2000) 'Biological markers and schizophrenia', *Australian and New Zealand Journal of Psychiatry*, Vol. 34, pp. S108–S112.

Courage, M. L. and Adams, R. J. (1990) 'The early development of visual acuity in the binocular and monocular peripheral fields', *Journal of Infant Behavior & Development*, Vol. 13, No. 1, pp. 123–128.

Courneya, K. S. and Carron, A. V. (1990) 'The home advantage: present status and future directions', *Annual Meeting of the Canadian Psychomotor Learning and Sport Psychology Society*, Windsor, Ontario, Canada.

Costa, G. (1999) 'Fatigue and biological rhythms', in: Garland, D. J. et al. (eds) *Handbook of Aviation Human Factors*, Lawrence Erlbaum Associates.

Costello, C. G. (1992) 'Research on symptoms versus research on syndromes: arguments in favour of allocating more research time to the study of symptoms', *British Journal of Psychiatry*, Vol. 160, pp. 304–308.

Cowan, J. (1989) *Mysteries of the Dreaming: The Spiritual Life of Australian Aborigines*, Prism Press.

Cramer, D. (1994) 'Personal relationships', in Tantam, D. and Birchwood, M. (eds) *Seminars in Psychology and the Social Sciences*, Gaskell Press.

Crespi, B. et al. (2007) 'Adaptive evolution of genes underlying schizophrenia', *Proc Biol Sci.*, Vol. 22, No. 1627, pp. 2801–10.

Crow, T. J. (1982) 'Two syndromes in schizophrenia?', *Trends in Neurosciences*, Vol. 5, No. 10, pp. 351–354.

Cruz, M. G. (1998) 'Explicit and implicit conclusions in persuasive messages', in Allen, M. and Preiss, R. W. (eds) *Persuasion: Advances through Meta-analysis*, Hampton Press.

Cunningham, M. (2001) 'The influence of parental attitudes and behaviors on children's attitudes toward gender and household labor in early adulthood', *Journal of Marriage & the Family*, Vol. 63, No. 1, pp. 111–122.

Curran, H. V. and Drummond, D. C. (2005) 'Psychological treatments for substance misuse and dependence',

in Robbins, T. et al. (eds) *Foresight Review of Addiction and Brain Science*, Department of Trade and Industry.

Dagnall, N. et al. (2007) 'Superstitious belief — negative and positive superstitions and psychological functioning', *European Journal of Parapsychology*, Vol. 22, No. 2, pp. 121–137.

Dalton, K. (1997) 'Is there a formula to success in the ganzfeld? Observations on predictors of psi-ganzfeld performance', *European Journal of Parapsychology*, Vol. 13, pp. 71–82.

Dalton, K. (1964) *The Premenstrual Syndrome*, Charles C. Thomas

Daly, M. and Wilson, M. (1988) 'Evolutionary social psychology and family homicide', *Science*, Vol. 242, No. 4878, pp. 519–524.

Daly, M. and Wilson, M. (1996) 'Violence against stepchildren', *Current Directions in Psychological Science*, Vol. 5, No. 3, pp. 77–81.

Daly, M. and Wilson, M. (1982) 'Whom are newborn babies said to resemble?', *Ethology and Sociobiology*, Vol. 3, pp. 69–78.

Damon, J. (2008) 'The impact of gender role on recovery from sexual trauma in women', *Dissertation Abstracts International: Section B: The Sciences and Engineering*, Vol. 68, No. 12-B, p. 8393.

Dapretto, M. et al. (2006) 'Understanding emotions in others: mirror neuron dysfunction in children with autism spectrum disorders', *Nature Neuroscience*, Vol. 9, No. 1, pp. 28–30.

Darwin, C. (1871) *On the Origin of Species*, Murray.

Dauncey, K. et al. (1993) 'Schizophrenia in Nottingham: lifelong residential mobility of a cohort', *British Journal of Psychiatry*, Vol. 163, pp. 613–619.

David, A. S. and Cutting, J. C. (1993) *The Neuropsychology of Schizophrenia*, Erlbaum.

Davies, P. and Lipsey, Z. (2003) 'Ana's gone surfing', *The Psychologist*, Vol. 16, No. 8.

Davis, K. L. et al. (1991) 'Dopamine in schizophrenia: a review and reconceptualization', *American Journal of Psychiatry*, Vol. 148, No. 11, pp. 1474–1486.

Davison, E. H. (2000) 'The interrelationships among subjective well-being, gender role flexibility, perceived sexism, and perceived ageism in older women', *Dissertation Abstracts International: Section B: The Sciences and Engineering*, Vol. 60, No. 12-B, pp. 6357.

Dawson, D. and Campbell, S. S. (1991) 'Time exposure to bright light improves sleep and alertness during simulated night shifts', *Sleep*, Vol. 14, pp. 511–516.

Day, R. H. (1989) 'Natural and artificial cues, perceptual compromise and the basis of veridical and illusory perception', in Vickers, D. and Smith, P. L. (eds) *Human Information Processing: Measures and Mechanisms*, Elsevier, pp. 107–109.

Dejanovic, S. D. et al. (2003) 'Aetiopathogenesis of `insomnia', *Psihijatrija Danas*, Vol. 35, pp. 5–21.

Delgado, G. (2005) 'A child and adolescent stalker prevention program', *Dissertation Abstracts International: Section B: The Sciences and Engineering*, Vol. 65, No. 10-B, p. 5395.

De Lecea, L. et al. (1998) 'The hypocretins: hypothalamus-specific peptides with neuroexcitatory activity', *Proc Natl Acad Sci*, Vol. 95, No. 1, pp. 322–327.

DeLoache, J. S. and Brown, A. L. (1987) 'Differences in the memory-based searching of delayed and normally developing young children', *Intelligence*, Vol. 11, pp. 277–289.

De Renzi, E. (1986) 'Prosopagnosia in two patients with CT scan: evidence of the damage confined to the right hemisphere', *Neuropsychologia*, Vol. 24, 385–389.

Dematteis, M. et al. (2001) 'Charcot-Marie-Tooth disease and sleep apnoea syndrome: a family study', *Lancet*, Vol. 357, No. 9252, pp. 267–72.

Dement, W. and Kleitman, N. (1957) 'The relation of eye movements during sleep to dream activity: an objective method for the study of dreaming', *Journal of Experimental Psychology*, Vol. 53, No. 5, pp. 339–346.

Deregowski, J. (1972) 'Pictorial perception and culture', *Scientific American*, Vol. 227, pp. 82–88.

Devaux, A. and Krebs, M. (2004) 'Factors involved in vulnerability to heroin dependence', *Annales Médico-Psychologiques*, Vol. 162, No. 4, pp. 307–310.

Dewitt, I. A. (2004) 'Peer influences on the attitudes of early adolescent girls', *Dissertation Abstracts International Section A: Humanities and Social Sciences*, Vol. 65, No. 5-A, pp. 1675.

Dickson, D. H. and Kelly, I. W. (1985) 'The "Barnum effect" in personality assessment: a review of the literature', *Psychological Reports*, Vol. 57, No. 2, pp. 367–382.

Diener, E. et al. (1976) 'Effects of deindividuation on stealing among Halloween trick or treaters', *Journal of Personality and Social Psychology*, Vol. 33, pp. 178–183.

Dill, K. E. and Thill, K. P. (2007) 'Video game characters and the socialization of gender roles: young people's perceptions mirror sexist media depictions', *Sex Roles*, Vol. 57, No. 11–12, pp. 851–864.

DiIorio, C. et al. (2009) 'Adherence to antiretroviral medication regimens: a test of a psychosocial model', *AIDS and Behavior*, Vol. 13, No. 1, pp. 10–22.

Dindia, K. and Baxter, L. A. (1987) 'Maintenance and repair strategies in marital relationships', *Journal of Social and Personal Relationships*, Vol. 14, pp. 143–158.

Dinstein, I. et al. (2008) 'A mirror up to nature', *Curr Biol* Vol. 18, No. 1, pp. 13–18.

Dion, K. and Dion, K. (1988) 'Romantic love: individual and cultural perspectives', in Sternberg, R. and Barnes, M. (eds) *The Psychology of Love*, Yale University Press.

Dirks, J. (1982) 'The effect of a commercial game on children's Block Design scores on the WISC-R IQ test', *Intelligence*, Vol. 6, No. 2, pp. 109–123.

Dishion, T. J. et al. (1994) 'Peer adaptations in the development of antisocial behavior: a confluence model', *Aggressive Behavior: Current Perspectives*, in Huesmann, L. R. (ed.) Plenum.

Dodge, K. A. et al. (1997) 'Reactive and proactive aggression in school children and psychiatrically impaired chronically assaultive youth', *Journal of Abnormal Psychology*, Vol. 106, No. 1, pp. 37–51.

Doise, W. and Mugny, G. (1984) *The Social Development of the Intellect*, Pergamon Press.

Dollard, J. et al. (1939) *Frustration and Aggression*, Yale University Press.

Donald, M. (2001) *A Mind So Rare: The Evolution of Human Consciousness*, Norton.

Donaldson, M. (1978) *Children's Minds*, Fontana.

Duck, S. (1992) *Human Relationships* (2nd edn), Sage.

Dunbar, R. (1995) 'Are you lonesome tonight?', *New Scientist*, Vol. 145, No. 1964, pp. 12–16.

Dunbar, R. et al. (1999) *The Evolution of Culture*, Edinburgh University Press.

Duncan, H. F. et al. (1973) *A Story of Pictorial Perception Among Bantu and White Primary School Children in South Africa*, Witwatersrand University Press.

Dunn, J. and Brown, J. (1994) 'Affect expression in the family, children's understanding of emotions, and their interactions with others', *Merrill-Palmer Quarterly*, Vol. 40, No. 1, pp. 120–137.

DuRan, R. H. et al. (1997) 'Tobacco and alcohol use behaviors portrayed in music videos: a content analysis', *American Journal of Public Health*, Vol. 87, No. 7, pp. 1131–1135.

Durkin, K. F. et al. (2005) 'College students and binge drinking: an evaluation of social learning theory', *Sociological Spectrum*, Vol. 25, No. 3, pp. 255–272.

Eadie, D. et al. (2008) 'A qualitative analysis of compliance with smoke-free legislation in community bars in Scotland: implications for public health', *Addiction*, Vol. 103, No. 6, pp. 1019–1026.

Eagly, A. (1997) 'On comparing women and men', *Feminism and Psychology*, Vol. 4, No. 4, pp. 513–522.

Eagly, A. H. and Chaiken, S. (1993) *The Psychology of Attitudes*, Harcourt Brace Jovanovich College Publishers.

Eccles, J. S. et al. (1990) 'Gender role stereotypes, expectancy effects, and parents' socialization of gender differences', *Journal of Social Issues*, Vol. 46, No. 2, pp. 183–201.

Eicher, W. et al. (1980) 'Transsexuality and X-Y antigen', *Geburtshilfe Frauenheilkd*, Vol. 40, No. 6, pp. 529–540.

Einon, D. (1988) 'How many children can one man have?', *Evolution and Human Behaviour*, Vol. 19, pp. 413–426.

Eisenberg, N. (1986) *Altruistic Emotion, Cognition and Behaviour*, Erlbaum.

Eisenberg, N. et al. (1987) 'Prosocial development in middle childhood: a longitudinal study', *Developmental Psychology*, Vol. 23, No. 5, pp. 712–718.

Eiser, J. R. et al. (1978) 'Consonant and dissonant smokers and the self-attribution of addiction', *Addictive Behaviors*, Vol. 3, No. 2, pp. 99–106.

Eisler, R. (1996) 'Human rights and violence: integrating the private and public spheres', in Turpin, J. E. and Kurtz, L. R. (eds) *The Web of Violence: From Interpersonal to Global*, University of Illinois Press.

Elliot, A. J. and Devine, P. G. (1994) 'On the motivational nature of cognitive dissonance: dissonance as psychological discomfort', *Journal of Personality and Social Psychology*, Vol. 67, No. 3, pp. 382–394.

Ellison, P. A. et al. (1995) 'Anonymity and aggressive driving behavior: a field study', *Journal of Social Behavior and Personality*, Vol. 10, No. 1, pp. 265–272.

Emmerlich, W. et al. (1977) 'Evidence for a transitional phase in the development of gender', *Child Development*, Vol. 48, pp. 930–936.

Emmons, C. F. and Sobal, J. (1981) 'Paranormal beliefs: testing the marginality hypothesis', *Sociological Focus*, Vol. 14, pp. 49–56.

Empson, J. A. S. C. and Clarke, P. R. F. (1970) 'Rapid eye movements and remembering', *Nature*, Vol. 228, pp. 287–288.

Enrile, A. and Agbayani, P. T. (2007) 'Differences in attitudes towards women among three groups of Filipinos: Filipinos in the Philippines, Filipino American immigrants, and U.S.-born Filipino Americans', *Journal of Ethnic & Cultural Diversity in Social Work*, Vol. 16, No. 1–2, pp. 1–25.

Epling, W. F. and Pierce, W. D. (1992) *Solving the Anorexia Puzzle*, Hogrefe & Huber.

Epstein, R. et al. (1984) '"Insight" in the pigeon: antecedents and determinants of an intelligent performance', *Nature*, Vol. 308, No. 5954, pp. 61–62.

Erikson, E. H. (1968) *Identity: Youth and Crisis*, Faber.

Estes, W. K. (1970) *Learning Theory and Mental Development*, Academic Press.

Etaugh, C. and Liss, M. B. (1992) 'Home, school, and playroom: training grounds for adult gender roles', *Sex Roles*, Vol. 26, No. 3–4, pp. 129–147.

Evans, J. R. and Claycomb, S. (1999) 'Abnormal QEEG patterns associated with dissociation and violence', *Journal of Neurotherapy*, Vol. 3, pp. 21–27.

Eysenck, H. J. (1971) *The IQ Argument: Race, Intelligence and Education*, Library Press.

Fantz, R. L. (1963) 'Pattern vision in newborn infants', *Science*, Vol. 140, pp. 296–297.

Farooqi, I. S. et al. (2007) 'Leptin regulates striatal regions and human eating behavior', *Science*, Vol. 317, No. 5843, p. 1355.

Feldman, M. B. and Meyer, I. H. (2007) 'Childhood abuse and eating disorders in gay and bisexual men', *International Journal of Eating Disorders*, Vol. 40, No. 5, pp. 418–423.

Felsher, J. R. (2007) 'Etiological factors related to gambling problems: the impact of childhood maltreatment and subsequent stressors', *Dissertation Abstracts International: Section B: The Sciences and Engineering*, Vol. 68, No. 3-B, p. 1923.

Ferguson, C. J. et al. (2008) 'Violent video games and aggression: causal relationship or byproduct of family violence and intrinsic violence motivation?', *Criminal Justice and Behavior*, Vol. 35, No. 3, pp. 311–332.

Festinger, L. (1957) *A Theory of Cognitive Dissonance*, Row, Peterson.

Festinger, L. and Carlsmith, J. M. (1959) 'Cognitive consequences of forced compliance', *Journal of Abnormal and Social Psychology*, Vol. 58, No. 2, pp. 203–210.

Feyerabend, P. (1975) *Against Method: Outline of an Anarchist Theory of Knowledge*, New Left Books.

Fidler, J. J. et al. (2008) 'Smoking status of step-parents as a risk factor for smoking in adolescence', *Addiction*, Vol. 103, No. 3, pp. 496–501.

Fishbein, M. and Ajzen, I. (1975) *Belief Attitude, Intention and Behavior. An Introduction to Theory and Research*, Addison-Wesley.

Fisher, H. E. (1992) *Anatomy of Love: the Natural History of Monogamy, Adultery and Divorce*, Norton.

Fleury, C. et al. (1997) 'Uncoupling protein-2: a novel gene linked to obesity and hyperinsulinemia', *Nat Genet.* Vol. 15, No. 3, pp. 269–72.

Flight, I. et al. (2008) 'Food neophobia and associations with cultural diversity and socio-economic status amongst rural and urban Australian adolescents', *Appetite*, Vol. 41, No. 1, pp. 51–59.

Floyd, J. A. et al. (2007) 'Changes in REM-sleep percentage over the adult lifespan', *Sleep,* Vol. 30, No. 7, pp. 829–836.

Foa, U. G. and Foa, E. B. (1975) *Social Structures of the Mind*, Thomas.

Fodor, J. A. and Pylyshyn, Z. W. (1981) 'How direct is visual perception? Some reflections on Gibson's "ecological approach"', *Cognition*, Vol. 9, pp. 139–196.

Foley, R. A. (1987) *Another Unique Species: Patterns of Human Evolutionary Ecology*, Longman.

Fontana, L. and Beckerman, A. (2004) 'Childhood violence prevention education using video games', *Information Technology in Childhood Education Annual*, Vol. 16, pp. 49–62.

Foster, G. M. and Anderson, B. (1978) *Medical Anthropology*, Wiley.

Fowkes, F. et al. (2008) 'Scottish smoke-free legislation and trends in smoking cessation', *Addiction*, Vol. 103, No. 11, pp. 1888–1895.

Fowler, T. et al. (2007) 'Exploring the relationship between genetic and environmental influences on initiation and progression of substance use', *Addiction*, Vol. 102, pp. 413–22.

Frank, F. (1966) 'On the conservation of liquids', in Bruner, J.S. et al. (eds) *Studies in Cognitive Growth*, Wiley.

French, J. (1957) 'The reticular formation', *Scientific American*, Vol. 196, No. 5, pp. 54–60.

French, S. A. et al. (1999) 'Is dieting good for you? Prevalence, duration and associated weight and behaviour changes for specific weight loss strategies over four years in US adults', *International Journal of Obesity*, Vol. 23, pp. 320–327.

Freud, S. (1889/1954) *The Origins of Psychoanalysis*, Basic Books.

Friedrich, L. K. and Stein, A. H. (1973) 'Aggressive and prosocial television programmes and the natural behaviour of preschool children', *Monographs of the Society for Research in Child Development*, Vol. 38, No. 4.

Frith, C. D. (1997) *Schizophrenia*, Psychology Press.

Furman, W. et al. (2002) 'Adolescents' working models and styles for relationships with parents, friends, and romantic partners', *Child Development*, Vol. 73, No. 1, pp. 241–255.

Galef, B. G. Jr (1988) 'Communication of information concerning diet in social central-place foraging species: *Rattus norvegicus*', in Zentall, T. R. and Galef, B. G. Jr (eds) *Social Learning Psychological and Biological Perspectives*, Lawrence Erlbaum.

Galef, B. G. Jr et al. (1998) 'Carbon disulfide: a semiochemical mediating socially induced diet choice in rats', *Physiology and Behaviour*, Vol. 42, pp. 119–124.

Gallup, G. (1970) 'Chimpanzees: self-recognition', *Science*, Vol. 167, pp. 86–87.

Gallup, G. (1983) 'Toward a comparative psychology of mind', in Mellgren, R.L. (ed.) *Animal Cognition and Behaviour*, North Holland Publishing Co.

Gallup, G. G. (1977) 'Self recognition in primates: a comparative approach to the bidirectional properties of consciousness', *American Psychologist*, Vol. 32, No. 5, pp. 329–338.

Gallup, G. and Newport, F. (1991) 'Belief in paranormal phenomena among adult Americans', *Skeptical Inquirer*, Vol. 15, pp.137–146.

Garcia, J. and Koelling, R. A. (1966) 'Relation of cue to consequence in avoidance learning', *Psychonomic Science*, Vol. 4, No. 3, pp. 123–124.

Garcia-Arraras, J. E. and Pappenheimer, J. R. (1983) 'Site of action of sleep-inducing muramyl peptide isolated from human urine: microinjection studies in rabbit brains', *Journal of Neurophysiology*, Vol. 49, No. 2, pp. 528–533.

Garden, G. M. and Rothery, D. J. (1992) 'A female monozygotic twin pair discordant for transsexualism: some theoretical implications', *British Journal of Psychiatry*, Vol. 161, pp. 852–854.

Gardner, H. (1983) *Frames of Mind: The Theory of Multiple Intelligences*, Basic Books.

Gardner, H. (1999) *Intelligence Reframed*, Basic Books.

Garfinkel, P. E., and Garner, D.M. (1982) *Anorexia Nervosa: A Multidimensional Perspective*, Brunner/Mazel.

Garner, D. M. et al. (1980) 'Cultural expectations of thinness in women', *Psychological Reports*, Vol. 47, No. 2, pp. 483–491.

Gaulin, S. J. C. and Robbins, C. J. (1992) 'Trivers-Willard effect in contemporary North American society', *American Journal of Physical Anthropology*, Vol. 86, pp. 61–69.

Gaunt, R. (2006) 'Couple similarity and marital satisfaction: are similar spouses happier?', *Journal of Personality*, Vol. 74, No. 5, pp. 1401–1420.

Gergen, K J. et al. (1973) 'Deviance in the dark', *Psychology Today*, Vol. 7, pp. 129–130.

Gibson, E. J. and Walk, R. D. (1960) 'The visual cliff', *Scientific American*, Vol. 202, pp. 64–71.

Gibson, E. L. (2006) 'Emotional influences on food choice: sensory, physiological and psychological pathways', *Physiology & Behavior*, Vol. 89, No. 1, pp. 53–61.

Gibson, J. J. (1950) *The Perception of the Visual World*, Houghton Mifflin.

Giesler-Petersen, I. (2008) 'Further commentary on "Induced OBEs"', *Journal of Near-Death Studies*, Vol. 26, No. 4, pp. 306–308.

Gilbert, E. (2007) 'Constructing "fashionable" youth identities: Australian young women cigarette smokers', *Journal of Youth Studies*, Vol. 10, No. 1, pp. 1–15.

Giles D. C. (2000) *Illusions of Immortality: A Psychology of Fame and Celebrity*, MacMillan.

Giles, D. and Maltby, J. (2004) 'Praying at the altar of the stars', *The Psychologist*, Vol. 19, No. 2, pp. 82–85.

Gilligan, C. (1977) 'In a different voice: Women's conceptions of self and of morality', *Harvard Educational Review*, Vol. 47, No. 4, pp. 481–517.

Gilligan, C. (1982) *In a Different Voice: Psychological Theory and Women's Development,* Harvard University Press.

Gilligan, C. and Attanucci, J. (1988) 'Two moral orientations: gender differences and similarities', *Merrill-Palmer Quarterly*, Vol. 34, No. 3, pp. 223–237.

Goddard, H. H. (1929) 'Hereditary mental aptitudes in man', *Eugenics*, 2, pp. 1–7.

Gold, D. R. et al. (1992) 'Rotating shift work, sleep and accidents related to sleepiness in hospital nurses', *American Journal of Public Health*, Vol. 82, pp. 1011–1014.

Goldman, D. et al. (2005) 'The genetics of addictions: uncovering the genes', *Nat Rev Genet*, Vol. 6, pp. 521–32.

Goldstein, J. (1993) 'Humor and comedy in mass media', *Zeitschrift für Medienpsychologie*, Vol. 5, No. 4, pp. 246–256.

Goldstein, J. H. and Arms, R. L. (1971) 'Effects of observing athletic contests on hostility', *Sociometry*, Vol. 34, No. 1, pp. 83–90.

Goldstein, W. N. and Anthony, R. N. (1988) 'The diagnosis of depression and the DSMs', *American Journal of Psychotherapy*, Vol. 42, No. 2, pp. 180–196.

Goldwyn, E. (1979) 'The fight to be male', *The Listener*, Vol. 24 May, pp. 709–712.

Goodwin, R. (1995) 'Personal relationships across cultures', *The Psychologist*, Vol. 8, No. 2, pp. 73–75.

Gopnik, A. and Astington, J. W. (1998) 'Children's understanding of representational change and its relation to the understanding of false belief and the appearance-reality distinction', *Child Development*, Vol. 59, No. 1, pp. 26–37.

Gottesman, I. I. (1991) *Schizophrenia Genesis: The Origins of Madness*, W H Freeman.

Gottesman, I. I. and Shields, J. (1972) *Schizophrenia and Genetics: A Twin Study Vantage Point*, Academic Press.

Gottesman, I. I. and Bertelson, A. (1989) 'Confirming unexpressed genotypes for schizophrenia: risks in the offspring of Fischer's Danish identical and fraternal discordant twins', *Archives of General Psychiatry*, Vol. 46, No. 10, pp. 867–872.

Gow, K. et al. (2001) 'Fantasy proneness and other psychological correlates of UFO experiences', *Queensland University of Technology*, Brisbane, Queensland, Australia, accessed May 24, 2009 from http://www.anomalistik.de/gow.pdf.

Granberg, D. and Holmberg, S. (1990) 'The intention-behavior relationship among U.S. and Swedish voters', *Social Psychology Quarterly*, Vol. 53, No. 1, pp. 44–54.

Grant, J. E. et al. (2004) 'Retrospective review of treatment retention in pathological gambling', *Comprehensive Psychiatry*, Vol. 45, No. 2, pp. 83–87.

Gray, T. (1987) 'Educational experience and belief in paranormal phenomena', in Harrold, F. B. and Eve, R. A. S. (eds) *Cult Archaeology and Creationism: Understanding Pseudoscientific Beliefs About the Past*, University of Iowa Press.

Gray, T. and Mill, D. (1990) 'Critical abilities, graduate education (Biology vs. English), and belief in unsubstantiated phenomena', *Canadian Journal of Behavioral Science*, Vol. 22, pp. 162–172.

Green, C. E. (1968) *Out-of-Body Experiences*, Institute of Psychophysical Research.

Green, R. (2000) 'Family coocurrence of gender dysphoria: ten siblings or parent-child pairs', *Archives of Sexual Behavior*, Vol. 29, No. 5, pp. 499–507.

Gregor, A. J. and McPherson, D. (1965) 'A study of susceptibility to geometric illusions among cultural outgroups of Australian aborigines', *Psychologia Africana*, Vol. 11, pp. 490–499.

Gregory, R. L. (1966) *Eye and Brain*, Weidenfeld and Nicholson.

Greyson, B. et al. (2008) 'Visualizing out-of-body experience in the brain', *New England Journal of Medicine*, Vol. 358, No. 8, pp. 855–856.

Griffiths, M. and Wood, R. (2000) 'Risk factors in adolescence: the case of gambling, videogame playing, and the Internet', *Journal of Gambling Studies*, Vol. 16, No. 2–3, pp. 199–225.

Grotevant, H. D. (1998) 'Adolescent development in family context', in Damon, W. and Eisenberg, N. (eds) *Handbook of Child Psychology: Vol. 3: Social, Personality and Emotional Development*, pp. 1097–1149, Wiley.

Groth-Marnat, G. and Pegden, J. A. (1998) 'Personality correlates of paranormal belief: locus of control and sensation seeking', *Social Behavior and Personality*, Vol. 26, No. 3, pp. 291–296.

Gruesser, S. M. et al. (2005) 'Pathological gambling: an empirical study of the desire for addictive substances', *Nervenarzt*, Vol. 76, No. 5, pp. 592–596.

Grunhaus, L. et al. (1994) 'Sleep electroencephalographic studies after ECT: age and clinical response', *American Journal of Geriatric Psychiatry*, Vol. 2, No. 1, pp. 39–51.

Gschwandtner, U. et al. (2001) 'Pathological gambling in patients with Parkinson's disease', *Clinical Neuropharmacology*, Vol. 24, No. 3, pp. 170–172.

Guilleminault, C. et al. (2005) 'Adult chronic sleepwalking and its treatment based on polysomnography', *Brain: A Journal of Neurology*, Vol. 128, No. 5, pp. 1062–1069.

Guisinger, S. (2003) 'Adapted to flee famine: adding an evolutionary perspective on anorexia nervosa', *Psychological Review*, Vol. 110, No. 4, pp. 745–761.

Gunn, S. R. and Gunn, W. S. (2007) 'Are we in the dark about sleepwalking's dangers?', in Read, C. A. (ed.) *Cerebrum 2007: Emerging Ideas in Brain Science*, Dana Press.

Gupta, U. and Singh, P. (1992) 'Exploratory study of love and liking and types of marriage', *Indian Journal of Applied Psychology*, Vol. 19, pp. 92–97.

Gur, R. C. et al. (2002) 'Sex differences in temporo-limbic and frontal brain volumes of healthy adults', *Cerebral Cortex*, Vol. 12, No. 9, pp. 998–1003.

Gutschoven, K. and van den Bulck, J. (2005) 'Television viewing and age at smoking initiation: does a relationship exist between higher levels of television viewing and earlier onset of smoking?', *Nicotine & Tobacco Research*, Vol. 7, No. 3, pp. 381–385.

Haig, D. (1993) *Quarterly Review of Biology*, Vol. 68, pp. 495–532.

Halaas, J. L. et al. (1995) 'Weight-reducing effects of the plasma protein encoded by the obese gene', *Science*, Vol. 269, No. 5223, pp. 543–546.

Hall, W. D. et al. (2008) 'The genetics of nicotine addiction liability: ethical and social policy implications', *Addiction*, Vol. 103, No. 3, pp. 350–359.

Halliday-Boykins, C. A. and Graham, S. (2001) 'At both ends of the gun: testing the relationship between community violence exposure and youth violent behavior', *Journal of Abnormal Child Psychology*, Vol. 29, No. 5, pp. 383–402.

Halmi, K. A. et al. (1977) 'Perceptual distortion of body image in adolescent girls: distortion of body image in adolescence', *Psychological Medicine*, Vol. 7, No. 2, pp. 253–257.

Halmi, K. A. (1992) 'The psychobiology of eating behavior', in K. A. Halmi (ed.) *The Psychobiology and Treatment of Anorexia Nervosa and Bulimia Nervosa*, American Psychiatric Press.

Halmi, K. A. and Yum, S. Y. (2007) 'Psychopharmacology of norepinephrine in eating disorders', in Ordway, G. A. et al. (eds) *Brain Norepinephrine: Neurobiology and Therapeutics*, Cambridge University Press, pp. 595–609.

Hamilton, W. D. (1964) 'The genetical evaluation of social behaviour', *Journal of Theoretical Biology*, Vol. 7, pp. 1–52.

Hampson, P. J. and Morris, P. E. (1996) 'Oestrogen-related variations in human spatial and articulatory-motor skills', *Psychoneuroendocrinology*, Vol. 15, pp. 97–111.

Hanassab, S. and Tidwell, R. (1989) 'Cross-cultural perspectives on dating relationships of young Iranian women: a pilot study', *Counselling Psychology Quarterly*, Vol. 2, pp. 113–121.

Hanlon, M. (2007) *10 Questions Science Can't Answer (Yet)*, Macmillan.

Haracz, J. L. (1982) 'The dopamine hypothesis: an overview of studies with schizophrenic patients', *Schizophr Bull*, Vol. 8, No. 3, pp. 438–69.

Harakeh, Z. et al. (2007) 'The influence of best friends and siblings on adolescent smoking: a longitudinal study', *Psychology & Health*, Vol. 22, No. 3, pp. 269–289.

Harrell, W. A. (1981) 'Verbal aggressiveness in spectators at professional hockey games: the effects of tolerance of violence and amount of exposure to hockey', *Human Relations*, Vol. 34, No. 8, pp. 643–655.

Harris, C. R. (2002) 'Sexual and romantic jealousy in heterosexual and homosexual adults', *Psychological Science*, Vol. 13, No. 1, pp. 7–12.

Harris, C. R. and Christenfeld, N. (1996) 'Gender, jealousy, and reason', *Psychological Science*, Vol. 7, pp. 364–366.

Harrison, P. (1995) 'Schizophrenia: a misunderstood disease', *Psychology Review*, Vol. 2, No. 2, pp. 2–6.

Hatgis, C. et al. (2008) 'Attributions of responsibility for addiction: the effects of gender and type of substance', *Substance Use & Misuse*, Vol. 43, No. 5, pp. 700–708.

Hauck, Y. et al. (2007) 'Prevalence, self-efficacy and perceptions of conflicting advice and self-management: effects of a breastfeeding journal', *Journal of Advanced Nursing*, Vol. 57, No. 3, pp. 306–317.

Hawkes, K. et al. (1982) 'Why hunters gather: optimal foraging and the Achè of eastern Paraguay', *American Ethnologist*, Vol. 9, pp. 379–398.

Hays, R. B. (1985) 'A longitudinal study of friendship development', *Journal of Personality and Social Psychology*, Vol. 48, No. 4, pp. 909–924.

Hazan, C. and Shaver, P. (1987) 'Romantic love conceptualized as an attachment process', *Journal of Personality and Social Psychology*, Vol. 52, pp. 511–524.

Hazan, C., and Shaver, P. (1987) 'Conceptualizing romantic love as an attachment process', *Journal of Personality and Social Psychology*, 52, pp. 511–524.

Heather, N. (1976) *Radical Perspectives in Psychology*, Methuen.

Heider, F. (1944) 'Social perception and phenomenal causality', *Psychological Review*, Vol. 57, pp. 358–378.

Hergovich, A. (2003) 'Field dependence, suggestibility and belief in paranormal phenomena', *Personality and Individual Differences*, Vol. 34, No. 2, pp. 195–209.

Herman, R. (1984) 'The genetic relationship between identical twins', *Early Child Development and Care*, Vol. 16, No. 3–4, pp. 265–275.

Hertel, G. and Fiedler, K. (1993) 'Affective and cognitive influences in social dilemma game', *European Journal of Soc. Psych.*, Vol. 24, No. 1, pp. 131–145.

Heston, L. L. (1966) 'Psychiatric disorders in foster home reared children of schizophrenic mothers', *British Journal of Psychiatry*, Vol. 112, No. 489, pp. 819–825.

Hetherington, A. W. and Ranson, S. W. (1942) 'The relation of various hypothalamic lesions to adiposity in the rat' *Journal of Comparative Neurology*, Vol. 76, pp. 475–499.

Heurtin-Roberts, S. et al. (1997) 'Expressions of anxiety in African-Americans: ethnography and the epidemiological catchment area studies', *Culture Medicine and Psychiatry*, Vol. 21, pp. 337–363.

Higuchi, S. et al. (2006) 'New findings on the genetic influences on alcohol use and dependence', *Current Opinion in Psychiatry*, Vol. 19, No. 3, pp. 253–265.

Hill, D. (1992) 'Major tranquillizers: a good buy?', *Clinical Psychology Forum*, Vol. 49, pp. 20–22.

Hittner, J. B. and Daniels, J. R. (2002) 'Gender-role orientation, creative accomplishments and cognitive styles', *Journal of Creative Behavior*, Vol. 36, No. 1, pp. 62–75.

Hoffner, C. (1996) 'Children's wishful identification and parasocial interaction with favorite television characters', *Journal of Broadcasting & Electronic Media*, Vol. 40, No. 3, pp. 389–402.

Hofling, K. C. et al. (1966) 'An experimental study in the nurse-physician relationship', *Journal of Nervous and Mental Disorders*, Vol. 143, pp. 171–180.

Hofstede, G. (1980) *Culture's Consequences: International Differences in Work-Related Values*, Sage.

Holland, A. J. et al. (1984) 'Anorexia nervosa: evidence for a genetic basis', *Journal of Psychosomatic Research*, Vol. 32, No. 6, pp. 561–571.

Hollingshead, A. B. and Redlich, F. C. (1958) *Social Class and Mental Illness: Community Study*, John Wiley & Sons.

Holub, A. et al. (2005) 'Development of the temptations for gambling questionnaire: a measure of temptation in recently quit gamblers', *Addiction Research & Theory*, Vol. 13, No. 2, pp. 179–191.

Honorton, C. (1985) 'Meta-analysis of psi ganzfeld research: a response to Hyman', *Journal of Parapsychology*, Vol. 49, No. 1, pp. 51–91.

Honorton, C. (1977) 'Effects of meditation and feedback on psychokinetic performance: a pilot study with an instructor of TM', in Morris, D. J. et al. (eds) *Research in Parapsychology 1976*, Scarecrow Press.

Honorton, C. and Harper, S. (1974) 'Psi-mediated imagery and ideation in an experimental procedure for regulating perceptual input', *Journal of the American Society for Psychical Research*, Vol. 68, No. 2, pp. 156–1.

Honorton, C. et al. (1990) 'Psi communication in the ganzfeld: experiments with an automated testing system and a comparison with a meta-analysis of earlier studies', *Journal of Parapsychology*, Vol. 54, No. 2, pp. 99–139.

Honzik, M. P. et al. (1948) 'The stability of mental test performance between two and eighteen years', *Journal of Experimental Education*, Vol. 17, pp. 309–324.

Hood, B. and Willats, P. (1986) 'Reaching in the dark to an object's remembered position: evidence of object permanence in 5-month-old infants', *British Journal of Developmental Psychology*, Vol. 4, pp. 57–65.

Hoogsteder, M. et al. (1998) 'Adult-child interaction, joint problem solving and the structure of cooperation', in Woodhead, M. et al. (eds) *Cultural Worlds of Early Childhood*, Routledge.

Horn, J. M. et al. (1979) 'Intellectual resemblance among adoptive and biological relatives: the Texas Adoption Project', *Behavior Genetics*, Vol. 9, No. 3, pp. 177–207.

Hovland, C. et al. (1949) *Experiments on Mass Communication*, Princeton University Press.

Howes, O. D. et al. (2007) 'Street slang and schizophrenia', *British Medical Journal*, Vol. 335, No. 7433, pp. 1–3.

Hsu, F. (1971) 'Psychosocial homeostasis and jen: conceptual tools for advancing psychological inquiry', *American Anthropologist*, Vol. 73, pp. 23–44.

Hsu, L. K. G. (1990) *Eating Disorders*, Guilford Press.

Hublin, C. et al. (1997) 'Prevalence and genetics of sleepwalking', *Neurology*, Vol. 48, pp. 177–181.

Hudson, W. (1960) 'Pictorial depth perception in subcultural groups in Africa', *Journal of Social Psychology*, Vol. 52, pp. 183–208.

Hughes, M. (1975) *Egocentrism in Preschool Children*, Edinburgh University: unpublished doctoral thesis.

Humphrey, N. (1976) 'The social function of intellect', in Bateson, P. and Hinde, R. (eds) *Growing Points in Ethology*, Cambridge University Press.

Hunt, K. et al. (2009) 'An examination of the association between seeing smoking in films and tobacco use in young adults in the west of Scotland: cross-sectional study', *Health Education Research*, Vol. 24, No. 1, pp. 22–31.

Huot, B. et al. (1989) 'Temporal lobes signs and Jungian dimensions of personality', *Perceptual and Motor Skills*, Vol. 69, No. 3,1, pp. 841–842.

Hurd, M. W. and Ralph, M. R. (1998) 'The significance of circadian organization for longevity in the golden hamster', *Journal of Biological Rhythms*, Vol. 13, No. 5, pp. 430–436.

Hust, S. (2006) 'From sports heroes and jackasses to sex in the city: boys' use of the media in constructions of masculinities', *Dissertation Abstracts International Section A: Humanities and Social Sciences*, Vol. 67, No. 1-A, pp. 18.

Hyland, M. E. (2003) 'Extended network generalized entanglement theory: therapeutic mechanisms, empirical predictions, and investigations', *Journal of Alternative and Complementary Medicine*, Vol. 9, No. 6, pp. 919–936.

Hyman, R. (1977) 'Cold reading: how to convince strangers that you know all about them', *The Zetetic (Skeptical Inquirer)*, Vol. 1, No. 2.

Hyman, R. (1985) 'The ganzfeld psi experiment: a critical appraisal', *Journal of Parapsychology*, Vol. 49, No. 1, pp. 3–49.

Hyman, R. and Honorton, C. (1986) 'A joint communiqué: the psi ganzfeld controversy', *Journal of Parapsychology*, Vol. 50, No. 4, pp. 351–364.

Iacoboni, M. et al. (1999) 'Cortical mechanisms of human imitation', *Science*, Vol. 286, No. 5449.

Ibuka, N. and Kawamura, H. (1975) 'Loss of circadian rhythm in sleep-wakefulness cycle in the rat by suprachiasmatic nucleus lesions', *Brain Research*, Vol. 96, pp. 76–81.

Imperato-McGinley, J. et al. (1974) 'Steroid 5-reductase deficiency in man: an inherited form of pseudohermaphroditism', *Science*, Vol. 186, pp. 1213–1216.

Inhelder, B. and Piaget, J. (1958) *The Growth of Logical Thinking*, Routledge and Kegan Paul.

Irwin, H. J. (1986) 'Personality and psi performance: directions of current research', *Parapsychology Review*, Vol. 17, No. 5, pp. 1–4.

Irwin, H. J. (1990) 'Fantasy proneness and paranormal beliefs', *Psychological Reports*, Vol. 66, No. 2, pp. 655–658.

Irwin, H. J. (1992) 'Origins and functions of paranormal belief: the role of childhood trauma and interpersonal control', *Journal of the American Society for Psychical Research*, Vol. 86, No. 3, pp. 199–208.

Irwin, H. J. (1985) 'Parapsychological phenomena and the absorption domain', *Journal of the American Society for Psychical Research*, Vol. 79, No. 1, pp. 1–11.

Irwin, H. J. (1993) 'The near-death experience as a dissociative phenomenon: an empirical assessment', *Journal of Near-Death Studies*, Vol. 12, No. 2, pp. 95–103.

Isaac, R. and Shah, A. (2004) 'Sex roles and marital adjustment in Indian couples', *International Journal of Social Psychiatry*, Vol. 50, No. 2, pp. 129–141.

Iverson, L. L. (1979) 'The chemistry of the brain', *Scientific American*, Vol. 241, pp. 134–149.

Jacobs, P. A. et al. (1965) 'Aggressive behaviour, mental abnormality and XXY male', *Nature*, Vol. 208, pp. 1351–1352.

Jacobsen, L. H. et al. (2007) 'An overview of cognitive mechanisms in pathological gambling', *Nordic Psychology*, Vol. 59, No. 4, pp. 347–361.

Jahoda, G. (1966) 'Geometric illusions and environment: a study in Ghana', *British Journal of Psychology*, Vol. 57, pp. 193–199.

James, D. (2004) 'Factors influencing food choices, dietary intake, and nutrition-related attitudes among African Americans: application of a culturally sensitive model', *Ethnicity & Health*, Vol. 9, No. 4, pp. 349–367.

Janis, I. L. and Feshbach, S. (1953) 'Effects of fear-arousing communications', *Journal of Abnormal and Social Psychology*, Vol. 48, No. 1, pp. 78–92.

Jankowski, M. K. et al. (1999) 'Intergenerational transmission of dating aggression as a function of witnessing only same sex parents vs. opposite sex parents vs. both parents as perpetrators of domestic violence', *Journal of Family Violence*, Vol. 14, No. 3, pp. 267–279.

Jansen, K. L. R. (2004) 'The ketamine model of the near-death experience: a central role for the n-methyl-D-aspartate receptor', *Journal of Near-Death Studies*, Vol. 16, No. 1, pp. 5–26.

Jansson-Fröjmark, M. and Lindblom, K. (2008) 'A bi-directional relationship between anxiety and depression, and insomnia? A prospective study in the general population', *Journal of Psychosomatic Research*, Vol. 64, No. 4, pp. 443–449.

Jauregui, C. E. (2008) 'Consumers' use of food labels: an application of ordered probit models', *Dissertation Abstracts International Section A: Humanities and Social Sciences*, Vol. 69, No. 2-A, pp. 695.

Jeffery, R. W. and Wing, R. R. (1995) 'Long-term effects of interventions for weight loss using food provision and monetary incentives', *Journal of Consulting and Clinical Psychology*, Vol. 63, pp. 793–796.

Jensen, A. R. (1980) 'Level I and Level II abilities in Asian, white, and black children', *Intelligence*, Vol. 4, No. 1, pp. 41–49.

Jensen, A. R. (1969) 'How much can we boost IQ and scholastic achievement?', *Harvard Educational Review*, Vol. 39, No. 1, pp. 1–123.

Jiang, M. et al. (2003) 'Study on mental health status, personality characteristics and coping styles in 40 medical students with insomnia', *Chinese Journal of Clinical Psychology*, Vol. 11, No. 4, pp. 289–291.

Jimenez-Murcia, S. et al. (2007) 'Cognitive-behavioral group treatment for pathological gambling: analysis of effectiveness and predictors of therapy outcome', *Psychotherapy Research*, Vol. 17, No. 5, pp. 544–552.

Joesting, J. and Joesting, R. (1969) 'Torrance's creative motivation inventory and its relationship to several personality variables', *Psychological Reports*, Vol. 24, No. 1, pp. 30.

John, J. et al. (2000) 'Systemic administration of hypocretin-1 reduces cataplexy and normalizes sleep and waking durations in narcoleptic dogs', *Sleep Res Online*, Vol. 3, No. 1, pp. 23–8.

Johnstone, E. C. and Frith, C. D. (1996) 'Validation of three dimensions of schizophrenic symptoms in a large unselected sample of patients', *Psychological Medicine*, Vol. 26, No. 4, pp. 669–679.

Jones, M. C. (1957) 'The later careers of boys who were early- or late-maturing', *Child Development*, Vol. 28, pp. 113–128.

Jones, S. L. and Tinker, D. (1982) 'Transsexualism and the family: an interactional explanation', *Journal of Family Therapy*, Vol. 4, No. 1, pp. 1–14.

Josephson, W. L. (1987) 'Television violence and children's aggression: testing the priming, social script, and disinhibition predictions', *Journal of Personality and Social Psychology*, Vol. 53, pp. 882–890.

Jouvet, M. (1967) 'Mechanisms of the state of sleep: a neuropharmacological approach', *Research Publications of the Association for the Research in Nervous and Mental Diseases*, Vol. 45, pp. 86–126.

Kail, R. and Park, Y. (1992) 'Global developmental change in processing time', *Merrill-Palmer Quarterly*, Vol. 38, No. 4, pp. 525–541.

Kalat, J. W. (1998) *Biological Psychology* (6th edn), Thomson Brooks.

Kales, A. et al. (1974) 'Chronic hypnotic-drug use: ineffectiveness, drug-withdrawal insomnia, and dependence', *JAMA*, Vol. 227, No. 5, pp. 513–517.

Kales, A. et al. (1983) 'Biopsychobehavioral correlates of insomnia II: Pattern specificity and consistency with the Minnesota Multiphasic Personality Inventory', *Psychosom Med*, Vol. 45, No. 4, pp. 341–56.

Kallucy, R. S. et al. (1977) 'A study of 56 families with anorexia nervosa', *British Journal of Medical Psychology*, Vol. 50, pp. 381–395.

Kamin, L. J. (1974) *The Science and Politics of I.Q*, Lawrence Erlbaum.

Kanasawa, S. (2002) 'Bowling with our imaginary friends', *Evolution and Human Behavior*, Vol. 23, pp. 167–171.

Kao, C. et al. (2008) 'Insomnia: prevalence and its impact on excessive daytime sleepiness and psychological well-being in the adult Taiwanese population', *Quality of Life Research: An International Journal of Quality of Life Aspects of Treatment, Care & Rehabilitation*, Vol. 17, No. 8, pp. 1073–1080.

Kassel, J. D. et al. (2007) 'Adult attachment security and college student substance use', *Addictive Behaviors*, Vol. 32, No. 6, pp. 1164–1176.

Katz, J. and Aspden, P. (1997) 'Motivations for and barriers to internet usage: results of a national public opinion survey', *Internet Research*, Vol. 7, pp. 170–188.

Kaufman, A. R. and Augustson, E. M. (2008) 'Predictors of regular cigarette smoking among adolescent females: does body image matter?', *Nicotine & Tobacco Research*, Vol. 10, No. 8, pp. 1301–1309.

Kaufman, R. M. and Heiman, M. (1964) *Evolution of Psychosomatic Concepts*, International Universities Press.

Kelman, H. C. and Hovland, C. I. (1953). '"Reinstatement" of the communicator in delayed measurement of opinion change', *Journal of Abnormal and Social Psychology*, Vol. 48, No. 3, pp. 327–335.

Kendler, K. S. et al. (2004) 'Level of family dysfunction and genetic influences on smoking in women', *Psychological Medicine*, Vol. 34, No. 7, pp. 1263–1269.

Kennedy, G. A. (2002) 'A review of hypnosis in the treatment of parasomnias: nightmare, sleepwalking, and sleep terror disorders', *Australian Journal of Clinical & Experimental Hypnosis*, Vol. 30, No. 2, pp. 99–155.

Kennedy, J. E. (2005) 'Personality and motivations to believe, misbelieve and disbelieve in paranormal phenomena', *Journal of Parapsychology*, Vol. 69, pp. 263–292.

Kennedy, J. E., and Kanthamani, H. (1995) 'An exploratory study of the effects of paranormal and spiritual experiences on peoples' lives and well-being', *Journal of the American Society for Psychical Research*, Vol. 89, pp. 249–264.

Kennedy, M. G. et al. (2004) 'Increases in calls to the CDC national STD and AIDS hotline following AIDS-related episodes in a soap opera', *Journal of Communication*, Vol. 54, No. 2, pp. 287–301.

Kenrick, D. and Simpson, J. (eds) (1997) *Evolutionary Social Psychology*, Erlbaum.

Kenton, S. B. (1989) 'Speaker credibility in persuasive business communication: a model which explains gender differences', *Journal of Business Communication*, Vol. 26, No. 2, pp. 143–157.

Kerckhoff, A. C. and Davis, K. E. (1962) 'Value consensus and need complementarity in mater selection', *American Sociological Review*, Vol. 27, pp. 295–303.

Kerckhoff, A. C. (1974) 'The social context of interpersonal attraction', in Huston, T.L. (ed.) *Foundations of Interpersonal Attraction*, Academic Press.

Kienlen, K. K. (1998) 'Developmental and social antecedents of stalking', in J.R. Meloy (ed.) *The Psychology of Stalking: Clinical and Forensic Perspectives*, Academic Press.

Killen, J. D. et al. (2008) 'Extended cognitive behavior therapy for cigarette smoking cessation', *Addiction*, Vol. 103, No. 8, pp. 1381–1390.

Kim, K. and Lowry, D. T. (2005) 'Television commercials as a lagging social indicator: gender role stereotypes in Korean television advertising', *Sex Roles*, Vol. 53, No. 11–12, pp. 901–910.

Kiminyo, D. M. (1977) 'A cross-cultural study of the development of conservation of mass, weight and volume among Kamba children', in Dasen, P. R. (ed.) *Piagetian Psychology*, Gardner Press.

King, K. M. and Chassin, L. (2008) 'Adolescent stressors, psychopathology, and young adult substance dependence: a prospective study', *Journal of Studies on Alcohol and Drugs*, Vol. 69, No. 5, pp. 629–638.

Kiss, C. G. et al. (2004) 'Informed Consent and Decision Making by Cataract Patients', *Arch Ophthalmol.*, Vol. 122, pp. 94–98.

Klem, M. L. et al. (1997) 'A descriptive study of individuals successful at long-term maintenance of substantial weight loss', *American Journal of Clinical Nutrition*, Vol. 66, 239–246.

Klinesmith, J. et al. (2006) 'Guns, Testosterone, and Aggression: an Experimental Test of a Mediational Hypothesis', *Psychological Science*, Vol. 17, pp. 568–571.

Klump, K. L. et al. (2006) 'Preliminary evidence that gonadal hormones organize and activate disordered eating', *Psychological Medicine*, Vol. 36, No. 4, pp. 539–546.

Klump, K. L. et al. (2001) 'Genetic and environmental influences on anorexia nervosa syndromes in a population-based twin sample', *Psychological Medicine*, Vol. 31, No. 4, pp. 737–740.

Klüver, H. and Bucy, P. C. (1939) 'Preliminary analysis of functions of the temporal lobes in monkeys', *Archives of Neurology and Psychiatry (Chicago)*, Vol. 42, pp. 979–1000.

Knight, R. A. (1984) 'Converging models of cognitive deficit in schizophrenia', in Spaulding, W. D. and Cole, J. K. (eds) *Theories of Schizophrenia and Psychosis*, University of Nebraska Press.

Kobak, R. R. and Sceery, A. (1988) 'Attachment in late adolescence: working models, affect regulation, and representations of self and others', *Child Development*, Vol. 59, No. 1, pp. 135–146.

Koehler, W. (1925) *The Mentality of Apes*, Routledge and Kegan Paul.

Koeppen-Schomerus, G. et al. (2001) 'A genetic analysis of weight and overweight in 4-year-old twin pairs', *Int. J Obes.* Vol. 25, pp. 838–844.

Kohlberg, L. (1963) 'The development of children's orientations toward a moral order', *Human Development*, Vol. 6, pp. 11–33.

Kohlberg, L. (1978) 'Revisions in the theory and practice of moral development', *Directions for Child Development*, Vol. 2, pp. 83–88.

Kohlberg, L. (1981) *Essays on Moral Develoment*, Vol.1, Harper and Row.

Kohlberg, L. (1969) 'Stage and sequence: the cognitive developmental approach to socialisation', in Goslin, D. A. (ed.) *Handbook of Socialisation Theory and Research*, Rand McNally.

Kohlberg, L. (1966) 'A cognitive-developmental analysis of children's sex-role concepts and attitudes', in Maccoby, E. E. (ed.) *The Development of Sex Differences*, Stanford University Press.

Kolakowski, D. and Malina, R. M. (1974) 'Spatial ability, throwing accuracy and man's hunting heritage', *Nature*, Vol. 251, No. 5474, pp. 410–412.

Koller, M. (1983) 'Health risks related to shift work: an example of time-contingent effects of long-term stress', *International Archives of Occupational and Environmental Health*, Vol. 53, No. 1, pp. 59–75.

Kraepelin, E. (1913) *Clinical Psychiatry: A Textbook for Physicians*, Macmillan.

Kraft, T. and Kraft, D. (2005) 'Covert sensitization revisited: six case studies', *Contemporary Hypnosis*, Vol. 22, No. 4, pp. 202–209.

Krampe, H. et al. (2006) Follow-up of 180 alcoholic patients for up to 7 years after outpatient treatment: impact of alcohol deterrents on outcome', *Alcoholism, Clinical and Experimental Research*, Vol. 30, No. 1, pp. 86–95.

Kraut, R. et al. (1998) 'Internet paradox: a social technology that reduces social involvement and psychological well-being?', *American Psychologist*, Vol. 53, No. 9, pp. 1017–1031.

Krishnan-Sarin, S. et al. (2006) 'Contingency management for smoking cessation in adolescent smokers', *Exp Clin Psychopharmacol*, Vol. 14, pp. 306–310.

Krucoff, M. et al. (2005) 'Music, imagery, touch, and prayer as adjuncts to interventional cardiac care: the monitoring and actualisation of noetic trainings (MANTRA) II: randomised study', *Lancet*, Vol. 366, No. 9481, pp. 211–217.

Kruijver, F. P. et al. (2000) 'Male-to-female transsexuals have female neuron numbers in a limbic nucleus', *J Clin Endocrinol Metab*, Vol. 85, No. 5, pp. 2034–41.

Kuhn, D. et al. (1978) 'Sex-role concepts of two- and three-year-olds', *Child Development*, Vol. 49, pp. 445–451.

Kuhn, T. S. (1962) *The Structure of Scientific Revolutions*, University of Chicago Press.

Kurtz, H. and Davidson, S. (1974) 'Psychic trauma in an Israeli child: relationship to environmental security', *American Journal of Psychotherapy*, Vol. 28, No. 3, pp. 438–444.

Kushner, M. et al. (2008) 'Urge to gamble in a simulated gambling environment', *Journal of Gambling Studies*, Vol. 24, No. 2, pp. 219–227.

Kutnik, P. (1986) 'The relationship of moral judgement and moral action: Kohlberg's theory, criticism and revision', in Modgil, S. and Modgil, C. (eds) *Lawrence Kohlberg: Consensus and Controversy*, The Falmer Press.

Kyes, R. et al. (1995) 'Aggression and brain serotonergic responsivity: response to slides in male macaques', *Physiology & Behaviour*, Vol. 57, No. 2.

Laing, R. D. and Esterson, A. (1964) *Sanity, Madness and the Family*, Penguin.

Laing, R. D. (1965) *The Divided Self*, Penguin.

Langer, E. J. (1975) 'The illusion of control', *Journal of Personality and Social Psychology*, Vol. 32, No. 2, pp. 311–328.

Langlois, J. H. and Downs, A. C. (1980) 'Mothers, fathers, and peers as socialization agents of sex-typed play behaviors in young children', *Child Development*, Vol. 51, No. 4, pp. 1237–1247.

Laroche, M. et al. (1998) 'Italian ethnic identity and its relative impact on the consumption of convenience and traditional foods', *Journal of Consumer Marketing*, Vol. 15, No. 2, pp. 125–151.

Lawick-Goodall, J. (1970) 'Tool-using in primates and other vertebrates', in Lehrman, D.S. et al. (eds) *Advances in the Study of Behaviour*, Vol. 3, Academic Press.

Lawrence, A. R. (1992) 'Gathering in the sheep and goats... a meta-analysis of forced-choice sheep-goat ESP studies, 1947–1993', in *Proceedings of the 36th Annual Convention of the Parapsychological Association*, pp. 75–86.

Leader, T. et al. (2007) 'Without mercy: the immediate impact of group size on lynch mob atrocity', *Personality and Social Psychology Bulletin*, Vol. 33, No. 10, pp. 1340–1352.

Leahy, A. M. (1935) 'A study of adopted children as a method of investigating nature-nurture', *Journal of the American Statistical Association*, Vol. 30, pp. 281–287.

Le Bon, G. (1895) *Psychologie des Foules*, Alcan.

Lee, L. (1984) 'Sequences in separation: a framework for investigating endings of the personal (romantic) relationship', *Journal of Social and Personal Relationships*, Vol. 1, pp. 49–74.

Leff, J. (1992) 'Schizophrenia and similar conditions', *International Journal of Mental Health*, Vol. 21, No. 2, p. 2.

Leff, J. (1982) 'A controlled trial of social intervention in the families of schizophrenic patients', *British Journal of Psychiatry*, Vol. 141, pp. 121–134.

Lefkowitz, E. S. and Zeldow, P. B. (2006) 'Masculinity and femininity predict optimal mental health: a belated test of the androgyny hypothesis', *Journal of Personality Assessment*, Vol. 87, No. 1, pp. 95–101.

Leser, M. S. et al. (2002) 'A low-fat intake and greater activity level are associated with lower weight regain 3 years after completing a very-low-calorie diet', *J Am Diet Assoc*, Vol. 102, No. 9, pp. 1252–6.

Leslie, A. M. (1987) 'Pretense and representation: the origins of "theory of mind"', *Psychological Review*, Vol. 94, No. 4, pp. 412–426.

Lethmate, J. and Ducke, G. (1973) 'Experiments on self-recognition in a mirror in orangutans, chimpanzees, gibbons and several monkey species', *Zeitschrift für Tierpsychologie*, Vol. 33, No. 3–4, pp. 248–269.

Letourneau, A. R. et al. (2007) 'Timing and predictors of postpartum return to smoking in a group of inner-city women: an exploratory pilot study', *Birth: Issues in Perinatal Care*, Vol. 34, No. 3, pp. 245–252.

Leucht, S. et al. (1999) 'Efficacy and extrapyramidal side-effects of the new antipsychotics olanzapine, quetiapine, risperidone, and sertindole compared to conventional antipsychotics and placebo: a meta-analysis of randomized controlled trials', *Schizophr Res*, Vol. 35, No. 1, pp. 51–68.

Lewis, R. A. (1972) 'A developmental framework for the analysis of premarital dyadic formation', *Family Process*, Vol. 2, pp.17–48.

Li, M. D. et al. 'A meta-analysis of estimated genetic and environmental effects on smoking behavior in male and female adult twins', *Addiction*, Vol. 98, pp. 23–31.

Liben, L. S. and Signorella, M. L. (1993) 'Gender-schematic processing in children: the role of initial interpretations of stimuli', *Developmental Psychology*, Vol. 29, No. 1, pp. 141–149.

Liddle, P. F. (1987) 'The symptoms of chronic schizophrenia: a re-examination of the positive–negative dichotomy', *British Journal of Psychiatry*, Vol. 151, pp. 145–151.

Light, P. et al. (1979) 'The conservation task as an interactional setting', *British Journal of Educational Psychology*, Vol. 49, No. 3, pp. 304–310.

Liou, D. and Contento, I. R. (2001) 'Usefulness of psychosocial theory variables in explaining fat-related dietary behavior in Chinese Americans: association with degree of acculturation', *Journal of Nutrition Education*, Vol. 33, No. 6, pp. 322–331.

Lloyd, P. (1995) *Cognitive and Language Development*, BPS Books.

Locke, T. P. and Shonz, F. C. (1983) 'Personality correlates of the near-death experience: a preliminary study', *Journal of the American Society for Psychical Research*, Vol. 77, No. 4, pp. 311–318.

Loessl, B. et al. (2008) 'Are adolescents chronically sleep-deprived? An investigation of sleep habits of adolescents in the southwest of Germany', *Child: Care, Health and Development*, Vol. 34, No. 5, pp. 549–556.

Logan, T. K. et al. (2000). Stalking as a variant of intimate violence: implications from a young adult sample', *Violence and Victims*, Vol. 15, pp. 91–111.

Lopera, F. and Ardila, A. (1992) 'Prosopamnesia and visuolimbic disconnection syndrome: a case study', *Neuropsychology*, Vol. 6, No. 1, pp. 3–12.

Lopez, S. and Hernandez, P. (1986) 'How culture is considered in evaluations of psychopathology', *Journal of Nervous and Mental Disease*, Vol. 174, No. 10, pp. 598–606.

Lorenz, K. (1965) *Evolution and Modification of Behaviour*, University of Chicago Press.

Lott, B. E. (1994) *Women's Lives: Themes and Variations in Gender Learning*, Brooks Cole.

Louis-Sylvestre, J. et al. (2003) 'Highlighting the positive impact of increasing feeding frequency on metabolism and weight management', *Forum Nutr*, pp. 126–8.

Luria, A. R. (1976) *The Mind of a Mnemonist*, Basic Books.

Luxen, M. F. (2005) 'Gender differences in dominance and affiliation during a demanding interaction', *J Psychol*, Vol. 139, No. 4, pp. 331–47.

Lytton, H. and Romney, D. M. (1991) 'Parents' differential socialization of boys and girls: a meta-analysis', *Psychological Bulletin*, Vol. 109, No. 2, pp. 267–296.

Lyver, M. et al. (2006) 'Effect of belief in "psychic healing" on self-reported pain in chronic pain sufferers', *Journal of Psychosomatic Research*, Vol. 60, No. 1, pp. 59–61.

MacArthur, R. H. and Pianka, E. R. (1966) 'On the optimal use of a patchy environment', *American Naturalist*, Vol. 100.

Macht, M. and Mueller, J. (2007) 'Immediate effects of chocolate on experimentally induced mood states', *Appetite*, Vol. 49, No. 3, pp. 667–674.

Mackintosh, N. J. and Mascie-Taylor, C. G. (1985) 'The IQ question', in *Report of Committee of Inquiry into Education of Children from Ethnic Minority Groups*, pp. 126–163, HMSO.

Maddux, J. E. and Rogers, R. W. (1983) 'Protection motivation and self-efficacy: a revised theory of fear appeals and attitude change', *Journal of Experimental Social Psychology*, Vol. 19, No. 5, pp. 469–479.

Maes, H. et al. (1997) 'Genetic and environmental factors in relative body weight and human adiposity', *Behavior Genetics*, Vol. 27, No. 4, pp. 325–351.

Maestripieri, D. (2007) *Macachiavellian Intelligence: How Rhesus Macaques and Humans Have Conquered the World*, Chicago University Press.

Main, M. and Solomon, J. (1990) 'Procedures for identifying infants as disorganised/disoriented during the Ainsworth Strange Situation', in Greenberg, M.T. et al. (eds) *Attachment in the Preschool Years*, University of Chicago Press.

Main, M. and Goldwyn, R. (1994) 'Predicting rejection of her infant from mother's representation of her own experience: implications for the abused–abusing inter-generational cycle', *Child Abuse and Neglect*, Vol. 8, pp. 203–217.

Maltby, J. et al. (2003) 'A clinical interpretation of attitudes and behaviors associated with celebrity worship', *Journal of Nervous and Mental Disease*, Vol. 191, pp. 25–29.

Maltby, J. et al. (2006) 'Extreme celebrity worship, fantasy proneness and dissociation: developing the measurement and understanding of celebrity worship within a clinical personality context', *Personality and Individual Differences*, Vol. 40, No. 2, pp. 273–283.

Maltby, J. et al. (2004) 'Celebrity worship, cognitive flexibility and social complexity', *Personality and Individual Differences*, Vol. 37, pp. 1475–1482.

Mann, T. et al. (2007) 'Medicare's search for effective obesity treatments: diets are not the answer', *American Psychologist*, Vol. 62, pp. 220–233.

Marazziti, D. et al. (2008) 'Decreased density of the platelet serotonin transporter in pathological gamblers', *Neuropsychobiology*, Vol. 57, No. 1–2, pp. 38–43.

Marcoux, B. C. and Shope, J. T. (1997) 'Application of the theory of planned behavior to adolescent use and misuse of alcohol', *Health Education Research Theory & Practice*, Vol. 12, No. 3, pp. 323–331.

Marder, S. R. et al. (1997) 'The effects of risperidone on the five dimensions of schizophrenia derived by factor analysis: combined results of the North American trials', *J Clin Psychiatry*, Vol. 58, No. 12, pp. 538–46.

Marlatt, G. A. et al. (1973) 'Loss of control drinking in alcoholics: an experimental analogue', *Journal of Abnormal Psychology*, Vol. 81, pp. 233–241.

Marlatt, G. A. and Gordon, J. R. (1980) 'Determinants of relapse: implications for the maintenance of behavior change', in Davidson, P.O. and Davidson, S.M. (eds) *Behavioral Medicine: Changing Health Lifestyle*, Brunner/Mazel.

Marlatt, G. A. and Gordon, J. R. (1985) (eds) *Relapse Prevention*. Guilford.

Martikainen, K. et al. (1994) 'Natural evolution of snoring: a 5-year follow-up study', *Acta Neurol Scand*, Vol. 90, No. 6, pp. 437–42.

Martin, C. and Halverson, C. (1983) 'Gender constancy: a methodological and theoretical analysis', *Sex Roles*, Vol. 9, pp. 775–790.

Martin, C. L. and Halverson, C. F. (1981) 'A schematic processing model of sex typing and stereotyping in children', *Child Development*, Vol. 52, No. 4, pp. 1119–1134.

Martin, C. L. (1989) 'Children's use of gender-related information in making social judgments', *Developmental Psychology*, Vol. 25, No. 1, pp. 80–88.

Martin, P. (2003) *Counting Sheep*, HarperCollins.

Marwick, B. (1978) 'The Soal-Goldney experiments with Basil Shackleton: new evidence of data manipulation', *Proceedings of the Society for Psychical Research*, Vol. 56, pp. 250–280.

Mathur, C. et al. (2008) 'Differences in prevalence of tobacco use among Indian urban youth: the role of socioeconomic status', *Nicotine & Tobacco Research*, Vol. 10, No. 1, pp. 109–116.

May, J. L. and Hamilton, P. A. (1980) 'Effects of musically evoked affect on women's interpersonal attraction toward and perceptual judgments of physical attractiveness of men', *Motivation and Emotion*, Vol. 4, No. 3, pp. 217–228.

Mazur, T. et al. (2004) 'Male pseudohermaphroditism: long-term quality of life outcome in five 46, XY individuals reared female', *J Pediatr Endocrinol Metab*, Vol. 17, No. 6, pp. 809–23.

McAllister, P. O. and Davies, J. B. (1992) 'Attributional shifts in smokers as a consequence of clinical classification', *Journal of Drug Issues*, Vol. 22, No. 1, pp. 139–153.

McAuliffe, W. E. and Gordon, R. A. (1974) 'A test of Lindesmith's theory of addiction: the frequency of euphoria among long-term addicts', *American Journal of Sociology*, Vol. 79, pp. 795–840.

McCaffery, J. M. et al. (2008) 'Educational attainment, smoking initiation and lifetime nicotine dependence

among male Vietnam-era twins', *Psychological Medicine*, Vol. 38, No. 9, pp. 1287–1297.

McCall, R. B. et al. 'Developmental changes in mental performance', *Monographs of the Society for Research in Child Development*, Vol. 38, No. 3, p. 83.

McCartney, K. et al. (1990) 'Growing up and growing apart: a developmental meta-analysis of twin studies', *Psychological Bulletin*, Vol. 107, No. 2, pp. 226–237.

McClearn, D. G. (2004) 'Interest in sports and belief in sports superstitions', *Psychological Reports*, Vol. 94, No. 3, pp. 1043–1047.

McClenon, J. (1994) *Wondrous Events: Foundations of Religious Beliefs*, University of Pennsylvania Press.

McClenon, J. (2002) *Wondrous Healing: Shamanism, Human Evolution, and the Origin of Religion*, Northern Illinois University Press.

McCutcheon, L. E. et al. (2002) 'Conceptualization and measurement of celebrity worship', *British Journal of Psychology*, Vol. 93, No. 1, pp. 67–87.

McCutcheon, L. E. et al. (2003) 'A cognitive profile of individuals who tend to worship celebrities', *Journal of Psychology*, Vol. 137, pp. 309–322.

McCutcheon, L. E. et al. (2006) 'Exploring the link between attachment and the inclination to obsess about or stalk celebrities', *North American Journal of Psychology*, Vol. 8, No. 2.

McGarrigle, J. and Donaldson, M. (1974) 'Conservation accidents', *Cognition: International Journal of Cognitive Psychology*, Vol. 3, No. 4, pp. 341–350.

McGarry, J. J. and Newberry, B. H. (1981) 'Beliefs in paranormal phenomena and locus of control: a field study', *Journal of Personality and Social Psychology*, Vol. 41, No. 4, pp. 725–736.

McGhie, A. and Chapman, J. S. (1961) 'Disorders of attention and perception in early schizophrenia', *British Journal of Medical Psychology*, Vol. 34, pp. 103–116.

McGue, M. et al. (1992) 'Personality stability and change in early adulthood: a behavioural genetic analysis', *Developmental Psychology*, Vol. 29, pp. 96–109.

McGuire, E. J. et al. (1992) 'Aggression as a potential mediator of the home advantage in professional ice hockey', *Journal of Sport and Exercise Psychology*, Vol. 14, No. 2, pp. 148–158.

McGuire, W. J. (1957) 'Order of presentation as a factor in "conditioning" persuasiveness', in Hovland, C. I. et al. (eds) *The Order of Presentation in Persuasion*, Yale University Press.

McGuire, W. J. (1969) 'The nature of attitudes and attitude change', in Lindzey, G. and Aronson, E. (eds) *The Handbook of Social Psychology,* Vol. 3, Addison-Wesley.

McGurk, H. (1975) *Growing and Changing*, Methuen.

McHale, S. M. et al. (2001) 'Sibling influences on gender development in middle childhood and early adolescence: a longitudinal study', *Developmental Psychology*, Vol. 37, No. 1, pp. 115–125.

McManus, K. et al. (2001) 'A randomized controlled trial of a moderate-fat, low-energy diet compared with a low-fat, low-energy diet for weight loss in overweight adults', *International Journal of Obesity,* Vol. 25, pp. 1503–1511.

McNeil, J. E. and Warrington, E. K. (1991) 'Prosopagnosia: a reclassification', *Quarterly Journal of Experimental Psychology A: Human Experimental Psychology*, Vol. 43A, No. 2, pp. 267–287.

McNeil, T. F. and Kaij, L. (1978) 'Obstetric factors in the development of schizophrenia: complications in the births of preschizophrenics and in reproduction by schizophrenic patients', in Wynne, L. C. et al. (eds) *The Nature of Schizophrenia: New Approaches to Research and Treatment*, Wiley.

McVey, D. and Stapleton, J. (2009) 'Can anti-smoking television advertising affect smoking behaviour? Controlled trial of the Health Education Authority for England's anti-smoking TV campaign', *Tobacco Control* 2000, No. 9, pp. 273–82.

Mead, M. (1935) *Sex and Temperament in Three Primitive Societies*, William Morrow.

Meadows, S. (1995) 'Cognitive development', in Bryant, P. E. and Colman, A. M. (eds) *Developmental Psychology*, Longmans.

Meddis, R. (1975) *The Sleep Instinct*, Routledge.

Mednick, S. A. et al. (1988) 'Adult schizophrenia following prenatal exposure to an influenza epidemic', *Archives of General Psychiatry*, Vol. 45, No. 2, pp. 189–192.

Mercer, J. D. et al. (2002) 'Insomniacs' perception of wake instead of sleep', *Sleep*, Vol. 25, No. 5, pp. 564–71.

Mercer, N. (2000) *The Guided Construction of Knowledge*, Multilingual Matters.

Mevarech, Z. et al. (1991) 'Learning with computers in small groups: cognitive and affective outcomes', *Journal of Educational Computing Research*, Vol. 7, No. 2, pp. 233–243.

Meyers, A. et al. (1976) 'Case study: use of covert self-instruction for the elimination of psychotic speech', *Journal of Consulting and Clinical Psychology*, Vol. 44, No. 3, pp. 480–482.

Michel, S. T. (2007) 'Psychosocial and behavioral factors associated with emotional eating in adolescents', *Dissertation Abstracts International: Section B: The Sciences and Engineering*, Vol. 68, No. 3-B, pp. 1593.

Milgram, S. (1963) 'Behavioral study of obedience', *Journal of Abnormal and Social Psychology*, Vol. 67, No. 4, pp. 371–378.

Miller, M. K. and Summers, A. (2007) 'Gender differences in video game characters' roles, appearances, and attire as portrayed in video game magazines', *Sex Roles*, Vol. 56, No. 9–10, pp. 733–742.

Miller, N. and Campbell, D. T. (1959) 'Recency and primacy in persuasion as a function of the timing of speeches and measurements', *Journal of Abnormal and Social Psychology*, Vol. 59, No. 1, pp. 1–9.

Miller, N. E. and Dollard, J. (1941) *Social Learning and Imitation*, Yale University Press.

Miller, T. J. et al. (2002) 'Prospective diagnosis of the initial prodrome for schizophrenia based on the Structured Interview for Prodromal Syndromes: preliminary evidence of interrater reliability and predictive validity', *Am J Psychiatry*, Vol. 159, No. 5, pp. 863–5.

Miller, W. R. et al. (2003) 'What works? A summary of alcohol treatment outcome research', in Hester, R. K. and Miller, W. R. (eds) *Handbook of Alcoholism Treatment Approaches: Effective Alternatives*, Allyn and Bacon.

Mills, J. and Clark, M. S. (1982) 'Exchange and communal relationships', *Review of Personality and Social Psychology*, Vol. 3, pp.121–144.

Milton, B. et al. (2008) 'Starting young? Children's experiences of trying smoking during pre-adolescence', *Health Education Research*, Vol. 23, No. 2, pp. 298–309.

Milton, J. and Wiseman, R. (1999) 'A meta-analysis of mass-media tests of extrasensory perception', *British Journal of Psychology*, Vol. 90, No. 2, pp. 235–240.

Mineka, S. and Cook, M. (1988) 'Social learning and the acquisition of snake fear in monkeys', in Zentall, T. and Galef, B. (eds) *Social Learning: Psychological and Biological Perspectives*, Lawrence Erlbaum Associates.

Minuchin, S. et al. (1978) *Psychosomatic Families: Anorexia Nervosa in Context*, Harvard University Press.

Moffitt, T. E. et al. (1998) 'Whole blood serotonin relates to violence in an epidemiological study', *Biological Psychiatry*, Vol. 43, No. 6, pp. 446–457.

Moghaddam, F. M. et al. (1993) *Social Psychology in Cross-Cultural Perspective*, W. H. Freeman.

Money, J. (1974) 'Pre-natal hormones and post-natal socialization in gender identity differentiation', in Cole, J. K. and Dienstbier, R. (eds) *Nebraska Symposium on Motivation*, University of Nebraska Press.

Money, J. and Ehrhardt, A. (1972) *Man and Woman, Boy and Girl*, Johns Hopkins University Press.

Monnier, M. and Hosli, L. (1964) 'Dialysis of sleep and waking factors in blood of the rabbit', *Science*, Vol. 146, pp. 796–797.

Moore, D. W. (2005) 'Three in four Americans believe in paranormal', *Gallup Poll News Service*, 16 June 2005.

Morphy, H. et al. (2007) 'Epidemiology of insomnia: a longitudinal study in a UK population', *Sleep*, Vol. 30, No. 3, pp. 274–280.

Morris, R. L. et al. (1995) 'Comparison of the sender/no sender condition in the Ganzfeld', *Proceedings of the 38th Annual Convention of the Parapsychological Association*, held in Durham, North Carolina, August 1995.

Morse, M. et al. (1989) 'Near-death experiences: a neurophysiologic explanatory model', *Journal of Near-Death Studies*, Vol. 8, No. 1, pp. 45–53.

Moruzzi, G. and Magoun, H.W. (1949) 'Brain stem reticular formation and activation of the EEG', *Electroencephalography and Clinical Neurophysiology*, Vol.1, pp. 455–473.

Moyer-Guse, E. (2008) 'Entertainment television and safe sex: understanding effects and overcoming resistance', *Dissertation Abstracts International Section A: Humanities and Social Sciences*, Vol. 68, No. 7-A, p. 2711.

Mrosovsky, N. and Sherry, D.F. (1980) 'Animal anorexias', *Science*, Vol. 207, pp. 837–842.

Mueller, U. (1993) 'Social status and sex', *Nature*, Vol. 363, p. 490.

Mullen, P.E. et al. (2000) *Stalkers and Their Victims*, Cambridge University Press.

Mukhametov, L. (1984) 'Sleep in marine animals', in Borbely, A. and Valatx, J. L. (eds) *Sleep Mechanisms*, Springer Verlag.

Mukherjee, S. (1983) 'Misdiagnosis of schizophrenia in bipolar patients: a multiethnic comparison', *American Journal of Psychiatry*, Vol. 140, No. 12, pp. 1571–1574.

Mulgrew, A.T. et al. (2008) 'Risk and severity of motor vehicle crashes in patients with obstructive sleep apnoea/hypopnoea', *Thorax*, Vol. 63, pp. 536–541.

Munsey, B. (1980) *Moral Development, Moral Education, and Kohlberg*, Religious Education Press.

Murstein, B.I. (1976) 'The stimulus-value-role theory of marital choice', in Grunebaum, H. and Christ, J. (eds) *Contemporary Marriage: Structures, Dynamics and Therapy*, Little, Brown.

Murstein, B. I. (1974) *Love, Sex, and Marriage Through the Ages,* Springer.

Neisser, U. (1976) *Cognition and Reality*, W. H. Freeman.

Newman, H. H. et al. (1937) *Twins: a Study of Heredity and Environment,* University of Chicago Press.

Norton, J. P. (1982) 'Expressed emotion, affective style, voice tone and communication deviance as predictors of offspring schizophrenia spectrum disorders', unpublished doctoral dissertation, University of California at Los Angeles.

Nyiti, R. M. (1976) 'The development of conservation in the Meru children of Tanzania', *Child Development*, Vol. 47, pp. 1622–1629.

Ogden, J. (2003) 'Some problems with social cognition models: a pragmatic and conceptual analysis', *Health Psychology*, Vol. 22, No. 4, pp. 424–428.

Ohayon, M. M. et al. (2004) 'Meta-analysis of quantitative sleep parameters from childhood to old age in healthy individuals: developing normative sleep values across the human lifespan', *Sleep*, Vol. 27, No. 7, p. 1255.

Ohayon, M. M. et al. (2005) Frequency of narcolepsy symptoms and other sleep disorders in narcoleptic patients and their first-degree relatives, *Journal of Sleep Research,* Vol. 14, No. 4, pp. 437–445.

Ohayon, M. M. et al. (1999) 'Night terrors, sleepwalking, and confusional arousals in the general population: their frequency and relationship to other sleep and mental disorders', *Journal of Clinical Psychiatry*, Vol. 60, No. 4, pp. 268–76.

O'Keefe, D. A. (1990) *Persuasion: Theory and Research*, Sage.

Olson, C. K. et al. (2008) 'The role of violent video game content in adolescent development: boys' perspectives', *Journal of Adolescent Research*, Vol. 23, No. 1, pp. 55–75.

Onyskiw, J. E. (2000) 'Processes underlying children's responses to witnessing physical aggression in their families', *Dissertation Abstracts International: Section B: The Sciences and Engineering*, Vol. 61, No. 3, p. 1620.

Oswald, I. (1966) *Sleep*, Penguin.

Otis, L. P. and Kuo, E. C. (1984) 'Extraordinary beliefs among students in Singapore and Canada', *Journal of Psychology: Interdisciplinary and Applied*, Vol. 116, No. 2, pp. 215–226.

Owen, H. M. (2001) 'Pharmacological aversion treatment of alcohol dependence I: Production and prediction of conditioned alcohol aversion', *American Journal of Drug and Alcohol Abuse*, Vol. 27, No. 3, pp. 561–585.

Owen, L. (2000) 'Impact of a telephone helpline for smokers who called during a mass media campaign', *Tobacco Control*, Vol. 9, pp. 148–154.

Palmer, J. (1978) 'The out-of-body experience: a psychological theory', *Parapsychology Review*, Vol. 9, pp. 19–22.

Pappenheimer, J. R. et al. (1975) 'Extraction of sleep-promoting factor S from cerebrospinal fluid and from brains of sleep-deprived animals', *Journal of Neurophysiology*, Vol. 38, No. 6, pp. 1299–1311.

Parke, J. and Griffiths, M. (2004) 'Gambling addiction and the evolution of the "near miss"', *Addiction Research & Theory*, Vol. 12, No. 5, pp. 407–411.

Parker, C. (2008) 'An examination of the interrelationship between social demographic factors and multiple intelligences among college students', *Dissertation Abstracts International Section A: Humanities and Social Sciences*, Vol. 69, No. 1-A, pp. 114.

Parkes, J. D. and Lock, C. B. (1989) 'Genetic factors in sleep disorders', *Journal of Neurology, Neurosurgery & Psychiatry*, Spec Suppl, June 1989. pp. 101–108.

Pathe, M. and Mullen, P. E. (1997) 'The impact of stalkers on their victims', *British Journal of Psychiatry*, Vol. 170, pp. 12–17.

Patterson, F. and Cohn, R. (1994) 'Self-recognition and self-awareness in lowland gorillas', in Parker, S. et al. (eds) *Self-Awareness in Animals and Humans: Developmental Perspectives*, Cambridge University Press.

Paul, G. H. and Lentz, R. (1977) *Psychosocial Treatment of the Chronic Mental Patient*, Harvard University Press.

Pavlov, I. P. (1927) *Conditioned Reflexes*, Oxford University Press.

Pawlowski, B. and Dunbar, R. I. M. (2005) 'Waist-to-hip ratio versus body mass index as predictors of fitness in women', *Human Nature*, Vol. 16, No. 2, pp. 164–177.

Pearlson, G. D. et al. (1989) 'Ventricle–brain ratio, computed tomographic density, and brain area in 50 schizophrenics', *Archives of General Psychiatry*, Vol. 46, No. 8, pp. 690–697.

Pedrosa, E. et al. (2009) 'Survey of schizophrenia and bipolar disorder candidate genes using chromatin immunoprecipitation and tiled microarrays (ChIP-chip)', *J Neurogenet*, 18 February, pp. 1–12.

Pepperburg, I. M. et al. (1995) 'Mirror use by African grey parrots (Psittacus erithracus)', *Journal of Comparative Psychology*, Vol. 109, pp. 182–195.

Perlman, D. and Duck, S. (eds) (1987) *Intimate Relationships: Development, Dynamics, and Deterioration*, Sage.

Perlis, M. L. et al. (2001) 'Beta/gamma EEG activity in patients with primary and secondary insomnia and good sleeper controls', *Sleep*, Vol. 24, No. 1, pp.110–117.

Perner, J. et al. (1989) 'Exploration of the autistic child's theory of mind: knowledge, belief, and communication', *Child Development*, Vol. 60, No. 3, pp. 689–700.

Perri, M. G. and Fuller, P. R. (1995) 'Success and failure in the treatment of obesity: where do we go from here?', *Medicine, Exercise, Nutrition, and Health*, Vol. 4, pp. 255–272.

Petry, N. M. et al. (2007) 'Do coping skills mediate the relationship between cognitive-behavioral therapy and reductions in gambling in pathological gamblers?', *Addiction*, Vol. 102, No. 8, pp. 1280–1291.

Pettigrew, S. (2007) 'A thematic content analysis of children's food advertising', *International Journal of Advertising*, Vol. 26, No. 3, pp. 357–367.

Petty, R. E. and Cacioppo, J. T. (1996) *The Elaboration Likelihood Model of Persuasion*, Academic Press.

Petty, R. E. and Cacioppo, J. T. (1981) *Attitudes and Persuasion: Classic and Contemporary Approaches*, William C. Brown.

Petty, R. E. et al. (1981) 'Personal involvement as a determinant of argument-based persuasion', *Journal of Personality and Social Psychology*, Vol. 41, pp. 847–55.

Piaget, J. (1963) *The Origins of Intelligence in Children*, Norton.

Piaget, J. and Inhelder, B. (1956) *The Child's Conception of Space*, Routledge and Kegan Paul.

Picchioni, D. et al. (2007) 'A case-control study of the environmental risk factors for narcolepsy', *Neuroepidemiology*, Vol. 29, Nos. 3–4, pp. 185–192.

Pinker, S. (1997) *How the Mind Works*, Norton.

Piran, N. et al. (1985) 'Affective disturbance in eating disorders', *Journal of Nervous and Mental Disease*, Vol. 173, No. 7, pp. 395–400.

Pisarski, A. et al. (2008) 'Organizational influences on the work–life conflict and health of shiftworkers', *Applied Ergonomics*, Vol. 39, No. 5, pp. 580–588.

Pizzagalli, D. et al. (2000) 'Brain electric correlates of strong belief in paranormal phenomena: intracerebral EEG source and regional omega complexity analyses', *Psychiatry Research: Neuroimaging*, Vol. 100, No. 3, pp. 139–154.

Platt, S. et al. (1997) 'Effectiveness of antismoking telephone helpline: follow-up survey', *BMJ*, Vol. 314, pp.1371.

Pliner, P. (1994) 'Development of measures of food neophobia in children', *Appetite*, Vol. 23, No. 2, pp. 147–163.

Plowden Report (1967) *Children and their Primary Schools*, Central Advisory Council for Education, HMSO.

Polman, H. et al. (2008) 'Experimental study of the differential effects of playing versus watching violent video games on children's aggressive behavior', *Aggressive Behavior*, Vol. 34, No. 3, pp. 256–264.

Pomerlau, A. et al. (1990) '"Pink or blue": environmental gender stereotypes in the first two years of life', *Sex Roles*, Vol. 22, pp. 359–367.

Popper, K. (1959) *The Logic of Scientific Discovery*, Hutchinson.

Povinelli, D. (1989) 'Failure to find self-recognition in Asian elephants (*Elephas maximus*) in contrast to their use of mirror cues to discover hidden food', *Journal of Comparative Psychology*, Vol. 103, No. 2, pp. 122–131.

Price, G.R. (1955) 'Science and the supernatural', *Science*, Vol. 122, pp. 359–367.

Profet, M. (1992) 'Pregnancy sickness as adaptation: a deterrent to maternal ingestion of teratogens', in Barkow, et al. (eds) *The Adapted Mind: Evolutionary Psychology and the Generation of Culture*, Oxford University Press.

Quigley, B. M. et al. (2003) 'Characteristics of violent bars and bar patrons', *Journal of Studies on Alcohol*, Vol. 64, No. 6, pp. 765–772.

Quinton, D. and Rutter, M. (1984) 'Parents with children in care II: intergenerational continuities', *Journal of Child Psychology and Psychiatry*, Vol. 25, No. 2, pp. 231–250.

Radin, D. I. and Ferrari, D. C. (1991) 'Effects of consciousness on the fall of dice: a meta-analysis', *Journal of Scientific Exploration*, Vol. 5, pp. 61–84.

Radin, D. I. and Nelson, R. D. (1989) *Replication in Random Event Generator Experiments: A Meta-Analysis and Quality Assessment*, Princeton University Human Information Processing Group.

Raine, A. et al. (1997) 'Brain abnormalities in murderers indicated by positron emission tomography', *Biological Psychiatry*, Vol. 42, No. 6, pp. 495–508.

Raistrick, D. et al. (2006) *Review of the Effectiveness of Alcohol Treatment*, National Treatment Agency.

Ralph, M. et al. (1990) 'Transplanted suprachiasmatic nucleus determines circadian period', *Science*, Vol. 247, pp. 975–978.

Ramachandran, V. S. (2000) 'Mirror neurons and imitation learning as the driving force behind "the great leap forward" in human evolution', *Edge*, No. 69, May 29.

Randall, J. L. (1974) 'An extended series of ESP and PK tests with three English schoolboys', *Journal of the Society for Psychical Research*, Vol. 47, No. 762, pp. 485–494.

Randarajan, S. and Kelly, L. (2006) 'Family communication patterns, family environment, and the impact of parental alcoholism on offspring self-esteem', *Journal of Social and Personal Relationships*, Vol. 23, No. 4, pp. 655–671.

Rechtschaffen, A. and Kales, A. (1968) 'A manual of standardised terminology, techniques, and scoring system for sleep stages of human subjects', *National Institute of Health Publication 204*, US Government printing Office.

Reed, T. M. (1998) 'Peer influence on the maintenance of gender roles', *Dissertation Abstracts International: Section B: The Sciences and Engineering*, Vol. 58, No. 8-B, p. 4494.

Reeves, A. G. and Plum, F. (1969) 'Hyperphagia, rage, and dementia accompanying a ventromedial hypothalamic neoplasm', *Archives of Neurology*, Vol. 20, No. 6, pp. 616–624.

Repacholi, B. M. and Gopnik, A. (1997) 'Early reasoning about desires: evidence from 14- and 18-month-olds', *Developmental Psychology*, Vol. 33, No. 1, pp. 12–21.

Rest, J. R. (1983) 'Morality', in Flavell, J. H. and Markman, E. (eds) *Handbook of Child Psychology*, Vol. 3, Wiley.

Rhee, S. and Waldman, I. D. (2002) 'Genetic and environmental influences on antisocial behavior: a meta-analysis of twin and adoption studies', *Psychological Bulletin*, Vol. 128, No. 3, pp. 490–529.

Rhine, J. B. (1947) *The `Reach of the Mind*, W. Sloane.

Richards, M. (1995) 'The international year of the family: family research', *The Psychologist*, Vol. 8, No. 1, pp. 17–20.

Ring, K. (1980) *Life at Death. A Scientific Investigation of the Near-Death Experience*', Coward McCann and Geoghenan.

Rivadeneyra, R. and Lebo, M. J. (2008) 'The association between television-viewing behaviors and adolescent dating role attitudes and behaviors', *Journal of Adolescence*, Vol. 31, No. 3, pp. 291–305.

Rivers, W. H. R. (1901) 'Vision', in Haddon, A.C. (ed.) *Reports of the Cambridge Anthropological Expedition to the Torres Straits*, Vol. 2, part 1, Cambridge University Press.

Rizzolatti, G. (1995) 'The mirror neuron system and its function in humans', *Anat Embryol*, Vol. 210, No. 5–6, pp. 419–421.

Roberts, G. W. (1991) 'Schizophrenia: a neuropathological perspective', *British Journal of Psychiatry*, Vol. 158, pp. 8–17.

Roberts, K. A. (2007) 'Relationship attachment and the behaviour of fans towards celebrities', *Applied Psychology in Criminal Justice*, Vol. 3, No. 1, pp. 54–74.

Robins, L. N. (1974) 'A follow-up study of Vietnam veterans' drug use', *Journal of Drug Issues*, Vol. 4, No. 1, pp. 61–63.

Roe, C. A. (1999) 'Critical thinking and belief in the paranormal: a re-evaluation', *British Journal of Psychology*, Vol. 90, No. 1, pp. 85–98.

Roe, C. A. (1994) 'Subjects' evaluations of a tarot reading', *Proceedings of the 37th Annual Parapsychological Association Convention*, pp. 323–334.

Rogers, P. et al. (2007) 'The mediating and moderating effects of loneliness and attachment style on belief in the paranormal', *European Journal of Parapsychology*, Vol. 2, No. 2, pp. 138–165.

Rogers, R. W. (1983) 'Cognitive and psychological process in fear appeals and attitude change: a revised theory of protection motivation', in Cacioppo, J. T. and Petty, R. E. (eds) *Social Psychophysiology: A Source Book*, Guilford.

Rose, R. J. and Dick, D. M. (2004–5) 'Gene-environment interplay in adolescent drinking behavior', *Alcohol Research & Health*, Vol. 28, No. 4, pp. 222–229.

Rosen, B. K. (1980) 'Kohlberg and the supposed mutual support of an ethical and psychological theory', *Journal for the Theory of Social Behaviour*, Vol. 10, No. 3, pp. 195–210.

Rosenhan, D. L. (1973) 'On being sane in insane places', *Science*, Vol. 179, pp. 365–369.

Rosenthal, R. and Lesieur, H. (1992) 'Self-reported withdrawal symptoms and pathological gambling', *American Journal of the Addictions*, Vol. 1, pp. 150–154.

Rubin, J. Z. et al. (1974) 'The eye of the beholder: parents' views on sex of newborns', *American Journal of Orthopsychiatry*, Vol. 44, pp. 512–519.

Ruble, D. N. (1988) 'Sex-role development', in Bornstein, M.H. and Lamb, M.E. (eds) *Developmental Psychology: An Advanced Textbook* (2nd edn), Lawrence Erlbaum Associates.

Ruble, D. N. and Martin, C. L. (1998) 'Gender development', in Damon, W. and Eisenberg, N. (eds) *Handbook of Child Psychology, Vol. 3: Social, Emotional, and Personality Development*, pp. 933–1016, John Wiley & Sons.

Ruble, D. N. et al. (2007) 'The role of gender constancy in early gender development', *Child Development*, Vol. 78, No. 4, pp. 1121–1136.

Rudski, J. (2004) 'The illusion of control, superstitious belief, and optimism', *Current Psychology*, Vol. 22, No. 4, pp. 306–315.

Rusak, B. and Groos, G. (1982) 'Suprachiasmatic stimulation phase shifts rodent circadian rhythms', *Science*, Vol. 215, No. 4538, pp. 1407–1409.

Rusbult, C. E. and Zembrodt, I. M. (1983) 'Responses to dissatisfaction in romantic involvements: a multidimensional scaling analysis', *Journal of Experimental Social Psychology*, Vol. 19, No. 3, pp. 274–293.

Rusbult, C. E. (1987) 'Responses to dissatisfaction in close relationships: the exit-voice-loyalty-neglect model', in Perlam, D. and Duck, S. (eds) *Intimate relationships: Development, Dynamics, Deterioration*, pp. 209–238, Sage.

Rusbult, C. E. et al. (1986) 'The impact of gender and sex-role orientation on responses to dissatisfaction in close relationships', *Sex Roles*, Vol. 15, No. 1–2, pp. 1–20.

Rusbult, C. E. and Zembrodt, I. M. (1983) 'Responses to dissatisfaction in romantic involvements: a multidimensional scaling analysis', *Journal of Experimental Social Psychology*, Vol. 19, No. 3, pp. 274–293.

Rush, B. R. et al. (2008) 'Influence of co-occurring mental and substance use disorders on the prevalence of problem gambling in Canada', *Addiction*, Vol. 103, No. 11, pp. 1847–1856.

Russek, M. (1971) 'Hepatic receptors and the neurophysiological mechanisms in controlling feeding behaviour', in Ehrenpreis, S. (ed.) *Neurosciences Research*, Vol. 4, Academic Press.

Russell, M. J. et al. (1980) 'Olfactory influences on the human menstrual cycle', *Pharmacology, Biochemistry and Behaviour*, Vol. 13, pp. 737–538.

Rutherford, J. et al. (1993) 'Genetic influences on eating attitudes in a normal female twin population', *Psychological Medicine*, Vol. 23, pp. 425–436.

Ryback, B. S. and Lewis, O. F. (1971) 'Effects of prolonged bed rest on EEG sleep patterns in young, healthy volunteers', *Electroencephalography and Clinical Neurophysiology*, Vol. 31, pp. 395–399.

Sameroff, A. J. and Seifer, R. (1983) 'Familial risk and child competence', *Child Development*, Vol. 54, No. 5, pp. 1254–1268.

Sanders, G. et al. (2005) 'The ratio of the 2nd to 4th finger length predicts spatial ability in men but not women', *Cortex*, Vol. 41, No. 6, pp. 789–795.

Sarafino, E. P. (1990) *Health Psychology: Biopsychosocial Interactions*, John Wiley & Sons.

Scarr-Salapatek, S. (1971) 'Race, social class, and IQ', *Science*, Vol.174, No. 4016, pp. 1285–1295.

Schachter, S. (1971) 'Some extraordinary facts about obese humans and rats', *American Psychologist*, Vol. 26, pp. 129–144.

Scharrer, E. et al. (2006) 'Working hard or hardly working? Gender, humor, and the performance of domestic chores in television commercials', *Mass Communication and Society*, Vol. 9, No. 2, pp. 215–238.

Schneider, K. (1959) *Clinical Psychopathology*, Grune and Shelton.

Schumaker, J. F. (1990) *Wings of Illusion: The Origin, Nature and Future of Paranormal Belief*, Prometheus Books.

Schumaker, J. F. (2001) *The Age of Insanity: Modernity and Mental Health*, Praeger.

Schwartz, B. and Barsky, S. F. (1977) 'The home advantage', *Social Forces*, Vol. 55, No. 3, pp. 641–661.

Segall, M. H. et al. (1963) 'Cultural differences in the perception of geometrical illusions', *Science*, Vol. 139, pp. 769–771.

Seid, R. P. (1994) 'Too "close to the bone."', in Fallon, P. et al. (eds) *Feminists' Perspectives on Eating Disorders*, Guilford Press.

Seidman, L. J. (1983) 'Schizophrenia and brain dysfunction: an integration of recent neurodiagnostic findings', *Psychological Bulletin*, Vol. 94, No. 2, pp. 195–238.

Selfe, L. (1977) *Nadia: A Case of Extraordinary Drawing Ability in an Autistic Child*, Academic Press.

Seligman, M. (1970) 'On the generality of the laws of learning', *Psychological Review*, Vol. 77, pp. 406–418.

Selman, R. L. (1980) *The Growth of Interpersonal Understandings*, Academic Press.

Selman, R. L. (1971) 'The relation of role taking to the development of moral judgment in children', *Child Development*, Vol. 42, No. 1, pp. 79–91.

Sen, M. G. H. et al. (2001) 'Development of infants' sensitivity to surface contour information for spatial layout', *Perception*, Vol. 30, pp. 167–176.

Seneviratne, H. and Saunders, B. (2000) 'An investigation of alcohol dependent respondents' attributions for their own and "others'" relapses', *Addiction Research*, Vol. 8, No. 5, pp. 439–453.

Serpell, R. S. (1976) *Culture's Influence on Behaviour*, Methuen.

Seyfarth, R. M. and Cheney, D.L. (1980) 'The ontogeny of vervet monkey alarm calling behaviour: a preliminary report', *Zeitschrift für Tierpsychologie*, Vol. 54, pp. 37–56.

Seyfarth, R. M. and Cheney, D. L. (1986) 'Vocal development in vervet monkeys', *Animal Behaviour*, Vol. 34, No. 6, pp. 1640–1658.

Sham, P. C. et al. (1993) 'Risk of schizophrenia and age difference with older siblings: evidence for a maternal viral infection hypothesis?', *British Journal of Psychiatry*, Vol. 163, pp. 627–633.

Shannon, B. et al. (1990) 'Self-efficacy: a contributor to the explanation of eating behavior', *Health Education Research*, Vol. 5, No. 4, pp. 395–407.

Shapiro, C. M. (1981) 'Slow-wave sleep: a recovery period after exercise', *Science*, Vol. 214, No. 4526, pp. 1253–1254.

Shapiro, J. S. (1999) 'Loneliness: paradox or artifact?', *American Psychologist*, Vol. 54, No. 9, pp. 782–783.

Sharif, Z. A. et al. (2000) 'Comparative efficacy of risperidone and clozapine in the treatment of patients with refractory schizophrenia or schizoaffective disorder: a retrospective analysis', *J Clin Psychiatry*, Vol. 61, No. 7, pp. 498–504.

Sherif, M. (1966) *The Psychology of Social Norms*, Harper Torchbooks.

Shields, J. (1962) *Monozygotic Twins Brought up Apart and Brought up Together*, Oxford University Press.

Shields, S. (1975) 'Functionalism, Darwinism, and the psychology of women', *American Psychologist*, Vol. 30, No. 7, pp. 739–754.

Shiffman, S. et al. (1996) 'First lapses to smoking: within-subjects analysis of real-time reports', *Journal of Consulting and Clinical Psychology*, Vol. 64, No. 2, pp. 366–379.

Shih, J. et al. (2000) '*Ginkgo biloba* abolishes aggression in mice lacking MAOA', *Antioxidants and Redox Signaling*, Vol. 2, No. 3, p. 467

Shillito, D. J. et al. (1999) 'Factors affecting mirror behaviour in western lowland gorillas, *Gorilla gorilla*', *Animal Behaviour*, Vol. 57, No. 5, pp. 999–1004.

Short, R. L. (1991) *The Differences Between the Sexes*, Cambridge University Press.

Shuey, A. M. (1966) *The Testing of Negro Intelligence* (2nd edn), Social Science Press.

Siegel, M. and Biener, L. (2000) 'The impact of an anti-smoking media campaign on progression to established smoking: results of a longitudinal youth study', *American Journal of Public Health*, Vol. 90, No. 3, pp. 380–386.

Siegel, S. et al. (1987) 'Anticipation of pharmacological and nonpharmacological events: classical conditioning and addictive behavior', *Journal of Drug Issues*, Vol. 17, No. 1–2, pp. 83–110.

Siegler, R. S. (1991) *Children's Thinking*, Prentice Hall.

Siffre, M. (1972), cited in Aschoff, J. (1979) 'Circadian rhythms: general features and endocrinological aspects', in Krieger, D. (ed.) *Endocrine Rhythms*, Raven.

Silverman, I. and Eals, M. (1992) 'Sex differences in spatial abilities: evolutionary theory and data', in Barkow, J. H. et al. (eds) *The Adapted Mind: Evolutionary Psychology and the Generation of Culture*, Oxford University Press.

Silverman, I. and Phillips, K. (1998) 'The evolutionary psychology of spatial sex differences', in Crawford, C. B. and Krebs, D. L. *Handbook of Evolutionary Psychology: Ideas, Issues, and Applications*, Lawrence Erlbaum Associates.

Simmons, R. G. et al. (1979) 'Entry into early adolescence: the impact of school structure, puberty, and early dating on self-esteem', *American Sociological Review*, Vol. 44, No. 6, pp. 948–967.

Singh, D. (1993) 'Adaptive significance of female attractiveness', *Journal of Personality and Social Psychology*, Vol. 65, pp. 295–307.

Skender, M. L. et al. (1996) 'Comparison of 2-year weight loss trends in behavioral treatments of obesity: diet, exercise, and combination interventions', *Journal of the American Dietetic Association*, Vol. 96, pp. 342–346.

Skodak, M. and Skeels, H. M. (1949) 'A final follow-up study of one hundred adopted children', *Journal of Genetic Psychology*, Vol. 75, pp. 85–125.

Skoe, E. et al. (2002) 'The influences of sex and gender-role identity on moral cognition and prosocial personality traits', *Sex Roles*, Vol. 46, No. 9–10, pp. 295–309.

Skumanich, S. A. and Kintsfather, D. P. (1996) 'Promoting the organ donor card: a causal model of persuasion effects', *Social Science & Medicine*, Vol. 43, No. 3, pp. 401–408.

Slaby, R. G. and Frey, K. S. (1975) 'Development of gender constancy and selective attention to same-sex models', *Child Development*, Vol. 46, No. 4, pp. 849–856.

Slater, A. et al. (1990) 'Size constancy at birth: newborn infants' responses to retinal and real size', *Journal of Experimental Child Psychology*, Vol. 49, pp. 314–322.

Slijper, F. (2007) 'Androgens and gender role behaviour in girls with congenital adrenal hyperplasia', in Einstein, G. (ed.) *Sex and the Brain*, MIT Press.

Sloan, R. P. and Ramakrishnan, R. (2006) 'Science, medicine, and intercessory prayer', *Perspectives in Biology and Medicine*, Vol. 49, No. 4, pp. 504–514.

Smallwood, K. (2008) 'Behavioral, attitudinal, and decision-altering effects of aggressive video games on young adults', *Dissertation Abstracts International: Section B: The Sciences and Engineering*, Vol. 69, No. 1-B, pp. 661.

Smith, C. (1948) *Mental Testing of Hebridean Children in Gaelic and English*, University of London Press.

Smith, C. and Lloyd, B. B. (1978) 'Maternal behaviour and perceived sex of infant', *Child Development*, Vol. 49, pp. 1263–1265.

Smith, J. et al. (1992) 'Informing people with schizophrenia about their illness: the effect of residual symptoms', *Journal of Mental Health*, Vol. 1, No. 1, pp. 61–70.

Smith, J. and Birchwood, M. (1987) 'Specific and non-specific effects of educational intervention with families living with a schizophrenic relative', *British Journal of Psychiatry*, Vol. 150, pp. 645–652.

Smith, M. D. (1978) 'Precipitants of crowd violence', *Sociological Inquiry*, Vol. 48, pp. 121–131.

Smith, P. K. (1982) 'Does play matter? Functional and evolutionary aspects of animal and human play', *Behavioral and Brain Sciences*, Vol. 5, No. 1, pp. 139–184.

Smith, Y. et al. (2005) 'Sex reassignment: outcomes and predictors of treatment for adolescent and adult transsexuals', *Psychological Medicine*, Vol. 35, No. 1, pp. 89–99.

Smyer, M. A. et al. (1982) 'A prevention approach to critical life events of the elderly', *Journal of Primary Prevention*, Vol. 2, No. 4, pp.195–204.

Snarey, J. R. (1985) 'Cross-cultural universality of social-moral development: a critical review of Kohlbergian research', *Psychological Bulletin*, Vol. 97, No. 2, pp. 202–232.

Snygg, D. (1938) 'The relation between the intelligence of mothers and of their children living in foster homes', *Journal of Genetic Psychology*, Vol. 52, pp. 401–406.

Soal, S. G. (1956) 'Some statistical aspects of ESP', in Wolstenholme, G.E.W. and Millar, E.C.P. (eds) *Extrasensory Perception: A Ciba Foundation Symposium*, Little, Brown.

Soal, S. G. and Goldney, K. M. (1960) 'The Shackleton report', *Journal of the Society for Psychical Research*, Vol. 40, pp. 378.

Soldatos, C. R. and Kales, A. (1982) 'Sleep disorders: research in psychopathology and its practical implications', *Acta Psychiatrica Scandinavica*, Vol. 65, No. 6, pp. 381–387.

Spence, J. T. and Helmreich, R.L. (1979) 'On assessing androgyny', *Sex Roles*, Vol. 5, No. 6, pp. 721–738.

Sprafkin, J. et al. (1975) 'Effects of a prosocial televised example on children's helping', *Journal of Experimental Child Psychology*, Vol. 20, No. 1, pp. 119–126.

Standing, L. (1973) 'Learning 10,000 pictures', *Quarterly Journal of Experimental Psychology*, Vol. 25, pp. 207–222.

Startup, M. et al. (2004) 'North Wales randomized controlled trial of cognitive behaviour therapy for acute schizophrenia spectrum disorders: outcomes at 6 and 12 months', *Psychological Medicine*, Vol. 34, No. 3, pp. 413–422.

Startup, M. et al. (2005) 'North Wales randomised controlled trial of cognitive behaviour therapy for acute schizophrenia spectrum disorders: two-year follow-up and economic evaluation', *Psychological Medicine*, Vol. 35, pp. 1307–1316.

Steiner, J. E. (1987) 'What the neonate can tell us about umami', in Kayamura, Y. and Kare, M. R. (eds) *Umami: A Basic Taste*, Marcel Dekker.

Stellefson, M. L. et al. (2006) 'Effects of cognitive dissonance on intentions to change diet and physical activity among college students', *American Journal of Health Studies*, Vol. 21, No. 4, pp. 219–227.

Sternberg, R. J. (1986) 'A triangular theory of love', *Psychological Review*, Vol. 93, pp. 119–135.

Stevenson, J. and Goodman, R. (2001) 'Association between behaviour at age 3 years and adult criminality', *British Journal of Psychiatry*, Vol. 179, No. 3, pp. 197–202.

Stokes, M. et al. (2007) 'Stalking, and social and romantic functioning among adolescents and adults with Autism Spectrum Disorder', *Journal of Autism and Developmental Disorders*, Vol. 37, No. 10, pp. 1969–1986.

Stoneman, Z. and Brody, G. H. (1981) 'Peers as mediators of television food advertisements aimed at children', *Developmental Psychology*, Vol. 17, No. 6, pp. 853–858.

Stradling, J. R. and Crosby, J. H. (1991) 'Predictors and prevalence of obstructive sleep apnoea and snoring in 1001 middle aged men', *Thorax*, Vol. 46, pp. 85–90.

Strassberg, D. S. and Holty, S. (2003) 'An experimental study of women's internet personal ads', *Archives of Sexual Behavior*, Vol. 32, No. 3, pp. 253–260.

Strong, D. A. (2008) 'Audience involvement with "Kushiko Sansar" — a children's TV show in Nepal: an entertainment-education initiative promoting positive attitudes and actions toward people with disabilities', *Dissertation Abstracts International Section A: Humanities and Social Sciences*, Vol. 69, No. 3-A, pp. 801.

Strough, J. et al. (2007) 'From adolescence to later adulthood: femininity, masculinity, and androgyny in six age groups', *Sex Roles*, Vol. 57, No. 5–6, pp. 385–396.

Sullivan, H. S. (1953) *The Interpersonal Theory of Psychiatry*, Norton.

Swaab, D. F. et al. (1995) 'Brain research, gender and sexual orientation', *Journal of Homosexuality*, Vol. 28, No. 3–4, pp. 283–301.

Swaim, R. C. et al. (2007) 'Gender differences in a comparison of two tested etiological models of cigarette smoking among elementary school students', *Journal of Applied Social Psychology*, Vol. 37, No. 8, pp. 1681–1696.

Swanson, D. W. and Dinello, F. A. (1970) 'Follow-up of patients starved for obesity', *Psychosomatic Medicine*, Vol. 32, No. 2, pp. 209–214.

Symington, A. (2008) 'Results of the first North American prescription heroin study are promising', *Policy Law Review*, Vol. 13, Nos. 2–3, pp. 11–12.

Symons, D. (1979) *The Evolution of Human Sexuality*, Oxford University Press.

Tager, D. and Good, G. E. (2005) 'Italian and American masculinities: a comparison of masculine gender role norms', *Psychology of Men & Masculinity*, Vol. 6, No. 4, pp. 264–274.

Tajfel, H. (ed.) (1978) *Differentiation Between Social Groups: Studies in the Social Psychology of Intergroup Relations*, Academic Press.

Tajfel, H. (1970) 'Experiments in intergroup discrimination', *Scientific American*, Vol. 223, pp. 96–102.

Tapper, K. et al. (2003) 'The Food Dudes to the rescue!', *The Psychologist*, Vol. 16, No. 1, pp. 18–21.

Targ, R. and Puthoff, H. (1974) 'Information transmission under conditions of sensory shielding', *Nature*, Vol. 251, No. 5476, pp. 602–607.

Tart, C. T. (2002) 'Parapsychology and transpersonal psychology: "anomalies" to be explained away or spirit to manifest?', *Journal of Parapsychology*, Vol. 66, pp. 31–47.

Tashakkori, A. and Thompson, V. (1991) 'Social change and change in intentions of Iranian youth regarding education, marriage and careers', *International Journal of Psychology*, Vol. 26, pp. 203–217.

Taylor, H. F. (1980) *The IQ Game: A Methodological Inquiry into the Heredity-Environment Controversy*, Harvester.

Taylor, S. E. and Thompson, S. C. (1982) 'Stalking the elusive "vividness" effect', *Psychological Review*, Vol. 89, pp. 155–181.

Teaford, M. F. and Ungar, P. S. (2000) 'Diet and the evolution of the earliest human ancestors', *Proc Natl Acad Sci USA*, Vol. 97, No. 25, pp. 13506–11.

Tedeschi, J. T. et al. (1971) 'Cognitive dissonance: private ratiocination or public spectacle?', *American Psychologist*, Vol. 26, No. 8, pp. 685–695.

Teitelbaum, P. and Stellar, E. (1954) 'Recovery from the failure to eat produced by hypothalamic lesions', *Science*, Vol. 120, pp. 894–895.

Temerline, M. K. (1970) 'Diagnostic bias in community mental health', *Community Mental Health Journal*, Vol. 6, pp. 110–117.

Terman, L. M. (1921) 'Mental growth and the IQ', *Journal of Educational Psychology*, Vol. 12, No. 7, pp. 401–407.

Thalbourne, M. A. and Haraldsson, E. (1980) 'Personality characteristics of sheep and goats', *Personality and Individual Differences*, Vol. 1, No. 2, pp. 180–185.

Thannickal, T. C. et al. (2000) 'Reduced number of hypocretin neurons in human narcolepsy', *Neuron*, Vol. 27, No. 3, pp. 469–74.

Thibaut, J. W. and Kelley, H. H. (1959) *The Social Psychology of Groups*, Wiley.

Tienari, P. et al. (2006) 'Finnish adoption study of schizophrenia: implications for family interventions', *Families, Systems & Health*, Vol. 24, No. 4, pp. 442–451.

Tiggemann, M. and Rüütel, E. (2004) 'Gender role concerns in Estonian and Australian young adults', *Journal of Social Psychology*, Vol. 144, No. 1, pp. 93–95.

Tobacyk, J. and Milford, G. (1983) 'Belief in paranormal phenomena: assessment instrument development and implications for personality functioning', *Journal of Personality and Social Psychology*, Vol. 44, pp. 1029–1037.

Tobacyk, J. J. and Mitchell, T. T. (1987) 'The out-of-body experience and personality adjustment', *Journal of Nervous and Mental Diseases*, Vol. 175, No. 6, pp. 367–370.

Tobacyk, J. J. and Pirttila-Backman, A. M. (1992) 'Paranormal beliefs and their implications in university students from Finland and the United States', *Journal of Cross-Cultural Psychology*, Vol. 23, No. 1, pp. 59–71.

Tobacyk, J. J. and Shrader, D. (1991) 'Superstition and self-efficacy', *Psychological Reports*, Vol. 68, No. 3, pp. 1387–1388.

Tolman, E. C. and Honzik, C. H. (1930) 'Introduction and removal of reward and maze learning in rats', *University of California Publications in Psychology*, Vol. 4, pp. 257–275.

Tomasello, M. and Call, J. (1997) *Primate Cognition*, Oxford University Press.

Tooby, J. and Cosmides, L. (1992) 'The psychological foundations of culture, part 1: theoretical considerations', *Ethology and Sociobiology*, Vol. 10, pp. 29–49.

Touitou, Y. and Bogdan, A. (2007) 'Promoting adjustment of the sleep-wake cycle by chronobiotics', *Physiology & Behavior*, Vol. 90, No. 2–3, pp. 294–300.

Tripathi, S. K. (2004) 'Anxiety as a function of experimental crowding', *Social Science International*, Vol. 20, No. 1, pp. 1–11.

Trivers, R. L. (1972) 'Parental investment and sexual selection', in Campbell, B. (ed.) *Sexual Selection and the Descent of Man*, Aldine.

Trivers, R. L. (1974) 'Parent-offspring conflict', *American Zoologist*, Vol. 14, No. 1, pp. 249–264

Trivers, R. L. and Willard, D. E. (1973) 'Natural selection of parental ability to vary the sex ratio of offspring', *Science*, Vol. 179, pp. 90–92.

Trucco, E. M. et al. (2007) 'The relationship of self-esteem and self-efficacy to treatment outcomes of alcohol-dependent men and women', *The American Journal on Addictions*, Vol. 16, No. 2, pp. 85–92.

Turner, N. E. et al. (2006) 'The experience of gambling and its role in problem gambling', *International Gambling Studies*, Vol. 6, No. 2, pp. 237–266.

Turner, R. H. and Killian, L. M. (1973) *Collective Behaviour* (2nd edn), Prentice Hall.

Tyler, L. E. (1965) *The Psychology of Human Differences*, Appleton-Century-Crofts.

Umiltà, M. A. et al. (2006) 'When pliers become fingers in the monkey motor system', *Journal of Neurophysiology*, Vol. 95, pp. 709–729.

US Bureau of the Census (1994) *Statistical Abstract of the United States* (114th edn), US Government Printing Office.

Valente, T. et al. (2007) 'Evaluating a minor storyline on ER about teen obesity, hypertension, and 5 a Day', *Journal of Health Communication*, Vol. 12, No. 6, pp. 551–566.

Valentine, E. R. (1982) *Conceptual Issues in Psychology*, Routledge.

van den Bulck, J. et al. (2006) 'Television and music video exposure and adolescent "alcopop" use', *International Journal of Adolescent Medicine and Health*, Vol. 18, No. 1, pp. 107–114.

van den Oord, E. J. et al. (1994) 'A study of problem behavior in 10- to 15-year-old biologically related and unrelated international adoptees', *Behavior Genetics*, Vol. 24, No. 3, pp. 193–205.

van der Vijver, F. (2007) 'Cultural and gender differences in gender-role beliefs, sharing household task and child-care responsibilities, and well-being among immigrants and majority members in the Netherlands', *Sex Roles*, Vol. 57, No. 11–12, pp. 813–824.

van Kammen, D. P. et al. (1977) 'Amphetamine-induced catecholamine activation in schizophrenia and depression: behavioral and physiological effects', *Adv Biochem Psychopharmacol*, Vol. 16, pp. 655–659.

van Lommel, P. et al. (2001) 'Near-death experience in survivors of cardiac arrest: a prospective study in the Netherlands', *Lancet*. Vol. 358, No. 9298, pp. 2039–2045.

Varca, P. E. (1980) 'An analysis of home and away game performance of a male college basketball team', *Journal of Sport Psychology*, Vol. 2, No. 3, pp. 245–257.

Vaughn, C. and Leff, J. (1976) 'The measurement of expressed emotion in the families of psychiatric patients', *British Journal of Social & Clinical Psychology*, Vol. 15, No. 2, pp. 157–165.

Vernon, P. A. et al. (1999) 'Individual differences in multiple dimensions of aggression: a univariate and multivariate genetic analysis', *Twin Research*, Vol. 2, pp.116–21.

Vernon, P. A. and Mori, M. (1992) 'Intelligence, reaction times, and peripheral nerve conduction velocity', *Intelligence*, Vol. 16, No. 3–4, pp. 273–288.

Vernon, P. E. (1950) *TheStructure of Human Abilities,* Wiley.

Veselska, Z. et al. (2009) 'Self-esteem and resilience: the connection with risky behavior among adolescents', *Addictive Behaviors*, Vol. 34, No. 3, pp. 287–291.

Virkkunen, M. E. et al. 1987) 'Plasma phospholipid essential fatty acids and prostaglandins in alcoholic, habitually violent, and impulsive offenders', *Biological Psychiatry*, Vol. 22, No. 9, pp. 1087–1096.

Visser, B. A. et al. (2006) 'Beyond g: putting multiple intelligences theory to the test', *Intelligence*, Vol. 34, No. 5, pp. 487–502.

Vondra, J. I. et al. (1995) 'Predicting infant attachment classification from multiple contemporaneous measures of maternal care', *Infant Behaviour and Development*, Vol. 18, pp. 215–225.

Wachtel, S. et al. (1986) 'On the expression of H-Y antigen in transsexuals', *Arch Sex Behav*, Vol. 15, No. 1, pp. 51–68.

Wade, C. and Tavris, C. (1993) *Psychology* (3rd edn), HarperCollins.

Wagner, M. W. and Monnet, M. (1979) 'Attitudes of college professors toward extrasensory perception', *Zetetic Scholar*, Vol. 5, pp. 7–17.

Walker, A. M. et al. (1997) 'Mortality in current and former users of clozapine', *Epidemiology*, Vol. 8, No. 6, pp. 671–677.

Wall, A. M. et al. (1998) 'Alcohol outcome expectancies, attitudes toward drinking and the theory of planned behavior', *Journal of Studies on Alcohol*, Vol. 59, No. 4, pp. 409–419.

Walster, E. et al. (1966) 'On increasing the persuasiveness of a low prestige communicator', *Journal of Experimental Social Psychology*, Vol. 2, No. 4, pp. 325–342.

Walster, E. et al. (1978) *Equity Theory and Research*, Allyn and Bacon.

Wang, W. et al. (2001) 'Mismatch negativity and personality traits in chronic primary insomniacs', *Funct Neurol*, Vol. 16, No. 1, pp. 3–10.

Wann, D. L. and Branscombe, N. R. (1990) 'Person perception when aggressive or nonaggressive sports are primed', *Aggressive Behaviour*, Vol. 16, pages 27–32.

Warburton, F. W. (1951) 'The ability of the Gurkha recruit', *British Journal of Psychology*, Vol. 42, pp. 123–133.

Warrington, E. K. and James, M. (1967) 'An experimental investigation of facial recognition in patients with unilateral cerebral lesions', *Cortex*, Vol. 3, 317–326.

Watson, J. B. (1913) 'Psychology as a behaviourist views it', *Psychological Review*, Vol. 20, pp. 158–177.

Webb, W. B. (1982) *Biological Rhythms, Sleep and Performance,* John Wiley and Sons.

Weber, R. et al. (2006) 'Does playing violent video games induce aggression? Empirical evidence of a functional magnetic resonance imaging study', *Media Psychology*, Vol. 8, No. 1, pp. 39–60.

Weisner, T. S. and Wilson-Mitchell, J. E. (1990) 'Nonconventional family life-styles and sex typing in six-year-olds', *Child Development*, Vol. 61, No. 6, pp. 1915–1933.

Wellman, H. M. and Bartsch, K. (1994) 'Before belief: children's early psychological theory', in Lewis, C. and Mirtchell, P. (eds) *Children's Early Understanding of Mind: Origins and Development*, Lawrence Erlbaum Associates.

Werner, N. E. (2001) 'Friends' influence on changes in externalizing behavior during middle childhood: a longitudinal study of relational and physical aggression', *Dissertation Abstracts International: Section B: The Sciences and Engineering*, Vol. 61, No. 10-B, p. 5603.

Westcombe, A. and Wardle, J. (1997) 'Influence of relative fat content information on responses to three foods', *Appetite*, Vol. 28, No. 1, pp. 49–62.

Whitaker, L. C. (2000) *Understanding and Preventing Violence: The Psychology of Human Destructiveness*, CRC Press.

Whiten, A. and Byrne, R. W. (1988) 'The manipulation of attention in primate tactical deception', in Byrne, R. W. and Whiten, A. (eds) *Machiavellian Intelligence: Social Expertise and the Evolution of Intellect in Monkeys, Apes, and Humans*, Clarendon Press/Oxford University Press.

Whiteside, U. et al. (2007) 'Difficulties regulating emotions: do binge eaters have fewer strategies to modulate and tolerate negative affect?', *Eating Behaviors*, Vol. 8, No. 2, pp. 162–169.

Wiederman, M. W. and Allgeier, E. R. (1992) 'Gender differences in mate selection criteria: sociobiological or socioeconomic explanation?', *Ethology & Sociobiology*, Vol. 13, No. 2, pp. 115–124.

Wiegman, O. and van Schie, E. (1998) 'Video game playing and its relations with aggressive and prosocial behaviour', *British Journal of Social Psychology*, Vol. 37, No. 3, pp. 367–378.

Wierzbicki, M. (1985) 'Reasoning errors and belief in the paranormal', *Journal of Social Psychology*, Vol. 125, No. 4, pp. 489–494.

Wikler, A. (1948) 'Recent progress in research on the neurophysiologic basis of morphine addiction', *American Journal of Psychiatry*, Vol. 105, pp. 329–338.

Williams, E. et al. (2007) 'Personality and paranormal belief: a study among adolescents', *Pastoral Psychology*, Vol. 56, No. 1, pp. 9–14.

Williams, R. L. (1972) 'The BITCH-100: a culture-specific test', *American Psychological Association Annual Convention*.

Williams, T. M. (1985) 'Implications of a natural experiment in the developed world for research on television in the developing world', *Journal of Cross-Cultural Psychology*, Vol. 16, No. 3, pp. 263–287.

Williamson, A. M. and Sanderson, J. W. (1986) 'Changing the speed of shift rotation: a field study', *Ergonomics*, Vol. 29, No. 9, pp. 1085–1096.

Wilson, K. and French, C. (2008/9) 'Misinformation effects for psychic readings and belief in the paranormal', *Imagination, Cognition and Personality*, Vol. 28, No. 2, pp. 155–171.

Wimmer, H. and Perner, J. (1983) 'Beliefs about beliefs: Representation and constraining function of wrong beliefs in young children's understanding of deception', *Cognition*, Vol. 13, No. 1, pp. 103–128.

Wing, J. K. et al. (1974) *Measurement and Classification of Psychiatric Symptoms: An Instruction Manual for the PSE and Catego Program*, Cambridge University Press.

Wing, R. R. et al. (2008) 'Maintaining large weight losses: the role of behavioral and psychological factors', *Journal of Consulting and Clinical Psychology*, Vol. 76, No. 6, pp. 1015–1021.

Wiseman, R. and Watt, C. (2002) 'Experimenter differences in cognitive correlates of paranormal belief and in psi', *Journal of Parapsychology*, Vol. 66, No. 4, pp. 371–385.

Wiseman, R. et al. (2003) 'An investigation into alleged "hauntings"', *British Journal of Psychology*, Vol. 94, pp. 195–211.

Wobber, V. et al. (2008) 'Great apes prefer cooked food', *J Hum Evol*, Vol. 55, pp. 340–348.

Wolburg, J. M. (2004) 'The need for new anti-smoking advertising strategies that do not provoke smoker defiance', *Journal of Consumer Marketing*, Vol. 21, No. 3, pp. 173–174.

Wong, D. F. et al. (1986) 'Positron emission tomography reveals elevated D2 dopamine receptors in drug-naive schizophrenics', *Science*, Vol. 234, No. 4783, pp. 1558–1563.

Woo, M. and Oei, T. (2006) 'The MMPI-2 gender-masculine and gender-feminine scales: gender roles as predictors of psychological health in clinical patients', *International Journal of Psychology*, Vol. 41, No. 5, pp. 413–422.

Wood, D. J. (1981) 'Problem-solving and creativity', in Howarth, C. I. and Gilham, W. E. C. *The Structure of Psychology: An Introductory Text*, George Allen & Unwin.

Wood, D. and Middleton, D. (1975) 'A study of assisted problem-solving', *British Journal of Psychology*, Vol. 66, No. 2, pp. 181–191.

Wood, D. et al. (1978) 'An experimental evaluation of our face-to-face teaching strategies', *International Journal of Behavioural Development*, Vol. 1, pp. 131–147.

Wright, A. J. et al. (2007) 'Is attributing smoking to genetic causes associated with a reduced probability of quit attempt success? A cohort study', *Addiction*, Vol. 102, No. 10, pp. 1657–1664.

Wright, S. H. (1999) 'Paranormal contact with the dying: 14 contemporary death coincidences', *Journal of the Society for Psychical Research*, Vol. 63, No. 857, pp. 258–267.

Yeates, K. O. and Selman, R. L. (1989) 'Social competence in the schools: toward an integrative develop-mental model for intervention', *Developmental Review*, Vol. 9, No. 1, pp. 64–100.

Yeates, K. O. et al. (1979) 'Maternal IQ and home environment as determinants of early childhood intellectual competence: a developmental analysis', *Developmental Psychology*, Vol. 15, pp. 731–739.

Young, A. W. et al. (1986) 'The faces that launched a thousand slips: everyday difficulties and errors in recognising people', *British Journal of Psychology*, Vol. 76, pp. 495–523.

Young, J. Z. (1981) *The Life of Vertebrates*, Oxford University Press.

Youngson, R. M. and Schott, I. (1996) *Medical Blunders*, NYU Press

Yovetich, N. A. and Rusbult, C. E. (1994) 'Accommodative behaviour in close relationships: exploring transformation of motivation', *Journal of Experimental Social Psychology*, Vol. 30, No. 2, pp. 138–164.

Zanna, M. P. and Cooper, J. (1974) 'Dissonance and the pill: an attribution approach to studying the arousal properties of dissonance', *Journal of Personality and Social Psychology*, Vol. 29, No. 5, pp. 703–709.

Zeigler, H. P. and Karten, H. J. (1974) 'Central trigeminal structures and the lateral hypothalamic syndrome in the rat', *Science*, Vol. 186, No. 4164, pp. 636–637.

Zigler, E. et al. (1973) 'Motivational factors in the performance of economically disadvantaged children on the Peabody Picture Vocabulary Test, *Child Development*, Vol. 44, No. 2, pp. 294–303.

Zillmann, D. (1999) 'Exemplification theory: judging the whole by some of its parts', *Media Psychology*, Vol. 1, pp. 69–94.

Zillmann, D. and Bryant, J. (1974) 'Effect of residual excitation on the emotional response to provocation and delayed aggressive behavior', *Journal of Personality and Social Psychology*, Vol. 30, pp. 782–791.

Zimbardo, P. G. (1969) 'The human choice: individuation, reason and versus deindividuation, impulse and chaos', in Arnold, W. J. and Levine, D. (eds) *Nebraska Symposium on Motivation*, University of Nebraska Press.

Zimmermann, P. et al. (2000) 'Longitudinal attachment development from infancy through adolescence', *Psychologie in Erziehung und Unterricht*, Vol. 47, pp. 99–117.

Zwarun, L. et al. (2006) 'Effects of showing risk in beer commercials to young drinkers', *Journal of Broadcasting & Electronic Media*, Vol. 50, No. 1, pp. 52–77.

Sample questions

Unit 3

In Unit 3, there are eight topics; on the exam paper there is one question on each topic. You are asked to answer three questions, so you will need to have studied at least three topics. The exam lasts 1 hour 30 minutes, so you have around 30 minutes to write each answer, including thinking time.

Each question is worth 25 marks. The questions may take the form of essays, or they may be in two or more parts; in this case, the marks awarded for each part are shown on the paper, and you should answer both or all the parts. The length of what you write for each part should reflect the number of marks available, so you should not spend so long on one part of a question that you do not have enough time to write answers for the other part(s).

In some cases, you may be asked to outline and/or evaluate **one or more** theories. You have the choice of looking at one theory in more detail, or two or more theories in less detail; both options are equally acceptable, but you should bear in mind the time available when making your decision.

In all the questions, the examiner will be looking for evidence of both AO1 (relevant information) and AO2 (evaluation and commentary). Words such as 'outline' and 'describe' are AO1 terms, while 'evaluate' is an AO2 term. 'Discuss' and 'explain' relate to both AO1 and AO2. Wherever possible, you should make brief reference to research studies to illustrate and support the points you are making.

Some questions may contain quotations, which you may wish to refer to in your answer.

Biological rhythms and sleep

(1) (a) Outline one or more theories relating to the functions of sleep.   *(9 marks)*
     (b) Evaluate one of the theories outlined in (a), making reference to relevant research studies.   *(16 marks)*

Perception

(2) Describe and evaluate Gregory's top down theory of perception.   *(25 marks)*

Relationships

(3) Discuss evolutionary explanations of parental investment, e.g. sex differences and parent-offspring conflict.   *(25 marks)*

Aggression

(4) (a) Outline what is meant by institutional aggression. (5 marks)

(b) Discuss evolutionary explanations of human aggression. (20 marks)

Eating behaviour

(5) 'Eating behaviour is not merely a matter of eating enough food of sufficient nutritional quality to keep us healthy; it is affected by a range of psychological factors.'

Discuss some of the psychological factors that influence eating behaviour. (25 marks)

Gender

(6) Describe and evaluate evolutionary explanations of gender roles. (25 marks)

Intelligence and learning

(7) Discuss the role of conditioning in the behaviour of non-human animals. (25 marks)

Cognition and development

(8) (a) Outline one theory of cognitive development. (9 marks)

(b) Discuss the application of theories of cognitive development to education. (16 marks)

Unit 4

Unit 4 has three sections. Each of the first two sections contains three questions that follow a similar format to those in Unit 3, and each is worth 25 marks. In the first section there is one question on each of the disorders covered in the specification: schizophrenia, depression, and anxiety disorders.

In the second section there is one question on each of the 'Psychology in action' topics: media psychology, addictive behaviour, and anomalistic psychology. You should answer one question from each section.

In the third section there is one compulsory structured question, which is worth 35 marks. This typically takes the form of a description of a study and its findings, followed by a number of methodological questions, and finishing with a longer question that asks you to design a study to test a particular idea. This is worth a good proportion of the marks, so a fair amount of detail is required. Suggestions as to what should be included are noted with the question. The marks awarded for each question are shown on the paper, and the amount you write should reflect the number of marks available.

Psychopathology

(1) Outline and evaluate one or more psychological explanations of one anxiety disorder. (25 marks)

(2) (a) Outline the clinical characteristics of schizophrenia. *(5 marks)*
  (b) Explain issues associated with the classification and diagnosis of schizophrenia. *(10 marks)*
  (c) Outline and evaluate one psychological explanation of schizophrenia. *(10 marks)*
(3) Outline and evaluate biological therapies for the treatment of depression. *(25 marks)*

Psychology in action

(4) (a) Outline the different components that make up an attitude. *(5 marks)*
  (b) Discuss some of the factors that make a communication effective in bringing about attitude change. *(20 marks)*
(5) Discuss some of the methods used to prevent and treat addictive behaviour. *(25 marks)*
(6) 'A distinction can be made between people who believe in the paranormal (sheep) and those who do not (goats). Surveys have repeatedly shown that sheep are not a small minority: belief in the paranormal is widespread.'

Discuss some of the ways in which people who believe in the paranormal may differ from those who do not. *(25 marks)*

Psychological research and scientific methods

(7) Based on findings from previous research, a psychologist is interested in whether the use of the keyword system helps students of a foreign language to learn vocabulary in that language. In this method, an English word that is similar to the foreign language word to be learned is identified. For example, the Spanish word for 'dog' is 'perro', which sounds similar to the English word 'pear'. An interactive image linking the two words is then formed, e.g. a dog carrying a pear in its mouth. When shown the foreign word and asked to give the English equivalent, the learner would need to recall the keyword ('pear') to access the image of the dog and the pear, and so retrieve the meaning of 'perro'.

In one condition (words only), 20 participants are shown a list of 30 German words and their English equivalents, e.g. 'Ente = duck'. In the other condition (keyword system), an image is suggested, e.g. 'Ente = duck. Imagine a duck entering a tunnel.' Both groups are given the same amount of time to attempt to learn the words. They are then asked to carry out a short distracter task before being given the list of German words and asked to write the English equivalents next to them. A statistical analysis is carried out on the data to find out if those in the 'keyword' condition remember significantly more words than those in the 'words only' condition. The test is significant at the 1% level for a one-tailed test ($p \leq 0.01$).

Table 1 *Average number of words remembered using the keyword system and words only*

	Keyword system	Words only
Words remembered	22	13
Standard deviation	3.2	6.8

(a) What is the experimental design in this study? *(1 mark)*

(b) Identify one possible confounding variable in this study, and suggest how it might be addressed. *(4 marks)*

(c) Why did the experimenters include a distracter task between the learning and recall phases of the study? *(2 marks)*

(d) Identify an appropriate statistical test for analysing these data, and explain why it would be suitable. *(4 marks)*

(e) Give one reason why a one-tailed test was used. *(2 marks)*

(f) Using the data in Table 1, outline and discuss the findings of the study. *(10 marks)*

(g) The psychologist decides to extend the research to see if the keyword system is more useful for people who could readily form visual images. She decides to test visual imagery by asking participants to spell 'social psychology' aloud, backwards and timing how long they take to do this.

Design a study to investigate the relationship between readiness in forming visual images and the usefulness of the keyword system. You should include sufficient detail to permit replication, for example a hypothesis, variables, detail of design and procedure and sampling. *(12 marks)*

Index